# JUDICIAL EXTERNSHIPS THE CLINIC INSIDE THE COURTHOUSE

(2016–Pub.3553)

# JUDICIAL EXTERNSHIPS
# THE CLINIC INSIDE THE
# COURTHOUSE

## FOURTH EDITION

**REBECCA A. COCHRAN**
*Professor of Law Emerita*
*University of Dayton School of Law*

CAROLINA ACADEMIC PRESS

Durham, North Carolina

Library of Congress Control Number: 2016937891

ISBN: 978-1-6328-4952-6

Carolina Academic Press, LLC
700 Kent Street
Durham, NC 27701
Telephone (919) 489-7486
Fax (919) 493-5668
www.caplaw.com
Printed in the United States of America

(2016–Pub.3553)

# Acknowledgments

I deeply appreciate the ideas, suggestions, and support provided me by Julie Bauer, Mary Boston, Jim Dare, Barbara Gorman, James Guthrie, Jenna Hosier, Staci Rucker, Melinda Warthman, and the students in my judicial externship courses.

# Dedication

To my co-clerks,
Marquerite M. Lloyd
Julie A. Bauer

# Preface

Many of my judicial extern students have noted for themselves that a judicial externship placement requires them to synthesize skills and knowledge from their entire law school curriculum. The process is never dull. Each week students report that their judge's needs and the demands imposed by a busy court's docket accelerate the rate at which they acquire knowledge in new areas of the law, as well as new analysis, research, and writing skills.

Some common discussion themes emerge: motion practice; statutory interpretation; the organization, operation and roles of the court; judicial selection, socialization and ethics. In addition, students explore the roles of the extern/clerk, develop research techniques, debate the reasoning and rhetoric of judicial opinions and other topics. The materials in this book are designed to provoke discussion, provide exercises, ask questions, and to provide selected bibliographies for further reading and study. The materials do not attempt to cover all possible issues which can arise during a judicial externship, but simply those which may most benefit law students.

The materials are ordered as I tended to follow them in my own class, but inevitably the topics are riddled with cross-references. The instructor may take them in any order. Some materials have been edited; footnotes have been eliminated, but where they survive, they have retained their original numbers.

The materials may serve as a focus for classroom discussion, as background reading, as material to be responded to in journal entries, as the starting point for more in-depth study or research on a topic. Students and instructors will and should use more than is contained in these printed pages. Instructors have used movies, works of fiction, trial and deposition transcripts, field trips, guest speakers, mock trials, and a number of other methods in the classroom component.

The Reports placed at the end of each chapter require students to look in two directions. The In Court Reports ask the externs to connect, as directly as possible, the chapter materials to the extern's assigned court or to courts in the area the extern can access. The Out of Court Reports focus on the chapter materials themselves by asking how they relate to each other and what questions they raise about judges and judicial processes. In addition, these Reports may suggest other issues to research or consider further.

My students kept journals throughout their judicial externship placement. I pull journal entries together anonymously in handouts at the start and the end of the term. Students' observations, which appear below, remind me again of the educational benefits of a judicial externship experience.

> "Working on the cases for the judge pulls together stuff from all these courses: research and writing, civil procedure, torts, contracts. You use all that knowledge at once and you have to use it QUICKLY."

> "Working on and seeing actual cases is more fun, but also more frustrating and frightening than law school courses."

> "I think that to be a good lawyer, you have got to put yourself in the judge's shoes. You need argue in a way that permits the court to rule easily in your favor. It's based on the law, yes, but also on the way you frame, order and argue the issues."

## *Preface*

"I have gained confidence from observing the docket call and watching the attorneys in my judge's courtroom. I will not be as intimidated when I walk into court for the first time as an attorney."

# Table of Contents

**Chapter 1**      **THE ROLE OF THE JUDICIAL CLERK OR EXTERN** . . . . . 1

I.      JUDICIAL CLERKS, EXTERNS & THEIR HISTORY . . . . . . . . . . . . . . . . 2

        J. Daniel Mahoney, *Law Clerks: For Better or for Worse?* . . . . . . . . . . . 2

II.     RESPONSIBILITIES OF JUDICIAL CLERKS AND EXTERNS . . . . . . . . . 5

        J. Daniel Mahoney, *Law Clerks: For Better or for Worse?* . . . . . . . . . . . 5

        Judicial Law Clerk-First Judicial District (Continual Posting) Hastings,

        Minnesota . . . . . . . . . . . . . . . . . . . . . . . . . . . . . . . . . . . . . . . . . . . 6

III.    ETHICS FOR JUDICIAL CLERKS AND EXTERNS . . . . . . . . . . . . . . . . 8

  A.      Confidentiality of Chambers . . . . . . . . . . . . . . . . . . . . . . . . . . . . . 8

        Model Confidentiality Statement . . . . . . . . . . . . . . . . . . . . . . . . . . 8

        John Paul Jones, *Some Ethical Considerations for Judicial Clerks* . . . . 11

        Rule 46 of the Supreme Court of the State of New Hampshire . . . . . . . . 13

    1.     Revealing Present Confidences . . . . . . . . . . . . . . . . . . . . . . . . . . . . 14

          *In re Corrugated Container Antitrust Litigation* . . . . . . . . . . . . . . . . 14

    2.     Revealing Past Confidences . . . . . . . . . . . . . . . . . . . . . . . . . . . . . . 15

          Thomas G. Krattenmaker, *Looking Back at Cohen v. California: A 40-*

          *Year Retrospective from Inside the Court* . . . . . . . . . . . . . . . . . . . . 15

    3.     Judicial Privilege . . . . . . . . . . . . . . . . . . . . . . . . . . . . . . . . . . . . 16

          *In the Matter of the Enforcement of a Subpoena* . . . . . . . . . . . . . . 16

          *Sheppard v. Beerman* . . . . . . . . . . . . . . . . . . . . . . . . . . . . . . . . . 21

  B.      Clerk or Extern's Conflict of Interest . . . . . . . . . . . . . . . . . . . . . . . 22

    1.     Future Employment & Family Relations . . . . . . . . . . . . . . . . . . . . . . 22

        John Paul Jones, *Some Ethical Considerations for Judicial Clerks* . . . 22

        Arizona Supreme Court Judicial Ethics Advisory Committee, *Ethical*

        *Issues Involving Prospective Employers of Law Clerks* . . . . . . . . . . . 25

    2.     Current Employment as Judicial Clerk . . . . . . . . . . . . . . . . . . . . . . . 28

          *Sallie v. State* . . . . . . . . . . . . . . . . . . . . . . . . . . . . . . . . . . . . . 28

          *Deyling v. Flowers* . . . . . . . . . . . . . . . . . . . . . . . . . . . . . . . . . . 30

          *Uniloc USA v. Microsoft Corp.* . . . . . . . . . . . . . . . . . . . . . . . . . . 33

    3.     Former Clerks and Externs as Counsel in Their Judges' Courts . . . . . . . 39

          *Fredonia Broadcasting Corp., Inc. v. RCA Corp.* . . . . . . . . . . . . . . 39

          *Smith v. Pepsico, Inc.* . . . . . . . . . . . . . . . . . . . . . . . . . . . . . . . . 40

  C.      Decision-Making on the Record . . . . . . . . . . . . . . . . . . . . . . . . . . 42

        John Paul Jones, *Some Ethical Considerations for Judicial Clerks* . . . . 42

        *Price Brothers Company v. Philadelphia Gear Corporation* . . . . . . . . 44

        *Lisson v. O'Hare* . . . . . . . . . . . . . . . . . . . . . . . . . . . . . . . . . . . 47

IV.    QUALIFICATIONS & SELECTION . . . . . . . . . . . . . . . . . . . . . . . . . 48

# Table of Contents

In Court Reports . . . . . . . . . . . . . . . . . . . . . . . . . . . . . . . . . . . . . . . . . 51

Out of Court Reports . . . . . . . . . . . . . . . . . . . . . . . . . . . . . . . . . . . . . . 51

Selected Bibliography . . . . . . . . . . . . . . . . . . . . . . . . . . . . . . . . . . . . . 53

**Chapter 2    JUDICIAL OPINIONS: DECISIONMAKING AND OPINION DRAFTING** . . . . . . . . . . . . . . . . . . . . . . . . . . . . . . . . . . **57**

I.      WRITTEN OPINIONS: WRITING WELL-REASONED JUDGMENTS . . . 58

      S.I. Strong, *Writing Reasoned Decision and Opinions* . . . . . . . . . . . . . 58

II.     JUDGES WRITING FOR MULTIPLE AUDIENCES . . . . . . . . . . . . . . . . . 77

      *Denny v. Radar Industries, Inc.* . . . . . . . . . . . . . . . . . . . . . . . . . . . . . 77

      *Gray v. State* . . . . . . . . . . . . . . . . . . . . . . . . . . . . . . . . . . . . . . . . . . 77

      *Russell v. State* . . . . . . . . . . . . . . . . . . . . . . . . . . . . . . . . . . . . . . . 78

      *Escola v. Coca Cola Bottling Co.* . . . . . . . . . . . . . . . . . . . . . . . . . . . 80

III.    WRITTEN OPINIONS: DRAFTING BY CLERK "GHOSTWRITERS," PUBLIC PERCEPTION & PUBLIC RECOGNITION . . . . . . . . . . . . . . . 83

      J. Daniel Mahoney, *Law Clerks: For Better or for Worse?* . . . . . . . . . . . 84

      *United States v. DiFrancesco* . . . . . . . . . . . . . . . . . . . . . . . . . . . . . . . 86

      *Parker v. Connors Steel Company* . . . . . . . . . . . . . . . . . . . . . . . . . . 91

      In Court Reports . . . . . . . . . . . . . . . . . . . . . . . . . . . . . . . . . . . . . . . 96

      Out of Court Reports . . . . . . . . . . . . . . . . . . . . . . . . . . . . . . . . . . . . 97

      Selected Bibliography . . . . . . . . . . . . . . . . . . . . . . . . . . . . . . . . . . . 98

**Chapter 3    JUDICIAL SELECTION, QUALIFICATIONS, AND TRAINING** . . . . . . . . . . . . . . . . . . . . . . . . . . . . . . . **101**

I.      JUDICIAL SELECTION METHODS . . . . . . . . . . . . . . . . . . . . . . . . . . . 102

  A.    Federal Court Selection . . . . . . . . . . . . . . . . . . . . . . . . . . . . . . . . . . 102

      2002 U.S. Senate Committee on the Judiciary Hearing on the Nomination of Miguel Estrada . . . . . . . . . . . . . . . . . . . . . . . . . . . . . . . . . . . . . . . . . 102

  B.    State Court Selection . . . . . . . . . . . . . . . . . . . . . . . . . . . . . . . . . . . 110

      Florida State Canons of Judicial Conduct Canon 7 . . . . . . . . . . . . . . 110

      *Williams-Yulee v. The Florida Bar*, Brief of *Amicus* Cameron A. Blau in Support of the Petitioner . . . . . . . . . . . . . . . . . . . . . . . . . . . . . . . . . 111

      *Williams-Yulee v. The Florida Bar*, Brief of *Amicus* Jed Shugerman in Support of the Petitioner . . . . . . . . . . . . . . . . . . . . . . . . . . . . . . . . . 117

II.     QUALIFICATIONS . . . . . . . . . . . . . . . . . . . . . . . . . . . . . . . . . . . . . . 126

  A.    Federal Court Qualifications . . . . . . . . . . . . . . . . . . . . . . . . . . . . . . 126

  B.    State Court Qualifications . . . . . . . . . . . . . . . . . . . . . . . . . . . . . . . . 126

      Ohio Rev. Code §§ 2301.01; 2501.02; 2503.01 . . . . . . . . . . . . . . . . 126

      Arizona Rev. Statutes § 11-402 . . . . . . . . . . . . . . . . . . . . . . . . . . . . 127

III.    JUDICIAL EVALUATION AND EDUCATION . . . . . . . . . . . . . . . . . . . 129

# Table of Contents

| | | |
|---|---|---|
| A. | Judicial Evaluation | 129 |
| | Federal Judicial Center, Judicial Evaluation Pilot Project Judicial Evaluation Questionnaire | 130 |
| B. | Judicial Education | 131 |
| IV. | THE RESULTS OF THE JUDICIAL SELECTION PROCESS: LACK OF DIVERSITY | 132 |
| A. | The Numbers of Women & Minority Judges | 132 |
| B. | The Numbers Create Issues of Legitimacy & Influence on Decisions | 133 |
| | In Court Reports | 135 |
| | Out of Court Reports | 135 |
| | Selected Bibliography | 137 |

| | | |
|---|---|---|
| **Chapter 4** | **JUDICIAL ETHICS: PERFORMING DUTIES IMPARTIALLY** | **141** |

| | | |
|---|---|---|
| I. | JUDICIAL RECUSAL AND DISQUALIFICATION | 142 |
| | *Callahan v. Callahan* | 142 |
| A. | JUDICIAL CONDUCT RULES OF RECUSAL AND DISQUALIFICATION | 145 |
| | ABA Code of Judicial Conduct, Canon 2 | 145 |
| | Ohio Code of Judicial Conduct | 150 |
| | 28 U.S.C. § 455 | 151 |
| | 28 U.S.C. § 144 | 152 |
| | 28 U.S.C. § 47 | 153 |
| B. | APPLYING RULES OF RECUSAL AND DISQUALIFICATION: JUDICIAL FRIENDSHIPS | 153 |
| | *United States v. Murphy* | 154 |
| | *Cheney v. United States District Court for the District of Columbia* | 163 |
| | *Domville v. State* | 174 |
| C. | APPLYING THE RULES OF RECUSAL & DISQUALIFICATION: TRIAL JUDGE AS APPELLATE JUDGE | 176 |
| | *Swann v. Charlotte-Mecklenburg Bd. of Educ.* | 176 |
| II. | IMPARTIAL JUDICIAL TREATMENT OF COUNSEL & PARTIES | 179 |
| | *In re Disqualification of Burge* | 179 |
| | *In re Complaint as to the Conduct of the Honorable Ronald D. Schenck* | 186 |
| | In Court Reports | 189 |
| | Out of Court Reports | 190 |
| | Selected Bibliography | 196 |

# Table of Contents

**Chapter 5**        **JUDICIAL ROLES: JUDGING AS CIVIL JURY TRIALS, APPELLATE BRIEFS & ORAL ARGUMENTS DECLINE . 199**

I.     THE CIVIL JURY TRIAL'S DECLINE . . . . . . . . . . . . . . . . . . . . . . . . . . . 201

          The Supreme Court of Ohio, 2014 Ohio Courts Statistical Summary . . . . 202

II.    SEVENTH AMENDMENT RIGHT TO A CIVIL JURY TRIAL . . . . . . . . 204

III.   COMPLEX LITIGATION & CIVIL JURY COMPETENCE . . . . . . . . . . . 205

    A.    Jury Competence in Complex Litigation: Federal Court . . . . . . . . . . . . . 205

          *In re Boise Cascade Securities Litigation* . . . . . . . . . . . . . . . . . . . . 205

          *Allianz Risk Transfer AG v. Paramount Pictures Corporation* . . . . . . . 211

    B.    Jury Competence in Complex Litigation: State Court . . . . . . . . . . . . . . 219

          *Rieff v. Evans* . . . . . . . . . . . . . . . . . . . . . . . . . . . . . . . . . . . . . . . 219

    C.    Civil Jury Trial: Accompanying "Burdens" . . . . . . . . . . . . . . . . . . . . . 223

          *Richardson v. Boddie-Noell Enterprises, Inc.* . . . . . . . . . . . . . . . . . . 223

IV.   THE RISE OF ALTERNATIVE DISPUTE RESOLUTION: ARBITRATION . . . . . . . . . . . . . . . . . . . . . . . . . . . . . . . . . . . . . . . . . . 229

          *Circuit City Stores, Inc. v. Adams,* . . . . . . . . . . . . . . . . . . . . . . . . . . 230

          *Arnold v. Burger King* . . . . . . . . . . . . . . . . . . . . . . . . . . . . . . . . . . 238

V.    APPELLATE JUGES: JUDGING AS APPELLATE PROCEDURES DECLINE . . . . . . . . . . . . . . . . . . . . . . . . . . . . . . . . . . . . . . . . . . . . . . 259

    A.    Appellate Courts: Settlement on Appeal Before Appellate Briefs . . . . . . . 259

          Twelfth District Court of Appeals of Ohio, *Prehearing Conference Procedures* . . . . . . . . . . . . . . . . . . . . . . . . . . . . . . . . . . . . . . . . . . 259

    B.    Appellate Courts: Decline in Oral Arguments . . . . . . . . . . . . . . . . . . . 262

          Federal Rules of Appellate Procedure, Rule 34 . . . . . . . . . . . . . . . . . 262

          United States Court of Appeals for the Eighth Circuit, Rule 34A . . . . . 263

          Appellants' Brief, *Two Rivers Bank & Trust v. Atanasova* . . . . . . . . . 264

          Appellees' Brief, *Two Rivers Bank & Trust v. Atanasova* . . . . . . . . . . 265

          In Court Reports . . . . . . . . . . . . . . . . . . . . . . . . . . . . . . . . . . . . . 265

          Out of Court Reports . . . . . . . . . . . . . . . . . . . . . . . . . . . . . . . . . . 267

          Selected Bibliography . . . . . . . . . . . . . . . . . . . . . . . . . . . . . . . . . . 268

**Chapter 6**        **JUDICIAL ROLES: THERAPEUTIC JURISPRUDENCE AND THE RISE OF SPECIALTY DOCKETS & PROBLEM-SOLVING COURTS . . . . . . . . . . . . . . . . . . . . . . . . . . . . . . 273**

I.     THE JUDGE IN TRADITIONAL AND PROBLEM-SOLVING COURTS . 275

          Roger K. Warren, *A Comparison of Transformed and Traditional Court Procedures* . . . . . . . . . . . . . . . . . . . . . . . . . . . . . . . . . . . . . . . . . . 275

II.    DRUG COURTS AS PROBLEM-SOLVING COURTS . . . . . . . . . . . . . 275

          Gordon M. Griller, *Key Drug Court Protocols* . . . . . . . . . . . . . . . . . 276

          Judge Kevin S. Burke, *Just What Made Drug Courts Successful?* . . . . . 276

# Table of Contents

III.   THE WORKING PARTS OF A DRUG COURT . . . . . . . . . . . . . . . . . . . . 288

Chief Justice Maureen O'Connor, *State of the Judiciary* . . . . . . . . . . . . 289

Ohio Supreme Court Rule 36.20 & Appendix I . . . . . . . . . . . . . . . . . 290

Montgomery County Drug Court, *Drug Court Participation Agreement* . 297

IV.   DRUG COURTS, THE ADVERSARIAL PROCESS, & DUE PROCESS . . 302

*State v. Shambley* . . . . . . . . . . . . . . . . . . . . . . . . . . . . . . . . . . . . . . 304

In Court Reports . . . . . . . . . . . . . . . . . . . . . . . . . . . . . . . . . . . . . . . 313

Out of Court Reports . . . . . . . . . . . . . . . . . . . . . . . . . . . . . . . . . . . . 314

Selected Bibliography . . . . . . . . . . . . . . . . . . . . . . . . . . . . . . . . . . . 315

**Chapter 7**      **JUDICIAL ROLES: TECHNOLOGY'S EFFECTS ON
                 JUDICIAL RESEARCH AND DECISION-MAKING . . . . . 319**

I.   JUDICIAL INTERNET FACT RESEARCH . . . . . . . . . . . . . . . . . . . . . . . 321

Federal Rule of Evidence 201 . . . . . . . . . . . . . . . . . . . . . . . . . . . . . . 322

Federal Rule of Appellate Procedure 10 . . . . . . . . . . . . . . . . . . . . . . . 323

ABA Model Code of Judicial Conduct Rule 2.9 . . . . . . . . . . . . . . . . . 324

*Fire Insurance Exchange v. Oltmanns* . . . . . . . . . . . . . . . . . . . . . . . 324

*Mendler v. Winterland Production, Ltd.* . . . . . . . . . . . . . . . . . . . . . . . 332

*Randy Disselkoen Properties v. Charter Twp. of Cascade* . . . . . . . . . . . 340

*In re Kogler* . . . . . . . . . . . . . . . . . . . . . . . . . . . . . . . . . . . . . . . . . . 341

II.   IMAGES IN THE JUDICIAL PROCESS . . . . . . . . . . . . . . . . . . . . . . . . 341

A.   Attorney-Created Images . . . . . . . . . . . . . . . . . . . . . . . . . . . . . . . . 341

*In re Glasmann* . . . . . . . . . . . . . . . . . . . . . . . . . . . . . . . . . . . . . . . 341

B.   Court-Created Images . . . . . . . . . . . . . . . . . . . . . . . . . . . . . . . . . . 350

*Sandifer v. U.S. Steel Corp.* (7th Cir.) . . . . . . . . . . . . . . . . . . . . . . . 350

*Sandifer v. United States Steel Corp.* (U.S. Supreme Court) . . . . . . . . 355

In Court Reports . . . . . . . . . . . . . . . . . . . . . . . . . . . . . . . . . . . . . . . 355

Out of Court Reports . . . . . . . . . . . . . . . . . . . . . . . . . . . . . . . . . . . . 356

Selected Bibliography . . . . . . . . . . . . . . . . . . . . . . . . . . . . . . . . . . . 360

**Index**      . . . . . . . . . . . . . . . . . . . . . . . . . . . . . . . . . . . . . . . . . . . . . . . **I-1**

# Chapter 1

## THE ROLE OF THE JUDICIAL CLERK OR EXTERN

There remains the fact that law school is needlessly abstract, and needlessly removed from life. There remains the fact that seeing-it-done gives reading-it-in-books new flavor, new perspective. If one afternoon a week, during one semester of one year, were free of other classes, and the students with an instructor should visit various courts; if written critiques of what had been observed were followed by the instructor's comment and criticism; if the lawyers concerned were invited to explain their own views on their strategy — or if law school would deliberately set to work to plan an interstitial relationship.

Karl N. Llewellyn, *On What Is Wrong with So-Called Legal Education*, 35 COLUM. L. REV. 651 (1935).

The [externship] program was the single most valuable experience of my law school career. [It] immersed me into a real life role. Accordingly, I found myself thinking more critically and researching more effectively . . . . In sum, my role in the program as participant-observer contributed significantly to bridging the chasm between law school and the practice of law.

Elizabeth A. Kovachevich, *Federal Judicial Internship Programs*, 41 FED. B. NEWS & J. 680 (1994).

The undersigned selects his clerks with care. Scholastic ability has its place, but the focus is on maturity and judgment. The Court prefers people who have been around the barn once or twice, and who know what is out there behind the barn.

*Bishop v. Albertson's, Inc.*, 806 F. Supp. 897 (E.D. Wash. 1992).

As a judicial clerk or student extern, a law student has many of the same responsibilities as a regular judicial clerk, such as evaluating pleadings and motions, listening to oral arguments, researching and analyzing legal issues, conferring with judges, and drafting bench memos or opinions. Given these responsibilities, a pre-graduation clerkship can significantly advance a student's legal career in a number of ways.

Anna E. McDowell & Pamela S. Mzembe, *Working in Chambers: The Rewards of a Pre-Graduation Judicial Clerkship*, 74 J. KAN. B. ASS'N. 7 (Aug. 2005).

> I want [my law clerks] to treat me as an equal, not as a superior. If they think I am wrong about something, I want them to tell me I'm wrong, with no pussy-footing. Often I *am* wrong, because my law clerks are very smart, and know things that I don't know; and because there are three of them and only one of me, so that they spend more time on each case than I do; and because their priors are often different from mine.

RICHARD A. POSNER, REFLECTIONS ON JUDGING 128 (2013).

Judicial clerks, joined by law student judicial externs, constitute a vital component of federal and state court processes. Each court and judge will define the roles assigned to the clerk and extern and any number of guides and manuals will assist. In this chapter, essential concerns are introduced, including a brief history of the clerk and extern entry into the courts, their often shared responsibilities, and the always shared ethical duties of operating within a judge's chambers.

# I. JUDICIAL CLERKS, EXTERNS & THEIR HISTORY

For over a hundred years, judicial clerks have served federal and state court judges as researchers, drafters, confidantes, and sounding boards. Along with providing a fresh perspective, a clerk's services are often needed to help "move" the cases on a judge's docket.

Judge Horace Gray is generally credited as the first judge to use a legal assistant or a law clerk to assist him as the Chief Justice of the Massachusetts Supreme Judicial Court of Errors. The judge and his clerks found the relationship enjoyable and effective; eventually, law clerks came to work for the United States Supreme Court, the Circuit Courts of Appeals, and the district courts, as well as state courts at all levels.

**J. Daniel Mahoney**
***Law Clerks: For Better or for Worse?**[*]*
54 BROOK. L. REV. 321 (1988)

* * * *

## I. HISTORICAL OVERVIEW

The institution of clerking began over a hundred years ago. It is largely undisputed that the first jurist to utilize legal assistants was Horace Gray. Upon becoming the Chief Justice of the Massachusetts Supreme Judicial Court of Errors in 1873, after spending many years as an associate justice, Gray assumed a greatly increased

---

[*] Copyright © 1988. Reprinted with permission of the Brooklyn Law Review and J. Daniel Mahoney.

workload. Amazingly, Gray authored approximately 25 percent of that court's opinions. In addition, he presided over the many trials then within the court's jurisdiction. It was undoubtedly the pressures associated with such a workload that led Gray to employ the services of a law assistant in the summer of 1875.

Gray's first law clerk, as well as all others that followed, was a recently graduated and highly ranked Harvard Law School student — a hiring practice that some judges follow, or attempt to follow, to this day. Each of these law clerks was referred to Gray by his half brother, Harvard professor John Chipman Gray. When Chief Justice Gray was appointed to the Supreme Court in 1882, he brought his personal assistant to Washington with him. Perhaps the most interesting aspect of Gray's use of these young clerks was the fact that he paid them from his own resources, a practice that has fallen into fortunate disuse.

The first official reference to the idea of employing assistants for the Supreme Court justices occurred in 1885, when Attorney General A. H. Garland suggested in his annual report that:

> [i]t would greatly facilitate the business of the Supreme Court if each justice was provided by law with a secretary or law clerk, to be a stenographer, to be paid an annual salary sufficient to obtain the requisite qualifications, whose duties shall be to assist in such clerical work as might be assigned to him.

The notion of clerical help was a direct result of the increased workload the Supreme Court faced at the time, and the associated delays in judicial action. On August 4, 1886, Congress acted upon Garland's recommendation and provided for a 'stenographic clerk' for each justice of the Supreme Court at a salary of $1,600 a year.

While it might appear from this legislative description that Congress intended to circumscribe the duties that law clerks were to perform by limiting them to clerical work, Justice Gray continued to use his clerks in the same manner as he had in the past, which envisioned a much broader role. According to Samuel Williston, who served as one of Gray's law clerks, Gray used his assistants to review newly filed cases and opinions proposed by Gray's colleagues on the Court, engaged his clerks in vigorous colloquy, and had real interest in and respect for their views. They were sometimes asked to draft opinions, although the drafts served only as sources of discussion. It is fair to say that Justice Gray was not only the founder of the institution of "law clerking," but also the draftsman of the role a law clerk was thereafter to perform.

Despite the initial hesitance of the justices, all nine were using the allotted "stenographic clerk" by 1888. The justices typically found their law clerks through friends or relatives, or from the bar and law schools of the District of Columbia.

In 1919, Congress provided the justices with another clerical assistant. After some initial confusion, it became clear that Congress was authorizing a "law clerk" in addition to the previously authorized "stenographic clerk." It was not until 1921, however, that Chief Justice Taft became the first member of the Court to use both assistants. The other justices were slow to follow, but by 1939 all the justices were using both assistants.

In 1941, Harlan F. Stone became chief justice and employed four personal assistants: two law clerks and two secretaries. Again, the increased personal staff was a direct consequence of the increased workload associated with the position. In addition to being the chief administrative officer of the federal judiciary, Chief Justice Stone dealt with all *in forma pauperis* petitions personally, and their number increased greatly while he was chief justice. It was also during this time that the terms senior and junior clerk came into vogue, since Stone was the first justice to employ his law clerks for two-year, overlapping terms. When Chief Justice Vinson replaced Stone in 1946, he employed seven assistants: three law clerks, three secretaries, and a messenger. Around that time, many of the associate justices added a second law clerk to their staffs. Chief Justice Warren continued the Vinson practice.

The institution of 'law clerking' became truly entrenched within the federal judiciary during the 1930s when law clerks were introduced to the lower federal courts. In 1930, Congress provided each circuit court judge with one law clerk, subject to the approval of the Attorney General. In 1936, district court judges were allowed to use law clerks, although the number of district court clerks was strictly limited until 1948, and required a certification of need by the appropriate senior circuit judge until 1959.

Since 1960, the approximate beginning of the 'caseload explosion' in the nation's federal courts, the number of law clerks has increased at what some believe is an alarming rate. The number of law clerks is not specified by statute; rather, a general provision for each court authorizes the hiring of law clerks, and the number of clerks is set in line items as a part of the annual judicial appropriations act. Currently, Supreme Court justices are entitled to four law clerks, circuit court judges to three, and district court judges to two. Further, the ratio of clerks to circuit court judges in the courts of appeals is actually four to one, if one counts the attorneys that make up each circuit's central staff.

---

By the 1970s, law students, serving as externs, joined the law clerks, in serving federal and state court judges. Law students serve as full- or part-time volunteer law clerks to judges. The law students volunteer their services and may also receive academic credit for their work. *See generally* JOHN B. OAKLEY & ROBERT S. THOMPSON, LAW CLERKS AND THE JUDICIAL PROCESS, 27–29 (1980) (describing the history and duties of externs or "quasi-clerks"). *See also* Paul R. Baier & T. John Lesinski, *In Aid of the Judicial Process: A Proposal for Law Curricular and Student Involvement*, 56 JUDICATURE 100 (1972); Jack B. Weinstein & William B. Bonvillian, *A Part-time Clerkship Program in the Federal Courts for Law Students*, 68 F.R.D. 265 (1975); Amany Ragab Hacking, *Jumpstarting the Judicial Externship Experience: Building Upon Common Themes for Student Success in the Classroom and in the Judge's Chambers*, 21 CLINICAL L. REV. 29 (2014).

## II.  RESPONSIBILITIES OF JUDICIAL CLERKS AND EXTERNS

Although the benefits of judicial clerking for the judges, the clerks, and the judicial system seem readily apparent, the clerk's responsibilities periodically receive comment and criticism. Debate over the proper limits to clerk and extern roles often focuses on the concern that their roles have grown too large or powerful. *See, e.g.*, Rick A. Swanson & Stephen L. Wasby, *Good Stewards: Law Clerk Influence in State High Courts*, 29 Just. Sys. J. 24 (2008).

### J. Daniel Mahoney
*Law Clerks: For Better or for Worse?*[*]
54 Brook. L. Rev. 321 (1988)

* * * *

### II. THE FUNCTIONS AND RESPONSIBILITIES OF LAW CLERKS

What is it that law clerks actually do? How do their actions affect the judicial process? In short, '[t]he law clerk has no statutorily defined duties but rather performs a broad range of functions to assist his judge.' As the Second Circuit recently noted:

> Law clerks are closely connected with the court's decision-making process. Law clerks are 'sounding boards for tentative opinions and legal researchers who seek the authorities that affect decisions. Clerks are privy to a judge's thoughts in a way that neither parties to the lawsuit nor his most intimate family members may be.' *Hall v. Small Business Admin.*, 695 F.2d 175, 179 (5th Cir. 1983). Moreover, the work done by law clerks is supervised, approved, and adopted by the judges who initially authorized it. A judicial opinion is not that of the law clerk, but of the judge. Law clerks are simply extensions of the judges at whose pleasure they serve.

It is indeed difficult to draw more specific conclusions. The functions of a law clerk vary from court to court and from judge to judge. There is little in the way of concrete evidence in the public domain that actually describes the duties and functions of a law clerk. This is undoubtedly due to the uniquely personal nature of the relationship.

Most of the available information on the role clerks play in the justice system comes from the personal reminiscences of former Supreme Court law clerks. In 1977, however, the Federal Judicial Center made an attempt to set forth in writing what a clerkship entails by publishing its Law Clerk Handbook. Despite the detailed and comprehensive nature of that publication, the authors could only agree to the following general job description for law clerks:

> The law clerk is an assistant to the judge and has no statutorily defined duties. Rather, the clerk serves at the direction of the judge and performs a broad

range of functions. Clerks are usually assigned legal research, drafting, editing, proofreading, and verification of citations. Frequently, clerks also have responsibility for library maintenance, document assembly, service as courtroom crier, and some personal errands for the judge. Clerks often attend conferences in chambers with the attorneys in a case and also engage in conferences and discussions with the judge regarding pending cases.

With respect to appellate clerks, the Law Clerk Handbook states that their primary function "is to research the issues of law and fact in an appeal and to draft a working opinion for the judge, pursuant to his directions." The problem with this broad assertion is self-evident. While it may be generally recognized that a majority of appellate law clerks today draft preliminary opinions, some may be confined to research, screening, and editorial or sounding board functions.

---

## Judicial Law Clerk-First Judicial District (Continual Posting) Hastings, Minnesota

https://www.governmentjobs.com/jobs/192842/judicial-law-clerk-first-judicial-district-continual-posting

### Description

The First Judicial District continually accepts applications for Judicial Law Clerk positions *(Applications will only be accepted 60 days prior to law school graduation date).* Judicial clerks work directly with a district court judge performing legal research and drafting memoranda and orders including civil, family and criminal. The First Judicial District operates on a daily calendar system, which means Law Clerks have the opportunity to work on a variety of assignments and observe many different types of court proceedings.

### Example of Duties

(Any one position may not include all of the duties listed, nor do the examples cover all the duties which may be performed.)

• Reviews, studies and researches laws, court decisions, documents, opinions, briefs, and related legal authorities.

• Prepares legal memoranda, statement of issues involved and proposed orders, including appropriate suggestions or recommendations to the judge.

• Compiles references on laws and decisions necessary for legal determinations.

• Confers with judge concerning legal questions, construction of documents and granting of orders.

• Attends court sessions to hear oral arguments.

• Prepares and summarizes case files in advance of hearings and monitors cases under advisement.

- Prepares jury instructions and verdict forms.
- Responds to phone calls and written inquiries from public and attorneys.

———————

In David Lat's 2015 novel, SUPREME AMBITIONS, readers learn, in great detail, the specific duties of a Ninth Circuit Court of Appeals clerk as experienced by the leading character, Audrey Coyne, who clerks for Judge Christina Wong Stinson. Both characters, however, have ambitions to reach the Supreme Court:

> First, in advance of each oral argument "calendar," or one-week period in which Judge Stinson would hear cases in court, I would help the judge get ready for the arguments. This would involve writing a "bench memorandum," a memo summarizing the facts and legal issues of a case and offering a recommendation for how the case should be decided, and preparing a "bench book," a binder containing the memo and various key legal documents relevant to the case. * * *

> Second, . . . after the completion of each oral argument calendar I would work with Judge Stinson on the opinion in the case. How much work this would involve would vary depending upon the judge's role in the case — writing the majority opinion, dissenting, or merely offering editorial suggestions on the opinion of a colleague — and whether the opinion was published or unpublished. * * *

> Third, I would assist Judge Stinson with "en banc" matters, an area where the judge was fairly active. This would involve reviewing the opinions generated by the other Ninth Circuit three-judge panels to see if they were problematic — for example, inconsistent with Ninth Circuit or Supreme Court precedent. If so, the judge might want to call for rehearing en banc, or a rehearing by a larger group of judges.

David Lat, SUPREME AMBITIONS 37, 38–39 (2015).

Details of the variety of tasks performed by law student externs appear in descriptions by the court for volunteers and in externship course descriptions where students receive academic credit. Often the externs report to the judge's law clerk, and the clerk and extern perform similar tasks. *See* Gerard J. Clark, *Supervising Judicial Interns: A Primer*, 36 SUFFOLK U. L. REV. 681 (2003); Stacy Caplow, *From Courtroom to Classroom: Creating an Academic Component to Enhance the Skills and Values Learned in a Student Judicial Clerkship Clinic*, 75 NEB. L. REV. 872 (1996); Richard L. Fruin, Jr. & Barbara A. Blanco, *Judicial Externs: Judicial Outreach to the Future*, 44 JUDGES' J. 44 (Spring 2005).

## III.  ETHICS FOR JUDICIAL CLERKS AND EXTERNS

Because judicial clerks and externs play important roles in the life of the court, their conduct reflects directly upon the judge and the court. Courts have variously found that clerks' ethical duties are "equivalent" to those of judges, *Miller Ind., Inc. v. Caterpillar Tractor Co.*, 516 F. Supp. 84 (S.D. Ala. 1980), or that clerks are bound by the same judicial canons that bind their judges, *United States v. Bronston*, 491 F. Supp. 593 (S.D.N.Y. 1980). The Federal Judicial Center's pamphlet describes in detail and with examples the judicial employees' obligations of confidentiality while performing their jobs. Federal Judicial Center, Maintaining the Public Trust: Ethics for Federal Judicial Law Clerks (4th ed. 2013). Available at http://www.fjc.gov/public/pdf.nsf/lookup/Maintaining-Public-Trust-4D-FJC-Public-2013.pdf/$file/Maintaining-Public-Trust-4D-FJC-Public-2013.pdf.

Three ethical obligations are essential for the judge, the judicial clerk, and the extern: (A) the confidentiality of chambers; (B) conflicts of interest; and (C) decision-making on the record.

### A.  Confidentiality of Chambers

Some courts and judges adopt the judicial employee Model Confidentiality Statement, Form AO-306, below and at http://jnet.ao.dcn/resources/forms/model-confidentiality-statement. Local court rules may also govern confidentiality of chambers.

> All courthouse personnel, including . . . law clerks . . . shall under no circumstances disclose to any person, without express authorization by the court, information relating to a pending criminal case or grand jury matter that is not a part of the public records of the court. This rule specifically forbids the divulgence of information concerning arguments and hearings held in chambers or otherwise outside the presence of the public.

U.S. Dist. Ct. Rules M.D. La. Local Crim. R. 53.8 (2002).

Read the Model Confidentiality Statement, "sign" it, and consider the specific obligations of confidentiality you would be undertaking as an extern governed by the Model Confidentiality Statement.

---

AO 306 (Rev. 10/11)

**MODEL CONFIDENTIALITY STATEMENT**

One of the most important obligations of judicial employees is to ensure that nonpublic information learned in the course of employment is kept confidential. In the performance of job duties, employees may have access to files, records, draft materials, and conversations that are, under the Code of Conduct for Judicial Employees or by practice of the court, confidential. Canon 3D of the Code sets forth the minimum standard:

A judicial employee should avoid making public comment on the merits of a pending or impending action and should require similar restraint by personnel subject to the judicial employee's direction and control. This proscription does not extend to public statements made in the course of official duties or to the explanation of court procedures. A judicial employee should never disclose any confidential information received in the course of official duties except as required in the performance of such duties, nor should a judicial employee employ such information for personal gain. A former judicial employee should observe the same restrictions on disclosure of confidential information that apply to a current judicial employee, except as modified by the appointing authority.

## 1. Confidential Information

Confidential information means information received in the course of judicial duties that is not public and is not authorized to be made public. This includes information received by the court pursuant to a protective order or under seal; expressly marked or designated by a judge to be kept confidential; or relating to the deliberative processes of the court or an individual judge. Examples of confidential information are:

(a) the substance of draft opinions or decisions;

(b) internal memoranda, in draft or final form, prepared in connection with matters before the court;

(c) the content or occurrence of conversations among judges or between a judge and judicial employees concerning matters before the court;

(d) the identity of panel members or of the authoring judge before release of this information is authorized by the court;

(e) the authorship of *per curiam* opinions or orders;

(f) the timing of a decision, order, or other judicial action, including the status of or progress on a judicial action not yet finalized (except as authorized in accordance with Section 2.C.);

(g) views expressed by a judge either in casual conversation or in the course of discussions about a particular matter before the court;

(h) any subject matter the appointing authority has indicated should not be revealed, such as internal office practices, informal court procedures, the content or occurrence of statements or conversations, and actions by a judge or staff; and

(i) any matter on which you have been, are, or will be working.

Information that is not considered confidential includes court rules, published court procedures, public court records including the case docket, and information disclosed in public court documents or proceedings. However, judicial employees should not disclose, or make public or private statements about the merits or decision making process concerning past, pending, or future cases even if those statements entail the use of only non-confidential materials.

## 2. Nondisclosure

**A. Unauthorized disclosure.** To promote public confidence in the integrity of the judicial system and to avoid impropriety, illegality, or favoritism, or any appearance thereof, it is critical that confidential information not be disclosed by a judicial employee. No past or present judicial employee may disclose or make available confidential information, except as authorized in accordance with Section 2.C.

**B. Inadvertent disclosure.** Sometimes breaches of confidentiality do not involve intentional disclosure but are the result of overheard remarks, casual comments, or inadequate shielding of sensitive materials. Judicial employees should take care to prevent inadvertent disclosure of confidential information by avoiding:

(1) case-related conversations and other discussions of confidential information in public places within the court, such as the library, hallways, elevators, and cafeteria, either in person or by telephone or cellular phone;

(2) case-related conversations and other discussions of confidential information at bar association meetings, law schools, other gatherings of noncourt persons, or in public places, either in person or by telephone or cellular phone;

(3) exposure of confidential documents to the view of noncourt persons;

(4) visible display of confidential documents in public places such as a library, on public transportation, or in a photocopier or scanner to which noncourt persons have access, and the internet;

(5) substantive discussions with counsel, litigants, or reporters about the merits of a matter before the court;

(6) use of writing samples from judicial employment without adequate redaction and approval of the appointing authority; and

(7) internet and other electronic exchanges (anonymously, pseudonymously, or otherwise) about the court or its cases, including email, instant messaging, social networking postings (such as Twitter and Facebook), blog posts, and other internet comments or postings.

**C. Authorized disclosure.** Confidential information is authorized to be disclosed in the following circumstances:

(1) pursuant to a statute, rule, or order of the court, or authorization from the appointing authority;

(2) pursuant to a valid subpoena issued by a court or other competent body; and

(3) to report an alleged criminal violation to the appointing authority or other appropriate government or law enforcement official.

**D. Continuing obligation.** Confidentiality obligations do not end when judicial employment ceases or when a matter is completed or a case is closed. Former judicial employees should observe the same restrictions on disclosure of confidential information that apply to current employees, except as modified in accordance with Section 2.C. Confidentiality restrictions continue to apply with respect to open as well as closed and completed matters.

Judicial employees should consult their appointing authority if there is any doubt whether a certain disclosure is authorized before any disclosure is made.

3. Individual courts, judges and/or other appointing authorities may institute stricter standards than those outlined herein. They may also limit who is authorized to speak for the court or agency and the topics that specific judicial employees are allowed to address. The policies described in this document do not supersede or in any way override any stricter disclosure standards that a court, a judge, or other appointing authority may institute.

4. This Model Confidentiality Statement does not address, and in no way limits, the remedy or penalty that a court, judge, or other appointing authority may impose for a breach of an employee's duties of confidentiality, but all judicial employees should be aware that the Judiciary considers all such breaches to be serious, given the need to maintain the public's confidence in the impartiality of the judicial system.

## 5. Acknowledgment

To emphasize the importance of the duty of confidentiality, the court asks that you sign this statement as an acknowledgment that you have read it, understand it, and agree to abide by it, and further that you understand violations of these confidentiality obligations may result in disciplinary action.

_____
Signature

_____
                                                                    Date

**John Paul Jones**
*Some Ethical Considerations for Judicial Clerks*
4 GEO. J. LEGAL ETHICS 771 (1991)*

* * * *

WHAT GOES ON IN CHAMBERS STAYS IN CHAMBERS

A judge is bound by Canon 3 of the *Code of Judicial Conduct* to perform her duties impartially. She must not only refrain from public comment about a pending or impending proceeding in any court, but must also require similar abstention by her

---

clerks. In 1919, a clerk for Justice McKenna of the United States Supreme Court used inside information about decisions not yet announced by the Court to speculate in the stock market.

* * * *

## WHAT GOES ON IN CHAMBERS STAYS IN CHAMBERS PART II

Aside from the law clerk's derivative duty to refrain from comments indicating pre-judgment or bias regarding pending cases, he has a duty to preserve the privacy of the court. Thus, long after the case has been completed, an obligation may still exist to keep confidential that information to which the clerk had been made privy only through the special access he acquired as a member of the chambers staff. The authors of *The Brethren: Inside the Supreme Court* bragged that more than 170 former law clerks had contributed inside information to their expose of the inner workings of the Supreme Court. When law clerks or former law clerks tattle about the off-bench remarks, behavior, or collegiality of their judges, they violate the trust placed in them when they are invited into the private world of the chambers.

Just as the cloak of confidentiality enhances the effectiveness of the relationship between attorney and client, it also enhances the effectiveness of the relationship between law clerk and judge. One judge has written:

> My relationship with my law clerks is a close and confidential one. If I cannot speak freely to them, they cannot do their job for me. And I could not speak freely to them if I thought that my questions, soul-searching, and opinions would be made matters of public record or private conversation. There is often a good deal of give and take and what finally emerges may not have been anyone's original thought. If my half-formed ideas or preliminary thoughts are not kept confidential by my law clerks — then I will have to keep them confidential myself — and that will seriously impair the decision-making process.

Telling tales out of court is incompatible with the clerk's role as confidant and sounding board. It also threatens a major benefit of the clerkship for future clerks, and it should raise questions among the clerk's observers about his capacity for protecting the secrets of his future law firm and its clients.

———

Breaches of confidentiality and other ethical violations may result in specific penalties for judicial clerks and externs working in the judicial system, including complaints against the clerk or extern brought before a court's Committee on Judicial Conduct.

# RULES OF THE SUPREME COURT OF THE STATE OF NEW HAMPSHIRE ADMINISTRATIVE RULES 35 TO 59

## Rule 46.　Law Clerk Code Of Conduct.
### Canon 7. Compliance

A person to whom this Code becomes applicable should arrange his affairs as soon as reasonably possible to comply with it or receive a waiver from the Supreme Court. This Code shall apply to all full- or part-time law clerks or interns in all courts. Violations shall be brought before the Committee on Judicial Conduct which shall have jurisdiction over any complaints arising under this Code. A law clerk should initially refer any ethical questions under this Code to the justice to whom he is regularly assigned. In the event that in a rare instance he feels dissatisfied with the decision of the justice he may solicit the opinion of all of the justices on the court which he is serving. Such recourse to the justices shall be used with circumspection and without the divulging of such procedure to any persons except to the justices on the court which the law clerk duly is serving. The words "he," "him" or "his" shall equally apply to the feminine gender. Nothing in this Code shall limit any court from having any further and additional requirements for employment as a law clerk so long as they are not less restrictive than this Code. All courts or justices employing a full- or part-time law clerk or intern must file the name and address of such persons with the Clerk of the Supreme Court within two weeks of any such employment.

----

Many judges report they have not experienced breaches of confidentiality by law clerks. Comment, *The Law Clerk's Duty of Confidentiality*, 129 U. PA. L. REV. 1230, 1236–38 (1981) (*citing* WILLIAM O. DOUGLAS, THE COURT YEARS: 1939–1975, at 174 (1980)) ("In the long years I served, there was never any suspicion that a clerk violated a confidence of the Court.").

As mentioned by Professor Jones in his article, a law clerk to U.S. Supreme Court Justice Joseph McKenna in 1919, disclosed confidential information he had gained from his clerkship position. He revealed his inside information not to the public, but to his two co-conspirators who planned to use the information about the upcoming Court decisions to make a profit on Wall Street. For details about Ashton Embry and the allegations concerning this "clerk leak," *see* John B. Owens, *The Clerk, The Thief, His Life as a Baker: Ashton Embry and the Supreme Court Leak Scandal of 1919*, 95 Nw. U. L. REV. 271 (2000).

## 1.  Revealing Present Confidences

## IN RE CORRUGATED CONTAINER ANTITRUST LITIGATION
### 614 F.2d 958 (5th Cir. 1980)

FRANK M. JOHNSON, JR., CIRCUIT JUDGE

\* \* \* \*

C. Actions of Judge Singleton's Law Clerk

Defendants' final contention that Judge Singleton is disqualified from presiding further in the litigation is derivative in nature. Defendants assert that the conduct of Judge Singleton's law clerk necessitates his disqualification.[1] Since this Court has held that ordinarily a judge's bias, to be disqualifying, must run to a party rather than merely to the attorney, *Davis v. Board of School Comm'rs*, 517 F.2d at 1050–51, we think it fitting to restrict those situations in which the bias of a law clerk will work to disqualify the clerk's employer. Clearly, a law clerk's views cannot be attributed to the judge for whom the clerk works. Moreover, even if law clerks' opinions accurately reflected the views of their employers, we could not hold Judge Singleton disqualified in the present case because of actions and statements attributed to his law clerk.

Defendants allege that the law clerk voiced her opinions on the resolution of the criminal case to one of Mead's lawyers. Setting aside questions, of which we have many,

---

[1] [20] Baker's affidavit filed in support of this contention states that: It is my understanding that Judge Singleton's law clerk . . . was hired specifically to assist Judge Singleton in the criminal corrugated cases and the related civil corrugated cases. (The clerk) on or about May 9, 1979, shortly after the not guilty verdicts were returned April 27, 1979, told an attorney representing Mead in substance that defendants did not deserve to win the criminal trial and that plaintiffs' counsel in the civil cases would do a better job than the government counsel did in the criminal cases. At some time prior to June 6, 1979, (she) was reportedly interviewed by, or talked to a representative of, a trade magazine for purchasing agents, a group which includes employees of the named plaintiffs and class members in the pending corrugated container proceedings. (The clerk) was quoted in Purchasing magazine, published on June 6, 1979, as saying that "Industrial buyers may choose not to participate in the settlement and press their own suit, seeking higher payment. If a large number of companies decide to file their own suits, then the amount left of the $295 million for the others will be higher." . . . The statements attributed to (her) in this trade magazine constitute a recommendation (or may be reasonably so interpreted) that purchasers of corrugated containers opt out of the classes established for settlement and file their own suits. These statements . . . are particularly prejudicial in light of (her) expressed, and I believe well known, bias against defendants. . . .

Her statements could have a substantial adverse impact on the ultimate dollar liability of Mead and defendants generally in this civil litigation. This is especially so since notices to the class are now being prepared and will, in the normal course of events, be sent to prospective class members. The law clerk's statements to counsel outside the courtroom, her interview and the substance of her remarks, I believe, constitute bias on her part and taint the appearance of impartiality required of Judge Singleton and his law clerk in this massive pending litigation. Whether or not Judge Singleton assented to the interview or whether or not (her) public statements reflect the judge's viewpoints, her comments raise serious questions concerning the appearance of this Court's impartiality in these civil corrugated container proceedings.

of the propriety of such comments, they are clearly based upon her observations made in connection with the case. If Judge Singleton cannot be found disqualified for opinions he developed in the course of the litigation, it is difficult to comprehend how he could be found disqualified because of the opinions his law clerk developed in a judicial setting.

The law clerk also allegedly gave a press interview and, of course, defendants also urge that as a ground for the disqualification. In giving an interview with the press, the clerk most likely breached duties imposed upon her by Canons 3 A(6), [footnote and citation omitted] and 3 B(2), of the Code of Judicial Conduct for United States Judges. Nevertheless, the statements attributed to the clerk constitute no basis for disqualification of Judge Singleton. Indeed the statements express no opinion whatsoever. Rather, they merely state obvious fact: If fewer members of the class elect to participate in the settlement, each claimant's share will increase. There is no basis on which Judge Singleton should be disqualified.

---

## 2.   Revealing Past Confidences

Although a clerk should not make public comments on a pending proceeding nor reveal confidences obtained in chambers, may a former clerk ever reveal such information? Some attorneys read codes of conduct governing law clerks to require confidentiality after the clerkship has ended. "Confidential relationships simply would not be confidential if confidences could be breached as soon as the relationship ended." Richard W. Painter, *Clerks Honor Bound to Keep Confidences*, WALL ST. J., May 8, 1998, at A15. Other observers argue that some knowledge obtained while clerking may eventually be made public. *See* Jeffrey B. Abramson, *Should a Clerk Ever Reveal Confidential Information?* 63 JUDICATURE 361 (1980).

### Thomas G. Krattenmaker,
### *Looking Back at Cohen v. California: A 40-Year Retrospective from Inside the Court,*[*]
20 WM. & MARY BILL RTS. J. 651 (2012)

* * * *

Candor, if not modesty, requires that I state at the outset that my perspective is not (solely) that of a disinterested academic. During the 1970 Term of the Supreme Court, I had the good luck and great privilege to serve as one of Justice Harlan's law clerks. One of my tasks that year was to draft, at his direction, an opinion for the court in *Cohen*. With two alterations, Justice Harlan filed the opinion as drafted.

---

\* \* \* \*

Most of what I recount there comes from public records, such as the briefs, transcripts of oral arguments, and public papers of the Justices. Some, however, are remembrances of conversations I had with Justice Harlan. I have no doubt that I was under a strict cloak of confidentiality when I had these conversations and that my obligation to keep quiet about them stayed with me after I finished my clerkship. I also believe, however, that this "law clerk privilege" does not survive forty years later, when all the participants are dead, and most of the participating Justices have left their working papers pertaining to this case in public libraries. At some point, it seems to me, the values of unobstructed historical inquiry outweigh the privacy or secrecy interests of deceased Justices. Just where this point arises probably varies with the matter under discussion. Here, I believe that the few incidents, not already in the public realm, that I reveal have no capacity to harm anyone and may help current readers understand some aspects of the process of case resolution at the Supreme Court forty years ago.

---

Many judges, when surveyed, reported that they had not experienced problems with breaches of confidentiality by their law clerks. Comment, *The Law Clerk's Duty of Confidentiality*, 129 U. Pa. L. Rev. 1230 (1981). Some survey respondents concluded "permanent clerks may become an attractive alternative, especially if the confidentiality problem is perceived as chronic."

## 3. Judicial Privilege

Confidentiality of chambers, including discussions among judges, their judicial clerks, and their externs may be protected from disclosure by asserting a "judicial privilege." The "judicial privilege protects a judge who withholds evidence or refrains from testifying in court on matters related to her decision-making process. Necessity mandates that this protection include conversations and correspondence with fellow judges, attorneys, law clerks and other support personnel. The privilege belongs to the judge and would extend to bar testimony by members of the judge's chambers staff." Robert S. Catz & Jill J. Lange, *Judicial Privilege*, 22 Ga. L. Rev. 89, 147 n.3 (1987).

# IN THE MATTER OF THE ENFORCEMENT OF A SUBPOENA
### 972 N.E.2d 1022 (Mass. 2012)

Cordy, J.

\* \* \* \*

[T]he subpoena calls on the judge to produce seven categories of documents. The present petition is most directly concerned with the first category: "Any notes, notebooks, bench books, diaries, memoranda, recordation or other written recollections of any of the cases described in the Complaint, cited in our letter to you of October 24th, or described in the Boston Globe articles."

In response, the petitioner filed a motion for a protective order and a motion to quash or modify the subpoena before a single justice in the county court. He also contends that he cannot be compelled to testify about the twenty-three additional cases identified by special counsel because he has not been given adequate notice of the misconduct of which he is accused in those cases. The single justice reserved and reported the matter, without decision, to the full court.

*Statutory scheme.* We begin by briefly reviewing the mandate and investigatory powers of the commission. Established by St. 1978, c. 478, § 114, the commission has the "authority to receive information, investigate, conduct hearings, and make recommendations to the supreme judicial court concerning allegations of judicial misconduct." G.L. c. 211C, § 2(1). The commission may recommend that a judge be disciplined for various categories of misconduct, including "any conduct that constitutes a violation of the code[ ] of judicial conduct," G.L. c. 211C, § 2(5)(*e*), a code that, among other things, obligates a judge to "perform judicial duties without bias or prejudice." S.J.C. Rule 3.09, Canon 3(B)(5), as appearing in 440 Mass. 1301 (2003). Commission proceedings are not, however, "a substitute for an appeal," and "[i]n the absence of fraud, corrupt motive, bad faith, or clear indication that the judge's conduct violates the code of judicial conduct, the commission shall not take action against a judge for making findings of fact, reaching a legal conclusion, or applying the law as he understands it." G.L. c. 211C, § 2(4). On receiving a complaint stating facts that, if true, would be grounds for discipline, the commission must notify the judge and "conduct a prompt, discreet and confidential inquiry, investigation and evaluation." G.L. c. 211C, § 5(1). The commission is vested with broad investigatory powers, including the ability "to compel by subpoena the attendance and testimony of witnesses, including the judge, and to provide for the inspection of documents, books, accounts, and other records." G.L. c. 211C, § 5(4). This investigatory power is not, however, unlimited, and "[a] witness at any stage of commission proceedings may rely on any privilege applicable to civil proceedings." G.L. c. 211C, § 3(5). If the subpoena seeks to invade a "privilege applicable to civil proceedings," the judge, as a witness, would be entitled to assert it.

The subpoena at issue here plainly and admittedly directs the judge to produce notes and other material concerning his decision-making in cases over which he presided. Special counsel concedes that he is "concerned with understanding [the judge's] processes, methodology, and conduct in adjudicating cases before him," and considers it necessary to delve into the judge's mental processes because of the "notoriously elusive" and "difficult" task of proving bias. Consequently, we must decide whether there exists a privilege that protects the deliberative process of judicial decision-making.

*Judicial deliberative privilege.* In general, no person has a privilege to refuse to be a witness, refuse to disclose any matter, refuse to produce a writing, or prevent another from doing the same. Mass. G. Evid. § 501 (2012). "Testimonial privileges are exceptions to the general duty imposed on all people to testify." *Commonwealth v. Corsetti,* 438 N.E.2d 805 (Mass. 1982). Thus, the recognition of privileges contravenes the "fundamental maxim that the public . . . has a right to every man's evidence." *United States v. Bryan,* 339 U.S. 323 (1950). When we recognize testimonial privileges, a power "that we have exercised sparingly," *Babets v. Secretary of Human Servs.,* 526

N.E.2d 1261 (Mass. 1988), we do so on the basis that "excluding relevant evidence has a public good transcending the normally predominant principle of utilizing all rational means for ascertaining truth." *Three Juveniles v. Commonwealth*, 455 N.E.2d 1203 (Mass. 1983), *cert. denied*, 465 U.S. 1068 (1984). Therefore, it is important to examine the purposes and interests furthered by the recognition of a judicial deliberative privilege that have formed the basis for its universal recognition by courts that have considered its application.

*Finality.* To ensure the finality of judgments, judges have long been barred from testifying to impeach their own verdicts. "A judgment is a solemn record. Parties have a right to rely upon it. It should not lightly be disturbed, and ought never to be overthrown or limited by the oral testimony of a judge or juror of what he had in mind at the time of the decision." *Fayerweather v. Ritch*, 195 U.S. 276 (1904). We have more recently affirmed the underlying importance of this rule to the integrity and finality of decision-making. In *Glenn v. Aiken*, 569 N.E.2d 783 (Mass. 1991), a trial attorney sought to defend against a claim of legal malpractice by introducing an affidavit prepared by the judge regarding his decision-making at a trial the attorney was alleged to have mishandled. Citing *Fayerweather v. Ritch, supra*, we held that "summoning judges to testify on such matters" was inappropriate and that "[p]robing the mental processes of a trial judge, that are not apparent on the record of the trial proceeding, is not permissible." *Glenn v. Aiken*, 569 N.E.2d 783. See *Day v. Crowley*, 172 N.E.2d 251 (Mass. 1961), quoting *Fayerweather v. Ritch* (judgment is solemn record not to be overthrown or limited by what judge "had in mind" at time of decision). We agreed with the reasoning of the United States Court of Appeals for the Fifth Circuit that thought processes reconstructed years after the fact are unlikely to be accurate, and that "the finality and integrity of judgments would be threatened by a rule that enabled parties to attack a judgment by probing the mental processes of a judge." [citations omitted].

* * * *

2. *Quality and integrity of decision-making.*

In addition to ensuring the finality of judgments, protecting judges from the post hoc probing of their mental processes also ensures the integrity and quality of judicial decision-making. Federal and State courts faced with requests to question judges or their law clerks regarding judicial deliberations have underscored the importance of protecting that process, not just for the sake of the judge's personal interests, but to ensure the quality and integrity of decision-making that benefits from the free and honest development of a judge's own thinking and candid communications among judges and between judges and the courts' staff in resolving cases before them. See *State ex rel. Kaufman v. Zakaib*, 535 S.E.2d 727 (W. Va. 2000) (shielding judges protects public more than judge because "judges could not do their jobs if their internal thought processes were subject to examination"). "If the rule were otherwise, the advice that judges receive and their exchange of views may not be as open and honest as the public good requires. . . . In order to protect the effectiveness of the judicial decision-making process, judges cannot be burdened with a suspicion that their deliberations and communications might be made public at a later date." *Thomas v. Page*, 837 N.E.2d 483 (Ill. App. Ct. 2005). See *Matter of Certain Complaints Under Investigation by an Investigating Comm. of the Judicial Council of the Eleventh Circuit*, 783 F.2d 1488, 1519–1520 (11th Cir.), *cert. denied*, 477 U.S. 904 (1986) (*Williams*) ("Judges . . . depend upon open and candid discourse with their colleagues and staff to promote the effective discharge of their duties").

This court has also censured attorneys who attempted to "pierce the confidential communications of a former law clerk and a judge in a pending matter to benefit one of the litigants." *Matter of Curry*, 880 N.E.2d 388 (Mass. 2008). We deemed such attempts to be "prejudicial to the administration of justice," which requires "respect for the internal deliberations and processes that form the basis of judicial decisions, at very least while the matter is still pending." *Id*. Confidentiality in the inner workings of the court is appropriate "in order to foster frank and open discussions between judges and clerks, which promote more effective decision-making." *Matter of Crossen*, 880 N.E.2d 352 (Mass. 2008).

### 3. *Independence and impartiality.*

The judiciary's independence from the other branches of government and from outside influences and extraneous concerns has been one of the cornerstones of our constitutional democracy, intended to ensure that judges will be free to decide cases on the law and the facts as their best judgment dictates, without fear or favor.

The writings of John Adams preceding the drafting and adoption of the Massachusetts Constitution developed and articulated the essential linkage between judicial independence and impartial decision-making:

> "[Judges'] minds should not be distracted with jarring interests; they should not be dependent upon any man, or body of men. To these ends, they should hold estates for life in their offices; or, in other words, their commissions should be during good behavior, and their salaries ascertained and established by law."

\* \* \* \*

### 4. *Recognition of privilege.*

As the foregoing makes clear, the need to protect judicial deliberations has been implicit in our view of the nature of the judicial enterprise since the founding. Consequently, we join other courts, State and Federal, that, when faced with attempts by third parties to extract from judges their deliberative thought processes, have uniformly recognized a judicial deliberative privilege. See *Williams, supra; Thomas v. Page*, 837 N.E.2d 483 (Ill. App. Ct. 2005); *In re Cohen's Estate*, 174 N.Y.S. 427, 428 (N.Y. Sur. 1919); *Leber v. Stretton*, 928 A.2d 262, 270 (Pa. Super. 2007); *State ex rel. Kaufman v. Zakaib*, 535 S.E.2d 727 (W. Va. 2000). See also *United States v. Morgan*, 313 U.S. 409 (1941) (mental processes of judge cannot be subjected to scrutiny; "[s]uch an examination of a judge would be destructive of judicial responsibility"); *Grant v. Shalala*, 989 F.2d 1332, 1344 (3d Cir. 1993) (noting threat to administrative law judges and serious interference with ability to decide cases solely on evidence and law if thought process subject to subsequent inquiry; "[i]t has long been recognized that attempts to probe the thought and decision making processes of judges . . . are generally improper"); *Nixon v. Sirica*, 487 F.2d 700, 740–742 (D.C. Cir. 1973) (MacKinnon, J., concurring) (source of judicial privilege "rooted in history and gains added force from the constitutional separation of powers.")

To the extent that "[e]xpress authorities sustaining [a judicial privilege] are minimal," it is "undoubtedly because its existence and validity has been so universally recognized." *Id.* At 740. [citations omitted] Special counsel has not cited, nor have we been able to locate, a single case rejecting the existence of a privilege for a judge's mental processes or intra-court deliberative communications.

*Scope of judicial privilege.* Having established that a judicial deliberative privilege exists and, consequently, that it applies to commission proceedings, see G.L. c. 211C, § 3(5), we turn to defining the privilege's scope. If the privilege is absolute, "the opposing party cannot defeat the privilege by an ad hoc, case-specific showing of need for the privileged information." *Thomas v. Page*, 837 N.E.2d 483, quoting E.J. Imwinkelried, *The New Wigmore: A Treatise on Evidence* § 3.2.4, at 139–140 (2002). A qualified privilege, on the other hand, does not prevent disclosure in every instance. "[T]he investigating party can attempt to show the importance of the inquiry for which the privileged information is sought; the relevance of that information to its inquiry; and the difficulty of obtaining the desired information through alternative means. The court then must weigh the investigating party's demonstrated need for the information against the degree of intrusion upon the confidentiality of privileged communications necessary to satisfy that need." [citation omitted]. If a sufficient showing of need is made, the qualified privilege can be overcome even if the information sought falls within its scope.

In light of the important interests served by the recognition of a judicial deliberative privilege, as discussed, *supra*, we agree with the Illinois Appeals Court and the West Virginia Supreme Court that the best approach is to consider this privilege narrowly tailored but absolute. [citations omitted]. This absolute privilege covers a judge's mental impressions and thought processes in reaching a judicial decision, whether harbored internally or memorialized in other nonpublic materials. The privilege also protects confidential communications among judges and between judges and court staff made in the course of and related to their deliberative processes in particular cases. *Thomas v. Page*, 837 N.E.2d 483.

It does not cover a judge's memory of nondeliberative events in connection with cases in which the judge participated. Nor does the privilege apply to inquiries into whether a judge was subjected to improper "extraneous influences" or ex parte communications during the deliberative process. By definition, such influences and communications lie outside the protected sphere of the judge's internal deliberations. As in jury deliberations, inquiry into extraneous influences does not probe into "subjective mental processes," and "[t]he existence of such influences often can be objectively ascertained, and many times the evidence can be corroborated." *Commonwealth v. Fidler*, 385 N.E.2d 513 (Mass. 1979).

In addition, the privilege does not apply when a judge is a witness to or was personally involved in a circumstance that later becomes the focus of a legal proceeding. These cases concerning "acts that simply happen to have been done by judges" do not implicate a judge's deliberative processes during the course of his official duties. *State ex rel. Kaufman v. Zakaib*, 535 S.E.2d 727 (W. Va. 2000); *Leber v. Stretton*, 928 A.2d 262, 270 n.12 (Pa. Super. 2007).

*Judicial investigations.* "[J]udges who do not abide by those high and well recognized standards of personal and judicial conduct to which they must be held cannot employ the argument of judicial independence as a shield when questionable practices on their part are challenged." *Matter of DeSaulnier*, 279 N.E.2d 296 (Mass. 1972). See *Matter of Troy*, 306 N.E.2d 203 (Mass. 1973). However, contrary to the special counsel's assertions, the recognition of a judicial deliberative privilege will not overly impede the commission's investigations. Indeed, in prior cases, the commission has never needed to use information falling within the scope of this privilege to conduct its proceedings.

\* \* \* \*

*Application.* In the present case, so much of the subpoena as relates to the judge's internal thought processes and deliberative communications, memorialized in notes, diaries, or otherwise, must be quashed. The remaining portions of the subpoena are not objectionable. Neither party has suggested the text of a revised subpoena that does not intrude on the judicial privilege we have recognized. We remand the matter to the single justice to oversee the issuance of a revised subpoena in the first instance.

## SHEPPARD v. BEERMAN
### 18 F.3d 147 (2d Cir. 1994)

ALTIMARI, CIRCUIT JUDGE:

[A former state court judicial clerk brought a civil rights action against his former employer. The clerk alleged that after a dispute and then dismissal over the clerk's accusations that the judge had made *ex parte* communications with counsel, the judge had violated the Fourth Amendment by searching the clerk's office, desk, and file cabinets.]

An "employee's expectation of privacy must be assessed in the context of the employment relation[ship]." The working relationship between a judge and her law clerk, as noted by the district court, is unique. Unlike a typical employment relationship where an employer may limit the information she wants to share with her employees, in order for a judicial chambers to function efficiently, an absolute free flow of information is usually necessary. Accordingly, the clerk has access to all the documents pertaining to a case. More importantly, clerks regularly have access to the judge's confidential thoughts on a case. The judge may discuss her feelings with her clerk, or may allow the clerk access to her personal notes. In turn, the judge necessarily has access to the files and papers kept by the clerk, which will often include the clerk's notes from discussions with the judge. Because of this distinctive open access to documents characteristic of judicial chambers, we agree with the district court's determination that Sheppard had "no reasonable expectation of privacy in chambers' appurtenances, embracing desks, file cabinets or other work areas."

Accordingly, the district court was correct in finding that there was no violation of Sheppard's Fourth Amendment rights.

## B.   Clerk or Extern's Conflict of Interest

## 1.   Future Employment & Family Relations

Current clerks and externs both must consider potential conflict of interests. When working on cases pending before the court, the clerk and extern should research the parties and attorneys appearing before the court. Clerks and externs may be applying for or have accepted work at legal employers appearing in court. Externs may be working in a law school clinic or in a part time position with a law firm or government employer such as a prosecutor's office. This law student work can also create conflicts of interest.

**John Paul Jones**
***Some Ethical Considerations for Judicial Clerks***
4 Geo. J. Legal Ethics 771 (1991)*

* * * *

POTENTIAL CONFLICTS ARISING FROM FUTURE
EMPLOYMENT AND FAMILY

The brief terms of most clerkships make possible conflicts of interest and the appearance of impropriety. A clerk who begins a term in chambers already assured of association afterwards with a particular law firm would face a conflict of interest were she to involve herself with a case in which her future employers appear. In *Oliva v. Heller*, a law clerk was sued for more than five million dollars in damages for working on a prisoner's petition for post-conviction relief after having accepted an offer from the U.S. Attorney's office. In *Miller Industries, Inc. v. Caterpillar Tractor Co.*, the court found that a law clerk's continued participation in a case in which the clerk's future employers were counsel required disqualification of his judge. In *Hall v. Small Business Administration*, the court found, relying on 28 U.S.C. § 455, that a magistrate should have recused himself when he learned on the first day of trial that his law clerk was a member of the plaintiff class in the sexual discrimination suit, and that she had left defendant's employ complaining of sexual discrimination, and that she had accepted a job offer from plaintiff's counsel.

Many judges make it known to applicants for their clerkships that they prefer lawyers who will join local firms after their stint with the judge. Such a preference increases the likelihood of conflicts involving law clerks, and such clerks ought to be retained by judges only after consideration of the concomitant risk to efficient chambers administration. In any case, decisions about what to do about apparent

---

conflict of interest, like most other decisions in his court, belongs to the judge, not the clerk. "Judges recuse themselves, not law clerks." Law clerks ought to heed the advice of Rule 1.12 of the Model Rules and keep their judges informed about employment interviews and offers.

Judge Alvin B. Rubin, who authored the opinion in *Hall v. Small Business Administration*, opined in a handbook for federal law clerks: "When a clerk has accepted a position with an attorney or with a firm, that clerk should cease further involvement in those cases in which the future employer has an interest." Judge Rubin's strict view of law clerk purity no doubt stems from his experience in an appellate court, in which several judges are each served by three law clerks. Withdrawal by one law clerk will be relatively painless for the appellate judge who can easily recruit a stand-in from his own or from another judge's chambers. However, many other courts lack such resources. Like federal magistrates, many state judges enjoy the services of but one clerk; indeed, some judges must share a single clerk. Substitutes can be hard to come by in rural courts.

The limitations of a small pool of available law clerks might seem well illustrated by the web of conflicts potentially handicapping Judge Raymond Acosta's use of his law clerks in mass tort litigation in Puerto Rico. Fifty-one Puerto Rican law firms appeared for 2,300 defendants at a time when less than 500 lawyers comprised the entire federal bar of the island. One clerk's brother was a partner in a San Juan law firm representing 58 plaintiffs; the other clerk's brother was a member of the firm representing the defendant corporation. In *In re Allied-Signal, Inc.*, the Court of Appeals declined to order a mistrial or disqualify Judge Acosta despite the potential appearance of impropriety presented by his clerk's family connections. Writing for the court, Judge Breyer took some pains to distinguish this case from others in which a law clerk's family connections create at least the appearance of impropriety. Recognizing that "the appearance of impropriety" has a relativist component, the Appeals Court noted that:

> The risk that a law clerk, or some other staff member, will have a brother or sister or some other family member involved in this case is a likely concomitant of trying such a large case in a small district. . . . [A] knowledgeable objective observer is therefore more likely to see the relation as implicit in the special circumstances than as an odd coincidence the failure to avoid which might suggest bias.

In addition to the external context in which the impropriety is tested, Judge Breyer noted that Judge Acosta had shown an appreciation for circumstances which demanded withdrawal by granting a recusal motion in an earlier case in which both a former law clerk and a brother of the only available current law clerk appeared as counsel. In a complex case such as *Allied Signal*, however, the benefit of the normally appropriate procedure of denying the clerk's participation in the case was outweighed by the potential contributions of two career law clerks that had been with Judge Acosta since the case began.

Judge Breyer appears not to have considered the relative ease with which substitutes untarnished by family connections could have been recruited for temporary assignment to Judge Acosta. Judge Breyer mistakenly measured the pool of available law clerks by the number on the island of Puerto Rico. Fixing the sum of available clerk resources at the number locally available arbitrarily overstated the burden on Judge Acosta of preventing even the appearance of impropriety. But judicial clerks ought to be at least as interchangeable as federal judges, when substitution is prompted by the appearance of impropriety. The pool of available substitutes should therefore be measured nationwide. Certainly volunteers among judicial clerks and staff attorneys unrelated to members of the law firms involved in the suit could have been found elsewhere in the First Circuit (if not elsewhere in the federal court system) willing to take an assignment to Judge Acosta's chambers in San Juan — particularly if they were approached in the wintertime. In declining to order Judge Acosta to remove his clerks from the case, Judge Breyer assigned too little weight to the importance of consistency in dealing with questions of judicial impropriety and too much weight, as did Judge Acosta, to the court's convenience. Whether real or imagined, the influence said by some to be exercised by law clerks over their judges makes the appearance of impropriety by a law clerk as serious as the appearance of impropriety by his judge. Rules and remedies for the former are reasonably drawn from among those for the latter.

As Judge Acosta's case illustrates, family relationships, like employment, can produce apparent conflicts of interest for the law clerk. In *Parker v. Connors Steel Co.*, the court found an appearance of partiality where the law clerk's father was a partner in the law firm representing a party. While the appellate court did not require the trial judge's recusal in either *Parker* or *Allied Signal*, the judges' handling of the issue came under close scrutiny on appeal. To avoid the necessity for such scrutiny, the law clerk owes the judge prompt notice of either family or career connections with a case in the judge's court.

Federal law prohibits the appointment of a federal judge's family member to "any office or duty in any [federal] court." The Comptroller General has stated that the position of law clerk is not an office or duty within the meaning of this prohibition, so the anti-nepotism statute apparently does not prevent a judge from appointing as a law clerk his own or a colleague's relative. The Judicial Conference's Advisory Committee on Codes of Conduct has announced, however, that the Code of Judicial Conduct sets a standard stricter than that of the nepotism statute, and prohibits a judge from hiring as her clerk the son or daughter of a judge sitting on the same court. The Committee relied upon Canons 2 and 3(B)(4) as the basis for its opinion. A similar limitation ought to bind every judge.

---

The "small pool of available law clerks" in Puerto Rico to serve Judge Acosta as he undertook in a massive tort litigation case created potential conflicts because of the many law firms serving as counsel. Those firms included family members of clerks and also could have represented future employers of those law clerks.

# ARIZONA SUPREME COURT
# JUDICIAL ETHICS ADVISORY COMMITTEE
# ETHICAL ISSUES IN CASES INVOLVING
# PROSPECTIVE EMPLOYERS OF LAW CLERKS
Opinion 01-02
December 31, 2001

## ISSUES

1. Must judges be informed of their law clerks' law-related job applications, interviews, and offers? **Answer**: Yes.

2. Is a judge required to screen a law clerk from cases involving a law firm, public agency, or other entity with whom the clerk obtains future employment? **Answer**: Yes, once the clerk accepts a job offer and, depending on the circumstances, perhaps even earlier in the process.

3. When a law clerk receives and accepts a job offer from a law firm, public agency, or other entity with matters pending before the judge, must the judge disqualify himself from such cases? **Answer**: Yes, with qualifications.

## FACTS

A law clerk employed by a superior court judge applied for a position with the local county attorney's office. He ultimately received a job offer and accepted a position with that office. Before his interviews, the clerk worked on a post-conviction relief petition that was pending before the judge. He performed legal research and wrote a partial draft minute entry. After the interview process began, the clerk edited his work in non-substantive ways but did not change his recommendations in the proposed minute entry. After the clerk resigned and began his new job, the judge prepared a final order denying relief to the petitioner. The judge relied on the clerk's work in preparing the order.

## DISCUSSION

Judges typically employ law school graduates as clerks for relatively brief periods of time. During their tenure with the court, clerks often apply for and negotiate employment with law firms or public agencies. This practice can raise questions about the judge's impartiality when prospective employers of the clerk have matters pending before the court in question. Judges routinely rely on law clerks' legal research and writing in making decisions, and there is a general consensus that "[r]egardless of actual influence, the perception of law clerks' influence on judges is present, even among lawyers." *Protecting the Appearance of Judicial Impartiality In the Face of Law Clerk Employment Negotiations*, 62 Wash. L. Rev. 813, 820 (1987). Recognizing that the pending inquiry is relatively narrow and fact-specific, this opinion will nevertheless address broader issues implicated by the job-seeking activities of law clerks.

Issue 1

Canon 3E(1) requires disqualification "in a proceeding in which the judge's impartiality might reasonably be questioned." Although the standard is an objective one, it is the appearance of partiality, more than the reality, that is at issue. *See Matter of Haddad*, 128 Ariz. 490, 627 P.2d 221 (1981) (judge is required not only to *be* impartial, but to *be seen* as impartial). *See also* Opinion 95-11 (test under Canon 3E(1) is "whether a person of ordinary prudence in the judge's position knowing all the facts known to the judge could find that there is a reasonable basis for questioning the judge's impartiality"). A judge who himself is negotiating for employment must recuse from any matters in which the prospective employer appears, absent full disclosure to the parties and counsel and waiver of any conflict. *See* Canon 3E(1), commentary.

Law clerks must comply with the Code of Conduct for Judicial Employees. Among other things, the code requires judicial staff to: (1) manage personal and business matters so as to avoid an appearance of conflict; (2) inform the appropriate supervisor of any potential conflict; and (3) withdraw from participation in any proceeding in which they have an interest that may appear to influence the outcome. Canon 4C.

The committee concludes that law clerks must advise their employing judges of all law-related job applications, interviews, and offers. They should take special care to inform (and remind) judges on a timely basis when a prospective employer has a matter pending before the court.

Issue 2

The next question is whether clerks must be screened from cases involving a prospective employer. Requiring automatic screening of cases based on any job application or interview could be problematic — especially for judges assigned to a criminal problematic — especially for judges assigned to a criminal calendar, where the number of prospective employers (particularly on the prosecution side) is limited. An excellent discussion of the legal and policy considerations relating to screening of clerks can be found in the comment cited above, "Protecting the Appearance of Judicial Impartiality in the Face of Law Clerk Employment Negotiations."

The comment advocates screening of clerks once a job offer is extended, but not before. It correctly notes that law clerks often apply with numerous prospective employers. At such a preliminary stage, any appearance of partiality by the judge is relatively attenuated and would not meet the "reasonably questioned" standard of Canon 3E(1). Moreover, mandating screening based merely on job applications, interviews, and even job offers would likely lead to significant restrictions on clerks' job-seeking activities and a corresponding difficulty in attracting talented, qualified law graduates. It also would unduly impede the swift and orderly disposition of cases in trial and appellate courts.

As the employment process progresses through the interview and into the negotiation and job offer phases, however, the appearance of conflict becomes more pronounced. Incentive for a clerk to consciously or unconsciously affect the outcome of a pending matter is enhanced. The committee concludes that once a clerk accepts a job offer, he or she should be screened from all cases involving the clerk's future employer. After that point, the clerk may not continue working on such matters, even if he or she has work in progress that started before the job offer was made and accepted.

Even before a law clerk actually accepts a job offer, the judge should take a close look at any pending matters that the clerk is working on and that involve a prospective employer that has interviewed or extended a job offer to the clerk. Depending on the nature and extent of any further work the clerk may need to do, the judge, in his or her discretion, may choose to screen the clerk from any further involvement in such matters. The judge probably should err on the side of caution in those situations, particularly in light of law clerks' obligation under Canon 4C(3) of the employee code to "withdraw from participating in a court proceeding" in which they have a personal or business interest "that may actually or appear to influence the outcome."

In addition, although the committee has established a law clerk's acceptance of a job offer as the point at which the clerk must be screened from any cases involving the future employer, courts may choose to adopt a more restrictive or stringent standard. *See* Arizona Code of Conduct for Judicial Employees, Preamble ("The minimum standards contained in this code do not preclude the adoption of more rigorous standards by law, court order or local rule."). For example, section 3D(4)(c) of the "Law Clerk Code of Conduct," adopted by the Arizona Supreme Court in 1984, does not require a law clerk's recusal from participation in a case involving a law firm to which an application for employment is pending. That same section, however, provides that "if serious or active negotiations are underway, the law clerk should so inform the judge, and volunteer to withdraw from the case."

Many courts have approved screening of clerks as an alternative to disqualification of judges. *See Hunt v. American Bank & Trust Co.*, 783 F.2d 1011 (11th Cir. 1986); *Bartel Dental Books Co., Inc. v. Schultz*, 786 F.2d 486 (2nd Cir. 1986); *Milgard Tempering, Inc. v. Selas Corp. of America*, 902 F.2d 703 (9th Cir. 1990); *In re Cooke*, 160 B.R. 701 (D. Conn. 1993). While the Arizona courts have not specifically addressed the issue, in an analogous context, our Rules of Professional Conduct allow screening of government lawyers who transfer to the private sector. *See* Rule 42, Ariz. R. S. Ct., ER 1.11. *See also State v. Superior Court*, 184 Ariz. 223, 708 P.2d 37 (App. 1995). Similar policy considerations support screening of law clerks versus *per se* disqualification of judges.

If prompt screening of a clerk does not occur once the law clerk has accepted a job offer, the judge must recuse himself unless the parties and counsel waive any conflict after full disclosure. *See, e.g., Miller Industries, Inc. v. Caterpillar Tractor Co.*, 516 F. Supp. 84 (S.D. Ala. 1980) (disqualification required when clerk accepted job with plaintiff's firm during trial but continued to work on case); *Hall v. Small Business Administration*, 695 F.2d 175 (5th Cir. 1983) (impermissible appearance of partiality where clerk accepted job with plaintiff's firm during class action litigation).

Issue 3

Based on the foregoing principles, after a law clerk accepts a job offer from a law firm, public agency, or other entity with matters pending or impending before the judge, disqualification is required unless the clerk is screened from any substantive work and discussion in such matters, or unless the parties and counsel waive the apparent conflict pursuant to Canon 3F. A party would likely question the judge's impartiality upon learning of the clerk's continued work on a case after having accepted a job offer from an adverse party or its legal representative. Even if a reasonable person would not necessarily question the judge's impartiality in such circumstances, the judge should disqualify himself or herself in the absence of the screening or waiver discussed above.

## CONCLUSION

Applying the foregoing analysis to the pending inquiry, the judge was not ethically required to disqualify from the case after the law clerk applied for and ultimately accepted a position with the county attorney's office. Nor was the judge ethically prohibited from using the law clerk's prior work product in preparing the final order. After interviewing with the county attorney's office, the clerk here performed only minor, editorial work on his existing draft and did not alter his prior recommended disposition of the pending matter. Under these circumstances, one cannot reasonably question the judge's impartiality in continuing on and disposing of the case after the clerk had resigned and begun his new job.

## 2.   Current Employment as Judicial Clerk

While future employment and employment negotiations raise difficult issues, even more serious conflicts can arise when a judicial clerk undertakes to represent parties in his or her judge's courtroom, while still serving as a judicial clerk to their judge.

## SALLIE v. STATE
### 499 S.E.2d 897 (Ga. 1998)

THOMPSON, JUSTICE.

This is a death penalty case. William C. Sallie was convicted of malice murder and other crimes, and the jury recommended a death sentence. Because one of Sallie's trial lawyers was laboring under a conflict of interest, we reverse the convictions and remand for a new trial.

1. Considered in the light most favorable to the verdict, the evidence showed that Sallie was embroiled in divorce proceedings with his wife, Robin. In the early morning hours of March 29, 1990, Sallie entered the home of his in-laws, where his wife and infant son were staying. He was armed with a pistol and carrying handcuffs, and he had also cut the telephone lines to the house. Sallie proceeded directly to the master bedroom and shot Robin's parents, killing his father-in-law and wounding his mother-in-law. Sallie then abducted his wife and her sister, took them to a trailer he had rented in Liberty County, and raped them. The evidence of Sallie's guilt is sufficient to support the convictions. *Jackson v. Virginia*, 443 U.S. 307 (1979).

2. Sallie contends that one of his appointed trial lawyers, Wendell Boyd English, was

operating under a conflict of interest that effectively denied Sallie his Sixth Amendment right to counsel. We agree. Shortly after his arrest, the trial court appointed Earl McRae to defend Sallie. McRae asked for assistance and the trial court appointed Boyd English as McRae's co-counsel in May 1990. English represented Sallie until the conclusion of his trial in March 1991.

The conflict arises from English's concurrent employment as the sole judicial law clerk for the Waycross Judicial Circuit. Employment records show that English was employed as the circuit's law clerk from April 1987 to May 1989, and from August to October 1990. He was rehired in December 1990, four months before Sallie's trial, and continued as the circuit's law clerk until 1996.

The state claims that English was a part-time law clerk who only worked for the chief judge of the circuit. English further states in his affidavit that he was hired by the chief judge as his personal law clerk and that he had no contact in his capacity as a law clerk with the other two superior court judges in the Waycross Circuit, including the trial judge. Payroll records, however, show that English was expected to work at least 40 hours per week and that his monthly pay ranged from about $1,800 in 1987 to $2,350 in 1996. In addition, English's personnel forms list his position as "Law Clerk-Waycross Judicial Circuit," and state that he serves the circuit. OCGA § 15-6-28(a), the statute which authorized English's position, provides that the chief judge of each judicial circuit can hire one law clerk or court administrator *for the circuit*. Thus, under state law, only one law clerk position per circuit may be compensated with state funds and English's payroll records clearly show that he was paid by the state. See OCGA § 15-6-28(a), (b), (h). Although English served at the pleasure of the chief judge of the Waycross Circuit, OCGA § 15-6-28I, it is clear that his position served the entire circuit and all three superior court judges in the circuit.

The federal and state constitutions guarantee criminal defendants the effective assistance of counsel. *Strickland v. Washington*, 466 U.S. 668 (1984); Ga. Const. Art. I, Sec. I. "Counsel's function is to assist the defendant, and hence counsel owes the client a duty of loyalty, a duty to avoid conflicts of interest." *Strickland*, supra at 688, citing *Cuyler v. Sullivan*, 446 U.S. 335, 346 (1980). Undivided loyalty is an essential element of the right to counsel. "Where a constitutional right to counsel exists, our Sixth Amendment cases hold that there is a correlative right to representation that is free from conflicts of interest." *Wood v. Georgia*, 450 U.S. 261, 271 (1981).

We have never before addressed a conflict of interest that arises from a lawyer's simultaneous role as criminal defense attorney and law clerk in the same court where he is trying the case. We have also not uncovered any cases in other jurisdictions that present the same issue. Most criminal conflict-of-interest cases involve one attorney representing multiple defendants. See e.g. *Meyers v. State*, 454 S.E.2d 490 (Ga. 1995); *Mitchell v. State*, 405 S.E.2d 38 (Ga. 1991); *Wilson v. State*, 359 S.E.2d 661 (Ga. 1987). A few cases involve law clerks, but are unlike the situation now before us. See *Todd v. State*, 410 S.E.2d 725 (Ga. 1991) (prosecutor employed by the district attorney's office during defendant's trial became law clerk for judicial circuit while motion for new trial was pending); *Potts v. State*, 376 S.E.2d 851 (Ga. 1989) (former law clerk became defendant's attorney); *Pope v. State*, 345 S.E.2d 831 (Ga. 1986) (prosecutor who worked on state's brief on direct appeal had been law clerk during defendant's trial). The situation in this case is unique because English occupied the job of criminal defense attorney and law clerk in the same court *at the same time.*

We conclude that an actual conflict of interest existed in this case and reverse the convictions. There is no need to embark on an analysis of *Cuyler,* supra, and its progeny: the conflict here is obvious and, given the enormity of the penalty in this case, completely impermissible. Sallie did not waive his right to conflict-free representation. The evidence is uncontroverted that he was never informed of English's role as the law clerk for the Waycross Judicial Circuit.

Sallie's lawyer represented a capital defendant in the same court in which he was a full-time law clerk. We cannot allow such a conflict of interest to exist in a death penalty case. See *Chapel v. State,* 443 S.E.2d 271 (Ga. 1994) (attorney disqualified in capital case due to conflict of interest and appearance of impropriety); *Fleming v. State,* 270 S.E.2d 185 (Ga. 1980) (slight conflict of interest not permitted in death penalty case); Code of Professional Responsibility, Canon 9. We therefore reverse and remand for a new trial.

3. Our disposition of the conflict-of-interest claim renders the consideration of Sallie's remaining enumerations of error unnecessary.

*Judgment reversed.*

# DEYLING v. FLOWERS
## 1979 Ohio App. LEXIS 12242 (Sept. 27, 1979)

STILLMAN, P.J.

This cause came on to be heard upon the pleading and the transcript of the evidence and record in the Common Pleas Court, and was argued by counsel; on consideration whereof, the court certifies that in its opinion substantial justice has not been done the party complaining, as shown by the record of the proceedings and judgment under review, and judgment of said Common Pleas Court is reversed. Each assignment of error was reviewed by the court and upon review the following disposition made.

This appeal arises from a judgment for plaintiffs-appellees in the Court of Common Pleas for Cuyahoga County. Kenneth and Yvonne Deyling filed a complaint against Stanley and Victoria Flowers alleging that they were the owners of an easement for roadway purposes over a strip of land running north from Pleasant Valley Road, Independence, along the eastern line of the Flowers' property to the Deylings' property and that the Flowers had obstructed and interfered with the claimed easement. Monetary damages and injunctive relief were sought. The Flowers filed counterclaims.

The case came before Judge James Kilbane. The trial was scheduled for March 20, 1978. The Deylings appeared in person and were represented by counsel. Mr. Flowers appeared in his own behalf, Mrs. Flowers was not in attendance or represented by counsel. The trial judge appointed his law clerk, Mr. Jerry Federman to assist in the presentation of defendant's case. Mr. Flowers was dismissed as a defendant as he had no interest in the real property at issue. Mr. Federman was asked by the court to represent the absentee Mrs. Flowers. Appellees, the Deylings, presented their case-in-chief. The trial continued until April 17, 1978, at which time Mrs. Flowers appeared, represented by counsel. Mrs. Flowers' attorney moved to strike the testimony offered on March 20, 1978, which motion was denied. The counterclaims were dismissed. Appellant presented her defense.

The trial court found that Mrs. Flowers' property was subject to an easement in favor of the Deylings' property and that the Flowers had obstructed the use of said easement; the obstruction was ordered removed. Further, the court found the Flowers had erected a corral in the rear of the property, extending onto the Deylings' property, and ordered it removed.

Mrs. Flowers has taken a timely appeal asserting three assignments of error:

I. THE TRIAL COURT ERRED BY FINDING AN EASEMENT FOR ROADWAY PURPOSES.

II. THE TRIAL COURT ERRED BY APPOINTING ITS LAW CLERK TO REPRESENT APPELLANT AND IN OVERRULING APPELLANT'S MOTION TO STRIKE THE TESTIMONY FROM THE HEARING WHEN THE LAW CLERK REPRESENTED APPELLANT.

III. THE TRIAL COURT ERRED IN FINDING THAT APPELLANT'S FENCE EXTENDED ONTO APPELLEES' PROPERTY AND ORDER-ING REMOVAL OF THE FENCE.

We will first consider Assignment of Error No. II as it is dispositive of this appeal. Apparently, in an effort to expedite the trial and give defendant-appellant a day in court, the trial judge appointed his law clerk to represent Mr. Flowers, and then when the latter was dismissed as a party defendant, to represent the absent Mrs. Flowers. The judge's explanation was that "Mr. Federman has researched the law for me. He knows the law." Although Mr. Flowers stated, "I don't think that Mr. Federman would know the case in detail because we have such short notice," he reluctantly agreed. Mrs. Flowers did not consent to Mr. Federman's representation of her interests after the dismissal of her husband from the case.

Plaintiffs' case was then presented. During Fred Deyling, Sr.'s testimony, numerous lengthy interjections were made by his sons, Fred Jr. and Kenneth Deyling, although they had not yet been sworn as witnesses. No objections were made to this informal testimony by the Deylings, or to drawings offered and comments on the documentary evidence. Deyling's counsel introduced a number of photographs of the alleged easement obstruction, but no documentary evidence. The only documents were introduced by Mr. Federman during his cross-examination of the plaintiffs' four witnesses. No exhibits were admitted into evidence during this stage of the proceedings. Plaintiffs' counsel rested; Mr. Federman made no motion at the close of the plaintiffs' case.

Mr. Federman's representation of Mrs. Flowers' interests is prohibited in R.C. § 4705.01, which provides in pertinent part:

No sheriff, deputy sheriff, or coroner shall practice as an attorney at law in any court of this state, and no clerk of the supreme court or court of common pleas, or the deputy of either, shall practice in the particular court of which he is clerk or deputy. . . .

In addition, two provisions of the Code of Professional Responsibility speak to such representation:

DR 5-101. Refusing Employment When the Interests of the Lawyer May Impair His Independent Professional Judgment

(A) Except with the consent of his client after full disclosure, a lawyer shall not accept employment if the exercise of his professional judgment on behalf of his client will be or reasonably may be affected by his own financial, business, property, or personal interests.

\* \* \* \*

DR 9-101. Avoiding Even the Appearance of Impropriety

\* \* \* \*

(B) A lawyer shall not accept private employment in a matter in which he had substantial responsibility while he was a public employee.

It is next to impossible for one to be employed by a judge, researching the law of a case, and represent the defendant in that case before that same judge. Inherent in such a dual representation is the likelihood that a clerk has already made recommendations on the legal issues before the trial and the secondary danger that the clerk, as attorney, will be more concerned with impressing the judge for whom he works than protecting the interests of his client.

Similarly, the Code of Judicial Conduct provides in pertinent part:

### CANON 2

#### A Judge Should Avoid Impropriety and the Appearance of Impropriety in All His Activities

A judge should respect and comply with the law and should conduct himself at all times in a manner that promotes public confidence in the integrity and impartiality of the judiciary.

Appointing one's law clerk to defend a client in one's court in derogation of R.C. § 4705.01 and then allowing the trial to progress without observation of the fundamental rule against unsworn testimony does little to promote public confidence in the integrity and impartiality of the judiciary.

In light of the above considerations, we find that by refusing to strike the testimony elicited while Mr. Federman represented Mrs. Flowers, Mrs. Flowers was denied a fair trial and this case should be reversed and remanded for a new trial.

For this reason, it is not necessary to discuss the merits of Assignments of Error

Nos. I and III, the court's finding of an easement for roadway purposes and the determination that the Flowers' fence extended onto the Deylings' property, respectively. However, we note that both findings rest in part upon the results of a survey conducted for the Deylings by a civil engineer. The record fails to reveal that this individual ever testified or that the survey was ever admitted into evidence despite the trial judge's recollection to the contrary.

Accordingly, Assignment of Error No. II is well taken and the case is reversed and remanded for a new trial in accordance with this opinion.

———————

Judicial externs may serve the court for a semester or two, but this is long enough to create the potential for conflict of interests, often because of an extern's past, present, or future employment — whether legal or non-legal.

# UNILOC USA v. MICROSOFT CORP.
### 2007 U.S. Dist. Ct. Motions LEXIS 5242 (D.R.I. May 11, 2007)

## MEMORANDUM OF LAW IN SUPPORT OF PLAINTIFFS' MOTION FOR RECUSAL

Plaintiffs, Uniloc USA, Inc. and Uniloc Singapore Private Limited (together, "Uniloc"), respectfully submit this Memorandum of Law in Support of their Motion for Recusal of District Judge William E. Smith pursuant to 28 U.S.C. § 455(a). For the reasons set forth below, Uniloc requests that this motion be granted.

## I. INTRODUCTION

At the hearing on May 2, 2007, Judge Smith directed that Uniloc either "accept on the record the fact that I'm going to continue to work on this case, and I'm going to do so with the assistance of Mr. Eddon, this intern, and you're going to place on the record that you have absolutely no objection to me doing that" or, in the alternative, file a motion to recuse Judge Smith. Ex. A, p. 8, 12.

Due to Mr. Eddon's financial, contractual, personal and legal relationships with defendant Microsoft and its employees, his contemplated engagement as an intern to assist the Court in resolving Microsoft's motion for summary judgment creates at least "an appearance of partiality."

## II. PROCEDURAL BACKGROUND

By a letter dated March 20, 2007, Judge Smith advised counsel that the Court had the opportunity to hire an intern and explained that, over the years, this individual had previous contacts with Microsoft Research, Microsoft Systems Journal and Microsoft Press, a division of defendant Microsoft. Ex. B, p. 1. The Court indicated that the prospective intern did not feel that these contacts would prevent him (the intern) from being impartial in this matter. *Id.* The Court requested counsel to express their views regarding the proposed intern:

I think it would be prudent to seek your views as to whether you believe any of these past (or present) involvements present a conflict of interest that would prevent his participation in this case.

Please communicate your views in writing to me within ten days of this letter.

*Id.* at 2.

Both parties responded to the Court's invitation. On March 29, 2007, counsel for Microsoft sent the Court a letter stating Microsoft's belief that the proposed intern's past connection with Microsoft would not present a conflict of interest. Ex. C. In view of the numerous connections between Microsoft and the proposed intern, on March 30, 2007, counsel for Uniloc sent the Court a letter stating, *inter alia,* that "the appearance and concomitant possibility of bias exists" regarding the proposed intern and citing *Reilly v. United States,* 863 F.2d 149, 159 (1st Cir. 1988) for the proposition that such an independent expert should be identified before he or she is appointed. Ex. D.

In a letter to counsel dated April 18, 2007, the Court identified the proposed intern as Mr. Eddon and expressed satisfaction that the appointment of Mr. Eddon to assist on this case would not pose any ethical problems, notwithstanding his past or present connections with Microsoft. Ex. E. In addition, the Court advised counsel that the parties could file a motion to recuse Judge Smith if they felt differently, although the Court did not feel a basis for recusal exists. *Id.* at 2.

Having received the proposed intern's name, Uniloc conducted additional research to determine whether this individual could objectively be seen to be impartial. On April 23, 2007, counsel for Uniloc submitted a letter detailing the significant connections between Mr. Eddon and Microsoft and stated that Uniloc maintained its objection to the proposed intern. *See,* Ex. F. Counsel for Uniloc also stated that, although Mr. Eddon should not be permitted to work on this case, Uniloc did not believe that Judge Smith should be recused. *Id.* at 2.

In response to Uniloc's April 23, 2007 letter, the Court scheduled a hearing, which took place in open court on May 3, 2007. Relevant to the present motion are the following comments by the Court at that hearing:

- "let me make it clear, I have hired Mr. Eddon, and he is coming to work for me" (Ex. A, at p. 7);

- "But you can't separate the intern from me. That's the thing you're trying to do. He is part of my staff. He is going to work on this case." (*id.* at 9) (*but, see,* footnote 2 below discussing recusal of clerk or intern);

- "And if you believe that [Mr. Eddon] has a bias, then that is the same as saying you believe I have a bias" (*id.* at 9);

- "it's not my practice, generally, to ask parties in a case whether they approve of the law clerks I hire or the interns I hire. You don't get that veto power" (*id.* at 11);

- "I want it very clear on the record, either that you are not moving to recuse with the full understanding that Mr. Eddon will work on this case as part of my staff, or that you are moving to recuse." (*id.* at p. 12).

## III. DISCUSSION

As previously indicated, Uniloc does not have any reason to question the impartiality of Judge Smith. Uniloc has been instructed, however, that it cannot maintain its objection to Mr. Eddon without filing a motion to recusal Judge Smith. Given this choice, Uniloc moves for recusal.[2]

### A. Legal Standard

Uniloc grounds its motion upon 28 U.S.C. § 455(a), which states as follows:

> Any justice, judge, or magistrate judge of the United States shall disqualify himself in any proceeding in which his impartiality might reasonably be questioned.

This provision "requires recusal wherever the objective circumstances create an *appearance* of partiality." *In re Martinez-Catala*, 129 F.3d 213, 220 (1st Cir. 1997) (emphasis in original). The test is whether "the facts provide what an objective, knowledgeable member of the public would find to be a *reasonable basis* for doubting the judge's impartiality." *In re United States*, 666 F.2d 690, 695 (1st Cir. 1981) (emphasis in original). "[D]oubts ordinarily ought to be resolved in favor of recusal." *In re United States*, 158 F.3d 26, 30 (1st Cir. 1998). The decision to grant a motion for recusal is committed largely to the discretion of the trial court. *United States v. Giorgi*, 840 F.2d 1022, 1034 (1st Cir. 1988).

### B. Objective Facts Supporting Recusal

The objective facts regarding Mr. Eddon — deemed by the Court to be one and the same with Judge Smith for the purposes of this motion — strongly support recusal. Uniloc respectfully submits that, if these connections between Mr. Eddon and Microsoft instead were between Judge Smith and Microsoft, they would instantly require recusal.

The connections between Mr. Eddon and Microsoft include at least the following:

---

[2] Authority exists wherein it has been recognized that a clerk or intern whose impartiality may be questioned should be recused, not the judge. *See e.g., In re* Allied Signal, Inc., 891 F.2d 967, 972–73 (1st Cir. 1989), *cert. denied*, 495 U.S. 957 (1990) ("[i]f a clerk has a possible conflict of interest, it is the clerk, not the judge who must be disqualified") (quoting Hunt v. Am. Bank & Trust Co., 783 F.2d 1011, 1016 (11th Cir. 1986)); Simonson v. General Motors Corp., 425 F. Supp. 574, 575–76 (E.D. Pa. 1976) (unpaid, part-time intern hired by the Court prohibited from working on case in which a possible appearance of partiality may exist but permitted to continue working on other cases).

1. Publishing Through Microsoft Press

Mr. Eddon has published the following books through Microsoft Press, a division of Microsoft:

- *Programming Components with Microsoft visual Basic 6.0 Second Edition;*
- *Active Visual Basic 5.0;*
- *Inside COM+Base Services;* and
- *Inside Distributed COM.*

Exs. G–J.

The retail price of these books, each of which runs to several hundred pages, was between $39.99–$49.99. *See,* Exs. G–J, last pages. It is fair for the objective observer to assume that Mr. Eddon received, and may still receive, royalties or other remuneration from Microsoft Press as a result of the sales of his books by Microsoft Press.

In view of Microsoft Press publishing numerous books for Mr. Eddon, and Mr. Eddon's assignment of copyright to Microsoft Press and joint copyright ownership with defendant Microsoft set forth below, it is inescapable that one or more publishing and/or assignment agreements (written or verbal) have been entered into by Mr. Eddon and Microsoft/Microsoft Press.

2. Mr. Eddon's "Indebtedness" To Microsoft

From the prefaces to these books, it is apparent that Mr. Eddon worked closely with Microsoft Press and Microsoft editors and related personnel in preparing these books. In the Preface to his book, *Programming Components with Microsoft Visual Basic 6.0,* Exhibit G, p. xi, Mr. Eddon expresses his indebtedness and gratitude for the "moral support" provided to him by his "friends" at Microsoft Press, a division of Microsoft:

> In writing this book we are indebted to many others. We thank our friends at Microsoft Press [a division of Microsoft], including Eric Stroo, who entrusted us with the project and provided moral support in times of need . . . and the rest of the gang at *Microsoft Systems Journal* and *Microsoft Interactive Developer.*

In *Inside Distributed COM,* Mr. Eddon likewise expresses his gratitude to Microsoft employees for supporting him with preparing the book:

> Mark Ryland, Charlie Kindel, Mary Kirtland, and Sanji Abraham of Microsoft Corporation supported us throughout this project by answering many questions. (We hope that this small token of gratitude will earn us some brownie points for future questions.)

Ex. J. Preface, p. xvi.

Similar statements appear in Mr. Eddon's other books published by Microsoft Press. Copies of the Prefaces are found in Exhibits G–J.

3. Assignment of Copyright

A search of the copyright office records reveals that Mr. Eddon has also assigned copyrights in at least two of the above-identified publications to Microsoft Press. A copy of the copyright office records disclosing these assignments is submitted herewith as Exhibit K. Thus, Mr. Eddon has had other contractual connections to Microsoft Press, "a division of [defendant] Microsoft Corporation." *Id.*

4. Mr. Eddon and Microsoft are Joint Copyright Owners

Each of Mr. Eddon's books published by Microsoft Press includes a CD to allow the purchaser to view the book's contents on a computer. Each of the CDs displays a copyright notice. The copyright notice for the CD sold with the book *Inside COM + Base Services* states as follows:

> Copyright (c) 1999 Microsoft Corporation
>
> Portions copyright (c) Guy Eddon and Henry Eddon
>
> All rights reserved.

*See,* Ex. L, p. 1.

The CDs sold with the books *Programming Components with Microsoft Visual Basic 6.0 Second Edition* and *Active Visual Basic 5.0* contain similar copyright notices. *Id.* at 2–3. Thus, as the copyright notices indicate, Microsoft is a joint owner with Mr. Eddon of the copyrights in at least these three CDs. Joint owners of a copyright are deemed to be tenants in common, with each owner having an undivided, independent right to use the work but with a duty to account for profits to each co-owner. *See, e.g.,* Berge v. Bd. of Trustees, Univ. of Alabama, 104 F.3d 1453, 1461 (4th Cir. 1997).

Microsoft's copyrights in these CDs have not expired and will not expire for approximately another 86 years. *See,* 17 U.S.C. § 302. Mr. Eddon's copyrights will likely extend beyond that. *Id.* Thus, Mr. Eddon and Microsoft will be joint owners and tenants in common with respect to these copyrights for many years to come. Clearly, were the Court a joint copyright owner and tenant in common with Microsoft, the Court would not have been able to sit on this case.

Mr. Eddon's four books published through Microsoft Press also include a license agreement for use of the CDs. The license agreement, however, is not between Mr. Eddon and the purchaser of the book. The agreement is entitled "MICROSOFT LICENSE AGREEMENT" and is between the purchaser of the book and defendant herein, Microsoft Corporation (as opposed to Microsoft Press). *See,* Exs. M–P. As a result, Mr. Eddon has entrusted defendant Microsoft to protect his joint copyright with Microsoft in the CDs.

5. Publishing Through Microsoft Systems Journal/MSDN

Over the years, in addition to his four books published by Microsoft Press, Mr. Eddon has published numerous articles through the *Microsoft Systems Journal* and MSDN. *See, e.g.,* Ex. Q. 4. In several of his publications, Mr. Eddon expresses his admiration for defendant Microsoft and its technology. For example, in *Inside*

*Distributed COM: Type Libraries and Language Integration,* Mr. Eddon states that:

> Visual J++ is Microsoft's answer to both of these ideas; it is a great Integrated Development Environment (IDE) for Java development and provides Java/COM integration features.

Ex. R, p. 23.

In *Internet Explorer Version 3.0: Not Just Another Web Browser,* Mr. Eddon discusses the "very cool" and "other neat features" of Microsoft's Internet Explorer product. Ex. S, pp. 2–3. Thus, Mr. Eddon has expressed a partiality for Microsoft's products.

6. Microsoft Funding for Mr. Eddon

In its letter to counsel dated March 20, 2007, the Court advised the parties that Mr. Eddon has "over the years, received funding from Microsoft Research grants." *See,* Ex. B., p. 1. The amount of such funding has not been disclosed. Uniloc submits that such funding to Mr. Eddon would cause a reasonable person objectively to doubt the impartiality of Mr. Eddon in a case in which Microsoft is a party.

7. Mr. Eddon's Subjective Belief

In the letters to counsel dated March 20 and April 18, 2007, the Court states that Mr. Eddon believes that he can be impartial in this matter and is not biased in favor of any party. *See,* Exs. B and E. The test, however, is an objective one, *In re Martinez-Catala,* 129 F.3d at 220, not whether Mr. Eddon subjectively believes he is impartial. Thus, Uniloc submits, Mr. Eddon's belief is not germane to this issue at hand.

C. The Factual Basis For Recusal Has Been Established

Recusal is required wherever the objective circumstances "create an *appearance* of partiality." *In re Martinez-Catala,* 129 F.3d at 200. Uniloc has been ordered by the Court to treat Judge Smith and Mr. Eddon as the same for the purpose of this motion to recuse. Uniloc respectfully submits that if Judge Smith himself had, *inter alia,* (1) published four separate books through Microsoft Press; (2) received royalties or other remuneration from Microsoft as a result of the sales of such books; (3) an ongoing contractual arrangement with Microsoft to pay to him royalties or other remuneration in the future; (4) joint copyright ownership with Microsoft; and (5) professed in at least two publications readily available to the public his "indebtedness" to Microsoft, such would, at the very least, create an *appearance* of partiality. Accordingly, Uniloc submits that recusal is appropriate.

## IV. CONCLUSION

For the reasons set forth above, Uniloc requests that this motion be granted.

## 3.    Former Clerks and Externs as Counsel in Their Judges' Courts

Even after a clerkship has ended, potential conflicts of interest may remain. Former clerks and externs appearing as practicing attorneys before the judges they had served as clerks can present a number of problems. Former clerks and externs may, as practicing attorneys, become involved in litigation which began while they were working as clerks.

# FREDONIA BROADCASTING CORP., INC. v. RCA CORP.
## 569 F.2d 251 (5th Cir. 1978)

TJOFLAT, CIRCUIT JUDGE

\* \* \* \*

Once it appeared that Fredonia might have an unfair advantage in the litigation because its counsel included a lawyer who had been exposed to the trial judge's innermost thoughts about the case, the trial judge had no alternative to disqualifying himself. No matter how many assurances were given by Fredonia's counsel that the former law clerk would withdraw from the case, we think it clear that the propriety of continuing the proceedings before this district judge had been irrevocably tainted, and the impartiality of the judge had been reasonably questioned.

\* \* \* \*

A law clerk, by virtue of his position, is obviously privy to his judge's thoughts in a way that the parties cannot be. We are not holding that a former law clerk may never practice before the judge for whom he clerked. Such a holding would clearly be unwarranted and would cast an undue burden on the law clerk. Moreover, it would hinder the courts in securing the best qualified people to serve as law clerks. What is offensive here is that the district judge seemed to countenance the notion that the law clerk could improperly use the specific knowledge gained from working with him on this particular case. The impartiality of a trial judge is seriously open to question when the judge refuses to recuse himself after being made aware that his former law clerk is actively involved as counsel for a party in a case in which the law clerk participated during his clerkship.

\* \* \* \*

Because of the nature of the judge-law clerk relationship, this trial judge invited serious questions to his impartiality when he refused to recuse himself.

\* \* \* \*

Section 455(a) is a general safeguard of the appearance of impartiality and establishes a "reasonable factual basis reasonable man" standard. *Parrish*, 524 F.2d at 103. We hold that a reasonable man, viewing the facts as they stood at the time of RCA's motion, would reasonably question this trial judge's impartiality and the integrity of the judicial system. The district judge could not remain in the case. Consequently, we find that we must remand this case once again, this time for a trial before a different judge.

We note here that nothing in the record before us would preclude the law firm representing Fredonia from continuing to serve as counsel before another district judge. Disqualification of counsel is a drastic measure and conceivably could have due process implications, especially when counsel has served throughout proceedings as involved and lengthy as these and the client's investment in legal representation is substantial.

---

# SMITH v. PEPSICO, INC.
### 434 F. Supp. 524 (S.D. Fla. 1977)

ROETTGER, DISTRICT JUDGE

Defendants have filed a joint motion for recusal based solely on the fact that plaintiff's attorney, Barbara Pariente, was a law clerk for this judge for a period of two years ending more than two years ago. Because no affidavit of bias or prejudice has been filed by the parties as required by 28 U.S.C. § 144, the court will treat this motion as having been brought pursuant to 28 U.S.C. § 455(a).[2] In determining whether a judge should disqualify himself under the latter provision the appropriate test is whether a reasonable person knowing all of the circumstances would be led to the conclusion that the judge's "impartiality might reasonably be questioned." 28 U.S.C. § 455(a); *see Parrish v. Board of Com'rs of Alabama State Bar,* 524 F.2d 98 (5th Cir. 1975); *Davis v. Board of School Com'rs of Mobile County,* 517 F.2d 1044 (5th Cir. 1975). This standard is sufficiently broad to require recusal both in those circumstances where partiality is in fact present and where only the appearance of partiality is present. *See Lawton v. Tarr,* 327 F. Supp. 670 (E.D.N.C. 1971). Nonetheless this standard is still one of reasonableness and should not be interpreted to require recusal on spurious or vague charges of partiality. *Mavis v. Commercial Carriers, Inc.,* 408 F. Supp. 55 (C.D. Cal. 1975).

---

[2] [1] The body of the motion is as follows: "COME NOW the defendants herein, by and through undersigned counsel, and move the Honorable Norman C. Roettger to recuse himself from the case herein and in support thereof state: 1. Plaintiff's attorney, Barbara Pariente, as (sic) the law clerk to the Honorable Norman C. Roettger for approximately two years. 2. Plaintiff's attorney, Barbara Pariente, left the court's employ approximately two years ago. 3. As law clerk to the Honorable Norman C. Roettger, Barbara Pariente had a close working relationship to the Honorable Norman C. Roettger, was privy to the bulk of his decisions, and was continuously relied upon by him. WHEREFORE, all defense counsel herein pray that the Honorable Norman C. Roettger will enter an order recusing himself from the within cause."

In the instant case there has been no suggestion that the court has obtained extra-judicial information as a result of any communication with his former law clerk. (There, of course, has been none.) *Cf. United States v. Sieffert*, 501 F.2d 974 (5th Cir. 1974). Nor has there been any suggestion that the court has violated any section of the Code of Judicial Conduct.

The use of law clerks, and even third-year law students as interns under a law school clinical program, has spawned a number of challenges to a District Judge. In each case the challenge has been rejected by the Court of Appeals or the motion to disqualify has been denied by the District Judge. *Wolfson v. Palmieri*, 396 F.2d 121 (2d Cir. 1968) (a former law clerk is an assistant prosecutor); *U.S. v. Trigg*, 392 F.2d 860 (7th Cir. 1968) (Judge's former law clerk was court-appointed trial counsel for the defendant who claimed the natural reaction of a former law clerk would prevent him from effectively representing his client); *Simonson v. General Motors Corp.*, 425 F. Supp. 574 (E.D. Pa. 1976) (Law student intern was also clerking on a part-time basis with law firm representing the defendant General Motors Corp.); and *Reddy v. Jones*, 419 F. Supp. 1391 (W.D.N.C. 1976) (One of the judge's present law clerks had accepted employment with law firm representing one of the parties). When one of the parties has been a former law clerk, recusal has occurred, apparently sua sponte. *Wall v. Coleman*, 393 F. Supp. 826 (S.D. Ga. 1975).

Although these decisions reveal no precedent in support of the motion, the court has additionally considered the most closely analogous situation: when the trial judge is a former law partner of a firm now appearing in litigation before the court. Such relationship in the past has been held an insufficient basis for recusal. *Bumpus v. Uniroyal Tire*, 385 F. Supp. 711 (E.D. Pa. 1974); *Cf. Broome v. Simon*, 255 F. Supp. 434 (W.D. La. 1965); Interim Advisory Committee on Judicial Activities, Advisory Opinion No. 24 (1972). Although the working relationships between a judge and the judge's law clerks are admittedly close and considerable mutual respect is traditionally the case, as was the case here, the past association by itself is less strong than the closeness of a law partnership which often endures for many years and entails mutually inherent risks to fortune and honor. Thus, accepting defendants' allegations as true there are insufficient facts for a reasonable person to question the court's impartiality and, therefore, for the court to recuse itself.

Inasmuch as "appearance of partiality" may vary from district to district it would seem appropriate to apply a "community standard" (if that principle may be borrowed from the obscenity field) to recusal questions under § 455(a). Several of the judges of the Southern District of Florida, including the undersigned, have recused themselves from cases involving their former law firms for a period of one year after becoming a judge, although at least two of the judges have continued to recuse themselves from all such cases.[3]

---

[3] [3] As reflected in *Bumpus v. Uniroyal Tire*, *supra*, the Eastern District of Pennsylvania follows a custom of recusal for a period of two years from cases involving the judge's former law firm. There is a paucity of reported decisions setting forth recusal periods in various districts. The larger incidence of recent decisions involving former law clerks vis-a-vis former law partners may reflect the bar's suspicion that law clerks exert an undue influence on judges compared with their acceptance, albeit unenthusiastic, of judges' former law firms practicing in the same court.

Even if a court were to recuse itself for the same length of time whether the cases involved former law clerks or former law partners, the prevailing custom in this district is for a recusal period of one year. Because Ms. Pariente left the court's employ more than two years ago that disqualifying period has long since passed.

The court observes in passing that some judges (but not the undersigned) employ law clerks with the specific expectation that the clerks will remain in that city or area to practice law. If a court were to accept the contention that recusal was necessary whenever any counsel had been a prior law clerk to a judge, this would be an unfair penalty placed upon former law clerks of Federal Judges. In addition, United States judges themselves would suffer an obvious limitation on their recruiting of talented law clerks in the future.

It is therefore ORDERED AND ADJUDGED that defendants' motion for recusal is hereby denied.

## C.   Decision-Making on the Record

**John Paul Jones**
***Some Ethical Considerations for Judicial Clerks***
4 GEO. J. LEGAL ETHICS 771 (1991)[*]

* * * *

### JUDGES AND THEIR CLERKS ARE CONSTRAINED BY THE RECORD

As the judge's research assistant, the law clerk is free to investigate as thoroughly as time permits the legal issues presented in a case before the court. The same is not true for issues of fact. A law clerk must curb her curiosity about matters of fact when it cannot be satisfied by what has been placed in the record. She is not free to do her own investigation to supplement facts provided by the parties, except as to facts of which the court is free to take judicial notice. Such facts generally include only those within everyday common knowledge and those readily ascertainable from indisputable sources. Otherwise, the law clerk must confine herself to the record, or else she and her judge can be accused of prejudice against a party.

* * * *

The obligation to remain within the scope of the record goes beyond refraining from inspections of the scene. It extends to *ex parte* communication to the judge of facts relevant to the disposition of the case. The law clerk's role as a judge's research assistant does not make every communication between judge and clerk proper. On the contrary, when a clerk offers a judge deciding a case information about anything but

---

[*] Copyright © 1991. Reprinted with permission of the publisher, Georgetown Journal of Legal Ethics.

law, the clerk usurps the role of counsel. Such communications are improper, only in part because they are typically *ex parte*.

As a judge's research assistant, a clerk is expected to discover relevant law in published cases and promulgated statutes or regulations. To discover the law itself, a clerk is often expected to add the gloss of its published interpretations by legal scholars. That the law clerk frequently delivers to the judge his findings about law only after the record is closed, and without particular notice to the attorneys, seems nevertheless fair for the parties because of a convention regarding accessibility: The law and its interpretation is presumed to be out there for every lawyer to find. Clearly, albeit curiously, this convention reaches not only law found in the public record, but also its interpretation, which is often found in privately published journals and treatises. In light of this convention, the clerk and his judge do not prejudice a party when the clerk delivers *ex parte* the results of legal research, even when such research includes cases or law review articles unmentioned by counsel in briefs or comments on the record. Indeed, a clerk's discovery of binding precedent not previously offered by counsel ought to be a moment of triumph for the clerk and satisfaction for his judge.

The same is not, and should not, be true for the clerk's report of facts other than law and its associated commentary. Here applies the court's obligation to consider and decide within the constraints of a record dictated by counsel. Just as a law clerk's visit to the scene breaches the record of the case, so should a law clerk's gleaning of facts by research other than legal libraries or databases. Where, for example, the record leaves the judge unclear about how a machine, a bank, a drug, or a culture operates, the clerk ought not to repair to the local library for a text on the subject. Neither the social nor the physical sciences ought to be presumed to be as accessible to the legally trained as the law and its interpretation. Thus, the convention regarding communications about law should not reach facts, and a law clerk generally ought not to engage in research to enlarge upon the non-legal facts of the record.

Judicial notice, as an alternative convention, permits a judge to introduce into the record certain facts, but only after alerting counsel and affording them the opportunity to challenge or qualify the source from which these facts are to be drawn. Thus, if a judge and her clerk conclude that research to produce additional facts is essential, the record should be reopened in order to record notice to counsel and their response to either the importance of the research or the validity of its results.

If supplementation of the facts in the record by a law clerk's research is normally to be discouraged and is only to be permitted in most instances after notice and comment by counsel, then it should follow with equal vigor that a clerk cannot offer his judge his expertise in matters other than law. Judges Levanthal and Wyzanski are both known to have engaged particular law clerks because of their non-legal expertise. Judge Wyzanski appointed a Harvard economist as his law clerk to assist with a difficult antitrust case. Judge Levanthal employed a scientifically trained clerk to help with difficult environmental cases. While Judge Wyzanski later admitted he would not make another such appointment, in part because of his concerns about the undue influence on the judge of an expert in chambers, Judge Levanthal called for special clerkships reserved for the scientifically trained. When a law clerk, also trained as an economist or a biologist, is available within chambers to offer economic or biologic information to a judge deciding factual issues of economics or biology, the parties' right to a decision on the record is violated. Affording notice and an opportunity for comment on the clerk's findings cannot alleviate the harm without leading inexorably to the law clerk's transmutation from chambers staff to witness.

Success in a field other than law ought not, however, create an obstacle to subsequent appointment as a law clerk by a judge overzealous to prevent the appearance of impropriety by the suggestion of *ex parte* fact finding or improper influence. Any limitation on the communications between a judge and her chambers staff must, in the end, be largely self-enforced. The judge who announces a preference for one or more non-legal backgrounds ought to make clear to her law clerks from the outset how the record must limit the clerk even in the field of his expertise. Just as a careful clerk working for a careful judge will always relate each proposed conclusion of law to a case or statute, a careful clerk working for a careful judge will always relate each finding of fact to the specific part of the record in which supporting evidence can be found. Such a practice is the best safeguard against extra-record fact finding.

\* \* \* \*

# PRICE BROTHERS COMPANY v. PHILADELPHIA GEAR CORPORATION
## 649 F.2d 416 (6th Cir. 1981)

JOHN W. PECK, SENIOR CIRCUIT JUDGE

This is an appeal from a judgment entered in a diversity action for breach of contract and breach of warranties. Plaintiff, Price Brothers Company, a manufacturer of reinforced concrete pipe, brought an action against Philadelphia Gear Corporation, claiming that machine components produced by the defendant and used in Price Brothers' pipe wrapping machine had failed to perform as represented. At the conclusion of a trial to the bench, the district court entered judgment for the plaintiff and awarded $125,864.15 in damages. The defendant appealed both the conclusion as to liability and the award of damages, and the plaintiff cross-appealed, asserting that the damage award was inadequate.

## I.

Among the issues raised by Philadelphia Gear's appeal is an assertion that the trial court relied on information outside the record in reaching its decision. As one basis of this contention, Philadelphia Gear alleged that prior to the trial the trial judge's law clerk had traveled from Dayton, Ohio, to Beacon, New York, and had observed the operation of the pipe wrapping machine that is at the center of this controversy. Philadelphia Gear argued that the law clerk's observations were presumably reported to the trial judge, and speculated that this report may have been relied on by the judge in making his findings. Philadelphia Gear asserted that it had no knowledge of the clerk's trip prior to its occurrence, that it therefore had no opportunity to be present when the clerk observed the machine, and that it had no opportunity to review or rebut any report made by the clerk to the judge. Philadelphia Gear argues that the fact finding potentially based on the nonevidentiary observation by the law clerk is clearly erroneous as a matter of law.

Philadelphia Gear first raised the issue of the law clerk's off-the-record involvement by a motion made after entry of judgment, pursuant to Fed. R. Civ. Pro. 59(c), asking the court to amend its findings to reflect the fact of the law clerk's visit. The district judge denied that motion without comment on the law clerk's involvement. With the record in the state just described, serious questions regarding the impartiality of the fact-finding were necessarily noted by this Court on appeal. *Price Bros. Co. v. Philadelphia Gear Corp.*, 629 F.2d 444 (6th Cir. 1980).

It is imperative that a finder of fact avoid off-the-record contacts that might bias its judgment or otherwise impair its ability to fairly and objectively weigh the evidence properly submitted at trial. A judge presiding at a bench trial may not directly or indirectly, through his law clerk or by any other means, conduct an investigation outside the record and use the results of that investigation in determining the facts of a case. It need hardly be mentioned that what a judge cannot do in person he may not do by proxy. The fact that the clerk rather than the judge made the trip and observed the machine in no way alters the problem. The fair and impartial administration of justice demands that facts be determined only upon the evidence properly presented on the record. Furthermore, it is incumbent on the finder of fact to protect the appearance, as well as the fact, or its impartiality. It is fundamental that no judgment can be maintained under circumstances that suggest that the fact finder may have relied on covert, personal knowledge rather than on the evidence produced in open court and subject to review by the parties, the public, and the appellate court.

A view by the fact finder of places or objects related to a lawsuit does not *per se* destroy the fact finder's impartiality. Where the purpose of a view is to assist the fact finder to better understand evidence properly introduced, and the view itself is not considered as evidence, then the potential for prejudice to a party not present at the view is minimized. In contrast, where the fact finder's observations upon a view are used as evidence to determine the facts, then the procedural safeguards of a trial, including the rules of evidence and the participation of the parties must apply.

Unfortunately, from the record originally presented to this Court it could not be determined if the trial judge's law clerk had observed the pipe wrapping machine, and if such an observation did occur, how it was used by the trial judge. Accordingly, we remanded for an evidentiary hearing on the questions of whether the law clerk had viewed the machine, what the law clerk reported to the trial judge, when the defendant learned of the view by the clerk, whether the defendant consented to the view, and, most importantly, what use the trial judge made in deciding the case of whatever the law clerk had observed.

On remand, a district judge not previously involved in this case conducted a hearing directed at the questions recited above. Testimony was elicited from the trial judge's law clerk and secretary, attorneys for both parties, and other witnesses. In addition, the trial judge submitted a statement concerning the matters that necessitated the remand.

The undisputed testimony from the hearing answers several of the questions presented. The law clerk did, at the direction of the trial judge, travel to New York and observed the operation of the pipe wrapping machine at the premises of the plaintiff. Counsel for neither party were present. The clerk's conversations with plaintiff's employees were limited to identifying the machine that the clerk had come to see and identifying a part of the machine in response to a question from the clerk.

It is unfortunate that our remand "for an evidentiary hearing and report" (629 F.2d at 447) was interpreted by the district judge conducting the hearing to mean that no findings of fact were required of him. We are unable, on the basis of the cold record of the hearing, to resolve conflicting testimony as to when the defendant first learned of the law clerk's view of the machine and whether defendant consented to it. Fortunately, however, the questions answered by the undisputed testimony produced at the hearing and by the trial judge's statement do permit us to resolve the issue of whether the trial judge's fact finding was critically impaired by his law clerk's off-the-record observations and report. Thus, whether the defendant consented to the view by the clerk and is thus estopped from asserting prejudice based on that view become irrelevant.

The view involved in this case was more than a simple observation of the place where a specified event was alleged to have occurred. The subject viewed here, the machine, was under the control of the plaintiff. The plaintiff had the opportunity to manipulate what the law clerk saw in order to present an image most favorable to the plaintiff. The defendant was not present to learn what the law clerk observed, what conversations the law clerk had with plaintiff's employees, or what impressions the law clerk conveyed to the trial judge. Obviously, the defendant could not rebut any of the off-the-record information that the trial judge received from this source. These factors created a presumption of prejudice to the defendant in the trial judge's determination of facts that must be rebutted before his decision can stand.

Based on the undisputed testimony produced at the hearing on remand, we conclude that the presumption of prejudice arising from the law clerk's report of off-the-record observations has been overcome. The law clerk's testimony and the statement of the trial judge establish that the sole purpose of the clerk's trip was to observe the operation of the pipe wrapping machine and describe it to the judge so that he might be better able to understand the evidence to be produced at trial. There is no indication that the trial judge considered the law clerk's report as evidence or that the judge was improperly influenced in his fact finding by the clerk's report. Since the trial judge's fact finding was not based on the off-the-record contact of the clerk's view, any error that may have occurred in not obtaining the parties' consent to that view did not result in prejudice and was harmless. We therefore conclude that the specter of prejudice created by the judge's off-the-record contact with material evidence has been removed, and that the trial judge's findings were not biased by his law clerk's view of the wrapping machine.

---

# LISSON v. O'HARE

2009 U.S. App. LEXIS 8039 (5th Cir. Apr. 16, 2009)

PER CURIAM:

Plaintiff-Appellant Stephen N. Lisson appeals the take-nothing judgment rendered against him in this action for copyright and trademark infringement and computer fraud. The district court entered judgment on the magistrate judge's recommendation after Lisson failed to file a timely objection to the magistrate judge's report. That recommendation had been entered after Lisson chose not to put on evidence of damages because he believed that the magistrate judge was required to recuse himself after his law clerk viewed publicly accessible portions of Lisson's website, InsiderCV-.com, which was the subject of Lisson's infringement and fraud claims.

If a case is assigned to a magistrate judge without a party's consent, as Lisson's was, that party is entitled to file objections within 10 days after receiving a copy of the magistrate judge's recommendation and to have those objections reviewed de novo by the district court. 28 U.S.C. § 636(b)(1)(C); Fed. R. Civ. P. 72(b). But a party's failure timely to file such written objection creates a bar to that party's "attacking on appeal the unobjected-to proposed factual findings and legal conclusions accepted by the district court," except for plain error, "provided that the party has been served with notice that such consequences will result from a failure to object." *Douglass v. United Services Auto. Ass'n*, 79 F.3d 1415, 1428–29 (5th Cir. 1996) (en banc). Lisson was served with such a notice. The plain error standard has application even if the district court has, as in Lisson's case, alternatively accepted the magistrate judge's recommendation on de novo review. *Id.* at 1429.

"To prevail on plain error review," a party must demonstrate an error that was clear or obvious, that the error affected his substantial rights, and that "the fairness, integrity, or public reputation of [his] judicial proceedings" would be seriously affected if the error were not corrected. *Norton v. Dimazana*, 122 F.3d 286, 289 (5th Cir. 1997). "It is the unusual case that will present [plain] error." *Highlands Ins. Co. v. National Union Fire Ins. Co. of Pittsburgh*, 27 F.3d 1027, 1032 (5th Cir. 1994).

An error is considered plain only if it is clear or obvious under existing law. *United States v. Olano*, 507 U.S. 725, 734 (1993). Whether entry of judgment on the magistrate judge's recommendation was plainly erroneous depends on how this court and other courts interpreted the law at the time the district court ruled. *See United States v. Garcia-Rodriguez*, 415 F.3d 452, 455 (5th Cir. 2005). If the law was unsettled, any error by the district court would not be clear or readily apparent. *United States v. Dupre*, 117 F.3d 810, 817 (5th Cir. 1997).

Lisson cites no case in which this court has made it plain that a judge must recuse himself simply because he or his law clerk has viewed a website that is the subject of default proceedings to prove damages. Although one case cited by Lisson, *Kennedy v. Great Atlantic & Pacific Tea Co.*, 551 F.2d 593, 596 (5th Cir. 1977), bears some superficial similarities to the facts in his case, it also presents significant differences. In *Kennedy*, a law clerk took a private view of evidence for purposes related to determining fault and then, on instruction of the district judge, communicated to defense counsel what he had seen, eventually resulting in (a) the district court's having to advise plaintiff of the viewing and of the ex-parte communication and (b) plaintiff's calling the clerk to testify. *See Kennedy,* 551 F.2d at 597. We held that "the potential for prejudice to the defendants' case was too great . . . to conclude that the . . . overruling of the defendants' motion to prohibit" the clerk from testifying before the jury "or, in the alternative, to disqualify [the district judge] from continuing in the trial was harmless error." *Id.* at 598–99. Here, however, there was no chance of prejudicing a jury, and Lisson adduced no admission or other proof that the law clerk ever related anything about the website to the magistrate judge other than the fact of his visit. Moreover, "[m]ere prior knowledge of some facts" germane to a suit "is not in itself necessarily sufficient to require disqualification." *United States v. Seiffert,* 501 F.2d 974, 978 (5th Cir. 1974).

Notably missing from Lisson's brief is any description of the damage he suffered, i.e., an explication of what of his was taken or otherwise harmed by the defendants. Section 455(b) dictates disqualification if the judicial officer has "personal knowledge of disputed evidentiary facts." § 455(b)(1) (emphasis added). Lisson has not shown what, if anything at all, about his website was *disputed* for purposes of a damages assessment. Consequently Lisson has not shown plain error. *See Garcia-Rodriguez,* 415 F.3d at 455; *Dupre,* 117 F.3d at 817.

AFFIRMED.

## IV.   QUALIFICATIONS & SELECTION

Although Justice Gray had no need to undertake an extensive search for his law clerks, the selection process for clerks now involves thousands of judges and law clerk positions. Trenton H. Norris, *The Judicial Clerkship Selection Process: An Applicant's Perspective on Bad Apples, Sour Grapes, and Fruitful Reform,* 81 CAL. L. REV. 765 (1993).

One critic described the judicial clerk hiring process in terms of a hypothetical report outlining the process:

> Two thousand federal jobs a year. Over $65 million in government salaries. Recent law school graduates, many not yet members of the bar, influence judges' decisions and draft opinions in thousands of cases that affect tens of thousands of lives, millions of dollars, and the development of important legal doctrines. They are chosen after only a year's worth of law classes in a frenzied competition among judges who are free to appoint based on hometown, alma mater, race, sex, or whether they know the student's family or teachers.

Norris, 81 CAL. L. REV. at 783.

In 2008, the hiring process for federal district court clerks was described as similar to the running of the bulls in Pamplona:

> Over the past two decades, the Judicial Conference, the body charged with determining the number of clerks that judges at each federal level may hire,

has wavered between controlling the timing of clerkship hiring and allowing a free market to prevail. Criticism of the hiring process increased when the Judicial Conference allowed judges free rein in determining when to begin the hiring process, an environment described as "a frenzied 'Pamplona-like' atmosphere" in which hiring decisions were based, at most, on only two semesters of law school grades and negligible extracurricular activities (like law review or moot court). Despite the unpopularity of a free market for clerkship hiring, each hiring plan and restriction introduced by the Judicial Conference has been similarly attacked, and authors have moved beyond criticism and offered their own suggestions as to how best to perfect the hiring process. While a few judges and legal commentators have expressed support for the free market clerkship hiring system, they are in the minority.

The current clerkship hiring process is guided by a Judicial Conference policy that has been in place since 2003. Termed the "Law Clerk Hiring Plan," the voluntary guideline specifies the dates when students can submit clerkship applications and the date when judges can give call-backs, interview, and make clerkship offers. The new plan, though still in place, has not curbed discourse on the clerk hiring process. Instead, the new plan has spawned debate over its fairness and efficacy, and the likelihood that it will or should ultimately survive.

Todd C. Peppers, Micheal W. Giles, Bridget Tainer-Parkins, *Inside Judicial Chambers: How Federal District Court Judges Select and Use Their Law Clerks*, 71 ALB. L. REV. 623, 630–31 (2008) (footnotes omitted).[*]

Despite the new guidelines for federal court clerk hiring, the practice proved uneven:

I received the offer via voicemail while I was in flight to my second interview. The judge actually left three messages. First, to make the offer. Second, to tell me that I should respond soon. Third, to rescind the offer. It was a 35 minute flight.

Christopher Avery, et. al, *The New Market for Federal Judicial Law Clerks*, 74 U. CHI. L. REV. 447, 448 (2007) (quoting 2005 applicant for federal judicial clerkships).

By January 2014, the Federal Law Clerk Hiring Plan, undertaken in 2003, "which sought to bring order to the process of hiring judges' law clerks, 'ha[d] been effectively discontinued, and no further dates are being set in connection with the plan,' according to a memo sent to all federal judges." The Third Branch News (Jan. 13, 2014). 112 MICH. L. REV. FIRST IMPRESSIONS 22 (2013). *See also* Aaron L. Nielson, *Reflections on the End of the Federal Law Clerk Hiring Plan.*

The outcomes of the judicial clerk selection process have too often resulted in rosters of law clerks that display little diversity. Several commentators have addressed the absence of women and minority judicial clerks, especially among the Supreme Court clerks. Christopher R. Benson, *A Renewed Call for Diversity Among Supreme*

---

[*] Copyright © 2008. Reprinted with permission of the Albany Law Review.

*Court Clerks: How a Diverse Body of Clerks Can Aid the High Court As an Institution*, 23 HARV. BLACKLETTER L.J. 23 (2007). "Somewhere between success in law school and Supreme Court clerkships, qualified women are being screened out." Mark R. Brown, *Gender Discrimination in the Supreme Court's Clerkship Selection Process*, 75 OR. L. REV. 359 (1996); *see also* Lynn K. Rhinehart, *Is There Gender Bias in the Judicial Law Clerk Selection Process?* 83 GEO. L.J. 575 (1994); David H. Kaye & Joseph L. Gastwirth, *Where Have All the Women Gone? The Gender Gap in Supreme Court Clerkships*, 49 JURIMETRICS J. 411 (Summer 2009).

One judge's former clerk cited her judge for his willingness to choose "clerks whose backgrounds, values, and viewpoints might not mirror his." The judge regularly hired "individuals of different backgrounds, genders, and ages . . . ." Geraldine Szott Moohr, *One Kind of Legacy: Judge Sprouse's Law Clerks*, 98 W. VA. L. REV. 17 (1995).

In November 1998, thousands gathered on the steps of the United States Supreme Court to protest against the lack of minority law clerks. Wu, *Examining the Supreme Court's Clerkship*, CHI. TRIB., 31 (Nov. 19, 1998). And this lack continues:

> A 2010 study conducted by the Judicial Conference of the United States found that fewer than 14% of all law clerks in the federal judiciary at that time were members of various racial and ethnic minority groups:
>
> > The assumption from critics of the lack of diversity among the law clerks at the Supreme Court seems to be that the presence of female and minority law clerks might change the way the justices approach cases regarding race and sex discrimination, among others. Jeffrey Toobin argues that the presence of another minority group among the clerks, gay and lesbian individuals, did change the way the justices approached gay rights cases. Writes Toobin: "The gay clerks changed the Court, not because of their advocacy but because of their existence. They were, of course, pretty much indistinguishable from their straight colleagues, and that was precisely the point."

Mark C. Miller, *Law Clerks and Their Influence at the US Supreme Court: Comments on Recent Works by Peppers and Ward*, 39 Law & Soc. Inquiry 741, 754 (2014) (citations omitted).

––––––––––

Judicial externs may be selected by law school personnel or by personnel working with the judge and the judges' law clerks. One survey showed that externs might later serve as law clerks for the judge they externed with, or, more likely, for a different judge. The majority of former externs surveyed, however, moved directly into practice after graduation. *See* John B. Oakley & Robert S. Thompson, *Law Clerks and the Judicial Process, Perceptions of the Qualities and Functions of Law Clerks in American Courts*, 29 n.2.74 (1980). Former law clerks may, in turn, become judges. One high-profile law clerk-turned-judge is Justice William Rehnquist. *See* Laura K. Ray, *A Law Clerk and His Justice: What William Rehnquist Did Not Learn From Robert Jackson*, 29 IND. L. REV. 535 (1996).

––––––––––

## In Court Reports

1.    Locate the rules of confidentiality that govern externs in your assigned court. In addition to any written rules, try to articulate any implied or "cultural" practices of confidentiality you observe.

2.    Identify settings where you will share space with people who are not part of chambers and thus may risk inadvertent breaches of confidentiality. These may include: elevators, hallways, restrooms, security screening areas, law libraries open to the legal community. Add to this list as other settings emerge during your time as an extern.

3.    Perform a personal "conflicts check" by documenting all legal contacts you have in the relevant legal community outside of the externship. Consider: A part time job with a law firm, work in the law school clinic, non-legal work before and during law school, relatives who work for or practice in the court. Keep this conflicts' check at hand and cross check it whenever you begin work on a new matter for the court.

4.    Describe the duties assigned you as a judicial extern in detail; write an extern job description for your placement that includes how hours are earned and credited; expected turnaround time of assigned tasks; sample documents of the type you are likely going to be assigned to research and/or draft.

5.    Research your working conditions and resources. Investigate work space in chambers or out; how docket sheets and files are accessed; legal research resources on line or in paper; courtroom protocols; policies in place for when juries are sitting, trials are conducted, or oral arguments heard.

6.    Identify court staff and their roles in chambers and in the courtroom. Research job postings within your court, if any, and the qualifications listed for the job.

7.    Place your court in full context in terms of vertical and horizontal hierarchy and precedential value and authority of case law. The federal court system may be familiar, but state court organization are often more complicated. The National Center for State Courts: http://www.ncsc.org/

8.    Locate the system of citation used in your court. Some states will have their unique citation rules. Many have adopted a "universal" or "public domain" citation format: "As states publish primary documents on their own web sites and researchers utilize a wide variety of options to access legal materials, it is necessary to have a universal system of citation that helps users locate information across all formats, platforms, and publishers." AALL Universal Citation Guide (Wm. S. Hein & Co. 2014).

9.    Understand the security precautions in place for your court and for the building that houses your court.

## Out of Court Reports

1.    What policies or rules govern confidentiality in the judicial externship class-room? Before discussing in class or writing in a paper or journal entry about your extern experiences, make sure you understand the policies in place in your classroom.

**2.** Consider the following scenarios that a fellow judicial extern or judicial clerk, serving in the same court with you, has raised with you. Draft a response to your classmate or co-clerk and refer to specific facts and to relevant sources from this book or your court's rules and practices.

**a.** Yesterday afternoon, I stayed past 4:30 to work on an assignment. While I was working, I heard a knock on the door to chambers, which had automatically locked at 4:30, and answered it. It was an attorney, actually a law school classmate who graduated a couple of years ahead of me. She desperately needed a copy of one of the documents from a case that is currently being briefed on summary judgment. The first floor clerk's office was closed, the court's website had crashed again, so she asked me to make her a copy from the chambers' file. I figured it couldn't hurt, so I made her a copy. Do you think that I made the right decision?

**b.** The chambers and hallways have been busy this whole semester because of this very long civil trial. I feel badly for the jurors, especially this one older juror who has been looking exhausted. During a break, she saw me in the hallway and asked me when I thought the trial would end. I gave her a ballpark estimate of three more weeks. Do you think telling her that is a problem?

**c.** This summary judgment motion I am working on is so interesting. The briefs are excellent. I am so impressed with the law firm representing the plaintiff. In fact, two weeks ago, I saw the firm had posted an opening, I applied and I have an interview next week. And I will also get to see this firm in action because arguments on the summary judgment motion are scheduled the same week. Most exciting.

**d.** I am working on the *Samuelson v. Huffy Corporation*, motion to dismiss. My ex-husband's family has run that company for generations. But, we were married out of high school and it's been six years since we divorced. Do you think I should mention this to the judge?

**e.** I think you know that Judge Chow is my uncle; he's a magistrate in the federal district court these days. Maybe it sounds like nepotism, but I would love to clerk for him after law school. Do you think that our family relationship would be an issue in working for him?

**f.** We are finally going to trial on that nuisance case between those adjoining landowners. It's the one where the concrete work on the one lot allegedly caused water to overflow onto and flood the neighbor's lot. But, there are some questions as to whether it floods every time it rains or just during heavy rains. Tomorrow is forecast for heavy rains and I am going to check this scene out. Then I can send pictures to the judge and she can get a clearer understanding of the problem. Want to come with me?

**g.** I have been working on a Social Security appeal. The medical jargon in the briefs is awful. But I have been helped greatly by the librarian at the medical school library and the resources he has provided to me. If you ever have to work on a Social Security case, I recommend this approach.

**h.** All week I have been reading the briefs on a post-conviction motion. Then, over the week end, I realized that this case was sounding familiar because I had seen that made-for-TV movie about it a couple of years ago. I pulled it up on Netflix and watched it again — very suspenseful. You should see it.

**i.** Remember when we clerked and the judge had that great case with "Ma Barker" who robbed banks robbery performed by a mother and her five children. I had people in stitches at the law firm holiday party and wanted to describe how the judge would recount to us each day the amazing characters who gave testimony. But then I decided not to — but is it really confidential when it happened two years ago?

**j.** Today the judge was in rare form during motion call and he actually referred to a scene in Star Wars while he was asking an attorney about why he filed a motion to reconsider. I think we should get the transcript and send it into the ABA Journal for the page devoted to humorous stories about the practice of law.

**k.** I always rely on the authority the attorneys cite in their briefs. But yesterday I decided to do some research on my own and I found a case on point, all fours, that is mandatory authority and neither of the parties cited in in their briefs. It seems odd that they didn't cite it, but I figured that's their choice. Do you think I need to cite it in the draft opinion?

**3.** How valid do you find a "judicial privilege"? Compare it to other long-recognized privileges: attorney-client; spousal privileges; priest-penitent; or others.

**4.** In *Deyling*, a judicial clerk experienced a baffling array of conflicts of interest. Consider various duties owed by the clerk, Mr. Jerry Federman, to both of his "employers": the judge and the client. Next, evaluate Mr. Federman's trial skills.

**5.** Compare the facts of *Fredonia* and *PepsiCo*. Consider how the facts in a particular case influence a recusal decision.

**6.** Draft the Memorandum in Opposition to Plaintiff's Motion for Recusal in *Uniloc USA v. Microsoft Corp.* Then undertake the role of the judge and decided the motion; should the judge recuse or not?

**7.** If a judicial clerkship is a goal, consult a resource that includes sections on the externship experience; court guides and directories; the clerk selection process; the clerk's role; writing and citation; opinion drafting; jury instruction drafting; ethics issues. Mary Dunnewold, Beth Honetschlager & Brenda Tofte, *Judicial Clerkships: A Bibliography*, 8 Legal Comm. & Rhetoric: JALWD 239 (2011).

## SELECTED BIBLIOGRAPHY

Ruggiero J. Aldisert, *Sample Instructions to Law Clerks Sample B: Duties of Law Clerks*, 26 Vand. L. Rev. 1251 (1973).

Alexis Anderson et al., *Ethics in Externships: Confidentiality, Conflicts, and Competence Issues in the Field and in the Classroom*, 10 Clinical L. Rev. 473 (2004).

Paul R. Baier, *The Law Clerks: Profile of an Institution*, 26 Vand. L. Rev. 1125 (1973).

Barbara A. Blanco & Sande L. Buhai, *Externship Field Supervision: Effective Techniques for Training Supervisors and Students*, 10 Clinical L. Rev. 611

(2004).

Arthur M. Boley, *Pretrial Motions in a U.S. District Court: The Role of the Law Clerk*, 74 JUDICATURE 44 (June–July 1990).

John Boudreau, et al., 8 Federal Procedure § 20:77 *Personal and Professional Acquaintanceships — Law Clerks* (2014).

CALVERT C. CHIPCASE, FEDERAL DISTRICT COURT LAW CLERK HANDBOOK (2007).

MARY L. DUNNEWOLD, BETH A. HONETSCHLAGER & BRENDA L. TOFTE, JUDICIAL CLERKSHIPS: A PRACTICAL GUIDE (2010).

YAIDA O. FORD, THE TIP BOOK: 18 PEARLS OF WISDOM FOR JUDICIAL LAW CLERKS (2010).

Ruth Bader Ginsburg, *Informing the Public About the U.S. Supreme Court's Work*, 29 LOY. U. CHI. L.J. 275 (1998).

Frederick G. Hamley, *Sample Instructions to Law Clerks, Sample A: Law Clerks for the Judges of the Ninth Circuit Court of Appeals*, 26 VAND. L. REV. 1241 (1973).

TONI JAEGER-FINE, AMERICAN LEGAL SYSTEMS: A RESOURCE AND REFERENCE GUIDE (2015).

Wesley Kobylak, Annotation, *Conduct or Bias of Law Clerk or Other Judicial Support Personnel as Warranting Recusal of Federal Judge or Magistrate*, 65 A.L.R. FED. 775 (1983).

EDWARD LAZARUS, CLOSED CHAMBERS (1998).

Gerald Lebovits, *Judges' Clerks Play Varied Roles in the Opinion Drafting Process*, 76 N.Y. ST. B.J. 34 (July/Aug. 2004).

JOSEPH L. LEMON, JR., FEDERAL APPELLATE LAW CLERK HANDBOOK (ABA 2007).

ALIZA MILNER, JUDICIAL CLERKSHIPS: LEGAL METHODS IN MOTION (2011).

Marie A. Monahan, *Towards a Theory of Assimilating Law Students into the Culture of the Legal Profession*, 51 CATH. U. L. REV. 215 (2001).

Chad Oldfather & Todd. C. Peppers, *Judicial Assistants or Junior Judges: The Hiring, Utilization, and Influence of Law Clerks*, 98 MARQ. L. REV. 1 (2014).

Parker B. Potter, Jr., *Law Clerks Gone Wild*, 34 SEATTLE U. L. REV. 173 (2010).

Parker B. Potter, Jr., *Law Clerks Gone Wild: The State-Court Report*, 38 OHIO N.U. L. REV. 19 (2011).

Todd C. Peppers et al., *Inside Judicial Chambers: How Federal District Court Judges Select and Use Their Law Clerks*, 71 ALB. L. REV. 623 (2008).

ALVIN B. RUBIN & LAURA B. BARTELL, LAW CLERK HANDBOOK (Fed. Jud. Ctr. 1989).

JENNIFER L. SHEPPARD, IN CHAMBERS A GUIDE FOR JUDICIAL CLERKS AND EXTERNS (2012).

Linda F. Smith, *The Judicial Clinic: Theory and Method in a Live Laboratory of*

*Law*, 1993 Utah L. Rev. 429.

Charles W. Sorenson Jr., *Adopting the Judicial Deliberations Privilege: Making Explicit What Has Been Implicit*, 95 Mass. L. Rev. 243 (2014).

Debra Strauss, Behind the Bench: The Guide to Judicial Clerkships (2002).

Patricia M. Wald, *Selecting Law Clerks*, 89 Mich. L. Rev. 152 (1990).

Stephen L. Wasby, *Clerking for an Appellate Judge: A Close Look*, 5 Seton Hall Circuit Rev. 19 (2008).

Charles Allen Wright et al., 13 Fed. Prac. & Proc. § 3511 *Support Personnel and Services for the Courts* (3d ed. 1998).

Charles Allen Wright et al., 13D Fed. Prac. & Proc. § 3543 *Grounds for Disqualification — Personal Knowledge of Disputed Facts* (3d ed. 1998).

# Chapter 2

# JUDICIAL OPINIONS: DECISIONMAKING AND OPINION DRAFTING

> [t]oo often . . . judges write as if only the writer counted. Too often they write as if to themselves and as if their only purpose were to provide a documentary history of having made a judgment. Instead, they must realize that the purpose of an opinion is to make a judgment credible to a diverse audience of readers.

Dwight W. Stevenson, *Writing Effective Opinions*, 59 JUDICATURE 134 (1975).

> The crisis I have in mind rarely is discussed because it raises too many embarrassing questions. I'm talking about the longstanding and well-established practice of having law clerks ghostwrite judges' legal opinions. We have become too comfortable with the troubling idea that judging does not require that judges do their own work.

William Domnarski, Op-Ed., *Judges Should Write Their Own Opinions*, N.Y. TIMES, May 31, 2012.

> If law schools really want to improve the writing of lawyers, they should make their students study briefs, complaints, newspapers, advertisements, even direct-mail letters. But no more opinions, please. No more opinions.

Steven Stark, *Why Judges Have Nothing to Tell Lawyers About Writing*, 1 SCRIBES J. OF LEGAL WRITING 25 (1990).

The judge wields final authority over the opinion drafting process and product. A judicial clerk or extern may often be trained to serve the judge by reviewing recently issued opinions and "reverse engineering" their structure, reasoning, tone, and writing style. Judicial clerk and extern drafting assignments may include drafting appellate opinions; appellate dissenting and concurring opinions; appellate court bench memoranda; trial court opinions on dispositive motions; bench trial findings of fact and conclusions of law; and other forms of court writing. These court orders and opinions may share similar forms across judges and courts. *See* ALIZA MILNER, JUDICIAL CLERKSHIPS: LEGAL METHODS IN MOTION (2011) (chapters addressing in detail drafting appellate opinions, trial court orders, including drafting checklists).

In this chapter, three major aspects of written judicial opinions are explored: [1] what reasoning and explanation a judge ethically owes to a wide and varied audience of opinion readers, [2] examining a sampling of written opinions while standing in the shoes of these readers; and [3] concerns that judicial opinions are declining in quality because increasingly they are drafted by court personnel, not the judge.

# I. WRITTEN OPINIONS: WRITING WELL-REASONED JUDGMENTS

Advice for writing judicial opinions abounds from all corners of the judicial system and beyond. In the article that follows, the author defines and provides context for the role of a well-reasoned judgment within the judicial system both at the trial and appellate court level. But she goes also further by "providing both experienced and novice judges with a structured and content-based method of writing fully reasoned decisions and opinions."

Her article also foreshadows and reflects many issues reflected in other chapters: The need for judicial education; how much judicial fact research is proper; the scope of judicial clerks and extern in opinion writing; as well as the rise of arbitration and the need for written arbitration opinions.

**S.I. Strong**

***Writing Reasoned Decision and Opinions: A Guide for
Novice, Experienced, and Foreign Judges***

2015 J. Disp. Resol. 93[*]

## I. INTRODUCTION

Producing well-written reasoned judgments (a term that is used herein to denote both trial court decisions and appellate opinions) is the goal of all members of the bench. Badly written rulings can have significant legal consequences for both the parties, who may incur costs as a result of a need to appeal a poorly worded decision or opinion, and society as a whole, since a poorly drafted precedent may drive the law in an unanticipated and unfortunate direction or lead to increased litigation as individuals attempt to define the parameters of an ambiguous new ruling. As a result, helping judges write decisions and opinions that are coherent and clear would appear fundamentally important to the proper administration of justice.

Good judicial writing is vital in common law countries like the United States, where the principle of *stare decisis* gives legal opinions the force of law. However, most common law countries, including the United States, do not have career judges who are given instruction in writing judicial rulings from the earliest days of their legal careers. Instead, most common law countries have inherited the English tradition of selecting judges from a pool of experienced lawyers who are considered competent to take up their judicial duties immediately upon ascending to the bench. However, the skills associated with judging are significantly different from those associated with advocacy, and new judges face a very steep learning curve. Nowhere is this more true than with respect to the task of learning to write well-reasoned decisions and opinions. As a result, many newly appointed judges find the "move from advocacy to decision, from

---

marshalling and presenting evidence to fact-finding and synthesizing," to be extremely challenging. Indeed, U.S. Supreme Court Justice Hugo Black, one of the most influential writers to ever grace the bench, once said that "the most difficult thing about coming on to the Court was learning to write."

This is not to say that new judges are entirely without resources. Judicial education opportunities abound at both the public, private, national and international levels, with numerous providers offering instruction in judicial writing. However, the current approach to judicial education faces several practical problems.

First, it is not clear how many judges take up the opportunity to study judicial writing, since the decision of whether and to what extent to seek judicial education is entirely optional in many jurisdictions. Given the punishing caseloads that currently exist in both state and federal courts, as well as the often overwhelming number of new skills that new judges need to master immediately upon taking the bench, it is perhaps understandable that writing is put on the back burner, particularly since many judges may feel that after decades of work as practicing attorneys, they are already competent writers. However, new judges may not appreciate the extent to which judicial writing differs from other forms of communication.

Second, judicial education programs face several significant structural challenges, particularly when it comes to courses on judicial writing. For example, most judicial education centers only ask judges to act as faculty, based on the fact that most judges prefer to be taught by other judges. This practice can result in a number of self-reinforcing behaviors as judges emphasize issues that they consider to be important with little input from external or empirical sources. Additional problems may arise because most judges are not especially qualified to teach writing, despite their experience on the bench. As a result, many judicial writing seminars end up focusing on personal anecdotes or basic writing techniques that do not address the deeper challenge of producing well-reasoned judgments.

These problems suggest that there is a critical need for further assistance regarding judicial writing techniques. Furthermore, it would appear that the judicial community would derive a significant benefit from information provided in published form, since that avoids the cost and time associated with in-person seminars. Written guides may be particularly appropriate, given that "[j]udges are generally autonomous [as learners], entirely self-directed, and exhibit an intensely short-term problem-orientation in their preferred learning practices."

This Article attempts to fill that need by providing both experienced and novice judges with a structured and content-based method of writing fully reasoned decisions and opinions. Although the current discussion is aimed primarily at judges sitting in U.S. state and federal courts, there are several other groups who can benefit from this analysis.

The first such group involves judges and others who are participating in judicial outreach efforts. Over the last few years, an increasing number of public and private organizations such as the American Bar Association (ABA) and the U.S. Agency for International Development (USAID) have implemented programs that seek to bolster the international rule of law through education. These programs strive to provide judges in countries with struggling judicial systems with information about alternative practices that could be suitable for adoption in those other nations. One popular area of discussion involves reasoned judgments. As a result, those who develop and serve as faculty on judicial outreach programs can benefit from a concise and practically oriented discussion of reasoned judgment.

The second group of persons who may appreciate information regarding reasoned judgments involves judicial law clerks who have been asked to write the first draft of a legal decision or opinion. Although the process of writing a ruling under the direction of a judge is somewhat different than the process of writing a decision or opinion on one's own behalf, there are nevertheless sufficient similarities to make this Article of interest to clerks.

The third group of persons who may benefit from this Article involves arbitrators who are asked to produce fully reasoned awards. Fully reasoned awards are now standard in a number of types of arbitration and optional in several others, which makes it necessary for arbitrators to understand how to draft such documents. Although various arbitral institutions around the world offer programs on how to write reasoned awards, such training is largely optional, just as it is in the judicial context. Since a fully reasoned arbitral award is in many ways analogous to a fully reasoned judicial decision, arbitrators can benefit from the principles identified in the current discussion.

The primary focus of this Article is on providing practical advice on how to write a reasoned decision or opinion (Section IV). However, experts in education theory have found that adult learners do best when they understand why certain information is being presented, so the discussion of how to write reasoned judgments will be preceded by a brief section on why such judgments are necessary or useful (Section III). This Article also considers what a reasoned decision or opinion actually is as a preliminary matter (Section II), since it is impossible to write such a document without a true appreciation for what is entailed in a well-reasoned ruling.

Before beginning, it is helpful to note a few basic points. First, reasoned judgments can vary a great deal in terms of form, tone and style. As a result, this Article does not suggest a single, formulaic model of judicial writing that should be followed in all cases, since the best writing occurs when the author is true to his or her own voice. However, those who seek to improve their writing often find it helpful to read a variety of types of good writing in order to develop a better appreciation of the effectiveness of certain writing techniques. Although good judicial writing can be found in many places, those seeking a quick and easy compilation should consider reviewing the annual list of exemplary judicial writing compiled by the editors of *The Green Bag Almanac & Reader*. The decisions and opinions contained on those lists are not only inspirational, they are also highly educational for anyone wishing to improve his or her own writing.

Second, in the interest of brevity, this Article does not address certain issues that are logically but tangentially related to reasoned judgments. For example, this Article does not discuss whether a particular decision or opinion should be written or oral or whether a particular ruling should be published. Furthermore, this Article does not address basic rules of good writing or elements of style. Although all of these matters are important, they are covered in detail elsewhere and need not be discussed herein.

## II. WHAT CONSTITUTES A REASONED DECISION OR OPINION

The first matter to consider involves the question of what constitutes a reasoned decision or opinion. Most lawyers can recite the standard definition of a reasoned ruling as one that includes "findings of fact and conclusions of law based upon the evidence as a whole . . . [and] clearly and concisely states and explains the rationale for the decisions so that all can determine why and how a particular result was reached." However, this definition only goes so far, particularly for those seeking to write such a ruling, since finding "the appropriate methodology for distinguishing questions of fact from questions of law [is], to say the least, elusive." Indeed, "the practical truth [is] that the decision to label an issue a 'question of law,' a 'question of fact,' or a 'mixed question of law and fact' is sometimes as much a matter of allocation as it is of analysis."

The difficulties associated with defining a reasoned judgment can lead some people to focus on various external attributes as a means of distinguishing a reasoned judgment from other types of written rulings. However, that approach is problematic, since principles of judicial independence preclude the use of a single, standard format for reasoned judgments. Furthermore, various differences arise according to whether the ruling was made by a trial court or an appellate court. As a result, external criteria are largely useless as definitional tools.

Instead, the best way to define a reasoned judgment is through a functional analysis that looks at how the opinion operates within the legal system. As it turns out, reasoned judgments arise in a limited category of cases that require a precedential ruling that is binding on more than the parties themselves, which suggests that the form and content of reasoned judgments are largely driven by the demands of the common law legal method. However, the common law has not always required written judgments, nor has the principle of precedent always been defined in the same way as it currently is. As a result, there appear to be other reasons why a reasoned judgment may be useful or necessary. These issues are taken up in the following section.

## III. WHY REASONED JUDGMENTS ARE NECESSARY OR USEFUL

### A. Structural Rationales for Reasoned Judgments

The best known rationale for reasoned judgments indicates that such rulings "serve as a statement of the necessary reasoning (the '*ratio decidendi*') for courts bound to adhere to precedent under *stare decisis*." The importance of stare decisis in the common law legal tradition means that courts must be clear when identifying the factual and legal basis of a particular decision. As a result, judges in the United States and other common law countries are frequently required to write reasoned judgments.

Although the principle of *stare decisis* is well-settled, opinions vary as to the particular matters that are to be considered precedential. Indeed, "[w]hat facts or statements actually constitute precedent is the subject of much scholarly debate: at one extreme, some scholars only give precedential weight to the critical facts of the case; at another extreme, some scholars give precedential weight to any judicial statement; other scholars provide for a mix of facts and statements." Judges demonstrate a similar range of opinions regarding the precedential value of earlier rulings. For example, when determining whether it is bound by an earlier decision, a court considers not merely the "reason and spirit of cases" but also "the letter of particular precedents." This includes not only the rule announced, but also the facts giving rise to the dispute, other rules considered and rejected and the views expressed in response to any dissent or concurrence. Thus, when crafting binding authority, the precise language employed is often crucial to the contours and scope of the rule announced.

The individualized nature of the interpretative process suggests that judges must be extremely careful in how they write reasoned judgments. Thus, Judge Alex Kozinski has stated:

> In writing an opinion, the court must be careful to recite all facts that are relevant to its ruling, while omitting facts that it considers irrelevant. Omitting relevant facts will make the ruling unintelligible to those not already familiar with the case; including inconsequential facts can provide a spurious basis for distinguishing the case in the future. The rule of decision cannot simply be announced, it must be selected after due consideration of the relevant legal and policy considerations. Where more than one rule could be followed — which is often the case — the court must explain why it is selecting one and rejecting the others. Moreover, the rule must be phrased with precision and with due regard to how it will be applied in future cases. A judge drafting a precedential opinion must not only consider the facts of the immediate case, but must also envision the countless permutations of facts that might arise in the universe of future cases. Modern opinions generally call for the most precise drafting and redrafting to ensure that the rule announced sweeps neither too broadly nor too narrowly, and that it does not collide with other binding precedent that bears on the issue. Writing a precedential opinion, thus, involves much more than deciding who wins and who loses in a particular case. It is a solemn judicial act that sets the course of the law for hundreds or thousands of litigants and potential litigants. When properly done, it is an exacting and extremely time-consuming task.

As important as precedent is in the common law legal method, *stare decisis* is not the only structural reason for writing fully reasoned judgments. A second structural rationale involves the role that reasoned judgments play in the appellate process. Reasoned decisions provide critical information as to why the trial court decided as it did and therefore to help appellate courts determine whether a lower court decision should be upheld. While the need for the lower court's rationale may not be necessary in situations when the appellate court considers issues *de novo*, judges in trial and intermediate appellate courts typically do not know whether and to what extent a particular matter will be appealed and what the relevant standard of review may be. Therefore, it is best for lower courts to err on the side of caution and provide a fully reasoned analysis for higher courts to consider.

## B. Non-Structural Rationales for Reasoned Judgments

The importance of the various structural rationales for reasoned judgments suggests that judges should always be aware of how a reasoned ruling may be interpreted and used by judges and lawyers in the future. However, there are also a number of non-structural rationales supporting the use of reasoned decisions and opinions. Not only do these rationales apply equally in both common law and civil law countries, they also provide useful information on how a judge can improve his or her writing.

First and perhaps most importantly, use of reasoned judgments improves the decision-making process, thereby improving the quality of the decision itself As Judge Richard Posner has noted, "[r]easoning that seemed sound when 'in the head' may seem half-baked when written down, especially since the written form of an argument encourages some degree of critical detachment in the writer, who in reading what he [or she] has written will be wondering how an audience would react." By encouraging judges to articulate their reasons for following a particular course of action, reasoned judgments help "rationalize the . . . process," "safeguard against arbitrary decisions," "prevent consideration of improper and irrelevant factors," "minimize the risk of reliance upon inaccurate information," and "attain[] . . . institutional objective[s] of dispensing equal and impartial justice" while simultaneously "demonstrat[ing] to society that these goals are being met."

Second, reasoned judgments provide various benefits to society at large. For example, "[r]equiring a trial court to provide a reasoned basis for the . . . [outcome] imposed may enhance the court's legitimacy as perceived by judges themselves and participants in the . . . justice system." Although this rationale may initially seem to be most relevant to countries with weak or struggling judiciaries, respect for the U.S. judiciary appears to have decreased in recent years. While most of the criticism has been aimed at the U.S. Supreme Court, which is increasingly seen as operating in a highly politicized manner, concerns are now also being raised about state courts and lower federal courts. One of the ways to offset any negative perceptions that may currently exist about the judicial branch would be to increase the number of well-written and well-reasoned judgments that were produced in state and federal courts.

Third, reasoned judgments may be easier to enforce internationally, since foreign courts can see that the judgment was reached in a logical and legally justifiable manner. Globalization has resulted in an ever-increasing amount of litigation involving foreign parties, which means that more judgments will be subject to international enforcement procedures in the coming years. As a result, judges around the world are perhaps under an increased duty to demonstrate the propriety of their rulings so as to promote international enforceability of judgments.

Fourth, reasoned judgments can act as persuasive authority in other courts, even if those rulings are not formally binding in those other jurisdictions. Judges in the United States are well versed in this kind of comparative analysis, at least with respect to decisions and opinions rendered by sister courts in the United States. However, persuasive authority can also operate internationally. Indeed, a number of courts, including those in England, Canada, Australia and New Zealand, routinely consider foreign legal sources, including those from the United States, when analyzing novel points of law. Although U.S. courts are often less inclined to look at foreign sources, some judges have been known to consult foreign or international law even in legal fields considered uniquely domestic, such as constitutional law. Some legal specialties, such as commercial law, derive particular benefits from international consistency.

Not every judge will find each of the preceding rationales equally persuasive. However, this brief analysis provides a strong foundation for the use of reasoned judgments, even in cases where stare decisis may not apply. Agreeing that reasoned judgments are beneficial is only the first step; the more important issue is how to write such documents.

## IV. HOW TO WRITE REASONED JUDGMENTS

Writing a reasoned judgment is a difficult and time-consuming task. However, both the process and the quality of writing can be greatly assisted by a deeper understanding of certain structural issues affecting both the shape and the content of the ruling. Therefore, this section considers issues relevant to the source of the judgment (i.e., whether the judgment comes from a trial court or an appellate court) and the method of writing the judgment (i.e., whether the judgment is written by a single person or a panel) before discussing a framework for drafting a reasoned judgment.

### A. Issues Relating to the Source of the Reasoned Judgment

Although decisions produced by trial courts are in many ways analogous to opinions produced by appellate courts, some differences nevertheless exist, primarily as a result of the different functions of the two types of rulings. These distinctions are outlined below.

### 1. Trial court decisions

"[M]ost judicial writing seminars hold up appellate opinions as the exemplars of 'good judicial writing,' " thereby leaving many "[i]mportant questions about the role of trial court judges as opinion writers" unexplored. As it turns out, trial court judges face a number of challenges not visited upon appellate court judges. For example, the trial court judge does not find the facts and evidence readily organized and the evidence logically sifted. The trial court opinion must create a coherent narrative from the raw source material — the evidence (witness testimony, depositions, exhibits, reports, demonstrative evidence) introduced at trial. The trial court is thus able to indulge less artistry (and sometimes license approaching manipulation) in the order and emphasis of presentation than appellate courts enjoy

When drafting a reasoned decision, a trial court judge should aim to include a full discussion of "the nature of the case, the issues, the facts, the law applicable to the facts, and the legal reasoning applied to resolve the controversy." This type of content is necessary because the trial court decision "is the authoritative answer to the questions raised by the litigation . . . [and] should explain the reasons upon which the judgment is to rest."

Trial courts have a unique perspective on the factual record in a particular case and therefore have a duty to report findings of fact accurately and completely, particularly with respect to witness credibility. Trial courts also have a responsibility to organize the factual record in such a way as to facilitate subsequent review by higher courts, even if most or all of the key documents will subsequently be made available to the appellate court.

When writing a reasoned decision, a trial judge must adopt an approach that minimizes the possibility of appeal. Badly written opinions (whether they are confusing, illogical or simply unsupported by legal or factual authority) may not only increase the possibility the decision will be overturned, they may make the parties more inclined to appeal a decision. Even if the litigation involves an issue on which an appeal is likely (due to its novel nature, for example), a well-written trial court decision can facilitate the appeals process by limiting the range of disputable issues. Since an appellate court can dispose of a narrowly tailored appeal more easily than one that is broadly framed, the trial court might well be said to have a duty to write a well-reasoned judgment as a matter of judicial efficiency.

Some questions can arise as to whether a trial judge should rule in the alternative. On the one hand, providing an alternative decision can be confusing and hence inefficient to the extent that parties and judges who read the decision are not able to discern the precise basis on which the holding is founded. On the other hand, reasoning in the alternative can also be said to increase efficiency, since an appellate court may uphold the decision on the alternative rationale, thereby avoiding the need to remand the case for rehearing.

## 2. Appellate court opinions

Appellate courts (a term that encompasses both intermediate courts and courts of final resort) fulfill a different function than trial courts and therefore require a different type of written ruling. Generally, an appellate "opinion provides a succinct statement of the facts with the major emphasis placed upon the law. The reasons should be set forth clearly so that the disposition is easily understandable."

When drafting reasoned opinions, appellate judges must keep several goals in minds. The first, of course, is the need to act justly, not only an individual level but also on a societal level. Appellate courts — particularly those of final recourse — have an obligation to achieve an outcome that is not only appropriate in the dispute at bar (justice *in personam*) but also in any similar cases that may arise in the future (justice *in rem*) Although this duty may be most apparent in common law jurisdictions as a result of the common law's ability to develop legal principles through judicial precedent, courts in civil law systems also strive towards consistency in their jurisprudence, particularly with respect to judgments from higher courts, and therefore must keep both individual and societal needs in mind when writing appellate opinions.

Appellate courts in the United States review lower court decisions for three reasons: (1) to correct the lower court; (2) to allow for the progressive development of the law; and (3) to ensure the uniformity of the law. While the question of whether to render a fully reasoned opinion in any particular case is a matter of judicial discretion, some commentators have suggested that reasoned opinions are most needed in cases involving the progressive development of the law.

Fully reasoned appellate opinions contain a number of features that are also seen in trial court decisions, as discussed further below. However, appellate court judges have a heightened duty to include a detailed description of the procedural history of the case so as to establish both the standard and propriety of appellate review.

Like trial courts, intermediate appellate courts need to consider whether to rule in the alternative. The issues at the appellate level are the same as at first instance, with judges needing to balance questions of efficiency against the possibility of confusion. Courts of last resort should avoid alternate holdings, since such rulings cannot be justified on the basis of efficiency and the likelihood of confusion is high.

Appellate courts also need to consider whether and to what extent to allow dissenting and concurring judgments. Some jurisdictions prohibit the use of individual opinions on the grounds the court should speak with one voice, while other jurisdictions allow judges to write individual opinions without even trying to obtain a single majority opinion. The preference in most U.S. jurisdictions is for a single majority opinion, although individual opinions are allowed if consensus cannot be reached. Thus, a judge may write a dissenting opinion if he or she cannot join the majority opinion as a matter of judicial integrity. A concurring opinion may be appropriate if a judge agrees with the outcome reached by the majority but arrives at that result through different analytical means.

Some people oppose the use of individual opinions because such opinions are said to threaten the legitimacy of both the court and the law by demonstrating a lack of unanimity among the members of the court. However, others believe that a well-written dissent or concurrence can increase the legitimacy of the law, particularly in cases where the majority decision is later overruled or abrogated, since the dissent or concurrence demonstrates longstanding judicial support for the "new" interpretation of the relevant principle.

Appellate judges also need to be aware of the possibility of "strategic" dissents in jurisdictions where a dissent at the intermediate appellate level automatically triggers review of the case by the highest court in that jurisdiction. In those cases, it is particularly important that both the majority and the dissenting opinions be well-written, since the scope for appeal to the high court may be set by the parameters of the dissenting opinion rather than by the parties, as would be true in situations where the highest court accepts an appeal on a discretionary basis.

Some courts view dissents as problematic because they diminish collegiality among members of the court. However, other courts consider a well-written dissent as advancing the legal debate, so long as the dissent is written in a respectful manner. Thus, sarcasm and ad hominem attacks should play no role in a dissent.

### B. Issues Relating to the Process of Writing A Reasoned Judgment

How a reasoned judgment is written can have a significant effect on its content and style. As a rule, trial judges have more flexibility than appellate judges in this regard, since trial judges work alone and have only their own consciences to consider. Because appellate courts involve multiple judges or justices, the drafting process often includes a certain amount of compromise and negotiation.

Every appellate court approaches the process of writing judgments differently. Sometimes, writing assignments are known from the very beginning, while at other times the primary author is not identified until after the hearing. In either case, [t]he writing judge has the responsibility of drafting the proposed opinion, which may be adopted by the other members of the panel and which ultimately speaks for the court. The writing judge . . . does not have the luxury of writing independently, but should approach the opinion-writing task so that it will reflect the collective mind of the collegial body that makes up the panel.

After the first draft is circulated, members of the court continue their deliberations by parsing through the language of the draft. Ideally, judges who disagree with portions of the draft opinion should not only identify the grounds for disagreement but should also "[o]ffer alternative solutions for the writing judge to consider." This process is critically important, since the opinion must reflect the views of a majority of the court. If the judges can reach only a narrow consensus, then the resulting opinion will have to be equally narrow.

One issue that is becoming increasingly important in both trial and appellate courts involves the role of law clerks in writing reasoned judgments. Judges in the United States have long used law clerks to help draft opinions, and the practice appears to be spreading to other jurisdictions. Commentators have expressed a variety of concerns about the extensive use of law clerks in U.S. courts, noting (among other things) the way in which the use of law clerks has affected the style of written decisions and opinions. The first change involved the number and style of footnotes, which were initially all that law clerks were asked to draft. However, as clerks became more extensively involved in the writing process, observers began to notice that an increasing number of reasoned decisions and opinions were taking on the character-istics of a law review article, which is the type of writing with which U.S. law clerks are most familiar.

The current practice in the United States is for clerks to write the first draft of a reasoned decision or opinion, although some judges have refused to relinquish that task. Editing someone else's work is obviously a very different task than writing the first draft oneself and one that judges should take seriously.

This Article does not discuss how best to instruct a clerk in the process of drafting an opinion, nor does this discussion consider the intricacies of editing one's own or others' work, although both issues are of great importance to the production of well-reasoned judgments. Fortunately, there are numerous resources available on these important subjects for those who are interested in learning more.

While it is important to recognize issues relating to authorship, such matters ultimately do not affect the core characteristics of a well-reasoned judgment. Regardless of who writes the document or how the process is managed, the elements of good judicial writing remain the same. The following sub-section therefore discusses the framework of a well-reasoned decision or opinion, including core considerations relating to scope, audience and structure.

## C. Issues Relating to the Framework for Reasoned Judgments

### 1. Scope

The process of drafting a reasoned judgment begins by considering questions of scope. Not every dispute merits a fully reasoned judgment, and judges must learn to differentiate between those matters that deserve a detailed legal analysis and those that do not

In *The Nature of the Judicial Process*, Justice Benjamin Cardozo suggests that there are three different categories of cases that can result in a judicial ruling.

The first category, the majority of the docket, is comprised of those cases where "[t]he law and its application alike are plain." Such cases "could not, with semblance of reason, be decided in any way but one. Such cases are predestined, so to speak, to affirmance without opinion." To publish an opinion in such cases would contribute nothing new to the body of law or to the reader. These cases do not merit even a non-precedential opinion. Instead, a plain judgment order or citation to the district court opinion in the appendix is sufficient.

Cardozo's second category of cases, a "considerable percentage" of the docket, is comprised of those cases where "the rule of law is certain, and the application alone doubtful." In such cases,

> [a] complicated record must be dissected, the narratives of witnesses, more or less incoherent and unintelligible, must be analyzed, to determine whether a given situation comes within one district or another upon the chart of rights and wrongs . . . . Often these cases . . . provoke difference of opinion among judges. Jurisprudence remains untouched, however, regardless of the outcome.

It is in this second category that a non-precedential opinion is legitimate. The rule of law is settled, and the only question is whether the facts come within the rule. Such fact-oriented opinions do not add to our jurisprudence and thus do not require publication.

It is only in Cardozo's third and final category where an opinion for publication should be written. "The final category . . . is comprised of cases 'where a decision one way or the other, will count for the future, will advance or retard, sometimes much, sometimes little, the development of the law.' . . . From such cases, each modestly articulating a narrow rule, emerge the principles that form the backbone of a court's jurisprudence and warrant [a] full-length, signed published opinion."

This taxonomy of judicial disputes helps explain the character of different judicial rulings. Summary orders (also known as summary judgment orders) are used in Justice Cardozo's first category of cases and usually run no more than a single page in length. Although a summary order may include a brief statement of the findings of fact and conclusions of law, it provides little or no explanation of why the court reached the outcome that it did.

Memoranda opinions are used in Cardozo's second category of cases. These documents, which are not considered precedential, are nevertheless slightly more fulsome than summary orders and therefore provide at least some description of how the court arrived at its decision. However, memoranda opinions do not qualify as fully reasoned judgments because they do not include either a detailed discussion of the facts or a comprehensive explanation of the legal rationales underlying the decision.

Both of these types of documents can be contrasted with fully reasoned opinions and decisions, which are generated by Justice Cardozo's third category of cases, i.e., "where a decision one way or the other, will count for the future, will advance or retard, sometimes much, sometimes little, the development of the law." Although Justice Cardozo believed that these types of cases arose relatively infrequently, he was writing prior to the adoption of various procedural rules promoting early settlement of civil litigation and the advent of alternative dispute resolution. As a result, the percentage of cases needed a reasoned judgment may be higher now than in Justice Cardozo's time, since the only disputes that currently make their way to final disposition by a court are those that are too difficult to settle as either a legal or factual matter.

The scope of the facts and law in contention define the focus of the reasoned judgment. For example, matters that are factually complex require courts, by necessity, to summarize and analyze factual issues in more depth. Disputes that turn on novel issues of law require courts to spend more time on both the governing law as well as the underlying policies that drive the law in a particular direction.

Novice judges can find it difficult to differentiate between a factual finding and a legal conclusion. "Findings of fact may be defined as those facts which are deduced from the evidence and which are found by the judge to be essential to the judgment rendered in the case." Conclusions of law, on the other hand, "are drawn by the judge through the exercise of her [or her] legal judgment from those facts he [or she] has found previously as the trier of fact."

The inductive nature of common law analysis requires judges in the United States to give due consideration to the factual basis of any legal claim that is made. Reasoned decisions and opinions must therefore provide a sufficient level of factual detail to identify the boundaries and context of the legal ruling so that parties can determine going forward whether their behavior falls into the category of conduct being regulated. Factual analyses can also help demonstrate why a particular outcome is appropriate as a matter of policy.

Although the scope of a judicial opinion is heavily affected by factual considerations, legal issues are equally important. "If the issue has been thoroughly discussed in prior opinions, the judge need not trace the origins of the law or elaborate on its interpretation." If, however, the case involves a legal issue that is less well-developed or a rule that will be modified or extended, then:

[t]he judge should discuss and analyze the precedents in the area, the new direction the law is taking, and the effect of the decision on existing law. Even if it appears that the litigants do not need a detailed statement of the facts, the opinion should present sufficient facts to define for other readers the precedent it creates and to delineate its boundaries. The relevant precedents — and the relevant policies — should be analyzed in sufficient detail to establish the rationale for the holding.

Finally, a well-reasoned judgment needs to weigh the conflicts involved in the dispute thoughtfully and disinterestedly (thereby demonstrating the reasonableness of the decision) while also demonstrating how fair and long-lasting the resolution of the conflict will be (thereby demonstrating the logic of the decision).153 Although this is a challenging goal, it is one to which all reasoned decisions and opinions should nevertheless aspire.

### 2. Audience

Knowing one's audience is one of the fundamental rules of good writing, regardless of context. Because "[t]he basic purpose of a judicial opinion is to tell participants in the lawsuit why the court acted the way it did," conventional wisdom suggests that judges should direct their statements to the parties, and, in cases that are being heard on appeal, to the court whose judgment is under review.

This advice is absolutely true, as far as it goes. Certainly the litigants must be able to understand the decision, since they "have an all-pervasive interest" in the outcome of the dispute. However, reasoned decisions and opinions are read by many different people and for many different purposes. Judges must therefore consider whether and to what extent they are also writing for the bar, the legislature, the media, other judges (including both future judges and in some cases other members of an appellate panel) and/or lay members of the public. Appellate courts must also think about "the effect the opinion will have on itself as an institution charged with responsibilities for setting precedent and for defining law."

Writing for such a diverse audience can be challenging. However, experts have suggested that "[t]he mark of a well-written opinion is that it is comprehensible to an intelligent layperson," since that standard will meet the needs of all possible audience members. As a result, decisions and opinions must be "clear, logical, unambiguous, and free of legal jargon while also reflecting consistency and coherence with existing legal authorities. Although a judge must always be true to his or her own beliefs, "[o]pinions should not . . . be turned into briefs or vehicles for advocacy."

### 3. Structure

As important as questions of scope and audience may be, the real challenge involves structure. Without a good structure, a writer cannot hope to persuade or even inform his or her reader.

Perhaps the most often-used and well-regarded structural framework for reasoned decisions and opinions is based on the classical principles of Greco-Roman rhetoric.

Although ancient theories of communication may initially appear irrelevant in the twenty-first century, the benefits of this approach have been well documented.

This model includes five different sections that are each set off by a header. Although the content of each section varies somewhat according to whether the ruling is from a trial court or an appellate court, the core elements remain the same. The five sections include:

- an opening paragraph or orientation (*exordium*);
- a summary of the issues to be discussed (*divisio*);
- a recitation of material adjudicative facts (*narratio*);
- an analysis of the legal issues (*confirmatio a confutatio*); and
- a conclusion (*peroratio*).

This model does not include headnotes and syllabi, since those features are not considered authoritative in many jurisdictions. However, some experts have suggested that judges who sit in jurisdictions that consider the syllabus be the authoritative statement of the holding of the case should write their own head-notes and syllabi.

### *i. Orientation*

Experts agree that every well-reasoned decision or opinion should begin with an opening or orientation section that puts the legal and factual discussion into context and lets the reader know what is to come. Although substance is more important than style, a good orientation paragraph should nevertheless attempt to "pique the opinion reader's interest with its language."

Even though the orientation section is only one or two paragraphs long, it serves two important purposes. First, this section describes the structure of the discussion so as to give readers a roadmap of where the author is going. Second, a good orientation paragraph provides readers with sufficient information to know whether they should continue reading. The most common consumers of reasoned judgments (typically lawyers and other judges) are often pressed for time and need to know immediately whether a decision or opinion is relevant to the issue they are researching. As a result, all of the critical information about the case should appear in the orientation section.

One way to approach an orientation section is by reference to the six questions posed by journalists: who, what, when, where, why and how. "Who" is perhaps the easiest of the questions to answer, since it simply requires the judge to identify the litigants and, if the case is being heard on appeal, who prevailed in the lower court.

"What" is also relatively straightforward. Here, the judge merely needs to identify the particular area of law that is addressed in the judgment and outline the specific legal issues at stake. Thus, a judge might indicate that the case involved a claim in negligence and that the primary issue in contention involved whether the defendant owed a legal duty to the plaintiff.

"When" is important in both trial-level and appellate courts, although the question may be framed in a slightly different manner, depending on the context. In trial courts, "when" would likely refer to the timing of the legal injury so as to establish whether the case was being brought in a timely manner and/or to ascertain the scope of any possible damages. In appellate courts, the question of "when" might refer to whether the appeal was raised within the proper period of time.

"Where" can relate to a variety of issues. For example, an appellate court might need to establish where the appeal is coming from so as to demonstrate that appellate jurisdiction exists. Trial judges may also frame the question of "where" as jurisdictional in nature, since courts are often only competent to hear matters that arise within their own particular territory. Although jurisdictional issues can be considered in response to a "where" question, there is no need to characterize jurisdictional matters in that particular light. However, judges should always indicate the basis for the court's jurisdiction over the matter at bar, regardless of how they frame the issue.

The next question relates to "why" a matter has been brought to the court's attention. Sometimes, this issue will have already been answered as a result of the "who," "what," "when," or "where" analyses. However, a judge should raise this matter independently if it has not already been addressed, since the question of "why is this matter being brought before this court at this time" is fundamental to every litigation.

"How" is primarily a procedural question relating to the way the issue reached the court. Thus, a trial court judge may wish to indicate whether a decision relates to a matter that was raised on motion or following a full trial. Similarly, an appellate court may wish to indicate whether the dispute was heard as of right or as a matter of discretion. In either case, it is important to know how the matter reached the court.

The "how" paragraph can also be interpreted as indicating how the court has decided to rule. While some judges believe that withholding the result until the end of the decision or opinion increases the reader's anticipation, there is little to be gained by not indicating the outcome in the orientation paragraph, since most readers who do not find the holding in the orientation paragraph simply turn to the end of the document to find out how the case was decided. In fact, numerous authorities suggest that the orientation paragraph should include a reference to the holding or disposition "as a guide to the intelligent reading of the opinion" or decision. When announcing the outcome of the dispute, judges should avoid using the passive tense or other indirect language (such as "I believe"), since such language "dilute[s] the vigor which should characterize the result."

A clear reference to the outcome of the case may be particularly important in "splintered" decisions, where a claim is denied in part and granted in part. Plurality decisions offer similar opportunities for confusion, which suggest a heightened need for well-written orientation paragraphs. Although the orientation section is comprehensive in scope, it should be very brief. In fact,

> [t]he simplest form of preview statement sets forth the legal issue and the answer to it in the most concise form possible. The following opening paragraph is a classic: "We are called upon to determine whether "attempted assault" is a crime in the state of California. We conclude that it is not."

Learning to write a good orientation section takes practice, and even experienced judges spend considerable time getting the wording just right. However, the benefits of a clear, concise opening justify the time spent on drafting.

### ii. Summary of legal issues

The second section of a reasoned decision or opinion involves a summary of the various legal issues that will be discussed in the body of the document. This section focuses exclusively on legal issues, since factual issues are considered separately.

Some writers worry about discussing legal issues outside their factual context, thinking that such an analysis is too academic and treatise-like. However, the goal in this subsection is not to discuss the law in a vacuum, but rather to provide a clear analysis of the legal dispute that will ultimately be informed by the material adjudicative facts. This technique not only brings the discussion of legal concerns down to a manageable size, it helps the reader better understand the materiality of the facts that are presented later in the decision or opinion. "The effect is like reading a review of a movie before seeing it, so that one knows what to look for in the theater."

Some disputes present more than one legal issue. However, this situation is not unduly problematic, since there are a number of ways of handling these types of complex matters. Some judges present all of the potential legal issues in a single summary paragraph while other judges split up the various issues and introduce them in separate paragraphs under topic sentences introducing individual sub-issues. Either technique is fine, so long as the approach is clear to the reader.

When discussing legal issues, it is usually not necessary to address everything raised by counsel in detail, since it is the court, not the parties, who control the scope and content of a legal ruling. While it is important to address any claim, defense, error or objection that has been properly raised or preserved on appeal, some concerns do not merit lengthy analysis and can be handled in a relatively succinct manner.

Although trial judges and appellate judges can usually approach the summary of legal issues in a relatively similar manner, appellate judges do need to be sure to include a separate paragraph describing the appropriate standard of review. That standard is usually determined by reference to the matter under review, with the three most frequently used standards — clear error, abuse of discretion and plenary (*de novo*) review — typically relating to evidentiary, discretionary and legal matters, respectively.

### iii. Statement of facts

A well-written factual analysis is critical to a well-reasoned decision or opinion, since the judge needs to demonstrate and discuss the interaction between the law and the facts. Therefore, a judge must include all the relevant facts, although he or she must simultaneously take care to avoid introducing any unnecessary facts, since additional elements not only slow the reader down but may cause confusion about the scope and future applicability of the legal principle enunciated in the judgment. As a result, "[o]nly material, adjudicative facts should be set forth in the opinion" or decision.

To determine what facts are material, judges look to the substantive law. Only "facts that might affect the outcome of the suit under the governing law" can be considered material. Focusing on facts "that are truly essential as opposed to those that are decorative and adventitious" allows the "conclusion . . . to follow so naturally and inevitably as almost to prove itself."

When summarizing the facts, judges must ensure the accuracy of each individual element. "While the author may interpret the law liberally or strictly, he [or she] must not take this kind of liberty with the facts." Experts suggest pulling the facts from the record itself rather than adopting the proposed findings of facts submitted by one of the parties, both to minimize error and to avoid claims that the judge has not exercised the requisite amount of independent judgment when reviewing the facts.

When describing the material facts, a judge needs to do more than simply recount the evidence. Instead, the decision or opinion must "set out express findings of fact showing how the judge reasoned from the evidentiary facts to the ultimate fact" that decides a particular legal issue. While it is often best to state the facts chronologically, some matters are better served by another type of organizational structure.

If witness testimony is discussed, the court of first instance should address issues of credibility. However, the judge does not need to list all of the witnesses who have appeared. Instead, it is sufficient to "identify the undisputed facts and make findings of those in dispute, all within the rubric of pertinence. It is important to make findings of credibility when establishing the probative force of a witness' testimony, and to give reasons."

Some authorities believe that the summary of the facts should precede the summary of the legal issues, although there is no consensus on that point. Ultimately, the order of the various sections is a matter of individual preference. However, most experts suggest writing the summary of the issues before writing the summary of the facts so as to avoid including immaterial factual information in the summary of the facts. Sections can be rearranged later, during the editing process.

### iv. Analysis of the legal issues

The fourth section constitutes the core of a reasoned decision or opinion. This section provides a detailed analysis of the legal issues and presents the rationale for reaching the outcome in question.

There are a variety of ways to organize this section. For example, if there is one issue dispositive of the dispute, then it is often best to begin with that issue. If there is no single issue that controls the outcome, then a judge may follow the order set forth by counsel or begin with either the easiest or the most difficult of the outstanding issues, whichever seems best. Regardless of the order adopted, "[t]here is but one obligation: to correctly describe the arguments in support of each party's position on each issue, and to give clear reasons justifying the result."

Reasoned judgments differ from written advocacy in several key ways. For example, reasoned decisions and opinions

> [r]esemble a form of justification . . . . [J]udges are not required to convince, but rather to make themselves understood. They must therefore express their

reasons in a fashion that will carry with them the support of the majority of the readers. The losing parties may never be convinced their cause was wrong but they are entitled to know why they lost and how the judge reached that result.

Judicial analyses should therefore be both thoughtful and neutral so as to give both the parties and society as a whole reason to trust in the integrity of the system. Furthermore, judges should be very careful about adopting any proposed conclusions of law submitted by a party, since that may cause doubts about whether the judge considered the case fully and independently. Functionally,

[j]udges must decide all the issues in a case on the basis of general principles that have legal relevance; the principles must be ones the judges would be willing to apply to the other situations that they reach; and the opinion justifying the decision should contain a full statement of those principles.

Although "[t]he legal conclusion should cover each of the legal elements required to decide the case," the goal is not to "state the law [as] fully and comprehensively . . . as might be expected in writing a law review" or "to resolve unasked questions or legal issues not yet in dispute." Indeed, it is generally considered "improper for the judge to state more in a decision/opinion than is necessary or to resolve or attempt to resolve future problems." While some courts (such as the court of last resort) might be inclined to suggest how the law might develop in the future, such statements are technically made *ober dicta* and can cause significant problems in the lower courts.

When undertaking a legal analysis, a judge faces three possible scenarios. First, after "identify[ing] the flash point of the conflict," the judge may find him or herself required to "choose among competing legal precepts to determine which should control." Once the controlling principle of law is determined, that principle must then be interpreted and applied to the facts of the case.

Second, the judge may not have any difficulties identifying which of several competing principles controls the issue but may nevertheless need to decide how to interpret that principle. This type of concern arises most frequently in cases involving statutory construction. In this situation, the judge does not need to discuss other potential legal principles at length but can focus only on the interpretation of the law and the application of that law to the facts.

Third, the judge may be faced with disputes that are primarily factual in nature. In this category of cases, the judge only needs to focus on the application of the governing law (as chosen and interpreted) to the facts that have been established by the finder of facts.

As helpful as it is to distinguish between different types of cases, judges must do more than apply the law mechanistically. Instead, reasoned judgments must "weigh the case for and against given rulings." Although some of the elements that go into a reasoned judgment require a value judgment, judges "must not rely on value judgments to the exclusion of reasoned analysis."

One question that is often raised involves the extent to which judges may conduct independent research. A number of courts have indicated that

[a] competent judge is not so naive to believe that briefs will always summarize the relevant facts and the applicable law in an accurate fashion. A competent judge uses the briefs as a starting line and not the finish line for his or her own independent research. Not only does a good judge confirm that the authorities cited actually support the legal propositions in the briefs, a good judge also makes sure that the authorities continue to represent a correct statement of the law. A member of the bench who fails to independently develop his or her own legal rationale does so at his or her own peril and the peril of the litigants.

Other authorities suggest precisely the opposite, based on the fact that independent judicial research denies the parties of "the opportunity for crossexamination, rebuttal, or the introduction of further testimony." However, commentators have concluded that "the prerogative of the judge to search the case law independently and to consult legal treatises is soundly entrenched, presumably to promote uniformity and accuracy in legal interpretation."

The situation is much more unsettled when it comes to independent factual research. Not only do surveys of state appellate judges suggest that the bench is sharply divided on this issue, but "the rules governing independent research are astonishingly unclear." Thus, commentators suggest that judges should conduct sua sponte research into factual matters very rarely and only in the interests of justice. As a practical matter, a judge who has discovered a factual issue of relevance should strongly consider asking the parties to provide written submissions concerning that issue so as to avoid the possibility of a subsequent appeal.

### v. Holding or disposition

The final section of a reasoned judgment involves the holding or disposition of the case. This section usually constitutes "a single paragraph or sentence at the end of the decision" and "is that portion of the decision that ultimately will be incorporated into the judgment."

The content of this section differs somewhat depending on the type of court involved. For example, trial courts should be sure to address all of the outstanding claims and defenses so as not to leave a gap that must later be remedied. Appellate courts should also take care to identify clearly which aspects of the lower court decision have been affirmed, reversed, vacated and remanded or modified, but should also indicate what obligations, if any, the court of first instance has with respect to the case at bar.

If a judge has not specifically discussed all of the issues presented in a civil dispute, then he or she should consider making a global statement indicating that all matters not explicitly addressed have been considered and determined to be without merit. If the dispute is criminal in nature, then it may be better for the judge to specify each issue that has been denied, even if the decision or award does not discuss that matter in detail.

## V. CONCLUSION

As the preceding discussion suggests, writing a well-reasoned judgment is a difficult and time-consuming task. Although the process may seem particularly daunting to those who are new to the bench, many experienced judges also struggle to convey their thoughts in a concise but coherent manner.

Ideally, every judge would be able to take advantage of one or more in-person seminars involving judicial writing. Although the need for assistance is perhaps most urgent when judges first take the bench, more experienced judges would also benefit from this sort of instruction, since they now have some first-hand experience with the difficulties associated with writing a reasoned decision or opinion. The problem, of course, is that many judges find it hard to make the time to attend in-person seminars, particularly given expanding workloads and decreasing budgets. For those people, a published guide on writing well-reasoned judicial decisions and opinions may be the best way to trigger new ways of thinking about judicial writing.

This Article has attempted to provide judges with precisely that type of assistance. Hopefully there will be more such efforts in the future, since a well-educated judiciary is critical to a well-functioning society.

## II.  JUDGES WRITING FOR MULTIPLE AUDIENCES

Using the author's concept of writing well-reasoned judgments for the parties, as well as the additional audiences of the lawyers, the general public, the legislature, the media, other judges, and future judges with similar cases coming before them, read the sample opinions that follow.

### DENNY v. RADAR INDUSTRIES, INC.
184 N.W.2d 289 (Mich. Ct. App. 1970)

Gillis, Judge

The appellant has attempted to distinguish the factual situation in this case from that in *Renfroe v. Higgins Rack Coating and Manufacturing Co., Inc.* 17 Mich. App. 259, 169 N.W.2d 326 (1969). He didn't. We couldn't.

Affirmed. Costs to appellee.

### GRAY v. STATE
456 A.2d 1290 (Md. Ct. Spec. App. 1983)

Moylan, Judge

In Paris at the height of the Reign of Terror, Sidney Carton visited a friend at the Bastille, where Charles Darnay awaited execution. Following a quick change of clothing, Darnay was spirited from the Bastille, posing as the visiting Sidney Carton. In Baltimore on August 19, 1981, the Appellant, Edward Gray, visited a friend at the

Maryland Penitentiary, where Steven Lloyd Everett was serving a lengthy sentence. Following a quick switch into similar clothing, Everett walked out of the Maryland Penitentiary, posing as the visiting Edward Gray. For his role in the Paris escape, Sidney Carton received immortality at the hands of Charles Dickens. For his role in the Baltimore escape, Edward Gray received a five-year sentence at the hands of Judge Paul Dorf. Heroically, Sidney Carton accepted his fate with the words, "It is a far, far better thing I do than I have ever done." Less heroically, the appellant Gray has taken the present appeal.

\* \* \* \*

# RUSSELL v. STATE
372 S.E.2d 445 (Ga. Ct. App. 1988)

Deen, Presiding Judge.

The events of the instant case dramatically illustrate the stark truth underlying the poetic adage, " . . . Hell [has no] fury like a woman scorned." Appellant Carol Star Russell, who admittedly believed that "diamonds are a girl's best friend" if and only if they are bought at Tiffany or Maier & Berkele, was rejected by her almost-fiance, David Roberson, after she had expressed in explicit terms her disdain for the engagement and wedding rings which he had proposed buying for her at Kay Jewelers. Roberson then met and subsequently married another young lady, Tammy, whose taste in jewelry was apparently not so elevated.

Approximately six weeks after her marriage to David, Tammy received, while on the job at a Gainesville, Ga., restaurant, a telephone call from appellant, who stated that she was at Tammy's residence in bed with David; she also allegedly threatened to kill Tammy. Knowing that her work telephone number was not listed in the telephone directory but was written down in her personal address book, which she kept at home, Tammy called the police and reported the likelihood that an intruder had entered her house. Police officers investigated and then summoned Tammy to the scene. As she approached the house, Tammy spotted Carol's car and alerted the police, who followed Carol and subsequently took her into custody. When Tammy entered the house she found the premises in considerable disarray: a light fixture had been broken; the bedspread had been cut to pieces; the waterbed was slashed in several places; broken pieces of wedding crystal floated on the water which had poured forth from the now eminently unseaworthy waterbed; and the bedroom carpet was soaked. She discovered that her address book, her wedding pictures, and the receipts for her wedding and engagement rings were missing. The police officer who apprehended appellant found in her possession not only Tammy's address book but also a bag containing a hammer, a pair of scissors, a knife, a pair of gloves, and two Bibles. The record is silent as to the ownership of the latter two items.

David Roberson testified, and proved by a canceled check, that he had paid $1,900 for the waterbed some sixteen months previously; he further testified that he had paid $500 for the carpeting. Both he and his wife testified that none of the damaged items had any value in their present conditions. At the close of the State's evidence defendant/appellant moved for a directed verdict of acquittal on the grounds that the State had not proven the ownership or the value of the damaged property; the motion was denied.

A Hall County jury convicted Russell of criminal damage to property in the second degree. She was sentenced to two years' imprisonment, with ten days to serve and the balance on probation, together with payment of $1,000 in restitution and mandatory participation in a mental health program. Russell appeals, enumerating as error the denial of her motion for directed verdict of acquittal on the basis of the alleged insufficiency of the evidence of ownership and the State's alleged failure to prove the value of the property. *Held:*

1. OCGA § 16-7-23 states in pertinent part: "(a) A person commits the offense of criminal damage to property in the second degree when he: (1) Intentionally damages any property of another person without his consent and the damage thereto exceeds $500.00." The victim's husband stated that he had purchased the waterbed and carpet and testified to the amount he had paid. He produced a canceled check for $1,900, with which he had paid for the waterbed. He further testified that the items were useless after Carol's depredations. This evidence established not only the ownership but the present value of the items, within the contemplation of the statute, which requires that they be worth more than $500.00 to warrant conviction. *Cf. Johnson v. State,* 156 Ga. App. 411, 274 S.E.2d 778 (1980), *cert. denied,* 451 U.S. 989, 101 S. Ct. 2327, 68 L. Ed. 2d 848 (1981), in which this court reversed a conviction for criminal damage to property because the owner of the damaged property offered only an opinion as to its value, unsupported by any documentation.

2. Examination of the transcript and the remainder of the record reveals that the evidence was more than sufficient to authorize a jury to find appellant guilty of the offense charged beyond a reasonable doubt. *Jackson v. Virginia,* 443 U.S. 307 (1979). Appellant's enumeration of error is without merit.


JUDGMENT AFFIRMED.


CARLEY and SOGNIER, JJ., concur specially.


CARLEY, JUDGE, concurring specially.

I agree that the judgment of conviction should be affirmed. However, I cannot join the majority opinion because I do not believe that humor has a place in an opinion which resolves legal issues affecting the rights, obligations, and, in this case, the liberty of citizens. The case certainly is not funny to the litigants. I concur in the judgment only.

I am authorized to state that JUDGE SOGNIER joins in this special concurrence.

# ESCOLA v. COCA COLA BOTTLING CO.
## 150 P.2d 436 (Cal. 1944)

GIBSON, CHIEF JUSTICE.

Plaintiff, a waitress in a restaurant, was injured when a bottle of Coca Cola broke in her hand. She alleged that defendant company, which had bottled and delivered the alleged defective bottle to her employer, was negligent in selling 'bottles containing said beverage which on account of excessive pressure of gas or by reason of some defect in the bottle was dangerous * * * and likely to explode.' This appeal is from a judgment upon a jury verdict in favor of plaintiff.

Defendant's driver delivered several cases of Coca Cola to the restaurant, placing them on the floor, one on top of the other, under and behind the counter, where they remained at least thirty-six hours. Immediately before the accident, plaintiff picked up the top case and set it upon a near-by ice cream cabinet in front of and about three feet from the refrigerator. She then proceeded to take the bottles from the case with her right hand, one at a time, and put them into the refrigerator. Plaintiff testified that after she had placed three bottles in the refrigerator and had moved the fourth bottle about 18 inches from the case 'it exploded in my hand.' The bottle broke into two jagged pieces and inflicted a deep five-inch cut, severing blood vessels, nerves and muscles of the thumb and palm of the hand. Plaintiff further testified that when the bottle exploded, 'It made a sound similar to an electric light bulb that would have dropped. It made a loud pop.' Plaintiff's employer testified, 'I was about twenty feet from where it actually happened and I heard the explosion.' A fellow employee, on the opposite side of the counter, testified that plaintiff 'had the bottle, I should judge, waist high, and I know that it didn't bang either the case or the door or another bottle * * * when it popped. It sounded just like a fruit jar would blow up * * *.' The witness further testified that the contents of the bottle 'flew all over herself and myself and the walls and one thing and another.'

The top portion of the bottle, with the cap, remained in plaintiff's hand, and the lower portion fell to the floor but did not break. The broken bottle was not produced at the trial, the pieces having been thrown away by an employee of the restaurant shortly after the accident. Plaintiff, however, described the broken pieces, and a diagram of the bottle was made showing the location of the 'fracture line' where the bottle broke in two.

One of defendant's drivers, called as a witness by plaintiff, testified that he had seen other bottles of Coca Cola in the past explode and had found broken bottles in the warehouse when he took the cases out, but that he did not know what made them blow up.

Plaintiff then rested her case, having announced to the court that being unable to show any specific acts of negligence she relied completely on the doctrine of res ipsa loquitur.

Defendant contends that the doctrine of res ipsa loquitur does not apply in this case, and that the evidence is insufficient to support the judgment.

Many jurisdictions have applied the doctrine in cases involving exploding bottles of carbonated beverages. [citations omitted] Other courts for varying reasons have refused to apply the doctrine in such cases. [citations omitted]. It would serve no useful purpose to discuss the reasoning of the foregoing cases in detail, since the problem is whether under the facts shown in the instant case the conditions warranting application of the doctrine have been satisfied.

Res ipsa loquitur does not apply unless (1) defendant had exclusive control of the thing causing the injury and (2) the accident is of such a nature that it ordinarily would not occur in the absence of negligence by the defendant. [citations omitted].

Many authorities state that the happening of the accident does not speak for itself where it took place some time after defendant had relinquished control of the instrumentality causing the injury. Under the more logical view, however, the doctrine may be applied upon the theory that defendant had control at the time of the alleged negligent act, although not at the time of the accident, *provided* plaintiff first proves that the condition of the instrumentality had not been changed after it left the defendant's possession. [citation omitted]. As said in *Dunn v. Hoffman Beverage Co.*, 126 N.J.L. 556, 20 A.2d 352, 354, 'defendant is not charged with the duty of showing affirmatively that something happened to the bottle after it left its control or management * * * to get to the jury the plaintiff must show that there was due care during that period.' Plaintiff must also prove that she handled the bottle carefully. The reason for this prerequisite is set forth in Prosser on Torts, . . . where the author states: 'Allied to the condition of exclusive control in the defendant is that of absence of any action on the part of the plaintiff contributing to the accident. Its purpose, of course, is to eliminate the possibility that it was the plaintiff who was responsible. If the boiler of a locomotive explodes while the plaintiff engineer is operating it, the inference of his own negligence is at least as great as that of the defendant, and res ipsa loquitur will not apply until he has accounted for his own conduct.' [citation omitted] It is not necessary, of course, that plaintiff eliminate every remote possibility of injury to the bottle after defendant lost control, and the requirement is satisfied if there is evidence permitting a reasonable inference that it was not accessible to extraneous harmful forces and that it was carefully handled by plaintiff or any third person who may have moved or touched it. [citation omitted]. If such evidence is presented, the question becomes one for the trier of fact (see, e. g., *MacPherson v. Canada Dry Ginger Ale, Inc.*, 129 N.J.L. 365, 29 A.2d 868, 869), and, accordingly, the issue should be submitted to the jury under proper instructions.

In the present case no instructions were requested or given on this phase of the case, although general instructions upon res ipsa loquitur were given. Defendant, however, has made no claim of error with reference thereto on this appeal.

Upon an examination of the record, the evidence appears sufficient to support a reasonable inference that the bottle here involved was not damaged by any extraneous force after delivery to the restaurant by defendant. It follows, therefore, that the bottle was in some manner defective at the time defendant relinquished control, because sound and properly prepared bottles of carbonated liquids do not ordinarily explode when carefully handled.

The next question, then, is whether plaintiff may rely upon the doctrine of res ipsa loquitur to supply an inference that defendant's negligence was responsible for the defective condition of the bottle at the time it was delivered to the restaurant. Under the general rules pertaining to the doctrine, as set forth above, it must appear that bottles of carbonated liquid are not ordinarily defective without negligence by the bottling company. . . . [I]t is stated that: 'The doctrine * * * requires evidence which shows at least the probability that a particular accident could not have occurred without legal wrong by the defendant.'

An explosion such as took place here might have been caused by an excessive internal pressure in a sound bottle, by a defect in the glass of a bottle containing a safe pressure, or by a combination of these two possible causes. The question is whether under the evidence there was a probability that defendant was negligent in any of these respects. If so, the doctrine of res ipsa loquitur applies.

The bottle was admittedly charged with gas under pressure, and the charging of the bottle was within the exclusive control of defendant. As it is a matter of common knowledge that an overcharge would not ordinarily result without negligence, it follows under the doctrine of res ipsa loquitur that if the bottle was in fact excessively charged an inference of defendant's negligence would arise. If the explosion resulted from a defective bottle containing a safe pressure, the defendant would be liable if it negligently failed to discover such flaw. If the defect were visible, an inference of negligence would arise from the failure of defendant to discover it. Where defects are discoverable, it may be assumed that they will not ordinarily escape detection if a reasonable inspection is made, and if such a defect is overlooked an inference arises that a proper inspection was not made. A difficult problem is presented where the defect is unknown and consequently might have been one not discoverable by a reasonable, practicable inspection. In the Honea case we refused to take judicial notice of the technical practices and information available to the bottling industry for finding defects which cannot be seen. In the present case, however, we are supplied with evidence of the standard methods used for testing bottles.

A chemical engineer for the Owens-Illinois Glass Company and its Pacific Coast subsidiary, maker of Coca Cola bottles, explained how glass is manufactured and the methods used in testing and inspecting bottles. He testified that his company is the largest manufacturer of glass containers in the United States, and that it uses the standard methods for testing bottles recommended by the glass containers association. A pressure test is made by taking a sample from each mold every three hours — approximately one out of every 600 bottles — and subjecting the sample to an internal pressure of 450 pounds per square inch, which is sustained for one minute. (The normal pressure in Coca Cola bottles is less than 50 pounds per square inch.) The sample bottles are also subjected to the standard thermal shock test. The witness stated that these tests are 'pretty near' infallible.

It thus appears that there is available to the industry a commonly-used method of testing bottles for defects not apparent to the eye, which is almost infallible. Since Coca Cola bottles are subjected to these tests by the manufacturer, it is not likely that they contain defects when delivered to the bottler which are not discoverable by visual inspection. Both new and used bottles are filled and distributed by defendant. The used bottles are not again subjected to the tests referred to above, and it may be inferred that defects not discoverable by visual inspection do not develop in bottles after they are manufactured. Obviously, if such defects do occur in used bottles there is a duty upon the bottler to make appropriate tests before they are refilled, and if such tests are not commercially practicable the bottles should not be re-used. This would seem to be particularly true where a charged liquid is placed in the bottle. It follows that a defect which would make the bottle unsound could be discovered by reasonable and practicable tests.

Although it is not clear in this case whether the explosion was caused by an excessive charge or a defect in the glass there is a sufficient showing that neither cause would ordinarily have been present if due care had been used. Further, defendant had exclusive control over both the charging and inspection of the bottles. Accordingly, all the requirements necessary to entitle plaintiff to rely on the doctrine of res ipsa loquitur to supply an inference of negligence are present.

It is true that defendant presented evidence tending to show that it exercised considerable precaution by carefully regulating and checking the pressure in the bottles and by making visual inspections for defects in the glass at several stages during the bottling process. It is well settled, however, that when a defendant produces evidence to rebut the inference of negligence which arises upon application of the doctrine of res ipsa loquitur, it is ordinarily a question of fact for the jury to determine whether the inference has been dispelled. [citations omitted].

The judgment is affirmed.

## III.   WRITTEN OPINIONS: DRAFTING BY CLERK "GHOSTWRITERS," PUBLIC PERCEPTION & PUBLIC RECOGNITION

The opinions in section II all tend to give the reader a sense of a judge's distinctive writing voice and personality. In 1944, Chief Justice Gibson of the California Supreme Court likely was the sole drafter of the *Escola* opinion, with law clerks typically supplying needed research. Sixty years later, the decisionmaking processes may remain with the judges, but it is undisputed that much of the initial drafting of opinions comes from the law clerks and externs. *See* Richard Posner, *Survival of the Federal Courts of Appeals*, 56 S. Cal. L. Rev. 761 (1983). These "ghostwriters" have been blamed for many of the defects critics cite in many written opinions.

## J. Daniel Mahoney
### *Law Clerks: For Better or for Worse?*
54 Brook. L. Rev. 321(1988)*

\* \* \* \*

This brings us to the strongest criticism leveled at the institution: law clerks write judicial opinions. '[C]lerks routinely now say in private that they were the ghostwriters of one or another important opinion and that it was published with hardly a change. . . . ' While this may overstate the case somewhat, it is widely known that law clerks play a substantial role in opinion writing. Law clerks are often responsible for a judge's first draft. Thus, at the very least, the judge has been transformed from a craftsman to an editor. And it is clear that the initial drafter will have a substantial influence on the ultimate work product, no matter how substantial the revisions may ultimately be, or how precise and detailed the instructions given prior to the inception of the clerk's effort.

Judge Posner has suggested that the law clerk's role in opinion writing has had a profound effect on the judicial process. Opinions drafted by law clerks differ in many ways, he asserts, from those initially drafted by judges. First, he claims that opinions written by clerks evince a wholly different style from those crafted by judges. They generally lack flavor, and evince a dull similarity that stems from the homogeneity of the law clerk pool and their similar educational experiences. As a result, he claims, the Federal Reporters are beginning to look more like the volumes of law reviews.

Another difference is that opinions are longer when written by law clerks. The greater number of law clerks in each judge's chambers provides clerks with a greater amount of time to work on opinions. Moreover, law clerks are hesitant to leave out even the smallest of details, since their inexperience precludes an ability to sift the relevant from the marginal. Further, their writing is replete with string cites and quotations that purport to dispose of the legal questions at issue, whether or not they are really on target.

Finally, if it becomes general knowledge that judges do not write their own opinions, it is allegedly less likely that, over time, these opinions will be regarded as authoritative by lawyers and other judges.

Original sources differ from judicial opinions. It has further been suggested that the increasing reliance on law clerks is at least partially responsible for doctrinal breakdown in the modern Supreme Court and the tendency toward separate opinions and plurality decisions: "Because each Justice has a number of law clerks and typically none serves more than one or two years, a heroic effort by a Justice would be required to impart unity of philosophy and authorship to the law clerks' drafts."

In discussing the Court's steadily increasing workload, the Freund Committee warned in 1972: "If trends continue, as there is every reason to believe they will, and if no relief is provided, the function of the Court must necessarily change." There are

---

\*  Copyright © 1988. Reprinted with permission of the Brooklyn Law Review and J. Daniel Mahoney.

increasing indications that the function of the Court has changed over time, and that one is no longer entitled to consider the work of a Justice as analogous to that of a poet or philosopher, i.e., as the intellectual product of a unified mind. In other words, at the same time that legal scholarship is becoming more ambitious, more theoretical, and more creative, Supreme Court opinions are becoming less so — less the product of an individual and powerful mind, less an original text or primary source providing a theoretical model for scholarship, and more the product of "bureaucratic writing" by law clerks. The point is not so much that the Justices have not written their opinions; no one has written them. They are the proverbial "work of many hands."

It is tempting to read the obscure, formulaic pronouncements of Supreme Court opinions as heavily freighted with deep significations that human language can only imperfectly capture. But perhaps a simpler interpretation is that:

> Most constitutional law casebooks are forced by coverage pressure to print only a small part of most opinions. The Court's formulas always survive the editing process. Supreme Court clerks mastered those formulas and were rewarded with high grades; the formulas may be the only way they know of doing constitutional law.

It is difficult, for example, to imagine a present-day law clerk drafting the following passage:

> A hypothetical claim resting on abstract assumptions is now for the first time made the basis for affording illusory relief for a particular evil even though it foreshadows deeper and more pervasive difficulties in consequence. The claim is hypothetical and the assumptions are abstract because the Court does not vouchsafe the lower courts — state and federal — guidelines for formulating specific, definite, wholly unprecedented remedies for the inevitable litigations that today's umbrageous disposition is bound to stimulate in connection with politically motivated reapportionments in so many States. In such a setting, to promulgate jurisdiction in the abstract is meaningless. It is as devoid of reality as "a brooding omnipresence in the sky," for it conveys no intimation what relief, if any, a District Court is capable of affording that would not invite legislatures to play ducks and drakes with the judiciary.

That passage is unmistakably the product of a brilliant, original (if somewhat egotistical) mind. The same inimitable judicial style and personal philosophy can be detected in Justice Frankfurter's *West Virginia State Board of Education v. Barnette* dissent, which he insisted on beginning with a personal statement about belonging to "the most vilified and persecuted minority in history."

In writing his *Barnette* dissent, Frankfurter included the passage quoted above against his law clerk's advice (reportedly with the reminder that "this is my opinion, not yours"). Frankfurter also disregarded similar advice from two of his fellow Justices, who "called formally on Frankfurter in his Chambers to plead with him to omit or soften this opening paragraph. They said it was too emotional and too personal for inclusion in a Supreme Court opinion. Frankfurter said they had given him very good reasons for taking these words out, but he had even better reasons for keeping them in; and in they stayed."

Robert Ferguson has also addressed some of the issues I have raised about the role of law clerks in the judicial process. In so doing, however, Ferguson only strengthens my case. He writes:

> As judges relinquish more and more aspects of the judicial opinion to their court clerks, or even to groups of clerks, there is some reason to qualify the designation of "personal" or "individual" writing. But to qualify does not mean to discard the idea altogether. As long as the actual written product remains "the self-conscious measure" of judicial performance, clerks will write with the style and philosophy of their judge in mind, and judges will monitor language and ideas to make sure that opinions remain in some sense their own. Clerks, in other words, work within the assumption of a personalized authority in the genre of the judicial opinion. The same assumption, that of a personal authority in the very form of the statement, also nourishes the interest and involvement of the imputed author, the judge who signs the opinion. * * *

---

The *DiFrancesco* opinion has been used to teach judges how NOT to write an appellate opinion. Charles G. Douglas, *How to Write a Concise Opinion*, 22 JUDGES' J. 4 (Spring 1983). These portions of the opinion summarize the lower courts' decisions and the applicable rules of law. As an opinion from the United States Supreme Court, some also view it as representing the influence of judicial clerks upon opinions issued by that court, such as length, word choice, extensive citations, and footnotes.

## UNITED STATES v. DIFRANCESCO
### 449 U.S. 117 (1980)

BLACKMUN, JUSTICE

The Organized Crime Control Act of 1970, Pub. L. 91-452, 84 Stat. 922, contains, among other things, a definition of "dangerous special offender," 18 U.S.C. § 3575(e) and (f); authorizes the imposition of an increased sentence upon a convicted dangerous special offender, § 3575(b); and grants the United States the right, under specified conditions, to take that sentence to the Court of Appeals for review, § 3576. The issue presented by this case is whether § 3576, authorizing the United States so to appeal, violates the Double Jeopardy Clause of the Fifth Amendment of the Constitution.

* * * *

## II

At the earlier racketeering trial, the evidence showed that respondent was involved in an arson-for-hire scheme in the Rochester, N.Y., area that was responsible for at least eight fires between 1970 and 1973; that the ring collaborated with property owners to set fire to buildings in return for shares of the insurance proceeds; and that insurers were defrauded of approximately $480,000 as a result of these fires. At the second trial, the evidence showed that respondent participated in the 1970 "Columbus

Day bombings," including the bombing of the federal building at Rochester.

Prior to the first trial, the Government, in accordance with § 3575(a), filed with the trial court a notice alleging that respondent was a dangerous special offender. This notice recited the Government's intention to seek enhanced sentences on the racketeering counts in the event respondent was convicted at that trial. After respondent was found guilty, a dangerous special offender hearing, pursuant to § 3575(b), was held. At the hearing, the Government relied upon the testimony adduced at the trial and upon public documents that attested to other convictions of respondent for the Columbus Day bombings, for loansharking, and for murder. App. 27–28, 30. The defense offered no evidence. It conceded the validity of the public records, *id.* at 31–32, but objected to any consideration of the murder offense because that conviction had been vacated on appeal. *Id.* at 28–29.

The District Court made findings of fact and ruled that respondent was a dangerous special offender within the meaning of the statute. The findings set forth respondent's criminal record and stated that that record revealed "virtually continuous criminal conduct over the past eight years, interrupted only by relatively brief periods of imprisonment in 1975, 1976 and 1977." *Id.* at 41. The court found, in addition, that respondent's "criminal history, based upon proven facts, reveals a pattern of habitual and knowing criminal conduct of the most violent and dangerous nature against the lives and property of the citizens of this community. It further shows the defendant's complete and utter disregard for the public safety. The defendant, by virtue of his own criminal record, has shown himself to be a hardened habitual criminal from whom the public must be protected for as long a period as possible. Only in that way can the public be protected from further violent and dangerous criminal conduct by the defendant." *Id.* at 43. The court thereupon sentenced respondent under § 3575(b) to the concurrent 10-year terms hereinabove described. App. 45–46.

The United States then took its appeal under § 3576, claiming that the District Court abused its discretion in imposing sentences that amounted to additional imprisonment of respondent for only one year, in the face of the findings the court made after the dangerous special offender hearing.[6] The dismissal of the Government's appeal by the Court of Appeals rested specifically upon its conclusion, which it described as "inescapable," that "to subject a defendant to the risk of substitution of a greater sentence, upon an appeal by the government is to place him a second time 'in jeopardy of life or limb.' " 604 F.2d at 783.

---

[6] [9] It was indicated at oral argument, Tr. of Oral Arg. 5, 37, 39, and in one of the briefs, Brief for Respondent 12, as well as in the opinion of the Court of Appeals, 604 F.2d at 781, and n.17, that this is the first case in which the United States specifically has sought review of a sentence under § 3576. Inasmuch as the statute was enacted a decade ago, this fact might be said to indicate either little use of the special offender statute by the United States, or prosecutorial concern about its constitutionality, or that federal trial judges are imposing sufficiently severe sentences on special offenders to make review unnecessary. No definitive explanation, however, has been offered. An attempt on the part of this Court to explain the nonuse of the statute would be speculation and we shall not indulge in it.

## III

While this Court, so far as we are able to ascertain, has never invalidated an Act of Congress on double jeopardy grounds, it has had frequent occasion recently to consider and pass upon double jeopardy claims raised in various contexts. *See United States v. Jorn*, 400 U.S. 470 (1971); *Colten v. Kentucky*, 407 U.S. 104 (1972); *Illinois v. Somerville*, 410 U.S. 458 (1973); *Chaffin v. Stynchcombe*, 412 U.S. 17 (1973); *United States v. Wilson*, 420 U.S. 332 (1975); *United States v. Jenkins*, 420 U.S. 358 (1975); *Serfass v. United States*, 420 U.S. 377 (1975); *Breed v. Jones*, 421 U.S. 519 (1975); *United States v. Dinitz*, 424 U.S. 600 (1976); *Ludwig v. Massachusetts*, 427 U.S. 618 (1976); *United States v. Martin Linen Supply Co.*, 430 U.S. 564 (1977); *Lee v. United States*, 432 U.S. 23 (1977); *Arizona v. Washington*, 434 U.S. 497 (1978); *Burks v. United States*, 437 U.S. 1 (1978); *Greene v. Massey*, 437 U.S. 19 (1978); *Crist v. Bretz*, 437 U.S. 28 (1978); *Sanabria v. United States*, 437 U.S. 54 (1978); *United States v. Scott*, 437 U.S. 82 (1978); *Swisher v. Brady*, 438 U.S. 204 (1978); *Whalen v. United States*, 445 U.S. 684 (1980); *Illinois v. Vitale*, 447 U.S. 410 (1980).

These cited cases are the additions of just the past decade to the less numerous list of well-known double jeopardy decisions of past years. Among those earlier cases are *United States v. Perez*, 6 L. Ed. 165, 9 Wheat. 579 (1824); *Ex parte Lange*, 21 L. Ed. 872, 18 Wall. 163 (1874); *United States v. Ball*, 163 U.S. 662 (1896); *Kepner v. United States*, 195 U.S. 100 (1904); *Green v. United States*, 355 U.S. 184 (1957); *Fong Foo v. United States*, 369 U.S. 141 (1962); *Downum v. United States*, 372 U.S. 734 (1963); *United States v. Tateo*, 377 U.S. 463 (1964).

That the Clause is important and vital in this day is demonstrated by the host of recent cases. That its application has not proved to be facile or routine is demonstrated by acknowledged changes in direction or in emphasis. *See, e.g., United States v. Scott, supra*, overruling *United States v. Jenkins, supra*; and *Burks v. United States*, 437 U.S. at 18, overruling at least in part, certain prior cases in the area. *See also* Note, 24 Minn. L. Rev. 522 (1940); Westen & Drubel, *Toward a General Theory of Double Jeopardy*, 1978 Sup. Ct. Rev. 81, 82. Nonetheless, the following general principles emerge from the Court's double jeopardy decisions and may be regarded as essentially settled:

— The general design of the Double Jeopardy Clause of the Fifth Amendment is that described in *Green v. United States*:

> "The constitutional prohibition against 'double jeopardy' was designed to protect an individual from being subjected to the hazards of trial and possible conviction more than once for an alleged offense. . . . The underlying idea, one that is deeply ingrained in at least the Anglo-American system of jurisprudence, is that the State with all its resources and power should not be allowed to make repeated attempts to convict an individual for an alleged offense, thereby subjecting him to embarrassment, expense and ordeal and compelling him to live in a continuing state of anxiety and insecurity, as well as enhancing the possibility that even though innocent he may be found guilty." 355 U.S. at 187–188.

*See also Serfass v. United States*, 420 U.S. at 387–388; *Crist v. Bretz*, 437 U.S. at 35.

This concept has ancient roots centering in the common-law pleas of autre fois acquit, autre fois convict, and pardon, 4 W. Blackstone, Commentaries 329–330 (1st ed. 1769), and found expression in the legal tradition of colonial America. *See Green v. United States*, 355 U.S. at 187; *id.* at 200 (dissenting opinion); *United States v. Wilson*, 420 U.S. at 339–342; *United States v. Scott*, 437 U.S. at 87.

— The stated design, in terms of specific purpose, has been expressed in various ways. It has been said that "a" or "the" "primary purpose" of the Clause was "to preserve the finality of judgments," *Crist v. Bretz*, 437 U.S. at 33, or the "integrity" of judgments, *United States v. Scott*, 437 U.S. at 92. But it has also been said that "central to the objective of the prohibition against successive trials" is the barrier to "affording the prosecution another opportunity to supply evidence which it failed to muster in the first proceeding." *Burks v. United States*, 437 U.S. at 11; *Swisher v. Brady*, 438 U.S. at 215–216. Implicit in this is the thought that if the Government may re-prosecute, it gains an advantage from what it learns at the first trial about the strengths of the defense case and the weaknesses of its own. *See United States v. Scott*, 437 U.S. at 105, n.4 (dissenting opinion); *United States v. Wilson*, 420 U.S. at 352.

Still consideration has been noted:

> "Because jeopardy attaches before the judgment becomes final, the constitutional protection also embraces the defendant's 'valued right to have his trial completed by a particular tribunal.' " *Arizona v. Washington*, 434 U.S. at 503, quoting from *Wade v. Hunter*, 336 U.S. 684, 689 (1949).

*See Swisher v. Brady*, 438 U.S. at 214–215; *Crist v. Bretz*, 437 U.S. at 36.

On occasion, stress has been placed upon punishment:

> "It is the punishment that would legally follow the second conviction which is the real danger guarded against by the Constitution." *Ex parte Lange*, 18 Wall. at 173.

— The Court has summarized:

> "That guarantee [against double jeopardy] has been said to consist of three separate constitutional protections. It protects against a second prosecution for the same offense after acquittal. It protects against a second prosecution for the same offense after conviction. And it protects against multiple punishments for the same offense." (Footnotes omitted.) *North Carolina v. Pearce*, 395 U.S. 711, 717 (1969).[7]

*See Illinois v. Vitale*, 447 US. at 415.

— An acquittal is accorded special weight. "The constitutional protection against double jeopardy unequivocally prohibits a second trial following an acquittal," for the "public interest in the finality of criminal judgments is so strong that an acquitted

---

[7] [10] This recital is described as this Court's "favorite saying about double jeopardy" and is the subject of comment, not uncritical, in Professor Westen's provocative and thoughtful article, *The Three Faces of Double Jeopardy: Reflections on Government Appeals of Criminal Sentences*, 78 MICH. L. REV. 1001, 1062–1063 (1980).

defendant may not be retried even though 'the acquittal was based upon an egregiously erroneous foundation.' " *See Fong Foo v. United States*, 369 U.S. 141, 143. If the innocence of the accused has been confirmed by a final judgment, the Constitution conclusively presumes that a second trial would be unfair." *Arizona v. Washington*, 434 U.S. at 503. The law "attaches particular significance to an acquittal." *United States v. Scott*, 437 U.S. at 91.

This is justified on the ground that, however mistaken the acquittal may have been, there would be an unacceptably high risk that the Government, with its superior resources, would wear down a defendant, thereby "enhancing the possibility that even though innocent he may be found guilty." *Green v. United States*, 355 U.S. at 188. *See also United States v. Martin Linen Supply Co.*, 430 U.S. at 571, 573, n.12. ("[W]e necessarily afford absolute finality to a jury's *verdict* of acquittal — no matter how erroneous its decision" (emphasis in original)); *Burks v. United States*, 437 U.S. at 16.[8]

— The result is definitely otherwise in cases where the trial has not ended in an acquittal. This Court has long recognized that the Government may bring a second prosecution where a mistrial has been occasioned by "manifest necessity." *United States v. Perez*, 9 Wheat. at 580. *See Arizona v. Washington*, 434 U.S. at 514–516; *Illinois v. Somerville*, 410 U.S. 458 (1973). Furthermore, re-prosecution of a defendant who has successfully moved for a mistrial is not barred, so long as the Government did not deliberately seek to provoke the mistrial request. *United States v. Dinitz*, 424 U.S. at 606–611.

Similarly, where the trial has been terminated prior to a jury verdict at the defendant's request on grounds unrelated to guilt or innocence, the Government may seek appellate review of that decision even though a second trial would be necessitated by a reversal. *See United States v. Scott*, 437 U.S. at 98–99. A fortiori, the Double Jeopardy Clause does not bar a Government appeal from a ruling in favor of the defendant after a guilty verdict has been entered by the trier of fact. *See United States v. Wilson, supra*; *United States v. Rojas*, 554 F.2d 938, 941 (CA9 1977); *United States v. De Garces*, 518 F.2d 1156, 1159 (CA2 1975).

Finally, if the first trial has ended in a conviction, the double jeopardy guarantee "imposes no limitations whatever upon the power to *retry* a defendant who has succeeded in getting his first conviction set aside" (emphasis in original). *North Carolina v. Pearce*, 395 U.S. at 720. "It would be a high price indeed for society to pay were every accused granted immunity from punishment because of any defect sufficient to constitute reversible error in the proceedings leading to conviction." *United States v. Tateo*, 377 U.S. at 466. "[T]o require a criminal defendant to stand trial again after he has successfully invoked a statutory right of appeal to upset his first conviction is not an act of governmental oppression of the sort against which the Double Jeopardy Clause was intended to protect." *United States v. Scott*, 437 U.S. at 91. There is, however, one exception to this rule: the Double Jeopardy Clause prohibits retrial after a conviction has been reversed because of insufficiency of the evidence. *Burks v. United States, supra*; *Greene v. Massey*, 437 U.S. at 24.

---

[8] [11] Professor Westen describes it succinctly this way: "The prohibition on retrial following an acquittal is based on a jury's prerogative to acquit against the evidence. . . . " *Id.* at 1012, 1063.

— Where the Clause does apply, "its sweep is absolute." *Burks v. United States*, 437 U.S. at 11, n.6.

— The United States "has no right of appeal in a criminal case, absent explicit statutory authority." *United States v. Scott*, 437 U.S. at 84–85. But with the enactment of the first paragraph of what is now 18 U.S.C. § 3731 by Pub. L. 91-644 in 1971, 84 Stat. 1890, permitting a Government appeal in a criminal case except "where the double jeopardy clause of the United States Constitution prohibits further prosecution," the Court necessarily concluded that "Congress intended to remove all statutory barriers to Government appeals and to allow appeals whenever the Constitution would permit." *United States v. Wilson*, 420 U.S. at 337. *See also United States v. Scott*, 437 U.S. at 85.[9]

\* \* \* \*

Reliance on judicial clerks and externs may not only create criticisms of written opinions, but may affect the public's perception of the judicial system and confidence in its impartiality. Recusal was mandated in the following opinion, where a judge's public recognition of his judicial clerk's research and drafting duties was held to create the public perception that the law clerk, not the judge, had decided the result and also drafted the case opinion. The judicial clerk also conducted a court hearing on the case with counsel, but without the judge. Finally, the judicial clerk had a conflict of interest with counsel for one of the parties. [*See* Chapter 1]. The judicial clerk's conduct created a public perception that his role in the case loomed too large.

## PARKER v. CONNORS STEEL COMPANY
### 855 F.2d 1510 (11th Cir. 1988)

Floyd R. Gibson, Senior Circuit Judge

Appellants, former employees of Connors Steel Company (Connors) and putative class representatives of approximately 600 former Connors employees, appeal an order of the district court granting summary judgment to Connors, H.K Porter Company, Inc. (H.K. Porter), and United Steelworkers of America, AFL-CIO, CLC (Union), in this complicated dispute which followed the closing of Connors's steel plant in Birmingham, Alabama. The employees sued Connors, its parent corporation H.K. Porter (Connors and H.K Porter are collectively referred to as the "Company"), and the Union alleging fraud, a hybrid § 301/fair representation claim, breach of the duty of fair representation, and breach of a collective bargaining agreement (CBA or agreement) and two concession agreements.

The district court concluded that the state law fraud claims were preempted by sections 7 and 8 of the National Labor Relations Act (NLRA or Labor Act). The district court also determined that there were no genuine issues of material fact and

---

[9] [12] And, of course, it is surely settled that the Double Jeopardy Clause of the Fifth Amendment has application to the States through the Fourteenth Amendment. *Benton v. Maryland*, 395 U.S. 784 (1969); *Illinois v. Vitale*, 447 U.S. 410, 415 (1980).

that the Union was entitled to summary judgment on the fair representation claim by the former employees as a matter of law. Finding that the Company's liability under section 301 of the Labor Management Relations Act (LMRA) was conditional on the Union's breaching its duty of fair representation, the district court granted the Company's motion for summary judgment. We affirm.

\* \* \* \*

D. Recusal

After the district court issued its decision, the employees filed a motion requesting the district judge to recuse himself from the case. The memorandum opinion issued by the district court contained a footnote that reads in relevant part:

> For the formulation of this opinion, the Court is indebted to its Law Clerk, William G. Somerville, III, for his careful analysis of the massive discovery materials and his countless discussions with the Court as to how the law should be applied to the material facts as to which there is no genuine issue.[1]

The employees argue that the district judge was required to recuse himself because his law clerk, William G. Somerville, III, was the son of William G. Somerville, Jr.,[2] a partner in the law firm of Lange, Simpson, Robinson & Somerville, the firm representing Connors and H.K Porter. The employees also allege that Somerville's participation in the decisional process was critical to the court's decision because it was Somerville who reviewed the voluminous discovery documents and determined that there were no material issues of fact that would prevent summary judgment disposition of the case.[3] Additionally, the employees allege that Somerville actually held a hearing with counsel in the absence of the district judge and later reported the results of the hearing to the judge. The employees argue that these circumstances violate 28 U.S.C. § 455 and thus require this court to reverse and reassign this case to another judge.

The Supreme Court very recently discussed § 455(a) and its goal of promoting public confidence in the integrity of the judicial process. In *Liljeberg v. Health Services Acquisition Corp.*, 108 S. Ct. 2194 (1988), the Supreme Court held that scienter is not required in order to find a violation of § 455(a). The Supreme Court stated:

---

[1] [8] We note that this is not an isolated case. The district judge has regularly included such footnotes in published opinions as far back as 1961. *See, e.g., Willoughby Roofing & Supply Co., Inc. v. Kajima Intern., Inc.*, 598 F. Supp. 353, 354 (N.D Ala. 1984), *aff'd*, 776 F.2d 269 (11th Cir. 1985) (per curiam); *United States Fidelity & Guaranty Co. v. Slifkin*, 200 F. Supp. 563, 582 (N.D. Ala. 1961).

[2] [9] William G. Somerville, Jr., is apparently a former law clerk to Judge Lynne. *See id.* at 582 ("Credit is due William G. Somerville, Jr., Law Clerk to the Court, for the preparation of this opinion.").

[3] [10] This argument is weakened somewhat by other language which also appears in the footnote crediting the assistance of Somerville. The district court stated: "More than two years ago the Court announced its tentative opinion that descendants were entitled to summary judgment but deferred to the request of plaintiffs' counsel that action be withheld pending the completion of discovery, which proved to be wide-sweeping." Thus, the district judge had tentatively ruled against the employees prior to Somerville's employment.

The judge's lack of knowledge of a disqualifying circumstance may bear on the question of remedy, but it does not eliminate the risk that 'his impartiality might reasonably be questioned' by other persons. . . . Moreover, advancement of the purpose of the provision — to promote public confidence in the integrity of the judicial process, . . . does not depend upon whether or not the judge actually knew of facts creating an appearance of impropriety, so long as the public might reasonably believe that he or she knew. [citations omitted].

Inherent in § 455(a)'s requirement that a judge disqualify himself if his impartiality might reasonably be questioned is the principle that our system of "justice must satisfy the appearance of justice." *Offutt v. United States*, 348 U.S. 11, 14 (1954). "The very purpose of § 455(a) is to promote confidence in the judiciary by avoiding even the appearance of impropriety whenever possible." *Liljeberg*, 108 S. Ct. at 2203–05.

Thus, section 455(a) embodies an objective standard. The test is whether an objective, disinterested, lay observer fully informed of the facts underlying the grounds on which recusal was sought would entertain a significant doubt about the judge's impartiality. *See Potashnick v. Port City Const. Co.*, 609 F.2d 1101, 1111 (5th Cir.), *cert. denied*, 449 U.S. 820 (1980).

We now turn to the objective facts that might reasonably cause an objective observer to question Judge Lynne's impartiality. First, the close familial relationship between Judge Lynne's law clerk and a senior partner in the firm representing Connors and H.K. Porter might lead an objective observer, especially a lay observer, to believe that Connors and H.K. Porter will receive favorable treatment from the district judge. This is compounded by the observation that William G. Somerville, Jr., is a former law clerk to Judge Lynne.[4]

Judge Lynne's practice of giving credit to his law clerk in a footnote may erroneously lead some to believe that the law clerk decided the case. While it has not been suggested that the decision in this case was made by Judge Lynne's law clerk and we have no reason to believe that it was, it is not unreasonable to believe that the public may come to this conclusion. *See, e.g., Acceptance Ins. Co. v. Schafner*, 651 F. Supp. 776, 778 (N.D. Ala. 1986) ("This Memorandum of Opinion was prepared by William G. Somerville, III, Law Clerk, in which the Court fully concurs.") . . . ; *Cone v. The Florida Bar*, 626 F. Supp. 132, 137 (M.D. Fla. 1985) (Judge Lynne, sitting by designation) ("This opinion is the product of exhaustive research and careful analysis by Luther M. Dorr, Jr., Law Clerk."). It goes without saying that it would be improper for a judge to delegate the adjudicative function of his office to one that was neither appointed by the President nor confirmed by the Senate.

Finally, we believe that when Somerville held a hearing in Judge Lynne's absence and later reported the results of the hearing to the judge this contributed to the appearance of impropriety.

---

**4** [13] We recognize, however, that ordinarily disqualification of an entire law firm is not required "when the propriety of a former law clerk's participation in a case is drawn in question." [citation omitted] William G. Somerville, Jr., did not actually participate in the instant case, but his relationship with Judge Lynne's law clerk and the fact that he is a former law clerk to Judge Lynne contribute to the appearance of impropriety.

We believe that these facts might cast doubt in the public's mind on Judge Lynne's ability to remain impartial and at a minimum these facts raise the appearance of impropriety. It has been stated on numerous occasions that when a judge harbors any doubts concerning whether his disqualification is required he should resolve the doubt in favor of disqualification. [citations omitted]

We express no opinion on whether any of the above facts standing alone would rise to the level of a § 455(a) violation. We merely conclude that all of these facts taken together raise the appearance of impropriety and may cause one to reasonably question Judge Lynne's impartiality.

In *Hall*, the Fifth Circuit found a violation of § 455(a) because a magistrate refused to disqualify himself after it was revealed that his law clerk was a member of the plaintiff class involved in the suit and had accepted employment with class counsel before judgment was rendered. The Fifth Circuit noted that:

> Law clerks are not merely the judge's errand runners.
>
> They are sounding boards for tentative opinions and legal researchers who seek the authorities that affect decision. Clerks are privy to the judge's thoughts in a way that neither parties to the lawsuit nor his most intimate family members may be.

*Id.* at 179.

This case was later characterized by the Second Circuit as involving actual bias on the part of the law clerk that was imputed to the court. *See United States v. Murphy*, 768 F.2d at 1539 n.3. Our decision in the instant case should not be interpreted as imputing to the district judge any appearance of impartiality on the part of the law clerk. [citations omitted] Similarly, when a judge's law clerk has a possible conflict of interest or knows of other disqualifying factors it is the clerk, not the judge, who must be disqualified. [citation omitted] This problem might have been avoided if Judge Lynne would have taken steps to isolate Somerville from this case.

A law clerk, as well as a judge, should stay informed of circumstances that may raise the appearance of impartiality or impropriety. And when such circumstances are present appropriate actions should be taken. In the instant case either Judge Lynne or his law clerk must have known of the grounds for disqualification and either of them should have raised the issue. If the issue had been raised and fully disclosed the employees may have waived the grounds for disqualification.

Having determined that a violation of § 455(a) is presented, we now must determine the proper remedy. In *Liljeberg* the Court noted that:

> As in other areas of the law, there is surely room for harmless error committed by busy judges who inadvertently overlook a disqualifying circumstance. There need not be a draconian remedy for every violation of § 455(a). 108 S. Ct. at 2202–03 (footnote omitted).

We believe that in this case Judge Lynne's refusal to disqualify himself was indeed harmless error. In determining the proper remedy for a § 455(a) violation the Supreme Court has suggested the following test. Consider: 1) the risk of injustice to the parties in the particular case; 2) the risk that the denial of relief will produce injustice in other cases; and 3) the risk of undermining the public's confidence in the judicial process. *Id.* at 2203–05. We believe that these factors weigh heavily in favor of our conclusion that Judge Lynne's decision not to recuse himself was harmless error.

First, the risk of injustice to the parties in this case if relief is denied is nonexistent. To the contrary, if we granted the employees relief for the § 455(a) violation and vacated the district court's decision then our action will create an injustice. The district court dismissed the case on summary judgment and therefore this court is in as good a position to determine the merits of the employees' claims as was the district court. [citation omitted] As discussed previously, we agree with the district court that summary judgment was proper. It would, therefore, be ridiculous to remand this case and reassign it to another judge after we have already exercised plenary review and have concluded that summary judgment was proper. We also note that Judge Lynne announced his tentative decision to grant the Company and the Union summary judgment prior to Somerville joining his staff. Therefore, the risk that Judge Lynne based his decision on Somerville's involvement is remote. *But see Hall*, 695 F.2d at 180 ("The judge's assertion that he had made up his mind immediately after hearing the case, without the law clerk's assistance, is immaterial. Every judge has suffered a change of heart after reaching a tentative decision. Much might happen during research and opinion writing to affect the decision.").

* * * *

Finally, we do not believe that the public's confidence in the judicial process will be undermined if we conclude that the § 455(a) violation was harmless error. Since we have determined that in fact a violation occurred and strongly urge Judge Lynne to discontinue his practice of crediting the work of his law clerks, we believe that our decision will instill greater confidence in our judiciary. To the extent that public confidence has already been undermined we do not believe that granting relief in this case will change the public's perception in any appreciable way. Such harm cannot be remedied by vacating the district court's decision and reassigning this case to a different judge. In fact, if we reverse and vacate a decision that we have already determined to be proper, the public will lose faith in our system of justice because the case will be overturned without regard to the merits of the employees' claims. Judicial decisions based on such technical arguments not relevant to the merits contribute to the public's distrust in our system of justice.

* * * *

---

The *Parker* case is not an isolated example of a judge crediting a clerk with contributing to a judicial opinion. Should there be any recognition at all or does the issue turn on the nature of the recognition?

Today, some judges continue to acknowledge their clerk or extern's research and writing assistance explicitly: "Drafted with the assistance of Ryan B. White, Esquire,

Law Clerk." *In re Excel Storage Products, L.P.*, 458 B.R. 175, 177 (Bankr. M.D. Pa. 2011); "The Court acknowledges the valuable contribution and assistance of judicial extern Benjamin J. Christoff of the University of Dayton School of Law in drafting this opinion." *Grisby v. Wilberforce Univ.*, 2012 U.S. Dist. LEXIS 14805 (S.D. Ohio).

Other judges and courts question this judicial recognition of law clerks and externs and at least one court expressly forbids it:

> Judges who thank their interns do so out of kindness to students who, mostly without pay, make a significant contribution. What is kind to the interns, however, is unkind to the litigants and the public. This is not to suggest that judges not use interns to help with opinions. To the contrary, judges and their law clerks improve legal education and sometimes their opinions when they assign research, writing, and editing tasks to interns, so long as the judge and the law clerk monitor all student work closely. But crediting the intern makes it appear that the court delegated its decision-making obligations to an unaccountable law student.
>
> A higher authority forbids what the *New York Law Journal* and the West Group permit. For the past decade, the New York State Law Reporting Bureau has put into effect a Court of Appeals policy in which the State Reporter will not print judicial acknowledgments to law clerks or interns. This policy suggests that judges who want to thank their clerks and interns reconsider their impulse, however well meaning.

Gerald Lebovits, *Judges' Clerks Play Varied Roles in the Opinion Drafting Process*, 76 N.Y. St. B.J. 34 (July/Aug. 2004).*

## In Court Reports

**1.**   Locate recent opinions from your judge and analyze them using the advice offered by Professor Strong in her article.

**2.**   Locate recent opinions from your judge and reverse engineer the organization, use of introductions, word choice, and the other criteria for effective opinion writing.

**3.**   Articulate your judge's advice on opinion writing from recent opinions or from materials provided to you by the judge or a judicial clerk during your externship.

**4.**   Track the actors — judge, clerk, extern, administrator — in the decisionmaking and opinion drafting processes in your court and assess each actor's contribution to the process:

**a.** Initial review of parties' brief on disputed motion/appeal.

**b.** Review and assessment of legal authorities cited in parties' briefs.

**c.** Reach or recommend initial decision on disposition of motion/appeal.

**d.** Reach or recommend final decision on disposition of motion/appeal.

---

**e.** Draft initial opinion on motion/appeal.

**f.** Proofread and cite-check initial and final opinions of motion/appeal.

**g.** Schedule docket call, hearings, oral argument.

**h.** Issue orders on "housekeeping" motions such as extension of time to file and others.

**i.** Conduct hearings, settlement, and other conferences.

**j.** Take notes at hearings, conferences, oral arguments; review transcripts of same.

**k.** Supervision of court staff — judicial clerks, externs.

**l.** Attend social and/or scholarly functions within the legal community.

**m.** Meet and consult with judges and staff from other chambers.

**5.** Do the roles and functions described in (4.) appear to have evolved, in whole or in part, as a response to an increase in filings or a crowded docket?

**6.** Observe counsel in court and assess their ability as an advocate to make vivid to the judge the effects of a decision on the litigant.

**7.** Similarly, assess this same type of advocacy in the written briefs filed by counsel. By envisioning the litigant as a reader or audience for an opinion, can you improve your advocacy?

**8.** Slip opinions and per curiam opinions are often the target of criticism and examples of "writing by committee." Locate these types of opinions, if issued by your court, and assess them. Compare them to full, published opinions issued by the court.

## Out of Court Reports

**1.** Using the *DiFrancesco* opinion, draft a short paragraph of rules of law for the concept of double jeopardy. Do not quote; put the law in your own words.

**2.** Read the entire opinion and then critique and/or defend the reasoning, research, citations, analysis, and writing in the *DiFrancesco* opinion.

**3.** Additional United States Supreme Court opinions under attack as "failures of rhetorical skill" and examples of the "decline of judicial writing" are: *Bush v. Gore*, 531 U.S. 98 (2000) and *Clinton v. Jones*, 520 U.S. 681 (1997). Read these opinions to decide if you agree with Judge Posner's evaluation. Richard A. Posner, *Legal Writing Today*, 8 Scribes J. Legal Writing 35 (2002).

**4.** In addition, Judge Posner takes on a re-write of the opinion in *United States v. Morris*, 977 F.2d 617 (D.C. Cir. 1992). Richard A. Posner, Reflections on Judging, Chapter 8: *Opinion Writing & Appellate Advocacy* (2013). He again expressed concern over symptoms in the writing indicating law clerk authorship: "I am guessing that the opinion was written by a law clerk, and edited but not rewritten extensively by the judge who was its nominal author. The opinion has the exhaustiveness of the anxious novice author . . . ."

Try a revision of the opinion yourself. Posner's version is the appendix of his book.

**5.**   Assess the *Escola* opinion: does it live up to its nomination as a decision that honestly provides the real reasons for its decision and also communicates effectively to its audiences?

**6.**   Judicial humor and cases using it have been collected and examined in several law review articles. Attitudes towards this practice divide sharply. Assess your own response to the *Denny, Gray,* and *Russell* opinions and consider the motivation of the judge and the responses of counsel, the parties, the public, and other judges on the same court.

## SELECTED BIBLIOGRAPHY

Douglas E. Abrams, *Judges and Their Editors*, 3 ALB. GOV'T L. REV. 392 (2010).

RUGGERO J. ALDISERT, OPINION WRITING (2d ed. 2009).

Ruggero J. Aldisert et al., *Opinion Writing and Opinion Readers*, 31 CARDOZO L. REV. 1 (2009).

Appellate Judges Conference, Judicial Opinion Writing Manual (1991).

Thomas E. Baker, *A Review of Corpus Juris Humorous*, 24 TEX. TECH. L. REV. 869 (1993).

John J. Brunetti, *Searching for Methods of Trial Court Fact-Finding and Decision-Making*, 49 HASTINGS L. J. 1491 (1998).

Richard B. Cappalli, *Improving Appellate Opinions*, 83 JUDICATURE 286 (May–June 2000).

Stephen J. Choi & G. Mitu Gulati, *Which Judges Write Their Opinions (and Should We Care)?*, 32 FLA. ST. U. L. REV. 1077 (2005).

Catherine Crowe, *Videri Quam Esse: The Role of Empathy in Judicial Discourse*, 34 LAW & PSYCHOL. REV. 121 (2010).

Michael D. Daneker, *Moral Reasoning and the Quest for Legitimacy*, 43 AM. U. L. REV. 49 (1993).

WILLIAM DOMNARSKI, IN THE OPINION OF THE COURT (1996).

FEDERAL JUDICIAL CENTER, JUDICIAL WRITING MANUAL: A POCKET GUIDE FOR JUDGES (2d ed. 2013).

Thomas Gibbs Gee, *A Few of Wisdom's Idiosyncrasies and of Few of Ignorance's: A Judicial Style Sheet*, 1 SCRIBES J. OF LEGAL WRITING 55 (1990).

JOYCE J. GEORGE, JUDICIAL OPINION WRITING HANDBOOK (3d ed. 2007).

Chris Guthrie et al., *Blinking on the Bench: How Judges Decide Cases*, 93 CORNELL L. REV. 1 (2007).

Lucas K. Hori, *Bons Mots, Buffoonery, and the Bench: The Role of Humor in Judicial Opinions*, 60 UCLA L. REV. DISCOURSE 16 (2012).

Peter J. Keane, *Legalese in Bankruptcy: How to Lose Cases and Alienate Judges*, 28 AM. BANKR. INST. J. 38 (Dec./Jan. 2010).

Mary Kate Kearney, *The Propriety of Poetry in Judicial Opinions*, 12 WIDENER L. J. 597 (2003)

Gerald Lebowitz, *Not Mere Rhetoric: Metaphors and Similes*, 74 N.Y. ST. BAR J. 64 (June 2002).

ROBERT A. LEFLAR, APPELLATE JUDICIAL OPINIONS (1974).

Robert A. Leflar, *Honest Judicial Opinions*, 74 NW. U. L. REV. 721 (1979).

Andrea McArdle, *Using a Narrative Lens to Understand Empathy and How It Matters in Judging*, 9 LEGAL COMM. & RHETORIC: JALWD 173 (2012).

David McGowan, *Judicial Writing and the Ethics of the Judicial Office*, 14 GEO. J. LEGAL ETHICS 509 (2001).

DAVID MELLINKOFF, LEGAL WRITING: SENSE AND NONSENSE (1982).

Abner J. Mikva, *For Whom Judges Write*, 61 S. CAL. L. REV. 1357 (1988).

Nicole E. Negowetti, *Judicial Decisionmaking, Empathy, and the Limits of Perception*, 47 AKRON L. REV. 693 (2014).

Anthony Niblett, *Do Judges Cherry Pick Precedents to Justify Extra-Legal Decisions?: A Statistical Examination*, 70 MD. L. REV. 234 (2010).

Martha C. Nussbaum, *Poets as Judges: Judicial Rhetoric and the Literary Imagination*, 62 U. CHI. L. REV. 1477 (1995).

Richard A. Posner, *Legal Writing Today*, 8 SCRIBES J. LEGAL WRITING 35 (2002).

Douglas R. Richmond, *Unoriginal Sin: The Problem of Judicial Plagiarism*, 45 ARIZ. ST. L.J. 1077 (2013).

Frederick Schauer, *The Failure of the Common Law*, 36 ARIZ. ST. L.J. 765 (2004).

Michael Serota, *Intelligible Justice*, 66 U. MIAMI L. REV. 649 (2012).

Daniel F. Solomon, *Crafting Substantial ALJ Decisions*, 43 JUDGES' J. 23 (Winter 2004).

Mary B. Trevor, *From Ostriches to Sci-Fi: A Social Science Analysis of the Impact of Humor in Judicial Opinions*, 45 U. TOL. L. REV. 291 (2014).

Ruth C. Vance, *Judicial Opinion Writing: An Annotated Bibliography*, 17 LEGAL WRITING: J. LEGAL WRITING INSTITUTE 197 (2011).

Patricia M. Wald, *The Rhetoric of Results and the Results of Rhetoric: Judicial Writing*, 62 U. CHI. L. REV. 1371 (1995).

Nancy A. Wanderer, *Writing Better Opinions: Communicating with Candor, Clarity, and Style*, 54 ME. L. REV. 47 (2002).

James Boyd White, *What's An Opinion For?*, 62 U. CHI. L. REV. 1363 (1995).

Nadine J. Wichern, *A Court of Clerks, Not of Men: Serving Justice in the Media Age*, 49 DEPAUL L. REV. 621 (1999).

JOSEPH M. WILLIAMS, STYLE: TEN LESSONS IN CLARITY AND GRACE (11th ed. 2013).

RICHARD C. WYDICK, PLAIN ENGLISH FOR LAWYERS (5th ed. 2005).

# Chapter 3

# JUDICIAL SELECTION, QUALIFICATIONS, AND TRAINING

The United States is the only country in the world that elects its judges, and for two-hundred years, we have been debating whether or not we should elect our judges.

Ric Simmons, *Chooseyourjudges.org: Treating Elected Judges as Politicians*, 45 AKRON L. REV. 1 (2012).

[T]he [Study] finds that elections produce a judiciary that is more beholden to interest groups than one generated through appointments. The consequence of this greater special interest involvement is an erosion of public trust and confidence in the judiciary.

Steven Zeidman, *To Elect or Not to Elect: A Case Study of Judicial Selection in New York City 1977–2002*, 37 U. MICH. J. L. REFORM 791 (2004).

In twenty-seven years of federal practice, I've never tried a case in front of a judge who was black, Hispanic, Asian, or American Indian.

Lawrence R. Baca, *Diversity Among Judges: Building a Better Bench*, 43 JUDGES' J. 30 (Spring 2004).

Highly qualified professionals have been targeted for attack almost randomly and then subjected to public character assassination and humiliation; all because they were among the relatively few talented lawyers willing to take a significant cut in pay in order to serve on the federal bench. The Senate's [confirmation] process has come to resemble not a deliberative function, but a spectacle like those at the Roman Coliseum where prisoners were thrown to wild beasts with only the barest tools of self-defense.

Edith H. Jones, *Observations on the Status and Impact of the Judicial Confirmation Process*, 39 U. RICH L. REV. 833 (2005).

The vast majority of people serving in the judiciary have no special credentials for the judicial role that set them apart from lawyers in general. Thus, other than a law school education, bar passage, and some amount of experience in the practice of law (typically, though not always, as litigators), there is no special training given to those who aspire to judicial office prior to their ascendancy to the bench

Keith R. Fisher, *Education for Judicial Aspirants*, 43 AKRON L. REV. 163 (2010).

> The training includes not only classroom instruction but also one-on-one mentoring, opportunities to observe, meetings with judges and justices who share responsibility for the system, and practical experience conducting mock trials, complete with the occasional sleeping juror, disruptive defendant, or objectionable lawyer.

Mary Vasaly, *Training the New Judge*, Bench & B. Minn., October 2011, 26.

This chapter addresses judicial selection, qualifications, education, and evaluation, as well as the results of the judicial selection process. First, judicial selection begins by appointment for federal judges at all levels, while state court judges are selected by a range of methods including different forms of election, appointment, and merit selections. Second, the qualifications to become a judicial candidate range from none in the federal courts to many among the state courts. Third, new judges require education to make the transition from lawyer to judge and need evaluation after they take the bench. Finally, no matter what the selection process employed, the results have created federal and state judiciaries with little diversity.

# I.  JUDICIAL SELECTION METHODS

## A.  Federal Court Selection

All Article III federal court judgeships are appointed for life, including appointments to the United States Supreme Court.

### How Are Supreme Court Justices Selected?

> The President nominates someone for a vacancy on the Court and the Senate votes to confirm the nominee, which requires a simple majority. In this way, both the Executive and Legislative Branches of the federal government have a voice in the composition of the Supreme Court.

http://www.supremecourt.gov/faq.aspx [website for United States Supreme Court]

For the past several decades, the Senate's federal judicial appointment confirmation process has become televised, controversial, bitter, prolonged by delay tactics, and divisive. The federal judge confirmation process has entered our popular culture and vocabulary:

> bork (bork), vb. Slang. 1. (Of the U.S. Senate) to reject a nominee, esp. for the U.S. Supreme Court, on grounds of the nominee's unorthodox political and legal philosophy. • The term derives from the name of Robert Bork, President Ronald Reagan's unsuccessful nominee for the Supreme Court in 1987. 2. (Of political and legal activists) to embark on a media campaign to pressure U.S. Senators into rejecting a President's nominee. 3. Generally, to smear a political opponent. BLACK'S LAW DICTIONARY (10th ed. 2014).

The attention focused on the confirmation process demonstrates that the stakes are high: the federal judges appointed by this process will decide issues that deeply divide Americans. For example, the Supreme Court has ruled on "gay rights, school vouchers, the environment, affirmative action, the Pledge of Allegiance, the war on terror, and abortion — just to name a few." William P. Marshall, *The Judicial Nominations Wars*, 39 U. RICH. L. REV. 819, 819–20 (2005).

The U.S. Senate Committee on the Judiciary convenes to question judicial nominees. Senators may also use the proceedings to comment on the nature of the nomination and confirmation process itself. One example of the Committee at work is this excerpt from the 2002 hearing on the nomination of Miguel Estrada to sit on the District of Columbia Circuit Court.

Senator Schumer of New York offered an "opening statement" referring to other nominee proceedings and expressing his desire to know the nominee's ideology and rejecting nominee responses that simply indicate he will follow the law.

———

Sen. Schumer:   Now, for the first time in a long time, there is balance on the D.C. Circuit: four Republican judges, four Democrats. That doesn't mean each case is always decided right down the middle, but there is balance. Some of us believe that this all important court should be kept in balance — not move too far left, not move too far right. Judicial nominees, we know, have worldviews they bring with them to the bench. They come to these positions of power with predilections, with leanings, with biases. Those biases influence the way they look at the law and at the facts of the cases coming before them. It is natural. And I am not saying there is anything nefarious or even wrong about this. It is just the way we all know how things are.

I wrote an op-ed piece in the New York Times a year ago suggesting we do away with "gotcha" politics and game-playing on this issue and that we be honest about our concerns. I published a report last week showing that the vast majority of the time that Democrats vote against the judicial nominee, it is a Republican nominee. And the vast majority of the time Republicans vote against a judicial nominee, it is a Democratic nominee.

Big shock, huh? But it is proof positive that ideology matters. If it didn't, if all we were looking at is legal excellence and judicial temperament, the votes against the nominees would be spread all over the place. Democrats would vote against an equal number of Democratic and Republican nominees, and the same with Republicans. That is not what happens, and we know that. Now, I have taken a lot of flack for saying this over and over again, but I think we have already proven the point.

Every single Senator on this side of the aisle has voted for conservative nominees. A lot of our friends are begging us to slow down. We are not going to slow down. Senator Leahy has done an admirable job of bringing nominees to the bench, as today's hearing shows. But we are also not going to speed things up and not give fair review to everybody, important review, important not just to the nominee, although that is important, but to the American people. We are going to take the time we need to review the records of all the nominees the President sends up here.

Conservative but non-ideological nominees, like Reena Raggi who last week was unanimously confirmed to the Second Circuit in near record time, will go through this committee with the greatest of ease. But those for whom red flags are raised will wait until we have done our due diligence. We owe the country, we owe the Constitution nothing less.

Ideology is not the only factor in determining how we vote, or most of us would have voted against just about every one of the judges who came forward. But for most of us, whether we want to admit it or not, it is a factor, and that is how it should be. And anyone who thinks it is okay for the President to consider ideology but not okay for the Senate is using double-think.

The White House is saying that they want to nominate conservatives in the mold of Scalia and Thomas. The President has said that. It is hard to believe that at least some of their nominees don't have a pretty strong agenda. Ideology is obviously being considered by the White House. When the White House starts nominating equal numbers of liberals and conservatives, equal numbers of Republicans and Democrats, that is when the Senate should ignore nominees' ideologies.

We had a hearing on Tuesday where Fred Fielding — a brilliant lawyer who served President Reagan well as counsel — testified. In his written testimony, he said that the administration never considered ideology when deciding whom to nominate to the bench. So I asked him if he could name five liberals that President Reagan nominated. After all, if he wasn't considering ideology, just temperament and legal excellence, you would get balance. His response was, "I certainly hope not. I hope we didn't nominate a single liberal nominee." I asked him to name one. He couldn't.

Of course that is true. I appreciate his candor. It proves that ideology plays a role when the President selects judges. I am befuddled by those who say the Senate shouldn't consider ideology when the President obviously does. It just doesn't make sense. So let's stop hurling invective and just be straight with each other.

Since we know that this is such an important court and since we know that ideology matters, whether we admit it or not, it is essential that this committee conduct a thorough and exhaustive examination of judicial nominees. Again, we would be derelict in our duty to the Constitution and our constituents if we did anything less.

We should demand that we hear more from nominees than the usual promises to follow the law as written. It is not enough to say, "I will follow the law, Senator," and expect us to just accept that. We need to be convinced that the nominees aren't far out of the mainstream. We need to be convinced that nominees will help maintain balance — not imbalance — on the courts.

A decade ago, our present President's father sent the Senate the nomination of Clarence Thomas. I wasn't in the Senate then, but I watched those hearings, and I have talked to a lot of my current colleagues who were here at that time. Clarence Thomas came before this distinguished committee and basically said he had no views on many important constitutional issues of the day. He said that he had never even discussed *Roe v. Wade* when he was in law school or since. But the minute Justice Thomas got to the Court, he was doctrinaire. Whether you agreed with him or not, he obviously had deeply held views that he shielded from the committee.

It wasn't a confirmation conversion. It was a confirmation subversion. And there is still a lot of simmering blood up here about that. We should do everything we can to prevent that from happening again.

We had a very good hearing last week on a very conservative nominee. Professor Michael McConnell has been nominated to the Tenth Circuit. He came before this committee and openly discussed his views — some of which I very much disagree with. But I will say this: He was candid with us about his beliefs, he engaged in honest discussion with us about his viewpoints, and he showed himself to be more of an iconoclast than an ideologue. I haven't made up my mind as to how I will vote on Professor McConnell, but by answering our questions, he put himself in a much better position, in my book.

The nominee before us today stands in contrast to Professor McConnell and to most other circuit court nominees for whom we have held hearings these past 14 months. Not his fault, but we know very little about who he is and what he thinks and how he arrives at his positions. There have been red flags raised by some who know him, but we don't know so far whether there is merit to those red flags or not. There is some support for him in the community and some opposition. We need to understand why.

As you know, a former supervisor of yours, Mr. Estrada, in the Office of Solicitor General has stated you were too much of an ideologue and do not have the temperament to merit confirmation. And you will be given the full opportunity to address those arguments.

Now, this committee has asked for the memos you wrote while you served in the Solicitor General's office. Everyone I have spoken with believes such memoranda will be useful in assessing how you approach the law. The role of the SG's office is to determine what positions the United States should take on important constitutional questions. The attorneys in that office engage in quintessentially judge-like behavior. So the memoranda will be illuminating.

There is ample historical precedent for the production of such memos. DOJ has routinely turned them over during the confirmation process. It was done for judicial nominees Bork, Rehnquist, and Easterbrook. They have been turned over for executive branch nominees Benjamin Civiletti and Bradford Reynolds.

And earlier this year, this White House — a White House more protective of executive privilege than any White House since the Nixon administration, I might note — turned over memoranda written by Jeffrey Holmstead, a nominee to a high post at the EPA. Mr. Holmstead's memoranda were from his years of service in the White House counsel's office, a more political and legally privileged post than the one you held when you were in the Department of Justice in the office charged with protecting and defending the Constitution.

I, for one, would think you would want the memoranda to be released so you could more ably defend your record. I know you haven't been blocking their release, but today you will have a chance to urge DOJ to make the record more complete by releasing the documents. I hope you will do so because from what I know thus far, I would have to say that I would be reluctant to support moving your nomination until we see those memoranda.

There is a lot we do not know about Miguel Estrada. Hopefully, we will take some meaningful steps today towards filling in the gaps in the record. Mr. Estrada, you are going to have a chance today to answer many of the questions regarding your views.

Some believe that once the President nominates a candidate, the burden falls on the Senate to prove why he shouldn't be confirmed.

I believe the burden is on the nominee, especially when it comes to a lifetime seat on the Nation's second-highest court to prove why he should be nominated or she should be nominated. Just as the nominees to the Supreme Court are subject to higher scrutiny, nominees to this unique and powerful circuit merit close and careful review. Our job is not just to rubber-stamp. Our job is to advise and to decide whether to consent.

---

The Estrada hearing continued, rather than ended, extensive nominee questioning on controversial issues and decisions. Estrada was asked to respond to questions concerning his views on *Roe v. Wade*, *Gideon v. Wainwright*, and *Romer v. Evans*, among other cases.

An issue concerning Estrada's service as a judicial clerk, however, came to dominate the hearing: the accusation that Estrada, who served as a clerk for Justice Kennedy, helped to screen clerk applicants for the Justice with the goal of "preventing liberal clerks from being hired." The extensive questions and responses given raised a set of judicial clerk-related issues, including the power of a law clerk to influence a judge's decision in a particular case — here, the gay rights decision of *Romer v. Evans*.

---

Sen. Schumer:    "Perhaps the most damaging evidence against Estrada comes from two lawyers he interviewed for Supreme Court clerkships. Both were unwilling to be identified for fear of reprisal. The first told me, and I quote, "Since I knew Miguel, I went to him to help me get a Supreme Court clerkship. I knew he was screening candidates for Justice Kennedy. And Miguel told me, "No way, you're way too liberal." I felt he was definitely submitting me to an ideological litmus test, and I am a moderate Democrat. When I asked him why I was being ruled out even without an interview, Miguel told me his job was to prevent liberal clerks from being hired. He told me he was screening out liberals because a liberal clerk had influenced Justice Kennedy to side with the majority and write a pro-gay rights decision in a case known as *Romer v. Evans*, which struck down a Colorado statute that discriminated against gays and lesbians." Did this happen?

Mr. Estrada:    Senator, let me — maybe I should explain what it is that I do from time to time for Justice Kennedy. Justice Kennedy picks his own clerks. As other judges and Justices, he will sometimes ask for help by former clerks with the interviewing of some candidates.

I have been asked to do that from time to time. I do not do it every year. I haven't done it for 2 or 3 years now, and sometimes I will get a file. It is in the nature of my role in the process that I could not do that which is alleged in the excerpt that you read since I don't have control over the pool of candidates.

Sen. Schumer:    I assume that you have read published reports that said that you attempted to block liberal applicants from clerking for your former boss, Justice Anthony Kennedy. I am sure you could understand why that would trouble people. If you are trying to preclude Justice Kennedy from hearing all sides argued in his chamber, it would suggest an ideological agenda when it comes to the courts. So I want to ask you a simple yes or no question.

Have you ever told anyone that you do not believe that any person should clerk for Justice Kennedy because that person is too liberal, not conservative enough, because that person did not have the appropriate ideology, politics, or judicial philosophy, or because you were concerned that person would influence Justice Kennedy to take positions you did not want him taking?

Let me repeat the question because it is an important one, at least to some of us.

Have you ever told anyone that you don't believe that any person should clerk for Justice Kennedy because that person is too liberal, not conservative enough, because that person did not have the appropriate ideology, politics, or judicial philosophy, or because you were concerned that person would influence Justice Kennedy to take positions you did not want him to be taking? Can you give us a yes or no to that, please?

Mr. Estrada:    Sen. Schumer, I have taken a cab up to Capitol Hill and sat in Justice Kennedy's office to make sure he hired people that I knew to be liberal.

Sen. Schumer:    But I am asking you yes or no in terms of the question I asked.

Mr. Estrada:    I don't believe I have. [shaking his head no.]

Sen. Schumer:    The answer is no. Thank you.

* * * *

Mr. Estrada:    And I realized as I was trying to drink my Coke that as she read a statement from a magazine which contained an implicit — I guess I will call it an assumption that I should have challenged out of deference and respect for Justice Kennedy.

Justice Kennedy is one of my mentors, and I have a great deal of personal affection for him. I would not want anybody to think that this man, who is at the pinnacle of his legal life, is a dupe who can be sort of moved one way or another by 22-year-olds. When I was his law clerk, I knew him as a man who knew his own mind, and when I have some role in talking to possible law clerk candidates for him, my view is to look for somebody who will work well with him and who will do his bidding after he comes to his own judgment.

And I mention that last point because I also—

Sen. Schumer:    I don't think anything you said before when you answered explicitly to me and then the same way to Senator Feinstein contradicted that in any way. You are welcome to make the record clear.

Mr. Estrada:    Right. But I also want to make clear that, as I thought about that and that premise, there is a set of circumstances in which I would consider somebody's ideology, if you want to call it that, in trying to interview somebody for Justice Kennedy, whether on the left or on the right. And that is to say, if I thought that there was somebody who had views that were so strongly held on any subject, whether, you know, the person thinks that there ought not to be the death penalty or whether the person thinks that the income tax ought not to be constitutional or anything, if I think that the person has some extreme view that he will not be willing to set aside in the service of Justice Kennedy, I would make sure that Justice Kennedy would know that. And I guess it is possible for somebody to think that he was turned down in a sense on the basis of his politics. But that would not be the case. It would be on the basis of a judgment that whatever class of politics he might have, he would not be willing to put him aside in the service of the Justice.

Sen. Schumer:   This morning, I asked you a question about that. You denied it unequivocally. Senator Feinstein went over it 2 hours later, read you this very passage, and you denied it unequivocally. Are you changing your answer now? Did you say, yes or no, to this clerk, "No way, you're way too liberal"? You have denied that twice.

Mr. Estrada:   Senator, I am certain that I never said that to anybody.

Sen. Schumer:   Thank you.

Mr. Estrada:   But I will not — but I have to tell you that it is possible that I said to somebody, including Justice Kennedy, Mr. "X" has an ideological view of this area of the law and, therefore, he would be unsuitable.

Sen. Schumer:   That is not the question I — I didn't ask you what you said to Justice Kennedy. You did not also say — you didn't tell this interviewee that you didn't like liberals — you didn't like it that a liberal clerk influenced Justice Kennedy to side with the majority and write a pro-gay-rights decision in *Romer v. Evans*?

Mr. Estrada:   Senator, I am certain that I don't know who was working for Justice Kennedy when Justice Kennedy had that case in front of him—

Sen. Schumer:   I didn't ask you that question, sir. I asked you if you said — you are a very accomplished man. You know the question I have asked. I said to you, did you say to this clerk — did you talk to him that you didn't like the fact that a liberal clerk had influenced Justice Kennedy to side with the majority and write a pro-gay-rights decision in a case known as *Romer v. Evans*? Yes or no. This does not take a peroration. This takes a yes or no answer if you are being truthful with this committee.

--------

Additional federal judicial appointments include bankruptcy judges and federal magistrates. A bankruptcy judge is a judicial officer of the federal district court; these judges are appointed by the majority of judges of the U.S. Court of Appeals to exercise jurisdiction over bankruptcy matters. Congress determines the number of bankruptcy judges. The Judicial Conference of the United States is required to submit recommendations from time to time regarding the number of bankruptcy judges needed. Bankruptcy judges are appointed for 14-year terms.

A magistrate judge is a judicial officer of a federal district court and is appointed by majority vote of the active district judges of the court. Magistrate judges exercise jurisdiction over matters assigned by statute, as well as matters delegated by the district judges. The number of magistrate judge positions is determined by the Judicial Conference of the United States, based on recommendations of the respective district courts, the judicial councils of the circuits, and the Director of the Administrative Office of the U.S. Courts. A full-time magistrate judge serves a term of eight years. Duties assigned to magistrate judges by district court judges may vary considerably from court to court.

## B.  State Court Selection

Judicial selection in state courts includes partisan and nonpartisan elections; appointment by governor or state assembly; merit selection through a nominating commission; and methods that combine merit selection with other methods. The "score card" or number of states using each method changes yearly. The National Center for the Study of State Courts keeps score. The ABA advocates "merit selection" and legal commentators often favor appointed judges because appointed judges are assumed to be less vulnerable to political pressures. However, some empirical research indicates that judicial selection methods are not always as they might appear:

> We began our research with the assumption that the data would demonstrate that appointed judges are better than elected judges. Our results suggest a more complicated story. It may be that elected judges are, indeed, superior to appointed judges. Or it may be that elected judges are superior to appointed judges *in small states only* and not necessarily in large states.

Stephen Choi, G. Mitu Gulati, & Eric A. Posner, *Professionals or Politicians*, 26 J. ECON. LAW & ORG. 290 (2010).

State judicial elections, and regulating the campaigns they require, have driven a series of state court decisions and United States Supreme Court decisions. Judicial candidates have challenged the limits placed on their campaign speech and fundraising efforts. Two amicus curiae briefs from *Williams-Yulee v. Florida Bar*, offer a quick course on the specifics of a challenge to a Florida canon that prevents a judge from personally soliciting for two items: (1.) monetary donations and (2.) statements of support from attorneys.

## FLORIDA STATE CANONS OF JUDICIAL CONDUCT CANON 7

### C.  Judges and Candidates Subject to Public Election

(1) A candidate, including an incumbent judge, for a judicial office that is filled by public election between competing candidates shall not personally solicit campaign funds, or solicit attorneys for publicly stated support, but may establish committees of responsible persons to secure and manage the expenditure of funds for the candidate's campaign and to obtain public statements of support for his or her candidacy. Such committees are not prohibited from soliciting campaign contributions and public support from any person or corporation authorized by law. A candidate shall not use or permit the use of campaign contributions for the private benefit of the candidate or members of the candidate's family.

# WILLIAMS-YULEE v. THE FLORIDA BAR
## No. 13-1499, 2014 U.S. S. Ct. Briefs LEXIS 4214

Supreme Court of the United States.
November 24, 2014

On Writ of Certiorari to the Supreme Court of Florida
Brief of Cameron A. Blau, Esq. as Amicus Curiae in Support of the Petitioner
[footnotes omitted]

\* \* \* \*

## STATEMENT OF INTEREST OF THE AMICUS CURIAE

*Amicus Curiae* Cameron Blau is a former candidate for District Judge for the November, 2014 election, and will be a candidate for District Judge in future elections, as well as an Intervening Plaintiff in the matter of *Winter, et. al. v. Wolnitzek, et. al.*, EDKY 2:14-cv-00119-ART-CJS, which involves challenges to various aspects of Kentucky's Judicial Canon 5, which governs political activities, including a prohibition upon personal solicitation.

*Amicus Curiae* seeks to engage in various activities that fall within the scope of the First Amendment, but is prohibited by certain Judicial Canons, in the course and scope of his campaigns, and has an interest aligned with many other potential and future judicial candidates. His interest in this matter includes both the narrow issue that certiorari was granted on — personal solicitation — and includes a much wider interest, since the decision in this matter could have a significant impact upon judicial candidates, judges, and the general public. *Amicus Curiae* adheres to the belief that a fully informed electorate is the best remedy and prevention to bad government, and that obtaining a fully informed electorate is best achieved not through more restrictions on speech and activities such as fundraising that implicate speech, but rather through more speech, and less restrictions.

This Court, in *Republican Party of Minnesota v. White*, 536 U.S. 765, 122 S. Ct. 2528, 153 L. Ed. 2d 694 (2002), first entered the fray of speech in judicial elections, and invalidated the so called "announce clause," determining that it was not narrowly tailored to advance a compelling state interest — namely the avoidance of bias against *parties*. Since *White*, the American Bar Association has failed to substantially revise their model canons, and, furthermore, certain state supreme courts have promulgated a series of rules that inhibit or restrict various aspects of speech in judicial campaigns. This has included limitations on fundraising, variations of the "announce clause" invalidated in *White*, participation in political parties, restrictions on disclosure of a candidate's political party affiliation and that of her opponent, prohibitions on the time such fundraising can occur, and, as is present in this matter, prohibitions on personal solicitation.

## SUMMARY OF THE ARGUMENT

Strict scrutiny applies. Thus, if a law does too little, or too much, to meet compelling state interests, it cannot stand. The canon at issue in this case, similar to canons that restrict party identification by candidates, limitations on speech of candidates, endorsements by candidates, and other provisions, are both overbroad and under-inclusive. As with any campaign related speech restriction, the prohibition on a judge's personal solicitation of campaign donors, as is the case with other canons, causes the general public to achieve a less than accurate picture of the candidate they are voting for. Furthermore, the canon is facially unconstitutional.

### I. Strict Scrutiny Applies and the Canon Is Not Narrowly Tailored to Achieve a Compelling State Interest

"A state sets itself on a collision course with the First Amendment when it chooses to popularly elect its judges but restricts a candidate's campaign speech." *Wolfson v. Concannon*, 750 F.3d 1145 (9th Cir. 2014), *Rehearing, en banc, granted by Wolfson v. Concannon*, 2014 U.S. App. LEXIS 18602 (9th Cir. Sept. 26, 2014). "The conflict arises from the fundamental tension between the ideal of apolitical judicial independence and the critical nature of unfettered speech in the electoral political process." *Id.*

To begin with, the solicitation ban-like all of the political activity prohibitions found within many states' judicial canons, is subject to strict scrutiny review. *Republican Party of Minn. v. White*, 536 U.S. 765, 788, 122 S. Ct. 2528, 153 L. Ed. 2d 694 (2002). Thus, the canon in question must be "(1) narrowly tailored, to serve (2) a compelling state interest." *Id.* at 775. The canon does not prohibit *any* communication to the public, would-be supporters, or even litigants from the judge or judicial candidate. Rather, it prohibits only a *specific kind of communication* — a solicitation for a donation of money. As this Court held in *Holder v. Humanitarian Law Project*, 561 U.S. 1 (2010), there is a content-based restriction, subject to strict scrutiny because "[p]laintiffs want to speak to [particular groups], and whether they may do so . . . depends on what they say." The same is true here: A judge can ask for help on the campaign, for instance, help with door-to-door canvassing, but cannot ask for a donation. The canon "focuses *only* on the content of the speech and the direct impact that speech has on its listeners." *United States v. Playboy Entm't Grp., Inc.*, 529 U.S. 803, 811 (2000) (internal quotation marks omitted). Strict scrutiny applies.

States have a recognized compelling interest in preventing bias against parties, which includes the prevention of so-called "*quid pro quo*" bias, in appearance and fact. *Carey v. Wolnitzek*, 614 F.3d 189, 198–99 (6th Cir. 2010).

Nevertheless, the existence of a compelling interest is not the end of the analysis. The canon must be narrowly tailored to meet that interest. Thus, if the "law does too much, or does too little, to advance the government's objectives, it will fail." *Carey*, 614 F.3d 189, 201. This canon does both.

Here, the canon at issue prevents a judge from personally soliciting for certain narrow things: *monetary donations* (and statements of support from attorneys). But it does not prevent the judge's campaign committee from doing so, nor does it prevent the judge's family and close friends from doing so. It also does not restrict the judge from receiving, or even litigants who are presently appearing before the court from offering to make a donation to a judge's campaign committee. It does not restrict the judge or judicial candidate from learning who donated — and who did not. And it does not restrict the judge from saying "thank you" for those same donations. *Carey*, 614 F.3d 189, 198–99. With the advent of online campaign finance reporting in most states, it does not keep the judge, or the public, from seeing who donated what to the judge. The canon permits a person - including a litigant - to approach the judge and offer a donation - but does not permit the judge to ask for it.

The canon does not prevent the potential judicial candidate from calling family, friends, and others, and asking the question "If I run, will you donate?" but after the candidate declares his or her candidacy that same call, email, or other action cannot be made.

Importantly, it does not restrict the judge from soliciting for non-monetary support. The judge or candidate can ask litigants in cases before the court, as well as the candidate's friends, family, or the general public for their votes, can ask these same persons to assist with the campaign by engaging in the time-honored tradition of door-to-door canvassing or campaigning, can ask these same persons to make phone calls for the judge, or even to record video endorsements of the judge or her campaign. In fact, the canon allows the judge or candidate to engage in every other form of campaigning, and to solicit others to help the judge, except for fundraising. Thus, the canon is under-inclusive.

There is yet another, equally problematic aspect of this matter: there is nothing that keeps political parties from raising funds to aid the judge, or political action committees from making independent expenditures in favor of bringing about the judge's election. Are we to presume that, merely because the judge cannot herself ask for a donation, we eliminate the possibility or appearance of *quid pro quo* corruption? If a political action committee were to invest millions in a judicial race at the behest of a litigant, is bias or its appearance eliminated? This Court has answered the question: "No." *Caperton v. A. T. Massey Coal Co.*, 556 U.S. 868 (2009).

The canon in question is also overbroad - "indirect methods of solicitation [such as speeches to large groups and signed mass mailings] present little or no risk of undue pressure or the appearance of a *quid pro quo*." *Carey*, 614 F.3d at 205. It also prohibits the judge or judicial candidate from asking for donations from persons who, if they were to appear before the judge, would require recusal. The judge is not permitted to solicit his or her parents, siblings, aunts, uncles, or in-laws. Yet if any of these persons appeared before the court, the judge would undoubtedly recuse herself. How does a prohibition that extends to such close family members avoid the appearance of bias, or actual bias, which likely exists in any event?

## II. The Canon Results in a Fraud Being Perpetuated on the Public

The canon is part of a larger problem: states insist on conducting judicial elections to achieve the imprimatur of the public's consent to the judge being a judge, but they then seek to take the "politics" — including fundraising, participation in parties, endorsements of, or by, other candidates, and a host of other activities — out of the political process. Furthermore, no sooner than a successful challenge is lodged in a piece of constitutional litigation, than the states attempt to end-run around such decisions. *See also, Winter v. Wolnitzek,* 2014 U.S. Dist. LEXIS 154287 (EDKY Oct. 29, 2014) ("Like a recurring bad dream, Kentucky's judicial canons keep getting struck down"). For instance, in *Carey,* 614 F.3d 189, the Sixth Circuit struck down certain provisions of Kentucky's Code of Judicial Conduct. Kentucky responded by re-promulgating various rules,

But to what end? *Amicus Curiae* suggests that the end result is a hiding of truth from the general public — and the restriction of speech by the government that would otherwise reveal truth. If the judge wants to solicit, allow him or her, and let the public see it. The judge most certainly provides the fundraising committee a list of friends, colleagues, and would-be supporters, and the committee then goes about the duties of solicitation. Why? So the judge does not do it himself or herself. But is this not the epitome of hypocrisy, with one goal in mind — the judge gets to fundraise, but does not *appear* get his or her hands dirty in the process (and receive any public backlash from any fundraising activities himself or herself)?

We preserve the *appearance* of judges and judicial candidates not involving themselves with the unseemly task of fundraising, even though they are very much involved. *United States v. Alvarez,* 132 S. Ct. 2537, 2547 (2012) ("Our constitutional tradition stands against the idea that we need Oceania's Ministry of Truth."). The Ministry of Truth, of course, is all for the notion that the judge herself is not engaged in fundraising - no how - no way. When the public raises questions about the solicitation of donations from high profile corporate executives, on one potential end of the political spectrum, or solicitation of trial lawyers, on the other, the judge or candidate can simply respond that she did not do the soliciting. Her "committee" did it. Orwell would certainly appreciate this "newspeak."

* * * *

As this Court noted in *Citizens United v. FEC,* 558 U.S. 310, 356 (2010), "[w]hen Government seeks to use its full power . . . to command where a person may get his or her information or what distrusted source he or she may not hear, it uses censorship to control thought. This is unlawful. The First Amendment confirms the freedom to think for ourselves."). Fundamentally, the solicitation ban prevents the public from learning, and attributing, fundraising activities to the judge or judicial candidate, even though that same candidate is almost certainly engaged — behind the scenes — in the fundraising.

This case has wider implications than solicitation. It is, at its core, the natural follow-on to this Court's determination in *White,* 536 U.S. 765, 788. The analysis employed, and determination of this matter, has implications on other issues now pending in constitutional challenges to various states' judicial canons throughout the country. Fundamentally, those cases come down to one key question: do we continue to pretend that politics do not exist in judicial races, or do we acknowledge that politics do exist, and sweep the issue into the light of day?

As Justice Brandeis said: "[s]unlight is said to be the best of disinfectants; electric light the most efficient policeman." *Buckley v. Am. Constitutional Law Found.*, 525 U.S. 182, 223 (1999) (O'Connor, J. and Breyer, J. dissenting in part and concurring in part).

States cannot pretend that the judges are not involved in fundraising — or that if we keep the candidates from doing the asking, that solves the underlying issue. We should not pretend that political parties do not work for, endorse, and get involved in judicial races; or that candidates for office — including judicial candidates — do not (though perhaps not publicly) endorse other candidates. Importantly, we should not adhere to the illusion that a candidate for office is not "political" as long as we do not allow that candidate to identify her political party and that of her opponent; or that we need to keep races "clean" and keep facts or opinions near the edges out of the races by banning "misleading" speech by judges (but allowing Political Action Committees and everyone else to make these same statements).

These questions arise in concrete challenges being raised across this nation to political speech regulations present in various states' judicial canons. They have one over-arching policy — and constitutional — question in common: Do we continue the mirage of a political-free state judiciary that is popularly elected, or acknowledge the fact that when we elect judges, we make them politicians, and, as such, operate in an environment of transparency and the disinfectant of sunlight?

"Knowledge will forever govern ignorance, and a people who mean to be their own governors, must arm themselves with the power knowledge gives. A popular government without popular information or the means of acquiring it, is but a prologue to a farce or a tragedy or perhaps both." James Madison to W. T. Barry, August 4, 1822, Writings 9:103-9.

### III. The Canon Does Not Further Any Due Process Interest, but Instead Frustrates It

The prevention of *quid pro quo* bias has been determined to be a compelling interest, which raises due process considerations. *Caperton*, 556 U.S. 868. The prohibition on personal solicitation of monetary contributions (but the allowance of solicitation of other non-monetary contributions and support), and the pushing of the task of fundraising to a committee does not further due process. If anything, a person seeking to engage in *quid pro quo activities* would be more likely to funnel significant funds to a political action committee, particularly one that is not subject to disclosure or other transparency requirements. The requirements "may in fact encourage the movement of money away from entities subject to disclosure." *McCutcheon v. FEC*, 134 S. Ct. 1434, 1460 (2014). This is because "[i]ndividuals can, for example, contribute unlimited amounts to 501(c) organizations, which are not required to publicly disclose their donors." *Id.*

If the judge — or her committee does the soliciting of those donations, those donations are subject to public disclosure requirements. This, in turn, allows parties to know whether or not a request for recusal may be appropriate. *Caperton*, 556 U.S. 868. Due process, of course, requires notice and an opportunity to be heard. *Mullane v. Central Hanover Trust Co.*, 339 U.S. 306, 314 (1950). There is no notice to a party or litigant if the campaign assistance comes from a political action committee that makes only independent expenditures. But the judge, or judicial candidate would likely know who was behind it — if only after-the-fact.

How is it that the recusal issue came about in *Caperton*, 556 U.S. 868? It was only because the company CEO's support of Justice Benjamin was widely known. How much more transparent, and how much better of a basis for recusal would have been presented, in *Caperton*, had proof been given that Justice Benjamin had solicited the same CEO of the coal company for the donations and support at issue? That did not occur, because the West Virginia Canon prevented it. But that simply demonstrates the issues with this canon — it sweeps potential bases for recusal into the darkness, instead of the light of day. In the process, it raises threats to the due process rights of litigants who may not even know it.

Thus, the canons work to make opaque potential violations of due process rights.

## IV. The Canon Is Facially Invalid

In the First Amendment context this Court recognizes "a second type of facial challenge," whereby a law may be invalidated as overbroad if "a substantial number of its applications are unconstitutional, judged in relation to the statute's plainly legitimate sweep." *Washington State Grange v. Washington State Republican Party*, 552 U.S. 442, 449, n.6, (2008); *United States v. Stevens*, 559 U.S. 460 (2010).

The under-inclusiveness and over-breadth of the canon, as discussed *infra*, creates just such a case. *Stevens*, 559 U.S. 460. Here, *Amicus Curiae* suggests there is no legitimate sweep to the canon at issue. That said, while the canon is certainly invalid as-applied to websites, emails, and other forms of solicitation, it is equally invalid in other contexts, because it is under-inclusive and overbroad. It should be declared invalid on its face.

## CONCLUSION

*Amicus Curiae* requests that this Court reverse the decision of the Florida Supreme Court, and declare Canon 7C(1) of the Florida Code of Judicial Conduct facially unconstitutional under the First Amendment of the Constitution.

# WILLIAMS-YULEE v. THE FLORIDA BAR
No. 13-1499, 2014 U.S. S. Ct. Briefs LEXIS 4528

Supreme Court of the United States.
December 22, 2014

On Writ of Certiorari To The Supreme Court of Florida
Brief of Amicus Curiae Professor Jed Shugerman in Support of Respondent
[footnotes omitted]

## INTEREST OF THE *AMICUS CURIAE*

*Amicus curiae* Professor Jed Shugerman is an expert on the history of judicial elections in America, and has written the only in-depth book on that topic, *The People's Courts: Pursuing Judicial Independence in America* (2012). Professor Shugerman's scholarship refutes the notion that States adopted judicial elections in an effort to turn judges into conventional politicians. Rather, history reveals that States adopted judicial elections in order to promote judicial independence and the rule of law, and to protect judges from special interests and the corruption endemic to the States' appointment systems. This pursuit of judicial independence from corrupting influences also drove each successive reform of their judicial-election systems.

Professor Shugerman files this brief to provide historical context relevant to the Court's consideration of the direct solicitation ban, which has been adopted by thirty of the thirty-nine States that elect their judges.

## SUMMARY OF ARGUMENT

Bans on direct solicitation of money by judicial candidates are part of a long history in which the States have adopted and reformed judicial elections for the express purpose of protecting courts against the reality and appearance of improper influence.

This historical reality is contrary to a perception that the adoption of judicial elections was an open abandonment of judicial independence and impartiality, in favor of treating judges like conventional politicians. Related to this misperception, there is an oft-expressed view that the only solution to the problems that elections pose is to abolish them. As Justice O'Connor put it in her concurrence in *Republican Party of Minnesota v. White*, "[i]f the State has a problem with judicial impartiality, it is largely one the State brought upon itself by continuing the practice of popularly electing judges." 536 U.S. 765, 792 (2002).

Plainly, the "States are free to choose [judicial elections] rather than, say, appointment and confirmation." *Id.* at 795 (Kennedy, J. concurring). And having done so, States may adapt their election rules to pursue judicial integrity, "despite the difficulties imposed by the election system." *Id.* at 796.

Thirty-nine States have adopted elections as the means for choosing judges, and the historical context of their adoptions bolsters the case for following the precedents of deference to State choices in judicial selection.

Parts I and II set out that history, culminating with the adoption, beginning in 1972, by thirty of the States with judicial elections, of the prohibition on direct solicitation of money by judicial candidates at issue in this case. The widespread adoption of this rule, in the face of the increasing importance that money has come to play in modern elections, reflects the States' pursuit of the "hard task" of "codify[ing] the essence of judicial integrity." Id. at 793 (Kennedy, J. concurring).

Part III concludes by discussing real-world instances of direct solicitation abuse, and suggesting that the very widespread adoption of the direct solicitation ban is a targeted rejection of conduct that invites actual corruption and the public appearance of improper influence.

## ARGUMENT

### I. THIRTY-NINE STATES HAVE TURNED TO JUDICIAL ELECTIONS IN ORDER TO PROTECT JUDICIAL INDEPENDENCE AND AVOID THE AP-PEARANCE AND REALITY OF IMPROPER INFLUENCE AND BIAS.

Historically, the States have exercised broad sovereign powers to protect the public integrity of their judiciaries against the probability and appearance of bias. Indeed, the history and evolution of state judicial systems exemplifies the States' critical " 'role as laboratories for experimentation to devise various solutions where the best solution is far from clear.' " *See Schuette v. Coalition to Defend Affirmative Action*, 134 S. Ct. 1623, 1630 (2014) (Kennedy, J., plurality op.) (quoting *United States v. Lopez*, 514 U.S. 549, 581 (1995) (Kennedy, J., concurring)).

### A. States Created Judicial Elections To Promote Judicial Independence From The Other Branches And From Special Interests.

Judicial independence has long been a central principle in the structure of state governments. Indeed, even during the colonial era, an independent judiciary was seen as an inalienable feature of republican government. *See, e.g.*, The Declaration of Independence para. 11 (U.S. 1776) ("[King George] has made Judges dependent on his Will alone, for the Tenure of their Offices, and the Amount and payment of their Salaries."). Once the colonies won their independence, the States sought to structure their judiciaries in a way that prevented this kind of judicial dependency and adopted varying models to achieve that end: four adopted a model of executive appointment and legislative consent, four others chose legislative election, three combined legislative election and tenure "at pleasure," and two provided judges with seven-year terms instead of life tenure. Evan Haynes, *The Selection and Tenure of Judges* 101–33 (1944).

Despite these initial efforts to guard against dependence upon and influence from a central power, by the early nineteenth century state judiciaries were beholden to the legislature, the executive, and, by extension, the parties that controlled each. Governors with the power of appointment typically nominated persons supporting their agendas, and then threatened those judges with removal if they behaved independently. *See, e.g., Report of the Debates and Proceedings of the Convention for the Revision of the Constitution of the State of New York* 613 (1846). Similarly, state legislatures controlled not only the salaries, fees, and removal of state judges, *see* Gordon S. Wood, *The Creation of the American Republic, 1776–1787*, at 161 (1969), but also the substance and finality of their judgments, *see* Edward S. Corwin, *The Progress of Constitutional Theory Between the Declaration of Independence and the Meeting of the Philadelphia Convention, in* The Constitution 93, 97 (James Morton Smith ed., 1971).

As one example, "[t]he New Hampshire legislature regularly vacated judicial proceedings, suspended judicial actions, annulled or modified judgments, cancelled executions, reopened controversies, authorized appeals, granted exemptions from the standing law, expounded the law for pending cases, and even determined the merits of disputes." *Id.* And in the 1820s, Missouri and Kentucky each removed their entire supreme courts prior to the expiration of their terms as a way of imposing shorter, unanticipated term limits upon what had become a disfavored bench. W.J. Hamilton, *The Relief Movement in Missouri, 1820–1822*, 22 Mo. Hist. Rev. 51, 89–90 (1927).

Against this backdrop, a severe economic depression in the 1840s precipitated a desire to free the judiciary of its dependence on the political branches. The 1840s depression led to the recognition that state legislatures had been overspending on canals, roads, and railroads - and often with political insiders and special interests corrupting the spending process. *See* Jed Shugerman, *Economic Crisis and the Rise of Judicial Elections and Judicial Review*, 123 Harv. L. Rev. 1061, 1076–80 (2010). This overspending drove nine States into default, and led to the closing of half of America's banks. Charles W. McCurdy, *The Anti-Rent Era in New York Law and Politics, 1839–1865*, at 75–76 (2001). Fiscally conservative reformers campaigned for constitutional conventions to impose new spending limits on legislatures. *See* Kermit L. Hall, *Mostly Anchor and Little Sail: The Evolution of American State Constitutions, in* Toward a Usable Past 388, 401 (Paul Finkelman & Stephen E. Gottlieb eds., 1991).

Legislative excess, however, was not the only target of public ire. Reformers partly blamed judges for having been captured by legislators and governors, so that they did not check the other branches sufficiently. *See, e.g., Debates and Proceedings in the New-York State Convention for the Revision of the Constitution* 651 (S. Croswell & R. Sutton reporters, Albany, Albany Argus 1846) (remarks of delegate Amos Wright) ("Who selects most of your judges now? The politicians of a party caucus."). As a result, the reformers sought to create a new state judiciary that would be more independent from governors and legislatures — and more independent from the forces of corruption. *See, e.g., The Constitutional Debates of 1847*, at 466 (Arthur Charles Cole ed., 1919) (remarks of delegate Archibald Williams).

To achieve such judicial independence, States began selecting judges through popular elections. Although a few States, including Georgia and Mississippi, experimented early on with judicial elections, it was not until New York debated the merits of, and ultimately adopted, judicial elections at its 1846 state constitutional convention that a national trend began. *The People's Courts, supra* at 57–86 (collecting authorities from each state); *see also* Shugerman, *Economic Crisis, supra* at 1096 (detailing the frequency of state constitutional conventions during the nineteenth century, through which the States addressed a broad array of problems, often "learn[ing] from one another's mistakes" in one decade and "borrow[ing] heavily from one another's constitutional innovations" in another).

Notably, the States adopted judicial elections for the express purpose of liberating judges from partisan interests and "increas[ing] fidelity" to the people. *See Report of New York Constitutional Convention, supra* at 645 (remarks of delegate Ira Harris); *see also The People's Courts, supra* at 104–116 (collecting state data). As one commentator put it, "make [judges] elective by the people, and then indeed will we have an independent judiciary." Veto, *Letter to the Editor, reprinted in* Samuel Medary, The New Constitution at 206, July 28, 1849.

For States in the early to mid-nineteenth century, therefore, "popular election was not viewed as inconsistent with the ideal of a powerful independent judiciary." Phillip L. Dubois, Special Issue, *Accountability, Independence and the Selection of State Judges: the Role of Popular Judicial Elections*, 40 S.W. L.J. 31, 35 (1987). To the contrary, judicial elections were seen as essential to an independent judiciary as well as the state constitutions' promises "to protect the rights of the people." 2 *Report of the Debates and Proceedings of the Convention for the Revision of the Constitution of the State of Indiana 1809* (H. Fowler ed., Indianapolis, A.H. Brown 1850) (remarks of Judge Borden). Ultimately, by 1860, eighteen of the thirty-one States in the Union elected all of their judges, and five additional States elected some of their judges. The People's Courts, supra at 105 (compiling state data).

It is important to note, however, that mid-nineteenth century campaigns generally did not rely on campaign donations. Judicial candidates ran on a partisan slate, and parties campaigned to get out the vote for their candidates. See Jed Shugerman, *The Twist of Long Terms*, 98 GEO. L.J. 1349, 1379–90 (2010). Parties raised the bulk of the money, rather than the candidates themselves, and moreover, parties raised a large amount of their money from their office-holders as part of the spoils system of kicking back public salaries to the local party. *Id.* Thus, the state reformers that adopted judicial elections were not embracing a system of direct judicial fundraising. *Id.*

B. States Have Enacted Wide-Ranging Reforms To Ensure The Public Legitimacy Of Their Judiciaries And Avoid The Probability Of Bias.

Although the turn to judicial elections largely succeeded in removing legislative and gubernatorial influence from the process of judicial selection, this change produced new threats of undue influence, or the appearance of such, over the state judiciaries. In response to these emerging sources of influence, States enacted a series of modest reforms aimed at ensuring the public legitimacy of their judiciaries and avoiding the appearance of partiality.

The initial concern facing States that adopted judicial elections was the significant role that political parties played in the elections and the corruption that ensued. As contemporaneous documentation and historical accounts show, judicial elections during this period were often close and hotly contested, which increased coalition politics and known corruption. In California, for instance, elections were swung by party machines more than the candidates themselves. 1 E.B. Willis & P.K. Stockton,

*Debates and Proceedings of the Constitutional Convention of the State of California* (1880). And in Pennsylvania, a brand of urban machine politics reigned, leading to the tyranny of local political bosses of the majority party. Mahlon H. Hellerich, *The Origin of the Pennsylvania Constitutional Convention of 1873*, 34 PENN. HIST. 158 (1967). That corruption increased over time is evidenced by the fact that more New York judges were awaiting trial for official corruption in 1872 alone than from 1777 to 1846. Renee Lettow Lerner, *From Popular Control to Independence: Reform of the Elected Judiciary in Boss Tweed's New York*, 15 GEO. MASON L. REV. 109, 157 (2007).

In the 1860s and 1870s, several States began extending judges' terms as a means to insulate judges from party machines and corruption and thus avoid the appearance of impropriety and risk of undue influence on their judiciaries. *The People's Courts, supra* at 144–54 (compiling state data). As explained by James Bryce, "short terms . . . oblige [the judge] to remember and keep on good terms with those who have made him what he is, and in whose hands his fortunes lie. They induce timidity, they discourage independence." James Bryce, 1 *The American Commonwealth* 455 (1906).

In the decades that followed, States continued to view party politics as a threat to the integrity of their judiciaries. Because party connections still determined the nominations process, elected judges were perceived as being beholden to partisan interests, and their independence and integrity were questioned once on the bench. *See, e.g.*, Robert Cushman, *Non-Partisan Nominations and Elections*, 106 ANNALS AM. ACAD. POL. & SOC. SCI. 83 (1923); Barry Friedman, *The Will of the People* 183 (2009) (citing a study by the National Economic League led by William Howard Taft). Even the Governor of Nebraska alleged that courts were "composed of lawyers who owe their position, not so much to legal attainment and profound learning, as they do to political service rendered." Gilbert E. Roe, *Our Judicial Oligarchy* 14 (1912) (quoting Gov. Aldrich).

Moreover, judicial elections remained hotly contested. For example, an 1889 Pennsylvania election for lower court seats was tainted by bribes, bitter personal fights, and a guerilla newspaper war waged in a way that lessened respect for the judiciary. *The Westmoreland Judgeship*, Pittsburgh Com. Gazette, Oct. 24, 1889; *The Thirty-Fifth Judicial District*, Pittsburgh Com. Gazette, Oct. 30, 1889. Likewise, in an 1894 New York election, partisan thugs and "gangs of rowdies" beat each other in a "free for all scuffle" at the ballot box. John Fabian Witt, *The Accidental Republic* 157, 281 n.22 (2004) (quoting *First Round for Warner*, N.Y. Herald, June 12, 1894).

In the 1910s, States began adopting non-partisan judicial elections to address these revitalized concerns of partisanship, special interests, and corruption. In 1911, Ohio passed the Non-Partisan Judiciary Act and then raised the issue again a year later at its high-profile 1912 convention, where it implemented direct party primaries to precede the nonpartisan election. Ohio Rev. Code Ann. 3505.04; *Proceedings and Debates of Ohio Constitutional Convention of 1912*, at 1051–52 (J.V. Smith reporter, 1851). By the end of the decade, eight other States followed Ohio's lead, with ten more adopting nonpartisan elections soon thereafter. *The People's Courts, supra* at 160 (collecting state data).

Once implemented, certain States concluded that nonpartisan elections were not as effective in protecting judicial independence as was desired. Instead, because judicial candidates could not rely on party organization to raise money, make connections, and get out the vote, candidates turned to special interest groups, including organized crime, for funding. 9 *Transactions of Commonwealth Club of California*, 311–12 (1914), *in* Lamar T. Beman, *Election versus Appointment of Judges*, 65 (1926). Moreover, observers recognized that as judicial candidates could no longer rely on party identification to get elected, these candidates had to raise even more money directly, and campaign even more aggressively. These problems set the stage for a sweeping new round of reforms in favor of judicial independence from financial corruption. *The People's Courts, supra* at 170–76 (collecting data).

In light of these challenges, in the 1920s and 1930s, the American Bar Association and the American Judicature Society proposed the adoption of what is now known as the merit selection system. Under this model, a nominating commission, which includes representatives of the state bar, selects a short slate of candidates, and the governor chooses one person from that slate. Once nominated, the judge sits an initial term and then runs in a yes-or-no retention election. *See, e.g., id.* at 185.

In 1937, the Missouri Bar Association grew tired of the political corruption that its judiciary faced and created the Missouri Institute for the Administration of Justice. This organization outlined a five-part merit selection process that was eventually passed by voters in 1940. Charles B. Blackmar, *Missouri's Nonpartisan Court Plan from 1942 to 2005*, 72 MO. L. REV. 199 (2007). Building upon this success, and the success of California a few years prior, many state and local reformers in the 1950s championed "The Missouri Plan" as a critical reform to address the difficulties that arose under partisan and nonpartisan election models. Ultimately, nineteen States adopted the merit selection system wholesale and another nine chose to incorporate certain parts of it. *The People's Courts, supra* at 208 (collecting data).

The nineteenth and twentieth centuries thus saw major reforms by the vast majority of States. Following the adoption of judicial elections, the States devised and employed widely diverse approaches to improving their judiciaries, each stage driven by the goal of protecting judges from corruption. By 1990, thirty-nine of the fifty States directly elected their judges: seven retained partisan elections; thirteen used nonpartisan elections and two more used nonpartisan elections after a partisan nomination; sixteen adopted retention elections; and the final two relied on legislative elections. *Carey v. Wolnitzek*, 614 F.3d 189, 211–13 (6th Cir. 2010) (compiling data on state elections in Appendix).

## II. SINCE 1972, THIRTY OF THE THIRTY-NINE STATES THAT ELECT THEIR JUDGES HAVE BANNED DIRECT SOLICITATION OF MONEY BY JUDGES AND CANDIDATES.

In recent decades, there have been vast increases in the amount of money spent on judicial elections. Between 1990 and 2008, States saw a 700% increase in the amount of money raised per election cycle by state supreme court candidates. Lawrence Lessig, *Republic, Lost* 229 (2011). In 2002 alone, Florida's judicial elections at the trial level alone cost $16 million — nearly half the amount spent that year collectively in state-wide legislative races. *See* Roy A. Schotland, *New Challenges to States' Judicial Selection*, 95 GEO. L.J. 1077, 1080 n.13 (2007).

These "growing sums of money" used to "influence the outcome of a judicial election" make it "hard to have faith that we are selecting judges who are fair and impartial." *See* Justice Sandra Day O'Connor, *How To Save Our Courts*, Parade, Feb. 24, 2008.

In view of the variations in the judicial electoral systems adopted by the States, it is notable that those States have responded with substantial consistency to these new challenges. In more than 75% of the States "with judicial elections, judicial candidates have been barred from *personally* soliciting campaign funds." Roy A. Schotland, *Six Fatal Flaws: A Comment On Bopp And Neeley*, 86 DENV. U. L. REV. 233, 235 (2008) (emphasis in original). At the outset certain States implemented a precatory approach to direct solicitation bans, as was initially suggested by the ABA in 1972. *See* American Bar Association, *Model Code of Judicial Conduct*, Canon 7(B)(2) (1972) (providing that a candidate "should not himself solicit or accept campaign funds"). As time passed, however, these States recognized the need for a clear prohibition on direct solicitations and adopted the mandatory language of the 1990 ABA Model Code of Judicial Conduct. *See* American Bar Association, *Code of Judicial Conduct*, Canon 5(C)(2) (1990).

By 2010, thirty States had adopted a mandatory prohibition on the direct solicitation of campaign funds by judicial candidates. *See Carey*, 614 F.3d at 211–13 (compiling then-current data on state elections).

## III. THE DECISION TO BAR DIRECT SOLICITATION OF MONEY BY JUDICIAL CANDIDATES ADVANCES THE VITAL INTEREST IN A FAIR, INDEPENDENT, AND IMPARTIAL JUDICIARY - AND ONE THAT APPEARS TO BE SUCH.

Viewed in historical context, in which most States decided to adopt judicial elections as a means of establishing judicial independence, and then to adopt various reforms aimed at curbing abuses and threats to the reality and perception of judicial integrity, the ban on personal solicitation of money is a rare instance in which the States have spoken almost with one voice. Indeed, this prohibition is an obvious step for States that have adopted electoral systems while remaining vigilant to defend against evolving threats of bias and corruption, and the appearance of such.

While "[t]o comprehend, then to codify, the essence of judicial integrity is a hard task," *White*, 536 U.S. at 793 (Kennedy, J., concurring), the decision to bar candidates from personally requesting money has not been a hard call. That is because the practice of personally asking for money tends inherently to create both the reality and the appearance of bias and undermines public confidence in judicial integrity. Justifiably, States have deemed that practice incongruous with their "vital" interest, recognized by all members of this Court in *Caperton v. A. T. Massey Coal Co.*, 556 U.S. 868, 889 (2009), in ensuring "public confidence in the fairness and integrity of the nation's elected judges." Allowing such bald, personal appeals for money is no way to "maintain a fair, independent, and impartial judiciary — and one that appears to be such." *Id.* at 890 (Roberts, C.J., dissenting).

As this Court has noted in a number of contexts, personal solicitation "exert [s] pressure" on recipients and "demands an immediate response, without providing an opportunity for comparison or reflection." *See Ohralik v. Ohio State Bar Ass'n*, 436 U.S. 447, 457 (1978) (upholding state bans on lawyer solicitation); *see also United States v. Kokinda*, 497 U.S. 720, 734 (1990) (plurality op.) (upholding a federal ban on political solicitation). If this is true of solicitation by lawyers, or advocates outside of a post office, it cannot be any less true of those who possess, or seek to possess, the power of a state-court judgeship. Indeed, in those jurisdictions without direct solicitation rules, lawyers know they must comply with a judge's demand for money as a "protection against ill fortune" in the courtroom. *See* Michael J. Goodman & William C. Rempel, *In Las Vegas, They're Playing With a Stacked Judicial Deck*, L.A. Times, June 8, 2006. According to one attorney in such a jurisdiction, "Giving money to a judge's campaign means you're less likely to get screwed" — otherwise, "bad things" can happen. *Id.*

Moreover, direct solicitation creates a greater probability of bias than do other fundraising methods. A "realistic appraisal of psychological tendencies and human weakness," *Caperton*, 556 U.S. at 883 (quoting *Withrow v. Larkin*, 421 U.S. 35, 47 (1975)), indicates that *personally* asking for money opens solicitors to greater opportunity for embarrassment or elation, depending on the success of their efforts. That being so, solicitors will undoubtedly have a greater personal stake in the success or failure of direct solicitation, and thus a concomitantly greater temptation "to disregard neutrality" based on the solicitee's response. *See id.* at 886.

Hence, direct solicitation poses a "regulable *quid pro quo* danger." *See McConnell v. FEC* 540 U.S. 93, 316–17 (2003) (Kennedy, J. concurring in the judgment in part and dissenting in part). Perhaps as importantly, the appearance of possible bias is enhanced materially by the fact that the personal nature of the request is perceived by others to give the candidate a more direct personal investment in the solicited party's decision to contribute or not.

The following reports of conduct by judges and judicial candidates suggest why the rule banning direct solicitation has been so universally adopted:

- Judges soliciting money from attorneys "in their chambers in the middle of presiding over their cases." *See, e.g., The People's Courts, supra* at 4.

- Soliciting money from attorneys by requiring them "to walk the gauntlet past [the] bailiff and make an appropriate campaign contribution before they could present their arguments." *See, e.g.*, Gerald F. Richman, *The Case For Merit Selection And Retention Of Trial Judges*, 72 Fla. Bar J. 71, 71 (1998).

- Soliciting money from attorneys during an in-chambers conference regarding a pending case and telling one that "he was f***ed because he hadn't contributed while the others had." *See, e.g., In re Sobel*, No. 0405-248 (Nev. Comm'n on Jud. Discipline Aug. 15, 2005).

- Soliciting money from attorneys in a bar by telling one that the "going rate for contributions from attorneys was $500 and that if he did not contribute, he would receive adverse rulings from the [judge] if he was elected." *See, e.g., In re Tennant*, 516 S.E.2d 496, 498 (W. Va. 1999).

- Soliciting money over the phone from an attorney in a pending case, and - after receiving several hundred dollars from the attorney - denying a motion to recuse and granting summary judgment in favor of the contributor's client. *See, e.g., Aguilar v. Anderson, 855 S.W.2d 799, 801 (Tex. App. 1993).*

- Soliciting money at a " 'testimonial' dinner" "from attorneys appearing before" the judge, and accepting $10,000 for "personal expenses" and $2,000 for the "re-election campaign." *See, e.g.*, Marie A. Failinger, *Can a Good Judge Be a Good Politician?*, 70 Mo. L. Rev. 433, 447 (2005).

- Soliciting money from citizens' groups while running for traffic-court judge, telling a motorcycle club: "There's going to be a basket going around because I'm running for Traffic Court Judge, right, and I need some money. I got some stuff that I got to do, but if you all can give me twenty ($20) dollars you're going to need me in Traffic Court, am I right about that?" *See, e.g., In re Singletary*, 967 A.2d 1094, 1096 (Pa. Commw. Ct. 2008).

- Soliciting and receiving $2,500 from an attorney, at a public fundraiser personally hosted by the judge, one day after ruling in favor of that attorney's clients. *See, e.g.*, Julie Fancher, *Dallas County's Judge Carlos Cortez Is Asked to Recuse Himself from Case Involving Campaign Donor*, The Dallas Morning News, Sept. 11, 2014, *available at* http://www.dallasnews.com/news/metro/20140911-judge-carlos-cortez-is-asked-to-recuse-himself-in-civil-case.ece.

These anecdotes underscore the extent to which direct solicitation by judges raises the same "specter of direct corruption," Failinger, *Can a Good Judge Be a Good Politician?, supra* at 490, that the States have struggled to eliminate since adopting judicial elections in the mid-nineteenth century.

They also demonstrate that disqualification and recusal are not adequate substitutes for direct solicitation rules. Disqualification and recusal are litigation-specific rules that address issues of bias piecemeal once "a proceeding" is initiated. *See, e.g.*, Fla. Code of Jud. Conduct, Canon 3(E)(1). But they do not address the probability of bias arising outside of discrete cases, and they do not address the corrosive, systemic effects that direct solicitation has on the public's confidence in the judiciary in general.

In fact, disqualification and recusal *exacerbate* the very problems direct solicitation rules guard against. As the *Caperton* opinions acknowledge, public confidence in the judiciary may be eroded by *either* the appearance that judges are biased, *see* 556 U.S. at 881–82 (maj. op.), or through "*allegations* that judges are biased, however groundless those charges may be," *see id.* at 891 (Roberts, C.J., dissenting) (emphasis added). Thus, by curtailing such ad-hoc accusations of bias before they can arise, direct solicitation rules not only enhance the appearance of impartiality before litigation begins, but they also reduce the incidence of *disqualification and recusal*, which themselves can "bring our judicial system into undeserved disrepute" *after* litigation begins. *See id.* at 902 (Roberts, C.J., dissenting).

CONCLUSION

For the reasons stated above, the Court should affirm the decision of the Supreme Court of Florida.

## II.  QUALIFICATIONS

Federal court appointments, including those to the United States Supreme Court, state no qualifications, while state courts often prefer practicing attorneys.

But does attending law school, passing a bar exam and practicing law provide the training and education needed to embark upon a judicial career? Some commentators suggest that pre-judicial education would be useful.

### A.  Federal Court Qualifications

**Are there qualifications to be a Justice? Do you have to be a lawyer or attend law school to be a Supreme Court Justice?**

The Constitution does not specify qualifications for Justices such as age, education, profession, or native-born citizenship. A Justice does not have to be a lawyer or a law school graduate, but all Justices have been trained in the law. Many of the 18th and 19th century Justices studied law under a mentor because there were few law schools in the country.

- The last Justice to be appointed who did not attend any law school was James F. Byrnes (1941–1942). He did not graduate from high school and taught himself law, passing the bar at the age of 23.

- Robert H. Jackson (1941–1954). While Jackson did not attend an undergraduate college, he did study law at Albany Law School in New York. At the time of his graduation, Jackson was only twenty years old and one of the requirements for a law degree was that students must be twenty-one years old. Thus rather than a law degree, Jackson was awarded with a "diploma of graduation." Twenty-nine years later, Albany Law School belatedly presented Jackson with a law degree noting his original graduating class of 1912.

http://www.supremecourt.gov/faq.aspx

### B.  State Court Qualifications

#### Ohio Revised Code

#### § 2301.01   Courts of common pleas.

There shall be a court of common pleas in each county held by one or more judges, each of whom has been admitted to practice as an attorney at law in this state and has, for a total of at least six years preceding his appointment or commencement of his term, engaged in the practice of law in this state or served as a judge of a court of record in any jurisdiction in the United States, or both, resides in said county, and is elected by the electors therein. Each judge shall be elected for six years at the general election next preceding the year in which the term, as provided in sections 2301.02 and 2301.03 of the Revised Code, commences, and his successor shall be elected at the general election next preceding the expiration of such term.

### § 2501.02   Qualifications and term of judge, jurisdiction.

Each judge of a court of appeals shall have been admitted to practice as an attorney at law in this state and have, for a total of six years preceding his appointment or commencement of his term, engaged in the practice of law in this state or served as a judge of a court of record in any jurisdiction in the United States, or both. One judge shall be chosen in each court of appeals district every two years, and shall hold office for six years, beginning on the ninth day of February next after his election.

### § 2503.01   Judges of supreme court.

The supreme court shall consist of a chief justice and six justices, each of whom has been admitted to practice as an attorney at law in this state and has, for a total of at least six years preceding his appointment or commencement of his term, engaged in the practice of law in this state or served as a judge of a court of record in any jurisdiction of the United States, or both.

### Arizona Revised Statutes

### § 11-402.   Qualifications

A person shall not be eligible for a county office, whether elective or appointive, nor shall a certificate of election or commission issue to any person, unless he is, at the time of his election or appointment, eighteen years of age or over, a resident of the state, an elector of the county or precinct in which the duties of the office are to be exercised and able to read and write the English language. The board of supervisors shall be the sole judge of such qualifications, subject to review by certiorari in the superior court.

* * * *

---

The justice of the peace courts serve a significant function in the Arizona judicial system. They process approximately 34% of all cases filed each year in the Arizona court system and are often the public's only point of contact with the judiciary. * * * By statute, a [Justice of the Peace] need only be eighteen years old, a resident of the state, an elector of the county, and able to read and write the English language.

Anne E. Nelson, *Fifty-Eight Years and Counting: The Elusive Quest to Reform Arizona's Justice of the Peace Courts*, 52 Ariz. L. Rev. 533, 538 (2010).

Some qualifications sought in judges may be difficult to assess or teach. Pre-judicial education for "judicial aspirants" could increase public confidence in judicial selection and improve the quality of judging. Training to be a judge is often gained by being a judge and learning on the job.

Proposals for "introductory judicial [training]" encompass a curriculum including "short courses" in these topics:

- developing listening skills;

- interpreting body language;

- judicial demeanor, and the proper treatment of court staff, attorneys, litigants, witnesses, and others;

- jury selection and selection of a foreperson;

- efficient, but appropriate, use of law clerks and staff attorneys;

- sensitivity training to help identify and cope with stereotyping and latent bias and prejudice, *e.g.*, those based (albeit with some overlap in many instances) on race, ethnicity, religion, gender, nationality, alienage, socio-economic status, prosecution or defense in criminal cases, and attitudes towards various organizations;

- identifying and dealing with personality conflicts (*e.g.*, with other judges, parties, or among lawyers, jurors, etc.);

- basic techniques of docket management;

- basic techniques of managing people, especially those with large personalities (including, but not limited to, lawyers) in the courtroom and in chambers;

- balancing the needs of judicial office with pre-existing friendships, family obligations, professional relationships, romantic attachments, and affiliations with or memberships in religious, professional, civic, and community organizations;

- some of the fine points of judicial ethics;

- balancing judicial independence and judicial restraint;

- financial planning: how to "afford" to be a judge;

- public perceptions and the importance of judicial decorum;

- dealing with threats to personal safety and security and that of court personnel and loved ones;

- determining when recusal is advisable, even where it is not mandatory;

- balancing First Amendment rights against the needs of judicial discretion in election campaigning, public speaking, relations with news media, and responding to public criticism of decisions.

Keith R. Fisher, *Education for Judicial Aspirants*, 43 AKRON L. REV. 163 (2010).

In addition to a specific pre-judicial course of study, qualifications to serve as a judge could also include time served on a lower court or served as a judicial clerk.

. . . if one wants seriously to treat fitness for judging as a matter determined primarily by professional qualification, then perhaps judging should be treated as an independent profession, rather than as an extension of lawyering, and judgeships awarded to those who have invested time and effort in preparing themselves for the role. The beginner might then learn how to judge in the tradition of apprenticeship, by sitting at the feet of the master, watching and, eventually, imitating when called upon to do some part of the work. The proper professional qualification for judging generally might then be apprentice judging — service as a law clerk. (The usual one- or two-year term of service might of course need to be extended.) The most important professional qualification for the highest form of judging — the judging that the Supreme Court does — would be service as a judge on a lower court.

Stephen Carter, *The Confirmation Mess*, 101 Harv. L. Rev. 1185 (1988) (footnotes omitted).

## III.  JUDICIAL EVALUATION AND EDUCATION

Once on the bench, judges need training and education to address the pressures and stresses of their new positions. The new judges need to know if they are being competent, effective, and fair. Often the local bar association performs the task of judging the judges.

### A.  Judicial Evaluation

The public and the bar may have the opportunity to evaluate judges once they are on the bench. A number of professional organizations and jurisdictions have implemented judicial evaluations. For example, the American Bar Association formed a committee to develop guidelines to assist jurisdictions in creating and performing effective judicial evaluation programs. The programs are designed to give judges feedback on their performance on the bench and a new perspective. ABA Black Letter Guidelines for the Evaluation of Judicial Performance (Feb. 2005).

The courts themselves also create and undertake judicial evaluations. The Federal Judicial Center undertook a pilot program for judicial evaluation in the U. S. District court for the Central District of Illinois. *Judicial Evaluation Pilot Project of the Judicial Conference Committee on the Judicial Branch* (Federal Judicial Center Aug. 1991). After asking the number of cases, contested motions and hours spent observing a judge, the Pilot Project Questionnaire asked these questions of attorneys concerning the judge:

## JUDICIAL EVALUATION QUESTIONNAIRE

* * * *

INTEGRITY (1-Strongly Agree, 2-Mildly Agree, 3-No Opinion, 4-Mildly Disagree, 5-Strongly Disagree)

4. His rulings are uninfluenced by the identity of the lawyers and parties involved.

5. His rulings are free from any predisposition to decide for a particular party.

6. His awards of costs are fair and reasonable.

7. His awards of attorney's fees in appropriate cases are fair and reasonable.

8. He refrains from ex parte communications.

COMMENTS:

JUDICIAL TEMPERAMENT (1-Strongly Agree, 2-Mildly Agree, 3-No Opinion, 4-Mildly Disagree, 5-Strongly Disagree)

9. He is courteous toward lawyers and litigants.

10. He conducts court proceedings with appropriate firmness.

11. He gives due consideration to the convenience of lawyers and litigants in scheduling proceedings.

12. He refrains from prejudging the outcome of a case during early proceedings.

13. He refrains from coercing settlements.

COMMENTS:

LEGAL ABILITY (1-Strongly Agree, 2-Mildly Agree, 3-No Opinion, 4-Mildly Disagree, 5-Strongly Disagree)

14. His written rulings are clearly expressed.

15. His oral rulings are clearly expressed.

16. His rulings on evidentiary questions reflect a current knowledge of the law and the case file.

COMMENTS:

DECISIVENESS (1-Strongly Agree, 2-Mildly Agree, 3-No Opinion, 4-Mildly Disagree, 5-Strongly Disagree)

17. He rules promptly on motions.

18. He insures steady progress of a case.

19. He is decisive in his rulings.

20. He decides cases with reasonable promptness.

21. He rules promptly on evidentiary questions.

COMMENTS:

DILIGENCE (1-Strongly Agree, 2-Mildly Agree, 3-No Opinion, 4-Mildly Disagree, 5-Strongly Disagree)

22. He convenes court punctually.

23. His hearings and pretrial conferences reflect adequate research and preparation regarding the facts of the case and the applicable law.

24. He deals with emergency matters expeditiously.

COMMENTS:

25. Does Judge _____ have any specific mannerisms or practices which you find irritating or distracting? If yes, please explain.

26. What positive statements can you make regarding how Judge _____ performs his official duties.

27. What are the areas in which you believe Judge _____ is in need of the most improvement regarding the performance of his official duties? Please explain.

28. Do you believe that Judge _____ should be more/less involved in settling cases. Please explain.

Attachment B Pilot District Evaluation Materials Mailed to Attorneys

The judges responded to the Pilot Program and evaluated the usefulness of the evaluation results:

> I have reviewed the results of the evaluation survey and I find them helpful. They are helpful because they are about as objective an evaluation as we can hope to get.

> 92% of the lawyers responding think that I am doing a good job. 3% believe I am an idiot or evil or both. The other 5% have the matter under advisement.

> Bottom line. It is good to know what the customers are thinking.

Federal Judicial Center Judicial Evaluation Pilot Project, p. 8.

## B.   Judicial Education

Once on the bench, the new judge faces a host of personal and professional challenges. Judicial education now encompasses case management procedures, hiring practices for court personnel, substantive legal learning, technology training, as well as managing the stresses that come with the position.

Traditional judge education programs addressed developments in statutory and case law, case management techniques, and such practical nuts-and-bolts subjects as evidence and procedure. These programs speak to a judge's professional skills and knowledge. For example, the National Judicial College in Reno, Nevada, offers new and experienced judges courses in a wide range of topics. Courses offered at the National Judicial College include: Special Problems in Criminal Evidence; Alternative

Dispute Resolution Methods; Basic Word Processing for Judges; Opinion Writing; The Decision Making Process; Children in Court; Ethics for Judges; Environmental Law; Effective Caseflow Management.

Other judicial programs introduce reading great works of literature and philosophy, understanding basic principles and new developments in science, political and cultural trends, lessons of history, and principles and values in ethics and religion. New topics now address the judge's whole person and the pressures of judging one's fellow human beings. *See* Charles S. Claxton, *Characteristics of Effective Judicial Education Programs*, 76 JUDICATURE 11 (1992).

Informal education and socialization also help educate new and established judges. Support networks have developed because of the potential for a judicial position to create both stress and isolation. *See, e.g.*, Celeste F. Bremer, *Reducing Judicial Stress Through Mentoring*, 87 JUDICATURE 244 (Mar.–Apr. 2004).

## IV.  THE RESULTS OF THE JUDICIAL SELECTION PROCESS: LACK OF DIVERSITY

Diversity among judges, including diversity in race, gender, religion, and practice experience, has been an elusive goal for decades in the federal and state court systems. Lack of diversity on the bench in turn influences a range of issues within a court's operations. These issues include: the notion of "legitimacy" in the eyes of citizens when benches do not reflect the diversity of the court's jurisdiction; lack of diversity among judges contradicts the established need for diversity among jurors; lack of diversity on the bench influences the decisions made on issues coming before the court.

Excerpts that follow reflect both the actual numbers of women and minority judges as well as the issues those numbers raise.

### A.  The Numbers of Women & Minority Judges

#### EIGHTH CIRCUIT

Up until 1978, all of the judges appointed to the court were white men, but since then, two black men and two white women have joined their ranks. The first African American judge on the court, Judge Theodore McMillan, was appointed in 1978 by President Jimmy Carter. Judge McMillan came to the Eighth Circuit form the Missouri Court of Appeals and served on the court until his death in 2006. I am the first woman to sit on the court, appointed by President William Clinton in 1994 when I was Chief Judge of the United States District court for the District of Minnesota (appointed in 1980 by President Jimmy Carter). Judge Lavenski R. Smith of Arkansas is the second African American to serve on the court, appointed by President George W. Bush in 2001 after serving our Arkansas courts. Judge Jane Kelly of the Northern District of Iowa is the second woman on the court and the first public defender, appointed by President Barack Obama in 2013.

Diana E. Murphy, *Diversity Within the Eighth Circuit*, 17 J. GENDER RACE & JUST. 435 (2014).

## ARIZONA

|  | Supreme Court | Court of Appeals | Superior Court |
|---|---|---|---|
| **Judgeships** | 5 | 22 | 193 |
| **Women Judges** | 1 | 5 | 62 |
| **African American/ Black Judges** | 0 | 1 | 2 |
| **Latino/Hispanic Judges** | 0 | 1 | 7 |
| **Native American Judges** | 0 | 0 | 0 |
| **Asian/Pacific Island Judges** | 0 | 1 | 2 |

National Center for State Courts [Figures were updated by AJS staff in September 2009. Gender figures for trial courts were derived from The American Bench's "Judges of the Nation Gender Ratio Summary," 20th ed (2010).]

The makeup of the current Supreme Court can be seen, in one way, as a big success story for certain minorities. It is a triumph, in fact, for two groups which have historically had to put up with a lot of discrimination and lack of political representation in America. These two groups are not defined by gender or race, but rather by religion. Broken down on religious lines, today's Supreme Court has members from just two religions, both of which had been historically underrepresented on the highest court: Roman Catholics and Jews. There are six Roman Catholics currently serving on the court (Samuel Alito, Anthony Kennedy, John Roberts, Antonin Scalia, Sonia Sotomayor, and Clarence Thomas) and three Jews (Stephen Breyer, Ruth Bader Ginsburg, and Elena Kagen). This is undoubtedly a story of rising up from underrepresentation. But, bearing in mind that America is a country with almost too many religions to count, have we actually moved into a problem of overrepresentation or lack of diversity?

Chris Weigant, *Supreme Court's Lack of Religious Diversity*, The Huffington Post (updated 8/30/14).

## B.    The Numbers Create Issues of Legitimacy & Influence on Decisions

Two issues have garnered special attention and research within the concerns over the lack of diversity in the court system. First, the concern for perceptions of legitimacy and second, the concern that lack of diversity will impact specific, identifiable decisions made by courts lacking diversity.

> Perhaps more important than its tangible impact on the decision in any particular case, racial exclusion of judges or jurors may adversely affect the perceived legitimacy of the judicial process. Decisions are more likely to

appear illegitimate if the decision-making body — be it a jury or judge — is homogeneous, exclusive, and not representative of a cross section of the community. The nation's stated commitment to representative juries reflects this understanding and led to a system that, in modern times, is designed to draw jurors from virtually all walks of life. In fact, the law requires that the jury pool include potential jurors from a cross section of the community.

Unlike the jury selection process, judicial selection at the federal and state levels in the United States generally lacks any institutional structure committed to ensuring diversity. Judges are selected on an ad hoc basis. In many instances, politicians, who by definition are beholden to the majority, select judges with relatively little oversight and without strong pressures to ensure that the judiciary reflects a cross section of the community.

Kevin R. Johnson & Luis Fuentes-Rohwer, *A Principled Approach to the Quest for Racial Diversity on the Judiciary*, 10 MICH. J. OF RACE & LAW 5 (2004) (footnotes omitted).

Empirical research identifies race and gender as influencing a judge's decision when addressing issues of race and gender in cases before the court.

This Article provides a status report on the reasonably clear conclusions that can be drawn from current empirical evidence in this area. To the extent that there is a difference between the way female judges and male judges resolve legal cases, the frequent hypothesis is that those differences would most likely appear in employment discrimination, particularly sex discrimination, cases. This macro review largely supports that hypothesis. Thus, it concludes that increasing gender diversity on the bench makes a substantive difference in how these kinds of cases are resolved. As the subject of the cases moves away from sex discrimination, however, the review of research indicates that the relationship of the judges' gender to case outcomes is less predictable.

Pat K. Chew, *Judges' Gender and Employment Discrimination Cases: Emerging Evidence-Based Empirical Conclusions*, 14 J. GENDER RACE & JUST. 359 (2011).

American society is becoming increasingly diverse. At the same time, the federal judiciary continues to be predominantly White. What difference does this make? This article offers an empirical answer to that question through an extensive study of workplace racial harassment cases. It finds that judges of different races reach different conclusions, with non-African American judges less likely to hold for the plaintiffs. It also finds that plaintiffs of different races fare differently, with African Americans the most likely to lose and Hispanics the most likely to be successful. Finally, countering the formalism model's tenet that judges are color-blind, the results suggest that judges of one race are more likely to hold for plaintiffs of the same race, suggesting a tendency toward insider group preferences. These findings illustrate the complex race dynamics in judicial decision-making and the consequences of a judiciary that does not reflect the citizenry's racial diversity. The article concludes that an integrated judiciary would be more responsive and accountable to society, while still exercising its principled decision-making.

Pat K. Chew & Robert E. Kelley, *The Realism of Race in Judicial Decision Making: An Empirical Analysis of Plaintiffs' Race and Judges' Race*, 28 Harv. J. Racial & Ethnic Just. 91 (2012).

## In Court Reports

**1.** Interview your judge or use judicial directories and databases to gather information about your judge's education and previous legal and non-legal experience before coming onto the bench.

**2.** What training and educational programs are offered to your judge? What topics are included? How often does your judge participate in such programs?

**3.** How long as your judge been on the bench? How does the length of time in office affect courtroom proceedings such as motion call or trials; appellate arguments; requirements for written materials submitted to the court? Have specific experiences created the need, over time, for specific rules or practices?

**4.** Evaluate and critique the methods used to appoint or elect judges to your court. If relevant, examine the state code of judicial conduct in light of campaign issues.

**5.** Has your state court system created a task force on bias in the courtroom? If so, find its report and conclusions concerning bias experienced by judges, litigants, attorneys, and court personnel. Has your federal circuit has created a similar task force? Can you see procedures or practices in your court which reflect an awareness of and respect for differences and diversity?

**6.** Research how judges' performances are evaluated in your court. Consider who is surveyed and what questions are asked.

**7.** Survey and evaluate the diversity of your court and those within your state and federal district and circuit. Consider diversity to include gender, race, practice experience, law school attended, family background.

**8.** How do you think your judge address issues often identified as the stresses and isolation of judges? These issues may include imposing criminal sentences, lengthy civil trials, discovery disputes, high profile cases, isolation from the practicing bar, workload, budget concerns.

## Out of Court Reports

**1.** What qualities would you seek in a judge? Draft a set of questions you would use in interviewing a judicial candidate to evaluate judicial qualities that would not be apparent from a resume.

**2.** How do you think the diversity of the judiciary affects the practice of law for attorneys and their clients? *See* Diana Pratt, *Representing Non Mainstream Clients to Mainstream Judges: A Challenge of Persuasion*, 4 Legal Writing: J. Legal Writing Inst. 79 (1998).

3. Select your own state or one of the 39 states that elect judges and locate the code of judicial conduct that governs judicial campaigns. Using that code of judicial conduct, evaluate these campaign statements made by Elizabeth Burdick, an attorney engaged in a judicial campaign against an incumbent judge. The incumbent judge had been appointed by the state's Supreme Court to fill a vacancy in the trial court:

a. "Less than one year ago the political bosses appointed a new judge to our courts."

b. "Elizabeth Burick will be a tough judge who supports the death penalty and isn't afraid to use it."

c. "Burick favors the death penalty for convicted murderers."

d. The insertion of the name "Elizabeth A. Burick" between the words "Common Pleas" and "Judge" in a campaign letter.

e. The statement in a campaign letter: "My goal as your Judge."

f. The statement "in my court there will be immediate punishment."

g. The statement "I will be creative with the use of community service and other programs, so that there is no longer a mockery of the courts."

h. The inadvertent placement of the word "judge" on her letterhead.

[See *In re Judicial Campaign Complaint Against Burick*, 705 N.E.2d 422 (Ohio Comm'n Judges 1999)].

4. If you live in a state where judges are elected, describe your voting history and your level of education concerning judicial candidates. What resources are available for learning about judicial candidates?

Traditionally the League of Women Voters supplied election information. In 2015, the Ohio State Bar Association, Ohio Supreme Court Justice Maureen O'Connor, the League of Women Voters of Ohio, the Bliss Institute at the University of Akron, the Ohio Newspaper Association and the Ohio Association of Broadcasters created a judicial voter education website called JudicialVotesCount.org.

The site is described as having information about every judicial office in the state and reliable background information about candidates running for judicial office. For the November 3, 2015 election, there were 55 municipal court judicial races in 28 counties in Ohio. The site provides: Comprehensive biographical information about the candidates; lists of candidates by county; each candidate provided their legal background; and why they were running for the judicial seat. Additional information on the website helped to explain the Ohio's court system and what judges do.

5. Having read the briefs in *Williams-Yulee v. Florida Bar*, draft an opinion that expresses your views of the issues. Then compare your reasoning to the several opinions issued: *Williams-Yulee v. Florida Bar*, 135 S. Ct. 1656 (2015).

## SELECTED BIBLIOGRAPHY

Gregory L. Acquaviva & John D. Castiglione, *Judicial Diversity on State Supreme Courts*, 39 Seton Hall L. Rev. 1203 (2009).

American Judicature Society, judicial selection in the states (www.ajs.org/js) (compilation of data on judicial selection in all states and District of Columbia).

Marc T. Amy, *Judiciary School: A Proposal for a Pre-Judicial LL.M. Degree*, 87 Judicature 30 (2003).

James M. Anderson & Eric Helland, *How Much Should Judges Be Paid? An Empirical Study on the Effect of Judicial Pay on the State Bench*, 64 Stan. L. Rev. 1277 (2012).

Seth Anderson, *Examining the Decline in Support for Merit Selection in the States*, 67 Alb. L. Rev. 793 (2004).

Orley Ashenfelter, Theodore Eisenberg & Stewart J. Schwab, *Politics and the Judiciary: The Influence of Judicial Background on Case Outcomes*, 24 J. Legal Stud. 257 (1995).

Larry Aspin, *Judicial Retention Election Trends 1964–2006*, 90 Judicature 208 (2007).

Dmitry Bam, *Voter Ignorance and Judicial Elections*, 102 Ky. L.J. 553 (2014).

Duane Benton & Jennifer A.L. Sheldon-Sherman, *What Judges Want and Need: User-Friendly Foundations for Effective Judicial Education*, 2015 J. Disp. Resol. 23 (2015).

Rebecca White Berch & Erin Norris Bass, *Judicial Performance Review in Arizona: A Critical Assessment*, 56 Ariz. L. Rev. 353 (2014).

Theresa M. Beiner, *How the Contentious Nature of Federal Judicial Appointments Affects "Diversity" on the Bench*, 39 U. Rich. L. Rev. 849 (2005).

Chris W. Bonneau & Melinda Gann Hall, In Defense of Judicial Elections (2009).

Darren M. Breslin, *Judicial Merit-Retention Elections in Pennsylvania*, 48 Duq. L. Rev. 891 (2010).

David C. Brody, *The Use of Judicial Performance Evaluations to Enhance Judicial Accountability, Judicial Independence, and Public Trust*, 86 Denv. U. L. Rev. 115 (2008).

Sande L. Buhai et. al., *The Role of Law Schools in Educating Judges to Increase Access to Justice*, 24 Pac. McGeorge Global Bus. & Dev. L.J. 161 (2011).

Suzanne L. Cassidy, *Judicial Selection: A Selective Bibliography*, 56 Mercer L. Rev. 1019 (2005).

Peter Chickris & Jack Turano III, *Integrity Is Their Portion and Proper Virtue: The Ethics of Funding Judicial Education*, 51 S. Tex. L. Rev. 869 (2009).

Stephen J. Choi, G. Mitu Gulati & Eric A. Posner, *Professionals or Politicians: The*

*Uncertain Empirical Case for an Elected Rather Than Appointed Judiciary*, 26 J. LAW ECON. & ORG. 290 (2010).

Stephen J. Choi & G. Mitu Gulati, *Choosing the Next Supreme Court Justice: An Empirical Ranking of Judge Performance*, 78 S. CAL. L. REV. 23 (2004).

Carmen Beauchamp Ciparick, *Judicial Independence: Is It Preserved or Impaired by the Election of Judges?* 77 ALB. L. REV. 1313 (2014).

MICHAEL COMISKEY, SEEKING JUSTICES: THE JUDGING OF SUPREME COURT NOMINEES (2004).

Diane E. Cowdrey, *Educating into the Future: Creating an Effective System of Judicial Education*, 51 S. TEX. L. REV. 885 (2010).

J. Andrew Crompton, *Pennsylvanians Should Adopt a Merit Selection System for State Appellate Court Judges*, 106 DICK. L. REV. 755 (2002).

Susanne DiPietro, Teresa W. Carns & William T. Cotton, *Judicial Qualifications and Judicial Performance: Is There a Relationship?*, 83 JUDICATURE 196 (Jan.–Feb. 2000).

William F. Dressel, *Judicial Recruitment, Competency, Retention, and Leadership: Critical Challenges Facing the Judiciary of Today, Tomorrow, and in 2030*, 51 S. TEX. L. REV. 905 (2010).

Jennifer K. Elek & David B. Rottman, *Improving Judicial-Performance Evaluation: Countering Bias and Exploring New Methods*, 49 COURT REV. 140 (2013).[*]

Jennifer K. Elek et al., *Judicial Performance Evaluation in the States: A Re-Examination*, 98 JUDICATURE 12 (2014).

Theodore Eisenberg, Talia Fisher & Issi Rosen-Zvi, *Actual Versus Perceived Performance of Judges*, 49 COURT REV. 146 (2013).

DION FARGANIS & JUSTIN WEDEKING, SUPREME COURT CONFIRMATION HEARINGS IN THE U.S. SENATE: RECONSIDERING THE CHARADE (2014).

Keith R. Fisher, *Education for Judicial Aspirants*, 43 AKRON L. REV. 163 (2010).

Amber Fricke & Angela Onwuachi-Willig, *Do Female "Firsts" Still Matter? Why They Do for Female Judges of Color*, 2012 MICH. ST. L. REV. 1529 (2012).

Rebecca D. Gill, Sylvia R. Lazos & Mallory M. Waters, *Are Judicial Performance Evaluations Fair to Women and Minorities? A Cautionary Tale from Clark County, Nevada*, 45 LAW & SOC'Y REV. 731 (2011).

Rebecca D. Gill, *Beyond High Hopes and Unmet Expectations: Judicial Selection Reforms in the States*, 96 JUDICATURE 278 (2013).

Sheldon Goldman, *The Politics of Appointing Catholics to the Federal Courts*, 4 U. ST. THOMAS L.J. 193 (2006).

---

[*] Court Review is published by the American Judges Association, aja.ncsc.dni.us/publications/court-review.html.

Paige E. Hoster, *Understanding the Value of Judicial Diversity Through the Native American Lens*, 36 AM. INDIAN L. REV. 457 (2012).

Mark S. Hurwitz & Drew Noble Lanier, *Judicial Diversity in Federal Courts: A Historical and Empirical Exploration*, 96 JUDICATURE 76 (2012).

Sherrilyn A. Ifill, *Judging the Judges: Racial Diversity, Impartiality and Representation on State Trial Courts*, 39 B.C. L. REV. 95 (1997).

Peter G. Jaffee et al., *Vicarious Trauma in Judges: The Personal Challenge of Dispensing Justice*, 45 JUDGES' J. 12 (Fall 2006).

Edith H. Jones, *Observations on the Status and Impact of the Judicial Confirmation Process*, 39 U. RICH L. REV. 833 (2005).

Emily Kadens, *The Puzzle of Judicial Education: The Case of Chief Justice William De Grey*, 75 BROOK. L. REV. 143 (2009).

John W. Kennedy, Jr., *Judging, Personality, and Gender: Not Just a Woman's Issue*, 36 U. TOL. L. REV. 905 (2005).

Sally J. Kenney, *Choosing Judges: A Bumpy Road to Women's Equality and a Long Way to Go*, 2012 MICH. ST. L. REV. 1499 (2012).

Rebecca Love Kourlis & Jordan M. Singer, *A Performance Evaluation Program for the Federal Judiciary*, 86 DENV. U. L. REV. 7 (2008).

David K. Kessler, *The More You Know: How 360-Degree Feedback Could Help Federal District Judges*, 62 RUTGERS L. REV. 687 (2010).

Douglas S. Lavine, *Practical Tips for New Judges Making the Transition to the Bench*, 48 JUDGES' J. 14 (Winter 2009).

Brian MacKenzie, *Judicial Stress*, 51 COURT REV. 3 (2015).

William P. Marshall, *The Judicial Nomination Wars*, 39 U. RICH. L. REV. 819 (2005).

Mary F. Moyer, *The Ohio Judicial Family Network* 45 JUDGES' J. 42 (Fall 2006).

Jonathan Remy Nash, *Judicial Election Versus Judicial Appointment: Evaluating the Potential for a Race to the Bottom*, 64 N.Y.U. ANN. SURV. AM. L. 617 (2009).

Peter Paul Olszewski, *Who's Judging Whom? Why Popular Elections Are Preferable to Merit Selection Systems*, 109 PENN. ST. L. REV. 1 (2004).

Malia Reddick, Michael J. Nelson & Rachel Paine Caulfield, *Racial and Gender Diversity on State Courts: An American Judicature Society Study*, 48 JUDGES' J. 28 (Summer 2009).

Alexis Resnick, Karen A. Myatt & Priscilla V. Marotta, *Surviving Bench Stress*, 49 FAM. CT. REV. 610 (2011).

Judith Resnick, *Judicial Selection and Democratic Theory: Demand, Supply, and Life Tenure*, 26 CARDOZO L. REV. 579 (2005).

Douglas R. Richmond, *Bullies on the Bench*, 72 LA. L. REV. 325 (2012).

Ronald D. Rotunda, *The Role of Ideology in Confirming Federal Court Judges*, 15 GEO. J. LEGAL ETHICS 127 (2001).

Gregory Sarno, *Election Campaign Activities as Grounds for Disciplining Attorney*, 26 A.L.R 4TH 170 (originally published 1983).

Robert O. Saunooke, *Native Americans and the Federal Bench: The Time Has Come*, 48 JUDGES' J. 25 (Fall 2009).

RALPH E. SHAFFER, THE BORK HEARINGS: HIGHLIGHTS FROM THE MOST CONTROVERSIAL CONFIRMATION BATTLE IN U.S. HISTORY (2005).

Jordon M. Singer, *Attorney Surveys of Judicial Performance: Impressionistic, Imperfect, Indispensable*, 98 JUDICATURE 20 (July–Aug. 2014).

Jordan M. Singer, *The Mind of the Judicial Voter*, 2011 MICH. ST. L. REV. 1443 (2011).

Danielle Sollars, *Gender Balance in the Judiciary: Why Does It Matter?*, 36 WM. MITCHELL L. REV. 1721 (2010).

Nicole A. Syzdek, *Gaining Cyberspace "Sea Legs": A Proposal for a Judicial Cyber Education Program in District Courts*, 48 U.S.F. L. REV. 559 (2014).

Ciara Torres-Spellecy, *A Bench That Looks Like America: Diversity Among Appointed State Court Judges*, 48 JUDGES' J. 12 (Summer 2009).

Sylvia R. Lazos Vargas, *Only Skin Deep?: The Cost of Partisan Politics on Minority Diversity of the Federal Bench*, 83 IND. L.J. 1423 (2008).

Stephen J. Ware, *Judicial Elections, Judicial Impartiality and Legitimate Judicial Lawmaking: Williams-Yulee v. The Florida Bar*, 68 VAND. L. REV. EN BANC 59 (2015).

Penny J. White, *Using Judicial Performance Evaluations to Supplement Inappropriate Voter Cues and Enhance Judicial Legitimacy*, 74 MO. L. REV. 635 (2009).

Nicholas H. Woolf & Jennifer MJ Yim, *The Courtroom-Observation Program of the Utah Judicial Performance Review Commission*, 47 COURT REV. 84 (2011).

Corey Rayburn Yung, *A Typology of Judging Styles*, 107 NW. U. L. REV. 1757 (2013).

# Chapter 4

# JUDICIAL ETHICS: PERFORMING DUTIES IMPARTIALLY

No bright line signals to a judge when a friendship with an attorney has gone from unremarkable to reasonably relevant to a possible motion for disqualification to raising reasonable questions about the judge's impartiality. Therefore, judicial ethics advisory opinions have identified numerous factors for a judge to consider in determining when a relationship needs to be disclosed and when it should prompt disqualification.

Cynthia Gray, *Judicial Disqualifications and Friendships with Attorneys*, 52 JUDGES' J. 20 (Summer 2013).

At the end of Roth's testimony, the court recessed. Before the jurors returned, defense counsel stated:

> Your Honor, before we go back on the record I need to make a record and I'm not sure it's going to be a record the Court will like but I'm sorry but Your Honor, I believe the Court's rolling of its eyes and the facial gestures the Court is making when I make my objections, I believe that's prejudicing my client[.]

*Tharpe v. State*, 955 N.E.2d 836 (Ind. Ct. App. 2011).

The specific comments made by the circuit court that Maiden claims constitute reversible error are as follows:

The Court:    I'm not going to make this speech again. If I cannot get people to stop talking at the same time, I'm going to let the jury go home and you all can just look at each other and talk together, but I'm not going to extend the trial past Thursday and I'm not going to hold the jury past 5:30. You're either going to learn how to obey the kindergarten rule that a five-year-old can obey or stop talking when witnesses are talking; is that clear?

Defense Counsel:    It's clear.

The Court:    Is it crystal clear?

Defense Counsel:    Yes, Your Honor.

The Court:    I want it to be real fast ball high and tight crystal clear. Mr. Smith—

Witness:    Yes, sir, Your Honor.

The Court:   [Defense counsel], when he's talking, don't say anything. When I'm talking, nobody says anything. Five-year-old children in a room with one person can obey this. It befuddles me that *people* who have gone to law school can't do it. Please prove *yourselves* capable of obeying what a five-year-old can do. *Both sides* have been doing this. Stop it. (emphasis in original)

*Maiden v. State*, 438 S.W.3d 263 (Ark. 2014), *reh'g denied*, (July 31, 2014).

The topic of judicial ethics is so broad that only two issues are addressed in the space of this chapter. Both topics relate to the need for an impartial judiciary: first, issues of judicial recusal and disqualification raised by a judge's friendship with counsel or a party in a case before the court; and second, arguments for reversal based on the court's alleged unfair or partial treatment of counsel and its adverse impact on counsel's clients. Both recusal required by friendships and challenges based on judicial temperament reflect the concern for judges to be impartial in their treatment of the parties and the attorneys appearing before them.

Judicial ethical issues are, of course, much broader than these two topics and may encompass *ex parte* communications with litigants and parties; abuse in issuing civil and criminal sanctions; public comments on pending cases; and conduct during judicial confirmation processes and election campaigns.

# I.   JUDICIAL RECUSAL AND DISQUALIFICATION

This first section considers judicial recusal or disqualification when a party questions a judge's impartiality to hear a case based upon the judge's friendship with counsel or friendship with the opposing party. In a legal world populated with former law school classmates, former colleagues at a law firm or government office, and former bar committee members, the issue of friendship and the degree of closeness of that friendship, questions of partiality emerge regularly. These issues arose before there were any efforts to create a model code of judicial conduct.

## CALLAHAN v. CALLAHAN
### 165 P. 1122 (Idaho 1917)

BUDGE, C.J.

Appellant instituted an action, in the district court for the First judicial district, in and for Shoshone County, for a decree of divorce from respondent. The respondent, after filing her answer and cross-complaint, made a motion for a change of venue, upon the ground that the Honorable William W. Woods, judge of said court, was disqualified, "because of the bias and prejudice of the said judge," and based her motion upon the records and files in the action, and upon her affidavit, in which she stated that she had been advised by certain residents of Shoshone county, and that she believed, and, therefore, alleged, that she could not have a fair and impartial trial before said judge, by reason of his friendship for appellant and prejudice against respondent; that appellant had on numerous occasions stated to her that he could win any case in which he was a party before said judge, because of their long friendship and the influence which appellant had over him; that in some actions decisions had been rendered favorable to him, by reason of such influence and friendship; that when decisions had been rendered against him he had lost solely on account of the misconduct of his counsel; that the judge had been for more than 30 years a close and intimate friend and political associate of appellant, and by reason thereof respondent could not have a fair and impartial trial; and that said judge was apprised of certain matters which had taken place between the parties to the action, looking to condonation [sic] and settlement, after the suit had been filed, and would be a material witness upon the trial.

At the hearing of the motion counter affidavits had not been filed, but the substance of the counter showing, thereafter made and filed, was stated to and considered by the court in making the following order, to wit:

> "* * * The court * * * being fully advised in the premises, and it satisfactorily appearing to the said judge that he is disqualified from trying the said cause, and that sufficient ground exists therefor: Now, therefore, it is ordered, a change of the place of trial of the said action be and the same hereby is granted, and that the said cause be and the same hereby is transferred to the district court of the Eighth judicial district of the state of Idaho, and to the Honorable Robert N. Dunn, one of the judges of the said district court."

On appeal from the above order, granting a change of the place of trial, appellant contends: First, that the showing made was insufficient to establish bias and prejudice; second, that if the showing was sufficient a change of venue should not have been granted, but that another district judge should have been called in to try the case; third, that if the showing was sufficient and the judge was within his rights in ordering a change of venue, that the order is void for insufficiency in that it should have specified the particular county to which the cause was transferred; fourth, that if the showing was sufficient the order was void for the reason that it designated the particular judge, there being two judges in the district to which it was transferred.

Upon the first proposition appellant relies mainly upon the decision of this court in *Bell v. Bell*, 18 Idaho, 636, 111 Pac. 1074, which reversed an order granting a change of venue under somewhat similar circumstances, upon the ground that the showing was insufficient in that it did not recite the facts which were relied upon to establish the existence of prejudice and bias on the part of the judge. In the instant case an examination of the affidavit discloses the facts relied upon to establish the existence of bias and prejudice on the part of the trial judge, which we think are sufficient. *Booren v. McWilliams*, 33 N.D. 339, 157 N.W. 117; *Faivre v. Mandercheid*, 117 Iowa, 724, 90 N.W. 76; *Morehouse v. Morehouse*, 136 Cal. 332, 68 Pac. 976. In the latter case it was said:

> "But here there is a direct allegation of the fact of prejudice and bias on the part of the judge; and, though the allegation is based — as in most cases it must be based — merely on the belief of the affiant, yet it is accompanied by a statement of the facts on which the belief is based, as complete as the nature of the case admitted of; and this was all that could reasonably be required."

The latter case was quoted with approval in *Bassford v. Earl*, 162 Cal. 115, 121, 121

Pac. 395–398, wherein the order denying the motion for a change of venue was reversed for the reason that there was no affidavit of the trial judge opposing the movant's showing, the court saying:

> "If such a statement was necessary in answer to the Bassford affidavit, and not only do we think it was, but from the affidavit of Mr. Wheeler it seems so to have been regarded by the respondents to that motion, the one person, who, with an informed mind, could make such a declaration, was the judge himself, and he does not do so."

The same rule was announced in *Keating v. Keating*, 169 Cal. 754, 147 Pac. 974; *Jones v. American Cent.* Ins. *Co.*, 83 Kan. 44, 109 Pac. 1077. Not only did the trial judge, in the case at bar, make no such affidavit, but on the contrary he expressly finds in his order that he is disqualified, and that sufficient ground exists for a change of venue. The order, therefore, was properly granted. Again referring to the Bell Case, it will also be noted that that case was decided in 1910, and that section 4125, Rev. Codes, has been amended by chapter 96, Sess. Laws 1913, p. 385, to read as follows:

> "The court or judge *must*, on motion, *when it appears by affidavit or other satisfactory proof*, change the place of trial in the following cases. * * *" (Italics ours.)

In this amendment "may" has been changed to "must," and the other italicized portion has been added. Just what the Legislature intended to include in the clause "other satisfactory proof" does not appear. But where the showing is such as appears in this record, and where the trial judge himself has expressly found that he was satisfied of his own disqualification and that sufficient grounds existed for a change of venue, it would not only be unjust to the parties litigant, but it would be an imposition upon the trial judge for this court to compel him to try the case under such circumstances.

The second point urged by appellant is equally without merit, in view of the language of section 4126, Rev. Codes, which provides that whenever the judge is disqualified in an action—

> "it must be transferred for trial to such other court of competent jurisdiction as may be agreed upon by the parties by stipulation in writing in open court, and entered in the minutes; or, if they do not so agree, then to the nearest court where the like objection or cause for making the order does not exist."

In other words, when a motion for a change of venue, on the ground of the bias and prejudice of the trial judge, is supported by a sufficient showing, it is the duty of such judge to grant a change of venue, and such duty is mandatory and not discretionary. Gordon v. Conor, 5 Idaho, 673, 51 Pac. 747.

Keeping the latter section in mind, appellant's third and fourth objections are readily disposed of. It is clear that the parties did not agree by stipulation in writing, entered in the minutes, or otherwise, that the cause should be transferred to any other court, and, failing in this, the judge being disqualified, the statute fixes the court to which the cause should be transferred, namely, to another district court and "to the nearest court where the like objection or cause for making the order does not exist."

What is the nearest court is a fact of which both the trial court and this court take judicial notice.

The order should have transferred the cause to the district court of the Eighth judicial district for Kootenai county, without designating what judge should try the case. That portion of the order which designated the particular judge must be regarded as mere surplusage, in view of section 3829, Rev. Codes, as amended by chapter 4, Sess. Laws 1911, p. 6, which provides that the senior judge shall apportion the business of such district among such judges as equally as may be.

The order appealed from is affirmed, and the trial judge who made the order is directed to amend the same in conformity with the views herein expressed. Costs awarded to respondent.


Morgan and Rice, JJ., concur.

## A.   JUDICIAL CONDUCT RULES OF RECUSAL AND DISQUALIFICATION

Model rules of judicial conduct, including those directed at judicial friendships, often derive from the ABA's Model Code of Judicial Conduct, created in 1972, revised in 1990, and now in the 2011 edition. State courts and legislatures have frequently adopted and tailored the ABA Model Code to suit their own goals and purposes.

## ABA MODEL CODE OF JUDICIAL CONDUCT [2011 EDITION]

### * indicates terms defined in terminology section

### CANON 2 A JUDGE SHALL PERFORM THE DUTIES OF JUDICIAL OFFICE IMPARTIALLY, COMPETENTLY, AND DILIGENTLY.

### RULE 2.2 Impartiality and Fairness.

A judge shall uphold and apply the law, and shall perform all duties of judicial office fairly and impartially.

### Comment on Rule 2.2

[1] To ensure impartiality and fairness to all parties, a judge must be objective and open-minded.

[2] Although each judge comes to the bench with a unique background and personal philosophy, a judge must interpret and apply the law without regard to whether the judge approves or disapproves of the law in question.

[3] When applying and interpreting the law, a judge sometimes may make good-faith errors of fact or law. Errors of this kind do not violate this Rule.

[4] It is not a violation of this Rule for a judge to make reasonable accommodations to ensure pro se litigants the opportunity to have their matters fairly heard.

## RULE 2.3 Bias, Prejudice and Harassment.

(A) A judge shall perform the duties of judicial office, including administrative duties, without bias or prejudice.

(B) A judge shall not, in the performance of judicial duties, by words or conduct manifest bias or prejudice, or engage in harassment, including but not limited to bias, prejudice, or harassment based upon race, sex, gender, religion, national origin, ethnicity, disability, age, sexual orientation, marital status, socioeconomic status, or political affiliation, and shall not permit court staff, court officials, or others subject to the judge's direction and control to do so.

(C) A judge shall require lawyers in proceedings before the court to refrain from manifesting bias or prejudice, or engaging in harassment, based upon attributes including but not limited to race, sex, gender, religion, national origin, ethnicity, disability, age, sexual orientation, marital status, socioeconomic status, or political affiliation, against parties, witnesses, lawyers, or others.

(D) The restrictions of paragraphs (B) and (C) do not preclude judges or lawyers from making legitimate reference to the listed factors, or similar factors, when they are relevant to an issue in a proceeding.

## Comment on Rule 2.3

[1] A judge who manifests bias or prejudice in a proceeding impairs the fairness of the proceeding and brings the judiciary into disrepute.

[2] Examples of manifestations of bias or prejudice include but are not limited to epithets; slurs; demeaning nicknames; negative stereotyping; attempted humor based upon stereotypes; threatening, intimidating, or hostile acts; suggestions of connections between race, ethnicity, or nationality and crime; and irrelevant references to personal characteristics. Even facial expressions and body language can convey to parties and lawyers in the proceeding, jurors, the media, and others an appearance of bias or prejudice. A judge must avoid conduct that may reasonably be perceived as prejudiced or biased.

[3] Harassment, as referred to in paragraphs (B) and (C), is verbal or physical conduct that denigrates or shows hostility or aversion toward a person on bases such as race, sex, gender, religion, national origin, ethnicity, disability, age, sexual orientation, marital status, socioeconomic status, or political affiliation.

[4] Sexual harassment includes but is not limited to sexual advances, requests for sexual favors, and other verbal or physical conduct of a sexual nature that is unwelcome.

## Rule 2.4: External Influences on Judicial Conduct

(A) A judge shall not be swayed by public clamor or fear of criticism.

(B) A judge shall not permit family, social, political, financial, or other interests or relationships to influence the judge's judicial conduct or judgment.

(C) A judge shall not convey or permit others to convey the impression that any person or organization is in a position to influence the judge.

## Comment on Rule 2.4

[1] An independent judiciary requires that judges decide cases according to the law and facts, without regard to whether particular laws or litigants are popular or unpopular with the public, the media, government officials, or the judge's friends or family. Confidence in the judiciary is eroded if judicial decision making is perceived to be subject to inappropriate outside influences.

\* \* \* \*

## RULE 2.7 Responsibility to Decide

A judge shall hear and decide matters assigned to the judge, except when disqualification is required by Rule 2.11 or other law.\*

## Comment on Rule 2.7

[1] Judges must be available to decide the matters that come before the court. Although there are times when disqualification is necessary to protect the rights of litigants and preserve public confidence in the independence, integrity, and impartiality of the judiciary, judges must be available to decide matters that come before the courts. Unwarranted disqualification may bring public disfavor to the court and to the judge personally. The dignity of the court, the judge's respect for fulfillment of judicial duties, and a proper concern for the burdens that may be imposed upon the judge's colleagues require that a judge not use disqualification to avoid cases that present difficult, controversial, or unpopular issues.

\* \* \* \*

## Rule 2.11: Disqualification

(A) A judge shall disqualify himself or herself in any proceeding in which the judge's impartiality\* might reasonably be questioned, including but not limited to the following circumstances:

(1) The judge has a personal bias or prejudice concerning a party or a party's lawyer, or personal knowledge\* of facts that are in dispute in the proceeding.

(2) The judge knows* that the judge, the judge's spouse or domestic partner,* or a person within the third degree of relationship* to either of them, or the spouse or domestic partner of such a person is:

> (a) a party to the proceeding, or an officer, director, general partner, managing member, or trustee of a party;

> (b) acting as a lawyer in the proceeding;

> (c) a person who has more than a de minimis* interest that could be substantially affected by the proceeding; or

> (d) likely to be a material witness in the proceeding.

(3) The judge knows that he or she, individually or as a fiduciary,* or the judge's spouse, domestic partner, parent, or child, or any other member of the judge's family residing in the judge's household,* has an economic interest* in the subject matter in controversy or is a party to the proceeding.

(4) The judge knows or learns by means of a timely motion that a party, a party's lawyer, or the law firm of a party's lawyer has within the previous [insert number] year[s] made aggregate* contributions* to the judge's campaign in an amount that [is greater than $[insert amount] for an individual or $[insert amount] for an entity] [is reasonable and appropriate for an individual or an entity].

(5) The judge, while a judge or a judicial candidate,* has made a public statement, other than in a court proceeding, judicial decision, or opinion, that commits or appears to commit the judge to reach a particular result or rule in a particular way in the proceeding or controversy.

(6) The judge:

> (a) served as a lawyer in the matter in controversy, or was associated with a lawyer who participated substantially as a lawyer in the matter during such association;

> (b) served in governmental employment, and in such capacity participated personally and substantially as a lawyer or public official concerning the proceeding, or has publicly expressed in such capacity an opinion concerning the merits of the particular matter in controversy;

> (c) was a material witness concerning the matter; or

> (d) previously presided as a judge over the matter in another court.

(B) A judge shall keep informed about the judge's personal and fiduciary economic interests, and make a reasonable effort to keep informed about the personal economic interests of the judge's spouse or domestic partner and minor children residing in the judge's household.

(C) A judge subject to disqualification under this Rule, other than for bias or prejudice under paragraph (A)(1), may disclose on the record the basis of the judge's disqualification and may ask the parties and their lawyers to consider, outside the presence of the judge and court personnel, whether to waive disqualification. If, following the disclosure, the parties and lawyers agree, without participation by the judge or court personnel, that the judge should not be disqualified, the judge may participate in the proceeding. The agreement shall be incorporated into the record of the proceeding.

### Comment on Rule 2.11

[1] Under this Rule, a judge is disqualified whenever the judge's impartiality might reasonably be questioned, regardless of whether any of the specific provisions of paragraphs (A)(1) through (6) apply. In many jurisdictions, the term "recusal" is used interchangeably with the term "disqualification."

[2] A judge's obligation not to hear or decide matters in which disqualification is required applies regardless of whether a motion to disqualify is filed.

[3] The rule of necessity may override the rule of disqualification. For example, a judge might be required to participate in judicial review of a judicial salary statute, or might be the only judge available in a matter requiring immediate judicial action, such as a hearing on probable cause or a temporary restraining order. In matters that require immediate action, the judge must disclose on the record the basis for possible disqualification and make reasonable efforts to transfer the matter to another judge as soon as practicable.

[4] The fact that a lawyer in a proceeding is affiliated with a law firm with which a relative of the judge is affiliated does not itself disqualify the judge. If, however, the judge's impartiality might reasonably be questioned under paragraph (A), or the relative is known by the judge to have an interest in the law firm that could be substantially affected by the proceeding under paragraph (A)(2)(c), the judge's disqualification is required.

[5] A judge should disclose on the record information that the judge believes the parties or their lawyers might reasonably consider relevant to a possible motion for disqualification, even if the judge believes there is no basis for disqualification.

[6] "Economic interest," as set forth in the Terminology section, means ownership of more than a de minimis legal or equitable interest. Except for situations in which a judge participates in the management of such a legal or equitable interest, or the interest could be substantially affected by the outcome of a proceeding before a judge, it does not include:

(1) an interest in the individual holdings within a mutual or common investment fund;

(2) an interest in securities held by an educational, religious, charitable, fraternal, or civic organization in which the judge or the judge's spouse, domestic partner, parent, or child serves as a director, officer, advisor, or other participant;

(3) a deposit in a financial institution or deposits or proprietary interests the judge may maintain as a member of a mutual savings association or credit union, or similar proprietary interests; or

(4) an interest in the issuer of government securities held by the judge.

* * * *

The ABA's Model Code of Judicial Conduct has been adopted and modified as needed, by 29 states. For example, in Ohio's Code of Judicial Conduct, effective March 1, 2009; amended November 18, 2014), each canon and comment is compared to the ABA Model Code of Judicial Conduct to note similarities and distinctions.

## OHIO CODE OF JUDICIAL CONDUCT

### Comparison to ABA Model Code of Judicial Conduct

Rule 2.4 is identical to Model Rule 2.4.

## Comparison to ABA Model Code of Judicial Conduct

With two exceptions, Rule 2.11 is comparable to Model Rule 2.11. Division (A)(4), relative to the disqualification of a judge who receives a campaign contribution in excess of a specific amount, is not adopted, in part because Rule 4.4 contains what are considered reasonable contribution limits applicable to individuals and organizations, including parties, lawyers, and law firms. Division (A)(6) is new language that addresses disqualification when a judge's spouse has previously acted as a judge in the same proceeding. This provision is comparable to Ohio Canon 3(E)(1)(d)(iii) but is not found in the Model Code. Comment [1] is modified to remove a reference to the fact that some jurisdictions use interchangeably the terms "recusal" and "disqualification" and to indicate that the mere receipt of a campaign contribution within the permissible limits set forth in Rule 4.4 is not grounds for disqualification. Comment [6] is stricken because it merely restates the definition of "economic interest" found in the Terminology section.

## FEDERAL STATUTES

Three specific federal statutes govern the federal courts on the issues of disqualification and recusal. In court opinions the two terms — disqualification and recusal — are often used interchangeably. The recusal statutes are 28 U.S.C. § 455, 28 U.S.C. § 144, and 28 U.S.C. § 47.

The statutes are related, but serve slightly different functions. The broadest statute is section 455; it no longer includes a "duty to sit," a view that favored hearing a case over recusal. Instead, the statute shifted its focus to the public perception of a fair and impartial judiciary.

## 28 U.S.C. § 455   Disqualification of justice, judge, or magistrate

(a) Any justice, judge, or magistrate of the United States shall disqualify himself in any proceeding in which his impartiality might reasonably be questioned.

(b) He shall also disqualify himself in the following circumstances:

(1) Where he has a personal bias or prejudice concerning a party, or personal knowledge of disputed evidentiary facts concerning the proceeding;

(2) Where in private practice he served as lawyer in the matter in controversy, or a lawyer with whom he previously practiced law served during such association as a lawyer concerning the matter, or the judge or such lawyer has been a material witness concerning it;

(3) Where he has served in governmental employment and in such capacity participated as counsel, adviser or material witness concerning the proceeding or expressed an opinion concerning the merits of the particular case in controversy;

(4) He knows that he, individually or as a fiduciary, or his spouse or minor child residing in his household, has a financial interest in the subject matter in controversy or in a party to the proceeding, or any other interest that could be substantially affected by the outcome of the proceeding;

(5) He or his spouse, or a person within the third degree of relationship to either of them, or the spouse of such a person:

(i) Is a party to the proceeding, or an officer, director, or trustee of a party;

(ii) Is acting as a lawyer in the proceeding;

(iii) Is known by the judge to have an interest that could be substantially affected by the outcome of the proceeding;

(iv) Is to the judge's knowledge likely to be a material witness in the proceeding.

(c) A judge should inform himself about his personal and fiduciary financial interests, and make a reasonable effort to inform himself about the personal financial interests of his spouse and minor children residing in his household.

(d) For the purposes of this section the following words or phrases shall have the meaning indicated:

(1) "proceeding" includes pretrial, trial, appellate review, or other stages of litigation;

(2) the degree of relationship is calculated according to the civil law system;

(3) "fiduciary" includes such relationships as executor, administrator, trustee, and guardian;

(4) "financial interest" means ownership of a legal or equitable interest, however small, or a relationship as director, adviser, or other active participant in the affairs of a party, except that:

(i) Ownership in a mutual or common investment fund that holds securities is not a "financial interest" in such securities unless the judge participates in the management of the fund;

(ii) An office in an educational, religious, charitable, fraternal, or civic organization is not a "financial interest" in securities held by the organization;

(iii) The proprietary interest of a policyholder in a mutual insurance company, of a depositor in a mutual savings association, or a similar proprietary interest, is a "financial interest" in the organization only if the outcome of the proceeding could substantially affect the value of the interest;

(iv) Ownership of government securities is a "financial interest" in the issuer only if the outcome of the proceeding could substantially affect the value of the securities.

(e) No justice, judge, or magistrate shall accept from the parties to the proceeding a waiver of any ground for disqualification enumerated in subsection (b). Where the ground for disqualification arises only under subsection (a), waiver may be accepted provided it is preceded by a full disclosure on the record of the basis for disqualification.

(f) Notwithstanding the preceding provisions of this section, if any justice, judge, magistrate, or bankruptcy judge to whom a matter has been assigned would be disqualified, after substantial judicial time has been devoted to the matter, because of the appearance or discovery, after the matter was assigned to him or her, that he or she individually or as a fiduciary, or his or her spouse or minor child residing in his or her household, has a financial interest in a party (other than an interest that could be substantially affected by the outcome), disqualification is not required if the justice, judge, magistrate, bankruptcy judge, spouse or minor child, as the case may be, divests himself or herself of the interest that provides the grounds for the disqualification.

---

Federal statute 28 U.S.C. § 144 requires recusal in the face of a party's "timely and sufficient" affidavit stating that the judge has a personal bias or prejudice against him or in favor of the opposing party.

## 28 U.S.C. § 144   (federal district court judges)

Whenever a party to any proceeding in a district court makes and files a timely and sufficient affidavit that the judge before whom the matter is pending has a personal bias or prejudice either against him or in favor of any adverse party, such judge shall proceed no further therein, but another judge shall be assigned to hear such proceeding.

The affidavit shall state the facts and the reasons for the belief that bias or prejudice exists, and shall be filed not less than ten days before the beginning of the term at which the proceeding is to be heard, or good cause shall be shown for failure to file it within such time. A party may file only one such affidavit in any case. It shall be accompanied by a certificate of counsel of record stating that it is made in good faith.

––––––––––

The third federal statute governing recusal and disqualification addresses appellate courts. While this disqualification rule may seem to be common sense, it was not always in place. When the Justices of the United States Supreme Court would "ride the circuits," at times, these justices heard the same cases on appeal that they had heard while on the circuit bench. *See* Joshua Glick, *On the Road: The Supreme Court and the History of Circuit Riding*, 24 CARDOZO L. REV. 1753 (2003).

### 28 U.S.C. § 47   Disqualification of trial judge to hear appeal

No judge shall hear or determine an appeal from the decision of a case or issue tried by him.

––––––––––

In addition to these federal statutes, federal court judges are also governed by the Code of Conduct for United States Judges. This Code re-enforces and supplements the requirements of the federal statutes. Guide to Judiciary Policy, Vol. 2 Ethics and Judicial Conduct, Pt A: Codes of Conduct (last revised March 20, 2014).

## B.   APPLYING RULES OF RECUSAL AND DISQUALIFICATION: JUDICIAL FRIENDSHIPS

Relationships made before and continuing after becoming a judge can provoke concerns about maintaining impartiality. While attorneys and judges may view these friendships without alarm, the test for an appearance of partiality is often framed as "whether an objective, disinterested observer fully informed of the facts underlying the grounds on which recusal was sought would entertain a significant doubt that justice would be done in the case." *United States v. Murphy* (text below). *Murphy* is frequently cited as the case most fully analyzing a judge's ability to disclose the relationship and to remain impartial where a close friend appears as counsel in the judge's court.

# UNITED STATES v. MURPHY
768 F.2d 1518 (7th Cir. 1985)

EASTERBROOK, CIRCUIT JUDGE

John M. Murphy was an Associate Judge of the Circuit Court of Cook County from 1972 until 1984. He was indicted in 1983 and charged with accepting bribes to fix the outcome of hundreds of cases, from drunk driving to battery to felony theft. Some of the counts on which he was convicted grew out of contrived cases staged by the FBI and federal prosecutors as part of Operation Greylord, an investigation of the Cook County courts.

The charges spanned many years and many statutes. Part I of this opinion sets out the background . . . and Part V [looks] at the decision of the district judge not to recuse himself.

## I.

The evidence at trial, which we now view in the light most favorable to the prosecution, showed several categories of cases in which Murphy took bribes. We separate the evidence into several groups: traffic court, "hustling," fixed felony offenses, and the cases that were contrived as part of the investigation. We omit a great deal of the evidence and describe only enough to give the general picture. Some of the events we recount are pertinent to other Greylord cases still in litigation. Our statement of the evidence and the inferences the jury could draw about Murphy's conduct is not meant to prejudge those cases.

*Traffic court.* The Cook County courts are organized into divisions, and supervisory judges assign other judges to particular divisions or courtrooms. From 1972 to early 1981 Murphy was assigned to traffic court, which has courtrooms for major offenses (driving while intoxicated, leaving the scene of an accident, and so on) and minor offenses (such as running a red light). Judge Richard LeFevour was the Supervising Judge of traffic court; he had the authority to decide whether Murphy and other judges would hear major or minor cases.

Officer James LeFevour of the Chicago police, Richard LeFevour's cousin, was assigned to traffic court from 1969 through 1980. James LeFevour testified for the prosecution as part of an agreement under which the Government limited its charges against him to three tax offenses. He testified that beginning in 1975 he met regularly with Melvin Cantor, who would give him a list of his cases that day. James LeFevour would take the list to Judge Richard LeFevour; Judge LeFevour would assign Murphy to hear some of Cantor's cases. James LeFevour would present Murphy the list of Cantor's cases. Murphy then would find the defendants not guilty or sentence them to "supervision," an outcome defendants favored. Later in each day Cantor would give James LeFevour money to pass to Judge LeFevour and some for James to keep for a "tip."

Although Richard LeFevour kept the bribes for these cases, he put Murphy in a position to "earn" his own bribes. Richard LeFevour would assign to major cases, on a regular basis, only those judges who would "see" James LeFevour. Lawyers then would bribe some of the judges assigned to the major courtrooms. Murphy was in a major courtroom more often than most other judges.

Lawyers known as "miracle workers" occasionally met with James LeFevour and with Joseph Trunzo, another police officer assigned to traffic court. The lawyers would tell Officer LeFevour or Officer Trunzo which defendants they represented; the officers would pass the information to Murphy; after the defendant had prevailed, the lawyer would hand an envelope to the officer with $100 per case for Murphy and another $10 or so for the officer; the officer would pass the envelope to Murphy. Prosecutors testified that although they won as many as 90% of their major traffic cases against public defenders, they almost never won a case in which the defendant was represented by one of the "miracle workers."

The testimony at the trial of this case concerned unidentified cases in traffic court. But some plays stood out, even though the players were anonymous. A prosecutor recalled one drunk driving case in which the defendant was represented by Harry Kleper, a miracle worker. The arresting police officer testified that the defendant failed the usual roadside tests of drunkenness and admitted drinking beer before driving. The defendant took the stand and did not deny imbibing; she said only that the liquor did not affect her ability to drive. Under cross-examination she admitted "feeling" the beer; the prosecutor then asked: "And don't you think it is fair to say that you were under the influence of intoxicating liquor?," to which she replied, "Yes, I guess that is a fair thing to say." Judge Murphy threw up his hands and called a recess, turning to Kleper with the remark: "Counselor, I suggest you talk to your client." As Murphy left the bench, the prosecutor heard Murphy yell down the hall to the judges' chambers: "You won't believe this. The State's Attorney just got the defendant to admit she was drunk." A few minutes later Murphy reconvened the court. Kleper asked the defendant whether she was drunk; she said no. In closing argument the prosecutor stressed the defendant's admission. Kleper did not give a closing argument. Murphy ruled: "I still have a reasonable doubt. Not guilty."

*Hustlers.* In 1981, Judge LeFevour became Presiding Judge for Cook County's First Municipal District court, which has a general jurisdiction. Many of the branch courts had been frequented by "hustlers." "Hustlers" are lawyers who stand outside the courtroom and solicit business from the people about to enter. Ethical rules long have prohibited such solicitation, and every appearance form in Circuit Court contains a representation that solicitation did not occur. Hustling is a profitable business nonetheless, and people find ways to pursue the profits of illegitimate enterprise with the same vigor they devote to lawful activities.

The profit in hustling comes from the bail system in Illinois. A defendant required to post bail may do so by depositing 10% of the bail in cash. If the defendant is discharged, the cash deposit (less the clerk's handling fee) is returned. This payment, called the cash bond refund (CBR), also may be assigned to the defendant's lawyer as compensation for legal services. Assignment requires the approval of the court. Hustlers make their money by persuading defendants to hire them and assign the CBR, then persuading the judge to release the CBR to them.

Judge Thaddeus L. Kowalski, who presided over the court known as Branch 29 from

June 1980 to March 1981, believed that hustlers cheated their clients at the same time as they violated ethical rules. Often the hustlers appeared as counsel only when the case was bound to be dismissed anyway, as they well knew. Their "representation" of the defendants simply diverted the CBRs from the defendants to the lawyers. Judge Kowalski addressed hustling in the most effective way — by eliminating its profitability. He refused to permit the hustlers to collect the CBRs. They soon deserted Branch 29. When Richard LeFevour became the presiding judge of the first district, Judge Kowalski explained to Judge LeFevour how he had cut down on hustling. Judge LeFevour praised Judge Kowalski and promptly transferred him from Branch 29 to the East Chicago Avenue Police Court, which handles criminal cases originating in the Cabrini Green housing project. Judge LeFevour replaced Kowalski with Murphy.

Hustlers flourished under Murphy, who routinely permitted them to collect the CBRs. The hustlers showed appropriate gratitude. Every month the lawyers, collectively known as the Hustlers Club, paid James LeFevour $2500. James kept $500 and gave the rest to Richard. (The sums were reduced for some months when the hustlers' take fell. Murphy was incapacitated by a broken ankle, and his replacement was apparently less compliant.) After a hustler made a certain amount, he paid an additional sum to the judge of the particular court. James LeFevour told Murphy of the Hustlers Club and Richard LeFevour's approval. Murphy told James LeFevour that he approved too.

Although Richard LeFevour kept the principal bribe, there were still rewards for Murphy. As at traffic court, Murphy was free to establish his own stable of bribe-givers. The Chicago Bar Association (CBA) maintains a Lawyer Referral Service. This service screens lawyers and assigns them to branch courtrooms to be of service to unrepresented defendants. These lawyers are potential competitors of the hustlers, and Murphy apparently cultivated them as independent sources of revenue.

Arthur Cirignani participated in the CBA's program. (The evidence at trial casts no shadows on the integrity of the CBA itself.) From June 1980 through the end of 1983 he was assigned to a courtroom three to four times a month. Whenever he was assigned to Branch 29, he paid Judge Murphy to assign cases to him rather than to continue the proceedings and allow the hustlers to claim the CBRs. For example, on June 21, 1982, Cirignani visited Murphy first thing in the morning and informed Murphy that he was there as the Bar's lawyer. Murphy referred thirteen cases to Cirignani that day and allowed Cirignani to collect CBRs totaling $1,010, a return Cirignani called "excellent." On June 22 Cirignani took $200 in cash to Murphy, who accepted the money without comment. Cirignani testified that he paid Murphy then and on other occasions to ensure referrals in the future.

*Fixed cases.* Murphy threw business to lawyers; he also threw cases. Cirignani, who testified under an arrangement that he would not be prosecuted if he told the truth, described one such case. Cirignani represented Arthur Best, charged with felony theft. The police had seized evidence from the grounds of Best's house under authority of a warrant, and Cirignani moved to suppress the evidence. On the day of the suppression hearing Cirignani visited Murphy's chambers before court began and while they were alone told Murphy that he had a "good" motion to suppress. Murphy promised to "take a look at it." Judge Murphy later granted the motion to suppress, giving no reasons.

The prosecutor then dismissed the case against Best. Before leaving the courthouse Cirignani gave Murphy an envelope containing $300. Cirignani received a CBR of $1800 in the case, and the client also paid $700 directly. (As it turned out, Cirignani's success was short-lived. The Appellate Court of Illinois reversed. *People v. Best*, 424 N.E.2d 29 (Ill. App. Ct. 1981).)

*Greylord cases.* Most of the evidence about fixed cases was presented by witnesses who had concocted the cases for the purpose of the Greylord investigation. Terrence Hake, an agent of the FBI posing as a corrupt lawyer, would represent the defendants in ghostwritten cases. Agents would file complaints and testify about made-up events.

In one case two agents of the FBI, posing as "Norman Johnson" and "John Stavros," claimed to have had a violent encounter in which Johnson injured Stavros. Hake represented Johnson, the "defendant." Wearing a tape recorder, Hake privately visited Judge Murphy's chambers on the morning the case was set for a hearing. He introduced himself as Johnson's lawyer and said he wanted a verdict of not guilty. Murphy replied: "I'll throw the fucker out the window." Hake mentioned dealings with Joseph Trunzo and suggested that Trunzo would make arrangements; Murphy said: "That's okay, everything's alright." Murphy found Johnson not guilty. But things were not well. After the trial Hake gave $300 to Officer Joseph Trunzo ($200 for Murphy, $100 for Joseph and his twin brother Jim). They did not deliver the $200 to Murphy, they apparently planned to fleece Hake (a novice at corruption) by keeping the money, leaving Hake to face an angry judge. Murphy told Hake the following week that he had not seen either Trunzo. A few days later Murphy visited traffic court, still the assignment of both Trunzos, looking for them. Joseph Trunzo then gave Murphy the $200 he had received from Hake, explaining to Murphy that "I got busy and forgot to call you." (In the other trials Joseph Trunzo kept Hake's money and Murphy did not get paid, but so far as the record shows Murphy did not know the money in these cases had been meant for him.)

Hake represented the "defendants" in several other cases fabricated by the FBI. The payoffs went more smoothly. On each occasion the "defendant" was discharged, and Hake paid Officer James LeFevour, apparently a more honest criminal than the brothers Trunzo. James LeFevour passed most of the money to Richard LeFevour and told Murphy that Judge LeFevour wanted verdicts of not guilty. Hake had some additional recorded ex parte conversations with Murphy. In one Hake conceded that his client was guilty but said he needed a verdict of not guilty, Murphy said "it'll be discharged that's all" and later acquitted the "defendant." During another meeting Murphy produced Hake's business card — a card given to James LeFevour on which Hake had written the names of cases he wanted dismissed. David Ries, another attorney and agent of the FBI, described two other concocted cases in which he represented "defendants" and paid a bribe through yet another police officer to obtain the desired deposition. See *United States v. Blackwood*, 768 F.2d 131 (7th Cir. 1985), affirming that officer's conviction.

*The outcome.* The jury convicted Murphy on 24 of the 27 counts in the indictment. The counts involved four legal theories. Some counts charged violations of the mail fraud statute, 18 U.S.C. § 1341. The checks constituting the CBRs were mailed to the attorneys, and each mail fraud count was based on the mailing of one CBR. The "fraud" was one committed by Murphy on the people of Cook County, who lost his honest services. Some counts were based on the Hobbs Act, 18 U.S.C. § 1951(a), which prohibits extortion affecting interstate commerce. The extortion lay in the solicitation and receipt of the bribes. Some counts were based on the theory that Murphy aided and abetted others who violated the Hobbs Act. The remaining count was based on the Racketeer Influenced and Corrupt Organizations Act (RICO), 18 U.S.C. § 1962(d), which prohibits the operation of an "enterprise" in interstate commerce through a "pattern" (two or more events) of "racketeering" (the violation of specified state or federal laws). The "enterprise" here was the Cook County Circuit Court.

The district court imposed 24 concurrent sentences. The longest, ten years, are based on the RICO and Hobbs Act counts. The court did not impose a fine or a forfeiture.

* * * *

V

This leaves for consideration the most difficult and troubling question: whether the district judge was required to recuse himself.

The principal lawyer for the United States at trial was Dan K. Webb, then the U.S. Attorney. Webb and Judge Kocoras [the federal judge presiding over the Murphy trial] are the best of friends. They met when both were Assistant United States Attorneys in Chicago between 1971 and 1975. Judge Kocoras stated that "our professional relationship developed into a social friendship as well." Immediately after Judge Kocoras sentenced Murphy on August 8, 1984, Judge Kocoras, Dan Webb, and the Kocoras and Webb families repaired to the Calloway Gardens Resort, Pine Mountain, Georgia. They resided there in adjoining cottages. The trip had been planned before the trial, and Judge Kocoras advanced the date of sentencing so that he could wrap up the Murphy case before going on vacation with the Webb family. This was not an isolated event. The Webbs and Kocorases had vacationed together at Calloway Gardens in 1982.

Counsel for Murphy learned of the 1984 vacation for the first time after Judge Kocoras had sentenced Murphy. In February 1985 counsel filed a motion seeking Judge Kocoras's recusal under 28 U.S.C. § 455(a), which provides that a judge "shall disqualify himself in any proceeding in which his impartiality might reasonably be questioned." *See also* Canon 3(C)(1) of the Code of Judicial Conduct. Judge Kocoras denied the motion.

Neither the close friendship between Kocoras and Webb nor either of the vacations was disclosed on the record. Yet the statute places on the judge a personal duty to disclose on the record any circumstances that may give rise to a reasonable question about his impartiality. Although a judge may accept a waiver of disqualification under § 455(a), the "waiver may be accepted [only if] it is preceded by a full disclosure on the record of the basis of the disqualification." 28 U.S.C. § 455(e).

Murphy contends that the vacation plans give rise to a reasonable question about any judge's ability to remain impartial. No one doubts that Judge Kocoras was in fact impartial; his reputation for integrity and impartiality is outstanding. Yet the statutory test is not actual impartiality but the existence of a reasonable question about impartiality. When a question arises about friendship between a judge and a lawyer, "[t]he twofold test is whether the judge feels capable of disregarding the relationship and whether others can reasonably be expected to believe that the relationship is disregarded." Advisory Opinion No. 11, Interim Advisory Committee on Judicial Activities (1970).

The statutory standard puts to the judge a question about the objective state of the legal and lay culture. The court must consider whether an astute observer in either culture would conclude that the relation between judge and lawyer (a) is very much out of the ordinary course, and (b) presents a potential for actual impropriety if the worst implications are realized. The inquiry is entirely objective, *see PepsiCo, Inc. v. McMillen*, 764 F.2d 458, 460–461 (7th Cir. 1985), and is divorced from questions about actual impropriety.

The existence of a "reasonable question" varies from time to time as ordinary conduct of lawyers and judges changes. When John Marshall was the Chief Justice, the Justices and many of the lawyers who practiced in the Supreme Court lived in the same boarding house and took their meals together. Washington, D.C., was still a small town and neither justices nor counsel lived there year-round. See G. Edward White, *The Working Life of the Marshall Court*, 1815–1835, 70 VA. L. REV. 1 (1984). It is accepted today for a judge in the United Kingdom to hear a case in which his sibling or child is an advocate. The ordinary standards of conduct of the legal profession reflect judgments about the likelihood of actual impropriety in a particular case. Unless the conduct is substantially out of the ordinary, it is unnecessary to pursue the further question whether the conduct presents the appearance of impropriety — although it is always possible to inquire into actual impropriety no matter how common the conduct may be.

In today's legal culture friendships among judges and lawyers are common. They are more than common; they are desirable. A judge need not cut himself off from the rest of the legal community. Social as well as official communications among judges and lawyers may improve the quality of legal decisions. Social interactions also make service on the bench, quite isolated as a rule, more tolerable to judges. Many well-qualified people would hesitate to become judges if they knew that wearing the robe meant either discharging one's friends or risking disqualification in substantial numbers of cases. Many courts therefore have held that a judge need not disqualify himself just because a friend — even a close friend — appears as a lawyer. [citations omitted]

These cases also suggest, however, that when the association exceeds "what might reasonably be expected" in light of the associational activities of an ordinary judge (*Parrish, supra*, 524 F.2d at 104), the unusual aspects of a social relation may give rise to a reasonable question about the judge's impartiality. The relation between Judge Kocoras and U.S. Attorney Webb was unusual. These close friends had made arrangements before the trial began to go off to a vacation hideaway immediately after sentencing.

Most people would be greatly surprised to learn that the judge and the prosecutor in a trial of political corruption had secret plans to take a joint vacation immediately after trial. An objective observer "might wonder whether the judge could decide the case with the requisite aloofness and disinterest" *(PepsiCo, supra,* 461). The test for an appearance of partiality in this circuit is "whether an objective, disinterested observer fully informed of the facts underlying the grounds on which recusal was sought would entertain a significant doubt that justice would be done in the case" *(id.* at 460). That hypothetical observer would be troubled by what happened in this case.

This is not an occasion on which to lay down rules for the permissible extent of social ties between judge and counsel. Social relations take so many forms that it would be imprudent to gauge all by a single test. We decide only the case before us. But with appreciation for both the difficulty of deciding how much is too much, and deference to the contrary judgment of a careful and upright judge, we conclude that an objective observer reasonably would doubt the ability of a judge to act with utter disinterest and aloofness when he was such a close friend of the prosecutor that the families of both were just about to take a joint vacation. A social relation of this sort implies extensive personal contacts between judge and prosecutor, perhaps a special willingness of the judge to accept and rely on the prosecutor's representations. The U.S. Attorney lays his own prestige, and that of his office, on the line in a special way when he elects to try a case himself. By acting as trial counsel he indicates the importance of the case and of a conviction, along with his belief in the strength of the Government's case. It is a particular blow for the U.S. Attorney personally to try a highly visible case such as this and lose. A judge could be concerned about handing his friend a galling defeat on the eve of a joint vacation. A defendant especially might perceive partiality on learning of such close ties between prosecutor and judge.

Yet this conclusion does not lead to a decision in Murphy's favor. Although perhaps 999 of 1000 observers would have been stunned to discover that judge and prosecutor were about to go on a joint vacation, the remaining one of the thousand was on Murphy's defense team. Matthias Lydon, the principal trial lawyer for Murphy, had been in the U.S. Attorney's office at the same time as Dan Webb and Judge Kocoras. Lydon and Webb later were partners in private practice. All three were friends and remained so. Judge Kocoras stated that "my professional relationship with [Lydon] developed into a social friendship as well, and no less than that with Mr. Webb. Those friendships developed [at the U.S. Attorney's office] and continue to the present day. The vacation at Calloway Gardens Resort in 1982 had included Lydon and his family as well as the Webb and Kocoras families. Although Lydon has filed an affidavit stating that he did not know of the plans for the 1984 vacation, he admitted that he knew of the close relation between Webb and Kocoras and did not deny the probability of future vacations at what is apparently the favorite resort of former members of the U.S. Attorney's office in Chicago. Murphy himself filed an affidavit conceding that he knew that Lydon, Webb, and Judge Kocoras are close friends, although Murphy denied knowledge of both vacations.

Lydon's friendship with Judge Kocoras removes some of the sting from the revelation about the vacation plans of the judge and the prosecutor. The defense camp's knowledge did not abrogate any obligation to spread the information on the record and seek Murphy's consent to his participation in the case, however. Section

455(e) requires waiver on the record, not waiver by implication. *Potashnick v Port City Construction Co.*, 609 F.2d 1101, 1114 (5th Cir.), *cert. denied*, 449 U.S. 820 (1980). This court said in *SCA Services, Inc. v Morgan*, 557 F.2d 110, 117–18 (7th Cir. 1977), that there is no time limit on a motion for recusal. The principal disqualification statute in effect before § 455 was amended in 1974 had contained a time limit for motions, and the Department of Justice asked Congress to put such a limit in the new § 455 as well. Congress did not, and the court concluded in *Morgan* that this implies the absence of a time limit.

Our decision stands alone, however. The Fifth Circuit has called the discussion in *Morgan* dicta and rejected the conclusion on the merits, reasoning that Congress did not put a time limit in § 455 because time limits were already so firmly fixed in both statute and common law that there was no need to add another. [Citations omitted.]

We need not decide whether to reconsider *Morgan* in light of *Delesdemier* and the cases that have followed *Delesdemier*. It would be difficult to find a "waiver" on this record because neither Murphy nor Lydon knew before sentencing of the vacation plans, the only source of the appearance of impropriety. We believe, however, that the absence of a waiver is not dispositive. The question here is not really whether Judge Kocoras was required to recuse himself when Murphy filed his motion. Judge Kocoras already had imposed sentence; there were no further proceedings from which Judge Kocoras could be recused. What Murphy wants is not recusal from future proceedings but the nullification of everything that went before. We conclude that this is not the appropriate consequence of a recusal for appearance of impropriety.

In cases decided under § 455(a), disqualification runs from the time the motion was made or granted. In *PepsiCo*, our most recent case under § 455(a), the court ordered the district judge to stand aside from the time a party filed the motion for recusal; we did not vacate all of the judge's earlier orders and require the new judge to start afresh. Our research has not turned up any case involving mere appearance of impropriety in which the court set aside decisions that had been taken by the district judge before any party asked for recusal.

The statute requiring recusal when the judge's impartiality might reasonably be questioned vindicates interests of the judicial system as a whole. It is important to the administration of justice that judges both be and appear to be impartial. When a question about impartiality reasonably arises, the judge must stand aside in order to preserve public confidence in the courts. But this does not imply that a judge who is a close friend of counsel will provide an unjust disposition; if it implied that, the question would be one of actual impropriety rather than the "appearance" of impropriety. No one thinks that Chief Justice Marshall acted with actual impropriety when he heard arguments from lawyers with whom he shared a boarding house. The rule of § 455(a) is designed to put an extra measure of safety into the system. When that extra measure fails, the result is regrettable, and the judicial system as a whole suffers, but this does not mean that the parties actually received an unjust trial. The waiver provision of § 455(e), which applies to the "appearance" of impropriety issues under § 455(a) but not to any actual conflict of interest under § 455(b), reinforces our conclusion that § 455(a) is concerned with perceptions rather than actual defects in the administration of justice. Under § 455(a) and (e) a party may stand on his right to a judge about whom no reasonable question may be asked; yet the possibility of waiver implies that the judge can provide a fair trial even if such questions may be asked. Section 455(e) gives a party an absolute right to remove a judge (by declining to waive), but it necessarily implies that conduct after a waiver (and therefore before one, too) does not automatically deprive the party of substantial personal rights. The many cases in other circuits holding that "appearance" questions are waived if not timely asserted — so the judge may continue to sit even after the motion — also show that appearance of impropriety does not undercut personal rights. And unless an error affects substantial rights, it is not a basis of reversal. 28 U.S.C. § 2111; FED. R. CRIM. P. 52(a).

It is important in criminal cases especially to induce defendants to present their claims in a timely fashion. A battery of rules — from contemporaneous objection rules to forfeiture rules such as Fed. R. Crim. P. 12(f) — requires defendants to present claims while there is still time to eliminate the problem and avoid a needless trial. If they fail to do so, the claim is forfeit. [Citations omitted.] Forfeiture may occur even in the absence of an explicit time limitation if the right is knowable in advance and exercise of the right would prevent repetitious litigation. [Citations omitted.] Only if the accused could not have known of the right or some other "cause" impedes a defendant from standing on his rights will a court permit the defendant to have two trials when a timely assertion of the right would have held the number to one. [Citations omitted.]

Certainly a request for recusal before trial would have avoided any possibility of retrial. Murphy might have given a formal waiver on the record; Judge Kocoras might have recused himself; U.S. Attorney Webb might have stepped aside and allowed the case to be tried by a member of his office. Murphy had all the information he needed to initiate inquiry. Although according to the affidavits of Lydon and Murphy the defense camp did not know of the vacation plans for 1984, Lydon knew of the actual vacation in 1982, and Murphy knew of the longstanding friendship among Lydon, Webb, and Judge Kocoras. This was more than enough to put a reasonable person on notice of the potential gains from further inquiry. The defense camp elected not to make any further inquiry, perhaps believing that an ethical judge such as Judge Kocoras would bend over backward to avoid favoring the prosecutor in such a case and that the defense therefore had more to gain from the Kocoras-Lydon friendship than it had to lose from the Kocoras-Webb friendship. The defendant is bound by a tactical choice such as this may have been, whether or not he participated personally in that choice. [Citations omitted.]

Ultimately, however, we do not rest on the fact that Lydon, Webb, and Judge Kocoras went on vacation together in 1982. A detailed inquiry into what the defense camp knew and when is not essential when the motion under § 455(a) is filed as late as this was. A criminal trial is too serious and too costly to permit a defendant to sit on possible errors, hoping to have a crack at an acquittal (or low sentence) and then still a second trial. If a defendant wants a judge to stand aside under § 455(a), he must make the appropriate motion. Judicial acts taken before the motion may not later be set aside unless the litigant shows actual impropriety or actual prejudice; appearance of impropriety is not enough to poison the prior acts. [Citations omitted.]

A judicial impropriety serious enough, and secret enough, to escape everyone's notice before trial probably also would be serious enough to create an actual conflict of interest. By the time the trial has been completed, an appearance of impropriety may have ripened into an actual impropriety. If it did not, and if no one asked for recusal before trial, then there is no need for still another trial to vindicate the concerns that underlie § 455(a).

It is regrettable that the vacation plans were not disclosed. This cast an unfortunate light on what was otherwise a well-handled trial. Judges and counsel should keep in mind the need to disclose unusual degrees of social as well as professional affiliation. The Webb-Kocoras vacation plans should have been disclosed. As it turns out, the silence did not adversely affect any substantial rights of Murphy. He could have protected himself fully by acting on the information he and Lydon possessed. At all events any appearance of impropriety under § 455(a) is not actual impropriety, so that recusal does not retroactively invalidate judicial acts that preceded the motion Murphy filed.

Both the circumstances concerning the vacation plans of the judge and the prosecutor, and the unavailability of a transcript of the conference on the jury instructions, have led us to resolve all ambiguities in favor of Murphy. After this review we are confident that Judge Kocoras was scrupulously impartial in fact and conducted this trial in accord with the highest standards of the bench. Murphy has had a fair trial, and the judgment is just.

AFFIRMED.

[Concurring opinion omitted.]

# CHENEY v. UNITED STATES DISTRICT COURT FOR THE DISTRICT OF COLUMBIA
## 541 U.S. 913 (2004)

Memorandum of JUSTICE SCALIA

I have before me a motion to recuse in these cases consolidated below. The motion is filed on behalf of respondent Sierra Club. The other private respondent, Judicial Watch, Inc., does not join the motion and has publicly stated that it "does not believe the presently-known facts about the hunting trip satisfy the legal standards requiring recusal." Judicial Watch Statement 2 (Feb. 13, 2004) (available in Clerk of Court's case file). (The District Court, a nominal party in this mandamus action, has of course made no appearance.) Since the cases have been consolidated, however, recusal in the one would entail recusal in the other.

I

The decision whether a judge's impartiality can " 'reasonably be questioned' " is to be made in light of the facts as they existed, and not as they were surmised or reported. *See Microsoft Corp. v. United States* (Rehnquist, C.J., respecting recusal). The facts here were as follows:

For five years or so, I have been going to Louisiana during the Court's long December–January recess, to the duck-hunting camp of a friend whom I met through two hunting companions from Baton Rouge, one a dentist and the other a worker in the field of handicapped rehabilitation. The last three years, I have been accompanied on this trip by a son-in-law who lives near me. Our friend and host, Wallace Carline, has never, as far as I know, had business before this Court. He is not, as some reports have described him, an "energy industry executive" in the sense that summons up boardrooms of Exxon Mobil or Con Edison. He runs his own company that provides services and equipment rental to oil rigs in the Gulf of Mexico.

During my December 2002 visit, I learned that Mr. Carline was an admirer of Vice President Cheney. Knowing that the Vice President, with whom I am well acquainted (from our years serving together in the Ford administration), is an enthusiastic duck hunter, I asked whether Mr. Carline would like to invite him to our next year's hunt. The answer was yes; I conveyed the invitation (with my own warm recommendation) in the spring of 2003 and received an acceptance (subject, of course, to any superseding demands on the Vice President's time) in the summer. The Vice President said that if he did go, I would be welcome to fly down to Louisiana with him. (Because of national security requirements, of course, he must fly in a Government plane.) That invitation was later extended — if space was available — to my son-in-law and to a son who was joining the hunt for the first time; they accepted. The trip was set long before the Court granted certiorari in the present case, and indeed before the petition for certiorari had even been filed.

We departed from Andrews Air Force Base at about 10 a.m. on Monday, January 5, flying in a Gulfstream jet owned by the Government. We landed in Patterson, Louisiana, and went by car to a dock where Mr. Carline met us, to take us on the 20-minute boat trip to his hunting camp. We arrived at about 2 p.m., the 5 of us joining about 8 other hunters, making about 13 hunters in all; also present during our time there were about 3 members of Mr. Carline's staff, and, of course, the Vice President's staff and security detail. It was not an intimate setting. The group hunted that afternoon and Tuesday and Wednesday mornings; it fished (in two boats) Tuesday afternoon. All meals were in common. Sleeping was in rooms of two or three, except for the Vice President, who had his own quarters. Hunting was in two- or three-man blinds. As it turned out, I never hunted in the same blind with the Vice President. Nor was I alone with him at any time during the trip, except, perhaps, for instances so brief and unintentional that I would not recall them — walking to or from a boat, perhaps, or going to or from dinner. Of course we said not a word about the present case. The Vice President left the camp Wednesday afternoon, about two days after our arrival. I stayed on to hunt (with my son and son-in-law) until late Friday morning, when the three of us returned to Washington on a commercial flight from New Orleans.

## II

Let me respond, at the outset, to Sierra Club's suggestion that I should "resolve any doubts in favor of recusal." Motion to Recuse 8. That might be sound advice if I were sitting on a Court of Appeals. But *see In re Aguinda*. There, my place would be taken by another judge, and the case would proceed normally. On the Supreme Court, however, the consequence is different: The Court proceeds with eight Justices, raising the possibility that, by reason of a tie vote, it will find itself unable to resolve the significant legal issue presented by the case. Thus, as Justices stated in their 1993 Statement of Recusal Policy: "We do not think it would serve the public interest to go beyond the requirements of the statute, and to recuse ourselves, out of an excess of caution, whenever a relative is a partner in the firm before us or acted as a lawyer at an earlier stage. Even one unnecessary recusal impairs the functioning of the Court." (Available in Clerk of Court's case file.) Moreover, granting the motion is (insofar as the outcome of the particular case is concerned) effectively the same as casting a vote against the petitioner. The petitioner needs five votes to overturn the judgment below, and it makes no difference whether the needed fifth vote is missing because it has been cast for the other side, or because it has not been cast at all.

Even so, recusal is the course I must take — and will take — when, on the basis of established principles and practices, I have said or done something which requires that course. I have recused for such a reason this very Term. *See Elk Grove Unified School Dist. v. Newdow*. I believe, however, that established principles and practices do not require (and thus do not permit) recusal in the present case.

## A

My recusal is required if, by reason of the actions described above, my "impartiality might reasonably be questioned." *28 U.S.C. 455(a)*. Why would that result follow from my being in a sizable group of persons, in a hunting camp with the Vice President, where I never hunted with him in the same blind or had other opportunity for private conversation? The only possibility is that it would suggest I am a friend of his. But while friendship is a ground for recusal of a Justice where the personal fortune or the personal freedom of the friend is at issue, it has traditionally *not* been a ground for recusal where *official action* is at issue, no matter how important the official action was to the ambitions or the reputation of the Government officer.

A rule that required Members of this Court to remove themselves from cases in which the official actions of friends were at issue would be utterly disabling. Many Justices have reached this Court precisely because they were friends of the incumbent President or other senior officials — and from the earliest days down to modern times Justices have had close personal relationships with the President and other officers of the Executive. John Quincy Adams hosted dinner parties featuring such luminaries as Chief Justice Marshall, Justices Johnson, Story, and Todd, Attorney General Wirt, and Daniel Webster. 5 Memoirs of John Quincy Adams 322–323 (C. Adams ed. 1875, reprint 1969) (Diary Entry of Mar. 8, 1821). Justice Harlan and his wife often " 'stopped in' " at the White House to see the Hayes family and pass a Sunday evening in a small group, visiting and singing hymns. M. Harlan, *Some Memories of a Long Life*,

1854–1911, p. 99 (2001). Justice Stone tossed around a medicine ball with members of the Hoover administration mornings outside the White House. 2 Memoirs of Herbert Hoover 327 (1952). Justice Douglas was a regular at President Franklin Roosevelt's poker parties; Chief Justice Vinson played poker with President Truman. J. Simon, Independent Journey: The Life of William O. Douglas 220–221 (1980); D. McCullough, Truman 511 (1992). A no-friends rule would have disqualified much of the Court in *Youngstown Sheet & Tube Co. v. Sawyer*, the case that challenged President Truman's seizure of the steel mills. Most of the Justices knew Truman well, and four had been appointed by him. A no-friends rule would surely have required Justice Holmes's recusal in *Northern Securities Co. v. United States*, the case that challenged President Theodore Roosevelt's trust-busting initiative. *See* S. Novick, HONORABLE JUSTICE: THE LIFE OF OLIVER WENDELL HOLMES 264 (1989) ("Holmes and Fanny dined at the White House every week or two . . . ").

It is said, however, that this case is different because the federal officer (Vice President Cheney) is actually a *named party*. That is by no means a rarity. At the beginning of the current Term, there were before the Court (excluding habeas actions) no fewer than 83 cases in which high-level federal Executive officers were named in their official capacity — more than 1 in every 10 federal civil cases then pending. That an officer is named has traditionally made no difference to the proposition that friendship is not considered to affect impartiality in official-action suits. Regardless of whom they name, such suits, when the officer is the plaintiff, seek relief not for him personally but for the Government; and, when the officer is the defendant, seek relief not against him personally, but against the Government. That is why federal law provides for *automatic substitution* of the new officer when the originally named officer has been replaced. *See* FED. RULE CIV. PROC. 25(d)(1); FED. RULE APP. PROC. 43(c)(2); this Court's Rule 35.3. The caption of Sierra Club's complaint in this action designates as a defendant "Vice President Richard Cheney, *in his official capacity* as Vice President of the United States and Chairman of the National Energy Policy Development Group." App. 139 (emphasis added). The body of the complaint repeats (in paragraph 6) that "Defendant Richard Cheney is sued *in his official capacity* as the Vice President of the United States and Chairman of the Cheney Energy Task Force." *Id.*, at 143 (emphasis added). Sierra Club has *relied* upon the fact that this is an official-action rather than a personal suit as a basis for denying the petition. It asserted in its brief in opposition that if there was no presidential immunity from discovery in *Clinton v. Jones*, 520 U.S. 681 (1997), which was a private suit, "[s]urely . . . the Vice President and subordinate White House officials have no greater immunity claim here, especially when the lawsuit relates to their official actions while in office and the primary relief sought is a declaratory judgment." Brief in Opposition 13.

Richard Cheney's name appears in this suit only because he was the head of a Government committee that allegedly did not comply with the Federal Advisory Committee Act (FACA), 5 U.S.C. App. § 2, p. 1, and because he may, by reason of his office, have custody of some or all of the Government documents that the plaintiffs seek. If some other person were to become head of that committee or to obtain custody of those documents, the plaintiffs would name that person and Cheney would be dismissed. Unlike the defendant in *United States v. Nixon*, 418 U.S. 683 (1974), or *Clinton v. Jones, supra*, Cheney is represented here, not by his personal attorney, but by the United States Department of Justice in the person of the Solicitor General. And the courts at all levels have referred to his arguments as (what they are) the arguments of "the government." *See In re Cheney*, 334 F.3d 1096, 1100 (D.C. Cir. 2003); *Judicial Watch, Inc. v. National Energy Policy Development Group*, 219 F. Supp. 2d 20, 25 (D.D.C. 2002).

The recusal motion, however, asserts the following:

> "Critical to the issue of Justice Scalia's recusal is understanding that this is not a run-of-the-mill legal dispute about an administrative decision. . . . Because his own conduct is central to this case, the Vice President's 'reputation and his integrity are on the line.' (Chicago Tribune.)" Motion to Recuse 9.

I think not. Certainly as far as the legal issues immediately presented to me are concerned, this *is* "a run-of-the-mill legal dispute about an administrative decision." I am asked to determine what powers the District Court possessed under FACA, and whether the Court of Appeals should have asserted mandamus or appellate jurisdiction over the District Court. [footnote omitted]. Nothing this Court says on those subjects will have any bearing upon the reputation and integrity of Richard Cheney. Moreover, even if this Court affirms the decision below and allows discovery to proceed in the District Court, the issue that would ultimately present itself *still* would have no bearing upon the reputation and integrity of Richard Cheney. That issue would be, quite simply, whether some private individuals were *de facto* members of the National Energy Policy Development Group (NEPDG). It matters not whether they were caused to be so by Cheney or someone else, or whether Cheney was even aware of their *de facto* status; if they *were de facto* members, then (according to D.C. Circuit law) the records and minutes of NEPDG must be made public.

The recusal motion asserts, however, that Richard Cheney's "reputation and his integrity are on the line" because "respondents have alleged, *inter alia*, that the Vice President, as the head of the Task Force and its subgroups, was responsible for the involvement of energy industry executives in the operations of the Task Force, as a result of which the Task Force and its subgroups became subject to FACA." *Ibid.*

As far as Sierra Club's *complaint* is concerned, it simply is not true that Vice President Cheney is singled out as having caused the involvement of energy executives. But even if the allegation had been made, it would be irrelevant to the case. FACA assertedly requires disclosure if there were private members of the task force, *no matter who* they were — "energy industry executives" or Ralph Nader; and *no matter who* was responsible for their membership — the Vice President or no one in particular. I do not see how the Vice President's' "reputation and . . . integrity are on the line" any more than the agency head's reputation and integrity are on the line in virtually all official-action suits, which accuse his agency of acting (to quote the Administrative Procedure Act) "arbitrar[ily], capricious[ly], [with] an abuse of discretion, or otherwise not in accordance with law." 5 U.S.C. § 706(2)(A). Beyond that always-present accusation, there is nothing illegal or immoral about making "energy industry executives" members of a task force on energy; some people probably think it would be a good idea. If, in doing so, or in allowing it to happen, the Vice President went beyond his assigned powers, that is no worse than what every agency head has done when his action is judicially set aside.

To be sure, there could be political consequences from disclosure of the fact (if it be so) that the Vice President favored business interests, and especially a sector of business with which he was formerly connected. But political consequences are not my concern, and the possibility of them does not convert an official suit into a private one. That possibility exists to a greater or lesser degree in virtually all suits involving agency action. To expect judges to take account of political consequences — and to assess the high or low degree of them — is to ask judges to do precisely what they should not do. It seems to me quite wrong (and quite impossible) to make recusal depend upon what degree of political damage a particular case can be expected to inflict.

In sum, I see nothing about this case which takes it out of the category of normal official-action litigation, where my friendship, or the appearance of my friendship, with one of the named officers does not require recusal.

B

The recusal motion claims that "the fact that Justice Scalia and his daughter [sic] were the Vice President's guest on Air Force Two on the flight down to Louisiana" means that I "accepted a sizable gift from a party in a pending case," a gift "measured in the thousands of dollars." Motion to Recuse 6 (footnote omitted).

Let me speak first to the value, though that is not the principal point. Our flight down cost the Government nothing, since space-available was the condition of our invitation. And, though our flight down on the Vice President's plane was indeed free, since we were not returning with him we purchased (because they were least expensive) round-trip tickets that cost precisely what we would have paid if we had gone both down and back on commercial flights. In other words, none of us saved a cent by flying on the Vice President's plane. The purpose of going with him was not saving money, but avoiding some inconvenience to ourselves (being taken by car from New Orleans to Morgan City) and considerable inconvenience to our friends, who would have had to meet our plane in New Orleans, and schedule separate boat trips to the hunting camp, for us and for the Vice President's party. (To be sure, flying on the Vice President's jet was more comfortable and more convenient than flying commercially; that accommodation is a matter I address in the next paragraph.) [footnote omitted.]

The principal point, however, is that social courtesies, provided at Government expense by officials whose only business before the Court is business in their official capacity, have not hitherto been thought prohibited. Members of Congress and others are frequently invited to accompany Executive Branch officials on Government planes, where space is available. That this is not the sort of gift thought likely to affect a judge's impartiality is suggested by the fact that the Ethics in Government Act of 1978, 5 U.S.C. App. § 101 *et seq.*, p. 38, which requires annual reporting of transportation provided or reimbursed, excludes from this requirement transportation provided by the United States. *See* § 109(5)(C); Committee on Financial Disclosure, Administrative Office of the U.S. Courts, Financial Disclosure Report: Filing Instructions for Judicial Officers and Employees, p. 25 (Jan. 2003). I daresay that, at a hypothetical charity auction, much more would be bid for dinner for two at the White House than for a one-way flight to Louisiana on the Vice President's jet. Justices accept the former with regularity. While this matter was pending, Justices and their spouses were invited (*all* of them, I believe) to a December 11, 2003, Christmas reception at the residence of the Vice President — which included an opportunity for a photograph with the Vice President and Mrs. Cheney. Several of the Justices attended, and in doing so they were fully in accord with the proprieties.

## III

When I learned that Sierra Club had filed a recusal motion in this case, I assumed that the motion would be replete with citations of legal authority, and would provide some instances of cases in which, because of activity similar to what occurred here, Justices have recused themselves or at least have been asked to do so. In fact, however, the motion cites only two Supreme Court cases assertedly relevant to the issue here discussed, [footnote omitted] and nine Court of Appeals cases. Not a single one of these even involves an official-action suit.[1] And the motion gives not a single instance in which, under even remotely similar circumstances, a Justice has recused or been asked to recuse. Instead, the argument section of the motion consists almost entirely of references to, and quotations from, newspaper editorials.

The core of Sierra Club's argument is as follows:

"Sierra Club makes this motion because . . . damage [to the integrity of the system] is being done right now. As of today, 8 of the 10 newspapers with the largest circulation in the United States, 14 of the largest 20, and 20 of the 30 largest have called on Justice Scalia to step aside. . . . Of equal import, there is no counterbalance or controversy: not a single newspaper has argued against recusal. Because the American public, as reflected in the nation's newspaper editorials, has unanimously concluded that there is an appearance of favoritism, any objective observer would be compelled to conclude that Justice Scalia's impartiality has been questioned. These facts more than satisfy Section 455(a), which mandates recusal merely when a Justice's impartiality 'might reasonably be questioned.' " Motion to Recuse 3–4.

The implications of this argument are staggering. I must recuse because a significant portion of the press, which is deemed to be the American public, demands it.

The motion attaches as exhibits the press editorials on which it relies. Many of them do not even have the facts right. The length of our hunting trip together was said to be several days (San Francisco Chronicle), four days (Boston Globe), or nine days (San Antonio Express-News). We spent about 48 hours together at the hunting camp. It was asserted that the Vice President and I "spent time alone in the rushes," "huddled

---

[1]  [4] *United States v. Murphy*, 768 F.2d 1518 (7th Cir. 1985), at least involved a judge's going on vacation — but not with the named defendant in an official-action suit. The judge had departed for a vacation with the prosecutor of Murphy's case, immediately after sentencing Murphy. Obviously, the prosecutor is personally involved in the outcome of the case in a way that the nominal defendant in an official-action suit is not.

together in a Louisiana marsh," where we had "plenty of time . . . to talk privately" (Los Angeles Times); that we "spent . . . quality time bonding [together] in a duck blind" (Atlanta Journal-Constitution); and that "[t]here is simply no reason to think these two did not discuss the pending case" (Buffalo News). As I have described, the Vice President and I were never in the same blind, and never discussed the case. (Washington officials know the rules, and know that discussing with judges pending cases — their own or anyone else's — is forbidden.) The Palm Beach Post stated that our "transportation [was] provided, appropriately, by an oil services company," and Newsday that a "private jet . . .whisked Scalia to Louisiana." The Vice President and I flew in a Government plane. The Cincinnati Enquirer said that "Scalia was Cheney's guest at a private duck-hunting camp in Louisiana." Cheney and I were Wallace Carline's guests. Various newspapers described Mr. Carline as "an energy company official" (Atlanta Journal-Constitution), an "oil industrialist" (Cincinnati Enquirer), an "oil company executive" (Contra Costa Times), an "oilman" (Minneapolis Star Tribune), and an "energy industry executive" (Washington Post). All of these descriptions are misleading.

And these are just the inaccuracies pertaining to the *facts*. With regard to the *law*, the vast majority of the editorials display no recognition of the central proposition that a federal officer is not ordinarily regarded to be a personal party in interest in an official-action suit. And those that do display such recognition facilely assume, contrary to all precedent, that in such suits mere political damage (which they characterize as a destruction of Cheney's reputation and integrity) is ground for recusal. Such a blast of largely inaccurate and uninformed opinion cannot determine the recusal question. It is well established that the recusal inquiry must be "made from the perspective of a *reasonable* observer who is *informed of all the surrounding facts* and circumstances." *Microsoft Corp. v. United States*, 530 U.S. at 1302 (Rehnquist, C.J., respecting recusal) (emphases added) (citing *Liteky v. United States*, 510 U.S. 540 (1994).

## IV

While Sierra Club was apparently unable to summon forth a single example of a Justice's recusal (or even motion for a Justice's recusal) under circumstances similar to those here, I have been able to accomplish the seemingly more difficult task of finding a couple of examples establishing the negative: that recusal or motion for recusal did *not* occur under circumstances similar to those here.

### Justice White and Robert Kennedy

The first example pertains to a Justice with whom I have sat, and who retired from the Court only 11 years ago, Byron R. White. Justice White was close friends with Attorney General Robert Kennedy from the days when White had served as Kennedy's Deputy Attorney General. In January 1963, the Justice went on a skiing vacation in Colorado with Robert Kennedy and his family, Secretary of Defense Robert McNamara and his family, and other members of the Kennedy family. Skiing Not The Best; McNamara Leaves Colorado, Terms Vacation "Marvelous," Denver Post, Jan. 2, 1963, p. 22; D. Hutchinson, The Man Who Once Was Whizzer White 342

(1998). (The skiing in Colorado, like my hunting in Louisiana, was not particularly successful.) At the time of this skiing vacation there were pending before the Court at least two cases in which Robert Kennedy, in his official capacity as Attorney General, was a party. *See Gastelum-Quinones v. Kennedy*, 374 U.S. 469 (1963); *Kennedy v. Mendoza-Martinez*, 372 U.S. 144 (1963). In the first of these, moreover, the press might have said, as plausibly as it has said here, that the reputation and integrity of the Attorney General were at issue. There the Department of Justice had decreed deportation of a resident alien on grounds that he had been a member of the Communist Party. (The Court found that the evidence adduced by the Department was inadequate.)

Besides these cases naming Kennedy, another case pending at the time of the skiing vacation was argued to the Court *by Kennedy* about two weeks later. *See Gray v. Sanders*, 372 U.S. 368 (1963). That case was important to the Kennedy administration, because by the time of its argument everybody knew that the apportionment cases were not far behind, and *Gray* was a significant step in the march toward *Reynolds v. Sims*, 377 U.S. 533 (1964). When the decision was announced, it was front-page news. *See* High Court Voids County Unit Vote, N.Y. Times, Mar. 19, 1963, p. 1, col. 2; Georgia's Unit Voting Voided, Washington Post, Mar. 19, 1963, p. A1, col. 5. Attorney General Kennedy argued for affirmance of a three-judge District Court's ruling that the Georgia Democratic Party's county-unit voting system violated the one-person, one-vote principle. This was Kennedy's only argument before the Court, and it certainly put "on the line" his reputation as a lawyer, as well as an important policy of his brother's administration.

### Justice Jackson and Franklin Roosevelt

The second example pertains to a Justice who was one of the most distinguished occupants of the seat to which I was appointed, Robert Jackson. Justice Jackson took the recusal obligation particularly seriously. *See, e.g., Jewell Ridge Coal Corp. v. United Mine Workers*, 325 U.S. 897 (1945) (Jackson, J., concurring in denial of rehearing) (oblique criticism of Justice Black's decision not to recuse himself from a case argued by his former law partner). Nonetheless, he saw nothing wrong with maintaining a close personal relationship, and engaging in " 'quite frequen[t]' " socializing with the President whose administration's acts came before him regularly. R. Jackson, *That Man: An Insider's Portrait of Franklin D. Roosevelt* 74 (J. Barrett ed. 2003) (footnote omitted).

In April 1942, the two "spent a weekend on a very delightful house party down at General Watson's in Charlottesville, Virginia. I had been invited to ride down with the President and to ride back with him." *Id.*, at 106 (footnote omitted). Pending at the time, and argued the next month, was one of the most important cases concerning the scope of permissible federal action under the Commerce Clause, *Wickard v. Filburn*, 317 U.S. 111 (1942). Justice Jackson wrote the opinion for the Court. Roosevelt's Secretary of Agriculture, rather than Roosevelt himself, was the named federal officer in the case, but there is no doubt that it was important to the President.

I see nothing wrong about Justice White's and Justice Jackson's socializing — including vacationing and accepting rides — with their friends. Nor, seemingly, did anyone else at the time. (The Denver Post, which has been critical of me, reported the White-Kennedy-McNamara skiing vacation with nothing but enthusiasm.) If friendship is basis for recusal (as it assuredly is when friends are sued personally) then activity which suggests close friendship must be avoided. But if friendship is *no* basis for recusal (as it is not in official-capacity suits) social contacts that do no more than evidence that friendship suggest no impropriety whatever.

Of course it can be claimed (as some editorials have claimed) that "times have changed," and what was once considered proper — even as recently as Byron White's day — is no longer so. That may be true with regard to the earlier rare phenomenon of a Supreme Court Justice's serving as advisor and confidant to the President — though that activity, so incompatible with the separation of powers, was not widely known when it was occurring, and can hardly be said to have been generally approved before it was properly abandoned. But the well-known and constant practice of Justices' enjoying friendship and social intercourse with Members of Congress and officers of the Executive Branch has *not* been abandoned, and ought not to be.

V

Since I do not believe my impartiality can reasonably be questioned, I do not think it would be proper for me to recuse. *See Microsoft*, 530 U.S. at 1302. That alone is conclusive; but another consideration moves me in the same direction: Recusal would in my judgment harm the Court. If I were to withdraw from this case, it would be because some of the press has argued that the Vice President would suffer political damage *if* he should lose this appeal, and *if*, on remand, discovery should establish that energy industry representatives were *de facto* members of NEPDG — and because some of the press has elevated that possible political damage to the status of an impending stain on the reputation and integrity of the Vice President. But since political damage often comes from the Government's losing official-action suits; and since political damage can readily be characterized as a stain on reputation and integrity; recusing in the face of such charges would give elements of the press a veto over participation of any Justices who had social contacts with, or were even known to be friends of, a named official. That is intolerable.

My recusal would also encourage so-called investigative journalists to suggest improprieties, and demand recusals, for other inappropriate (and increasingly silly) reasons. The Los Angeles Times has already suggested that it was improper for me to sit on a case argued by a law school dean whose school I had visited several weeks before — visited not at his invitation, but at his predecessor's. *See* New Trip Trouble for Scalia, Feb. 28, 2004, p. B22. The same paper has asserted that it was improper for me to speak at a dinner honoring Cardinal Bevilacqua given by the Urban Family Council of Philadelphia because (according to the Times's false report) [footnote omitted] that organization was engaged in litigation seeking to prevent same-sex civil unions, and I had before me a case presenting the question (whether same-sex civil unions were lawful? — no) whether homosexual sodomy could constitutionally be *criminalized. See Lawrence v. Texas*, 539 U.S. 558 (2003). While the political branches can perhaps survive the constant baseless allegations of impropriety that have become the staple of Washington reportage, this Court cannot. The people must have confidence in the integrity of the Justices, and that cannot exist in a system that assumes them to be corruptible by the slightest friendship or favor, and in an atmosphere where the press will be eager to find foot-faults.

* * * *

As I noted at the outset, one of the private respondents in this case has not called for my recusal, and has expressed confidence that I will rule impartially, as indeed I will. Counsel for the other private respondent seek to impose, it seems to me, a standard regarding friendship, the appearance of friendship, and the acceptance of social favors, that is more stringent than what they themselves observe. Two days before the brief in opposition to the petition in this case was filed, lead counsel for Sierra Club, a friend, wrote me a warm note inviting me to come to Stanford Law School to speak to one of his classes. (Available in Clerk of Court's case file.) (Judges teaching classes at law schools normally have their transportation and expenses paid.) I saw nothing amiss in that friendly letter and invitation. I surely would have thought otherwise if I had applied the standards urged in the present motion.

There are, I am sure, those who believe that my friendship with persons in the current administration might cause me to favor the Government in cases brought against it. That is not the issue here. Nor is the issue whether personal friendship with the Vice President might cause me to favor the Government in cases in which *he* is named. None of those suspicions regarding my impartiality (erroneous suspicions, I hasten to protest) bears upon recusal here. The question, simply put, is whether someone who thought I could decide this case impartially despite my friendship with the Vice President would reasonably believe that I *cannot* decide it impartially because I went hunting with that friend and accepted an invitation to fly there with him on a Government plane. If it is reasonable to think that a Supreme Court Justice can be bought so cheap, the Nation is in deeper trouble than I had imagined.

As the newspaper editorials appended to the motion make clear, I have received a good deal of embarrassing criticism and adverse publicity in connection with the matters at issue here — even to the point of becoming (as the motion cruelly but accurately states) "fodder for late-night comedians." Motion to Recuse 6. If I could have done so in good conscience, I would have been pleased to demonstrate my integrity, and immediately silence the criticism, by getting off the case. Since I believe there is no basis for recusal, I cannot. The motion is *Denied*.

* * * *

Friendship between the judge deciding a case and a prosecutor (*Murphy*) and a party (*Cheney*) are inevitable; practicing lawyers typically form the pool for judicial appointments or elections. More recently, the issue and the meaning of "friendship" has taken on new dimensions in the world of social media.

# DOMVILLE v. STATE
103 So. 3d 184 (Fla. Dist. Ct. App. 2012),
110 So. 3d 441 (Fla. 2013) (petition for review denied)

PER CURIAM.

In this case we consider a criminal defendant's effort to disqualify a judge whom the defendant alleges is a Facebook friend of the prosecutor assigned to his case. Finding that grounds for disqualification exist, we grant the petition for writ of prohibition.

Petitioner Pierre Domville moved to disqualify the trial judge. The motion was supported by an affidavit averring that the prosecutor handling the case and the trial judge are Facebook "friends." This relationship caused Domville to believe that the judge could not "be fair and impartial." Domville explained that he was a Facebook user and that his "friends" consisted "only of [his] closest friends and associates, persons whom [he] could not perceive with anything but favor, loyalty and partiality." The affidavit attributed adverse rulings to the judge's Facebook relationship with the prosecutor. The trial judge denied the motion as "legally insufficient."

In determining the legal sufficiency of a motion to disqualify the trial judge, this court reviews the motion's allegations under a de novo standard. *See Peterson v. Asklipious*, 833 So. 2d 262, 263 (Fla. 4th DCA 2002). Florida Rule of Judicial Administration 2.330(f) requires a judge to grant disqualification if the motion to disqualify is "legally sufficient." A motion is legally sufficient if " 'the facts alleged (which must be taken as true) would prompt a reasonably prudent person to fear that he could not get a fair and impartial trial.' " *Brofman v. Fla. Hearing Care Ctr., Inc.*, 703 So. 2d 1191, 1192 (Fla. 4th DCA 1997) (*quoting Hayslip v. Douglas*, 400 So. 2d 553, 556 (Fla. 4th DCA 1981)). A mere "subjective fear[ ]" of bias will not be legally sufficient; rather, the fear must be objectively reasonable. *Fischer v. Knuck*, 497 So. 2d 240, 242 (Fla. 1986).

We find an opinion of the Judicial Ethics Advisory Committee to be instructive. *See* Fla. JEAC Op. 2009-20 (Nov. 17, 2009). There, the Committee concluded that the Florida Code of Judicial Conduct precludes a judge from both adding lawyers who appear before the judge as "friends" on a social networking site and allowing such lawyers to add the judge as their "friend." The Committee determined that a judge's listing of a lawyer as a "friend" on the judge's social networking page — "[t]o the extent that such identification is available for any other person to view" — would violate Florida Code of Judicial Conduct Canon 2B ("A judge shall not . . . convey or permit others to convey the impression that they are in a special position to influence the judge."). *See* Fla. JEAC Op. 2009-20. The committee found that three elements are necessary in order to fall within the prohibition of Canon 2B:

> 1. The judge must establish the social networking page.

> 2. The site must afford the judge the right to accept or reject contacts or "friends" on the judge's page, or denominate the judge as a "friend" on another member's page.

3. The identity of the "friends" or contacts selected by the judge, and the judge's having denominated himself or herself as a "friend" on another's page must then be communicated to others.

*Id.* The committee noted that:

Typically, [the] third element is fulfilled because each of a judge's "friends" may see on the judge's page who the judge's other "friends" are. Similarly, all "friends" of another user may see that the judge is also a "friend" of that user. It is this selection and communication process, the Committee believes, that violates Canon 2B, because the judge, by so doing, conveys or permits others to convey the impression that they are in a special position to influence the judge.

*Id.*

Further, the Committee concluded that when a judge lists a lawyer who appears before him as a "friend" on his social networking page this "reasonably conveys to others the impression that these lawyer 'friends' are in a special position to influence the judge." *Id. See also* Fla. Code Jud. Conduct, Canon 5A.

The issue, however, is not whether the lawyer actually is in a position to influence the judge, but instead whether the proposed conduct, the identification of the lawyer as a "friend" on the social networking site, conveys the impression that the lawyer is in a position to influence the judge. The Committee concludes that such identification in a public forum of a lawyer who may appear before the judge does convey this impression and therefore is not permitted.

Fla. JEAC Op. 2009-20. Thus, as the Committee recognized, a judge's activity on a social networking site may undermine confidence in the judge's neutrality. Judges must be vigilant in monitoring their public conduct so as to avoid situations that will compromise the appearance of impartiality. The Commentary to Canon 2A explains that being a judge necessarily limits a judge's personal freedom:

A judge must avoid all impropriety and the appearance of impropriety. A judge must expect to be the subject of constant public scrutiny. A judge must therefore accept restrictions on the judge's conduct that might be viewed as burdensome by the ordinary citizen and should do so freely and willingly.

Fla. Code Jud. Conduct, Canon 2A, cmt.

Because Domville has alleged facts that would create in a reasonably prudent person a well-founded fear of not receiving a fair and impartial trial, we quash the order denying disqualification of the trial judge and remand to the circuit court for further proceedings consistent with this opinion.

GROSS, GERBER and LEVINE, JJ., concur.

## C. APPLYING THE RULES OF RECUSAL & DISQUALIFICATION: TRIAL JUDGE AS APPELLATE JUDGE

## SWANN v. CHARLOTTE-MECKLENBURG BD. OF EDUC.
### 431 F.2d 135 (4th Cir. 1970)

CRAVEN, CIRCUIT JUDGE

This is an appeal from orders of the United States District Court for the Western District of North Carolina entered in 1969 and 1970 requiring the Charlotte-Mecklenburg School Board to implement in various ways its constitutional duty to establish a unitary school system. I have previously treated a letter to me from one of counsel in the case as a motion to consider whether or not I am disqualified by 28 U.S.C. § 47 from participating as a member of the United States Court of Appeals for the Fourth Circuit in the hearing and disposition of the appeal. After careful consideration, I conclude that I am disqualified by the statute.

In 1965 I was one of the judges of the United States District Court for the Western District of North Carolina. In that capacity, I heard and determined the case of *Swann et al. v. Charlotte-Mecklenburg Board of Education*, Civil No. 1974, and filed an opinion in the case on July 14, 1965, 243 F. Supp. 667, affirmed, 369 F.2d 29. The questions before me then were whether certain school zones had been gerrymandered to prevent the mixing of races, whether there was justification for delaying geographical zoning with respect to ten schools, whether the desegregation of teachers and staff ought to be accomplished at once, and the validity of a freedom-of-choice option engrafted on top of a zoning plan.

In my published opinion discussing these questions, I said, among many other things,

> "It is undoubtedly true that one could deliberately sit down with a purpose in mind to change lines in order to increase mixing of the races and accomplish the same with some degree of success. I know of no such duty upon either the School Board or the District Court. . ."

> "The question before the District Court is not whether a 'better' zone might be established but simply whether the zone which was established is an arbitrary and unreasonable one based on race and without regard to natural boundary lines. Thus far it has not been held unconstitutional to assign children to a school on the basis of their residences in a cohesive and contiguous geographical area. . . ."

*Swann v. Charlotte-Mecklenburg Board of Education*, 243 F. Supp. 667, 670 (1965).

I found as a fact that the school board had rezoned Crestdale and Morgan Schools for the purpose of achieving a racial mix and concluded, 'This does not sound like a School Board bent upon maintaining a segregated system. *Id.* at 671.

My ultimate conclusion was that the plan proposed by the board in 1965, as amended with respect to teachers and staff, 'is a sufficient compliance with the duty imposed upon the board by the Constitution as interpreted in *Brown v. Board of Education of Topeka, Shawnee County, Kansas*, 347 U.S. 483 . . . and subsequent decisions.' *Id.* at 671.

The present case on appeal is facially the same case I decided in 1965: it bears the same Western North Carolina number, Civil No. 1974, and is between the same parties involving the desegregation of the same schools. The matters recently decided by Judge McMillan were brought before him by motion in the cause. The questions that are now to be determined on appeal from Judge McMillan include this one: whether the present Mecklenburg school system is unconstitutional in that it is illegally segregated according to race, or, conversely, whether the school board has been and is now operating a unitary school system.

The statute I must apply is the following one:

> 28 U.S.C. § 47, Disqualification of Trial Judge to Hear Appeal. "No judge shall hear or determine an appeal from the decision of a case or issue tried by him."

This statute has not been construed by the Supreme Court, but it appears to be a simplified version of a portion of the Evarts Act of March 3, 1891, 26 Stat. 826. Professor Wright notes that an important change made by the Evarts Act was 'the provision that no judge was to sit on an appeal in a case that he heard below. Prior to 1891 it happened not infrequently that on appeal from the district court to the circuit court the district judge who had decided against appellant in the district court would be found hearing the appeal.' Wright, Federal Courts, 2nd ed. Section 1, p. 5.

Every time the Supreme Court has had occasion to look at the predecessor statute to 28 U.S.C. § 47 it has been strictly construed. In *Rexford v. Brunswick-Balke-Collender Co.*, 228 U.S. 339 (1913), the Court interpreted the statute as follows:

> "The terms of the statute, before quoted, are both direct and comprehensive. Its manifest purpose is to require that the circuit court of appeals be composed in every hearing of judges none of whom will be in the attitude of passing upon the propriety, scope, or effect of any ruling of his own made in the progress of the cause in the court of first instance, and to this end the disqualification is made to arise, not only when the judge has tried or heard the whole cause in the court below, but also when he has tried or heard any question therein which it is the duty of the circuit court of appeals to consider and pass upon. *American Const. Co. v. Jacksonville*, T. & K.W.R. Co., 148 U.S. 372, 387, 492; *Moran v. Dillingham*, 174 U.S. 153. That the question may be easy of solution, or that the parties may consent to the judge's participation in its decision, can make no difference, for the sole criterion under the statute is, does the case in the circuit court of appeals involve a question which the judge has tried or heard in the course of the proceedings in the court below?"

In *Moran v. Dillingham*, 174 U.S. 153 (1899), the Court said this about the predecessor statute:

"The intention of congress, in enacting that no judge before whom 'a cause or question may have been tried or heard,' in a district or circuit court, 'shall sit on the trial or hearing of such cause or question,' in the circuit court of appeals, manifestly was to require that court to be constituted of judges uncommitted and uninfluenced by having expressed or formed an opinion in the court of the first instance. Whatever may be thought of the policy of this enactment, it is not for the judiciary to disregard or to fritter away the positive prohibition of the legislature.

The enactment, alike by its language and by its purpose, is not restricted to the case of a judge's sitting on a direct appeal from his own decree upon a whole cause, or upon a single question. A judge who has sat at the hearing below of a whole cause at any stage thereof is undoubtedly disqualified to sit on the circuit court of appeals at the hearing of the whole cause at the same or at any later stage. And, as 'a cause,' in its usual and natural meaning, includes all questions that have arisen or may arise in it, there is strong reason for holding that a judge who has once heard the cause, either upon the law or upon the facts, in the court of first instance, is thenceforth disqualified to take part, in the circuit court of appeals, at the hearing and decision of the cause or of any question arising therein. But, however that may be, a judge who has once heard the cause upon its merits in the court of first instance is certainly disqualified from sitting in the circuit court of appeals on the hearing and decision of any question, in the same cause, which involves in any degree matter upon which he had occasion to pass in the lower court."

I believe the interpretations of the predecessor statute by the Supreme Court bear strongly upon the present version codified as 28 U.S.C. § 47. It is true that inferior federal courts have more loosely construed Section 47 (and its predecessors) but I think, with Professor Wright, that such constructions seem to depart from "what might appear from the face of the statute." 2B Barron & Holtzoff, Federal Practice and Procedure, 89 (Wright ed. 1961). A decision such as *United States v. Perlstein*, 126 F.2d 789, 806 (3d Cir. 1942), is, to say the least, hard to reconcile with the flat language of the statute.

The questions before me in 1965 were similar to those before Judge McMillan in 1968 and 1969. Indeed, it seems to me the ultimate question was the same: what may a school board be compelled to do to dismantle a dual system and implement a unitary one, or how much school board action is enough?

The sense and purpose of the disqualifying statute was dramatically expressed many years ago: 'Such an appeal is not from Phillip drunk to Phillip sober, but from Phillip sober to Phillip intoxicated with the vanity of a matured opinion and doubtless also a published decision.'

I believe the statute prevents my sitting on this appeal, and I therefore enter this order of disqualification and decline to serve.

## II.  IMPARTIAL JUDICIAL TREATMENT OF COUNSEL & PARTIES

Just as a judge's friendship outside the courthouse with counsel or a party may raise questions of partiality, a judge's conduct inside the courthouse toward parties, counsel, jurors, and others may raise similar concerns of partiality. The attorney faced with hostility from a judge is placed in an impossible position of ensuring the judge's wrath at counsel does not impair the client's right to a fair and impartial judge.

### Model Code of Judicial Conduct, Canon 3(B)(4)

A judge shall be patient, dignified and courteous to litigants, jurors, witnesses, lawyers and others with whom the judge deals in an official capacity, and shall require similar conduct of lawyers, and of staff, court officials and others subject to the judge's direction and control.

### IN RE DISQUALIFICATION OF BURGE
28 N.E.3d 48 (Ohio 2014)

O'CONNOR, C.J.

Dennis P. Will, the Lorain County Prosecuting Attorney, has filed an affidavit with the clerk of this court under R.C. 2701.03 seeking to disqualify Judge James M. Burge from all matters in which Will or one of his assistant prosecutors appears as counsel of record. This would currently include 276 pending criminal cases and four civil matters. This is the sixth affidavit of disqualification that Will has filed or approved for filing against Judge Burge. One of Will's previous disqualification requests was granted; one was granted in part and denied in part; one was denied; and in the two other disqualification matters, Judge Burge voluntarily recused himself before the request was decided. *See* case Nos. 08-AP-057, 09-AP-106, 13-AP-027, 13-AP-065, and 14-AP-010. In his current 68-page affidavit, Will sets forth an assortment of allegations to support his position that Judge Burge is biased and prejudiced against the prosecutor's office and has violated various rules of the Code of Judicial Conduct.

Judge Burge has responded in writing to the allegations, denying any bias against Will and his assistant prosecutors. In addition to Will's initial affidavit and the judge's response, Will and Judge Burge have also submitted supplemental filings, and several members of the Lorain County bar, including assistant prosecutors and local defense attorneys, have submitted affidavits as well.

For the reasons explained below, Will has not established that he is entitled to the extraordinary relief requested in his affidavit.

### Scope of affidavit-of-disqualification proceedings

Much of Will's affidavit is devoted to proving that Judge Burge has violated the Code of Judicial Conduct. However, the issue before the chief justice in disqualification proceedings is a narrow one: "[t]he constitutional and statutory responsibility of the Chief Justice in ruling on an affidavit of disqualification is limited to determining whether a judge in a pending case has a bias, prejudice, or other disqualifying interest that mandates the judge's disqualification from that case." *In re Disqualification of Kate*, 88 Ohio St. 3d 1208, 1209–1210, 723 N.E.2d 1098 (1999). *See also In re Disqualification of Sutula*, 105 Ohio St. 3d 1237, 2004-Ohio-7351, 826 N.E.2d 297, ¶ 5 (the chief justice's "review of an affidavit of disqualification focuses not simply on the level of civility shown by judges and lawyers to each other, however, but rather more broadly on the judge's willingness and ability to serve fairly and impartially on a particular case"). Thus, affidavit-of-disqualification proceedings are "not the appropriate mechanism for determining whether a judge has followed the Code of Judicial Conduct." *In re Disqualification of Capper*, 134 Ohio St. 3d 1271, 2012-Ohio-6287, 984 N.E.2d 1082, ¶ 19. Judicial-misconduct complaints are heard by the Board of Commissioners on Grievances and Discipline and ultimately decided by the full court.

Moreover, many of Will's alleged judicial-rule violations are irrelevant to the issue whether Judge Burge is biased against the prosecutor's office. For example, Will claims that Judge Burge has used profanity during court proceedings; he has communicated with defendants using racially derogatory terms, such as "cracker" and "homeboy"; he has given preferential treatment to certain defense attorneys over other defense counsel; during the 2008 presidential election, he made sexually degrading comments about Hillary Clinton and racially harassed her supporters; he once threatened to "choke" a defendant; he has made inappropriate comments about other Lorain County judges; he has misused his position as administrative judge by attempting to block vacation- and sick-time payouts to former employees of the court; he has retaliated against other public officials, including judges, for their refusal to hire his wife; and he has been known to improperly "shake down" attorneys for campaign contributions.

Because these allegations of judicial misconduct do not support a conclusion that Judge Burge is biased against the prosecutor's office, they are outside the scope of this proceeding. Accordingly, only Will's specific bias allegations involving either himself or an assistant prosecutor will be addressed in this entry.

## Waiver

An affidavit of disqualification must be filed "as soon as possible after the incident giving rise to the claim of bias and prejudice occurred," and failure to do so may result in waiver of the objection, especially when "the facts underlying the objection have been known to the party for some time." *In re Disqualification of O'Grady*, 77 Ohio St. 3d 1240, 1241, 674 N.E.2d 353 (1996). And in affidavit-of-disqualification proceedings, "the affiant has the burden to demonstrate that the affidavit is timely filed." *In re Disqualification of Carr*, 138 Ohio St. 3d 1237, 2013-Ohio-5927, 5 N.E.3d 1278, ¶ 4.

Here, Will claims that Judge Burge has made various prejudicial comments to and about his assistant prosecutors. But many of the judge's alleged comments were made years ago, and Will offers no reason for presenting them now. For example, Will claims that in 2008, Judge Burge attempted to intimidate assistant prosecutor Richard Gronsky and called another former assistant prosecutor a liar. And Will claims that in 2010, Judge Burge made derogatory and inappropriate comments to assistant prosecutor Christopher Pierre about another assistant prosecutor and Pierre's supervisors. Will also asserts that during one criminal trial, assistant prosecutor Nick Hanek made an objection, to which Judge Burge responded by becoming visibly upset, slamming his fists on the bench, and scowling at Hanek. Yet Will offers no time frame for the judge's alleged prejudicial conduct towards Hanek. If Will believed that the judge's comments and conduct from years ago reflected bias against his office, he should have timely sought disqualification. Accordingly, Will waived the right to object to these alleged comments occurring years ago that Will failed to identify when he learned of the conduct.

## Merits of the affidavit of disqualification

### Applicable precedent and the standard for disqualification

"The statutory right to seek disqualification of a judge is an extraordinary remedy." *In re Disqualification of George*, 100 Ohio St. 3d 1241, 2003-Ohio-5489, 798 N.E.2d 23, ¶ 5. The relief requested by Will, however, differs from most disqualification requests. Will's affidavit does not involve one underlying case; instead, he requests the disqualification of a duly elected judge from his *entire* criminal docket *and* those civil cases in which the prosecutor is required by law to represent a party. As precedent confirms, Will has a heavy burden to show he is entitled to such extraordinary relief.

Prosecutors have sought similar relief in at least two previous disqualification matters. In *In re Disqualification of Olivito*, 74 Ohio St. 3d 1261, 657 N.E.2d 1361 (1994), the Jefferson County prosecuting attorney alleged that Judge Dominick E. Olivito had made disparaging public comments about the prosecutor and his assistants, among other allegations. *Id.* at 1262, 657 N.E.2d 1361. The chief justice first noted that the standard for disqualification must be necessarily high where the relief requested involves removal of the judge from his entire criminal docket. *Id.* at 1263, 657 N.E.2d 1361. Notwithstanding Judge Olivito's "rather egregious" public comments about the prosecutor, the chief justice denied the affidavit because Judge Olivito's feelings towards the prosecutor had not "manifested themselves in [the judge's] official duties to the extent that his disqualification from all criminal cases [was] warranted." *Id.* That is, despite Judge Olivito's "unworthy" language, the citizens of Jefferson County were not being deprived of their right to the fair and impartial administration of justice. *Id.*

The chief justice denied a similar affidavit brought by the Adams County prosecuting attorney against Judge Elmer Spencer in *In re Disqualification of Spencer*, case No. 94-AP-179 (Dec. 23, 1994). That prosecutor complained about Judge Spencer's disparaging comments about the prosecutor's office and the judge's pervasive use of profanity, among other allegations. The chief justice again noted that the standard for a blanket order of disqualification from all criminal cases "must necessarily be high." On the merits, the chief justice found that Judge Spencer's public comments about the prosecutor and his assistants were "regrettable" but that the comments had not "materially impact[ed] the fair administration of justice in Adams County." Similarly, Judge Spencer's pervasive use of profanity was "personally distasteful" to the chief justice, but there was insufficient evidence to conclude that the profanity affected "the judge's official duties or illustrate[d] bias or prejudice to the prosecutor's office that require[d] disqualification."

Consistent with *Olivito* and *Spencer*, the standard for disqualification of Judge Burge must necessarily be high. In order for Judge Burge to be removed from all cases involving the prosecutor's office, Will must demonstrate that Judge Burge has illustrated bias toward Will that manifests itself in the judge's official duties, thereby materially impacting the fair and impartial administration of justice in Lorain County. Will has not met his burden.

### *Alleged physically threatening behavior*

Will first claims that his employees "are in fear for their physical safety in Burge's courtroom." As support, Will recites two recent incidents between assistant prosecutor Jennifer Riedthaler and Judge Burge. First, Will claims that in March 2014, Judge Burge yelled at Riedthaler in his chambers for making him "look bad in the newspaper." According to Will, Judge Burge's "tone was extremely angry," and the judge was gripping the handles of his chair "as if to restrain himself." At one point, Judge Burge recalled a fact that he had apparently forgotten, and the judge "proceeded to slam his head against the wall." Riedthaler believed that Judge Burge might throw his chair, but instead he "angrily slammed the chair back down and walked into the hallway."

The second incident occurred in May 2014. Riedthaler was waiting in Judge Burge's courtroom at counsel table with a police detective. Before proceedings began, Judge Burge entered the room and announced that he felt "shitty." After Riedthaler asked the judge what was wrong, he "proceeded to walk over and position himself directly across the trial table" from her. He then "slammed his hands down on the table, shoulder-width apart, leaned over to APA Riedthaler and sternly said, 'You will know in about two minutes. I don't want to yell at you in front of everyone.' " Judge Burge then moved behind Riedthaler "and began pacing back and forth." Riedthaler felt upset and frightened, but the judge never told her what was wrong. Instead, the judge indicated that he was "over it," while grinning. Based on these two incidents, Will claims that Riedthaler "can no longer complete her functions in Judge Burge's courtroom," his "employees are in fear for their physical safety," and he is forced to staff Judge Burge's courtroom with two assistant prosecutors.

For his part, Judge Burge states that he was upset with Riedthaler during the May 2014 incident because she belatedly changed her position on an issue. However, Judge Burge denies threatening her or any other attorney. Jenifer Berki, a local defense attorney, also submitted an affidavit in support of Judge Burge. Berki claims that she was present for the recent allegation of Judge Burge threatening a prosecutor, and Berki avers that she did not feel that she was in a threatening environment at that time.

A video of the May 2014 incident has been submitted. The video image is grainy and does not have sound, but it shows Judge Burge with his hands on counsel table leaning towards Riedthaler, who is seated at the table with other people. After about a minute, Judge Burge moved behind Riedthaler and appeared to lean against the railing between counsel table and the galley. The judge stayed there for about six minutes while Riedthaler appeared to converse with others in the courtroom, and at one point, Riedthaler moved to retrieve something from another area in the courtroom. Judge Burge then left the room. Contrary to Will's affidavit, the video does not show Judge Burge "pac[ing] back and forth" behind Riedthaler.

Riedthaler may have reasonably felt intimidated by some of Judge Burge's alleged actions, such as yelling at her, slamming his head against a wall, or slamming his chair down. But these two incidents alone do not necessarily show that Judge Burge has threatened Will's employees with physical harm. Nor do the two incidents illustrate a bias against the prosecutor's office. That is, Will has not established that Judge Burge intimidated Riedthaler *because* she worked for Will. The judge's conduct could have been caused by his intemperate nature. But the issue here is bias, and these two incidents alone do not prove that Judge Burge has a bias against the prosecutor's office warranting the extraordinary relief requested by Will in his affidavit.

### Judge Burge's string of letters to Will

Will next claims that after Judge Burge's "threatening actions" toward Riedthaler, Will met with two other Lorain County common pleas court judges and requested that the general division judges remove Judge Burge as administrative judge and strip him of his criminal docket. Will claims that after Judge Burge learned of these meetings, the judge sent Will eight unsolicited letters over five business days. Will claims that these letters "reflect the depths of the hatred and animosity that Burge holds against" Will and his office.

Judge Burge's letters cover a variety of topics, and they definitely demonstrate a deteriorated relationship between the two public officials, as both sides feel that the other has made threatening comments. Nonetheless, the letters do not prove that Judge Burge cannot be fair and impartial in any matter involving an assistant prosecutor, nor do the letters show that Judge Burge's differences with Will have affected the judge's official duties.

### Sexual harassment

Will claims that there are "numerous instances" when his female employees have "felt that Judge Burge has committed sexual harassment." Will identifies two assistant prosecutors who have been subjected to this alleged harassment: Donna Freeman and Sherry Glass.

As for Freeman, Will claims that Judge Burge expressed a "professionally inappropriate interest" in her, but Will did not further elaborate on this allegation. In response, Judge Burge claims that he recently offered Freeman the position as his bailiff, which she declined, but he is unaware of any other interest that he has shown in her that could have given rise to a belief that his concern for her was other than as a lawyer and new mother. Without more from Will, this vague allegation is insufficient to constitute bias or prejudice, let alone to prove that Judge Burge sexually harassed Freeman. *See, e.g., In re Disqualification of Walker*, 36 Ohio St. 3d 606, 522 N.E.2d 460

(1988) ("vague, unsubstantiated allegations of the affidavit are insufficient on their face for a finding of bias or prejudice").

As for assistant prosecutor Glass, Will claims that Glass has been subjected to "many embarrassing and demeaning comments about her appearance, as well as sexual references." For example, Will claims that Judge Burge has referred to Glass as a "blond bombshell" and a "looker." In addition, Will claims that Judge Burge has mocked Glass by repeating what she says in a soft, exaggerated, feminine voice. Will further claims that during one September 2012 hearing, Glass asked to approach the bench with defense attorney Andy Robinson. Judge Burge commented on Glass's "librarian look" and "indicated that if she took off her glasses and let down her hair, 'Wow, what I would do to you.'" Glass was flustered and embarrassed by these degrading comments, which were allegedly loud enough to be heard by the entire courtroom. Will claims that he was just made aware of the judge's inappropriate comments to Glass while preparing this affidavit of disqualification.

Several people have submitted affidavits regarding the September 2012 hearing. Glass submitted an affidavit attesting to the truth of Will's allegations. In addition, Amanda Thomas, a paralegal in Will's office, submitted an affidavit averring that she also heard the judge's inappropriate comments to Glass. However, Andrew Robinson, the defense attorney named in Will's affidavit as witnessing the inappropriate comments, submitted an affidavit averring that he had no recollection of the judge making such comments to Glass, and if Robinson had heard the comments, he claims that he would have remembered them. In addition, the court reporter for that hearing averred in her affidavit that she did not recall Judge Burge saying anything inappropriate to Glass.

For his part, Judge Burge acknowledges occasionally commenting on Glass's appearance and referring to her as a "blond bombshell," which he claims was meant to characterize Glass as an aggressive prosecutor. Judge Burge does not recall making any statements similar to the remarks attributed to him at the September 2012 hearing.

Judge Burge should not be commenting on the appearance of attorneys or referring to any individuals in his courtroom as "blond bombshells." Such comments are undignified, unprofessional, and offensive. However, the record otherwise contains conflicting evidence regarding the September 2012 hearing. If Judge Burge made the alleged comments to Glass, his behavior is indefensible. Nevertheless, the issue here is not whether Judge Burge should be disciplined for making sexually inappropriate comments. The issue is whether Judge Burge has a bias against Will's office and whether that bias has materially affected the judge's official duties so that he must be removed from any case involving an assistant prosecutor. Based on this record, Will has not established that the judge's behavior towards Glass is a product of bias toward Will or that it reflects bias against Will and his office.

### Disparaging comments

Will also claims that Judge Burge has made disparaging comments about Will and his management team. Many of these comments were allegedly made by Judge Burge to his former bailiff, who had a falling-out with Judge Burge and now works for Will. Vulgar and offensive language about other public officials — whether made on the bench, in public, or in chambers — is inconsistent with proper judicial demeanor and decorum. Given some of the comments attributed to Judge Burge in Will's affidavit, Will's concerns are understandable. However, as in *Olivito* and *Spencer*, regardless of whether the judge's comments reflect his personal feelings toward Will, there is insufficient evidence to conclude that the judge's feelings have "manifested themselves in his official duties to the extent that his disqualification from all criminal cases is warranted." *Olivito*, 74 Ohio St. 3d at 1263, 657 N.E.2d 1361.

### *Professionalism*

Tension between a judge and a county prosecutor is bound to occur in our adversary system. Both sides seek to attain justice, but they do not always agree on what that means. However, principles of professionalism require judges and prosecutors to give proper respect to each other and to treat each other with the dignity and courtesy that each office deserves. The relationship between Will and Judge Burge has reached an unprofessional level and is less than the public deserves from these two veteran lawyers. Both parties must work to improve their professional relationship. The citizens of Lorain County deserve a civil working relationship between the prosecutor's office and the administrative judge of the common pleas court.

Finally, although Will's affidavit is being denied at this time, many of the allegations raised in his affidavit — especially those regarding Judge Burge's generally offensive language and conduct — are a cause for concern. Judge Burge is reminded of the "Judicial Creed," which the Supreme Court of Ohio adopted in 2001 in recognition of the unique standards of professionalism required of judges. Three provisions of that creed bear repeating:

I believe that my role requires scholarship, diligence, personal integrity and a dedication to the attainment of justice.

\* \* \* \*

I recognize that the dignity of my office requires the highest level of judicial demeanor.

\* \* \* \*

I will treat all persons, including litigants, lawyers, witnesses, jurors, judicial colleagues and court staff with dignity and courtesy and insist that others do likewise.

### Conclusion

For the reasons stated above, the affidavit of disqualification is denied. The visiting-judge assignment relating to Will's affidavit of disqualification is withdrawn, and Judge Burge may commence hearing cases assigned to him in which the Lorain County Prosecuting Attorney's office appears as counsel of record.

While many cases have focused on the judge's interactions with counsel in court and their adverse effects upon counsel's client, *In re Schenck* presents the case of a judge publishing a critique of the lawyer's skills in the local newspaper.

# IN RE COMPLAINT AS TO THE CONDUCT OF THE HONORABLE RONALD D. SCHENCK
### 870 P.2d 185 (Or. 1994)

\* \* \* \*

APPENDIX

\* \* \* \*

Wallowa County Chieftain
Guest editorial
October 1, 1992

*A judge's evaluation of the district attorney*

This is a report on my observations and evaluation of the performance of Mary Goebel as District Attorney for Wallowa County.

This is not something I would do in the ordinary course. However, Ms. Goebel's recent decision to disqualify me in every case she files leaves me with no alternative.

In my letter to you regarding the disqualification issue dated August 31, 1992, I stated that I would set forth specifics upon which I based my opinion that Ms. Goebel does not have the capability, experience or maturity to handle the duties of District Attorney. I do that now.

Since we both took office at the same time, I have worked with Ms. Goebel during the entire period of her performance in office.

She ha[s] not won one felony jury trial.

She still does not have a grasp of how to present a witness.

She does not as yet have the ability to differentiate between what evidence should be presented in the State's case in chief as opposed to rebuttal.

She does not understand the purpose of expert testimony in sex abuse cases or how to lay the proper foundation to get it admitted.

In one sex abuse case, she had to dismiss the case three times and take the indictment back to the grand jury the fourth time before she got it right. That case has been delayed for trial for over a year because she simply did not know how to get it prepared for trial.

She dismissed a felony sex abuse case based on an experienced defense attorney's assertion that the statute of limitation had ran [sic] out when in fact it had not.

The District Attorney always prepares the Sentence Order and Judgment. I have had to revise every sentence order she has presented to me. Some were seriously defective.

In two major felony cases, I have had to reject plea bargains which she agreed to. In both cases, she would have permitted the defendant to be sentenced to optional probation for serious felony crimes — one for dealing in controlled substances and having 90 pounds of marijuana in possession, and another for assault on his wife which almost killed her. I ended up sentencing both to maximum terms in state prison.

In the first nine months or so she was consistently late to court. I finally had to reprimand her in open court.

If you speak to her critically, even in a positive vein, she cries.

She has no comprehension of what a case (work) load is. She spoke to me about applying to the Court for inclusion in her budget of money to hire a deputy to help her.

The fact of the matter is that she has a workload (caseload) which is not more than 20 percent and probably closer to 10 percent of the caseload carried by the attorneys in the District Attorney's office in La Grande. There are three attorneys in La Grande, and over 200 felony cases were filed in 1991. Ms. Goebel filed eight felony cases in Wallowa County in 1991. The same percentages would hold for District Court.

Ms. Goebel, straight out of law school is being paid around $50,000 per year with benefits above that of $10,000 per year. She should be able to do the county's civil work for nothing and still have less than a 50 percent workload. She resigned from doing the civil work even though she was getting paid.

She accuses me of being biased against the State. The problem is really the opposite for me as judge. The real problem I face with Ms. Goebel representing the State is how do I insure [sic] that the State gets a fair trial? How do I insure [sic] that the people of Wallowa County have their case against the criminal defendant properly and competently presented — when it is obvious that the people's prosecutor often does not have a clue as to how to proceed?

The judge's hands are tied for the most part. The judge must maintain impartiality, especially in criminal trials and cannot help either side present their case.

I could go on, but I think you have the picture by now. Putting an attorney right out of law school into the courtroom trying felony jury cases is like putting a medical student fresh out of medical school into the operating room to do complex surgery.

Unfortunately, Ms. Goebel is the sole attorney in the Wallowa County District Attorney's office. She had no one to guide her on a daily basis. Her caseload is not sufficient for her to gain experience rapidly.

I spent several years going to court with an experienced attorney, as his assistant, before I tried a case.

Ms. Goebel is a lovely young lady. But she has placed herself in a position for which she has neither the training or experience to perform the duties competently.

Unfortunately, in this instance, it is the public that will get the short end of the stick. It may also be that Ms. Goebel will be seriously damaged in her career. She has a lot of potential if she was in a position where she could be properly trained.

The position of the District Attorney in Wallowa County has had its problems for as long as I can remember. No energetic, experienced, young career-minded attorney wants to take the job because it really offers little challenge and little opportunity for advancement. So the county has been saddled with older attorneys who were, in fact, not all that energetic or younger attorneys who were not all that experienced.

Perhaps the county court needs to investigate what alternatives might be available to ensure the county has a vigorous, competent prosecutor.

*Editor's note: Ronald D. Schenck is the circuit Court judge for Union and Wallowa counties.*

---

As the materials indicate, the stresses of the courtroom can weigh on both counsel and the judges. Consider these additional examples of judicial conduct toward attorneys in the courtroom and whether they are found to meet the standard for judicial disqualification or judicial misconduct.

> . . . Cutting comments to counsel, particularly those relating to skill rather than good faith or integrity, will not generally mandate reversal. [Citation omitted.] . . .

> For example, in response to their counsel's inquiry into why the court was sustaining defense counsel objection, the judge stated, "Counsel, I didn't realize I had to conduct a law school class, but I guess I do." . . .

> . . . At times the judge was gruff with the [plaintiffs'] counsel; but there are also incidents in the record where the judge was equally gruff with [defense] counsel. While we do not condone the heavy-handed style of the judge in this case, his conduct does not warrant retrial.

*Pau v. Yosemite Park & Curry Co.*, 928 F.2d 880 (9th Cir. 1991).

> The second ground which the Gregorys offer in support of their motion to recuse is my statement, which was directed to counsel, "I hope you choke on it." The circumstances surrounding this statement are not as insidious as the defendants argue. The request by counsel for a copy of my financial disclosure statement touched an exposed nerve. Like many other judges and public officials, I dislike being required to disclose my personal finances. My dislike is strong. Disclosure is, in my opinion, an unwarranted and unjustifiable invasion [into] my right [of] privacy. My reaction to the request by counsel for the Gregorys that I disclose my financial statement was sharp. I admit that.

> But a judge is not required to disqualify himself unless "his impartiality might reasonably be questioned." "Use of the word 'might' in the statute was intended to indicate that disqualification should follow if the reasonable man,

were he to know all the circumstances, would harbor doubts about the judge's impartiality." . . . I do not believe that a reasonable person who understood my sensitivity about disclosing my financial statement and the interplay between a judge and counsel which normally accompanies any lengthy proceeding would harbor doubts about my impartiality. There is no question in my mind about the propriety of my sitting on this case.

*United States v. Gregory*, 508 F. Supp. 1218 (S.D. Ala. 1980) (citations omitted).

MR. STORMENT:    Your Honor, I'd like to make an offer of proof, need to make an offer of proof. . . .

THE COURT:    Paul, the direct examination took about thirty minutes, you've taken an hour so far. Sit down. Go back to the cross-examination properly.

MR. STORMENT:    May I please make an offer of proof?

THE COURT:    No, you can't approach the bench. I don't want you up here.

MR. STORMENT:    Can I make an offer of proof?

THE COURT:    Turned off my hearing aid, can't hear a word you are saying.

MR. STORMENT:    Your Honor, I think I have to protect the record and make an offer of proof. I think it's a matter of right for this defendant to make an offer of proof in this case.

THE COURT:    Paul, I'm deaf and getting deafer.

*Illinois v. Eckert*, 551 N.E.2d 820, 822 (Ill. App. Ct. 1990) (reversing and remanding the defendant's conviction, finding that the judge's behavior did not constitute harmless error; "The record in the instant case, considered in its entirety, shows that the trial judge's conduct in the presence of the jury denied defendant a fair and impartial trial.").

## In Court Reports

1.    Identify the rules governing recusal and disqualification in your court. Compare them to the ABA Model Rules in this chapter. Analyze any distinctions between them as well as the rationale underlying any changes or modification to the Rules.

2.    Research if your court has a local rule requiring attorneys to file a disclosure statement. Such a statement lists names attorneys and law firms and alerts the court to possible recusal issues. For example, the Seventh Circuit Court of Appeals, Circuit Rule 26.1(b) lists the content of such a statement:

The statement must disclose the names of all law firms whose partners or associates have appeared for the party or amicus in the case (including proceedings in the district court or before an administrative agency) or are expected to appear in this court. If any litigant is using a pseudonym, the statement must disclose the litigant's true name. A disclosure required by the preceding sentence will be kept under seal.

**3.** Research recusal opinions in your court and determine if there are any recurring patterns among them or specific judicial attitudes expressed in the recusal opinions.

**4.** After courtroom observations, describe the different attitudes, tones, and styles of communication that judges express toward counsel during docket call, motion hearings, trials, settlement conferences, or other proceedings.

**5.** Does your court operate within a large or small legal community? Does this size make a difference in creating issue of partiality in terms of judicial friendship, former associations with practicing lawyers? Do large law firms tend to create such issues? Do graduates of a single law school who are now in practice create recusal problems?

**6.** Using your judge or another judge's biography, diagram the professional and personal relationships that he or she has formed before and after becoming a judge. Rate the "intensity" or degree of these relationships. How might these relationships become grounds for recusal? Have the relationships actually become the basis for motions to recuse? With what result?

**7.** Does your court or jurisdiction have specific rules governing judges' use of social media? Does your judge or other judges on your court use social media? In addition to the *Domville* case, another Florida appellate court held that trial judge's *ex parte* communication with a party in a case pending before him presented a legally sufficient claim for disqualification of judge. On advice of counsel, the party did not respond to judge's social media "friend" request, and thus, the party reasonably felt a fear of offending judge. *Chace v. Loisel*, 170 So. 3d 802 (Fla. Dist. Ct. App. 2014).

## Out of Court Reports

### 1. Motions to Recuse

In each of these fact scenarios, you are a federal district court judge who has received a timely motion to recuse from a litigant in a case pending before you. Review the three federal recusal and disqualification statutes, the cases in this chapter, and decide if you will grant or deny the motion. Consider any additional dispositive facts you might deem necessary to your decision. Cite to the statute or case precedent reasoning and facts, where available, to support your decision.

**a.** You are a graduate of Harvard Law School. You are presiding over a suit brought by plaintiff against the Harvard Law School alleging he was denied a position as a librarian as a result of age discrimination.

[*Brody v. President & Fellows of Harvard College*, 664 F.2d 10 (1st Cir. 1981)]

**b.** You were appointed to the bench by President Reagan. You are presiding over a case where the defendant has been charged with making threats against now former President Reagan. Reagan is both the victim and a potential witness in the case.

[*United States v. Gordon*, 974 F.2d 1110 (9th Cir. 1992)]

**c.** Your former law clerk gave testimony for the grand jury. The truthfulness of this testimony is crucial to an issue in the criminal case which is now pending before you.

[*United States v. Ferguson*, 550 F. Supp. 1256 (S.D.N.Y. 1982)]

**d.**  You own a home and therefore are a consumer and customer using natural gas to heat and cool your home. You are presiding over a case which alleges the state natural gas company unlawfully fixed the price of natural gas. A potential result of the litigation is that you and the other members of the public would receive an annual bill increase of $31.00.

[*In re New Mexico Natural Gas Antitrust Litigation*, 620 F.2d 794 (10th Cir. 1980)]

**e.**  You are presiding over a plaintiff class action brought against the electric utility. Treble damages are sought and as a customer of the utility, whether part of the class or not, you could benefit in amounts that exceed $7,200.

[*Gordon v. Reliant Energy, Inc.*, 141 F. Supp. 2d 1041 (S.D. Cal. 2001)]

**f.**  You presided over a criminal trial which resulted in a conviction. You have before you now the post-conviction motions from that trial. The defendant has expressed the intent to kill you and has let a contract to that effect.

[*United States v. Cerrella*, 529 F. Supp. 1373 (S.D. Fla. 1982)]

**g.**  At some point during the proceedings in this case, the criminal defendant obtained your home telephone number, which he called, leaving more than one threatening message on an answering machine. Before sentencing, you revealed that you had received these threatening messages from defendant. You, however, dismissed them as attempts to "manipulate the system" and proceeded to sentence the defendant.

[*United States v. Holland*, 519 F.3d 909 (9th Cir. 2008) (listing factors for judge to consider in face of a threat)].

**h.**  You presided over a criminal case where a jury found the defendant guilty of rape. Immediately after the verdict was read, the defendant assaulted you as you sat on the bench. Before sentencing, defendant sought your recusal arguing that because of the assault on you, you would not give him a fair and impartial hearing at his sentencing.

[*State v. Bilal*, 893 P.2d 674 (Wash. Ct. App. 1995)]

**i.**  You are presiding over a criminal case. Thirteen years ago you wrote a law review article and in a footnote stated: "I gratefully acknowledge helpful comments from . . . Veda Travis. . . ." The footnote also gives thanks to 12 other people and participants in a faculty colloquium. Veda Travis is the prosecutor in the criminal case before you.

[*United States v. Mendoza*, 468 F.3d 1256 (10th Cir. 2006)]

**j.**  Your son, currently a law student, worked as a summer associate and has a tentative job offer from a firm which represents a party in a case pending before you.

[*Wilmington Towing Co., Inc. v. Cape Fear Towing Co., Inc.*, 624 F. Supp. 1210 (E.D.N.C. 1986)]

**k.**   On appeal, a convicted criminal defendant has moved for reversal because you participated in a nonjudicial decision to reject the defendant's application to a bridge league because of his prior tax evasion convictions and his ownership of a house of prostitution. Defendant knew of your participation in the bridge club decision when the criminal trial began.

[*United States v. Conforte*, 624 F.2d 869 (9th Cir. 1980)]

**l.**   You are trying a criminal case where the defendant confessed to a robbery and admitted he carried a gun during the offense. You notice, however, that no firearm count was included in the indictment. At a status conference, you question why the Government failed to include such a count and opine it was "absurd" and "assinine" to fail to include a firearm count. You invite the Government attorney to share your opinion with the head of the criminal division. You also commentary that your role includes "represent[ing] the community" and that the community was "tired" of armed robbery The Government adds a firearm count; defendant moves for recusal.

[*United States v. Wilkerson*, 208 F.3d 794 (9th Cir. 2000)]

**m.**   Your law clerk is married to a named defendant in a case pending before you. Your other law clerk, however, has always been assigned to the case. The clerk's husband has been named in the case in his official capacity only and has no personal stake in the outcome.

[*Baugh v. City of Milwaukee*, 829 F. Supp. 274 (E.D. Wis. 1993)]

**n.**   You receive a motion to recuse based on comments made by one of your law clerks. The law clerk insinuated in jest to members of defense counsel's law firm, including an attorney who has made an appearance in the case on behalf of the defendant, that she influenced the Court's decisionmaking process with respect to certain discovery rulings in this case. Specifically, the law clerk sent a text message to an associate at defense counsel's law firm that "as of 3:34 [p.m.] today," when the Court issued its order, the associate "owe[d] [her] a beer [(or wine)!]".

[*Doe v. Cabrera*, 2015 U.S. Dist. LEXIS 132364 (D.D.C. Sept. 30, 2015)]

**o.**   You resolved a scheduling conflict in favor of the prosecutor in a post-trial proceeding in a criminal case. When defense counsel complained about your decision to grant the prosecutor an extension of time, you explained:

> "The prosecutor in this case is a friend of mine, as you know, *a dear friend*. He was my law clerk for a while. And such is the juxtaposition of the people in this building that I don't get to see him indeed nearly as often as I'd like to. But I hear from the grapevine that he really is being shoved around up there. He's being worked very, very hard. I don't think I've had a long talk with him in months. And he's under a lot of stress. *And just out of humanitarian milk of kindness I want to make things easier for him*, if that's possible. . . . He is one of the brightest lawyers I've ever met in my life . . . ."

[*United States v. Bosch*, 951 F.2d 1546 (9th Cir. 1991)]

**p.**   You appeared on a national television program. You spoke about abortion protests which were taking place despite your own court order concerning the protests. You expressed strong opinions. You stated that if abortion protesters planned to come to your jurisdiction, they had better bring their toothbrushes. You are hearing the charges lodged against the protesters. The defendant protesters file a motion for recusal.

[*United States v. Cooley*, 1 F.3d 985 (10th Cir. 1993)]

**q.**    You become annoyed at defendant's sentencing hearing because the defendant's testimony proves incredible and unbelievable. Defense counsel protests after you stop the testimony and tell the defendant you're not believing anything that he says. You tell defense counsel that you're the judge and you can "badger the witness," "use whatever tone you like," and when counsel moves for recusal, you deny the motion. You also inform him the defendant's testimony at the hearing was "just a crock of baloney."

[*United States v. Martin*, 278 F.3d 988 (9th Cir. 2002)]

**r.**    You conducted a civil bench trial, with intentional tort claims, on February 24, and completed the memorandum decision on March 26. Five days later, your father died. The mortuary which made the funeral arrangements asked you if there were any attorneys you wanted to serve as pallbearers at your father's funeral. You agreed and the funeral director suggested that at least two attorneys be named. You considered both of the attorneys involved in the case you had just tried, but named only one, the plaintiff's attorney. The funeral home then contacted plaintiff's attorney who served as a pallbearer on April 3. On April 5, the memorandum of opinion was filed and on April 9 the judgment was entered in favor of plaintiff, awarding both compensatory and punitive damages. Thus, plaintiff's attorney served as pallbearer eight days after the decision had been made but two days before it was communicated to the parties.

You issued this statement when asked about this choice of appellee's counsel as a pallbearer:

> Well, I would like the record to reflect that when the funeral arrangements were made for my father, I'm the one who made them, and because my mother was simply not able to do so, when Mr. Hale at [the funeral home] inquired about pallbearers, I asked him if it were necessary and he said, "Well, it would look better." I said, "Okay." Then he said, "Do you have any names?" So, I gave him a list of names and I started to give him Mr. Cole's [defendant's attorney] name but I didn't think I could get him from Malvern over here [to Hot Springs]. But, nevertheless, I just simply gave a list of names and they did the calling. I told him if he needed any additional names to give me a call, and that's the way it was . . .

[*Matthews v. Rogers*, 651 S.W.2d 453 (Ark. 1983)]

**s.**    You are presiding over a criminal drug case. Defendant questions your impartiality based on a law-review article you wrote 13 years ago. A footnote in the article states: "I gratefully acknowledge helpful comments from . . . Veda Travis . . . ." (the footnote also thanks 12 other people and the participants in a faculty colloquium). Ms. Travis is the prosecutor in the case before you.

[*United States v. Mendoza*, 468 F.3d 1256 (10th Cir. 2006)]

**2.** For a set of hypotheticals testing the definition of a friend distinguished from an acquaintance, see Jeremy M. Miller, *Judicial Recusal and Disqualification: The Need for a Per Se Rule on Friendship (Not Acquaintance)*, 33 PEPP. L. REV. 575 (2006).

### 3. United States v. Murphy & Operation Greylord

**a.** Corruption and bribery is not the focus of this chapter on judicial ethics, but consider and research how corruption takes hold in a particular court system.

The background in the *Murphy* recusal decision is Operation Greylord, the federal government's investigation of judicial and attorney corruption in Cook County Circuit Court. The investigation rested in part on the work of Judge Brocton Lockwood, a visiting judge from southern Illinois who rotated into the Cook County courts in an effort to reduce the backlog of cases there. Judge Lockwood discovered the activities described in the *Murphy* case. Lockwood went undercover to help in the investigation and later prosecution and conviction of his fellow judges. Judge Lockwood tells his story in his book, *Operation Greylord: Brocton Lockwood's Story* (1989). For an additional account of the investigation, apart from the published legal opinions, see ROB WARDEN, GREYLORD: JUSTICE, CHICAGO STYLE (1989).

The extent of judicial corruption and the means of uncovering it seen in Operation Greylord continues to attract attention decades later. TERRENCE HAKE, OPERATION GREYLORD: THE TRUE STORY OF AN UNTRAINED UNDERCOVER AGENT AND AMERICA'S BIGGEST CORRUPTION BUST (2015).

**b.** Consider the factor of backlog and a burdensome docket in corruption growing within a court system. What role might it play? Try a firsthand experience by attending a docket like the one described below to get a sense of its effects upon the judge, the attorneys, and the parties. The heavy workload in the Cook County Circuit Court may have been a factor in the corruption which took root there. Judge Lockwood described his early days on the bench in Cook County Traffic Court:

> Housing court was one thing, but when it came to judicial mockery, it couldn't hold a candle to traffic court. Six hours! That's 360 minutes to try six hundred cases — about one every thirty seconds.

> We called the speeders up in groups of ten to twenty. I gave each group a short lecture about slowing down and then sent them to Room 19 where they were "punished" by sitting through a boring fifteen minute movie.

> We moved through the cases quickly. Handling 600 cases a day is one hectic job! Everyone in the system had to work like crazy to put on even a facade of justice. As in housing court, all of the entries were made on computer sheets, with 35 or so lines of case names and numbers. And again, it was easy to get on the wrong line. But if I did, what the Hell? I was probably going to discharge the case or send the people to the movie anyway. Even so, it was still a lot of work, frantically trying to find the right line and make the appropriate entry in thirty seconds. I felt like I was being punished more than the defendants.

BROCKTON LOCKWOOD, OPERATION GREYLORD: BROCTON LOCKWOOD'S STORY 7, 8–9 (1989).

#### 4.   Gender & Other Bias in the Courtroom

Judge Schenck's treatment of Attorney Goebel and his public statements exhibited a "maliciousness" which was "remarkable in its intensity." The statements, including the judge's description of Goebel as a "lovely young lady," also may constitute gender bias in the courtroom. How do Schenck's remarks compare to those by the judge in the *Burge* case, decided 20 years later?

For a further discussion of the issue of gender bias and the use of judicial canons to address the issue, see Kittie D. Warshawsky, *The Judicial Canons: A First Step in Addressing Gender Bias in the Courtroom*, 7 GEO. J. LEGAL ETHICS 1047 (1994). For a judge's perspective on gender bias in the courtroom, see Shirley S. Abrahamson, *Toward a Courtroom of One's Own: An Appellate Court Judge Looks at Gender Bias*, 61 U. CIN. L. REV. 1209 (1993).

Unfortunately many other examples of gender or racial bias in judicial behavior can be found:

> In addition to referring to juveniles as "little peckerheads," Judge Fuller admits that he made disparaging remarks about women in the legal profession, Native Americans, and law enforcement. * * * The walls in Judge Fuller's courtroom are lined with photographs and artwork. In order to accommodate the audio-visual system, if needed in his courtroom, Judge Fuller would remove three pieces depicting Native Americans. When the trial was over, Judge Fuller would hang the artwork back on the wall. When doing so he admits "saying, again in a smart aleck deal, this is where I hang my Indians." Judge Fuller admits that the remark was completely inappropriate and claims that he apologized. He testified that the pictures of Native Americans in his courtroom were to demonstrate to Native American juveniles respect for their leaders.

*In re Fuller*, 798 N.W.2d 408 (S.D. 2011).

**5.**   Note the *Cheney* opinion's citation to *U.S. v. Murphy*. Do you agree that the two cases are readily distinguishable?

**6.**   Why does the *Murphy* court distinguish between the effects of § 455(a) and § 455(b)? Where no actual prejudice is found, the previous rulings stand; only actions taken after the recusal motion need be set aside. Do you agree with this result?

**7.**   In *Cheney*, Justice Scalia relies upon citations to friendships between Presidents and Justices. His media critics, however, claimed that times have changed and such relationships are no longer proper. Have times changed? Does the current public's perception of these friendships between a President and a Supreme Court Justice more likely lead them to conclude that a judge's impartiality can "reasonably be questioned" under these circumstances?

**8.**   Compare the consequences of recusal in *Swann* and in *Cheney*. Scalia stated in *Cheney* that if he were sitting on a Court of Appeals, as Judge Craven sat on the Fourth Circuit in *Swann*, he could resolve doubts in favor of recusal because another judge could take his place. However, on the Supreme Court, the court would have to proceed with eight Justices and risk a tie vote. Not noted by Scalia is the additional dimension that his own recusal decision would not be reviewed further.

The November 1, 1993 Statement of Recusal Policy, cited in *Cheney*, was issued by seven justices, explicitly recognizing the heightened impact of recusal by the Court: "In this Court, where the absence of one judge cannot be made up by another, needless recusal deprives litigants of the nine Justices to which they are entitled, produces the possibility of an even division of the merits of the case, and has a distorting effect upon the certiorari process, requiring the petitioner to obtain (under our current practice) four votes out of eight instead of four out of nine."

**9.** In the *Burge* case and the *Schenck* case, the judges and counsel — both counsel are prosecuting attorneys — are locked in ongoing encounters as they each attempt to perform their jobs. What advice would you give these attorneys, or any attorney practicing before judges who make disparaging or demeaning remarks? Do you agree that "[t]ension between a judge and a county prosecutor is bound to occur in our adversary system."?

## SELECTED BIBLIOGRAPHY

Leslie W. Abramson, *The Judge's Relative Is Affiliated with Counsel of Record: The Ethical Dilemma*, 32 HOFSTRA L. REV. 1181 (2004).

Sanaz Alempour, *Judicial Recusal & Disqualification: Is Sexual Orientation a Valid Cause in Florida?*, 32 NOVA L. REV. 609 (2008).

Dimtry Bam, *Making Appearances Matter: Recusal and the Appearance of Bias*, 2011 B.Y.U. L. REV. 943.

Deborah Lyn Bassett & Rex. R. Perschbacher, *The Elusive Goal of Impartiality*, 97 IOWA L. REV. 181 (2011).

John G. Browning, *Why Can't We Be Friends? Judges' Use of Social Media*, 68 U. MIAMI L. REV. 487 (2014).

Sande L. Buhai, *Federal Disqualification: A Behavioral and Quantitative Analysis*, 90 OR. L. REV. 69 (2011).

Sarah M. R. Cravens, *In Pursuit of Actual Justice*, 59 ALA. L. REV. 1 (2007).

Craig Estlinbaum, *Social Networking and Judicial Ethics*, 2 ST. MARY'S J. LEGAL MAL. & ETHICS 2 (2012).

FEDERAL JUDICIAL CENTER, RECUSAL: ANALYSIS OF CASE LAW UNDER 28 U.S.C. §§ 455 & 144 (2d ed. 2010).

Richard E. Flamm, *History of and Problems with the Federal Disqualification Framework*, 58 DRAKE L. REV. 751 (2010).

Charles Gardner Geyh, *The Dimensions of Judicial Impartiality*, 65 FLA. L. REV. 493 (2013).

Diana Gillis, *Closing an Administrative Loophole: Ethics for the Administrative Judiciary*, 31 J. NAT'L ASS'N ADMIN. L. JUDICIARY 149 (Spring 2011).

Maxine Goodman, *Three Likely Causes of Judicial Misbehavior and How These Causes Should Inform Judicial Discipline*, 41 CAP. U. L. REV. 949 (2013).

Cynthia Gray, *The Center for Judicial Ethics*, 96 JUDICATURE 305 (2013).

Cynthia Gray, *Judicial Disqualification and Friendships with Attorneys*, 52 JUDGES' J. 20 (2013).

Jeffrey M. Hayes, *To Recuse or To Refuse: Self-Judging and the Reasonable Person Problem*, 33 J. LEGAL PROF. 85 (2008).

Samuel Vincent Jones, *Judges, Friends and Facebook: The Ethics of Prohibition*, 24 GEO. J. LEGAL ETHICS 281 (2011).

JUDICIAL CONDUCT REPORTER (published quarterly by the Am. Jud. Soc'y Center).

M. Margaret McKeown, *To Judge or Not to Judge: Transparency and Recusal in the Federal System*, 30 REV. LITIG. 653 (2011).

Raymond J. McKoski, *Disqualifying Judges When Their Impartiality Might Reasonably Be Questioned: Moving Beyond a Failed Standard*, 56 ARIZ. L. REV. 411 (2014).

Terry A. Maroney, *Emotional Regulation and Judicial Behavior*, 99 CAL. L. REV. 1485 (2011).

Terry A. Maroney, *Angry Judges*, 65 VAND. L. REV. 1207 (2012).

Geoffrey P. Miller, *Bad Judges*, 83 TEX. L. REV. 431 (2004).

Jeremy M. Miller, *Judicial Recusal and Disqualification: The Need for a Per Se Rule on Friendship (Not Acquaintance)*, 33 PEPP. L. REV. 575 (2006).

Nicole E. Negowetti, *Judicial Decisionmaking, Empathy, and the Limits of Perception*, 47 AKRON L. REV. 693 (2014).

Stratos Pahis, *Corruption in Our Courts: What It Looks Like and Where It Is Hidden*, 118 YALE L. J. 1900 (2009).

James Sample, *Supreme Court Recusal from Marbury to Modern Day*, 26 GEO. J. LEGAL ETHICS 95 (2013).

James Sample & Michael Young, *Invigorating Judicial Disqualification: Ten Potential Reforms*, 92 Judicature 26 (July–Aug. 2008).

Jeffrey W. Stempel, *In Praise of Procedurally Centered Judicial Disqualification — And a Stronger Conception of the Appearance Standard: Better Acknowledging and Adjusting to Cognitive Bias, Spoliation, and Perceptual Realities*, 30 REV. LITIG. 733 (2011).

Jeffrey W. Stempel, *Chief William's Ghost: The Problematic Persistence of the Duty to Sit*, 57 BUFF. L. REV. 813 (2009).

Richard C. Tinney, Annotation, *Disqualification of Judge Because of Assault or Threat Against Him by Party or Person Associated with Party*, 25 A.L.R. 4TH 923 (Originally published in 1983).

Andrew J. Wistrich, Jeffrey J. Rachlinski & Chris Guthrie, *Heart Versus Head: Do Judges Follow the Law or Follow Their Feelings?*, 93 TEX. L. REV. 855 (2015).

# Chapter 5

# JUDICIAL ROLES: JUDGING AS CIVIL JURY TRIALS, APPELLATE BRIEFS & ORAL ARGUMENTS DECLINE

I will argue that federal trial courts are now more like administrative agencies than trial courts in their present efforts to discharge their duty to decide cases or controversies, and that we are witnessing the death of an institution whose structure is as old as the Republic.

*United States v. Massachusetts*, 781 F. Supp. 2d 1 (D. Mass. 2011).

In this court's view, the longstanding federal policy favoring arbitration should be revisited. The policy arose during a time when a reasonable percentage of federal cases went to trial and a burgeoning federal case load made arbitration an attractive, less expensive, and quicker form of dispute resolution. Today, it appears that the arbitration dockets may be more congested than the dockets of most federal district courts.

*Cox v. Time Warner Cable, Inc.*, 2013 U.S. Dist. LEXIS 140602, fn 1 (D.S.C. Sept. 30, 2013).

For a number of reasons, it makes sense to mandate the use of appellate mediation services as opposed to making them voluntary. First, many lawyers at the appellate level take the position that there is "no way" their case can settle. Yet, a significant number of these "no way" cases can and do settle. Without court-mandated mediation in these cases, the parties would not have had the opportunity to reach an amicable solution.

Joseph A. Torregrossa, *Appellate Mediation in the Third Circuit-Program Operations: Nuts, Bolts and Practice Tips*, 47 Vill. L. Rev. 1059 (2002).

The drastic reduction in the frequency of oral argument . . . has been driven largely by considerations of efficiency as reflected in the universal adoption of case-screening methods that shunt aside the majority of cases to a summary or non-argument calendar. This separate decisional track involves "a significantly lesser degree of personal attention by judges" by placing "primary reliance for the operation of the screening process on a centrally-organized, parajudicially-supervised group of staff attorneys."

David R. Cleveland & Steven Wisotsky, *The Decline of Oral Argument in the Federal Courts of Appeals: A Modest Proposal for Reform*, 13 J. App. Prac. & Process 119 (2012) (citations omitted).

———

The job description of judges has changed. In the trial court, the trial judge now conducts few civil jury trials. The appellate judge's staff now screens cases before briefs are submitted in mandatory appellate mediation programs. The appellate judge less frequently hears appellate oral arguments. The loss of such traditional judicial roles may be mourned, but others view the changes as a benefit that brings efficiency and savings in time and money and helps to avoid abusive, adversarial practices.

The obituary for the civil jury trials has been written and published widely in court opinions, bar journals, and law reviews over the last few decades. Charts, graphs, and court data all confirm that the number of civil jury trials has diminished in the last decades. Criminal trials and bench trial have declined as well. The "usual suspects" accused of causing this demise of the civil jury trial are typically listed as: alternative dispute resolution, especially arbitration; generous summary judgment standards; the expense of civil discovery and of jury trials; crowded dockets and need for efficiency; poorly conducted jury trials; over-zealous pre-trial litigation; complex litigation likely to overwhelm a jury of lay people; a concern that civil jury trial results are too often unpredictable. Some observers characterize the decline of the civil jury trial as the loss of a uniquely American form of justice, but others view it as a much needed change to an inefficient, overly adversarial system with unreliable results.

In this chapter, a few topics within the decline of the civil jury trial are highlighted. The prominent history and honored place of the American civil jury trial is compared with the concerns of allowing juries to decide complex civil cases. These complex cases and some of the resulting jury verdicts imply to some the incompetence of juries to make reasoned, predictable decisions in the face of, among other cases, complex financial, accounting, and technology issues and intellectual property disputes.

Complex cases and a jury's ability to comprehend the law and facts are one burden or concern raised when a trial judge conducts a civil jury trial rather than conducting a bench trial or enlisting some form of alternative dispute resolution. The "burdens" of the civil jury trial include the costs of empaneling a jury, but also the chores of jury instructions, protecting jurors from outside influences and media, ruling upon evidentiary matters where the rules of evidence are designed to control the jury's passions and prejudices which could result in unsupportable or excessive damages awards.

Thus, one factor in the decline of the civil jury trial is the desire to avoid these burdens of the civil jury trial and save costs through alternative dispute resolution, especially arbitration under the Federal Arbitration Act [FAA] and its state counterparts. *See* Unif. Arbitration Act (2000), 7 U.L.A. (Part IA) (2009). When court systems embraced the FAA and arbitration, however, a range of new concerns emerged. As demonstrated by recent, repeated efforts to enact an Arbitration Fairness Act, "forced" pre-dispute arbitration provisions in employment and consumer disputes may deprive workers and consumers of the benefits of the civil justice system, including a jury trial.

In addition, this chapter traces the thread of alternative dispute resolution and efficiency, as superior to jury trials, into the appellate process. At the appellate level, as well as the trial court level, these goals have changed the role of the appellate judge. Appellate briefs need not be filed and read nor appellate opinions issued if the case is settled on appeal through mediation. Even when an appeal is briefed, appellate oral arguments are the exception, not the rule, in many federal appellate courts and in some state courts as well.

## I.  THE CIVIL JURY TRIAL'S DECLINE

### The Road to Extinction?

* * * *

Although the rates of decline [in civil jury trials] vary from one case type to another, decline is general. There is no major category of cases that is exempt. We think it is fair to say that decline has become institutionalized in the practices and expectations of judges, administrators, lawyers, and parties.

The decline is accompanied by an ideology that explains and promotes it to judges, administrators, lawyers, clients, and policy-makers. Some of the expressions of this ideology are: that the role of judges is to manage and resolve disputes; that adjudication is only one — and not always the optimal — way to do that; that trials are expensive and wasteful; that that ordinarily disputes are preferably resolved by mutual concessions; that settlement benefits parties and the courts themselves; that outsourcing disputes to ADR institutions benefits courts without detriment to parties, and so forth. The trial-avoidance justified by this wisdom is seen to fit the interest of judges in keeping abreast of dockets and the interests of lawyers — both corporate lawyers who can minimize the risk of loss that might discredit them with clients and plaintiff lawyers who want to avoid the pro-defendant tilt of the appellate process.

The decline is self-perpetuating. There are fewer lawyers with extensive trial experience and new lawyers have fewer opportunities to gain such experience (hence, the rise of the trial skills training industry, NITA). As lawyers who ascend into decisionmaking positions have less trial experience, the discomfort and risk of trials looms larger in their decisions. Judges, too, accumulate less trial experience and, in many cases, less appetite for trials.
* * *

Marc Galanter & Angela Frozena, The Continuing Decline of Civil Trials in American Courts, 2011 Forum for State Appellate Court Judges, *The Jury Trial Implosion: The Decline of Trial by Jury and Its Significance for Appellate Courts, Executive Summary* (citations omitted).

# The Supreme Court of Ohio
## 2014 Ohio Courts Statistical Summary

\* \* \* \*

### Courts of Common Pleas

The court of common pleas, the only trial court created by the Ohio Constitution, is established by Article IV, Section 1, of the Constitution and its duties are outlined in Article IV, Section 4.

There is a court of common pleas in each of Ohio's 88 counties. The courts of common pleas have original jurisdiction in all criminal felony cases and original jurisdiction in all civil cases in which the amount in controversy is generally more than $15,000. Courts of common pleas have appellate jurisdiction over the decisions of some state administrative agencies.

Common pleas judges are elected to six-year terms on a nonpartisan ballot. A person must be an attorney with at least six years of experience in the practice of law to be elected or appointed to the court.

The courts of common pleas in most counties across the state have specialized divisions created by statute to which judges are specifically elected in order to hear criminal and civil, domestic relations, juvenile, or probate cases — or some combination of those categories. The use of the term "division" when describing the jurisdictional structure of the various counties' common pleas courts sometimes is at odds with how that term is applied when describing caseload statistics. For ease of description, it is common to group cases by their overall type — that is, by division. For example, when describing caseloads of matters generally grouped together as "domestic relations cases," they may be referred to as "domestic relations division" cases, even though a particular county may not technically have a domestic relations division. The courts of common pleas in Adams, Morgan, Morrow, Noble and Wyandot counties have no divisions and the judges elected to those courts have responsibility over all types of cases that come before the common pleas court. Summary at p. 23.

\* \* \* \*

The complex litigation case type is a special category reserved for civil cases involving novel or complicated issues of law and fact that are not likely to be resolved within the time guidelines established for other cases. A judge assigned to a civil case that meets the criteria prescribed under Sup. R. 42 may reclassify a civil case as a complex litigation case. Accordingly, no cases are filed with the courts as complex litigation cases. Instead, civil cases are first classified under their appropriate case types and then, if applicable, are reclassified as complex litigation cases. Complex litigation cases are rare. Since 2003, on average, approximately one out of every 1,500 civil cases (0.07 percent) in the general divisions of Ohio's common pleas courts are classified each year as complex litigation matters. Summary at p. 25.

* * * *

## Trial Rates

The rate of trials occurring in a court is a useful statistic when assisting courts in understanding the fundamentals of effective caseflow management. Although it is not a measure of a court's performance, per se, this statistic routinely is used by the Supreme Court of Ohio Case Management Section as part of its caseflow management training curriculum.

In order to calculate trial rates, the various termination categories reported by the courts first are separated into termination categories that are truly dispositive of the case and categories that instead simply render the case no longer active for reporting purposes. The number of dispositive terminations are then summed. The resulting sum is divided into the number of trials (either by jury, by court, or both) to produce the trial rate, expressed as a percentage.

It is conventionally understood among court observers at the national level that approximately 2 percent of civil cases and 5 percent of criminal cases ultimately go to trial.

Ohio trial rates fall below those figures. As shown in **Figure 3**, the trial rate for civil cases heard in the common pleas, general division courts in 2014 was 1.3 percent and 2.4 percent for criminal cases. When viewed over the last 10 years, the rates of civil and criminal cases proceeding to trial have declined considerably. Although the overall rates are certainly small regardless of the year, the generally continuing year-to-year decreases can be clearly seen. Summary at p. 29.

FIGURE 3

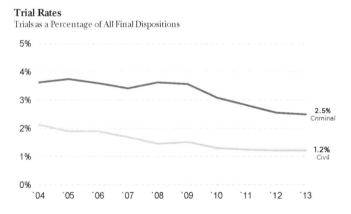

**Trial Rates**
Trials as a Percentage of All Final Dispositions

## II.   SEVENTH AMENDMENT RIGHT TO A CIVIL JURY TRIAL

The loss of the civil jury trial implicates the failure to exercise a right that was vitally important to the founding of the country. The text of the Seventh Amendment reads: "In Suits at common law, where the value in controversy shall exceed twenty dollars, the right of trial by jury shall be preserved, and no fact tried by a jury, shall be otherwise reexamined in any Court of the United States, than according to the rules of the common law." The American civil jury trial was essential to Americans because it mitigated the bias of judges and others who held powerful positions.

\* \* \* \*

### A. The American Commitment to Civil Juries

The comments of the Founders in the late eighteenth century provide repeated reference to the importance early Americans placed on the ideal of the civil jury as a critical check on the power of government. Patrick Henry, speaking in the Virginia Constitutional Convention, called civil juries the "best appendage of freedom," one "which our ancestors secured [with] their lives and property." Thomas Jefferson remarked, "I consider trial by jury as the only anchor ever yet imagined by man, by which a government can be held to the principles of its constitution." Thomas Paine felt civil juries were an extension of a natural right.

\* \* \* \*

"The Federalists opined that eliminating civil jury rights could lead to insurrection. In sum, there was consensus on the importance of civil juries." Kenneth S. Klein, *Is Ashcroft v. Iqbal the Death (Finally) of the "Historical Test" for Interpreting the Seventh Amendment?*, 88 NEB. L. REV. 467 (2010) (citations omitted).

While reverence for the civil jury trial remains, its glory has become tarnished in recent assessments of its value:

> In the United States, there are two very different views of the value of the civil jury. The first is that the civil jury is a cornerstone of democratic government, a protection against incompetent or oppressive judges, and a way for the people to have an active role in the process of justice. The second is that civil juries are inefficient, unpredictable, swayed by sympathy, and incompetent to decide complex cases.

Margaret L. Moses, *What the Jury Must Hear: The Supreme Court's Evolving Seventh Amendment Jurisprudence*, 68 GEO. WASH. L. REV. 183 (2000) (citations omitted).

Over time, the civil jury trial has become more uniquely American because its use in England has been much reduced: "During the twentieth century, the role of the jury was greatly limited in England. The role of the jury in civil cases was severely curtailed in 1933 when the English effectively abolished civil jury trials." Douglas G. Smith, *The Historical and Constitutional Context of Jury Reform*, 25 HOFSTRA L. REV. 377, 417

(1997). Because of this development in England, "the United States presently conducts almost all of the world's civil jury trials." *Id.* at fn 159.

# III.  COMPLEX LITIGATION & CIVIL JURY COMPETENCE

Beginning by the 1970s, large and complex cases began to crowd court dockets. These cases spurred concerns over a "litigation explosion" — an onslaught of cases that were large, in that they involved many parties, and because they arose from complicated business and financial matters, emerging scientific and environmental issues, intellectual property and new technologies, and other issues requiring lengthy discovery and battling experts. Further, such cases could take weeks or months to try and would tie up a jury for so long that few qualified jurors could be retained. The *Boise Cascade* case remains the most frequently cited case on juror competence for its creation of a three-part test to determine the need for a civil jury trial. Most notably, its third part: "the practical abilities and limitations of juries," is a factor listed in *Boise Cascade*, but cited without supporting precedent.

## A.  Jury Competence in Complex Litigation: Federal Court

### IN RE BOISE CASCADE SECURITIES LITIGATION
420 F. Supp. 99 (W.D. Wash. 1976)

SHARP, DISTRICT JUDGE

Before the Court are defendants' motions to strike plaintiffs' jury demands in this securities fraud litigation. The question before the Court is whether these jury demands may be stricken without conflicting with the Seventh Amendment. The Court is of the opinion that the answer is in the affirmative.

I

In simplest terms, this case centers around the acquisition of West Tacoma Newsprint Co. by Boise Cascade Corporation in November 1969. In return for their shares in Newsprint, the stockholders, various publishing companies, received shares of Boise which were listed on the New York Stock Exchange and showed a per share market value at that time of approximately $75.

In 1971 and 1972, Boise was forced to write down its assets for a variety of reasons. The alleged partial effect of these write-downs was a drastic reduction in the price of Boise's shares, to approximately $12.00 per share. In 1972, the Tribune Publishing Co., one of the former shareholders in Newsprint, instituted a civil action alleging various violations of federal and state securities laws by Boise, its accountant, Arthur Andersen & Co., its inside directors and officers and the outside directors. Specifically, plaintiffs charged violations of §§ 12(2) and 17(a) of the Securities Act of 1933, 15 U.S.C.A. §§ 77l (2) and 77q(a); §§ 10(b) and 13(a) of the Securities Exchange Act of 1934, 15 U.S.C.A. §§ 78j(b) and 78m(a) and Rule 10b-5, 17 C.F.R. 240.10b-5; and R.C.W.A. 21.20.010 and 21.20.430. A short time later, similar civil actions were filed by the McClatchy newspapers and the Chronicle Publishing Co. On September 10, 1973, the Judicial Panel on Multi district Litigation ordered these three cases, the West Tacoma Newsprint cases, consolidated for pretrial purposes together with a case from the Eastern District of Missouri, *Lewin, et al. v. Boise Cascade Corp., et al. Lewin* involves a merger of a corporation into Boise at almost the same time Newsprint was acquired and involving the same financial statements of Boise. Most of the claims in *Lewin* are identical to the claims in the West Tacoma Newsprint cases.

Still another civil action was filed in this district in June 1974, by the Longview and World Publishing companies against the same corporate and individual defendants. The allegations in this action are the same as in the other West Tacoma Newsprint cases.

In April 1973, the Court appointed a Special Master to supervise discovery in the West Tacoma Newsprint cases. After the opinion of the Judicial Panel on Multi district Litigation in September 1973, the order of reference was declared to be in full force and effect as to all the cases.

By Order of March 19, 1976, motions by defendants to sever the various cases for trial were denied. The Court granted motions by plaintiffs to consolidate the West Tacoma Newsprint cases for trial but reserved ruling on whether to consolidate the *Lewin* case until the completion of discovery.

Amended complaints were filed in May and June of 1975 in most of the cases. As of this date, it appears that all counsel have expended over 50,000 lawyer man hours in this litigation and that in excess of 900,000 documents have been produced.

A summary of the relevant allegations of misrepresentation and omission would be inadequate in order to show the true nature of this litigation. Instead, the most relevant portion of the complaint in the Chronicle case, paragraph 21, is set forth in full in the Appendix to this Opinion and Order.

## II

Defendants see the number of plaintiffs as a primary problem in managing the trial. They feel that each plaintiff has a different measure of reliance and that it will be necessary to contain the proof of each plaintiff to that particular plaintiff.

The question of reliance is, of course, a vital one in establishing liability under both the state and federal securities laws. This is particularly true under Section 10(b) of the Securities Exchange Act of 1934, 15 U.S.C.A. § 78j(b) and S.E.C. Rule 10b-5. An examination of that factor provides some idea of the difficulties facing the trier of facts in this case.

The materiality of an omission has been held to create a presumption of reliance, or causation, in a securities fraud case. *See Affiliated Ute Citizens of Utah v. United States*, 406 U.S. 128, 153–54 (1972). While reliance may be disproved, the burden placed upon defendants to do so varies according to the context of the transaction. The Ninth Circuit advanced the following rationale for not requiring proof of reliance in an open-market situation:

> Materiality circumstantially establishes the reliance of some market traders and hence the inflation in the stock price when the purchase is made the causational chain between defendant's conduct and plaintiff's loss is sufficiently established to make out a prima facie case.

*Blackie v. Barrack*, 524 F.2d 891, 906 (9th Cir. 1976). Thus, if deception affected the market resulting in damage to a plaintiff, the opportunity to rebut presumed causation has been found to be "virtually meaningless." *Little, et al. v. First California Company, et al.*, 532 F.2d 1302, 1304 (9th Cir. 1976). If presumed causation exists with respect to any facet of this complaint, it will be necessary to determine the character of the transaction in order to determine whether and to what extent the presumption may be disproved.

Both misrepresentations and omissions are alleged in this case, and while the two are not mutually exclusive, *see Little, et al. v. First California Company, et al., supra*, at 1304, the trier of fact may have to analyze each of the allegations in paragraph 21 with respect to each of the parties to determine the character of each transaction.

Other portions of the complaints present complicated concepts that will involve lengthy explanation and documentary evidence.

For example, the complaints allege that Boise failed to make proper provision for discount reserves with respect to its land sales. These reserves would reflect the difference between the interest charged on the unpaid balances on the notes of land purchasers and the then current market rate of interest. The foundation for this will likely require proof that a market rate of interest existed with respect to the land sales in question; the rate or rates charged by Boise; the amount of time that the market rate exceeded the rate actually charged and the amount of interest outstanding at various times. It may also be necessary to present evidence regarding the reasonableness of the rate or rates charged by Boise as well as proof relating to usury laws and state regulations, if any, of land sales and installment purchase contracts.

As another example, plaintiffs claim that Boise chose improper bases for the valuation of assets acquired in corporate acquisitions effected under 26 U.S.C.A. § 334(b)(2). As a result, it is alleged that Boise failed to note that it could be liable for up to $5,000,000 in federal income taxes. One of the issues here would be whether Boise properly accrued potential judgments resulting from litigation with the Internal Revenue Service before a United States District Court and the United States Tax Court. From the testimony produced at a hearing before the Court, it appears the potential tax liabilities may not have been accrued at one time. Rather, a portion of each liability may have been accrued during various stages of the litigations in question in the form of an unpaid tax obligation. It may have been reasonable and proper to determine at the outset of the litigation that it would be likely that no tax would be found owing, but to accrue a portion after an adverse judgment and to accrue the remainder after an unsuccessful appeal. Or, it may be that the entire amount was accrued in increments at various times throughout the litigation.

Other portions of the complaints which present unique and difficult accounting concepts are the following:

> Boise improperly allocated unit land costs to the costs of goods sold so as to understate the costs of goods sold for more desirable lots, overstate the value of the remaining land inventory, and consequently to overstate profits derived from the sale of recreational land.

And also:

> Boise's quarterly financial statements for the first three quarters of each year, including 1969, failed to recognize ratably and proportionately various adjustments made in the fourth quarter and therefore overstated net income for the first three quarters accordingly. The effect of said fourth quarter adjustments was concealed by the device of pooling the financial results of profitable companies acquired by merger during the year.

In addition to the complex accounting and proof questions, there is the very real possibility of substantial prejudice to the defendants due to evidence that Boise settled numerous civil actions brought by the State of California and others alleging improper land development and marketing practices. It is alleged that Boise knew of these practices and their nature and that it failed to maintain a reserve fund to satisfy potential judgments and settlements, as well as also failing to disclose the nature of the practices. Previously, the Court ruled that:

> (p)laintiffs are entitled to prove the cause of the write-down in question. Without proof of the settlement, the precise amount of the write-down itself could not be shown. In this case, the amount of the settlement constitutes a material portion of the write-down and its existence in fact cannot be denied or ignored.

Order of June 23, 1976, at p. 2.

Two questions are presented by this portion of the complaint: First, whether jurors will consider settlement of the California lawsuits in the amount of approximately $50,000,000 an admission of liability and second, if they do, whether they will speculate that liability there is tantamount to proof of fraud with respect to these plaintiffs. The answer to these questions can only be stated with qualification.

Finally, and most important, in order to determine whether liability exists, the fact finder will have to analyze the Boise accounting, not only of the accounts as they existed at the time of the merger, but as the plaintiffs claim they should have existed. It is anticipated that experts for each side will have to go through the accounting techniques and resulting figures in each of the areas complained of in paragraph 21. In all, assets and liabilities in excess of a billion dollars are involved and a period of more than five years will have to be examined.

The validity of the accounting practices will undoubtedly require evidence extrinsic to the accounting sheets. For example, it is alleged that Boise failed to maintain adequate reserves for bad debts in connection with the retail sales of recreational property. It is alleged that those sales were booked for the total purchase price although a minimal down payment was paid by the purchaser. The rest was covered by a note. Deposition testimony indicates that the national recession in the early part of this decade forced many purchasers to default. Thus, the truth or falsity of many of the allegations may have to be determined in the light of economic conditions as they existed a decade ago.

Competing theories of accounting will be presented for all of these matters. It has been suggested that more than one "generally accepted accounting principle" can be applied to a particular booking problem but that not all of those principles fairly reflect the financial condition of the corporation.

In sum, it appears to this Court that the scope of the problems presented by this case is immense. The factual issues, the complexity of the evidence that will be required to explore those issues, and the time required to do so leads to the conclusion that a jury would not be a rational and capable fact finder.

\* \* \* \*

## III

There can be no doubt that jury trials are favored in civil litigation in this country. The combination of the Seventh Amendment and the merger of actions at law and in equity into a single civil action under the Federal Rules of Civil Procedure encourages the use of juries to determine facts. [citations omitted]

However broad this policy may be, the Supreme Court has recognized that the use of juries is not without limits. In *Ross v. Bernard*, the Court set forth three factors which determine the susceptibility of a claim to trial by jury:

> [F]irst, the pre-merger custom with reference to such questions; second the remedy sought; and third, the practical abilities and limitations of juries.

No authority was cited for these three factors. As for the first two, Supreme Court precedent appears so clear as to be obvious. *See, e. g.*, *Parsons v. Bedford*, 28 U.S. (3 Pet.) 433, 447, 7 L. Ed. 732 (1830) (Story, J.). The third part is not explicit from previous opinions.

The procedural safeguards inherent in our legal system provide the impression and fact of fairness to the litigants and society. This is necessary in order to assure obedience to judgments and resort to the legal system as the only sanctioned means of settling disputes in a complex civilized society. Indeed, under the Fifth and Fourteenth Amendments, the legitimacy of government action is measured in terms of fairness.

Central to the fairness which must attend the resolution of a civil action is an impartial and capable fact finder. A properly selected panel of veniremen must generally be presumed to yield an impartial and capable jury. However, at some point, it must be recognized that the complexity of a case may exceed the ability of a jury to decide the facts in an informed and capable manner. When that occurs, the question arises as to whether the right and necessity of fairness is defeated by relegating fact finding to a body not qualified to determine the facts. The third part of the analysis in footnote 10 to the majority opinion in *Ross v. Bernard, supra*, directly recognizes this.

*See also* Kirkham, *Complex Civil Litigation — Have Good Intentions Gone Awry?* 70 F.R.D. 199, 208 (1976).

Of course, the point at which a jury's limitations exceed its abilities is not precise nor is it easy of definition. No single factor alone can dictate that a jury should not hear a case. As in this case, a number of factors must combine to convince the Court that a jury would be incapable of fairly deciding the case.

## IV

It must be apparent that any jury chosen to hear this case will not be a fair cross section of the community at large because of the estimated trial time of four to six months. It would not be unreasonable to excuse prospective jurors from serving in this civil case if they believe that service for that period of time would impair their employment. At the outset, then, the availability of employed persons to serve on this jury is limited. This suggests that at least the appearance of fairness would be diminished, if not eliminated, when a lengthy civil action involving millions of dollars in potential damages in a commercial setting would be heard by jurors who have not had exposure to a contemporary commercial or business environment. This should not be taken to mean that a non-employed person is somehow less able to determine facts. Rather, a basic purpose of the jury, the determination of facts by impartial minds of diverse backgrounds, is defeated if a sizable and significant portion of the community must be excluded from service.

Pointing out the limits of a jury to hear an extended civil action does not answer the problems presented by a particular case unless it can be shown that trial to the Court would be superior.

In addition to the Court's experience in presiding over other complicated cases involving commercial matters, the Court has available to it tools that are unwieldy in the possession of a jury. Among these tools are review of daily transcripts; admission of depositions into evidence instead of reading relevant portions aloud; review of selected portions of testimony from the reporter's notes and flexibility in scheduling trial activities. In addition, the Court is able to study exhibits in depth and carry on colloquies with witnesses, expert and non-expert alike, in an orderly and systematic manner. Of course, this is in addition to the Court's knowledge of the litigation resulting from its review of the record since the cases were filed.

In the light of the limitation of a jury to determine the facts in an informed manner and the ability of the Court to hear and review the evidence in an efficient and effective manner, the Court believes that it would be more capable of fairly deciding the facts.

## V

The Court is of the opinion that the third part to footnote 10 in *Ross v. Bernard*, is of constitutional dimensions. It must be seen as a limitation to or interpretation of the Seventh Amendment. Furthermore, the Court is of the opinion that there is no conflict in this case with any statutory policy favoring trial by jury, 28 U.S.C.A. § 1861, or the Federal Rules of Civil Procedure.

The explosion of litigation in the past two decades in terms both of number of filings and the complexity and scope of many of those cases has led thoughtful minds to wonder whether the judicial system as we now know it can cope with some of these cases. *See, e.g.*, Rifkind, *Are We Asking Too Much of Our Courts?* 70 F.R.D. 96 (1976).

Similarly, thoughtful minds have questioned the expansion of the right to jury trial in complex commercial civil actions. *See* Redish, 70 Nw. U. L. Rev. 486 at 514–530: It has been observed that:

> Any close question and sometimes one that is not so close is resolved in favor of the jury trial right without serious analysis of history, precedent, or policy. Shapiro and Coquillette, *The Fetish of Jury Trial in Civil Cases: A Comment on Rachal v. Hill*, 85 Harv. L. Rev. 442 (1971).

While it is true that the Supreme Court has favored jury trial in the cases where it has reviewed the issue, the opinions are not totally consistent. *Compare Ross v. Bernard, supra, with Katchen v. Landy*, 382 U.S. 323, 339 (1966).

With these thoughts in mind, the necessity for the appearance and fact of fairness dictate that the motions now before the Court be GRANTED.

\* \* \* \*

The *Boise Cascade* court found the complex issues arising from federal securities fraud litigation would surpass a jury's competence over the course of a four to six months trial. At times, however, such complex, large securities fraud actions do go to the jury. Thus, the lawyers and judges must take on the burdens of a civil jury trial, including drafting jury instructions that the jury will comprehend.

What follows is a one set of instructions out of 39 proposed jury instructions for a litigation that like *Boise* Cascade, was also based upon alleged false or misleading statements under Section 10(b) of the Securities Exchange Act.

## ALLIANZ RISK TRANSFER AG v. PARAMOUNT PICTURES CORPORATION

No. 1:08-CV-10420 (TPG) (S.D.N.Y. Oct. 7, 2014)

Defendant's Proposed Jury Instructions

\* \* \* \*

Proposed Instruction No. 18

Introduction to Plaintiffs' Claims

I will now instruct you on the law that governs Plaintiffs' claims in this case.

Plaintiffs seek to recover money damages related to their lending money to, and receiving interests in, an entity called Melrose Investors LLC, which I will refer to simply as "Melrose." Melrose invested the funds lent to it by the Plaintiffs and other lenders in 25 films produced and distributed by Paramount between April 2004 and March 2006. I will refer to the slate of films in which Melrose invested Plaintiffs' funds as the "Melrose Slate."

Plaintiffs loaned money to Melrose by purchasing Class B Bonds, and two of the four Plaintiffs also purchased membership interests in Melrose. Because bonds and membership interests are both kinds of securities, I will refer to Plaintiffs' interests in Melrose as the "Melrose Securities." Plaintiffs claim that in order to induce Paramount to purchase the Melrose Securities, Paramount made false statements regarding the manner in which the films in the Melrose Slate would be financed. In particular, Plaintiffs allege that Paramount misrepresented its intentions to seek co-financing in the form of foreign pre-sales for the films in a manner consistent with its historical practice.

Paramount argues that it did not make any false or misleading statements regarding co-financing of the films or foreign pre-sales and that, in any event, Plaintiffs could not have relied on any such statements because, among other things, Plaintiffs received accurate information about the actual levels of co-financing and foreign pre-sales before making their investments. Paramount also argues that, even if it had engaged in co-financing, including foreign pre-sales, for the Melrose Slate at the levels Plaintiffs urge they should have, the Plaintiffs would not have recouped any more money because the films in the slate were unsuccessful at the box office.

Plaintiffs have brought two claims against Paramount. They allege that Paramount defrauded them in violation of Section 10(b) of the Securities Exchange Act of 1934, a federal statute, and New York State law.

It is for you, the Jury, to decide whether each of the Plaintiffs has proven its claims against Paramount. I will now describe the elements of these claims in greater detail.

PROPOSED INSTRUCTION NO. 19

Burden of Proof — Section 10(b)

As I mentioned to you, Plaintiffs have brought two claims against Paramount. For each of the claims, Plaintiffs have the burden of proof. I'll explain to you the burden of proof that Plaintiffs must meet for each of their claims.

Plaintiffs first claim is that Paramount violated Section 10(b) of the Securities Exchange Act of 1934 and Rule 10b-5 of the Securities and Exchange Commission. I will use "Section 10(b)" to refer to this claim.

Plaintiffs have the burden of proving each element of their Section 10(b) claim by a preponderance of the evidence. This means that Plaintiffs have the burden of proving by a preponderance of the evidence each and every disputed element of their claim under the federal securities laws. If you find that Plaintiffs have failed to establish any element of their Section 10(b) claim by a preponderance of the evidence, you must decide against them on that claim.

To establish a fact by a preponderance of the evidence means to prove that the fact is more likely true than not true. A preponderance of the evidence means the greater weight of the evidence. It does not mean the greater number of witnesses or the greater length of time taken by either side. This phrase refers to the quality of the evidence, that is, its persuasiveness, the weight, and the effect that it has on your minds. In determining whether a claim has been proven by a preponderance of the evidence, you may consider the relevant testimony of all witnesses, regardless of who may have called them, and all the relevant exhibits received in evidence, regardless of who may have produced them.

The concept of preponderance of the evidence is often illustrated with the idea of scales. In considering whether Plaintiffs have met their burden of proof on a claim, you put on one side all of the credible evidence favoring the Plaintiffs and on the other side all the credible evidence favoring the Defendant. If the scales tip towards the Plaintiffs because Plaintiffs' evidence is weightier, you must find in the Plaintiffs' favor. But if the scales are evenly balanced (maybe yes or maybe no), or if they tip in the Defendant's favor, then you must find for the Defendant.

* * * *

## PROPOSED INSTRUCTION NO. 20

### Elements of Section 10(b) Claim

To prevail on their Section 10(b) claim against Paramount, Plaintiffs must prove each of the following elements by a preponderance of the evidence in connection with their purchase of Melrose Securities:

*First*, that the Defendant made an untrue statement of fact.

*Second*, that the Defendant's misstatement was material.

*Third*, that the material misstatement was made with a particular state of mind, called "scienter," which means that the Defendant acted with an intent to defraud.

*Fourth*, that the Plaintiffs justifiably relied upon Defendant's material misstatement when deciding to buy Melrose Securities.

*Fifth*, that Defendant's material misstatement directly, or proximately, caused Plaintiffs' losses.

*Sixth*, that Plaintiffs suffered damages.

If any of the four Plaintiffs fails to prove any one of these elements, then you must return a verdict against that particular Plaintiff.

PROPOSED INSTRUCTION NO. 21

Element One: Misstatement

To satisfy the first element of their Section 10(b) claim against the Defendant, Plaintiffs must prove by a preponderance of the evidence that the Defendant made a false or misleading statement of fact.

A misstatement is a statement of fact to investors that was false or misleading at the time it was made. Even if subsequent events render a past statement to be incorrect with the benefit of hindsight, that does not mean the statement was false or misleading when it was made.

You will be asked if the Defendant, as to each of the Plaintiffs, made an untrue statement of fact. You should only answer "Yes" if you unanimously find that at least one statement was untrue. Further, you must unanimously agree on which statement(s) meets this criteria. If you do not unanimously agree on a particular statement, then the Plaintiffs have not met their burden of proof and you must find that the Defendant did not violate the securities laws.

PROPOSED INSTRUCTION NO. 22

The Making of a Misstatement — Section 10(b)

Paramount may only be liable for a misstatement that Paramount made.

To satisfy the misstatement element of their claim against Paramount, Plaintiffs must show that Paramount actually made a misstatement to the Plaintiffs or that Paramount had ultimate authority or control over a false statement that was correctly attributed to Paramount at the time of its dissemination to Plaintiffs.

One example that judges have used to describe this second principle (where Paramount itself did not speak directly to a Plaintiff) is to point to the relationship between a speechwriter and a speaker. Even though the speechwriter is the one who drafts a speech ahead of time, the person who delivers the speech — the speaker — is the one who has control over what is ultimately said. For the purposes of Section 10(b), then, it is the speaker who "makes" the statements in the speech, not the speechwriter. Thus again, if Paramount did not actually make the false statement to a Plaintiff, it can only be liable for it if the statement was directly attributed to Paramount and Paramount had the ultimate authority or control over it.

Paramount and Melrose are two separate and independent companies. Therefore, statements made by Melrose and over which Paramount did not have ultimate control cannot be attributed to Paramount. The same is true as to Merrill Lynch. Statements made by Merrill Lynch over which Paramount did not have ultimate control cannot be attributed to Paramount.

\* \* \* \*

## PROPOSED INSTRUCTION NO. 24

### Element Two: Materiality

If you find that Plaintiffs have established by a preponderance of the evidence that Paramount made a misstatement of fact, you must next determine whether Plaintiffs have established by a preponderance of the evidence that the misstatement was material.

In determining whether a misstatement of fact is material, you should consider whether there is a substantial likelihood that a reasonable lender would have considered it important when deciding to buy Melrose Securities. Notice that you are being asked to think about what would be important to a reasonable lender and not necessarily to Plaintiffs. If you believe that Plaintiffs would have considered a misstatement of fact material but you do not believe a reasonable lender would have, then the misstatement is not material. In other words, each Plaintiff must show that disclosure of the information would have significantly altered the total mix of information made available and assumed actual significance in the deliberations of reasonable lenders when deciding to purchase Melrose Securities. You may consider each Plaintiff's conduct in determining whether information would have been material to reasonable lenders in deciding whether to purchase Melrose Securities.

The total mix of information includes information reasonably available to purchasers of securities, such as newspaper articles, public reports, websites, information from their advisors, and data provided to Plaintiffs by Merrill Lynch. If you find that correct information was already available to Plaintiffs with enough intensity and credibility to counter-balance any misleading impression of the alleged misstatement, then the allegedly misstatement cannot be material.

In addition, vague, broad, or non-specific statements of optimism are too general for a reasonable lender to rely on and are not material. General statements that a company is "optimistic" about its products, or that it has a "positive outlook and remains confident," are examples of "puffery" that cannot form the basis of a fraud claim under the federal securities laws.

You will be asked if any statement which you found to be false or misleading was also material. You should only answer "Yes" as to a misstatement if you unanimously agree that such misstatement was material. If you do not unanimously agree that a particular misstatement was material, then Plaintiffs have not met their burden of proof and you must find that the Defendant did not violate the securities laws.

## PROPOSED INSTRUCTION NO. 25

### Element Three: State of Mind or "Scienter"

To satisfy the third element of their Section 10(b) claim, Plaintiffs must prove by a preponderance of evidence that the Defendant acted with a particular state of mind, known as "scienter."

Scienter is a mental state embracing the intent to deceive, manipulate, or defraud. To show scienter, Plaintiffs must prove by a preponderance of the evidence that Paramount made a material misstatement with either: (a) actual knowledge that the statement was false or misleading, or (b) reckless disregard for whether the statement was true.

"Actual knowledge" means to act intentionally and deliberately. "Reckless disregard" means to engage in conduct that is highly unreasonable and represents an extreme departure from the standards of ordinary care. A person acts in reckless disregard if the falsity of the statement was either known to him at the time, or so obvious that it must have been known. Recklessness is more than simple, or even inexcusable, gross negligence. Therefore, it is not enough for Plaintiffs to show that a Defendant acted accidentally, mistakenly, or negligently. Instead, recklessness requires a state of mind approximating actual intent.

Even if a statement turns out to be false or misleading with the benefit of hindsight, the statement cannot have been made with intent to defraud if the Defendant had a good faith belief in the truth of the statement when it was made. In order for Plaintiffs to meet their burden, they must identify specific information that Paramount had at the time it made an alleged misstatement that contradicted the statement. Plaintiffs cannot carry their burden by showing that further investigation would have produced new data that contradicted Defendant's statements.

Similarly, the fact that a Defendant's interpretation of information or data may have differed from other reasonable interpretations is insufficient to prove scienter. To establish fraud, Plaintiffs must prove that Paramount believed it was making a false or misleading statement about the existing information or data. If Paramount's interpretation of data was made in good faith, the fact that the interpretation differed from other reasonable (or even better) interpretations is not enough to show fraud.

For you to find that Paramount, a corporation, had the required state of mind, Plaintiffs must prove that a natural person who is acting on behalf of Paramount made a material misrepresentation with scienter while acting within the scope of his or her authority, and that the act (and accompanying mental state) are attributable to Paramount. To meet this standard, the individual must have been a significant participant in the decision-making process at Paramount that was the subject of the statement. The mental state of others who were not acting on behalf of Paramount is not attributable to Paramount. If you do not find that at least one natural person had the required state of mind when making a materially false or misleading statement to the Plaintiffs, you must return a verdict for the Defendant.

PROPOSED INSTRUCTION NO. 26

Element Four: Justifiable Reliance

To establish the fourth element of their Section 10(b) claim, the reliance requirement, Plaintiffs must prove by a preponderance of the evidence that they both actually and justifiably relied on Defendant's alleged material misstatements.

In order to establish this element, each Plaintiff must prove that it was aware of Paramount's alleged misstatement, and purchased Melrose Securities based on that specific statement. If you find that Plaintiffs would have engaged in the transaction anyway, such that the alleged misrepresentation had no effect on each Plaintiff's decision to purchase the Melrose Securities, then there was no reliance and there can be no recovery.

Plaintiffs' reliance also must be reasonable or justified. Plaintiffs cannot satisfy this element if they acted unjustifiably in that they knew the truth or knew that the statement was false, or if Plaintiffs refused to investigate concerning the circumstances of the transaction in disregard of a known risk.

In assessing the reasonableness of a Plaintiff's alleged reliance, you should consider the entire context of the transaction, including factors such as the transaction's complexity and magnitude, the sophistication of the parties, and the content of any agreements between them. No single factor is determinative and all the relevant factors should be considered in determining whether Plaintiffs' reliance was justified.

If you find that Plaintiffs failed to prove either actual or justifiable reliance by a preponderance of the evidence, or if Paramount rebutted Plaintiffs' claim of reliance, then Plaintiffs have not met their burden of proof and you must return a verdict for the Defendant.

## PROPOSED INSTRUCTION NO. 27

### Element Five: Loss Causation

To satisfy the fifth element of their Section 10(b) claim, known as "loss causation," Plaintiffs must prove by a preponderance of the evidence that there was a direct causal link between a material misstatement made with intent to defraud and Plaintiffs' economic loss. Plaintiffs must establish that the losses suffered by Plaintiffs was either a direct result or foreseeable consequence of the materialization of a risk concealed by a material misstatement — here, an alleged misstatement about the use of a particular type of co-financing for the Melrose Slate known as foreign pre-sales.

It is not enough for Plaintiffs to recover if they merely show that Paramount's actions caused them to purchase Melrose Securities, or that they would have acted differently had they know the truth. In particular, if you determine that Paramount's level of use of foreign pre-sales did not cause Plaintiffs' losses, or that factors other than Paramount's level of use of foreign pre-sales caused Plaintiffs' losses, then those losses cannot be said to have occurred by reason of Paramount's actions, and Plaintiffs have not satisfied this element.

If Plaintiffs have failed to show loss causation, or if Paramount rebutted Plaintiffs' claim of loss causation, then Plaintiffs have not met their burden of proof and you must return a verdict for Paramount.

PROPOSED INSTRUCTION NO. 28

Element Six: Damages

If you find that Plaintiffs have not proven each and every one of the previous five elements of their Section 10(b) claim with respect to any statement made by Paramount, then you must return a verdict for Paramount and should not consider damages. If you find that Plaintiffs have proven each of the previous five elements against Paramount, then you will need to consider the question of damages. I will now instruct you how to calculate damages with the express caution that you must not understand this to be any indication from me that you should award any damages.

Plaintiffs have the burden of proving damages by a preponderance of the evidence. Any damages awarded to Plaintiffs must be limited to the direct and foreseeable results of the alleged fraudulent conduct, and must be limited to the actual damages suffered by Plaintiffs. In other words, damages are limited to those resulting from the injury alleged and proved (here, Paramount's level of use of foreign pre-sales), and the amount awarded should be precisely commensurate with the injury suffered.

The typical calculation for damages under Section 10(b) is the out-of-pocket calculation, which measures actual damages to Plaintiffs. To determine Plaintiffs' out-of-pocket damages, you must calculate the difference between the amount of money that Plaintiffs lost and the amount they would have lost if Paramount had engaged in the level of foreign pre-sales that Plaintiffs assert Paramount stated it would engage in. Plaintiffs are not entitled to recover damages for loss that was not caused by Paramount's failure to engage in foreign pre-sales to the level Plaintiffs claim it should have.

Please remember: the mere fact that I am instructing you how to calculate damages should not be taken as an indication in any way that I believe the Plaintiffs are entitled to damages, or that you should in fact make such an award.

\* \* \* \*

Two weeks after the proposed jury instructions were submitted, the judge ruled upon several motions *in limine* at the eve of the civil jury trial. *Allianz Risk Transfer AG v. Paramount Pictures Corp.*, 2014 U.S. Dist. LEXIS 152973, n.1 (S.D.N.Y. Oct. 21, 2014). In ruling, the judge noted that the motions *in limine* were "briefed on the basis that the matter would be tried before a jury." Yet, "[n]o timely jury demand had, in fact, been made, and plaintiffs contractually waived their right to a jury trial in a Subscription Agreement. Accordingly, this matter will proceed before the bench."

Once the "burden" of a civil jury trial was lifted, the judge indicated that other burdens of time pressure and pending motions were eliminated. The fact that there would be a bench trial, "renders some of what is covered in the *in limine* motions irrelevant, and eliminates the immediate time pressure as to other motions (because, in effect, the Court can admit the evidence and sort through it as the case proceeds, based on a fuller record)." *Id.*

## B.   Jury Competence in Complex Litigation: State Court

Federal courts were not alone in facing the onslaught of complex litigation. State constitutions, like the federal constitution, guarantee the right to a civil jury trial. In both court systems, the analysis frequently compares the abilities and competencies of the jury with those of the judge. Both systems must calibrate how great their level of trust is in the ordinary citizen juror to hear and determine complicated issues over the course of a long trial.

### RIEFF v. EVANS
672 N.W.2d 728 (Iowa 2003)

LARSON, JUSTICE.

The defendants appeal and the plaintiff cross-appeals from a district court ruling on the plaintiff's demand for a jury trial. The district court granted a jury trial as to one issue, but denied it as to another. The defendants were granted an interlocutory appeal, and the plaintiff cross-appealed. We affirm on the defendants' appeal, reverse on the plaintiff's cross-appeal, and remand for further proceedings.

I. *Facts and Prior Proceedings.*

This plaintiff, representing shareholders of Allied Mutual Insurance Company (Mutual), sued various parties, including Allied Group, Inc. (Group), and several individuals for damages arising out of alleged mismanagement of Mutual's financial affairs. According to the petition, Mutual conveyed to Group assets worth more than $900,000,000 for $126,000,000. Until 1985 Group was a totally dependent subsidiary of Mutual. However, in 1985 a transaction began a process that "would ultimately result in a role reversal between Mutual and Group." The plaintiff contends this role reversal benefited the directors, Group, and Group's shareholders at the expense of Mutual's shareholders and policyholders.

The plaintiff's petition asserted both direct and derivative claims. Counts I through V are clearly derivative claims, as to which there is no right to a jury trial, and those counts are not involved in this appeal. Count VI incorporated by reference the factual allegations of the first five counts and asserted a class-action claim for "de facto" conversion by the defendants. Count VII is a class-action claim for breach of fiduciary duty. The defendants filed motions to dismiss, which the court sustained as to all eight counts. We reversed as to Counts I to VII in *Rieff v. Evans*, 630 N.W.2d 278, 295 (Iowa 2001) (*Rieff I*), and remanded the case to the district court.

Following the remand, the defendants filed a motion to strike the plaintiff's jury demand under Counts VI and VII. They argue first that these counts raise equitable issues, as to which the plaintiff has no right to a jury trial. They further argue that, even if those counts are at law, they present such complexity that any right to a jury trial must yield to the defendants' right to due process. They base this argument on their interpretation of *Weltzin v. Nail*, 618 N.W.2d 293 (Iowa 2000). The district court denied the motion to strike the jury demand on Count VI, but sustained it as to Count VII.

## II. *The Complexity Issue.*

The defendants contend the claims in this case are so complex they cannot competently be resolved by a jury, despite this constitutional assurance of jury trials:

> The right of trial by jury shall remain inviolate; but the general assembly may authorize trial by a jury of a less number than twelve in inferior courts; but no person may be deprived of life, liberty, or property, without due process of law.

Iowa Const. art. I, § 9. A comparable right to a jury trial is found in the Seventh Amendment of the United States Constitution: "The right of trial by jury shall be preserved . . . ."

We said in *Rieff* I that "[t]his appeal is from a case with many issues, parties, attorneys, claims, counts, and legal theories." *Rieff* I, 630 N.W.2d at 282. The defendants portray an even more daunting picture of the case:

> In her 36-page, 104-paragraph Amended Petition, Plaintiff challenges in excess of ten separate, complex financial transactions that took place over an eight-year period between 1985 and 1993. These challenged transactions include a "pooling agreement" between Allied Mutual, Allied Group, and other affiliated organizations; administration of the pooling agreement; a leveraged employee stock ownership plan (ESOP); executive equity incentive plans; stock options; the formation and acquisition of various business entities; "corporate opportunities;" and restructuring. The various complex concepts foreign to lay people encompassed in these transactions include mutual insurance company governance issues, corporate debt, funding and initial public offerings, equity, premium to surplus and gross leverage ratios, expense ratios, loss ratios, combined ratios, underwriting, pooling and inter-company operating agreements, conflicts of interest, corporate restructuring, tender offers, return on premium, risk-based capital, and preferred versus common stock. As to each of the challenged transactions, Plaintiff seeks an accounting to determine the consideration exchanged between the parties.

The defendants add that, because the plaintiff seeks over $500,000,000 in damages, complex valuations at various times during an eight-year time period would be required. They estimate they alone have produced more than 100,000 pages of documents; the plaintiff has issued subpoenas to eight nonparty actuarial and accounting entities, and additional voluminous documents will be produced. They estimate the trial will last at least twelve weeks. In view of these assertions, we assume, for purposes of this appeal, this is truly a "complex" case.

We first address the claim by the defendants that we have already recognized a complex-litigation exception in *Weltzin* in which we said:

> [T]his court recognizes that in a shareholder's derivative suit a judge is simply better equipped to hear the complicated corporation and duty claims
>     . . . .

> . . . Moreover, allowing this type of complex case to be adjudicated by a jury may actually *offend* Iowa's constitutional mandate of due process under article I, section 9 [of the Iowa Constitution].

618 N.W.2d at 301–02 (citations omitted).

*Weltzin* did not, as the defendants urge, establish a general complexity exception to the constitutional right to a jury trial. In *Weltzin* we said, "[t]he derivative suit exists only in equity." 618 N.W.2d at 297. The statement from *Weltzin* about complexity gives additional reasons why bench trials might be better than jury trials in derivative actions. This language merely supports what was already the rule: derivative actions are to be tried in equity. It was not necessary to the holding of the case and was therefore dictum. Although we reject the argument that *Weltzin* establishes a general complex-litigation exception to the constitutional right to a jury trial, the question remains whether we will, independently of the *Weltzin* language, adopt a complexity exception.

As one court has observed, the "practical considerations [presented in complex litigation] diminish in importance when they come in conflict with the constitutional right to a jury in civil cases." *In re U.S. Financial Securities Litigation*, 609 F.2d 411, 416 (9th Cir. 1979) (applying Seventh Amendment right to jury under Federal Constitution). Cases recognizing a complex-litigation exception to the right to a jury trial sometimes rely on this language in a footnote in *Ross v. Bernhard*, 396 U.S. 531 (1970):

> As our cases indicate, the "legal" nature of an issue is determined by considering, first, the pre-merger custom with reference to such questions; second, the remedy sought; and, third, *the practical abilities and limitations of juries*. Of these factors, the first, requiring extensive and possibly abstruse historical inquiry, is obviously the most difficult to apply.

*Ross*, 396 U.S. at 538 n.10 (emphasis added). In *In re Financial Securities*, 609 F.2d at 425–26, the court discussed the general criticism that has been levied against the *Ross* footnote and noted widespread refusal of courts to follow it. The court said:

> While the Supreme Court has never specifically repudiated the third factor in the *Ross* footnote, it has never met with general acceptance by the courts. In the *Ross* decision itself, the court did not consider the practical abilities and limitations of juries. And, although the Supreme Court has considered the Seventh Amendment question in depth on at least five occasions since *Ross*, the abilities of juries have never been considered. The subsequent decisions have all relied upon the traditional historical test.

*Id.* (footnotes omitted).

We believe *Financial Securities* accurately assessed the *Ross* footnote. The court in *Financial Securities* said:

> While it is unclear as to what was meant by the inclusion of the third factor [in *Ross*, "the practical abilities and limitations of juries"], we do not believe that it stated a rule of constitutional dimensions. After employing an historical test

for almost 200 years, it is doubtful that the Supreme Court would attempt to make such a radical departure from its prior interpretation of a constitutional provision in a footnote.

*In re U.S. Financial Securities*, 609 F.2d at 425.

The Supreme Court's great solicitude for jury trials is illustrated by this language in *Dimick v. Schiedt*, 293 U.S. 474, 486 (1935):

> Maintenance of the jury as a fact-finding body is of such importance and occupies so firm a place in our history and jurisprudence that any seeming curtailment of the right to a jury trial should be scrutinized with the utmost care.

Of course, the footnote in *Ross*, which considered the United States Constitution's Seventh Amendment, is not binding on us in our assessment of Iowa's constitution. Nevertheless, we have considered these federal cases interpreting the Seventh Amendment with respect to a complexity exception, and we adopt the reasoning of cases such as *In re Financial Securities* in applying our own jury-trial constitutional provision.

The defendants have not demonstrated that, as a general rule, a judge may be expected to do a better job of trying the issues in a complex case. In fact, as the court said in *Financial Securities*:

> The assumption that attorneys cannot develop and present complex cases to a jury underestimates the abilities of the bar, especially the experienced and capable counsel associated with the present litigation. Whether a case is tried to a jury or to a judge, the task of the attorney remains the same. The attorney must organize and assemble a complex mass of information into a form which is understandable to the uninitiated. In fact, one judge has suggested attorneys may do a better job of trying complex cases to a jury than to a judge.

*In re U.S. Financial Securities*, 609 F.2d at 427 (citing Patrick E. Higginbotham, *Continuing the Dialogue: Civil Juries and the Allocation of Judicial Power*, 56 Tex. L. Rev. 47, 54–55 (1977)). Oversight by a judge is available in various ways, including summary judgments, directed verdicts, new trials, judgments notwithstanding the verdict, and orders for remittitur and additur. In addition, no definitive criteria for boundaries are established to identify "simple," "complex but not too complex," and "too complex" for juries. *See SRI Int'l v. Matsushita Elec. Corp.*, 775 F.2d 1107, 1127 n.3 (Fed. Cir. 1985). Based on these reasons and the weight of authority in other jurisdictions, we reject the defendants' request for recognition of a "complex litigation" exception to the constitutional right to a trial by jury. We affirm on the defendants' appeal.

* * * *

The *Boise Cascade* and *Weitzen* cases both admit the difficulty of defining "complex litigation" that places a case beyond the reach of a jury. Both cases would present a jury with financial computations and with "unique and difficult" accounting issues. The federal court decision considered the inability to retain a cross section of jurors able to serve for an extended time and also to be capable of comprehending the nature of commercial business accounting. The Iowa court found a jury was as capable as a judge in rendering a decision on complex financial computations and concluded that no definitive criteria existed to recognize when a case is "too complex."

## C.   Civil Jury Trial: Accompanying "Burdens"

A jury facing complex cases beyond their capability is one of many problems derived from conducting a civil trial using a jury. Juries and jurors create a host of additional responsibilities. These responsibilities create new realities, distinct from a bench trial or granting a dispositive motion. They include the costs of seating a jury, disputes arising from jury selection, the need for proper jury instructions, the protections afforded juries through rules of evidence, juries, swayed by emotion, may award excessive damages; juries may be improperly "tainted" by using social media during the trial.

In the case that follow, "a simple slip-and-fall negligence action" tried to a civil jury created nearly a dozen grounds for appeal. These grounds were all related to conducting a civil jury trial.

* * * *

## RICHARDSON v. BODDIE-NOELL ENTERPRISES, INC.
### 2003 U.S. App. LEXIS 21860 (4th Cir. Oct. 27, 2003)

PER CURIAM.

This appeal arises from a simple slip-and-fall negligence action. After a trial, a jury awarded Ernest E. Richardson $647,000 in compensatory damages for injuries that he sustained when he fell on a wet tile floor in a Hardee's restaurant owned by Boddie-Noell, Incorporated. Boddie-Noell appeals several of the district court's rulings. We affirm.

I.

On July 25, 2000, Richardson slipped on some wet tile in the entrance of a Hardee's restaurant in Louisa, Virginia. Richardson fell and severely injured his back and left shoulder. Richardson filed suit in Virginia state court, and Boddie-Noell removed the case to the United States District Court for the Western District of Virginia, based on the parties' diverse citizenship. See 28 U.S.C.A. §§ 1332 (West 1993), 1441 (West 1994).

During voir dire, Richardson used all four of his peremptory challenges to exclude men from the venire. Boddie-Noell objected, claiming that Richardson was unconstitutionally striking men from the venire solely because of their gender. At the district court's request, Richardson offered gender-neutral explanations for the use of his challenges. Richardson explained that he challenged two of the men because they were engineers, who, in his experience, tend to recreate evidence rather than evaluate the evidence produced at trial. He challenged a third man because the man had once slipped and fallen in the parking lot of a business without commencing a lawsuit. The final challenge was against a man who did not make eye contact with trial counsel and who seemed disinterested in the proceedings. Boddie-Noell alleged that these reasons were pretextual but presented no evidence of pretext except that Richardson had challenged only men. The district court accepted Richardson's explanations and allowed the case to proceed to trial, stating that "nongender reason[s] [had been] given."

In a pretrial order, the district court granted Boddie-Noell partial summary judgment, ruling that Richardson could not recover damages for lost profits from his genetic cattle business or for a diminution in the sale price of his tractor business, because those damages were not proximately caused by his fall. During the trial, when Boddie-Noell was presenting its defense, a Boddie-Noell employee testified that he had placed an orange cone in the area of the accident *before* mopping it. The district court had earlier sustained an objection and refused to let Richardson testify that he had observed the Boddie-Noell employee place a warning sign in the area of the accident *after* his fall. In rebuttal, Richardson renewed his effort to admit that testimony. Boddie-Noell again objected, but this time the district court overruled the objection and allowed the testimony. The district court gave the jury the following limiting instruction:

> I caution you that the evidence at this point is admitted only insofar as it goes to the credibility of previous — maybe it would go to whether previous witnesses were telling the truth. It may not be considered by you as evidence that there was any danger out there or not. You can only consider whether or not you use this evidence coming in now as to whether a previous witness was telling the truth, and it has to do with when the cones were there.
>
> You can't decide the cones were not there based on this evidence.

(J.A. at 185–86.)

During the course of the trial, Boddie-Noell also objected to testimony related to Richardson's inability to work at his tractor business and his farm. The district court excluded evidence related to Richardson's loss of income, but allowed Richardson to testify about the various physical activities that he no longer could perform.

Richardson's counsel made several procedural errors during the trial, made inappropriate comments and gestures in the presence of the jury, and attempted to elicit inadmissible testimony from multiple witnesses. The district court repeatedly reprimanded Richardson's trial counsel for his inappropriate behavior and instructed the jury to disregard counsel's inappropriate questions and comments. At one point, Boddie-Noell moved for dismissal because of Richardson's counsel's misconduct. The district court apparently took the motion under advisement, without ruling on it, and the trial continued.

After the jury returned its verdict for Richardson, Boddie-Noell moved for a new trial, relief from the verdict, and renewed its motion for dismissal of the action, alleging that Richardson's misconduct had inflamed the jury. Boddie-Noell also alleged that the damage award was excessive. The district court denied the motions, and Boddie-Noell now appeals to this court. We have jurisdiction to hear Boddie-Noell's appeal from the district court's final judgment. 28 U.S.C.A. § 1291 (West 1993). We address each of Boddie-Noell's arguments in turn.

## II.

### A.

Boddie-Noell first requests a new trial on the basis that Richardson used his peremptory challenges to remove only men from the venire in violation of Boddie-Noell's constitutional rights as recognized in *J.E.B. v. Alabama ex rel. T.B.*, 511 U.S. 127, 130–31(1994). *See United States v. Tipton*, 90 F.3d 861, 881 (4th Cir. 1996) (recognizing that Fifth Amendment provides comparable protections in federal court); *Edmonson v. Leesville Concrete Co., Inc.*, 500 U.S. 614, 623–27 (1991) (holding that private litigants in civil cases may not use peremptory challenges in a discriminatory manner). Because *J.E.B.* is based on the same logic and reasoning as *Batson v. Kentucky*, 476 U.S. 79 (1986), our cases addressing *Batson* claims are instructive here.

We have held that once a litigant offers a legitimate gender-neutral explanation for the use of his peremptory strikes, the burden lies with the party challenging the strikes "to show *both* that these reasons were merely pretextual *and* that [gender] was the real reason for the strike." *United States v. McMillon*, 14 F.3d 948, 953 (4th Cir. 1994).

"A trial court's determination regarding the exercise of a peremptory challenge for allegedly . . . discriminatory reasons is accorded great deference on appeal." *Davis v. Baltimore Gas & Elec. Co.*, 160 F.3d 1023, 1026–27 (4th Cir. 1998). "In the typical peremptory challenge inquiry, the decisive question will be whether counsel's [gender]-neutral explanation for a peremptory challenge should be believed." *Hernandez v. New York*, 500 U.S. 352, 365 (1991) (plurality opinion). Assessing the credibility of a litigant's gender-neutral explanation is "peculiarly within the trial judge's province." *Id.; accord McMillon*, 14 F.3d at 953. Accordingly, we will not disturb a district court's *Batson* ruling unless it is clearly erroneous. *Davis*, 160 F.3d at 1026.

In this case, Boddie-Noell asserts that the district court clearly erred when it denied Boddie-Noell's challenge to Richardson's use of his peremptory strikes. Upon a review of the record, we disagree. After following the requisite procedure, the district court accepted Richardson's gender-neutral explanations as non-pretextual. Boddie-Noell points to nothing in the record, other than the statistical fact that Richardson challenged only men, to support its assertion that a contrary finding was required. Given Boddie-Noell's inability to produce evidence demonstrating that gender-based discrimination was the motivating force for the strike, the district court's rejection of the discrimination challenge was not clearly erroneous. *See McMillon*, 14 F.3d at 953.

### B.

Boddie-Noell next argues that the district court made two separate evidentiary errors. We review a district court's rulings on the admissibility of evidence for abuse of discretion. *United States v. Whittington*, 26 F.3d 456, 465 (4th Cir. 1994).

Boddie-Noell first claims that the district court erred by allowing Richardson to testify that he observed a Boddie-Noell employee placing a warning sign in the area where he had fallen after the accident. They argue that this evidence of a subsequent remedial measure was offered to prove that Boddie-Noell was negligent, and thus should have been excluded under Federal Rule of Evidence 407. Rule 407 prohibits the admission of evidence of remedial measures taken after an accident "to prove negligence, culpable conduct, . . . or a need for a warning or instruction." Fed. R. Evid. 407. Such evidence is admissible, however, if "offered for another purpose, such as . . . impeachment." *Id.*

Boddie-Noell's argument ignores the limiting instruction given by the court prior to Richardson's testimony. The court admonished the jury that it could consider the evidence only to determine "whether previous witnesses were telling the truth," and not as evidence of whether "there was any danger out there or not." Rule 407 explicitly endorses the admission of evidence of subsequent remedial measures for impeachment purposes, and Richardson's testimony clearly impeached the testimony of a Boddie-Noell employee who claimed to have installed a warning cone *before* Richardson fell. As "[w]e must presume that the jury heeded [the limiting] instruction," *United States v. Silva*, 745 F.2d 840, 844 (4th Cir. 1984), we hold that the district court's admission of Richardson's testimony for impeachment purposes was not an abuse of discretion.

Boddie-Noell also avers that the district court improperly admitted irrelevant and prejudicial evidence of Richardson's inability to perform certain work-related activities. Richardson testified about his inability to perform various physical activities, such as breaking cattle and loading and unloading tractors from the back of a truck, since the accident. (J.A. at 78–79.) Boddie-Noell argues that this testimony was irrelevant because it only showed economic losses to Richardson's tractor and genetic cattle businesses, losses that the district court excluded as items of damage in a summary judgment. This argument has no merit. Richardson's testimony tended to show the extent of his physical injuries and his mental suffering, both of which are appropriate items of damage under Virginia law. *See, e.g., Chesapeake & Potomac Tel. Co. of Va. v. Carless*, 127 Va. 5, 102 S.E. 569, 572 (1920). The testimony was thus clearly relevant, *see* Fed. R. Evid. 401, and had little tendency, if any, to result in "unfair prejudice, confusion of the issues, or misleading the jury." Fed. R. Evid. 403. The district court therefore did not abuse its discretion by finding as much.

C.

Boddie-Noell also challenges the district court's denial of its motion to dismiss Richardson's claim because of his attorney's misconduct at trial. Federal Rule of Civil Procedure 41(b) gives district courts the power to involuntarily dismiss an action" [f]or failure of the plaintiff . . . to comply with [the Federal R]ules [of Civil Procedure] or any order of court." Fed. R. Civ. P. 41(b). We have noted that involuntary dismissal under Rule 41(b) "is such a harsh sanction . . . [that] it should be resorted to only in extreme cases." *McCargo v. Hedrick*, 545 F.2d 393, 396 (4th Cir. 1976) (quotation marks omitted). We thus require a district court to consider four factors when deciding whether to involuntarily dismiss an action for attorney misconduct. *Id.* First, the court must consider the "degree of personal responsibility on the part of the plaintiff." *Id.* Second, it must determine the "amount of prejudice to the defendant." *Id.* Third, it must look to the record to see if it indicates "a drawn out history of deliberately proceeding in a dilatory fashion." *Id.* Finally, the court must consider whether "sanctions less drastic than dismissal" will be effective. *Id.* Applying these factors, the district court concluded "that this case is not a situation which warrants the severe sanction of involuntary dismissal." (J.A. at 203.) We review a district court's denial of a Rule 41(b) motion to dismiss for abuse of discretion. *See McCargo*, 545 F.2d at 396.

Richardson's trial counsel admitted that he did not "know the Federal Rules of Civil Procedure, or the Federal Rules of Evidence, as well as [he] should." (J.A. at 200). We agree with the district court that counsel's errors were "frustrating," to say the least. (J.A. at 203). Despite the bungling, Richardson's trial counsel's misconduct was not so egregious as to warrant the severe sanction of dismissal. *See McCargo*, 545 F.2d at 396. The district court reprimanded Richardson's counsel after each misstep, and when necessary, instructed the jury to disregard his inappropriate questions and comments. The district court concluded that, by taking these actions, it had "adequately dealt with counsel's behavior," (J.A. at 203), and we agree. District Judge Moon did an extraordinary job of dealing with a difficult attorney, and, rather than demonstrating an abuse of discretion, his rulings and admonitions demonstrate an admirable balance of sternness and patience. We hold that the district court did not abuse his discretion by using "sanctions less drastic than dismissal" to remedy Richardson's trial counsel's misconduct. *See McCargo*, 545 F.2d at 396.

### D.

Boddie-Noell also assigns as error the district court's refusal to relieve it from the jury's verdict in light of the misconduct of Richardson's counsel. Federal Rule of Civil Procedure 60(b)(3) gives district courts the power to relieve a party from an adverse judgment because of "fraud . . . misrepresentation, or other misconduct of an adverse party." Fed. R. Civ. P. 60(b)(3). To prevail on a Rule 60(b)(3) motion, "the moving party must have a meritorious defense; . . . the moving party must prove misconduct by clear and convincing evidence; and . . . the misconduct [must have] prevented the moving party from fully presenting its case." *Schultz v. Butcher*, 24 F.3d 626, 630 (4th Cir. 1994). For example, we have granted Rule 60(b)(3) motions in cases in which one party failed to produce evidence essential to an adversary's position. *See id.; Green v. Foley*, 856 F.2d 660 (4th Cir. 1988); *Square Constr. Co. v. Wash. Metro. Area Transit Auth.*, 657 F.2d 68 (4th Cir. 1981). We review a district court's denial of a Rule 60(b)(3) motion for abuse of discretion. *Schultz*, 24 F.3d at 630.

The district court properly refused to relieve Boddie-Noell from the jury's verdict. Although Richardson's counsel behaved inappropriately, his misconduct did not prevent Boddie-Noell from fully presenting its case. *See Schultz*, 24 F.3d at 630. In short, the district court properly concluded that Richardson's misconduct was not the type that justifies relief under Rule 60(b)(3), because it did not "metaphorically tie one hand behind the back of the defendant." (J.A. at 204–205.)

E.

Finally, Boddie-Noell contends that the district court erred by refusing to set aside the jury's verdict as excessive and order a new trial. Because Virginia substantive law governed Richardson's claim for relief, we also apply Virginia law to determine whether the jury award was excessive. *Gasperini v. Ctr. for Humanities*, 518 U.S. 415, 437–438 (1996); *Steinke v. Beach Bungee, Inc.*, 105 F.3d 192, 197 (4th Cir. 1997). "[C]ourts of appeals engage in review of district court excessiveness determinations applying 'abuse of discretion' as their standard." *Gasperini*, 518 U.S. at 435, 116 S. Ct. 2211.

Under Virginia law, jury verdicts are excessive if they " 'shock the conscience of the court and . . . create the impression that the jury has been influenced by passion, corruption or prejudice, or has misconceived or misunderstood the facts or the law, or if the award is so out of proportion to the injuries suffered to suggest that it is not the product of a fair and impartial decision.' " *Norfolk Beverage Co. v. Cho*, 259 Va. 348, 354, 525 S.E.2d 287 (2000) (quoting *Smithey v. Sinclair Refining Co.*, 203 Va. 142, 122 S.E.2d 872, 875–76 (1961)). " 'If the verdict merely appears to be large and more than the trial judge would have awarded had he been a member of the jury, it ought not to be disturbed, for to do so the judge must then do what he may not legally do, that is, substitute his judgment for that of the jury.' " *Id.* (quoting *Smithey*, 122 S.E.2d at 875–76). "[T]here is no exact method by which to measure and value in monetary terms the degree of pain and anguish of a suffering human being, and, unless the jury's verdict is so great as to indicate its judgment was actuated by partiality or prejudice, the court should not disturb the verdict." *Virginia Elec. and Power Co. v. Dungee*, 258 Va. 235, 520 S.E.2d 164, 180 (1999).

In light of Richardson's injuries, we cannot say that the district court abused its discretion by finding that the jury's verdict did not shock its conscience. At trial, the evidence demonstrated that Richardson had permanently lost some range of motion in his arm. Richardson testified that he had been in constant, substantial pain since the fall and was planning on having corrective surgery because he could no longer deal with the pain. The surgery would leave him unable to engage in strenuous physical activity and unable fully to turn his head. Richardson is no longer able to work in the tractor business or to raise and break cattle.

Although we recognize that the verdict in this case is substantial, our job is not to review the record and come to an independent conclusion about how much damage Richardson sustained. The district court was not permitted to "substitute [its] judgment for that of the jury," *Norfolk Beverage*, 525 S.E.2d at 290, and neither are we. In light of the Virginia Supreme Court's recent decision upholding a jury verdict of $20,000,000 in favor of a burn victim who had incurred no medical expenses,3 the jury's $647,000 verdict in this case "is [not] so great as to indicate its judgment was actuated by partiality or prejudice." *Virginia Elec.*, 520 S.E.2d at 180; *see also Salih v. Lane*, 244 Va. 436, 423 S.E.2d 192, 197 (1992) (upholding a compensatory damage award of $1,200,000 to a woman who suffered "irreparable damage to some of the nerves that c[a]me out of [her] neck and [went] . . . down into [her] arm" and heart arrhythmia). We conclude that the district court did not abuse its discretion in finding that the award was not excessive.

III.

For the foregoing reasons, we affirm the judgment of the district court.

[footnotes omitted]

----------

Although not articulated in the *Richardson* opinion, the costs of "hosting" a jury is also a burden. One cost-cutting solution is to reduce the size of the jury:

> Because of dire economic conditions, the court system in California is facing drastic cuts. Governor Brown's May revision of 2012 calls for the court system to endure $544 million in cuts. The effects of these cuts have already been dramatic and devastating. Los Angeles County has closed 56 courtrooms and laid off numerous employees, including long-time court referees. San Diego has likewise announced the closing of branch courtrooms and the laying-off of 250 employees. Bailiffs in civil courtrooms have been replaced by courtroom attendants in Los Angeles and Orange counties. The court system is in turmoil.

> In light of the demands placed upon the court system, this article explores the possibility of reducing the size of civil and misdemeanor juries in California. The historical and legal bases of the twelve-person jury are discussed, and the ramifications of such a change are provided.

Kirk H. Nakamura, *Six Happy Jurors*, 54 Orange County Law. 20 (Nov. 2012).

## IV.    THE RISE OF ALTERNATIVE DISPUTE RESOLUTION: ARBITRATION

Alternative dispute resolution is a broad term and can simply be defined as resolving a dispute outside the court system. Many alternative processes are included, but in recent decades, arbitration and mediation have emerged as the dominant forms.

What began as "widespread judicial hostility" toward arbitration at the start of the twentieth century steadily evolved into favoritism toward arbitration by the start of the twenty-first century. The Federal Arbitration Act [FAA] began to combat this hostility through the Act's broad scope of coverage. State courts also saw the movement to arbitration as a majority of state legislatures adopted a form of the Uniform Arbitration Act.

> The FAA was enacted in 1925 in response to widespread judicial hostility to arbitration agreements. Section 2, the "primary substantive provision of the Act," provides, in relevant part, as follows:

> > "A written provision in any maritime transaction or a contract evidencing a transaction involving commerce to settle by arbitration a controversy thereafter arising out of such contract or transaction . . . shall be valid, irrevocable, and enforceable, save upon such grounds as exist at law or in equity for the revocation of any contract." 9 U.S.C. § 2.

We have described this provision as reflecting both a "liberal federal policy favoring arbitration," and the "fundamental principle that arbitration is a matter of contract."

*AT & T Mobility v. Concepcion*, 563 U.S. 333 (2012) (citations omitted).

The embrace of arbitration appears most prominently in contractual agreements that govern employment and consumer goods. Typically, the agreement to arbitrate disputes is in place well before any dispute arises.

# CIRCUIT CITY STORES, INC. v. ADAMS
## 532 U.S. 105 (2001)

Justice Kennedy delivered the opinion of the Court.

Section 1 of the Federal Arbitration Act (FAA or Act) excludes from the Act's coverage "contracts of employment of seamen, railroad employees, or any other class of workers engaged in foreign or interstate commerce." 9 U.S.C. § 1. All but one of the Courts of Appeals which have addressed the issue interpret this provision as exempting contracts of employment of transportation workers, but not other employment contracts, from the FAA's coverage. A different interpretation has been adopted by the Court of Appeals for the Ninth Circuit, which construes the exemption so that all contracts of employment are beyond the FAA's reach, whether or not the worker is engaged in transportation. It applied that rule to the instant case. We now decide that the better interpretation is to construe the statute, as most of the Courts of Appeals have done, to confine the exemption to transportation workers.

I

In October 1995, respondent Saint Clair Adams applied for a job at petitioner Circuit City Stores, Inc., a national retailer of consumer electronics. Adams signed an employment application which included the following provision:

"I agree that I will settle any and all previously unasserted claims, disputes or controversies arising out of or relating to my application or candidacy for employment, employment and/or cessation of employment with Circuit City, *exclusively* by final and binding *arbitration* before a neutral Arbitrator. By way of example only, such claims include claims under federal, state, and local statutory or common law, such as the Age Discrimination in Employment Act, Title VII of the Civil Rights Act of 1964, as amended, including the amendments of the Civil Rights Act of 1991, the Americans with Disabilities Act, the law of contract and [the] law of tort." App. 13 (emphasis in original).

Adams was hired as a sales counselor in Circuit City's store in Santa Rosa, California.

Two years later, Adams filed an employment discrimination lawsuit against Circuit City in state court, asserting claims under California's Fair Employment and Housing Act, Cal. Govt. Code Ann. § 12900 *et seq.* (West 1992 and Supp. 1997), and other claims based on general tort theories under California law. Circuit City filed suit in the United States District Court for the Northern District of California, seeking to enjoin the state-court action and to compel arbitration of respondent's claims pursuant to the FAA, 9 U.S.C. §§ 1–16. The District Court entered the requested order. Respondent, the court concluded, was obligated by the arbitration agreement to submit his claims against the employer to binding arbitration. An appeal followed.

While respondent's appeal was pending in the Court of Appeals for the Ninth Circuit, the court ruled on the key issue in an unrelated case. The court held the FAA does not apply to contracts of employment. See *Craft v. Campbell Soup Co.*, 177 F.3d 1083 (C.A.9 1999). In the instant case, following the rule announced in *Craft*, the Court of Appeals held the arbitration agreement between Adams and Circuit City was contained in a "contract of employment," and so was not subject to the FAA. 194 F.3d 1070 (C.A.9 1999). Circuit City petitioned this Court, noting that the Ninth Circuit's conclusion that all employment contracts are excluded from the FAA conflicts with every other Court of Appeals to have addressed the question. [citations omitted] We granted certiorari to resolve the issue. 529 U.S. 1129 (2000).

## II

### A.

Congress enacted the FAA in 1925. As the Court has explained, the FAA was a response to hostility of American courts to the enforcement of arbitration agreements, a judicial disposition inherited from then-longstanding English practice.[citations omitted] To give effect to this purpose, the FAA compels judicial enforcement of a wide range of written arbitration agreements. The FAA's coverage provision, § 2, provides that:

> "[a] written provision in any maritime transaction or a contract evidencing a transaction involving commerce to settle by arbitration a controversy thereafter arising out of such contract or transaction, or the refusal to perform the whole or any part thereof, or an agreement in writing to submit to arbitration an existing controversy arising out of such a contract, transaction, or refusal, shall be valid, irrevocable, and enforceable, save upon such grounds as exist at law or in equity for the revocation of any contract." 9 U.S.C. § 2.

We had occasion in *Allied-Bruce, supra*, at 273–277, to consider the significance of Congress' use of the words "involving commerce" in § 2. The analysis began with a reaffirmation of earlier decisions concluding that the FAA was enacted pursuant to Congress' substantive power to regulate interstate commerce and admiralty, see *Prima Paint Corp. v. Flood & Conklin Mfg. Co.*, 388 U.S. 395, 405 (1967), and that the Act was applicable in state courts and pre-emptive of state laws hostile to arbitration, see *Southland Corp. v. Keating*, 465 U.S. 1 (1984). Relying upon these background principles and upon the evident reach of the words "involving commerce," the Court interpreted § 2 as implementing Congress' intent "to exercise [its] commerce power to the full." *Allied-Bruce, supra*, at 277.

The instant case, of course, involves not the basic coverage authorization under § 2 of the Act, but the exemption from coverage under § 1. The exemption clause provides the Act shall not apply "to contracts of employment of seamen, railroad employees, or any other class of workers engaged in foreign or interstate commerce." 9 U.S.C. § 1. Most Courts of Appeals conclude the exclusion provision is limited to transportation workers, defined, for instance, as those workers " 'actually engaged in the movement of goods in interstate commerce.' " *Cole, supra*, at 1471. As we stated at the outset, the Court of Appeals for the Ninth Circuit takes a different view and interprets the § 1 exception to exclude all contracts of employment from the reach of the FAA. This comprehensive exemption had been advocated by *amici curiae* in *Gilmer*, where we addressed the question whether a registered securities representative's employment discrimination claim under the Age Discrimination in Employment Act of 1967, 81 Stat. 602, as amended, 29 U.S.C. § 621 *et seq.*, could be submitted to arbitration pursuant to an agreement in his securities registration application. Concluding that the application was not a "contract of employment" at all, we found it unnecessary to reach the meaning of § 1. See *Gilmer, supra*, at 25, n.2. There is no such dispute in this case; while Circuit City argued in its petition for certiorari that the employment application signed by Adams was not a "contract of employment," we declined to grant certiorari on this point. So the issue reserved in *Gilmer* is presented here.

### B.

Respondent, at the outset, contends that we need not address the meaning of the § 1 exclusion provision to decide the case in his favor. In his view, an employment contract is not a "contract evidencing a transaction involving interstate commerce" at all, since the word "transaction" in § 2 extends only to commercial contracts. See *Craft*, 177 F.3d at 1085 (concluding that § 2 covers only "commercial deal[s] or merchant's sale[s]"). This line of reasoning proves too much, for it would make the § 1 exclusion provision superfluous. If all contracts of employment are beyond the scope of the Act under the § 2 coverage provision, the separate exemption for "contracts of employment of seamen, railroad employees, or any other class of workers engaged in . . . interstate commerce" would be pointless. See, *e.g.*, *Pennsylvania Dept. of Public Welfare v. Davenport*, 495 U.S. 552, 562 (1990) ("Our cases express a deep reluctance to interpret a statutory provision so as to render superfluous other provisions in the same enactment"). The proffered interpretation of "evidencing a transaction involving commerce," furthermore, would be inconsistent with *Gilmer v. Interstate/Johnson Lane Corp.*, 500 U.S. 20 (1991), where we held that § 2 required the arbitration of an age discrimination claim based on an agreement in a securities registration application, a dispute that did not arise from a "commercial deal or merchant's sale." Nor could respondent's construction of § 2 be reconciled with the expansive reading of those words adopted in *Allied-Bruce*, 513 U.S., at 277, 279–280. If, then, there is an argument to be made that arbitration agreements in employment contracts are not covered by the Act, it must be premised on the language of the § 1 exclusion provision itself.

Respondent, endorsing the reasoning of the Court of Appeals for the Ninth Circuit that the provision excludes all employment contracts, relies on the asserted breadth of the words "contracts of employment of . . . any other class of workers engaged in . . . commerce." Referring to our construction of § 2's coverage provision in *Allied-Bruce*

— concluding that the words "involving commerce" evidence the congressional intent to regulate to the full extent of its commerce power — respondent contends § 1's interpretation should have a like reach, thus exempting all employment contracts. The two provisions, it is argued, are coterminous; under this view the "involving commerce" provision brings within the FAA's scope all contracts within the Congress' commerce power, and the "engaged in . . . commerce" language in § 1 in turn exempts from the FAA all employment contracts falling within that authority.

This reading of § 1, however, runs into an immediate and, in our view, insurmountable textual obstacle. Unlike the "involving commerce" language in § 2, the words "any other class of workers engaged in . . . commerce" constitute a residual phrase, following, in the same sentence, explicit reference to "seamen" and "railroad employees." Construing the residual phrase to exclude all employment contracts fails to give independent effect to the statute's enumeration of the specific categories of workers which precedes it; there would be no need for Congress to use the phrases "seamen" and "railroad employees" if those same classes of workers were subsumed within the meaning of the "engaged in . . . commerce" residual clause. The wording of § 1 calls for the application of the maxim *ejusdem generis*, the statutory canon that "[w]here general words follow specific words in a statutory enumeration, the general words are construed to embrace only objects similar in nature to those objects enumerated by the preceding specific words." 2A N. Singer, Sutherland on Statutes and Statutory Construction § 47.17 (1991); see also *Norfolk & Western R. Co. v. Train Dispatchers*, 499 U.S. 117, 129 (1991). Under this rule of construction the residual clause should be read to give effect to the terms "seamen" and "railroad employees," and should itself be controlled and defined by reference to the enumerated categories of workers which are recited just before it; the interpretation of the clause pressed by respondent fails to produce these results.

Canons of construction need not be conclusive and are often countered, of course, by some maxim pointing in a different direction. The application of the rule *ejusdem generis* in this case, however, is in full accord with other sound considerations bearing upon the proper interpretation of the clause. For even if the term "engaged in commerce" stood alone in § 1, we would not construe the provision to exclude all contracts of employment from the FAA. Congress uses different modifiers to the word "commerce" in the design and enactment of its statutes. The phrase "affecting commerce" indicates Congress' intent to regulate to the outer limits of its authority under the Commerce Clause. See, *e.g., Allied-Bruce*, 513 U.S. at 277. The "involving commerce" phrase, the operative words for the reach of the basic coverage provision in § 2, was at issue in *Allied-Bruce*. That particular phrase had not been interpreted before by this Court. Considering the usual meaning of the word "involving," and the pro-arbitration purposes of the FAA, *Allied-Bruce* held the "word 'involving,' like 'affecting,' signals an intent to exercise Congress' commerce power to the full." *Ibid.* Unlike those phrases, however, the general words "in commerce" and the specific phrase "engaged in commerce" are understood to have a more limited reach. In *Allied-Bruce* itself the Court said the words "in commerce" are "often-found words of art" that we have not read as expressing congressional intent to regulate to the outer limits of authority under the Commerce Clause. *Id.*, at 273; see also *United States v. American Building Maintenance Industries*, 422 U.S. 271, 279–280 (1975) (phrase "engaged in commerce" is "a term of art, indicating a limited assertion of federal jurisdiction"); *Jones v. United States*, 529 U.S. 848, 855 (2000) (phrase "used in commerce" "is most sensibly read to mean active employment for commercial purposes, and not merely a passive, passing, or past connection to commerce").

It is argued that we should assess the meaning of the phrase "engaged in commerce" in a different manner here, because the FAA was enacted when congressional authority to regulate under the commerce power was to a large extent confined by our decisions. See *United States v. Lopez*, 514 U.S. 549, 556 (1995) (noting that Supreme Court decisions beginning in 1937 "ushered in an era of Commerce Clause jurisprudence that greatly expanded the previously defined authority of Congress under that Clause"). When the FAA was enacted in 1925, respondent reasons, the phrase "engaged in commerce" was not a term of art indicating a limited assertion of congressional jurisdiction; to the contrary, it is said, the formulation came close to expressing the outer limits of Congress' power as then understood. [citations omitted]. Were this mode of interpretation to prevail, we would take into account the scope of the Commerce Clause, as then elaborated by the Court, at the date of the FAA's enactment in order to interpret what the statute means now.

A variable standard for interpreting common, jurisdictional phrases would contradict our earlier cases and bring instability to statutory interpretation. The Court has declined in past cases to afford significance, in construing the meaning of the statutory jurisdictional provisions "in commerce" and "engaged in commerce," to the circumstance that the statute predated shifts in the Court's Commerce Clause cases. In *FTC v. Bunte Brothers, Inc.*, 312 U.S. 349 (1941), the Court rejected the contention that the phrase "in commerce" in § 5 of the Federal Trade Commission Act, 38 Stat. 719, 15 U.S.C. § 45, a provision enacted by Congress in 1914, should be read in as expansive a manner as "affecting commerce." See *Bunte Bros., supra*, at 350–351. We entertained a similar argument in a pair of cases decided in the 1974 Term concerning the meaning of the phrase "engaged in commerce" in § 7 of the Clayton Act, 38 Stat. 731, 15 U.S.C. § 18, another 1914 congressional enactment. See *American Building Maintenance, supra*, at 277–283; *Gulf Oil Corp. v. Copp Paving Co.*, 419 U.S. 186, 199–202 (1974). We held that the phrase "engaged in commerce" in § 7 "means engaged in the flow of interstate commerce, and was not intended to reach all corporations engaged in activities subject to the federal commerce power." *American Building Maintenance, supra*, at 283, 95 S. Ct. 2150; cf. *Gulf Oil, supra*, at 202 (expressing doubt as to whether an "argument from the history and practical purposes of the Clayton Act" could justify "radical expansion of the Clayton Act's scope beyond that which the statutory language defines").

The Court's reluctance to accept contentions that Congress used the words "in commerce" or "engaged in commerce" to regulate to the full extent of its commerce power rests on sound foundation, as it affords objective and consistent significance to the meaning of the words Congress uses when it defines the reach of a statute. To say that the statutory words "engaged in commerce" are subject to variable interpretations depending upon the date of adoption, even a date before the phrase became a term of art, ignores the reason why the formulation became a term of art in the first place: The plain meaning of the words "engaged in commerce" is narrower than the more open-ended formulations "affecting commerce" and "involving commerce." See, *e.g., Gulf Oil, supra,* at 195 (phrase "engaged in commerce" "appears to denote only persons or activities within the flow of interstate commerce"). It would be unwieldy for Congress, for the Court, and for litigants to be required to deconstruct statutory Commerce Clause phrases depending upon the year of a particular statutory enactment.

In rejecting the contention that the meaning of the phrase "engaged in commerce" in § 1 of the FAA should be given a broader construction than justified by its evident language simply because it was enacted in 1925 rather than 1938, we do not mean to suggest that statutory jurisdictional formulations "necessarily have a uniform meaning whenever used by Congress." *American Building Maintenance Industries, supra,* at 277. As the Court has noted: "The judicial task in marking out the extent to which Congress has exercised its constitutional power over commerce is not that of devising an abstract formula." *A.B. Kirschbaum Co. v. Walling,* 316 U.S. 517, 520 (1942). We must, of course, construe the "engaged in commerce" language in the FAA with reference to the statutory context in which it is found and in a manner consistent with the FAA's purpose. These considerations, however, further compel that the § 1 exclusion provision be afforded a narrow construction. As discussed above, the location of the phrase "any other class of workers engaged in . . . commerce" in a residual provision, after specific categories of workers have been enumerated, undermines any attempt to give the provision a sweeping, open-ended construction. And the fact that the provision is contained in a statute that "seeks broadly to overcome judicial hostility to arbitration agreements," *Allied-Bruce,* 513 U.S., at 272–273, which the Court concluded in *Allied-Bruce* counseled in favor of an expansive reading of § 2, gives no reason to abandon the precise reading of a provision that exempts contracts from the FAA's coverage.

In sum, the text of the FAA forecloses the construction of § 1 followed by the Court of Appeals in the case under review, a construction which would exclude all employment contracts from the FAA. While the historical arguments respecting Congress' understanding of its power in 1925 are not insubstantial, this fact alone does not give us basis to adopt, "by judicial decision rather than amendatory legislation," *Gulf Oil, supra,* at 202, an expansive construction of the FAA's exclusion provision that goes beyond the meaning of the words Congress used. While it is of course possible to speculate that Congress might have chosen a different jurisdictional formulation had it known that the Court would soon embrace a less restrictive reading of the Commerce Clause, the text of § 1 precludes interpreting the exclusion provision to defeat the language of § 2 as to all employment contracts. Section 1 exempts from the FAA only contracts of employment of transportation workers.

C.

As the conclusion we reach today is directed by the text of § 1, we need not assess the legislative history of the exclusion provision. See *Ratzlaf v. United States,* 510 U.S. 135, 147–148 (1994) ("[W]e do not resort to legislative history to cloud a statutory text that is clear"). We do note, however, that the legislative record on the § 1 exemption is quite sparse. Respondent points to no language in either Committee Report addressing the meaning of the provision, nor to any mention of the § 1 exclusion during debate on the FAA on the floor of the House or Senate. Instead, respondent places greatest reliance upon testimony before a Senate subcommittee hearing suggesting that the exception may have been added in response to the objections of the president of the International Seamen's Union of America. See Hearing on S. 4213 and S. 4214 before a Subcommittee of the Senate Committee on the Judiciary, 67th Cong., 4th Sess., 9 (1923). Legislative history is problematic even when the attempt is to draw inferences from the intent of duly appointed committees of the Congress. It becomes far more so when we consult sources still more steps removed from the full Congress and speculate upon the significance of the fact that a certain interest group sponsored or opposed particular legislation. Cf. *Kelly v. Robinson,* 479 U.S. 36, 51, n.13 (1986) ("[N]one of those statements was made by a Member of Congress, nor were they included in the official Senate and House Reports. We decline to accord any significance to these statements"). We ought not attribute to Congress an official purpose based on the motives of a particular group that lobbied for or against a certain proposal — even assuming the precise intent of the group can be determined, a point doubtful both as a general rule and in the instant case. It is for the Congress, not the courts, to consult political forces and then decide how best to resolve conflicts in the course of writing the objective embodiments of law we know as statutes.

Nor can we accept respondent's argument that our holding attributes an irrational intent to Congress. "Under petitioner's reading of § 1," he contends, "those employment contracts *most* involving interstate commerce, and thus most assuredly within the Commerce Clause power in 1925 . . . are *excluded* from [the] Act's coverage; while those employment contracts having a less direct and less certain connection to interstate commerce . . . would come *within* the Act's affirmative coverage and would not be excluded." Brief for Respondent 38 (emphases in original).

We see no paradox in the congressional decision to exempt the workers over whom the commerce power was most apparent. To the contrary, it is a permissible inference that the employment contracts of the classes of workers in § 1 were excluded from the FAA precisely because of Congress' undoubted authority to govern the employment relationships at issue by the enactment of statutes specific to them. By the time the FAA was passed, Congress had already enacted federal legislation providing for the arbitration of disputes between seamen and their employers, see Shipping Commissioners Act of 1872, 17 Stat. 262. When the FAA was adopted, moreover, grievance procedures existed for railroad employees under federal law, see Transportation Act of 1920, §§ 300–316, 41 Stat. 456, and the passage of a more comprehensive statute providing for the mediation and arbitration of railroad labor disputes was imminent, see Railway Labor Act of 1926, 44 Stat. 577, 46 U.S.C. § 651 (repealed). It is reasonable to assume that Congress excluded "seamen" and "railroad employees" from the FAA for the simple reason that it did not wish to unsettle established or developing statutory dispute resolution schemes covering specific workers.

As for the residual exclusion of "any other class of workers engaged in foreign or interstate commerce," Congress' demonstrated concern with transportation workers and their necessary role in the free flow of goods explains the linkage to the two specific, enumerated types of workers identified in the preceding portion of the sentence. It would be rational for Congress to ensure that workers in general would be covered by the provisions of the FAA, while reserving for itself more specific legislation for those engaged in transportation. See *Pryner v. Tractor Supply Co.*, 109 F.3d at 358 (Posner, C. J.). Indeed, such legislation was soon to follow, with the amendment of the Railway Labor Act in 1936 to include air carriers and their employees, see 49 Stat. 1189, 45 U.S.C. §§ 181–188.

### III

Various *amici*, including the attorneys general of 21 States, object that the reading of the § 1 exclusion provision adopted today intrudes upon the policies of the separate States. They point out that, by requiring arbitration agreements in most employment contracts to be covered by the FAA, the statute in effect pre-empts those state employment laws which restrict or limit the ability of employees and employers to enter into arbitration agreements. It is argued that States should be permitted, pursuant to their traditional role in regulating employment relationships, to prohibit employees like respondent from contracting away their right to pursue state-law discrimination claims in court.

It is not our holding today which is the proper target of this criticism. The line of argument is relevant instead to the Court's decision in *Southland Corp. v. Keating*, 465 U.S. 1 (1984), holding that Congress intended the FAA to apply in state courts, and to pre-empt state antiarbitration laws to the contrary. See *id.*, at 16.

The question of *Southland's* continuing vitality was given explicit consideration in *Allied-Bruce*, and the Court declined to overrule it. 513 U.S., at 272; see also *id.*, at 282 (O'CONNOR, J., concurring). The decision, furthermore, is not directly implicated in this case, which concerns the application of the FAA in a federal, rather than in a state, court. The Court should not chip away at *Southland* by indirection, especially by the adoption of the variable statutory interpretation theory advanced by the respondent in the instant case. Not all of the Justices who join today's holding agreed with *Allied-Bruce*, see 513 U.S., at 284 (SCALIA, J., dissenting); *id.*, at 285 (THOMAS, J., dissenting), but it would be incongruous to adopt, as we did in *Allied-Bruce*, a conventional reading of the FAA's coverage in § 2 in order to implement proarbitration policies and an unconventional reading of the reach of § 1 in order to undo the same coverage. In *Allied-Bruce* the Court noted that Congress had not moved to overturn *Southland*, see 513 U.S., at 272; and we now note that it has not done so in response to *Allied-Bruce* itself.

Furthermore, for parties to employment contracts not involving the specific exempted categories set forth in § 1, it is true here, just as it was for the parties to the contract at issue in *Allied-Bruce*, that there are real benefits to the enforcement of arbitration provisions. We have been clear in rejecting the supposition that the advantages of the arbitration process somehow disappear when transferred to the employment context. See *Gilmer*, 500 U.S., at 30–32. Arbitration agreements allow parties to avoid the costs of litigation, a benefit that may be of particular importance in employment litigation, which often involves smaller sums of money than disputes concerning commercial contracts. These litigation costs to parties (and the accompanying burden to the courts) would be compounded by the difficult choice-of-law questions that are often presented in disputes arising from the employment relationship, cf. *Egelhoff v. Egelhoff, post*, at 1316–1317 (2001) (noting possible "choice-of-law problems" presented by state laws affecting administration of Employment Retirement Income Security Act of 1974 plans), and the necessity of bifurcation of proceedings in those cases where state law precludes arbitration of certain types of employment claims but not others. The considerable complexity and uncertainty that the construction of § 1 urged by respondent would introduce into the enforceability of arbitration agreements in employment contracts would call into doubt the efficacy of alternative dispute resolution procedures adopted by many of the Nation's employers, in the process undermining the FAA's proarbitration purposes and "breeding litigation from a statute that seeks to avoid it." *Allied-Bruce, supra*, at 275. The Court has been quite specific in holding that arbitration agreements can be enforced under the FAA without contravening the policies of congressional enactments giving employees specific protection against discrimination prohibited by federal law; as we noted in *Gilmer*, " '[b]y agreeing to arbitrate a statutory claim, a party does not forgo the substantive rights afforded by the statute; it only submits to their resolution in an arbitral, rather than a judicial, forum.' " 500 U.S., at 26, 111 S. Ct. 1647 (quoting *Mitsubishi Motors Corp. v. Soler Chrysler-Plymouth, Inc.*, 473 U.S. 614, 628 (1985)). *Gilmer*, of course, involved a federal statute, while the argument here is that a state statute ought not be denied state judicial enforcement while awaiting the outcome of arbitration. That matter, though, was addressed in *Southland* and *Allied-Bruce*, and we do not revisit the question here.

\* \* \* \*

For the foregoing reasons, the judgment of the Court of Appeals for the Ninth Circuit is reversed, and the case is remanded for further proceedings consistent with this opinion.

*It is so ordered.*

[dissenting opinions omitted]

# ARNOLD v. BURGER KING
2015-Ohio-4485, 2015 Ohio App. LEXIS 4383 (Ohio Ct. App. 2015)

## ON RECONSIDERATION

Anita Laster Mays, J.

### I. FACTS AND PROCEDURE

Defendant-appellant Carrols L.L.C. ("Carrols"), which owns and operates Burger King restaurant franchises, appeals from the trial court order that denied its motion to either compel arbitration and to dismiss the complaint or to stay the proceedings filed against it by plaintiff-appellee, its former entry-level employee, Shannon Arnold ("Arnold").

Upon a review of the record, we disagree with Carrols' assertions. Consequently, the trial court order is affirmed, and this case is remanded for further proceedings consistent with this opinion.

This employment dispute arises from the alleged rape of Arnold by her supervisor in the men's bathroom at a Burger King restaurant during working hours. She subsequently filed suit alleging the rape and that she was harassed and sexually abused by her supervisor over a period of time.

As a term of her employment, Arnold executed a mandatory arbitration agreement ("MAA"). The agreement provides that Arnold is to submit to JAMS, Inc. ("JAMS"), a national arbitration association, "any and all disputes, claims or controversies for monetary or equitable relief arising out of or relating to [Arnold's] employment" as well as "claims or controversies relating to events *outside the scope of your employment*." (Emphasis added.)

Arnold filed her complaint against Burger King, Carrols, and the individual, Terry Matthews ("Matthews"), on March 13, 2014. She alleged that she had been employed by Burger King and Carrols from May 2012 until August 2012 and that Matthews had been her supervisor. She further alleged that on July 21, 2012, as she "was cleaning the restrooms as part of her duties as an employee" of the defendants, Matthews followed her, grabbed her, "pushed her against the door, and forced her to give him oral sex." Arnold presented six (6) causes of action against the defendants collectively: (1) sexual harassment; (2) respondent superior/negligent retention; (3) emotional distress; (4) assault; (5) intentional tort; and (6) employment discrimination.

In lieu of an answer, Carrols filed a motion to compel arbitration pursuant to the MAA. It argued that the Federal Arbitration Act ("FAA") governed the dispute because Carrols is engaged in interstate commerce. It also asserted that the Burger King restaurant where Arnold was raped is one of over 500 franchises owned and operated by Carrols entities, which operates in 13 different states with more than 17,000 employees. Carrols further argued that the plain language of the MAA dictates that Arnold's claims be resolved in arbitration.

In Arnold's response, she conceded that she signed the MAA but argued she was unaware that she was agreeing to arbitrate with anyone other than Carrols Corporation ("Corporation"). She asserted that because Carrols was not a party to the MAA, Carrols could not enforce it. She further argued that her claims fell outside the scope of the MAA agreement and that the agreement was unenforceable because it is overly broad and unconscionable.

The trial court denied the motion to compel arbitration without opinion. Carrols now appeals and raises two assignments of error.

## II. ASSIGNMENTS OF ERROR

In the first assignment of error, Carrols argues the trial court erred in denying its motion to stay pending arbitration because the parties had a valid agreement to arbitrate, and Arnold's claims were within the scope of the MAA. In the second assignment of error, Carrols argues that the arbitration clause must be enforced because it is not unconscionable.

We find that both asserted errors lack merit. We affirm.

## III. STANDARD OF REVIEW

The question of whether a party has agreed to submit an issue to arbitration is reviewed under a de novo standard. *Hedeen v. Autos Direct Online, Inc.*, 8th Dist. Cuyahoga No. 100582, 2014-Ohio-4200, ¶ 9, 19 N.E.3d 957, citing *McCaskey v. Sanford-Brown College*, 8th Dist. Cuyahoga No. 97261, 2012-Ohio-1543, ¶ 7; and *Taylor Bldg. Corp. of Am. v. Benfield*, 117 Ohio St. 3d 352, 2008-Ohio-938, 884 N.E.2d 12. Under a de novo standard of review, we give no deference to a trial court's decision. *Hedeen* at ¶ 9, citing *Brownlee v. Cleveland Clinic Found.*, 8th Dist. Cuyahoga No. 97707, 2012-Ohio-2212, ¶ 9; *Akron v. Frazier*, 142 Ohio App. 3d 718, 721, 756 N.E.2d 1258 (9th Dist. 2001).

## IV. ANALYSIS

Carrols argues that Arnold's claims are subject to arbitration under the MAA because they arise out of Arnold's employment. Arnold responds that Carrols cannot enforce the MAA against her because the corporate employer named party in the MAA is not Carrols but Burger King and that her claims did not fall under the scope of the MAA.

We find that Carrols is a proper party to the MAA; however, we also find merit in Arnold's assertion that her claims do not fall under the scope of the MAA. Therefore, we affirm the trial court's denial of Carrols' motion to compel arbitration.

A. Enforceability by Carrols as a Party to the Agreement

Arnold's arbitration agreement provides, in plain language:

> My agreement to arbitrate Claims extends to Claims against Carrols' officers, directors, managers, employees, owners, attorneys and *agents*, as well as to any dispute you have with *any entity owned, controlled or operated by Carrols Corporation*.

(Emphasis added.)

Attached to Carrols' motion to compel arbitration was the affidavit of Gerald DiGenova ("DiGenova"), Vice President of the Human Resources Department of Carrols Restaurant Group, Inc., and copies of several documents. DiGenova explained the corporate relationship between Carrols Restaurant Group, Inc., Carrols L.L.C., and Burger King restaurants. He averred that Carrols adopted the MAA for all employees as of August 1, 2006, and that Arnold executed the MAA at the time she was hired as an employee.

DiGenova verified the motion's attached documents that included (1) a copy of the MAA signed by Arnold on May 10, 2012; (2) information about JAMS, the alternative dispute resolution provider named in the MAA; and (3) a "complete copy" of the JAMS employment arbitration rules and procedures.

DiGenova's affidavit states that the Corporation is the sole member of Carrols. Therefore, although Carrols is not "a signatory" to the agreement, we agree that it may enforce the agreement as an owner or agent of the Corporation, unless there exists some common law justification to void the contract. *Javitch v. First Union Sec., Inc.*, 315 F.3d 619, 629 (6th Cir. 2003).

## B. Enforceability of the MAA

### 1. Scope of the Agreement (Assignment of Error I)

Carrols relies on the United States Supreme Court's decision in *Marmet Health Care Ctr., Inc. v. Brown*, 565 U.S. __, 132 S. Ct. 1201, 1203, 182 L. Ed. 2d 42 (2012), in support of its argument that the MAA should be enforced whenever Ohio law conflicts with the FAA.[4]

In reversing the West Virginia Supreme Court's decision, the U.S. Supreme Court, quoting the FAA, explained:

> The FAA provides that a "written provision in * * * a contract evidencing a transaction involving commerce to settle by arbitration a controversy thereafter arising out of such contract or transaction * * * shall be valid, irrevocable, and enforceable, save upon such grounds as exist at law or in equity for the revocation of any contract.

*Marmet* at 1203, quoting 9 U.S.C. 2. Based on this provision, the *Marmet* court held that "'[w]hen state law prohibits outright the arbitration of a particular type of claim, the analysis is straightforward: The conflicting rule is displaced by the FAA.'" *Id.*, quoting *AT&T Mobility v. Concepcion*, 563 U.S. 333, 131 S. Ct. 1740, 1747, 179 L. Ed. 2d 742 (2011).

Accordingly, the *Marmet* court concluded that "West Virginia's prohibition against predispute agreements to arbitrate personal-injury or wrongful-death claims against nursing homes is a categorical rule prohibiting arbitration of a particular type of claim, and that rule is contrary to the terms and coverage of the FAA." *Marmet*, 565 U.S. __, 132 S. Ct. at 1204, 182 L. Ed. 2d 42. However, *Marmet* is not determinative here.

The *Marmet* court made the threshold finding that the plaintiffs' claims fell within the scope of the arbitration agreement, in contrast to the instant case. In addition, the court acknowledged that the West Virginia court also had to "consider whether, absent

---

[4] We recognize that the FAA was created in 1925 to address business-to-business arbitration agreements involving equally sophisticated parties. The scope of the FAA has been expanded over the years to encompass consumers, employees, nursing home residents, and civil rights actions. Grassroots and federal legislative efforts have been underway to address the rights of individuals subject to mandatory arbitration in noncommercial areas. *See, e.g.,* the Arbitration Fairness Act of 2015, S. 1133, 114th Cong. (2015); Arbitration Fairness Act of 2013, S. 878, 113th Cong. (2013); H.R. 1844, 113th Cong. (2013) (bills are identical). See also, Sen. Al Franken's (D-MN) amendment to H.R. 3326, the "Department of Defense Appropriations Act, 2010," which prohibits defense contractors from restricting their employees' abilities to take workplace discrimination, battery, and sexual assault cases to court versus arbitration. Pub. L. 111-118, § 8116, 123 Stat. 3409, 19 Dec. 2009.

th[e] general policy, the arbitration clauses in [plaintiff's cases] are unenforceable under state common law principles that are not specific to arbitration and pre-empted by the FAA." *Id.* In other words, the West Virginia court was free to find the arbitration agreement unenforceable for common law reasons, such as invalid formation of the contract or unconscionability.

Generally speaking, Ohio's public policy encourages arbitration as a method to settle disputes. *Schaefer v. Allstate Ins. Co.*, 63 Ohio St. 3d 708, 711–712, 590 N.E.2d 1242 (1992); and the Ohio Arbitration Act, R.C. Chapter 2711 (a trial court, "shall on application of one of the parties stay the trial of the action until the arbitration of the issue has been had in accordance with the agreement." R.C. 2711.02).

As a result of Ohio's pro-arbitration stance, courts indulge a strong presumption in favor of arbitration when the disputed issue falls within the scope of the arbitration agreement. *Williams v. Aetna Fin. Co.*, 83 Ohio St. 3d 464, 471, 1998-Ohio-294, 700 N.E.2d 859 (1998); *Taylor Bldg.*, 117 Ohio St. 3d 352, 2008-Ohio-938, 884 N.E.2d 12, at ¶ 27. Ohio also holds that arbitration agreements are, " 'valid, irrevocable, and enforceable, except upon grounds that exist at law or in equity for the revocation of any contract.' " *Taylor Bldg.* at ¶ 33, quoting R.C. 2711.01(A); *Marmet*, 565 U.S. __, 132 S. Ct. at 1204, 182 L. Ed. 2d 42.

Though guided by a strong presumption, Ohio also recognizes that principles of equity and fairness require that greater scrutiny be given to arbitration provisions that do not involve parties of equal sophistication and bargaining power:

> To be sure, an arbitration clause in a consumer contract with some characteristics of an adhesion contract "necessarily engenders more reservations than an arbitration clause in a different setting," such as a collective-bargaining agreement or a commercial contract between two businesses.

*Taylor Bldg., infra*, at ¶ 49, quoting *Williams* at 464.

This court has embraced the need for increased scrutiny in such cases:

> This court has previously emphasized the need for scrutiny arising from the uneven field upon which the consumer and business operate. "An arbitration agreement should only be enforceable when it was freely entered into, and the circumstances should be scrutinized where a consumer is confronted with a sophisticated lending institution, and waives the constitutional right of trial. * * *" *Miller v. Household Realty Corp.*, 8th Dist. Cuyahoga No. 81968, 2003-Ohio-3359, ¶ 40; *Hampton v. Swad*, 10th Dist. Franklin No. 03AP-294, 2003-Ohio-6655, ¶ 10.

*Olah v. Ganley Chevrolet, Inc.*, 8th Dist. Cuyahoga No. 86132, 2006-Ohio-694, ¶ 13.

The Ohio Supreme Court has steadfastly maintained that, " ' 'arbitration is a matter of contract and a party cannot be required to submit to arbitration any dispute which [it] has not agreed so to submit.' " *Taylor v. Ernst & Young, L.L.P.*, 130 Ohio St. 3d 411, 2011-Ohio-5262, 958 N.E.2d 1203, ¶ 20, quoting *AT&T Technologies, Inc. v. Communications Workers of America*, 475 U.S. 643, 648–649, 106 S. Ct. 1415, 89 L. Ed. 2d 648 (1986). *See also Acad. of Med. v. Aetna Health, Inc.*, 108 Ohio St. 3d 185, 2006-Ohio-657, 842 N.E.2d 488, ¶ 11–14 (in order for an arbitration agreement to be enforceable, the agreement must apply to the disputed issue), and *Ghanem v. Am. Greetings Corp.*, 8th Dist. Cuyahoga No. 82316, 2003-Ohio-5935, ¶ 12.

The *Taylor* court explained:

> Accordingly, when deciding motions to compel arbitration, the proper focus is whether the parties actually agreed to arbitrate the issue, i.e., the scope of the arbitration clause, not the general policies of the arbitration statutes. [*EEOC v.*] *Waffle House*[*, Inc.*], 534 U.S. [279] at 294[, 122 S. Ct. 754, 151 L. Ed. 2d 755 (2002)]. It follows that although any ambiguities in the language of a contract containing an arbitration provision should be resolved in favor of arbitration, the courts must not "override the clear intent of the parties, or reach a result inconsistent with the plain text of the contract, simply because the policy favoring arbitration is implicated." *Id.*

*Taylor, infra*, at ¶ 20; *Marks v. Morgan Stanley Dean Witter Commer. Fin. Servs.*, 8th Dist. Cuyahoga No. 88948, 2008-Ohio-1820, ¶ 15 ("parties cannot be compelled to arbitrate a dispute in which they have not agreed to submit to arbitration").

The Ohio Supreme Court stated that, in determining arbitrability, a court must be guided by the following analysis:

> (1) "[A]rbitration is a matter of contract and a party cannot be required to so submit to arbitration any dispute which he has not agreed to so submit"; (2) that the question whether a particular claim is arbitrable is one of law for the court to decide; (3) that when deciding whether the parties have agreed to submit a particular claim to arbitration, a court may not rule on the potential merits of the underlying claim; and (4) that when a "contract contains an arbitration provision, there is a presumption of arbitrability in the sense that '[a]n order to arbitrate the particular grievance should not be denied unless it may be said with positive assurance that the arbitration clause is not susceptible of an interpretation that covers the asserted dispute.' " [*Academy of Medicine of Cincinnati v. Aetna Health, Inc.*], 155 Ohio App. 3d 310, 2003-Ohio-6194, 800 N.E.2d 1185, P12, quoting *Cohen v. PaineWebber, Inc.*, Hamilton App. No. C-010312, 2002-Ohio-196, 2002 WL 63578, quoting *Council of Smaller Enters.*, 80 Ohio St. 3d at 665-666, 687 N.E.2d 1352, quoting *AT&T Technologies, Inc. v. Communications Workers of Am. (1986)*, 475 U.S. 643, 650, 106 S. Ct. 1415, 89 L. Ed. 2d 648.

*Academy of Medicine* at ¶ 5.

Ohio courts are guided in this analysis by the federal standard set forth in *Fazio v. Lehman Bros., Inc.*, 340 F.3d 386 (6th Cir. 2003), in determining whether a cause of action is within the scope of an arbitration agreement. "A proper method of analysis here is to ask if an action could be maintained without reference to the contract or relationship at issue. If it could, it is likely outside the scope of the arbitration agreement." *Acad. of Med.*, 108 Ohio St. 3d 185, 2006-Ohio-657, 842 N.E.2d 488 at ¶ 35 (adopting *Fazio* protocol for state court arbitrability analysis). *See also Complete Personnel Logistics, Inc. v. Patton*, 8th Dist. Cuyahoga No. 86857, 2006-Ohio-3356, ¶ 15 ("tort claims that may be asserted independently, without reference to the contract, fall outside the scope of the arbitration provision").

The *Academy of Medicine* court elaborated on the propriety of employing the *Fazio* test in light of the presumption of arbitrability in Ohio:

> The *Fazio* test does not act as a detriment to arbitration. It functions as a tool to determine a key question of arbitrability — whether the parties agreed to arbitrate the question at issue. It prevents the absurdity of an arbitration clause barring a party to the agreement from litigating any matter against the other party, regardless of how unrelated to the subject of the agreement. *It allows courts to make determinations of arbitrability based upon the factual allegations in the complaint instead of on the legal theories presented. It also establishes that the existence of a contract between the parties does not mean that every dispute between the parties is arbitrable.*

(Emphasis added.) *Academy of Medicine* at ¶ 29.

*Academy of Medicine* agreed with *Fazio*'s observation that, while torts may sometimes be covered by arbitration clauses where the allegations underlying the claims touch matters covered by the arbitration agreement, tort claims that may be asserted independently, without reference to the contract, fall outside of the scope of an arbitration provision. *Fazio* at ¶ 6. The court emphasized:

> "We are, however, aware of the Supreme Court's warning against 'forcing unwilling parties to arbitrate a matter they reasonably would have thought a judge, not an arbitrator, would decide.' *First Options [of Chicago, Inc. v. Kaplan* (1995)], 514 U.S. [938] at 945, [115 S. Ct. 1920, 131 L. Ed. 2d 985]." (Emphasis added.) *Fazio*[ ] at 395.

*Academy of Medicine, infra*, at ¶ 35.

The *Academy of Medicine* court also was also persuaded by the logic of the Tenth Circuit's determination of the scope of an arbitration provision in *Coors Brewing Co. v. Molson Breweries*, 51 F.3d 1511 (10th Cir. 1995). Coors and Molson had a licensing agreement to exclusively distribute Coors products in North America. Molson entered into a similar contract with Miller Brewing Company. Coors sued Molson for antitrust violations.

Finding that the claims were outside of the scope of a broadly drafted arbitration clause contained in the licensing agreement, the *Coors* court recognized:

> The existence of a contractual relationship between Coors and Molson did not mean that every conceivable claim between the two was arbitrable.

> \* \* \* \*

> "A dispute within the scope of the contract is still a condition precedent to the involuntary arbitration of antitrust claims. \* \* \* For example, if two small business owners execute a sales contract including a general arbitration clause, and one assaults the other, we would think it elementary that the sales contract did not require the victim to arbitrate the tort claim because the tort claim is not related to the sales contract. In other words, with respect to the alleged wrong, it is simply fortuitous that the parties happened to have a

contractual relationship."

*Acad. of Med. v. Aetna Health, Inc.*, 108 Ohio St. 3d 185, 2006-Ohio-657, 842 N.E.2d 488, ¶ 21–23, quoting *Coors* at 1516.

The South Carolina Supreme Court considered arbitration of an intentional tort in *Aiken v. World Fin. Corp.*, 373 S.C. 144, 644 S.E.2d 705 (2007). The question in *Aiken* was whether a lender could require a consumer to be bound by an arbitration clause contained in the loan documents where the consumer was damaged by the intentional tort of identity theft conducted by the lender's employees:

> Both state and federal policy favor arbitration of disputes and unless a court can say with positive assurance that the arbitration clause is not susceptible to any interpretation that covers the dispute, arbitration should generally be ordered. *Zabinski v. Bright Acres Assocs.*, 346 S.C. 580, 596–97, 553 S.E.2d 110, 118–19 (2001). However, arbitration is a matter of contract and a party cannot be required to submit to arbitration any dispute which he has not agreed to submit. *Id.* at 596, 553 S.E.2d at 118. Given these principles, courts generally hold that broadly-worded arbitration agreements apply to disputes in which a "significant relationship" exists between the asserted claims and the contract in which the arbitration clause is contained. *Id.* at 598, 553 S.E.2d at 119 (quoting *Long v. Silver*, 248 F.3d 309 (4th Cir. 2001)).

> * * * Applying what amounts to a "but-for" causation standard essentially includes every dispute imaginable between the parties, which greatly over-simplifies the parties' agreement to arbitrate claims between them. Such a result is illogical and unconscionable. *See Seifert v. U.S. Home Corp.*, 750 So. 2d 633, 638 (Fla. 1999)

* * * *

> * * * *Because even the most broadly-worded arbitration agreements still have limits founded in general principles of contract law, this Court will refuse to interpret any arbitration agreement as applying to outrageous torts that are unforeseeable to a reasonable consumer in the context of normal business dealings.*

* * * *

> In establishing the line for claims subject to arbitration, this Court does not seek to exclude all intentional torts from the scope of arbitration. * * * We only seek to distinguish those *outrageous torts*, which although factually related to the performance of the contract, are legally distinct from the contractual relationship between the parties. *See McMahon v. RMS Electronics, Inc.*, 618 F. Supp. 189, 191 (S.D.N.Y. 1985).

> Our decision today does not ignore the state and federal policies favoring arbitration as a less formal and more efficient means for resolving disputes. *See Lackey v. Green Tree Fin. Corp.*, 330 S.C. 388, 396, 498 S.E.2d 898, 902 (Ct. App. 1998). This Court merely seeks, as a matter of public policy, to promote

the procurement of arbitration in a commercially reasonable manner. *To interpret an arbitration agreement to apply to actions completely outside the expectations of the parties would be inconsistent with this goal.*

(Emphasis added and fns. omitted.) *Aiken* at 149-152. *See also Woda Constr., Inc. v. Miles-McClellan Constr. Co.*, Franklin C.P. Nos. 11CVH-04-4582 and 11CVH-04-4584 (Consolidated), 2012 Ohio Misc. LEXIS 189 (Dec. 6, 2012), citing *Aiken* for the premise that tort claim that is completely independent of a contract and may be maintained without reference to the contract is not arbitrable. Clearly, a lawsuit arising from a rape is an outrageous tort that is legally distinct from the contractual relationship between the parties.

While there are a number of cases on the enforceability of arbitration agreements and clauses, particularly in the consumer and employment realm, there are distinctly fewer on claims involving coworker criminal violence such as sexual assault. There are, however, several cases that are instructive here.

In *Smith v. Captain D's, LLC*, 963 So.2d 1116 (Miss. 2007), the Mississippi Supreme Court found a similar broadly drafted provision unconscionable where the employee's claims arose from a rape that was related to, but fell outside of the scope of, the employee's work. Smith was allegedly raped by her manager at the restaurant during working hours. The Mississippi Supreme Court held that an employee's sexual assault claim, as well as negligent hiring, retention, and supervision of her manager, did not fall within the scope of the arbitration agreement even though the agreement broadly covered "any and all * * * disputes, or controversies arising out of or relating to my employment."

In reaching this conclusion, the court explained:

> "[W]hile there is a strong and 'liberal policy favoring arbitration agreements,' such agreements must not be so broadly construed as to encompass claims and parties that were not intended by the original contract."

*Id.* at 1119, quoting *Thomson-CSF, S.A. v. Am. Arbitration Assoc.*, 64 F.3d 773, 776 (2d Cir. 1995), quoting *Mitsubishi Motors Corp. v. Soler Chrysler-Plymouth, Inc.*, 473 U.S. 614, 624 n.13, 105 S. Ct. 3346, 87 L. Ed. 2d 444 (1985). The Mississippi court concluded that, because the plaintiff's claims involved rape, they fell outside of the scope of employment even though the rape occurred at work during working hours. "[A] claim of sexual assault neither pertains to nor has a connection with [plaintiff]'s employment." *Id.* at 1121. *See also Niolet v. Rice*, 20 So.3d 31 (Miss. App. 2009), holding employee's claims of sexual assault and battery against her supervisor were not directly or indirectly related to her employment.

The widely publicized case of *Jones v. Halliburton*, 583 F.3d 228 (5th Cir. 2009), involved a gang rape of a federal contractor's employee by coworkers. Jones's employment agreement included the provision of overseas housing. She was placed in barracks occupied predominantly by male employees and promptly requested new housing due to the sexual harassment. *Id.* ¶ at 231.

The morning after a social event outside of the barracks area, an event that involved alcohol, Jones awakened to discover that she had been drugged, beaten, and gang raped by several coworkers. She suffered injuries including torn pectoral muscles. *Id.*

Jones allegedly reported the rape to another coworker and stated that her employer mishandled the rape kit, placed her under armed guard in a container, and was not permitted to leave or contact her family until she convinced one of her guards to allow her to telephone her father. Jones also stated she met with her supervisor and human resource personnel and was given the option, "to stay and 'get over it'; or to return home without the 'guarantee' of a job on return." *Id.* at ¶ 232. Her father was able to obtain congressional assistance to secure her return to the United States. *Id.*

The court considered whether the events arose out of the employment relationship and therefore were subject to arbitration. The Fifth Circuit held that Jones did not agree to arbitrate her claims for false imprisonment, assault and battery, negligent supervision, hiring and retention, and intentional infliction of emotional distress as the events did not arise within the scope of the relationship:

> Of course, although this reach [the language in the agreement] is broad, it is not unbounded. *Pennzoil [Exploration & Prod. Co. v. Ramco Energy*, 139 F.3d 1061, 1067 (5th Cir.1998)] recognized that a dispute need only " 'touch' matters covered by" the arbitration agreement to be arbitrable, *id.* at 1068 (quoting *Mitsubishi Motors Corp. v. Soler Chrysler-Plymouth, Inc.*, 473 U.S. 614, 624 n.13, 105 S. Ct. 3346, 87 L. Ed. 2d 444 (1985)); in the same discussion, however, it defined an arbitrable dispute under a broad clause as one "having a significant relationship to the contract" — here, Jones' employment contract — "regardless of the label attached to the dispute." *Pennzoil*, 139 F.3d at 1067. It further noted: "[E]ven broad clauses have their limits." *Id.* at 1067 n.8.

*Jones*, 583 F.3d at 235. The court further stated that, "Jones' allegations do not 'touch matters' related to her employment, let alone have a 'significant relationship' to her employment contract." *Id.* at 241 (i.e., the *Fazio* test).

The Eleventh Circuit entertained the question of whether a broadly drafted arbitration clause encompassed an employee being drugged and sexually assaulted by her cruise ship coworkers in *Doe v. Princess Cruise Lines, Ltd.*, 657 F.3d 1204 (11th Cir. 2011). Doe's claims included a refusal by the cruise ship supervisors to allow her to seek medical attention when docked at ports.

She filed five claims under the Jones Act, 46 U.S.C. § 30104 and Seaman's Wage Act, 46 U.S.C. § 10313 and five common law tort claims. Doe appealed the trial court's refusal to stay arbitration of the claims. *Doe* at 1211. The court reversed and remanded the common law tort claims and, construing a broadly drafted clause, held that the claims for false imprisonment, intentional infliction of emotional distress, invasion of privacy, spoliation of evidence, and fraudulent misrepresentation were not connected to, did not relate to, and did not arise out of her employment:

> The term "arising out of" is broad, but it is not all encompassing. In construing that same term to determine whether a dispute arises out of a contract, we have explained that the focus is on "whether the tort or breach in question was an immediate, foreseeable result of the performance of contractual duties." *Telecom Italia, SPA [v. Wholesale Telecom Corp.]*, 248 F.3d [1109] at 1116 [(11th Cir. 2001)]; *see also Hemispherx Biopharma [v. Johannesburg*

*Consol. Invs.*], 553 F.3d 1351, 1367 ("We have previously focused on foreseeability as [the] proper standard for resolving the scope of an arbitration clause that covers disputes 'arising out of or pursuant to' the contract between the parties."). "Arising out of" requires the existence of some direct relationship between the dispute and the performance of duties specified by the contract. *See Telecom Italia*, 248 F.3d at 1116 ("Disputes that are not related — with at least some directness — to performance of duties specified by the contract do not count as disputes 'arising out of' the contract, and are not covered by the standard arbitration clause.").

Similarly, "related to" marks a boundary by indicating some direct relationship; otherwise, the term would stretch to the horizon and beyond. As the Supreme Court has explained in the ERISA pre-emption context, "related to" is limiting language and "[i]f 'relate to' were taken to extend to the furthest stretch of its indeterminacy," it would have no limiting purpose because "really, universally, relations stop nowhere." *N.Y. State Conference of Blue Cross & Blue Shield Plans v. Travelers Ins. Co.*, 514 U.S. 645, 655, 115 S.Ct. 1671, 1677, 131 L. Ed. 2d 695 (1995) (quotation marks omitted). The same rationale applies here.

"Connected with" also connotes the necessity of some direct connection; if it did not, the term would be meaningless. *Cf. Ethicon Endo-Surgery, Inc. v. U.S. Surgical Corp.*, 93 F.3d 1572, 1578 (Fed. Cir. 1996) (construing a patent claim and stating that "[i]f, as Ethicon argues, 'connected to' should be read broadly to include elements which are connected directly or indirectly, then * * * the 'connected to' limitation would be meaninglessly empty").

*Doe* at 1218–1219. The court held that the claims were not an immediately, foreseeable result of the employment and thus, were not within the scope of the clause. *Id.* at 1219.

The " 'overarching issue is whether the parties agreed to arbitrate the issue.' " *Academy of Medicine*, 108 Ohio St. 3d 185, 2006-Ohio-657, 842 N.E.2d 488 at ¶ 19 quoting *Mitsubishi Motors Corp.*, 473 U.S. at 626, 105 S. Ct. 3346, 87 L. Ed. 2d 444. Was it reasonably foreseeable that the arbitration contract encompassed the conduct in question? *See Fazio*, 340 F.3d 386 at ¶ 395.

Foreseeability embraces the knowledge, sophistication and expectations of the parties at the time of contracting. This is not a case where an employee whose claims arose directly out of the employment relationship, was a professional with a negotiated contract of employment whose education, experience, and marketability provided an option to seek another position instead of accepting employment that required arbitration. *See, e.g., Short v. Resource Title Agency, Inc.*, 8th Dist. Cuyahoga No. 95839, 2011-Ohio-1577. Nor is this a case where a lower level employee appealed the arbitrability of an agreement where she testified that she simply failed to read it. *See Butcher v. Bally Total Fitness Corp.*, 8th Dist. Cuyahoga No. 81593, 2003-Ohio-1734, ¶ 41 ("The crux of appellant's appeal here centers around the unavoidable fact of 'the naked truth that she did not read the contract. It drives a stake into the heart of her claim.* * *'*ABM Farms* [*v. Woods*, 81 Ohio St. 3d 498, 1998-Ohio-612, 692 N.E.2d 574 (1998).]")

Further to the question of foreseeability and expectations, Carrols possessed unique and superior knowledge of the employment environment at the time the MAA was executed. In 1998, the EEOC filed suit in the Northern District of New York against Carrols on behalf of a class of 511 female employees, including teenaged employees, who were allegedly subjected to discrimination involving, "(1) hostile work environment sexual harassment; (2) failure to remedy alleged instances of sexual harassment; (3) retaliation against employees who complained about sexual harassment; and (4) constructive discharge of employees by failing to remedy a hostile work environment." *EEOC v. Carolls Corp.*, N.D.New York No. 5:98-CV-1772 (FJS/GHL), 2011 U.S. Dist. LEXIS 20972, at *2–3 (Mar. 2, 2011).

In 2005, the year prior to the launch of the Carrols mandatory arbitration program, the court dismissed the pattern and practice charges under 42 U.S.C. § 2000e-6 (§ 707 of Title VII). *EEOC v. Carrols Corp.*, N.D.New York No. 5:98-CV-1772 (FJS/GHL), 2005 U.S. Dist. LEXIS 8337 (Apr. 20, 2005).

In 2011, Carrols filed for summary judgment on the remaining charge brought in the name of the EEOC on behalf of the individual female employees (42 U.S.C. § 2000e-5(f)(1) (§ 706 of Title VII)). *Carrols Corp.*, 2011 U.S. Dist. LEXIS 20972, at *2.

Carrols sought dismissal on various grounds:

> "Untimely: Did not file charge and unrelated to timely charge," "Untimely: Failure to exercise right to sue," "Untimely: alleged [sexual harassment and/or retaliation] occurred prior to May 29, 1997," "Not supported by admissible evidence," "Non-actionable sexual harassment," "Non-actionable retaliation," "Bound by prior determination of charge/claim," and "EEOC failed to exercise discretion [with regard to] charge."

*Id.* at *13–14.

The court summarized the factual grounds underlying the EEOC's charges:

> Although the conduct differs in type and severity, running the gambit from repeatedly standing uncomfortably close to, rubbing up against, and offensively touching the bodies of these individuals to incidents of serious physical assault and rape, in addition to a constant barrage of sexually charged and offensive comments that were on-going * * *.

*Id.* at *33.

The court found that a number of claims failed due to procedural reasons such as employees who, "failed to avail themselves of the opportunity to seek Plaintiff's review of the state agency's decision or failed to file a suit within ninety days of receiving a right-to-sue letter from Plaintiff." *Id.* at *15. Another individual filed a civil suit and settled with a general release of claims. *Id.* at *16. An additional group was dismissed due to staleness because the acts occurred before May 29, 1997. *Id.*

A number of complainants were dismissed for failure to support the claims with admissible evidence, "the only material in the record that supports their claims is an unsigned and/or undated summary of what their testimony would be regarding the alleged harassment that they suffered." *Id.* at *19. The court dismissed the claims of another group, finding that the claims failed as a matter of law to establish a claim of hostile work environment/sexual harassment. *Id.* at *25.

Finally, the court held that the remaining 89 parties could proceed with the suit due to issues of fact precluding summary judgment for hostile work environment/sexual harassment. Three of the 89 moved forward because Carrols did not challenge their claims. *Id.* at *28.

In 2013, the parties entered into a settlement Consent Decree, which included payment of $2.5 million to the remaining 89 and requiring Carrols to take a number of steps to address the issue including increasing employees' awareness of Carrols' anti-harassment policies, responding to related complaints, providing enhanced training for managers, posting notices and issuance of an injunction against further retaliation and harassment. *See* Consent Decree, *infra, generally*; Equal Employment Opportunity Commission Press Release, *Carrols Corp. To Pay $2.5 Million to Settle EEOC Sexual Harassment and Retaliation Lawsuit*, issued January 9, 2013, http://www.eeoc.gov/eeoc/newsroom/release/1-9-13.cfm.

The lawsuit had been pending for more than ten (10) years at the time Arnold executed the MAA. Carrols was on notice of the allegations of sexual assault, including rape accusations, involving coworkers and restaurant supervisors in multiple restaurant locations at that time and had a unique knowledge of the environment and special challenges that may have been involved. Arnold did not have that knowledge.

Ambiguity of the agreement is an additional factor that impedes foreseeability:

> While ambiguities in the language of the agreement should be resolved in favor of arbitration, we do not override the clear intent of the parties, or reach a result inconsistent with the plain text of the contract, simply because the policy favoring arbitration is implicated. "Arbitration under the [FAA] is a matter of consent, not coercion."

(Citations omitted.) *EEOC v. Waffle House, Inc.*, 534 U.S. 279, 294, 122 S. Ct. 754, 151 L. Ed. 2d 755 (2002), quoting *Volt Information Sciences, Inc. v. Bd. of Trustees*, 489 U.S. 468, 479, 109 S. Ct. 1248, 103 L. Ed. 2d 488 (1989). Contractual terms are ambiguous if the meaning of the terms cannot be deciphered from reading the entire contract, or if the terms are reasonably susceptible to more than one interpretation. *Willard Constr. Co. v. Olmsted Falls*, 8th Dist. Cuyahoga No. 81551, 2003-Ohio-3018, ¶ 17.

Carrol's argues the MAA only applies to claims arising out of the scope of employment, but that is not how Carrols defined "Claims" in the MAA. Ambiguities are generally construed against the drafter where the parties have unequal bargaining power to select the contract language. *Michael A. Gerard, Inc. v. Haffke*, 8th Dist. Cuyahoga No. 98488, 2013-Ohio-168, ¶ 14. This is particularly true where, as here, Carrols effectively acknowledges the ambiguity by arguing that the MAA language does not actually mean what it says, i.e., that it also covers acts outside of the scope of the agreement.

Additionally relevant to assessing foreseeability and expectations is whether there was an understanding of what the parties understood the MAA language to mean. The

MAA provides a list of legal causes of actions and laws, in legal terminology, such as strict liability, Family Medical Leave Act, and Employee Retirement Income Security Act.

The MAA's sole listed exceptions to coverage are the "exclusive remedies under either workers compensation law or employee injury benefit plan." The MAA includes arbitration of "personal or emotional injury to you or your family." The agreement does not, in any way, explain the tremendously overreaching impact of its terms on the employee's life both within and outside the scope of employment. There is no bold language such as is required in consumer agreements putting the employee on notice of the extensive abrogation of rights.

The JAMS provisions are not attached to the MAA but are incorporated by reference to the website. Carrols did, however, provide a copy of the rather detailed 2009 terms and conditions to its motion to compel arbitration in the trial court. The documents contain rules and regulations governing subject areas such as ex parte communications, e-filing, summary dispositions, rules of evidence, privilege and work product. It is also observed that the JAMS rules that will apply are the "then current" rules that are subject to change at any time. There is no indication that there would be further notice to the employee accompanied by a choice of opting out at that point.

We proceed to apply the foregoing analysis to the instant case. Arnold's causes of actions are for: (1) sexual harassment; (2) respondeat superior/negligent retention; (3) emotional distress; (4) assault; (5) intentional tort; and (6) employment discrimination. Per *Academy of Medicine*, 108 Ohio St. 3d 185, 2006-Ohio-657, 842 N.E.2d 488, we examine the factual allegations underlying Arnold's claim, and not the causes of action, to determine whether arbitration of the claims may be independently maintained without reference to the contract or relationship at issue, bringing them outside of the scope of arbitration. *Academy of Medicine* at ¶ 35. Secondly, we determine whether the acts complained of were a foreseeable result of Arnold's employment. *Doe*, 657 F.3d at 1218–1219.

The complaint states that Arnold was constantly subjected to ongoing verbal and unwanted physical conduct that culminated in rape. On July 21, 2012, Arnold was cleaning the men's restroom when Matthews entered, grabbed Arnold by her hair, pushed her against the door and forced her to give him oral sex. She has incurred and believes she will continue to incur treatment for her medical and psychological injuries. The complaint also states that Carrols had actual or constructive knowledge of Matthews' tendencies and that he posed a hazard.

The complaint further provides that Carrols and supervisor Matthews retaliated or threatened to retaliate against Arnold, including termination, due to her attempt to enforce her rights; that she suffered unrelenting abuse, torment, harassment, threats, and embarrassment; and that she will require medical care and psychiatric counseling. It is also asserted that Carrols aided, abetted, incited, compelled, and coerced others to engage in unlawful discriminatory practices and/or interfere with or to obstruct Arnold.

Based on the underlying facts, we find that Arnold's claims relating to and arising from the sexual assault exist independent of the employment relationship as they may be "maintained without reference to the contract or relationship at issue." *Academy of Medicine*, 108 Ohio St. 3d 185, 2006-Ohio-657, 842 N.E.2d 488, at ¶ 24; *Fazio*, 340 F.3d 386, at ¶ 395, and *Winters Law Firm. L.L.C. v. Groedel*, 8th Dist. Cuyahoga No. 99922, 2013-Ohio-5260, ¶ 14. Any individual could assert the same causes of action based on the underlying facts.

A patron may, for example based on the asserted facts, pursue an action for sexual harassment per the Ohio Civil Rights Act that prohibits discriminatory practices by a proprietor, employer, keeper, or manager of a place of public accommodation (R.C. 4112.02(G)) that includes a restaurant. R.C. 4112.02(H)(9). In addition, R.C. 4112.02(I) prohibits unlawful discrimination for opposing unlawful discriminatory practices.

The second step of our scope of agreement analysis is to inquire whether the claims are a forseeable result of the employment. *Doe*, 657 F.3d at 1218–1219. We find that ongoing verbal and physical contact culminating in sexual assault as well as retaliation, harassment, or other detrimental acts against Arnold based on the unlawful conduct is not a foreseeable result of the employment.

## 2. Unconscionability (Assignment of Error II)

Carrols asserts in its second assignment of error that the MAA is enforceable and is not unconscionable. We disagree.

Unconscionability embodies two separate concepts: (1) unfair and unreasonable contract terms, i.e., substantive unconscionability; and (2) an absence of meaningful choice on the part of one of the parties, i.e., procedural unconscionability. *Taylor Bldg.*, 117 Ohio St. 3d 352, 2008-Ohio-938, 884 N.E.2d 12, at ¶ 34. A party asserting the unconscionabilty of a contract must prove a quantum of both substantive and procedural unconscionability. *Hayes v. Oakridge Home*, 122 Ohio St. 3d 63, 2009-Ohio-2054, 908 N.E.2d 408, ¶ 30; *Taylor Bldg.* at ¶ 34. In other words, these two concepts create a two-prong conjunctive test for unconscionability. *Gates v. Ohio Sav. Ass'n*, 11th Dist. Geauga No. 2009-G-2881, 2009-Ohio-6230, ¶ 47; *Strack v. Pelton*, 70 Ohio St. 3d 172, 1994 Ohio 107, 637 N.E.2d 914 (1994).

An unconscionable agreement has been described by the United States Supreme Court:

> [A]s one " 'such as no man in his senses and not under delusion would make on the one hand, and as no honest and fair man would accept on the other.' " *Thonen v. McNeil-Akron, Inc.*, 661 F. Supp. 1252 (N.D.Ohio 1986), quoting *Hume v. United States*, 132 U.S. 406, 411, 10 S. Ct. 134, 33 L. Ed. 393 (1889).

*Devito v. Autos Direct Online, Inc.*, 8th Dist. Cuyahoga No. 100831, 2015-Ohio-3336, ¶ 14, 37 N.E.3d 194.

### 1. Procedural Unconscionability

In determining whether an agreement is procedurally unconscionable, courts consider the relative bargaining positions of the parties including each party's age, education, intelligence, experience, and who drafted the contract. *Taylor Bldg.* at ¶ 44. *See also Johnson v. Mobil Oil Corp.*, 415 F. Supp. 264 (E.D. Michigan 1976); *Lake*

*Ridge Academy v. Carney*, 66 Ohio St. 3d 376, 383, 613 N.E.2d 183 (1993). "Procedural unconscionability concerns the formation of the agreement and occurs when no *voluntary* meeting of the minds is possible." (Emphasis added.) *Bayes v. Merle's Metro Builders/Blvd. Constr.*, 11th Dist. Lake No. 2007-L-067, 2007-Ohio-7125, ¶ 11.

An important consideration is, "whether 'each party to the contract, considering his obvious education or lack of it, [had] a reasonable opportunity to understand the terms of the contract, or were the important terms hidden in a maze of fine print?'" *Blackburn v. Ronald Kluchin Architects, Inc.*, 8th Dist. Cuyahoga No. 89203, 2007-Ohio-6647, ¶ 29, quoting *Vanyo v. Clear Channel Worldwide*, 156 Ohio App. 3d 706, 2004-Ohio-1793, 808 N.E.2d 482, ¶ 18 (8th Dist.). "[A] determination of unconscionability is a fact-sensitive question that requires a case-by-case review of the surrounding circumstances." *Brunke v. Ohio State Home Servs., Inc.*, 9th Dist. Lorain No. 08CA009320, 2008-Ohio-5394, ¶ 8. *Wallace v. Ganley Auto Group.*, 8th Dist. Cuyahoga No. 95081, 2011-Ohio-2909, ¶ 44.

As the Ohio Supreme Court explained:

> Procedural unconscionability considers the circumstances surrounding the contracting parties' bargaining, such as the parties' " 'age, education, intelligence, business acumen and experience, * * * who drafted the contract, * * * whether alterations in the printed terms were possible, [and] whether there were alternative sources of supply for the goods in question.'" *Collins [v. Click Camera & Video]*, 86 Ohio App. 3d [826,] 834, 621 N.E.2d 1294 [(2d Dist. 1993)]. "Factors which may contribute to a finding of unconscionability in the bargaining process [i.e., procedural unconscionability] include the following: belief by the stronger party that there is no reasonable probability that the weaker party will fully perform the contract; knowledge of the stronger party that the weaker party will be unable to receive substantial benefits from the contract; knowledge of the stronger party that the weaker party is unable reasonably to protect his interests by reason of physical or mental infirmities, ignorance, illiteracy or inability to understand the language of the agreement, or similar factors." Restatement of the Law 2d, Contracts (1981), Section 208, Comment d.

*Taylor Bldg.*, 117 Ohio St. 3d 352, 2008-Ohio-938, 884 N.E.2d 12, at ¶ 43.

It is clear that there was a disparity in bargaining power between Carrols and Arnold. Carrols wrote the MAA as well as the Policy Notice poster regarding the MAA that was posted at the Burger King location. Arnold was an individual seeking an entry level "team member" position.

Further, as we discussed in detail under the scope of the agreement analysis herein, Carrols possessed unique and superior knowledge of the employment environment at the time the MAA was executed. *See Taylor Bldg., infra* at ¶ 43. In *EEOC v. Carrols, infra*, involving sexual harassment charges, including sexual assault allegations, filed by the EEOC in 1998 and which were ongoing for more than a decade.

Courts will also consider, on the issue of procedural unconscionability, "whether alterations in the printed terms were possible," *Hayes*, 122 Ohio St. 3d 63, 2009-Ohio-2054, 908 N.E.2d 408, at ¶ 23, and whether the parties had alternatives to entering into the contract. *Rupert v. Macy's Inc.*, N.D. Ohio No. 1:09CV2763, 2010 U.S. Dist. LEXIS 54050 (June 2, 2010).

Arnold applied for employment in May 2012 and signed the MAA at the time she was hired. The MAA is dated May 12, 2012. Carrols drafted the MAA and presented it to Arnold as a condition for hiring her at a Burger King restaurant. As for Arnold's bargaining power, the choice was either sign it or remain unemployed. There is no evidence that Arnold could alter any of its terms.

Prior to moving forward with our analysis and as a point of clarification, we address a line of cases that have been erroneously advanced for the per se premise that signing an arbitration agreement instead of seeking other employment (or resigning from employment), negates any possibility of procedural unconscionability. Such an interpretation is a misconstruction of the case law.

First of all, such a broad interpretation provides an absurb result as no signed agreement could ever be procedurally unconscionable. In addition, this court has recently restated the obvious which is that no single factor alone determines whether a contract is procedurally unconscionable; a court must consider the totality of the circumstances. *Murea v. Pulte Group, Inc.*, 8th Dist. Cuyahoga No. 100127, 2014-Ohio-398, citing *Hayes*, 122 Ohio St. 3d 63, 2009-Ohio-2054, 908 N.E.2d 408, at ¶ 29–30; *Rude v. NUCO Edn. Corp.*, 9th Dist. Summit No. 25549, 2011-Ohio-6789.

The great disparity in bargaining power, by itself, would not be sufficient to rescind the MAA. Carrols drafted the misleading MAA and the Policy Notice that would give an ordinary reasonable person a false sense of security. Comprehension of the terms of the agreement is an element of both procedural and substantive unconscionability, the latter of which is addressed in greater detail below.

There can be no true meeting of the minds when a party is unable to understand the agreement. We restate that the MAA not only defines "Claims" as events arising out of the employment as well as outside of the scope of employment, it provides a laundry list of legal causes of actions and laws, in legal terminology, such as strict liability, Family Medical Leave Act, and Employee Retirement Income Security Act. The exceptions to coverage are the "exclusive remedies under either workers compensation law or employee injury benefit plan." The MAA includes arbitration of "personal or emotional injury to you or your family." The agreement does not, in any way, explain the tremendously overreaching impact of its terms on the employee's life both within and outside the scope of employment.

The Policy Notice is also misleading because it contradicts the terms of the MAA. The Policy Notice states, "employment related disputes that cannot be resolved internally will proceed to arbitration rather than in a lawsuit." The Policy Notice does not say that disputes arising outside the scope of employment are also required to proceed to arbitration. One may be willing to arbitrate disputes that arise in the course of employment. It is an entirely different scenario when one agrees to arbitrate claims that arise outside the scope of employment because the variety of potential claims is practically infinite and unforeseeable.

Based on the totality of the factors numerated herein, we find that the agreement is procedurally unconscionable. We next consider the second facet of the analysis, substantive unconscionability.

## 2. Substantive Unconscionability

The MAA's terms were not only procedurally unconscionable but also substantively unconscionable. As stated herein under our procedural unconscionability analysis, inasmuch as the MAA sought to include every possible situation that might arise in an employee's life, the clause is substantively unconscionable as the arbitrator would be resolving disputes unrelated to employment. *See, e.g., Drake v. Barclays Bank Del., Inc.*, 8th Dist. Cuyahoga No. 96451, 2011-Ohio-5275.

The Policy Notice states that arbitration is "quicker and less expensive for both sides." That is not always the case, particularly for the employee. For example, employment attorneys typically represent plaintiffs on a contingency basis so there is often no cost to the employee until success or settlement. Court filing fees are usually lower than the fees to initiate arbitration. Arbitration is generally beneficial for employers because it is, as opposed to litigation, less expensive due to brevity and lack of appeal rights. It is also advantageous to the employer where, as in this case, the agreement limits the worker's recovery of damages otherwise available via litigation, "[i]n the event you prevail, [the arbitrator] will limit your relief to compensation for demonstrated and actual injury to the extent consistent with the Procedural Standards [that are not attached to the MAA]."

To file a request for arbitration, an employee must send the request to the listed JAMS New York City office with a copy to the Legal Department in Syracuse, New York address with an explanation of the issue. The request must be sent via "U.S. mail or a reputable overnight delivery service." There is no mention of registered or certified mail to verify timeliness.

The MAA also states, reassuring the employee of the minimal cost and promoting the cooperative effort, that "Carrols will reimburse you 50% of any JAMS filing fee, *if* within two weeks after your request for arbitration, proof of payment is delivered to and received by Carrols at the above address." (Emphasis added.) What constitutes proof of payment is not described. There is no statement of the cost of arbitration.

If the employee submits the documents properly along with the unidentified fee amount, and if Carrols actually receives "proof of payment" (acceptable proof is not defined) within two weeks after the request for arbitration (the agreement does not state when the two weeks begins), Carrols will reimburse the employee for 50% of the unstated filing fee amount. The employee also bears any other costs, none of which are in the agreement. If the employee is able to determine the cost and initiate an arbitration, she must also craft an effective complaint and set forth arguments, unless she can afford to hire an attorney.

Ohio cases have considered whether the prohibitive costs of initiating arbitration constitute a deterrent to obtaining arbitration relief. In *Taylor Bldg., infra*, the Ohio Supreme Court stated that there is a point at which the costs of arbitration could render a clause unconscionable as a matter of law. *Taylor Bldg.* at ¶ 60.

This court, as well as the court in *Rude v. NUCO Edn. Corp.*, 9th Dist. Summit No. 25549, 2011-Ohio-6789, *infra*, concurs:

> Although silence of an arbitration clause with respect to costs does not, by itself, make the clause unconscionable, "if the costs associated with the arbitration effectively deny a claimant the right to a hearing or an adequate remedy in an efficient and cost-effective manner," then the clause is invalid.

*Rude* at ¶ 24, quoting *Felix v. Ganley Chevrolet Inc.*, 8th Dist. No. 86990, 86991, 2006-Ohio-4500, ¶ 21.

In *U.S. Bank N.A. v. Wilkens*, 8th Dist. Cuyahoga No. 96617, 2012-Ohio-1038, we considered the unconscionability of arguably prohibitive costs to which a consumer might be subjected to pursue arbitration. We were guided by the Ohio Supreme Court in *Williams*, 83 Ohio St. 3d 464, 1998-Ohio-294, 700 N.E.2d 859, where the court considered the unconscionability of arbitration for small consumer loans:

> "'The likely effect of these procedures is to deny a borrower against whom a claim has been brought any opportunity to a hearing, much less a hearing held where the contract was signed, unless the borrower has considerable legal expertise or the money to hire a lawyer and/or prepay substantial hearing fees. * * * In a dispute over a loan of $2,000 it would scarcely make sense to spend a minimum of $850 just to obtain a participatory hearing.' [*Williams v. Aetna Fin. Co.*, 83 Ohio St. 3d 464, 1998-Ohio-294, 700 N.E.2d 859], quoting *Patterson v. ITT Consumer Fin. Corp.*, 14 Cal. App. 4th 1659, 18 Cal. Rptr. 2d 563 (1993)."

*U.S. Bank* at ¶ 36.

The MAA refers the employee to the JAMS website, provides a generic link, and incorporates the terms and conditions by reference. This court observes that, instead of referring the trial court to the JAMS website to navigate its way through the information and determine the terms and conditions underlying the agreement since employment arbitration is just a portion of JAMS's services, Carrols provided the court with copies of the information. Glaringly absent from the submission, however, was a schedule of fees reflecting the cost to file as well as to maintain an action.

> Since:
>
> [t]he arbitration agreement does not set forth applicable rules or costs of arbitration but simply refers the consumer to the rules of the American Arbitration Association ("AAA")[,] [w]e therefore find it necessary to delve deeply into the voluminous rules and procedure to discern the resultant costs governing the instant consumer dispute.

*Devito*, 8th Dist. Cuyahoga No. 100831, 2015-Ohio-3336, at ¶ 22.

An examination of the JAMS website, which again is incorporated by reference into the MAA, reveals a wealth of information about JAMS which includes that JAMS is involved with a variety of practice areas and lists 45. The arbitration link directs the reader to the types of arbitration services JAMS provides in various disciplines, including consumer, expedited, and international.

There is a true labyrinth of information with links to rules, forms, ethics, discovery protocols, etc. There is nothing to direct an arguably unsophisticated individual through the maze of information in order to ascertain which of the multiple documents apply to pursuing arbitration against Carrols.

The MAA provides that an employee is to send a complaint to JAMS with a copy to Carrols' legal department. The JAMS website contains a six page form entitled "Demand for Arbitration" that was last updated "11/24/14." It is unknown whether a similar form was required to be filed to initiate arbitration via the MAA. To fill out the form, a party must know whether they are pursuing arbitration on a predispute, post dispute, oral dispute, or court order. A $400 nonrefundable "Case Management Fee" is also required. There is no schedule of fees contained in the document, just as there was none provided to the trial court via Carrols' submission of the applicable rules and regulations. In fact, this court's attempt to ascertain the costs attendant to pursuit of arbitration applicable to this case was an exercise in futility.

The MAA provides that an aggrieved employee will be subject to the "then current" JAMS terms and conditions. Therefore, the employee (even if they possessed the level of sophistication required to navigate the JAMS website), would not, at the time of signing, be able to identify the applicable rules and regulations or know what terms and conditions applied if an arbitration was filed since the rules could be revised at any time without notice.

In *Post*, 8th Dist. No. Cuyahoga 87646, 2007-Ohio-2106, this court found a provision unconscionable that resulted in a stated advantage to the employer:

> The imbalance of the respective rights of the parties to the employment agreement demonstrates the unconscionability of the arbitration clause. While [the employee] is limited to mandatory arbitration regarding any employment dispute, the agreement provides that [the employer] may bypass arbitration and seek judicial remedies in court in order to obtain injunctive relief for any breach or threatened breach by [the employee] of the covenants contained in the non-competition and confidentiality provisions of the employment agreement. We are not persuaded by [the employer's] assertion that this provision, which allows [the employer] to use a judicial forum when it is the plaintiff, but limits [the employee] to arbitration when he is the plaintiff, is not unconscionable.

*Id.* at ¶ 17.

The MAA provides that the "parties reserve the right to go to court if they are faced with the risk of irreparable harm, such as the disclosure of confidential information." Since the MAA attempts to cover "Claims" relating to almost every cause of action available to Arnold, the attempt at mutuality is misleading and arguably illusory. To the extent some degree of mutuality is deemed to be present, Arnold may be "irreparably harmed" if she is forced to defend herself at arbitration on a sensitive and emotionally scarring subject involving explicit personal details.

The MAA states that, "[t]he arbitrator will strictly apply relevant law and, in the event you prevail, will limit your relief to compensation for demonstrated and actual injury to the extent consistent with the Procedural Standards." There is no mention of attorney fees.

The JAMS documents delivered to the trial court by Carrols, the JAMS Policy on Employment Arbitration Minimum Standards of Procedural Fairness effective July 15, 2009 ("Procedural Standards") provide:

> All remedies that would be available under the applicable law in a court proceeding, including attorneys fees and exemplary damages, as well as statutes of limitations, must remain available in the arbitration. Post-arbitration remedies, if any, must remain available to an employee.

> Comment: This standard does not make any change in the remedies available. Its purpose is to ensure that the remedies available in arbitrations and court proceedings are the same. *JAMS does not object if an employer chooses to limit its own post-arbitration remedies.*

(Emphasis added).

The MAA says compensation is limited to "demonstrated and actual injury to the extent consistent with the Procedural Standards." The 2009 standards say that all remedies, including exemplary damages, are available. This language is ambiguous. Are remedies fully available to the employee or are they limited by the MAA? Ambiguities are generally construed against the drafter where the parties have unequal bargaining power to select the contract language. *Michael A. Gerard, Inc.*, 8th Dist. Cuyahoga No. 98488, 2013-Ohio-168, at ¶ 14.

It is also observed that there is no choice of law provision or waiver clause in the MAA and, as to forum, the location "will be convenient to the employee." There is also no severability provision declaring that, if any portion of the contract is declared to be invalid, the remainder may still be enforced.

We find that the MAA is also substantively unconscionable.

### V. Conclusion

This court finds that Arnold's claims are not only outside of the scope of the MAA but that the MAA is unconscionable as applied to this case.

The trial court appropriately denied Carrols' motion to either compel arbitration and dismiss the case or stay litigation pending arbitration. Carrols' assignments of error are overruled.

The trial court's order is affirmed, and this case is remanded for further proceedings consistent with this opinion.

It is ordered that appellee recover from appellant costs herein taxed.

The court finds there were reasonable grounds for this appeal.

It is ordered that a special mandate be sent to said court to carry this judgment into execution.

A certified copy of this entry shall constitute the mandate pursuant to Rule 27 of the Rules of Appellate Procedure.

Eileen T. Gallagher, J., dissenting. [Omitted.]

# V.   APPELLATE JUGES: JUDGING AS APPELLATE PROCEDURES DECLINE

Arbitration, mediation, and other alternative dispute resolution techniques now extend beyond trial courts. While the "decline in trials" grabs the attention of many judges, practitioners and academics, at the appellate level, a similar movement exists to "short circuit" the appellate process in a similar way, with similar goals — to avoid the "burden" of a full blown appellate process by limiting or eliminating traditional roles of appellate judges.

While the focus in trial courts is to avoid the burdens of a jury trial, on appeal, appellate courts use alternative dispute resolution techniques in the hopes of avoiding delay; clarifying issues, and therefore, will explore the possibility of "settlement on appeal" through mediation. Many federal and state appellate courts have created such settlement on appeal programs. Thus, while civil jury trials and the skills accompanying them decline, it may also be said that the skills of appellate briefing and appellate oral argument are also in decline.

The decline in civil trial juries and the decline in appellate oral argument touch on similar concerns.

> Both are public venues that offer citizens a window into the functioning of the judicial branch, which traditionally has been seen in operation at trials — civil and criminal — as well as in appellate oral arguments. The loss of these opportunities may be crucial to public perception and respect for the court system. As one appellate judge observed, ". . . [O]ral argument is the only opportunity the public has to observe the decision-making process at work; every other aspect of appellate opinion-making is secret."

Susan Larsen, *Wanna Talk? No, Not Really*, The Texas Blue, Jan. 15, 2007, www.thetexasblue.com/wanna-talk-no-not-really.

## A.   Appellate Courts: Settlement on Appeal Before Appellate Briefs

### Court of Appeals of Ohio
### Twelfth District Court of Appeals
### Prehearing Conference Procedures

Pursuant to App. R. 20 and Loc. R. 12, the Court conducts a prehearing mediation conference to offer participants a confidential, risk-free opportunity to candidly evaluate their case with an informed neutral and explore possibilities for voluntary resolution of the litigation. For your assistance, the following are answers to some commonly asked questions:

* **How are cases selected for prehearing mediation conferences?** All civil and administrative appeals and all original actions are eligible for mediation. Cases are selected specifically or at random by the Court. Counsel may also confidentially request a prehearing conference, which the Court may grant in its discretion.

* **Why are conferences scheduled shortly after the notice of appeal is filed?** Prehearing conferences are held quickly so that resolution can be explored prior to the parties incurring further cost and expense. Experience has shown that the filing of briefs dramatically reduces the likelihood that the parties will be able to reach a mutual resolution.

* **What if the record or brief is due shortly?** The mere setting of a prehearing conference date does not suspend other appeal deadlines. A request for a continuance can be made by written motion or merely by contacting the conference attorney . . . . The Court may grant the request if it is deemed to be conducive to the mediation process.

* * * *

* **Is participation in prehearing conference optional?** No. Participation is mandatory.

* **Must each party's lead attorney attend conference?** Yes. It is critical that each party be represented at the prehearing conference by the attorney who is conversant with the case, but is also the attorney on whose advice the client chiefly relies.

* **Are clients required to attend?** Clients are usually required to attend the initial conference. At any prehearing conference in which client attendance is not required, clients or their designated representatives with full settlement authority shall be available by telephone for the duration of the conference to facilitate the settlement discussions. The conference attorney encourages active client participation when helpful to the settlement discussions.

* **How long do the conferences last?** On average, prehearing conferences typically last approximately three hours. It is not unusual, however, for conferences to go beyond that. The conference attorney will afford counsel and the parties as much time as necessary to accomplish the purposes of the prehearing conferences.

* **What preparation is required of counsel?** Counsel are to consult with their clients prior to the conference and obtain the requisite settlement authority. Care should be taken to include the necessary "decision makers." Counsel are to be prepared to fully explore in good faith all options, avenues, and possibilities which might lead to a mutually acceptable resolution of the case. Counsel should also review their factual and legal interests prior to conference. Discussion of settlement is not necessarily limited to the appeal itself. If settlement of the appeal will not dispose of the entire case, or, if related litigation is pending or anticipated in other forums, counsel are encouraged to explore the possibility of a global settlement.

* **What takes place at the prehearing conference?** While prehearing conference procedures are official proceedings of the Court, they are conducted in a relatively informal manner. Discussions are typically conversational rather than argumentative. Initially, procedural issues and questions are addressed. The primary substantive issues and anticipated assignments of error are then discussed. Thereafter, resolution is actively explored through the mediation process. The mediation focuses on the possible outcomes on appeal, the risks and costs of further litigation, the interests and motivations of the parties, and the potential benefits gained by resolution of the appeal or settlement of the entire case. The conference attorney typically meets jointly with counsel and the parties and then meets separately with each side in his role as mediator. Settlement options and proposals are thoroughly discussed. Resolution may or may not be reached during the initial conference. Following an initial conference, the conference attorney typically initiates further discussions by telephone or will schedule follow-up conferences if helpful. By the conclusions of the prehearing conference process, the parties have either reached a resolution or have identified the remaining obstacles and areas of impasse.

* **What is the role of the conference attorney in the prehearing conference?** The conference attorney serves as a neutral and impartial mediator and may perform a variety of roles as may be conducive to the settlement process. He may act as a facilitator, moderator, or intermediator. He may act as a sounding board or as a reality check. Typically he will encourage neutral analysis rather than arguments and accusations. He will assist as needed in the generation of possible for resolution and encourage collaborative problem-solving in the search for mutually agreeable terms. Throughout the mediation process, he will maintain the confidence of the parties and make not recommendation to the Court on the merits of the case.

* **Are prehearing conferences confidential?** Yes. By rule and by agreement of counsel, prehearing conference proceedings are confidential and off the record. The conversations are also protected by the mediation privilege statute, R.C. § 2710.03. Nothing said by the participants, including the conference attorney, may be disclosed to anyone on the Twelfth District Court of Appeals or with any other court that might ever deal with the case on the merits.

* **Do judges of the Court of Appeals know what transpires at prehearing conferences?** No. Any settlement discussions or negotiations which have taken place at a prehearing conference remain confidential and are not revealed to the Court. The prehearing conference process provides appellate counsel and the parties with a confidential and credible, no risk and low cost environment in which they can actively explore options and avenues of resolution which are consistent with their best interests. If no agreements are reached, the case is absolutely unaffected and those in the decisional process that follows know nothing about the mediation discussions. The conference attorney's notes and documents created for settlement purposes will not become a part of the Court's file.

* **How can I best use the prehearing conference to benefit my client?** Recognize that the prehearing conference procedures provide a short window of opportunity to achieve a favorable outcome consistent with your client's overall interests and risks. While maintaining your role as advocate, understand that the appellate mediation

conference is essentially cooperative rather than adversarial. Take advantage of the opportunity to talk constructively and confidentially with counsel for the other parties. Listen closely to what the other participants have to say. Try to be as candid as possible without posturing. Be persuasive yet open to persuasion. Keep in mind that rigidly adhering to a predetermined "bottom line" is usually unproductive because your views about the case, based on new insights and information, often change during the course of the mediation process. This may lead to additional and unanticipated avenues and options for resolution and mutual gain.

\* \* \* \*

## B.  Appellate Courts: Decline in Oral Arguments

The chance to be heard in appellate argument is shrinking. Just as civil jury trials have been in decline in the name of efficiency, so too the efficiency of reducing or eliminating time spent in appellate oral argument has become an attractive option. In the federal circuit courts, the percentage of appeals terminated on the merits after oral argument has declined: in 1971, 65.8% of appeals were decided after oral argument and 34.2% on the briefs only; in 2011, 25.1% of appeals were decided after oral argument and 74.9% on the briefs only. David R. Cleveland & Steven Wisotsky, *The Decline of Oral Argument in the Federal Courts of Appeals: A Modest Proposal for Reform*, 13 J. App. Prac. & Process 119 (2012) (Table 2).

Moreover, even when oral argument is granted, the traditional allotment of 30 minutes per side has also been diminished as the majority of federal circuits average around 10 to 20 minutes each side. *Id.* at Table 1.

Like the decline in civil jury trials, the loss of appellate oral argument affects citizens' ability to see the court system in action. A jury trial and an appellate oral argument are increasingly rare opportunities for the public to observe what is otherwise a closed system.

## Federal Rules of Appellate Procedure Rule 34, 28 U.S.C.

### Rule 34. Oral Argument

**(a) In General.**

**(1) Party's Statement.** Any party may file, or a court may require by local rule, a statement explaining why oral argument should, or need not, be permitted.

**(2) Standards.** Oral argument must be allowed in every case unless a panel of three judges who have examined the briefs and record unanimously agrees that oral argument is unnecessary for any of the following reasons:

   **(A)** the appeal is frivolous;

   **(B)** the dispositive issue or issues have been authoritatively decided; or

(C) the facts and legal arguments are adequately presented in the briefs and record, and the decisional process would not be significantly aided by oral argument.

(b) **Notice of Argument; Postponement.** The clerk must advise all parties whether oral argument will be scheduled, and, if so, the date, time, and place for it, and the time allowed for each side. A motion to postpone the argument or to allow longer argument must be filed reasonably in advance of the hearing date.

(c) **Order and Contents of Argument.** The appellant opens and concludes the argument. Counsel must not read at length from briefs, records, or authorities.

(d) **Cross-Appeals and Separate Appeals.** If there is a cross-appeal, Rule 28.1(b) determines which party is the appellant and which is the appellee for purposes of oral argument. Unless the court directs otherwise, a cross-appeal or separate appeal must be argued when the initial appeal is argued. Separate parties should avoid duplicative argument.

(e) **Nonappearance of a Party.** If the appellee fails to appear for argument, the court must hear appellant's argument. If the appellant fails to appear for argument, the court may hear the appellee's argument. If neither party appears, the case will be decided on the briefs, unless the court orders otherwise.

(f) **Submission on Briefs.** The parties may agree to submit a case for decision on the briefs, but the court may direct that the case be argued.

(g) **Use of Physical Exhibits at Argument; Removal.** Counsel intending to use physical exhibits other than documents at the argument must arrange to place them in the courtroom on the day of the argument before the court convenes. After the argument, counsel must remove the exhibits from the courtroom, unless the court directs otherwise. The clerk may destroy or dispose of the exhibits if counsel does not reclaim them within a reasonable time after the clerk gives notice to remove them.

## United States Court of Appeals for the Eighth Circuit

**Rule 34A. Screening for Oral Argument**

(a) **Assignment of Screening Function.** The chief judge may appoint the clerk, the senior staff attorney, or a panel or panels of judges of the court to screen cases awaiting disposition.

(b) **Screening Categories.** Cases may be screened for disposition without oral argument, for abbreviated argument, or for full argument. Cases screened for full oral argument usually will be allotted 10, 15 or 20 minutes per side. Extended argument of 30 minutes or more per side occasionally will be allotted.

(c) **Reclassification by Hearing Panel.** The panel assigned to dispose of a case may alter time allocations for oral argument or reclassify the case as suitable for disposition without oral argument.

(d) **Disposition Without Oral Argument.** The clerk will notify the parties when a case has been classified as suitable for disposition without argument. Any party may ask the court to reconsider the case for oral argument by filing a written request for reclassification within seven days after receiving notice.

**(e) Calendar Designation.** The clerk will indicate on the calendar the time allocated for argument of each case.

**Cross-Reference:** FRAP 34.

# TWO RIVERS BANK & TRUST v. ATANASOVA
No. 11-2977
Eighth Circuit Court of Appeals

Appellants' Brief

(Nov. 23, 2011)

* * * *

## I. SUMMARY OF THE CASE AND STATEMENT REGARDING ORAL ARGUMENT

Defendants Vanya Atanasova and Venture One, Inc. appeal from a final judgment entered by the Honorable Harold D. Vietor on July 1, 2011 and from the trial court's ruling denying Defendants' post-trial motions entered on August 26, 2011. Defendant suffered an adverse verdict in a jury trial of personal injury and wrongful death claims arising out of a collision on February 20, 2008 on Highway 218 in rural Henry County, Iowa, in which a car being driven by Plaintiff Kala Holtkamp struck the rear of Defendants' truck.

Pursuant to Federal Rule of Appellate Procedure 34 and Eighth Circuit Rule 34A, Defendants respectfully request oral argument in this matter. Oral argument is necessary because the eight-day trial of the case resulted in a large verdict and because the factual and legal record is complex. In particular, the trial court's error in submitting claims to the jury which lacked sufficient evidence, and the court's errors in evidentiary rulings and submission of jury instructions that adversely affected the substantial rights of the Defendants resulted in a judgment for Plaintiffs of nearly $3.7 million. The importance of preserving fundamental fairness in trials and the need to overturn a manifestly unjust result unsupported by proper evidence necessitates oral argument. Counsel anticipates that 20 minutes will be necessary to present Defendant-Appellants' oral argument.

\* \* \* \*

# TWO RIVERS BANK AND TRUST v. ATANASOVA
No. 11-2977
(8th Cir. February 7, 2012)

Appellees' Brief

\* \* \* \*

## II SUMMARY OF THE CASE

The instant case is a diversity action arising out of motor vehicle accident taking place on southbound Highway 218, Mount Pleasant, Iowa, on February 20, 2008. Plaintiff, Kala Holtkamp, was the driver of a 2002 Ford Escort traveling southbound on Highway 218 toward exit 45, near Mount Pleasant, Iowa. Decedent, Christopher Davis, Kala's fiancé, was the front seat passenger, and her son, two-year-old, K.H., was secured in a child seat in the rear passenger-side of her vehicle.

At 7:03 p.m., the Holtkamp vehicle collided with the rear end of tractor trailer when it pulled out in front of them from the shoulder of the highway. The tractor was being operated by Defendant, Vanya Atanasova, and was owned by Defendant, Venture One, Inc. The case was tried to a jury, and following an 8-day trial, the jury returned a verdict in favor of all Plaintiffs totaling $4,088,139.75; $400,915.76 to Kala Holtkamp; $3,190,852.40 to K.H.; $71,371.59 to the Estate of Christopher Davis; $400,000.00 to Tia Hamm Individually; and $25,000 to Nicholas Finley. Plaintiff, Kala Holtkamp was determined to be 10% at fault and Defendant Atanasova was assigned 90% fault. Consequently the final judgment entered against Defendants was $3,679,325.77. Defendants now appeal claiming numerous errors.

## III STATEMENT REGARDING ORAL ARGUMENT

Appellees do not believe oral argument is necessary and suggest the briefs and record adequately present the facts and legal arguments. If the Court grants oral argument, the Appellees request permission to participate and believe 15 minutes per side would be sufficient.

\* \* \* \*

## In Court Reports

1.   The civil jury trial is reported to be in decline; assess your trial court's docket to determine if this trend is supported or contradicted. Consult annual court or state court reports and data collected to find relevant evidence on the possible decline in jury civil trials. The Ohio Courts Statistical Summary in this chapter provides an example of such a report.

**2.** If a decline is present, then consider and research the possible causes. Consider those causes reported elsewhere, such as costs to the court of a jury, any court-related ADR programs, costs of a trial to the litigants, complex issues more suited to a bench trial, any history of well-known "excessive" jury verdicts, increased use of summary judgment. If possible, investigate the issues from several perspectives, including those of the judge, court staff, and local practitioners.

**3.** Undertake research and interview court personnel and practitioners to discern their attitudes toward a decline in civil jury trials. Is a decline viewed as a loss to the court system? Is there a preference for bench trials?

**4.** Studies show that trial judges almost unanimously believe that juries reach fair verdicts; most trial judges report that if they personally were involved in a criminal or civil case they would want it to be decided by a jury. Judge William L. Dwyer . . . considered jurors his "courtroom companions" who routinely produced "fair and honest verdicts." Chief Judge Mark W. Bennett . . . states that it would be "catastrophic for the nation" if civil juries were to disappear. According to . . . trial judge Lyle Strom: "Out of hundreds of jury trials, I can count on fewer than the fingers of one hand the verdicts that I thought made no sense."

Jason Mazzone, *The Justice and the Jury*, 72 BROOK. L. REV. 35 (2006) (citations omitted).

Would the judges in your jurisdiction agree with these trial judges' view that jurors rarely go wrong in their deliberations and verdicts?

**5.** Determine if trial courts in your jurisdiction have created court-annexed mediation. Find the local or other rules that create these mediation court practices at the trial court level.

Many communities have mediation centers that will train law students, lawyers, and other citizens in the techniques of mediation. For example, the City of Dayton, Ohio, funds the Dayton Mediation Center and local police refer neighborhood disputes to the Center. http://daytonmediationcenter.org

After observing courtroom proceedings, contrast that experience by observing mediation procedures or participating in mediation training that may be available to you.

**6.** Search for cases in your court or jurisdiction for any concerning arbitration clauses or use of other ADR measures that gave rise to disputes and litigation over their enforceability. Categorize the fact settings — are they similar to those targeted in the proposed Arbitration Fairness Act noted in the *Arnold* case?

**7.** Participate in a jury instruction conference, if available. Or, draft jury instructions for a jury trial — if you can find one either in your on court or another in your community. Or take a hand at revising for clarity those submitted in *Allianz Risk Transfer*.

Evaluate the ability of a non-lawyer to comprehend and use the jury instructions. Or, sit in court when jurors are being instructed and consider comprehension of jury instructions when read aloud at a single sitting.

8.  Consider the expenses incurred if a jury trial were held in a trial court in your jurisdiction. Federal jurors are paid $40.00 a day for jury service; their transportation costs to and from court are covered; food and housing may be covered if they remain on site during the trial and deliberations. Multiply these daily costs by the average length of a jury trial in your court. Have jury costs been a factor in the trial court's view of civil jury trials?

9.  The value in a jury trial relies on the honest, unbiased judgment of the jurors who are protected from influences from outside of the courtroom. Increasingly, great efforts are taken to protect jurors from the outside influences of not only traditional print media, but social media. Does a trial court in your jurisdiction issue jury instructions concerning social media? How effective do you judge them to be?

10.  Investigate appellate courts in your jurisdiction to determine if they have created a settlement on appeal program. If so, what has the response been to the program by judges, by those staff conducting the settlement or mediation conferences, by attorneys and their clients.

11.  Investigate the oral argument rules in appellate courts in your jurisdiction. Have the rules changed to limit oral arguments or remained the same, but oral arguments have declined? Again, how do judges, their staff, practicing attorneys and their clients view a decline, if one is present. Appellate judges vary in the importance and weight they give to oral arguments in making their decisions.

12.  With the loss of traditional judicial roles such as trying cases, reading appellate briefs, and hearing oral arguments, some argue that judges are now more like administrators than judges because they are focused on hiring and supervising staff and clerks who perform various tasks like screening cases, mediating and settling cases, and drafting opinions.

Does this assessment ring true in your court?

## Out of Court Reports

1.  Jury trials traditionally held a place of honor in American history and culture, but John Grisham's The Runaway Jury, first published in 1996, provides a dark view as civil jurors in a "Big Tobacco" torts trial compete to be bribed or bought off by the opposing litigants. Research other works of fiction or popular culture that portray civil trial juries. What, if any, basis, do these portrayals have in reality?

2.  The movie, *12 Angry Men* (1957), defined the jury's place of honor and has achieved legendary status for many. Judge Kozinski of the Ninth Circuit Court of Appeals was dismayed when learned that his judicial clerks "had a troubling gap in their education: They hadn't seen *12 Angry Men*." 101 A.B.A. J. 9 (Aug. 15, 2015). The film portrays jurors deliberating over a criminal case, a murder, not a civil case, but the "star" is the American jury system.

View the film and consider: Does the portrayal of the jurors and their deliberations still ring true today? How does research on the composition of juries today compare with the jurors portrayed in the movie?

3.  After examining the Federal Rules of Evidence, consider if excluding evidence

that may arouse prejudice or passion in a jury is necessary. Are jurors more vulnerable to emotion and prejudice than judges? Consider any research supporting these Rules that prevent the jury from hearing or seeing certain evidence.

4.    Explore the language of arbitration clauses simply as a consumer. "If you have a national bank-issued credit card, a cell phone services contract, or you have borrowed from a payday or auto title lender, purchased a new or used car, or signed a home improvement contract, your contracts may contain binding arbitration clauses." Linda Cook, *"Law You Can Use"* Ohio State Bar Ass'n (5/20/2014).

5.    Should the decline of full blown civil jury trials and the possible decline of a full blown appellate court process with appellate briefs and oral arguments affect law school education? What lawyering skills are needed in a practice setting that is less adversarial and where a lawyer is advised to be "cooperative rather than adversarial" and to "[b]e persuasive yet open to persuasion"?

Or could courses be modified to reflect current practices? Perhaps requiring student appellate briefs to include sections in support of or opposition to oral argument or in requiring a mediation on appeal session?

6.    In *Two Rivers Bank and Trust*, both sides briefed the issue and oral argument was granted. Docket, *Order Setting Oral Argument* (April 13, 2012). Oral argument was held May 15, 2012. The Eighth Circuit provides MP3's of the oral arguments, including the one in Two *Rivers*, on its website: www.ca8.uscourts.gov/oral-arguments.

7.    Analyze the many "burdens" that the *Richardson* trial court judge took on when it held a civil jury trial for three days — May 29, 30, and 31, 2002 — contrasted with a bench trial or settlement. These jury trial burdens begin with jury selection and only end with the jury's verdict.

The *Richardson* appellate court granted the parties an oral argument. Based on the appellate opinion, make the arguments in favor of and opposed to oral argument.

8.    Despite drafting and submitting proposed jury instructions on the eve of a scheduled civil jury trial, the parties in *Allianz* had both failed to request a jury trial.

How might this omission have happened? When and how does an attorney request a civil jury trial?

## SELECTED BIBLIOGRAPHY

Richard M. Alderman, *Consumer Arbitration: The Destruction of the Common Law*, 2 J. AM. ARB. (July 2011)

Joseph F. Anderson, Jr., *Where Have You Gone Spot Mozingo? A Trial Judge's Lament over the Demise of the Civil Jury Trial*, 4 FED. CTS. L. REV. 99 (2010).

Theresa M. Beiner, *The Many Lanes Out of Court: Against Privatization of Employment Discrimination Disputes*, 73 MD. L. REV. 837 (2014).

Joe S. Cecil, Valerie P. Hans & Elizabeth C. Wiggins, *Citizen Comprehension of Difficult Issues: Lessons from Civil Jury Trials*, 40 AM. U. L. REV. 727 (1991).

George K. Chamberlin, *Complexity of Civil Action as Affecting Seventh*

*Amendment Right to Trial by Jury*, 54 A.L.R. Fed. 733 (Originally published 1981).

David R. Cleveland & Steven Witosky, *The Decline of Oral Argument in the Federal Courts of Appeals: A Modest Proposal for Reform*, 13 J. App. Prac. & Process 119 (2012).

Carmen Comsti, *A Metamorphosis: How Forced Arbitration Arrived in the Workplace*, 35 Berkeley J. Emp. & Lab. L. 5 (2014).

Shari Seidman Diamond & Andrea Ryken, *The Modern American Jury*, 96 Judicature 315 (2013).

Barry Edwards, *Renovating the Multi-Door Courthouse: Designing Trial Court Dispute Resolution Systems to Improve Results and Control Costs*, 18 Harv. Negot. L. Rev. 281 (2013).

Jennifer Walker Elrod, *Is the Jury Still Out? A Case for the Continued Viability of the American Jury*, 44 Tex. Tech. L. Rev. 303 (2012).

Royal Furgeson, *Civil Jury Trials R.I.P.? Can it Actually Happen in America?*, 40 St. Mary's L.J. 795 (2009).

Marc Galanter & Angela Frozena, *The Jury Trial Implosion: The Decline of Trial by Jury and Its Significance for the Appellate Courts*, Pound Civil Justice Institute (2011 Forum for State Appellate Court Judges).

Marc Galanter, *The Hundred-Year Decline of Trials and the Thirty Years War*, 57 Stan. L. Rev. 1255 (2005).

Patrick E. Higginbotham, *The Present Plight of the United States District Courts*, 60 Duke L.J. 745 (2010).

Stacy A. Hickox, *Ensuring Enforceability and Fairness in the Arbitration of Employment Disputes*, 16 Widener L. Rev. 101 (2010).

James F. Holderman, *As Generations X, Y, and Z Determine the Jury's Verdict, What is the Judge's Role?*, 58 DePaul L. Rev. 343 (2009).

D. Brock Hornby, *The Business of the U.S. District Courts*, 10 Green Bag 2d 453 (2007).

Kenneth F. Hunt, *Saving Time or Killing Time: How the Use of Unpublished Opinions Accelerates the Drain on Federal Judicial* Resources, 61 Syracuse L. Rev. 315 (2011).

Eric Koplowitz, *"I Didn't Agree to Arbitrate That!" — How Courts Determine If Employees' Sexual Assault and Sexual Harassment Claims Fall Within the Scope of Broad Mandatory Arbitration Clauses*, 13 Cardozo J. Conflict Resol. 565 (2012).

John Lande, *The Movement Toward Early Case Handling in Courts and Private Dispute Resolution*, 24 Ohio St. J. on Disp. Resol. 81 (2008).

Graham C. Lilly, *The Decline of the American Jury*, 72 U. Colo. L. Rev. 53 (2001).

Bobbi McAdoo & Nancy A. Welsh, *Look Before You Leap and Keep on Looking: Lessons from the Institutionalization of Court-Connected Mediation*, 5 NEV. L.J. 399 (2005).

Tracy W. McCormack, Susan Schultz & James McCormack, *Probing the Legitimacy of Mandatory Mediation: New Roles for Judges, Mediators and Lawyers*, 1 ST. MARY'S J. LEGAL MAL. & ETHICS 150 (2011).

Arthur R. Miller, *The Pretrial Rush to Judgment: Are the "Litigation Explosion," "Liability Crisis," and Efficiency Clichés Eroding Our Day in Court and Jury Trial Commitments?*, 78 N.Y.U. L. REV. 982 (2003).

Jennifer F. Miller, *Should Juries Hear Complex Patent Cases?*, 2004 DUKE L. & TECH. REV. 4.

Blake D. Morant, *The Declining Prevalence of Trials as a Dispute Resolution Device: Implications for the Academy*, 38 WM. MITCHELL L. REV. 1123 (2012).

Jacqueline Nolan-Haley, *Mediation: The Best and Worst of Times*, 16 CARDOZO J. CONFLICT RESOL. 731 (2015).

Arthur Pearlstein, *Foreward: Pretrial Litigation, Dispute Resolution, and the Rarity of Trial*, 40 CREIGHTON L. REV. 651 (2007).

Todd E. Pettys, *The Emotional Juror*, 76 FORDHAM L. REV. 1609 (2007).

Michael W. Pfautz, *What Would a Reasonable Jury Do? Jury Verdicts Following Summary Judgment Reversals*, 115 COLUM. L. REV. 1255 (2015).

Judith Resnick, *Whither and Whether Adjudication?*, 86 B.U. L. REV. 1101 (2006).

Willy E. Rice, *Courts Gone "Irrationally Biased" in Favor of the Federal Arbitration Act? — Enforcing Arbitration Provisions in Standardized Applications and Marginalizing Consumer-Protection, Anti-Discrimination, and States' Contract Laws: A 1925–2014 Legal and Empirical Analysis*, 6 WM. & MARY BUS. L. REV. 405 (2015).

Anna Roberts, *(Re)forming the Jury: Detection and Disinfection of Implicit Juror Bias*, 44 CONN. L. REV. 827 (2012).

Frederic N. Smalkin & Frederick N.C. Smalkin, *The Market for Justice, the "Litigation Explosion," and the "Verdict Bubble": A Closer Look at Vanishing Trials*, 2005 FED. CTS. L. REV. 8.

Mark Spottswood, *Emotional Fact-Finding*, 63 U. KAN. L. REV. 41 (2014).

Amy J. St. Eve & Michael A. Zuckerman, *Ensuring an Impartial Jury in the Age of Social Media*, 11 DUKE L. & TECH. REV. 1 (2012).

Richard L. Steagall, *The Recent Explosion in Summary Judgments Entered by the Federal Courts Has Eliminated the Jury from the Judicial Power*, 33 S. ILL. U. L.J. 469 (2009).

Thomas J. Stipanowich, *Arbitration: "The New Litigation,"* 2010 U. ILL. L. REV. 1 (2010).

Stephen N. Subrin, *A Traditionalist Looks at Mediation: It's Here to Stay and Much Better Than I Thought*, 3 NEV. L.J. 196 (2003).

Stephen D. Susman & Thomas M. Melsheimer, *Trial by Agreement: How Trial Lawyers Hold the Key to Improving Jury Trials in Civil Cases*, 32 Rev. Litig. 431 (2013).

Elizabeth G. Thornburg, *The Managerial Judge Goes to Trial*, 44 U. RICH. L. REV. 1261 (2010).

Roselle L. Wissler, *Court-Connected Mediation in General Civil Cases: What We Know from Empirical Research*, 17 OHIO ST. J. ON DISP. RESOL. 641 (2002).

Andrew J. Wilhelm, *Complex Litigation in the New Era of the iJury*, 41 PEPP. L. REV. 817 (2014).

William G. Young, *Vanishing Trials, Vanishing Juries, Vanishing Constitution*, 40 SUFFOLK U. L. REV. 67 (2006).

# Chapter 6

# JUDICIAL ROLES: THERAPEUTIC JURISPRUDENCE AND THE RISE OF SPECIALTY DOCKETS & PROBLEM-SOLVING COURTS

Problem-solving courts have emerged in the United States as a significant feature on the criminal justice landscape. There are now well over 3,000 specialized courts in the United States that pursue a problem-solving approach.

Richard C. Boldt, *Problem-Solving Courts and Pragmatism*, 73 Md. L. Rev. 1120 (2014).

[Defense counsel] in specialty courts becomes, in most instances, a collaborator. He collaborates with the judge and prosecutors, thereby taking on a role that works to diminish the effectiveness of the defender overall, decreases the confidence defendants have in the outcome, and supports a culture of ineffectiveness and under-representation. . . . [C]itizens most in need of justice and traditionally overrepresented in the criminal justice system may be adversely affected the most by this turn of events. Statistics and research from specialty courts indicate that indigent criminal defendants and those from racial and ethnic minority groups are often over-represented in specialty courts, thus bearing more than their fair share of the danger of indifferent representation.

Tamar M. Meekins, *"Specialized Justice": The Over-Emergence of Specialty Courts and the Threat of a New Criminal Defense Paradigm*, 40 Suffolk U. L. Rev. 1 (2006).

The war on drugs and subsequent implementation of zero tolerance approaches to drug use dramatically increased arrests and incarceration for drug offenses as early as the 1960s. . . . Because traditional courts lacked effective tools to deal with the underlying nature of severe substance use disorder, drug courts emerged to fill the missing niche in the correctional system.

Caitlinrose Fisher, *Treating the Disease or Punishing the Criminal?: Effectively Using Drug Court Sanctions to Treat Substance Use Disorder and Decrease Criminal Conduct*, 99 MINN. L. REV. 747 (2014).

> The scandal of America's drug courts is that we have rushed headlong into them — driven by politics, judicial pop-psychopharmacology, fuzzy-headed notions about "restorative justice" and "therapeutic jurisprudence . . . "

Morris B. Hoffman, *The Drug Court Scandal*, 78 N.C. L. REV. 1437 (2000).

> These [specialized] courts grow out of a recognition that traditional justice approaches have failed, at least in the areas of substance abuse, domestic violence, certain kinds of criminality, child abuse and neglect, and mental illness. . . . The traditional judicial model addressed the symptoms, but not the underlying problem.

BRUCE WINICK & DAVID B. WEXLER, EDS., JUDGING IN A THERAPEUTIC KEY, *Introduction* (2003).

Therapeutic jurisprudence revises a judge's role within the criminal justice system and revises the criminal justice system itself. Those who advocate for problem-solving courts view them as transforming court procedures. Critics view these courts as undermining the criminal justice system by relinquishing or at least sharing decision making with nonlegal treatment professionals, by changing the traditional roles of the prosecutor and defense counsel, and denying the offender-participants due process.

This chapter introduces the basic concepts underpinning the development of therapeutic justice. Then it focuses on a single, long established problem-solving court — the drug courts. Begun during the 1970s and 1980s "War on Drugs," drug courts are now widespread and have been studied, analyzed, and compared to the more traditional forms of criminal justice. Drug courts hoped to address the "revolving door" effect of seeing offenders arrested, jailed, released, and arrested again. The experience gained from drug courts has often formed the basis for starting other problem-solving courts addressing a range of issues with similar problems of repeat offenders cycling through the courtroom and jail. These courts include juvenile drug court, veterans' court, domestic violence court, and others.

Next, a specific drug court, operating in the Montgomery County Court of Common Pleas, Dayton, Ohio, is examined. The drug court's details include the relevant Ohio state statutes, the local court rules, and court processes needed in a drug court. This material includes the contract required to participate in the drug court program and statistics gathered during the drug court's operation, which began in 1997.

Finally, two documents — a hypothetical fact pattern and a judicial opinion — illustrate the potential risks created by drug courts and other problem-solving courts.

# I. THE JUDGE IN TRADITIONAL AND PROBLEM-SOLVING COURTS

### A Comparison of Transformed and Traditional Court Procedures

| *Traditional Process* | *Transformed Process* |
|---|---|
| Dispute Resolution | Problem-solving dispute avoidance |
| Legal outcome | Therapeutic outcome |
| Adversarial process | Collaborative process |
| Claim- or case-oriented | People-oriented |
| Rights-based | Interest or needs-based |
| Emphasis placed on adjudication | Emphasis placed on post-adjudication and |
| | Alternative dispute resolution |
| Interpretation and application of law | Interpretation and application of social science |
| Judge as arbiter | Judge as coach |
| Backward looking | Forward looking |
| Precedent-based | Planning-based |
| Few participants and stakeholders | Wide range of participants and stakeholders |
| Individualistic | Interdependent |
| Legalistic | Common-sensical |
| Formal | Informal |
| Efficient | Effective |

Judge Roger K. Warren, A Comparison of Transformed and Traditional Court Procedures, National Center for State Courts, PowerPoint presentation.

# II. DRUG COURTS AS PROBLEM-SOLVING COURTS

The widespread enthusiasm for problem-solving courts is rooted in judicial frustration with traditional sentencing of criminal defendants to jail time. Faced, for example, with non-violent drug addicted offenders in court during the 1980s "War on Drugs," judges came to recognize a revolving door effect "in which offenders typically resumed their drug-abusing behavior after release from prison." BRUCE WINICK & DAVID B. WEXLER, EDS., JUDGING IN A THERAPEUTIC KEY at 4.

Drug treatment courts emerged in Miami in 1989, but a problem-solving approach could be credited initially to the first juvenile courts that developed in Chicago during the 1870s. Current problem-solving courts address offenders with issues similar to drug addiction, that is, offenders with problems that tend to recur post-release and result in repeated convictions: domestic violence courts; mental health courts, problem gambling courts, veterans' courts, DWI court, homeless courts, gun courts, and truancy court. *See* West Huddleston & Douglas B. Marlowe, *Painting the Current Picture: A National Report on Drug Courts and Other Problem-Solving Court Programs in the United States* (National Drug Court Institute July 2011). As the list suggests, these courts "share a common commitment to the core principles of therapeutic jurisprudence, and recognize the important role of the court system in addressing and resolving some of society's major ills. . . . they all seek to solve problems rather than merely adjudicate controversies or punish malfeasance." *Id.* at 37.

---

**Key Drug Court Protocols**

**Multidisciplinary Teams** involving the judge and other justice system players;

**Judicial Status Hearings** repeatedly with the offender present during the first few months and less frequently as participants achieve sobriety;

**Drug Testing** on a frequent, random basis during the first several months and less frequently later in the program;

**Graduated Sanctions and Rewards** with swift punishment for infractions (brief jail detention) coupled with incentives for good performance; and

**Substance Abuse Treatment** conforming to standardized, evidence-based regimens.

---

Gordon M. Griller, *The Quiet Battle for Problem-Solving Courts*, National Center for State Courts, Future Trends in State Courts (2011).

## Judge Kevin S. Burke
### *Just What Made Drug Courts Successful?*[1]
36 NEW ENGLAND J. ON CRIM. & CIV. CONFINEMENT 39 (2010)

In the early 1970s, the United States saw a wave of new laws imposing dramatically harsher penalties for drug convictions. Court systems already inundated with serious offenses were flooded with drug cases as arrests for drug-related crimes in the United States jumped from 322,000 in 1970 to more than 1.3 million in 1998. Recidivism rates were horrible. Those recidivism rates contributed to giving the United States the highest incarceration rate in the world.

In response to the influx of drug cases, New York City created specialized "narcotics courts" to help manage the growing caseload. New York City's narcotics courts became known as "N Parts" and functioned as "specialized case management courts designed to handle a high volume of drug cases in a traditional manner." The "N Parts," however, had no additional treatment component for drug offenders.

The country's first treatment-based drug court was established in 1989 in Miami-Dade County, Florida. Judge Herbert M. Klein, along with the Dade County Attorney, Janet Reno, and a number of other officials, including Hillary Clinton's brother who was then a public defender, designed the court to introduce supervised drug treatment into the criminal justice system.

---

[1] Reprinted by permission of the New England Journal on Criminal and Civil Confinement.

Recognizing the need for treatment and believing the first drug courts to be successful, officials around the country began establishing treatment-based drug courts to deal with offenders through individualized treatment and monitoring programs. As United States Attorney General, Janet Reno became a champion of drug courts and paved the way for an influx of federal funds to plan and start the effort. There are currently more than 1600 drug courts operating in fifty states, as well as in the District of Columbia, Puerto Rico, Guam, and a number of Native American Tribal Courts.

Drug courts around the country operate in different ways and achieve a wide variety of outcomes. If there is any singular description of these drug courts, it is that each operates according to its own unique protocol. They have their own local legal culture. However, the theory behind their operation is largely the same: drug courts use the criminal justice system to treat drug addiction through judicially monitored treatment rather than mere incarceration or probation. Judges supervise the defendants in a more intense fashion than traditional courts and develop interpersonal relationships with defendants that would rarely occur in a more traditional court. The National Drug Court Institute describes drug courts as follows: "Drug courts represent the coordinated efforts of the judiciary, prosecution, defense bar, probation, law enforcement, mental health, social service, and treatment communities to actively and forcefully intervene and break the cycle of substance abuse, addiction, and crime."

In most instances, drug courts accept defendants who have been charged with drug possession or another non-violent offense and who either tested positive for drugs or had a known substance abuse problem at the time of their arrest. Many drug courts exclude defendants with current or prior violent offenses. Persons "who are currently facing charges for a drug offense may be denied entry into the drug court because of a past, wholly unrelated offense." Also, those drug courts that receive federal funding through the Bureau of Justice Assistance are required to accept only defendants who meet certain criteria.

Drug courts generally operate under one of two models: deferred prosecution programs or post-adjudication programs. Deferred prosecution programs divert certain eligible defendants to the drug-court system before they plead to a charge. Post-adjudication programs, on the other hand, require a defendant to first plead guilty to the charge before making treatment options available. The drug court then defers or suspends the defendant's sentence while he or she participates in a drug-court program. If the defendant successfully completes the program, the sentence may be waived and the offense may even be expunged. Defendants who fail to complete drug-court programs usually must return to the traditional criminal court for disposition of their criminal case.

Most drug courts in the United States require that participants remain drug-free and without arrests for a period of time, usually ranging from six months to one year, in order to complete the program. The progress of individual participants is monitored by judges, who interact frequently with participants, as well as by clinical staff. Participants who miss hearings or fail drug tests may be sanctioned through more frequent hearings or drug tests, admonishments in open court, or even jail time.

Participants may be required to obtain a GED, hold a job, make child-support and drug-court fee payments, and have a sponsor in the community. Some courts also require participants to complete community-service hours. These additional requirements may serve to reestablish a participant's ties to a community, which can then serve as a support network and as an incentive to maintain sobriety.

## I. DRUG COURTS TODAY

Today, the National Association of Drug Court Professionals aims to establish a sustainable drug-court program in each of the United States' 3143 counties. Its goal is to take drug courts to scale in order to "transform communities nationwide by fostering systemic change in the way addicted persons are treated in the adult, juvenile, and family justice systems." While the goal is noble, it is clear that even if achieved, there is a decent prospect that the result will be 3143 drug courts that act in different ways.

The U.S. Department of Justice has published what it calls the "key components" of successful drug courts. According to advocates, the key components are not to serve as a rigid list of procedures or regulations, but rather as an example of what the "best practices" to strive for are, even though each court will attempt to accomplish its task through different means.

There are ten key components. First, drug courts are encouraged to "integrate alcohol and other drug treatment services with justice system case processing." The purpose of this component is to have the justice system persuade or compel addicts to participate in treatment options because "a person coerced to enter treatment by the criminal justice system is likely to do as well as one who volunteers." Even outside of the criminal justice system, many people are coerced into treatment. Spouses threaten each other with divorce, employers threaten discharge if an employee does not go to treatment, and parents cart their children off to treatment kicking and screaming. Coercion begins the road to recovery for a number of people.

Second, the prosecution and defense counsel are urged to promote public safety and protect due-process rights by using a non-adversarial approach. This component envisions a prosecutor and defense counsel working as a team in order to screen cases for potential participants, and "encourage" defendants to enter the drug-court programs. Perhaps more than any other of the ten key components, this approach raises concerns, which will be discussed in greater depth later in this article.

Third, drug courts are encouraged to identify and place eligible participants in the drug-court program early and promptly. Action taken promptly after arrest is designed to take advantage of the shock of arrest felt by the defendant and to increase public confidence in the system. People have gone to treatment and continue to do so as part of probation even when there is no drug court. Many drug courts, however, emphasize the speed in which defendants are placed in treatment as a goal of the court. Since chemical dependency is a chronic progressive disease, presumably the quicker the intervention, the better the outcome.

Fourth, drug courts are to provide access to a continuum of alcohol, drug and other treatment and rehabilitation services. For the drug court to be effective, the system must consider problems that co-occur with drug addiction, including mental illness, homelessness, unemployment, and other health problems.

Because the drugs themselves may not be the only factor feeding the defendant's addiction, the treatment options must be able to treat the entire patient, rather than simply the physical manifestation of the illness that resulted in arrest for breaking the law.

The degree of serious mental health issues many drug-court defendants have is illustrated in a study of the defendants in the Hennepin County, Minnesota, drug court conducted by Doctors Hildi Hagedorn and Mark L. Willenbring. In their study, sixty drug-court defendants completed a demographic interview, the Beck Depression and Anxiety Inventories, and an examination of their medical quality of life. The study found that serious mental illness was common among the participants; the most common of which was post-traumatic stress disorder. Most of the individuals interviewed had not previously been identified as requiring psychiatric treatment. The study suggests that more frequent and thorough screening for psychiatric illness is necessary in drug courts to provide participants with all the tools needed to fight their addictions.

Fifth, the key components encourage frequent alcohol and drug tests to monitor a participant's abstinence. Testing programs are the only objective and efficient way to monitor a participant's progress and their compliance with the program. Testing usually occurs frequently at first and may taper off as the participant progresses, but additional testing may be ordered if a participant fails a test or refuses to take a test. Some but not all drug courts require the defendant to pay for the drug testing.

Sixth, a coordinated strategy is suggested to define court responses to a participant's compliance. Traditional criminal courts use negative consequences as the singular motivator. "Obey my order or I'll revoke your probation and send you to prison." Drug courts reward cooperation through methods such as praise from the bench, reduced supervision, dismissal or reduction of criminal charges, and graduation. If a participant does not comply, for example by failing a drug test, they are not immediately kicked out of the program and sent back into the general criminal justice docket, but they may be reprimanded through admonishments in open court, increased testing, fines, mandatory community service, and escalating periods of jail confinement. To their credit, drug court judges recognize that relapse is part of the disease of chemical dependency.

Seventh, the key components recognize that "[o]ngoing judicial interaction with each drug court participant is essential." The idea is that a relationship with the court increases the likelihood the participant will remain in treatment and increases the chances of success. Having a powerful authority figure such as a judge care about you can be a huge motivation to change. But caring takes an investment of passion and time. Unless there is a demonstrable decrease in recidivism, the requirement of a continued and ongoing relationship with the judge raises questions of how to best use the judicial resources of the court. That time investment has led to the demise of many drug courts. Despite the time commitment by judges and the experience that some drug courts ceased because of that commitment, there are strong proponents for using court hearings in all types of courts to motivate offender behavior change.

Eighth, the key components encourage monitoring and evaluation to measure the effectiveness of the program. The only way for a drug court to be effective is to monitor the progress of participants and adapt the program to ensure the most people will remain in treatment. Not every idea that has been tried in drug courts has worked; some ideas worked in one court and were a miserable failure in another. But to their credit, all of the drug courts embraced evaluation and change to a far greater degree than traditional criminal courts.

Ninth, interdisciplinary education is encouraged in order to promote effective planning, implementation, and operations. Educating the attorneys involved in drug courts in the areas of psychology and addiction help develop an understanding of the values, goals, and operating procedures of the treatment process. Similarly, educating the treatment providers about the criminal justice system helps them understand the procedures involved. Given the dominance of chemical dependency and mental health issues among defendants, it is almost bewildering why the criminal justice system as a whole, let alone drug courts, have not been more sophisticated in their understanding of the need for collaboration. For drug courts to be effective, they need to create a collaborative mentality between the courts and the treatment providers.

Tenth, drug-court programs are designed to forge partnerships among the courts, public agencies, and community-based organizations to generate local support and enhance effectiveness. Developing coalitions with community organizations, criminal justice agencies, and treatment providers creates greater access to services for participants and informs the community about drug court processes.

There is one major aspect missing from the Department of Justice's key components. Nowhere in the key components are the court or court officials encouraged to talk with the participant about what he or she wants. The defense counsel is supposed to encourage the offender's participation, but the participant is not necessarily encouraged to participate in the planning or implementation of his own treatment program. The court and attorneys decide what to do with the participant, and the participant is expected to obey a treatment program that is thrust upon him or her. Giving the participant the opportunity to be heard and to participate in the process — a key factor in the effectiveness of the early drug courts — regrettably has been lost in many drug courts. That failure to embrace the importance of voice and participation can create the perception of procedural unfairness, where the participant may feel that no one is listening to him. The adversarial system may not be perfect, but when the system works at its best it ensures a voice to the people.

## II. CRITIQUES OF DRUG COURTS

### A. Drug Courts Fail to Reduce Costs

A multitude of studies examining the effectiveness and efficiency of drug courts have been conducted over the last twenty years. Several have suggested that drug courts are effective when it comes to reducing recidivism and saving money. For example, in 2005 the Government Accountability Office found that drug-court participants had lower recidivism rates than comparison group members. Recidivism rates among drug-court participants have been reported at 5% to 28%, and at less than 4% for drug-court graduates. The Drug Court Clearinghouse and Technical Assistance Project boasts that of the more than 100,000 drug-dependent offenders who have entered drug court programs, more than 70% are either still enrolled or have graduated the program. According to the National Association of Drug Court Professionals, "for every dollar invested in drug court, nearly ten dollars are saved by corrections." However, given the diversity of the protocols of many drug courts, there are few, if any, studies that have been able to identify why they work.

Drug courts are not without skeptics. Some drug-court supporters have an almost evangelical passion for, and commitment to, the drug-court system, which make some people uncomfortable. Critics of drug courts argue that the impact of drug courts on prison populations may not be as positive as claimed, especially when jail time imposed as a sanction exceeds jail time that would have been imposed in traditional criminal court.

Drug courts are designed to incentivize compliance with the program and to disincentive failures. If the penalty for failure is no worse than what would have happened had the offender not participated, there is no real incentive to take the program seriously and to strive for graduation. As a result, the critics argue, many drug-court participants are convicted of non-violent offenses and would not have been sentenced to long prison stays if they had not been a part of the drug-court program.

In their critique of drug courts, Ryan S. King and Jill Pasquarella of the Sentencing Project further note that "there is a growing concern that instead of providing an alternative sentencing route for arrestees, drug courts actually increase the number of people arrested on drug charges." They suggest that law enforcement officials make more arrests of low-level offenders because drug courts allow for additional judges to deal with low-level drug offenders.

Former Denver District Court Judge William G. Meyer and Colorado Governor A. William Ritter, on the other hand, call accusations that drug courts "net widen" and increase the prison population "fallacious." They note that "[t]he research on almost one hundred drug courts fails to establish any pattern where the drug courts are actually sending more people to prison than a traditional sentencing program."

## B. Drug Courts Fail to Treat Serious Drug Use

Another common critique of drug courts is that they fail to treat serious drug addiction. The Drug Court Clearinghouse points out that "[m]ost drug court participants have been using drugs for many, many years; many are polydrug users. Most have never been exposed to treatment previously although a large portion have already served jail or prison time for drug related offenses." The National Drug Court Institute boasts that in treating these participants, drug courts provide "closer, more comprehensive supervision and much more frequent drug testing and monitoring during the program than other forms of community supervision."

Drug courts have opened new avenues for accessing chemical dependency treatment, but budget constraints frequently limit the treatment options. For example, criminologists Faith Lutze and Jacqueline van Wormer argue that drug courts may not provide effective treatment for participants with serious drug-addiction problems. They suggest that for seriously addicted individuals, long-term inpatient treatment would be a more effective strategy. The issue of the type of treatment available becomes even more critical because drug-court defendants all too often suffer not just from chemical dependency but from major mental illnesses as well.

Critics note that defendants with serious histories of drug use are often excluded from drug-court participation due to their criminal records. As a result, drug courts in many cases do not have the opportunity to work with the most seriously addicted offenders. Even so, drug courts at least leave open the option of helping those with serious addiction problems, whereas a pure incarceration model leaves no such opportunity, and can actually exacerbate addiction among inmates.

## C. Drug Courts Exacerbate Racial Disparities in the Prison System

Critics of drug courts further argue that drug courts serve to exacerbate the problem of racial disparities in the prison system. Marquette Law School Professor Michael O'Hear argues that "the war on drugs, and particularly the special intensity with which it has been waged against open-air drug dealing and crack cocaine, has fueled a massive and demographically disproportionate increase in the number of black males held in the nation's prisons." O'Hear suggests that the drug courts exacerbate rather than ameliorate the problem because evidence shows that white drug offenders are more likely than African-American offenders to benefit from the "pathway out" of the traditional criminal justice system provided by drug courts.

O'Hear suggests four reasons why drug courts may exacerbate racial disparities in the prison system: First, because a defendant must be arrested in order to participate in a drug-court program, the drug courts do not improve racial disparities in arrest patterns. In fact, the argument was that drug courts create an incentive to make arrests. Second, the eligibility requirements tend to "screen out the prison-bound," thus disadvantaging African-American offenders. Third, drug-court programs have a high failure rate, and African-Americans are more likely to fail than whites. Finally, participants who fail to complete drug-court programs may be subject to even longer sentences than they would have faced had they not entered the drug-court program. The fear that drug courts might exacerbate the problem of over-incarceration of chemically dependent people is not an unreasonable concern. One study found that drug court dropouts were sentenced to prison terms two to five times longer than those whose cases were processed entirely in traditional criminal court.

O'Hear argues that drug courts are unlikely to affect the stigma placed on African-American communities as a result of drug-related arrests. In fact, O'Hear notes that problems of stigma may be exacerbated by "a drug court culture that relies heavily on public shaming rituals." In the final analysis, perhaps what critics such as O'Hear fail to fully account for is the fact that drug courts simply are not capable of creating system-wide criminal justice reform. The purpose of the early drug courts was to get treatment for as many addicts as possible, no matter their race. The alternative of not having any drug courts creates an even bleaker alternative for those with addiction problems. Any reasoned and objective analysis of drug courts will not conclude that they are perfect, but when good becomes the enemy of perfect, the result will not be positive.

## D. Drug Courts Violate Defendants' Due Process Rights

The role of the adversary system in the context of drug courts is hotly debated. Among the most vocal critics are public defenders, private defense counsel and advocates for sentencing reform; the very people one might have expected to be ardent supporters of the effort. As reflected in the key components, many of drug courts' most ardent supporters argue that the courts cannot operate with a traditional criminal courts' adversarial system. Critics of drug courts suggest that by asking prosecutors to identify defendants who would benefit from drug-court programs and to assist in the defendants' recovery, drug courts interfere with the adversarial process.

The war on drugs created many casualties of war. Racial profiling of minorities occurred in some instances. By requiring a guilty plea before treatment is offered, some drug courts put the victims of racial profiling in between the proverbial rock and a hard place. They force the victims to choose to either litigate their legitimate constitutional rights or avail themselves of needed treatment. Critics question whether defendants can knowingly and voluntarily consent to drug-court programs "without duress or coercion," whether court officials avoid bias and conflicts of interest, and whether a stigma occurs when a defendant decides to participate in the drug court program or to go forward in the traditional criminal court system. Furthermore, there is concern that drug courts may violate the equal protection rights of certain defendants, since many drug-court programs are not available statewide.

The Bureau of Justice Assistance argues that drug courts are consistent with the adversarial process. In its publication *Defining Drug Courts: The Key Components*, the Bureau states that "[u]sing a nonadversarial approach, prosecution and defense counsel promote public safety while protecting participants' due process rights." The Bureau suggests that prosecutors and defense counsel should work together to design policies and procedures that safeguard the due process rights of drug court participants. As an aspiration of the legal profession, it is impossible to argue that the goal is not noble even if there is a practical problem of implementation. The problem with this aspiration is that it may not be easy to protect a defendant's due process rights if the prosecutor and defense counsel are working together outside of the adversarial process. Professor David Wexler argues that the defense counsel cannot operate solely as a member of the team, but must be permitted to confer with his client about what goes on in the pre-hearing conferences and make arguments on behalf of the client where appropriate.

One of the main aspects of due process is the opportunity to be heard in court. If the prosecution and defense are working together to get the defendant into treatment, his or her right to be heard in court may be stripped from him. An opportunity for one's lawyer to speak eloquently is important, but it is not always a satisfactory replacement for the ability to speak for oneself. Judge John Parnham, retired, states that pre-hearing conferences' ability to develop strategies for the participant would be hampered if the participant were present; however if the judge and attorneys decide beforehand what is going to happen to the defendant, the defendant has completely lost his or her chance to be heard. There are legitimate fiduciary-duty concerns by having defense counsel working and sharing information with the prosecution.

## III. IF THE DRUG COURTS ARE SO DIFFERENT, WHAT MAKES DRUG COURTS SUCCESSFUL?

Despite even the most valiant attempt to adhere to the key components, there were and remain differences among the drug courts in this country. How one gets into a drug court varies, as do the services available. Yet most of the initial drug courts were very successful, and many remain so today. The key to understanding why that is may well lie in understanding procedural fairness.

Professor Tom Tyler has called procedural fairness the most powerful explanatory concept for why people obey rules that restrict their behavior in ways they would otherwise find unacceptable. Procedural fairness is one explanation why drug courts which are so different are effective. And the failure to maintain an abiding commitment to procedural fairness may also be the best explanation for why some drug courts became less effective over time.

Former Congresswoman Barbara Jordan once said, "[w]hat the people want is an America as good as its promise." That is what the people want of courts: courts that are as good as their promise; fair, efficient, and effective. Virtually all of the initial evaluations of drug courts reported that they were effective, and most reported that they were efficient, particularly if the definition of efficient was cost effective. Few, if any, of the evaluations addressed whether or not they were procedurally fair. Fairness should be one of the driving forces of all courts, but particularly those that portray that they are problem-solving courts.

Professor Tyler wrote:

> A goal of the courts is to handle people's problems in ways that lead them to accept and be willing to abide by the decisions made by the courts. The effectiveness of the courts in managing social conflicts depends upon their ability to issue decisions that are authoritative, i.e., that shape the conduct of the parties that come before them. Courts want that deference to continue over time, with people adhering to court judgments long after their case, so that the parties are not continually bringing the issues back into the courts for re-litigation. Finally, the courts want to retain and even enhance public trust and confidence in the courts, judges, and the law. Such public trust is the key to maintaining the legitimacy of the legal system.

Procedural fairness does not suggest that people are happy if they lose. No drug-court defendants want to be in drug court — they "volunteered" to get into drug court by being arrested, and as a result from the inception of the prosecution they lost at some level. No one likes to lose, but litigants recognize that they cannot always win. They accept losing more willingly if the procedure used is fair. Change in human behavior or creating the motivation to successfully deal with chemical dependency does not come easily. It comes easier if there is an atmosphere of hope and support. Likewise, success comes easier in courtrooms where there is a sustained commitment to procedural fairness.

The essential elements of procedural fairness are voice, neutrality, respect, and trustworthy authorities. These elements of fairness dominate people's reaction to the legal system across ethnic groups, across income and educational levels, and across genders.

The element of voice refers to the fact that when people come to court, they want the opportunity to tell their story and explain their views to a judge who listens carefully. Voice in a drug-court setting is the embodiment of a courtroom that promotes conversation. Voice is not simply the technical decision of a defendant to make important decisions such as how to plead. Voice is the ability of a person to express their concerns, even if from a technical legal point of view the concern is not particularly relevant. Voice is also delivering the implied promise that the judge will in fact listen carefully.

In the early drug courts there were few, if any, available protocols. Judges, lawyers, probation officers and treatment providers appeared in court, listened to what was said and then the judge made a decision. Over time the concept that "we" need to preconference the defendant's court appearance became more prevalent. The judge and others would meet and decide what to do with the defendant before the defendant appeared. A non-adversarial approach with everyone working toward the common goal was, after all, one of the key components. The logic seems at first blush unassailable. Preparation is good. A lot of the second, third, and fourth generation drug-court judges were new to the drug-court experience and less comfortable with improvisation. The preconference meeting helps those judges.

Although the logic seems sound, without care it can create a major impediment. The danger of pre-conferencing before the judge hears from the defendant is that it can lead to early hypothesis generation, where a judge may then go on the bench thinking that the case is the same as a hundred other cases he has heard or thinking about what the decision in the preconference was, and then only look for the information that confirms the early hypothesis. Early hypothesis generation is not peculiar to drug courts. It can happen in any courtroom, but may be more likely where there is an over commitment to the idea that the adversarial system is inappropriate.

In drug cases, frequently the outcome is driven by the constitutionality of the search. Since criminal court defendants are represented by attorneys, their ability to express themselves vocally during court proceedings is frequently limited. Drug courts, on the other hand, provided a unique opportunity for defendants to have a forum to express themselves. For people who self-medicate pain through drugs or are hopeless, the judge can be an important person who cares about them and offers hope. The early drug courts were successful in part because they put an emphasis on voice.

The element of neutrality refers to the fact that people are more likely to accept a court decision when they feel they have been treated equally and fairly. One of the ways courts can show this is by clearly explaining the reasons for a decision and by emphasizing the importance of facts. Litigants respond more positively to court decisions when the importance of facts is emphasized and the reasons for a decision have been clearly explained. Neutrality is important to the judiciary. Neutrality is critical if courts are to be perceived as legitimate. But neutrality can mask that a judge cares. A good judge understands that you can both care and be neutral. A good judge understands that you can be neutral and engaged.

The element of respect refers to the fact that people react positively when they feel they are treated with politeness, dignity, and respect. This can be done through explaining how things work and what a party must do. Perhaps because of volume many criminal courts have ended up depersonalizing the defendant. There is a theater aspect of drug courts. Defendants see others who have succeeded and presumably can be motivated by their support. But respect is even more critical if the courtroom is going to be a semi-support group. Respect in a drug-court setting is a place where there is no threatening, lecturing, blaming, or shaming of defendants.

The final element of procedural fairness is a trustworthy authority. This element deals with the perception a person has of the official presiding over the case. People look for actions to indicate they can trust the character and sincerity of those in authority. They also look for signs that the judge is sincerely concerned with the person's needs. If the actions or body language of the judge conveys a message different from what the judge is saying, the person will not trust the judge and will be less likely to accept the outcome.

Too often, courts have not viewed themselves from the customers' perspective. Indeed, the word "customer" sometimes actually offends some judges, prosecutors, and public defenders. But the word frames an important self-analysis courts must undertake. What do the court customers look for from their courts? What do the defendants in a drug court look for from the drug court? What happens when the defendant in a drug court is not effectively listened to? Is the defendant satisfied simply with the favorable outcome?

A goal of the judicial system is to handle problems that lead litigants to accept and abide by decisions and retain and even enhance their trust and confidence in the justice system. Factors that could matter include outcome favorability: Did I win? Outcome fairness: Did I get what I deserve? Procedural fairness: Was my case handled with fair procedures?

The current emphasis of many courts and commentators on procedural fairness develops from research showing that how disputes are handled has an important influence upon people's evaluation of their experience in the court system. Procedural fairness is important because it encourages decision acceptance and it leads to positive views about the legal system. Those are precisely the goals that are integral for the success of a drug court.

Early social-science research on procedural fairness focused upon the theory that respectful and dignified treatment of defendants would lead to the perception that the judge is a trustworthy authority and foster a belief in unbiased decision-making by the judge. Other early procedural-justice research focused upon the importance of a judge providing explanations for the decision. Research showed that explanations to a litigant fosters a sense of legitimacy and results in higher compliance with court orders.

Although the academic research on procedural fairness is robust, there is little evidence that the early pioneers of drug courts consciously practiced that academic research as applied science in a courtroom. But, those early pioneers of drug courts were probably intuitively effective at running courtrooms that embodied the concepts. Not all judges and attorneys are as intuitive, and effective courtroom management has not always occurred in crowded criminal courts.

Because of their training, judges and lawyers focus on the fairness of case outcomes instead of the process. As the chart below illustrates, judges and lawyers focus on the importance of case outcomes as the measure of "success" of the justice system far more than the public or litigants do.

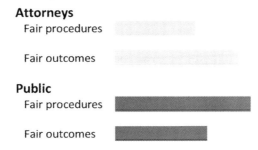

The impact procedural fairness has is not momentary. Research has shown that procedural fairness influences a person's acceptance of the decision over time. For example, there was a study done in Australia on a re-integrative shaming experiment in which researchers examined how 900 adults charged with drunk driving felt about the procedures they encountered, and then tracked their acceptance of the decision and their re-offense rate years down the road. Following a decision, the defendants were asked if the procedures were fair and the law legitimate. The researchers then looked at re-offense rates three and four years down the line. The study found that fairness of the legal procedure was related to the legitimacy of the legal system. Where the defendant believed the procedure was fair and the process was legitimate, the re-arrest rate for the same crime was 3.3%. Where the defendant believed the procedure was unfair and the process not legitimate, the re-arrest rate was 15.6%.

This Australian study shows that achieving procedural fairness creates greater compliance with court orders. The study dealt with a defendant population that is similar to a drug court, at least if you view alcohol abuse as similar to drug use. Unlike those in drug courts, however, these defendants were not all ordered to treatment, nor did they have the type of judicial supervision that a drug-court defendant has. But it makes sense that if the party feels the process was fair, even if the party loses, the party is more likely to accept and comply with the result. If people feel the procedures are not fair, then they are less likely to accept the result and are more likely to question the legitimacy of the legal system. It seems elementary then that judges should seek at all costs to achieve procedural fairness in their courtrooms.

## IV. CONCLUSION

The proper role of a judge has been a troubling aspect of drug courts for many. There is a perception among some that drug court judges hug the defendants and interact with defendants in inappropriate ways. Neutrality is important for judges, but if applied improperly it can mask that the judge cares. Neutrality requires judges to be transparent and open about how decisions were made, to give an explanation in terms understandable by a layperson, and to frequently cite to relevant statutes, rules or court policies. Many of the judges who engaged in the early generation of drug courts were quite transparent and open in how decisions were made and they gave explanations to the defendants as opposed to their lawyers. Their orders were understandable to defendants.

Respect in a courtroom is also important because subtle clues about people in a courthouse are important. The early drug courts took defendant's concerns seriously. Early drug-court judges made clear that they had heard the needs and concerns of the people and explained why those concerns could or could not be accommodated in a legal setting. Courtesy, politeness, and respect for people were important aspects of the drug courts. People come to court about issues that are important to them irrespective of whether they have a strong legal case. Giving people information about their rights and telling them how to complain to higher authorities were important parts of early drug courts.

There may come a day when there are 3143 drug courts in our country. More likely there will be a difficult effort to bring many of the existing drug courts to scale in order to permit them to survive. These are difficult budget times for state courts and corrections agencies. Some good drug courts may not make it. But, regardless of whether you are an optimist, pessimist, or somewhere in the middle, voice, respect, neutrality, and trust must be seen as key components of a successful drug court. Voice, respect, neutrality and trust, indeed, must be seen as the key component of all courts.

## III.  THE WORKING PARTS OF A DRUG COURT

To gain more than a general notion of how drug courts operate, drug court rules, regulations, and operating documents are offered here to present the specific parameters of highly regulated "specialized docket" court operating in Ohio state court.

Ohio is known nationally as a state court system that has encouraged, supported, and now regulates through a certification process, problem-solving courts. The Ohio Supreme Court created standards for certifying "specialized dockets," offering grants, hosting conferences and working in many ways to develop expertise in not only drug courts, but veterans' courts and human trafficking courts.

In her State of the Judiciary speech, September 2015, Ohio Supreme Court Chief Justice Maureen O'Connor celebrated the ongoing work of the Ohio specialized dockets, and in particular, of drug courts.

## State of the Judiciary
## Chief Justice Maureen O'Connor
## September 3, 2015

\* \* \* \*

Just two weeks ago, we hosted a forum that brought together judges, public health specialists, and addiction specialists to discuss how we could better respond to our state's opiate abuse problems.

Twenty-five years ago we could boil dockets down to essentially four areas: domestic relations, juvenile, civil and criminal.

Today's dockets are very different. Today we speak of specialized dockets such as drug courts, veteran's courts, mental health courts and the like.

We talk of problem-solving courts and therapeutic courts.

Specialized dockets represent silo-breaking within the justice system at its best and have found success because of the willingness of judges to accept new roles and new responsibilities in our communities.

\* \* \* \*

The original specialized docket — Drug Courts — continue to be crucial to the state's efforts to combat opiate addiction.

Perhaps the most significant involvement for Ohio's judicial branch in this area is the medication assisted treatment pilot program that began in January 2014, and was recently extended for another two years with a total investment of $16 million.

The intended outcome is critical: connecting high-need, high-risk defendants in the criminal justice system with the treatment they need for opiate and alcohol addictions and reintegrating them back in the community as productive citizens.

Drug courts in 15 designated counties administer the treatment programs.

Supreme Court staff work with these counties to ensure their drug courts meet all the requirements to be officially certified and operate within minimum standards as mandated by the Supreme Court.

We continue to support these courts throughout the project.

The judges in these courts order assessments to determine which addicted individuals in the criminal justice system meet the legal and clinical criteria to participate in the docket and seek treatment through the program.

Case Western Reserve has studied the original MAT [Medically Assisted Treatment] pilot courts that are providing medication assisted treatment to opiate and heroin addicted drug court participants in six Ohio counties.

Preliminary results indicate that medication assisted treatment is associated with decreased substance use, increased employment, and increased voluntary participation in self help groups like Alcoholics Anonymous and Narcotics Anonymous.

These studies prove the effectiveness of utilizing specialized dockets. It's no wonder that the Supreme Court has a total of 189 specialized dockets in the certification process.

While there is a cost-savings aspect to this approach to justice administration — we cannot afford to incarcerate or institutionalize our way out of some problems — it is most importantly an approach that focuses on helping people succeed and become productive members of society.

\* \* \* \*

## Ohio Supreme Court Rule 36.20.   Specialized Docket Certification

### (A)   Procedure for certification

A court of common pleas, municipal court, or county court or division of the court operating or establishing a particular session of court that offers a therapeutically oriented judicial approach to providing court supervision and appropriate treatment to individuals may receive certification of the session from the Supreme Court by doing both of the following:

(1) Complying with and adopting a local rule or issuing an administrative order implementing the "Specialized Docket Standards," as set forth in Appendix I to this rule;

(2) Successfully completing the certification application process pursuant to Sup. R. 36.21 through 36.26.

### (B)   Application

Division (A) of this rule shall not apply to a commercial docket of a court of common pleas or a housing or environmental division of a municipal court.

## Ohio Supreme Court Rule Appendix I.   Specialized Docket Standards

**Overview.**

The following standards are established to guide courts of common pleas, municipal courts, and county courts and divisions of these courts in the planning and implementation of all specialized dockets. The standards set forth minimum requirements for the certification and operation of all specialized dockets. Accompanying the standards are recommended practices that each specialized docket is encouraged to follow. While the standards seek to create a minimum level of uniform practices for specialized dockets, they still allow local specialized dockets to innovate and tailor their specialized docket to respond to local needs and resources.

**Standard 1.   Planning Process.**

A specialized docket shall utilize a comprehensive and collaborative planning process that results in all of the following:

(A) An agreement among relevant parties setting forth the terms of the specialized docket operations. Relevant parties may include, but are not limited to, the specialized docket judge; the court; the prosecutor; defense counsel; licensed treatment providers; children services for family dependency treatment dockets; and, for criminal and juvenile specialized dockets, the probation department, the parole authority, and law enforcement agencies.

(B) An advisory committee and a treatment team. The specialized docket judge shall attend and chair advisory committee and treatment team meetings.

(C) A program description that contains written policies and procedures defining the goals and objectives for the specialized docket, identifying the target population, detailing program entry and case flow, and providing written roles and responsibilities of each treatment team member;

(D) A written participation agreement and participant handbook detailing the rights and responsibilities of participants in the specialized docket.

### Standard 2.   Non-Adversarial Approach.

A specialized docket shall incorporate a non-adversarial approach while recognizing all of the following:

(A) A prosecutor's distinct role in pursuing justice and protecting public safety and victim's rights;

(B) A defense counsel's distinct role in preserving the constitutional rights of the specialized docket participant;

(C) The participant's right to request the attendance of defense counsel during the portion of a specialized docket treatment team meeting concerning the participant;

(D) A participant's right to a detailed, written participation agreement and participant handbook outlining the requirements and process of the specialized docket.

### Standard 3.   Legal and Clinical Eligibility and Termination.

#### (A) Criteria

A specialized docket shall have written legal and clinical eligibility, completion, termination, and neutral discharge criteria that have been collaboratively developed, reviewed, and agreed upon by the relevant parties identified in Standard 1(A) of these standards.

#### (B) Decision on admission or termination

A **specialized docket** judge shall have discretion to decide the admission into and termination from a **specialized docket** in accordance with the written criteria for the specialized docket.

**(C) No right to participate**

The written legal and clinical eligibility and termination criteria do not create a right to participation in a specialized docket.

**Standard 4.     Assessment and Referral.**

A specialized docket shall promptly assess individuals and refer them to the appropriate services. The assessment and referral shall meet all of the following requirements:

(A) All chemical dependency, mental health, and other programming assessments shall include available collateral information to ensure the accuracy of the assessment;

(B) The participant or the participant's guardian shall complete a release of information form to provide for communication about confidential information, participation/progress in treatment, and compliance with the provisions of relevant law, including the "Health Insurance Portability and Accountability Act of 1996," 42 U.S.C. 300gg-42, as amended, and R.C. 2151.421 and 2152.99;

(C) Participants shall be placed as soon as possible in appropriate treatment services and programs and under reporting supervision to monitor compliance with court requirements;

(D) All screenings and assessments for treatment determinations shall be provided by programs or persons who are appropriately licensed and trained to deliver such services according to the standards of the profession.

**Standard 5.     Individualized Needs and Evidence-Based Practices.**

A specialized docket shall have a plan to provide services that meet the individualized needs of each participant and incorporate evidence-based strategies for the participant population. Such plans shall take into consideration services that are gender-responsive and culturally appropriate and that effectively address co-occurring disorders.

**Standard 6.     Participant Monitoring.**

A specialized docket shall monitor each participant's performance and progress and incorporate all of the following:

(A) Regular treatment team meetings prior to the status review hearings;

(B) Status review hearings, as established by Standard 7 of these standards;

(C) Ongoing communication among the treatment team members, including frequent exchanges of timely and accurate information about the participant's overall performance;

(D) Progression through the specialized docket based upon the participant's performance in the treatment plan and compliance with requirements of the specialized docket phases. A participant's progress through the specialized docket phases is not to be based solely upon preset timelines.

(E) Explanation to the participant of responses to compliance and noncompliance, including criteria for termination.

### Standard 7.    Status Review Hearings.

#### (A) Ongoing judicial interaction

A specialized docket shall incorporate ongoing judicial interaction with each participant as an essential component of the docket.

#### (B) Appearance before specialized docket judge

(1) At a minimum, a specialized docket participant shall appear before the specialized docket judge at least twice monthly during the initial phase of the specialized docket.

(2) Thereafter, a specialized docket participant shall regularly appear before the specialized docket judge to review the participant's progress through the specialized docket.

### Standard 8.    Substance Monitoring.

A specialized docket shall monitor a specialized docket participant's substance use by random, frequent, and observed alcohol and other drug testing protocols which include all of the following:

(A) Written policies and procedures for sample collection, sample analysis, and result reporting. The testing policies and procedures shall address elements that contribute to the reliability and validity of the testing process.

(B) Individualized drug and alcohol testing plans. All testing shall be random, frequent, and observed.

(C) Clearly established plans for addressing a participant who tests positive at intake or who relapses. The plans shall include treatment guidelines and sanctions, when appropriate, that are enforced and reinforced by the specialized docket judge.

(D) Immediate notification of the court when the participant tests positive, fails to submit to testing, submits an adulterated sample or the sample of another individual, or dilutes the sample. Failure to submit to testing, submitting an adulterated sample or the sample of another individual, or diluting the sample shall be treated as positive tests and immediately sanctioned.

(E) Testing sufficient to include the participant's primary substance of dependence, as well as a sufficient range of other common substances.

**Standard 9.    Treatment and other Rehabilitation Services.**

### (A) Prompt access

A specialized docket shall provide prompt access to a continuum of approved treatment and other rehabilitation services.

### (B) Treatment plan and activities record

A specialized docket shall maintain a current treatment plan and record of activities.

### (C) Licensing and training

All required treatment and programming shall be provided by programs or persons who are appropriately licensed and trained to deliver such services according to the standards of their profession.

**Standard 10.    Incentives and Sanctions.**

Immediate, graduated, and individualized incentives and sanctions shall govern the responses of a specialized docket to a specialized docket participant's compliance or noncompliance.

**Recommended Practices**

\* \* \* \*

### (C) Incentives for compliance

Incentives for a specialized docket participant's compliance vary in intensity and may include, but are not limited to, the following:

(1) Encouragement and praise from the specialized docket judge;

(2) Ceremonies and tokens of progress, including advancement in specialized docket phases;

(3) Reduced supervision contacts;

(4) Decreased frequency of court appearances;

(5) Reduced fines or fees;

(6) Increased or expanded privileges;

(7) Encouragement to increase participation in positive activities the participant finds pleasurable, such as writing, art work, or other positive hobbies;

(8) Gifts of inspirational items, including books, pictures, and framed quotes;

(9) Assistance with purchasing clothing for job interviews;

(10) Gift cards for restaurants, movie theaters, recreational activities, or personal care services;

(11) Gifts of small personal care items, hobby or pet supplies, plants, or small household items;

(12) Dismissal of criminal charges or a reduction in the term of probation;

(13) Reduced or suspended jail, prison, or juvenile detention days;

(14) Graduation from the specialized docket.

**(D) Sanctions for noncompliance**

Sanctions for a specialized docket participant's noncompliance vary in intensity and may include, but are not limited to, the following:

(1) Warnings and admonishment from the specialized docket judge;

(2) Demotion to an earlier specialized docket phase;

(3) Increased frequency of drug or alcohol testing and court appearances;

(4) Refusal of specific requests, such as permission to travel;

(5) Denial of additional or expanded privileges or rescinding privileges previously granted;

(6) Increased supervision contacts and monitoring;

(7) Individualized sanctions, such as writing essays, reading books, or performing other activities to reflect upon unacceptable behavior;

(8) Imposition of suspended fines and costs;

(9) Community service or work programs;

(10) Jail or out-of-home placement, including detention for juveniles;

(11) Community control or probation violation;

(12) Termination from the specialized docket.

## Standard 11.    Professional Education.

A specialized docket shall assure continuing interdisciplinary education of treatment team members to promote effective specialized docket planning, implementation, and operations.

Practitioner Network by attending sub-network meetings, trainings, and the annual conference.

## Standard 12.    Effectiveness Evaluation.

A specialized docket judge shall evaluate the effectiveness of the specialized docket by doing each of the following:

(A) Reporting data as required by the Supreme Court, including information to assess compliance with these standards;

(B) Engaging in on-going data collection in order to evaluate whether the specialized docket is meeting its goals and objectives.

## Ohio Code of Judicial Conduct

### Rule 2.9.  *Ex Parte* Contacts and Communications with Others

(A) A judge shall not initiate, receive, permit, or consider *ex parte* communications, except as follows:

(1) When circumstances require it, an *ex parte* communication for scheduling, administrative, or emergency purposes, that does not address substantive matters or issues on the merits, is permitted, provided the judge reasonably believes that no party will gain a procedural, substantive, or tactical advantage as a result of the *ex parte* communication;

(2) A judge may obtain the advice of a disinterested expert on the *law* applicable to a proceeding before the judge, if the judge gives notice to the parties of the person consulted and the subject-matter of the advice solicited, and affords the parties a reasonable opportunity to object or respond to the advice received;

(3) A judge may consult with court staff and court officials whose functions are to aid the judge in carrying out the judge's adjudicative responsibilities, or with other judges, provided the judge makes reasonable efforts to avoid receiving factual information that is not part of the record and does not abrogate the responsibility personally to decide the matter;

(4) A judge, with the consent of the parties, may confer separately with the parties and their lawyers in an effort to settle matters pending before the judge;

(5) A judge may initiate, receive, permit, or consider an *ex parte* communication when expressly authorized by *law* to do so;

(6) A judge may initiate, receive, permit, or consider an *ex parte* communication when administering a *specialized docket*, provided the judge reasonably believes that no party will gain a procedural, substantive, or tactical advantage while in the specialized docket program as a result of the *ex parte* communication.

(B) If a judge receives an unauthorized *ex parte* communication bearing upon the substance of a matter, the judge shall make provision promptly to notify the parties of the substance of the communication and provide the parties with an opportunity to respond.

(C) A judge shall not investigate facts in a matter independently, and shall consider only the evidence presented and any facts that may properly be judicially noticed.

(D) A judge shall make reasonable efforts, including providing appropriate supervision, to ensure that this rule is not violated by court staff, court officials, and others subject to the judge's direction and control.

## Montgomery County Court of Common Pleas

### Rule 3.12 —   Drug Court

A.   CREATION OF SPECIALIZED DOCKET — "DRUG COURT":

Drug court is created pursuant to the specialized docket standards set forth in Sup. R. 36.20–36.28, including Appendix I. The purpose of Drug Court is to facilitate efficient and effective treatment of drug addicted or drug abusing offenders. Eligible offenders as defined in Subsection © of this Rule shall be supervised by the Montgomery County Adult Probation Department ("Probation Department") to ensure compliance with community control sanctions and to assist with criminogenic needs.

B.   DRUG COURT TEAM:

The "Drug Court Team" shall consist of the Judge assigned to Drug Court ("Drug Court Judge"), Adult Probation Department Manager and staff, Probation Officers, licensed treatment providers, community based employment program personnel, the Assistant Prosecuting Attorney, and Defense Counsel. The Drug Court Team shall convene weekly to discuss the progress and status of individual offenders, apply sanctions as needed, and for any other matters.

C.   ELIGIBILITY CRITERIA FOR DRUG COURT ADMISSION:

1. The assigned judge may order a defendant to Drug Court through a guilty or no contest plea, probation violation, judicial release, other early release options, or Intervention in Lieu of Conviction pursuant to R.C. § 2951.041 ("ILC").

2. In order for a defendant to be eligible for Drug Court the defendant shall:

a. Be amenable to community control;

b. Be charged with a third, fourth, or fifth degree felony;

c. Be a resident of Ohio;

d. Have little or no history of violent behavior;

e. Have a chemical abuse addiction in which the defendant's current or past criminal behavior has been alcohol or drug driven;

f. Have no acute health condition;

g. Demonstrate a sincere willingness to participate in a long term treatment process.

D.   REFERRING DEFENDANTS TO DRUG COURT

1. Drug Court receives referrals from the assigned Judge. The Drug

Court Team shall review the case for legal and clinical eligibility as identified in Subsection (c)(2)(a)–(g) of this Rule.

2. The assigned Judge shall have final discretion to decide if the defendant is ordered to Drug Court.

E.  SENTENCING:

After a defendant is ordered to Drug Court as a community control or ILC sanction, along with any other appropriate sanctions, the case shall be transferred to the Drug Court Judge for any and all further court proceedings. The Drug Court Judge shall have the authority to conduct arraignments, accept pleas, enter findings and dispositions, revoke community control or ILC, and order or modify community control or ILC sanctions.

F.  TREATMENT PHASES:

Drug Court offenders shall be required to complete phases of treatment as individually necessary and complete all other requirements as identified in the *Drug Court Participant Handbook* and the *Drug Court Participation Agreement*. Drug Court offenders shall comply with all the rules indicated to them by the Drug Court Judge at their initial appearance. While in Drug Court, the offender shall receive services to assist in meeting criminogenic needs. Upon graduation from Drug Court, the offender may be required to remain under community control or ILC sanctions to ensure continued compliance and success.

G.  SANCTIONS FOR NON-COMPLIANCE:

Sanctions for a Drug Court offender's non-compliance vary in intensity and may include, but are not limited to, the following:

1. Warning and admonition from the Drug Court Judge;

2. Demotion to an earlier Drug Court phase;

3. Increased frequency of drug or alcohol testing and court appearances;

4. Increased supervision contacts and monitoring;

5. Community service or work program;

6. Jail or out of home placement;

7. Community control or ILC violation;

8. Termination from Drug Court; and

9. Commitment to the Secure Transitional Offender Program ("S.T.O.P."), the MonDay Community Correctional Facility, or any other community based facility approved by the Court.

H.  UNSUCCESSFUL TERMINATIONS:

1. Reasons for termination from Drug Court include, but are not limited to:

a. Failure to remain clean from illegal substances or alcohol;

b. Violation of the *General Conditions of Supervision*;

c. Violation of any community control or ILC sanctions; and

d. Failure to comply with the Drug Court Participation Agreement or any other orders of the Drug Court Judge.

2. If an offender is terminated from Drug Court for reasons stated in Subsection (H)(1) of this Rule, or for any other reason as determined by the Drug Court Judge, the offender may be subject to a community control or ILC revocation hearing.

3. If a hearing is required pursuant to Subsection (H)(2) of this Rule:

a. The Drug Court Judge shall adjudicate the proceedings;

b. The offender may have his or her community control or ILC sanctions modified. Modifications include, but are not limited to, commitment to a Community Based Correctional Facility ("CBCF"), revocation of community control or ILC, or termination from Drug Court;

c. The Drug Court Judge shall have the sole discretion to refer an offender to the original assigned Judge for further proceedings; and

d. The law governing revocation apply, and the offender has a right to counsel.

I. STATISTICAL REPORTS

For purposes of Supreme Court statistical reports, the case shall be considered disposed by the assigned Judge when the defendant is sentenced to Drug Court or the defendant is ordered into Drug Court as a condition of ILC.

---

## DRUG COURT PARTICIPATION AGREEMENT

You have been ordered to complete the Montgomery County Drug Court as a result of the criminal activity which you were involved with and your abuse of or addiction to drugs. The purpose of Drug Court is to assist you in learning how to live a sober lifestyle and avoid violations of the law. You have been provided with the General Conditions of Supervision that apply to all offenders under supervision of the Court, as well as the Drug Court Handbook containing the rules and expectations of Drug Court. The Drug Court is a voluntary program, and you have the right to refuse participation in this program.

By agreeing to participate in the Drug Court, I acknowledge the following:

I understand that I have the right to a revocation hearing before the Court. At that hearing, the Judge would determine by a preponderance of the evidence whether I violated a condition of my Community Control or Intervention in Lieu of Conviction (ILC).

At the revocation hearing, I would have the right to be represented by a lawyer. If I am unable to afford a lawyer, the Court would appoint a lawyer to represent me at no cost to myself.

I understand that I have the right to request the attendance of defense counsel during the portion of the specialized docket team meeting concerning my case.

At the hearing, I would have the right to confront and cross exam the witnesses who are testifying against me. Also, I would have the right to present witnesses and evidence favorable to my defense.

At the hearing, I would have the right to remain silent and the right against self incrimination.

I agree to allow the Drug Court Judge to impose immediate and graduated sanctions, including periods of local incarceration (including a community-based correctional facility not to exceed the maximum six (6) months allowed by law), without a formal hearing and without my attorney present. The total amount of local incarceration imposed may not exceed the maximum sentence designated in my Termination Entry (Community Control) or for my offense(s) (ILC). I understand that I may also be placed in an Alternative Residential Program such as STOP or the VOA if necessary.

I agree to follow all rules of Drug Court as outlined in the Drug Court Handbook. This includes all General Conditions of Supervision and all policies of any treatment agency where I have been referred. I agree to be honest and to self-report any violations of the Drug Court Rules. I understand that I will be in Drug Court for a minimum of six months, up to my maximum expiration date of supervision.

I agree to participate in any treatment program that I am referred to. I agree to sign and keep current a Release of Information to allow unrestricted communication between my treatment provider and the Drug Court Team. I agree to keep confidential all information regarding other program participants that is shared during Drug Court. I understand that I will be placed in treatment as soon as possible, based on the availability of the treatment agency.

I agree to attend Drug Court as ordered, and will report to my assigned Probation Officer for monitoring of my substance use and treatment compliance, as well as to all other conditions of supervision and court ordered sanctions, including payment of my financial obligations. I will appear weekly for Drug Court during Phase I, and will be appearing regularly as ordered during Phases II and III. I understand that my Probation Officer will be communicating regularly with my treatment provider regarding my performance on supervision and in treatment. I understand that non-compliance with supervision or with treatment will result in a sanction as outlined in the Drug Court Handbook. If I wish to be represented by counsel at any portion of drug court, I will notify my Probation Officer of this request.

I understand that I will be randomly drug tested, at the request for the Court or my probation officer, for alcohol and other substance abuse, and that such testing will be random, frequent and observed. These requests may be made during an office visit or the probation officer may contact me at any time by telephone. If I am contacted by telephone, I am required to report within 24 hours to submit to drug testing. Any positive test will result in an immediate sanction. I agree to report any substance use immediately to my Probation Officer, including any lawful substances that are prescribed to me. I understand that I am not permitted to use any medications containing opiate, benzodiazepine, or amphetamine based compounds unless prescribed by an approved physician and approved by the treatment team. I understand that it is my responsibility to discuss this with my physician or dentist prior to taking any prescribed medications. I understand that any attempt to falsify a urinalysis sample by providing an adulterated or diluted sample, or a sample from another person, will result in my immediate arrest and appearance at a Revocation Hearing. In addition, failure to submit a sample as ordered will be considered a positive test and will result in an immediate sanction. Any positive test will result in an immediate sanction. I agree to report any substance use immediately to my Probation Officer, including any lawful substances that are prescribed to me.

I understand that successful completion of Drug Court requires completion of all three phases, and a minimum of six months of program attendance. Graduation requires completion of all court ordered sanctions, completion of treatment, payment of all financial obligations, and verification of lawful income unless waived by the Court.

I understand that if I am unsuccessfully terminated from Drug Court, I will appear before the Court for a Revocation / Violation hearing. At this hearing, the Judge may impose a prison sentence up to the amount specified in my Termination Entry (for Community Control) or the maximum term allowed for my offense(s) (for Intervention in Lieu of Conviction). I will be eligible for Jail Time Credit for any time I was confined for sanctions occurring during Drug Court and time that I accrued prior to Drug Court. I have the right to be represented by counsel at this hearing.

I ACKNOWLEDGE THAT I HAVE READ AND UNDERSTAND THIS AGREEMENT, FREELY AND VOLUNTARILY RELINQUISH THE RIGHTS DISCUSSED HEREIN, AND AGREE TO ABIDE BY ALL OF THE RULES AND CONDITIONS OF THE DRUG COURT. I ACKNOWL-EDGE THAT I MAY RESCIND ANY RIGHTS THAT I HAVE WAIVED AT ANY TIME. IF I CHOOSE TO DO SO, I WILL BE UNSUCCESFULLY TERMINATED FROM DRUG COURT AND WILL BE SCHEDULED FOR A REVOCATION / VIOLATION HEARING.

[Signatures: Drug Court Participant; Intensive Probation Officer; Drug Court Judge]

## DRUG COURT PROGRAM
### December 2014

|  | Month | Year-to-date | Percentage | Program-to-date |
|---|---|---|---|---|
| New Referrals | 11 | 58 | N/A | 3,583 |
| Successful Terms | 3 | 19 | 76% | 1,983 (74%) |
| Unsuccessful Terms | 1 | 10 | 12% | 649 (25%) |
| Admin. Terms | 0 | 1 | 1% | 41 (1%) |
| Absconders | 8 | 50 | N/A | 1,466 |
| Reinstatements | 1 | 33 | N/A | 1,121 |
| Transfer Outs | 2 | 59 | N/A | 498 |

Drug Court Program began in 1997.

Key to Terms:

Successful Terminations include dismissal/Complete/Incomplete Terminations.

Unsuccessful Terminations refer to revocations filed.

Administrative Terminations the original case was terminated administratively as the offender was sentenced on a new charge.

Absconders are offenders who stopped reporting and a warrant was issued for their arrest.

Reinstatements are offenders arrested on a warrant or the offender was continued on from a Violation Hearing (Revocation).

Transfer Outs is a term for transferring cases internally between probation officers.

## IV. DRUG COURTS, THE ADVERSARIAL PROCESS, & DUE PROCESS

Drug courts typically adopt "a non-adversarial approach" [Ohio Supreme Court Rule Appendix I Specialized Docket Standard 2] which requires the prosecutor, the defense counsel, the judge, and social service case managers to work together closely and cooperatively. For some observers, this team work in the courtroom is viewed as a threat that undermines the essential adversarial nature of criminal proceedings.

These threats are illustrated in a hypothetical exchange between court-appointed defense counsel and a defendant charged with a misdemeanor drug offense, with a 180 jail days as its maximum penalty:

Attorney:    Hello Mr. Defendant. My name is Attorney Advocate and the court has appointed me to represent you. To get done with this charge quickly, I think the best thing for you to do right away is to enter the community court program of community service and drug treatment. I've already talked to the prosecutor and he is willing to let you enter the program as long as you plead guilty to the charge and abide by the conditions of the program. You've been through this before, so let's just go in and plead . . .

Defendant:    You want me to plead guilty right now? I don't even know what evidence they have against me. How can I make that decision right now? Don't you have to get discovery or something? What am I charged with?

Attorney:    Well, you know you were picked up for drugs. We don't really need to do any discovery right now because you've been offered this really good new program. You can go into a treatment program, and get off the drugs. You'll have to do some community service too, but that's not much. Not many people get this opportunity and we have to jump on it fast, because you might not get this offered to you later on. All we have to do is go in there and let the judge know that you want the program. Then she'll take your plea, you get released and start your treatment and community service.

Defendant:    You're sure I'll get released if I enter the plea? You know I have a record.

Attorney:    Well, all I know is that the prosecutor told me you have a prior felony drug conviction. The program works just like I told you. You have to be released to get the treatment.

Defendant:    You keep saying treatment, treatment, treatment. What kind of treatment is it? How long is it? Do I go every day? I have two small kids to take care of. I can't do community service every day.

Attorney:    Its drug treatment. They do an assessment and decide what kind you need — what's appropriate for you.

Defendant:    Who is "they"? Will it be group meetings, outpatient or what? I don't really need treatment; I'm not addicted. I was just caught holding some marijuana.

Attorney:    Well, they always order treatment in these cases, so you're gonna have to do it anyway. The case will be called soon, so you have to sign this guilty plea form and waiver of jury trial. Take it and sign it. I have to go talk to some other clients that I have. I'll be back.

Defendant:    But wait! Aren't we going to talk about the evidence they have against me? I think the police violated my rights when they stormed into my house.

Attorney:    We can't get into that right now. We don't have time. If you don't want the program, then we can see if they violated your rights, but my experience in these cases is you do better if you just take the program. My advice is this is the best way to insure that you get out and don't get a bond today.

Defendant:    I don't know. This is a big decision to make in just a few minutes. So, I won't get stepped back anytime in the program?

Attorney:       Well, if you test positive or don't do the community service, there are sanctions, but not much. At most it's just a few days in jail.

Defendant:      A few days in jail is a lot to me! I told you I have kids and I can't afford a babysitter.

Attorney:       Well, we have about ten minutes before the case is called. I'll go talk to my other clients and you can talk to that program counselor over there (pointing). She can probably answer your questions and go over the forms with you.

Defendant:      Okay. I can still challenge what the police did, right?

Attorney:       No, because you have to plead guilty for the program. Just talk to the counselor, first. I'll be right back.

\* \* \* \*

Tamar M. Meekins, *"Specialized Justice": The Over-Emergence of Specialty Courts and the Threat of a New Criminal Defense Paradigm*, 40 SUFFOLK U. L. REV. 1, 4–6 (2006).

## STATE v. SHAMBLEY
### 795 N.W.2d 884 (Neb. 2011)

McCORMACK, J.

### NATURE OF CASE

This case presents an appeal from a participant's discharge from the drug court program. The participant argues she was denied her rights to due process and confrontation when no adverse witnesses were available for cross-examination and the only evidence considered in support of the alleged violations of her drug court contract was a letter, written to the judge by the drug court coordinator, and its attachments. This is the first time we consider what process is due in drug court termination proceedings.

### BACKGROUND

On December 23, 2008, Samantha A. Shambley pled guilty to possession of a controlled substance, a Class IV felony, in violation of Neb. Rev. Stat. § 28-416(3) (Reissue 2008). The district court accepted the plea and adjudged her guilty of the offense. In lieu of sentencing at that time, the court transferred the case to the drug court program.

The drug court program is a postplea or postadjudicatory intensive supervision drug and alcohol treatment program for eligible offenders. The purpose of the program is to reduce offender recidivism by fostering a comprehensive and coordinated court response composed of early intervention, appropriate treatment, intensive supervision, and consistent judicial oversight. A drug court program participant pleads guilty and agrees to the terms and conditions of the program in exchange for the possibility of avoiding sentencing and, oftentimes, being allowed to withdraw the plea upon successful completion of the program. If the participant is terminated from the program or withdraws before successful completion, then the conviction stands and the case is transferred back to the district court for sentencing. Throughout this opinion, we have, for convenience, used the term "drug court." In this case, when the term is used, it refers to the district court. There is not a separate drug court under the Nebraska Constitution, and when the term "drug court" is used, it simply refers to a program of the district court, county court, or juvenile court, rather than to a separate court.

The parties agree that Shambley signed a drug court contract which, among other things, required that she stay drug free. On August 28, 2009, Shambley appeared before a judge of the drug court after reports that she had used marijuana. Shambley admitted that she had used. Shambley promised to try harder to comply with the terms and conditions of the program. She was not represented by counsel, and no evidence was adduced or specific findings made. In a written order, the judge revoked Shambley's bond for 72 hours, during which time she was ordered incarcerated "for violations of [her] Drug Court program."

Similar proceedings occurred on November 13 and December 4, 2009. At the November 13 proceeding, the judge told Shambley that she could not smoke marijuana and referred to the fact that she had missed drug tests. Shambley neither specifically admitted nor denied having done so. Shambley again told the judge that she wanted to stay in the program. The judge revoked her bond for 72 hours and sent Shambley to jail "for violations of [her] Drug Court program." Shambley was told that thereafter, she was to report to the drug court weekly. These meetings are not in the record.

During her appearance on December 4, 2009, Shambley admitted to having had another "setback." She was sent to spend the weekend in jail "for violations of [her] Drug Court program." She was ordered to report back on December 18, but there is no record of any meeting on that date.

On February 5, 2010, Shambley appeared to discuss yet another report of drug usage, which she neither admitted nor denied. The judge warned Shambley that she was at risk for termination from the drug court program.

On March 12, 2010, the judge again told Shambley that she had tested positive for drugs. Shambley, however, denied that she had used on the occasion in question. The judge informed Shambley that this time, the drug court team had recommended that she be terminated from the program. The judge scheduled an informal hearing to determine the issue of the recommended termination.

The hearing on termination was held on March 25, 2010. For the first time, Shambley appeared with counsel. The court explained that it was Shambley's burden to go forward with showing why she should not be terminated from the program, stating:

> We have a termination hearing from the drug court. And this is a non — I guess the term is informal hearing to address that under our policy. And under the policy I believe that [Shambley] has the responsibility of going forward

with that. Any evidence to remain as the recommendation of the drug court team has been to terminate her from the drug court, and I've received a report. Have you folks seen that . . . ?

The State did not argue any position as to the termination and did not present any evidence or call witnesses. The judge noted that he had received the letter from the drug court coordinator recommending Shambley's termination. The letter and its attachments were the only evidence in support of termination.

In the letter, the drug court coordinator alleged three instances of drug usage for the court to consider at the termination hearing: (1) February 5, 2010, (2) March 11, 2010, and (3) March 19, 2010. The coordinator made a brief synopsis of Shambley's recent difficulties in following the drug court contract and included five attachments as proof of those difficulties.

The first attachment was a discharge summary report from the rehabilitation center where Shambley stayed from December 2009 to January 2010. The report summarized that Shambley had relapsed three times while at a previous center and that that was the reason for her transfer. The report stated that Shambley made good progress at the center. She was discharged, with a favorable prognosis, to a halfway house.

According to the drug court coordinator's letter, the placement at the halfway house was unsuccessful. The second attachment was a letter written by a therapist of a therapeutic community where Shambley was admitted on February 9, 2010, apparently after her discharge from the halfway house. The therapist stated that Shambley was admitted "due to her continued substance use." The therapist also stated that while at the community, Shambley violated the conditions of a pass when she skipped an appointment to go shopping and she tested positive for marijuana on March 8, 2010.

The third and fourth attachments were printouts from a toxicology laboratory. Under the "result" column, one printout showed "25.5 mg/dL" of creatinine from a sample collected from Shambley on February 24, 2010. The other printout showed "209.6 mg/dL" of creatinine and an indication in the "positives" column adjacent to a result of "404 ng/mL" of "THC" from a sample collected on March 8.

The final attachment, a printout of an e-mail from an unidentified author to an unidentified recipient, discussed the fact that a February 24, 2010, drug test of Shambley was negative with a weak concentration, but should nevertheless be considered a positive result.

Shambley's counsel objected to the court's consideration of the letter and its attachments on the grounds of hearsay and lack of foundation. Counsel also argued that the manner in which the report was received and in which the proceedings were being conducted violated Shambley's rights to due process and confrontation. Counsel argued that he was neither able to adequately question the veracity of the unsworn hearsay allegations contained in the letter and its attachments nor able to effectively examine the meaning and reliability of the unauthenticated laboratory printouts.

The court overruled all objections. Shambley testified at the hearing that she did not use illegal drugs on March 11, 2010. She was not asked and did not discuss whether she had used drugs on the other two occasions alleged by the drug court coordinator as grounds for termination from the program.

The judge concluded that he agreed with the letter and its attachments outlining Shambley's "difficulties." Apparently in reference to prior meetings with Shambley and ex parte meetings with the drug court team, the judge said he was "certainly . . . familiar with" these difficulties. He also observed that the letter now "indicate[d] a positive test, which [he had] no reason to dispute."

Based on this evidence, the judge agreed with the drug court team's recommendation to discharge Shambley from the program. The judge found that keeping Shambley in the drug court would not be in her best interests and would erode the integrity of the drug court program. In light of Shambley's discharge from the drug court program, the court scheduled a hearing in the district court to determine Shambley's sentence on the possession of a controlled substance conviction.

At the sentencing hearing, the same judge, now acting as a judge of the district court, sentenced Shambley to 90 days' incarceration with credit for 9 days served while awaiting sentence. Shambley appeals her termination from the drug court program.

## ASSIGNMENTS OF ERROR

Shambley assigns that the lower court erred in (1) terminating Shambley from the drug court program without affording her due process of law, in violation of the 14th Amendment to the U.S. Constitution and corresponding sections of Nebraska law; (2) placing the burden of proof on Shambley to go forward and show why she should not be terminated from the drug court program, thereby violating her rights to due process as guaranteed to her under the 14th Amendment to the U.S. Constitution and corresponding sections of Nebraska law; (3) receiving into evidence the probation report over Shambley's objections, thereby denying her the right to confront and cross-examine witnesses against her; and (4) finding sufficient evidence to terminate Shambley from the drug court program, insofar as the inadmissible report was the only evidence against her.

## STANDARD OF REVIEW

The determination of whether the procedures afforded an individual comport with the constitutional requirements for procedural due process presents a question of law.

## ANALYSIS

In considering claims under the Due Process Clause of the 14th Amendment, we first consider whether the nature of the interest is one within the contemplation of the liberty or property language of the 14th Amendment. If it is, we must then determine what procedural protections the particular situation demands, for "not all situations calling for procedural safeguards call for the same kind of procedure." Applying the Due Process Clause to the facts of any given case is an "uncertain enterprise which must discover what 'fundamental fairness' consists of in a particular situation by first considering any relevant precedents and then by assessing the several interests that are at stake." Consideration of what procedures due process may require under any given set of circumstances must begin with a determination of the precise nature of the government function involved as well as of the private interest that has been affected by governmental action.

## CONDITIONAL LIBERTY INTEREST

The U.S. Supreme Court has not had occasion to address due process in the context of termination from problem-solving diversion programs such as the drug court program. The Court has, however, examined what procedures due process requires in the revocation of parole or probation. In *Morrissey v. Brewer* and *Gagnon v. Scarpelli*, the Court explained that revocations of parole or probation deprive an individual of the "conditional liberty properly dependent on observance of special . . . restrictions."

The Court said that such liberty, although indeterminate and perhaps a "'privilege,'" includes many of the core values of unqualified liberty and is, therefore, an interest within the contemplation of the liberty or property language of the 14th Amendment. It is a condition very different from confinement in a prison; the parolee or probationer is still able to do "a wide range of things." For instance, subject to conditions, the parolee or probationer may be "gainfully employed and is free to be with family and friends and to form the other enduring attachments of normal life." Termination of this conditional liberty inflicts a " 'grievous loss' " and "calls for some orderly process."

To determine exactly what process is due, the Court balanced the individual's interest in his or her conditional liberty with the interests of the State. Because the termination of parole or probation does not deprive an individual of the absolute liberty to which every citizen is entitled, that having already been taken away upon conviction, the Court held that the process a parolee or probationer is due does not include "the full panoply of rights due a defendant in [a criminal prosecution]." The Court described that the State has "an overwhelming interest in being able to return the individual to imprisonment without the burden of a new adversary criminal trial if in fact he has failed to abide by the conditions of his parole." A full-blown adversary process, moreover, may be "less attuned to the rehabilitative needs of the individual proba-tioner or parolee."

On the other hand, the Court concluded that there is no necessity for summary treatment of the parolee or probationer and that revocation is not such a discretionary matter that some form of hearing would be "administratively intolerable." Further-more, "[s]ociety has a stake in whatever may be the chance of restoring [the parolee or probationer] to normal and useful life within the law." To this extent, the State shares the parolee's or probationer's "interest in not having parole [or probation] revoked because of erroneous information or because of an erroneous evaluation of the need to revoke parole [or probation], given the breach of . . . conditions."

Having considered the weight of the relative interests at stake, the Court concluded that before a parolee or probationer is deprived of his or her conditional liberty, there must be "an informal hearing structured to assure that the finding of a . . . violation will be based on verified facts and that the exercise of discretion will be informed by an accurate knowledge" of the parolee's or probationer's behavior. At such a hearing, the parolee or probationer is entitled to an opportunity to show that he or she did not violate the conditions and, where discretion exists, that there was a justifiable excuse for any violation or that revocation is not the appropriate disposition.

More specifically, the Court held that due process requires, at a minimum, both a preliminary hearing at or near the time of arrest, to determine whether there is probable cause or reasonable ground to believe that the parolee or probationer has committed acts that would constitute a violation of his or her conditions, and another opportunity for a hearing before the final finding of a violation and decision of evocation. In both hearings, the following minimum due process protections apply: (1) written notice of the time and place of the hearing; (2) disclosure of evidence; (3) a neutral factfinding body or person, who should not be the officer directly involved in making recommendations; (4) opportunity to be heard in person and to present witnesses and documentary evidence; (5) the right to cross-examine adverse witnesses, unless the hearing officer determines that an informant would be subjected to risk of harm if his or her identity were disclosed or unless the officer otherwise " 'specifically finds good cause for not allowing confrontation' "; and (6) a written statement by the fact finder as to the evidence relied on and the reasons for revoking the conditional liberty. In addition, the parolee or probationer has a right to the assistance of counsel in some circumstances where the parolee's or probationer's version of a disputed issue can fairly be represented only by a trained advocate.

Beyond this, the Court described the required procedure as "flexible" and subject to further refinement by the states. The Court reiterated that a parole or probation revocation hearing is not "a criminal prosecution" and that the process should be "flexible enough to consider evidence including letters, affidavits, and other material that would not be admissible in an adversary criminal trial." In *Morrissey*, the Court also noted that if it turned out that the parolee had admitted parole violations to the parole board, and if those violations were found to be reasonable grounds for revoking parole under state standards, then that "would end the matter." In *Young v. Harper*, the U.S. Supreme Court held that preparole, early release programs were sufficiently similar to parole and probation to require the same due process protections.

## APPLICATION OF *MORRISSEY* AND *GAGNON* TO DRUG COURTS

Shambley argues that a participant in the drug court program has a conditional liberty interest in continuing in the program similar to the conditional liberty interests of participants in preparole, early release programs; parolees; and probationers. She asserts that she should thus be afforded the same due process protections and that those protections were not afforded in this case.

We have never directly addressed this question. In *In re Interest of Tyler T.*, we were asked to consider whether the State complied with due process in revoking the probation of a juvenile adjudicated delinquent and sent to a drug treatment court program as a condition of his probation. The revocation was based on an alleged positive drug test. We vacated the detention order because of the absence of either a verbatim record of the hearing or a written order. We held that due process requires a written record when a judge of a problem-solving court conducts a hearing and enters an order affecting the terms of the juvenile's probation. "[W]here a liberty interest is implicated in problem-solving-court proceedings, an individual's due process rights must be respected."

The majority of other courts considering the issue have determined that participants facing termination from postplea diversion programs, such as the drug court program, are entitled to the same due process protections as persons facing termination of parole or probation. We agree. While restrictions upon the liberty of drug court participants may depend on their individual program plans, participants are not imprisoned, and, like parolees or probationers, they may still do a wide range of things. Participants are generally allowed to live at home and maintain gainful employment. They are allowed to be with family and friends and form the other enduring attachments of normal life, so long as these relationships are not a detriment to their rehabilitation. The termination of the conditional liberty granted drug court participants inflicts a " 'grievous loss' " similar to the loss of parole or probation.

The State's interests, as in parole or probation, include an interest in being able to terminate participation in the program without the burden of a full adversary criminal trial. But perhaps even more so than in parole or probation, the State has little necessity for summary treatment. Drug court participants must generally plead guilty in order to qualify for the program, and the State thereby avoids the burden of a full adversary trial in the first instance. Furthermore, in order to qualify for the program, the crime cannot be a crime of violence and the offender must not have a significant criminal history of crimes of violence. Thus, the risk inherent to any delay caused by conducting a termination hearing is minimal.

As with parole and probation, it is in the State's interests that drug court participants are restored to a normal and useful life. This is, after all, the point of the program. Accordingly, the State, like the participant, has an interest in seeing that there is a termination process which ensures participants are not terminated from the program because of erroneous information or because of an erroneous evaluation of the need to terminate.

Considering the relative interests in the drug court program together with those of parole or probation, their balance is essentially the same. Therefore, the minimal due process to which a parolee or probationer is entitled under *Morrissey* and *Gagnon* also applies to participants in the drug court program. Case law decided in Nebraska setting forth minimum due process for parolees and probationers is equally applicable to our drug courts. We expect drug court termination proceedings to be conducted similarly to hearings terminating parole or probation.

## TERMINATION HEARING VIOLATED DUE PROCESS

Applying these standards, we conclude that Shambley's termination hearing did not comport with the minimal due process to which a drug court participant is entitled. The drug court coordinator's letter and its attachments, considered without establishing foundation or reliability and containing statements made without personal knowledge, were insufficient to sustain the State's burden of proof. In addition, the failure to proffer any witness for Shambley to cross-examine as to the veracity of those statements, and the soundness of the recommendation to terminate, violated Shamb-ley's right to cross-examination as set forth in *Morrissey* and *Gagnon*.

In *State v. Mosley* and *State v. Clark*, our courts addressed the *Morrissey/Gagnon* right to cross-examine. In *Mosley*, we reversed an order revoking probation, because the probationer was denied his right to confront and cross-examine the informant regarding his alleged probation violation. The probationer was alleged to have robbed a store. The evidence of the robbery consisted of the testimony of the investigating officer at the hearing, who related the hearsay statements of a store clerk describing the robbers and suggesting that one of them might have left a fingerprint on a freezer door. The State also presented a technician's testimony that a fingerprint in the store matched the probationer's fingerprints. We observed that there was no finding, as required by *Morrissey*, of good cause for denying the probationer his right to confront the store clerk. Therefore, the court could not deny the defendant his right to cross-examination:

> The *Morrissey* requirement [of the right to confront and cross-examine adverse witnesses unless the hearing officer specifically finds good cause for not allowing confrontation] reserves to the defendant the right to confront and cross-examine adverse witnesses unless the hearing officer specifically finds good cause for not allowing confrontation. In *State v. Kartman*, [192 Neb. 803, 224 N.W.2d 753 (1975)], this court stated: "Persons who have given adverse information should be available for questioning unless the hearing officer determines that they would be subjected to risk of harm if their identity were disclosed."

The probationer's objection at the hearing claiming hearsay and the right to confrontation was sufficient to preserve these rights.

Subsequently, in *Clark*, the Nebraska Court of Appeals reversed an order revoking probation, when the State failed to present the laboratory technician to establish foundation for the urine screening test upon which the revocation was based. At the hearing, the probation officer testified that he had conducted the test on the probationer and sent the specimen to a laboratory for analysis, and the State offered a copy of the laboratory test result showing positive for marijuana. The district court overruled the probationer's objection that there was no evidence as to the specific procedures followed or the specific tests done and no opportunity to cross-examine the person who conducted the test. The Court of Appeals held that by denying the probationer his right to confront the technician who conducted the test, the district court denied the probationer's rights to due process as stated in *Gagnon*. While the court acknowledged that the Nebraska Evidence Rules do not apply to proceedings for revocation of probation, minimum due process, the court explained, includes the right to confront and cross-examine adverse witnesses unless the hearing officer specifically finds good cause for not allowing confrontation.

Despite the flexible standard which allows the consideration of hearsay evidence inadmissible under the rules of evidence, absent a showing of good cause, the drug court participant, parolee, or probationer has the right to confront adverse witnesses with personal knowledge of the evidence upon which the termination or revocation is based. Not a single adverse witness was available for Shambley to cross-examine, despite her protests that she was thus unable to adequately challenge the evidence against her. The drug court denied Shambley her right to cross-examination without making any findings that there was good cause to disallow it. In this manner, she was deprived of her right to procedural due process.

In addition, we agree with Shambley that the State failed to sustain its burden of proof when the sole evidence against her was the drug court coordinator's letter and its accompanying attachments, consisting of hearsay and hearsay within hearsay and considered without specific findings of reliability. While the burden of proof is not a point specifically discussed in *Morrissey* or *Gagnon*, it is understood that the State carried a greater burden of proof at the final revocation hearing than at the preliminary "probable cause" hearing. Other jurisdictions specifically hold that minimal due process demands that the State bear the burden of showing the grounds for revocation of parole or probation by a preponderance of the evidence. While the Nebraska Legislature, through Neb. Rev. Stat. § 29-2267 (Reissue 2008), has set forth a higher standard of proof in the case of violations of probation, we agree that the minimal standard under the Due Process Clause is a preponderance of the evidence. Having found no significant variance between the respective interests in parole and probation and those involved in postplea diversion, we conclude that the minimal preponderance of the evidence standard should also apply to demonstrating the alleged grounds for terminating a participant from the drug court program. The State and Shambley agree that this is the proper standard.

The U.S. Supreme Court has said that the required procedure is flexible enough to allow consideration of evidence, including letters, affidavits, and other material that would not be admissible in an adversary criminal trial. Nevertheless, the *sole* reliance on hearsay evidence in parole and probation hearings, especially when no findings of substantial reliability are made, is generally considered a failure of proof. No lesser standard should be applied to drug court termination proceedings. As one court said,

> Although evidentiary rules may be relaxed somewhat at a revocation hearing, . . . they cannot be relaxed to the point where a parole violation may be proved entirely by unsubstantiated hearsay testimony.

Few instances can be found, such as the one with which we are now presented, where the only evidence against the participant is letters and printouts with not even a single witness testifying in support of these documents. Needless to say, courts confronted with such a record find the evidence insufficient. The State here, in fact, did not present a case. It did not proffer evidence, call any witnesses, or make any argument as to its position at the discharge hearing. Yet the drug court imposed upon Shambley the burden to show that the statements against her were untrue and that she had not violated the conditions of her liberty.

We disagree with the State's argument that it made a prima facie case and that the drug court was merely shifting the burden to Shambley to rebut it. A prima facie case is made by an amount of evidence sufficient to counterbalance the general presumptions of innocence if not overthrown by evidence contradicting it. There was very little in the way of "evidence" at Shambley's hearing — certainly not enough to make a prima facie case. While we understand that the judge was familiar with Shambley's history, this does not diminish Shambley's right to have a hearing "structured to assure that the finding of a . . . violation will be . . . informed by an accurate knowledge" of her behavior. In this case, the court conducted something more akin to a summary procedure than a hearing commensurate with the interests at stake in depriving a person of conditional liberty.

While we acknowledge, as the State points out, that on some prior occasions before the drug court, Shambley appeared to admit certain acts of drug usage, we note that she was less clear on other occasions. Most importantly, she adamantly denied having used drugs on the occasion for which the drug court team finally recommended her termination. Therefore, Shambley did not waive her due process right to have the State prove by a preponderance of the evidence the alleged drug court contract violations for which her participation was to be terminated, at a hearing conducted in accordance with the principles set forth in *Morrissey* and *Gagnon*. The drug court failed to conduct such a hearing, and we must reverse.

## CONCLUSION

We reverse the order of termination and vacate Shambley's sentence, which was imposed after her termination from the program. We remand the cause for a new hearing before the drug court, conducted in accordance with the principles set forth above, to determine the extent to which Shambley violated the terms of the drug court contract and the appropriate action to be taken.

VACATED IN PART, AND IN PART REVERSED AND REMANDED WITH DIRECTIONS.

## In Court Reports

1.    Research a local problem-solving court or specialized docket. You could include the courts formed nearly a century ago that addressed particular populations, such as juvenile court or family court. Or, locate more recently formed courts such as drug courts, domestic violence court, DIU court, support court, veterans' court, and others.

For each court analyze:

a.    the state or federal statutes enacted to create the courts

b.    the local court rules governing the courts

c.    the duties and collaboration among legal and non-legal professionals staffing the courts

d.    the required records or data kept on the outcome of participation in the courts

e.    the participation agreement and other documents defining relationship between court and offender

f.    the protections in place for *ex parte* communications in the courts

g.    the protections in place for the offender's due process rights

h.    the economic or other benefits to the criminal justice system from the problem-solving courts

2.  What community programs or other volunteer activities are associated with your local problem-solving court? Some courts have attracted strong community support and donations of time, resources, and money. *See* Paul W. Shapiro, *Volunteers Are Vital to the Success of the Collaborative Courts*, 50 Orange County Law. 10 (2008).

3.  Many problem-solving courts hold graduation ceremonies for participants when they complete the required program. These celebrations are open to the public; see if any problem-solving courts in your jurisdiction hold these ceremonies and attend one. Critics have countered the success of graduates with the total numbers of those referred to drug courts. But, drug court graduates themselves will give compelling stories of success:

> I am not the same person I was three years ago. I received the most amazing gifts in drug court — things like insight to my fears, understanding of my disease, confidence, and self-esteem. . . . Drug court does amazing things with very limited resources. . . . [N]o one involved in drug court wants to see you fail. They don't do it for the money, or for the hours, or for the weekends off. They don't do it for the glamour and prestige that comes from working with a bunch of addicts. They do it because they truly care. To them, we are not bad people trying to get good, but, rather, sick people trying to get well.

Anonymous, *To the Outside World My Life Must Have Seemed Perfect: A Graduate's Perspective*, 51 ADVOCATE (IDAHO) 19 (2008).

4.  If your courthouse operates several different specialized dockets, consider why the judges in your community chose to create those specific courts for specific offenders, and not others. For example, the Montgomery County Court of Common Pleas has two drug courts — one for men and one for women — and a veterans' court. Other Ohio Common Pleas Courts made different choices: Cuyahoga County has a re-entry court, a drug court, and a mental health court. Summit County has a domestic violence court, a re-entry court, a drug court, and a veterans' court.

5.  Not all specialized dockets address criminal matters. Do any courts in your courthouse or jurisdiction operate a "specialized docket" for civil matters? In addition to family courts, new specialized courts for civil matters have developed. For example, in Ohio, the Lucas County Court of Common Pleas runs a commercial docket; commercial dockets are used to resolve business-to-business disputes more quickly and to provide consistency to the process by having judges develop expertise in this area of the law. *See* Rules 49–49.12, Rules of Superintendence for the Courts of Ohio.

## Out of Court Reports

1.  Develop further the critiques of drug courts suggested by the readings in this chapter. The "War on Drugs" placed the problems of drug and substance abuse squarely in the criminal justice system. Drug courts developed in these courtrooms to combat the repeated arrests and re-arrests by collaborating with treatment providers. However, some critics argue this means that drug courts are integrating drug abuse treatment into the criminal justice system, rather than viewing and approaching it as a public health issue.

2.  Drug courts are based on a non-adversarial approach. Gather arguments in

support of this approach and also in support of the traditional adversarial criminal process. Can a defendant's rights be fully protected when the prosecutor and defense counsel are working together?

3.   Pre-docket hearing conferences among the drug court team members — judge, probation officer, prosecutor, defense counsel, treatment professionals — are a fixture in many drug courts. What are the benefits and dangers created by this practice of shared assessment and decision-making among judges, lawyers, and non lawyers?

4.   How do drug courts and other problem-solving courts change the role of the judge? Be specific. If you were to clerk for a judge, would you prefer a traditional court or a problem-solving court setting?

5.   Ohio specialized dockets are highly regulated, subject to certification, data collection, and inspections or visits. Evaluate this approach and compare with other jurisdictions where problem-solving courts are less regulated. Would less regulation allow for more experimentation and further development?

6.   Identify an issue or a target population that you find would be appropriate for a specialized criminal or civil docket in state or federal court. Sketch out how and why this issue, subject matter or population would be amenable to a problem-solving court, rather than a traditional court. Recently developed courts include, for example, gambling courts and courts addressing human trafficking and prostitution.

7.   State courts are not alone in developing specialty courts. Federal specialty courts include both trial and appellate courts, such as the Court of Federal Claims, the Veterans Appeals Court, the Military Appeals Court, the Tax Court, the International Trade Court, and Bankruptcy Courts. What might be some additional federal specialty courts? One popular suggestion has been science and technology. For example, in the 1970s and again more recently, federal court observers have proposed a subject-matter specialty court with expertise in complex science and technology. *See* Justin Sevier, *Redesigning the Science Court*, 73 Md. L. Rev. 770 (2014); Andrew W. Jurs, *Science Court: Past Proposals, Current Considerations, and a Suggested Structure*, 15 Va. J.L. & Tech. 1 (2010).

### Selected Bibliography

Kimberly M. Baker, *Decision Making in a Hybrid Organization: A Case Study of a Southwestern Drug Court Treatment Program*, 38 Law & Soc. Inquiry 27 (2013).

Christopher P. Bellmore, *State v. Shambley and the Nebraska Supreme Court's Conclusory Approach Defining a Standard of Proof for Drug Court Termination Hearings*, 47 Creighton L. Rev. 1 (2013).

Richard C. Boldt, *Problem-Solving Courts and Pragmatism*, 73 Md. L. Rev. 1120 (2014).

Richard C. Boldt, *The "Tomahawk" and the "Healing Balm": Drug Treatment Courts in Theory and Practice*, 10 U. Md. L.J. Race, Religion, Gender & Class 45 (2010).

Josh Bowers, *Contraindicated Drug Courts*, 55 Ucla L. Rev. 783 (2008).

Pamela M. Casey & David B. Rottman, *Problem-Solving Courts: Models and Trends*, 26 JUST. SYS. J. 35 (2005).

Blake Courlang, *The War on Drugs Is Over (If You Want It): State Drug Courts as an Alternative to Criminal Courts for Low-Level, Nonviolent Drug Offenders*, 16 CARDOZO J. CONFLICT RESOL. 265 (2014).

John F. Coyle, *Business Courts and Interstate Competition*, 53 WM. & MARY L. REV. 1915 (2012).

Kevin Davis, *Just a Click Away: Training for Drug Court Professionals Goes Online*, 99 A.B.A. J. 12 (Mar. 2013).

Donald Dowd, *Suspicious of Drug Courts? Don't Be*, 77 TEX. B.J. 310 (2014).

Christopher C. Edward, *A Call to End Prospective Waivers of Judicial Disqualification in Accountability Courts*, 38 CHAMPION 34 (2014).

Sarah W. Ellis, *Drug Courts Impact Participants, Courts, and Communities*, 59 BOSTON B.J. 12 (2015).

Caitlinrose Fisher, *Treating the Disease or Punishing the Criminal?: Effectively Using Drug Court Sanctions to Treat Substance Abuse Disorder and Decrease Criminal Conduct*, 99 MINN. L. REV. 747 (2014).

Andrew Fulkerson, *How Much Process Is Due in the Drug Court?*, 48 No. 4 Crim. Law Bulletin ART 3 (2012).

Philip D. Gould & Patricia H. Murrell, *Therapeutic Jurisprudence and Cognitive Complexity: An Overview*, 29 FORDHAM URB. L.J. 2117 (2002).

Joel Gross, *The Effects of Net-Widening on Minority and Indigent Drug Offenders: A Critique of Drug Courts*, 10 U. MD. L.J. RACE, RELIGION, GENDER & CLASS 161 (2010).

Amaia Guenaga, *Improving the Odds: Changing the Perception of Problem Gambling and Supporting the Growth of Problem Gambling Courts*, 2 UNLV GAMING L. J. 133 (2011).

Cynthia Gray, *When Roles Collide: Judicial Ethics and Problem-Solving Judges*, 24 No. 1 Experience 38 (2014).

Kaitlyn Griffin, *Answering the Critics: How Judges' Adherence to High Ethical Standards Increases Drug Courts' Effectiveness*, 36 J. LEGAL PROF. 545 (2012).

Michael Daly Hawkins, *Coming Home: Accommodating the Special Needs of Military Veterans to the Criminal Justice System*, 7 OHIO ST. J. CRIM. L. 563 (2010).

Kimberly Y.W. Holst, *A Good Score?: Examining Twenty Years of Drug Courts in the United States and Abroad*, 45 VAL. U. L. REV. 73 (2010).

Peggy Fulton Hora & Theodore Stalcup, *Drug Treatment Courts in the Twenty-First Century: The Evolution of the Revolution in Problem-Solving Courts*, 42 GA. L. REV. 717 (2008).

West Huddleston & Douglas B. Marlowe, *Painting the Current Picture: A National Report on Drug Courts and Other Problem-Solving Court Programs in the United States*, National Drug Court Institute (2011).

Andrew R. Jones, *Toward a Stronger Economic Future for North Carolina: Precedent and the Opinions of the North Carolina Business Court*, 6 ELON L. REV. 189 (2014).

Fern L. Kletter, Annotation, *Due Process Afforded in Drug Court Proceedings*, 78 A.L.R. 6th 1 (originally published 2012).

Edward J. Latessa & Angela K. Reitler, *What Works in Reducing Recidivism and How Does It Relate to Drug Courts?*, 41 OHIO N.U. L. REV. 757 (2015).

Angel Lopez, *My Two Years in Drug Court*, 73 OR. ST. B. BULL. 62 (2013).

Douglas B. Marlowe, *Achieving Racial and Ethnic Fairness in Drug Courts*, 49 COURT REV. 40 (2013).

Douglas B. Marlowe, David S. DeMatteo & David S. Festinger, *A Sober Assessment of Drug Courts*, 16 FED. SENT. R. 153 (2003).

Eric J. Miller, *Drugs, Courts and the New Penology*, 20 STAN. L. & POL'Y REV. 417 (2009).

Eric J. Miller, *Embracing Addiction: Drug Courts and the False Promise of Judicial Interventionism*, 65 OHIO ST. L. J. 1479 (2004).

Liz Moore, *International Best Practice in Drug Courts*, 7 ARIZ. SUMMIT L. REV. 481 (2014).

Emily R. Murphy, *Paved With Good Intentions: Sentencing Alternatives from Neuroscience and the Policy of Problem-Solving Courts*, 37 LAW & PSYCHOL. REV. 83 (2013).

Patricia H. Murrell & Philip D. Gould, *Educating for Therapeutic Judging: Strategies, Concepts, and Outcomes*, 78 REV. JUR. U.P.R. 129 (2009).

Michael M. O'Hear, *Rethinking Drug Courts: Restorative Justice as a Response to Racial Injustice*, 20 STAN. L. & POL'Y REV. 463 (2009).

Melinda R. Roberts et al., *A Social Worker's Role in Drug Court*, SAGE OPEN (May 14, 2014).

Brian D. Shannon, *Specialty Courts, Ex Parte Communications, and the Need to Revise the Texas Code of Judicial Conduct*, 66 BAYLOR L. REV. 127 (2014).

Salmon A. Shomade, *Sentencing Patterns: Drug Court Judges Serving in Conventional Criminal Courts*, 96 JUDICATURE 36 (2012).

Katie Smith, *Fifty-Six Percent Success Is Still a Failing Grade: Reducing Recidivism and Ensuring Due Process Rights in Drug Courts*, 35 U. LA VERNE L. REV. 315 (2014).

REBECCA TIGER, JUDGING ADDICTS: DRUG COURTS AND COERCION IN THE JUSTICE SYSTEM (2013).

Andrew Wasicek, *Palliative Exceptions: Substance Abuse, Mental Illness, and Drug Courts*, 10 CONN. PUB. INT. L.J. 199 (2010).

Nancy Neal Yeend, *Tips for Facilitating Problem-Solving Court Teams*, 48 JUDGES' J. 20 (Spring 2004).

# Chapter 7

# JUDICIAL ROLES: TECHNOLOGY'S EFFECTS ON JUDICIAL RESEARCH AND DECISION-MAKING

> The cornerstones of that [judicial] system are that the lawyers have the ability to choose which facts they bring before the tribunal and an extensive code of evidentiary rules assist in sorting out the evidence that the tribunal may or may not consider. But what happens to that system when the world of factual information is just a mouse click away? Stated another way, may a judge conduct independent Internet research on something more than the law?

Eric J. Magnuson & Michael W. Kaphing, *No Longer a Luxury: Ethical Issues on Appeal in a Technological World*, 55 No. 11 DRI For Def. 18 (2013).

> Judicial Internet research, however, remains controversial. While the controversy in part reflects a more general ongoing debate about judicial factual research, the recasting of this age-old debate in a new technological sphere has created some additional wrinkles. Judicial Internet use is irreversibly altering our legal system and judicial decision-making processes.

Layne S. Keele, *When the Mountain Goes to Mohammed: The Internet and Judicial Decision-Making*, 45 N.M.L. Rev. 125 (2014).

> It is not uncommon for [Justice Breyer] to quiz an advocate at oral argument with extra-record statistics which he openly admits were gathered through an in-chambers Google search. And in [a] decision striking down a law which restricted the sale of violent video games to minors, [he] . . . compiled an appendix to his dissent of academic journals weighing in on the debate that violent video games cause psychological harm to children. Citing a YouTube video, he explained that filters on these video games are easy to evade . . . . Much of this research was not in the record and did not come from any of the briefs.

Allison Orr Larsen, *Confronting Supreme Court Fact Finding*, 98 Va. L. Rev. 1255 (2012).

> In addition to violating . . . legal and ethical rules, ex parte sua sponte judicial research is simply un-American. . . . Judges should not search blogs for information about the facts of the cases before them unless the parties are given notice and an opportunity to comment on any information the judges discovers.

Lee F. Peoples, *The Citation of Blogs in Judicial Opinions*, 13 Tul. J. Tech. & In-tell. Prop. 39 (2010).

> [W]hen did a Web site that any Internet surfer can edit become an authoritative source by which law students could write passing papers, experts could provide credible testimony, lawyers could craft legal arguments, and judges could issue precedents?

*Badasa v. Mukasey*, 540 F.3d 909 (8th Cir. 2008) (quoting R. Jason Richards, *Courting Wikipedi*a, 44 Trial 62 (Apr. 2008)).

> We propose that it is appropriate to cite Wikipedia when it is suitable to cite the wisdom of the crowd.

Jason C. Miller & Hannah B. Murray, *Wikipedia in Court: When and How Citing Wikipedia and Other Consensus Websites Is Appropriate*, 84 St. John's L. Rev. 633 (2010).

Describing the impact of "technology" on a judge's role at the trial court or appellate level is beyond the scope of this chapter, this book and likely many other books, websites, and blogs combined. Applied to the judicial process, any number of modern advances in technology affecting judges, parties, jurors, and attorneys may come to mind.

In his *2014 Year -End Report on the Federal Judiciary*, Chief Justice Roberts described the technology issues he finds have shaped the federal courts. These include: computer-assisted legal research; modern courtroom technologies used to introduce evidence; electronic case filing and management which allows public access. No doubt, the advance of technology will continue to be featured in future yearly reports.

In this chapter, however, the focus on technology in the court system narrows to two technology topics visible in courtrooms and written opinions. First, technology has created ready access to the Internet, making available to the courts not just legal resources, but an expanding array of "factual" information. This access has proven irresistible to some judges. Judges have begun to rely upon and cite to Internet resources — Wikipedia, blogs, hyperlinks to websites, Google maps, and others. This use is seen in trial courts and appellate courts where it goes by names such as "fact-finding on appeal," "in-house fact-finding," "judicial Internet fact gathering," "independent research," or "ex parte sua sponte judicial research." In particular, the specific reliance on and citation to Wikipedia, a collaborative on-line encyclopedia for legislative and adjudicative facts has stirred debate and alarm.

A second focus is technology's effect upon images that enter both trial and appellate courts as cases are tried and opinions published. Like Wikipedia and other Internet resources, images and video are now freely exchanged on the Internet. These images may be created, altered, photo-shopped. Such powerful images now play new roles in trial proceedings and opinions.

# I.  JUDICIAL INTERNET FACT RESEARCH

Much of the debate concerning the court's use of independent judicial factual research stems from judges' decisions to rely upon information gleaned from Internet resources. This judicial use triggers several concerns, including the use of judicial notice, the creation of a record, and ethical codes of judicial conduct. These rules reflect the court system's adversarial nature, the ability of parties to receive notice and an opportunity to challenge the accuracy, and the ethical implications of a court's reliance on Internet fact-finding research to reach its decisions.

The courts' use of Wikipedia triggers the issue of judicial notice, which is governed by Federal Rule of Evidence 201 and its state counterparts. Under the Rule, judicial notice of an adjudicative fact requires certain procedures to allow notice and a chance to be heard to the parties. Judicial notice of a legislative fact falls outside of Federal Rule of Evidence 201 and is governed instead by common law principles.

The definitions and distinctions between adjudicative and legislative facts do not appear in the Rule and this has led to trouble for judges and attorneys in answering the question what sort of fact is being given judicial notice.

> Indeed, the question has been described by courts and commentators as 'baffling.' Because of this difficulty, it is not unusual for a court to simply apply the restrictive provisions of Rule 201 without first determining whether the fact to be judicially noticed is adjudicative and subject to Rule 201 or legislative and not subject to Rule 201. Adding to the confusion, some courts have applied Rule 201(b) in determining the propriety of taking judicial notice of legislative facts.

Kurtis A. Kemper, Annotation, *What Constitutes "Adjudicative Facts" Within Meaning of Rule 201 of Federal Rules of Evidence Concerning Judicial Notice of Adjudicative Facts*, 150 A.L.R. Fed. 543 (originally published 1998) (citations omitted).

Courts offer further definitions for the two terms. Under Rule 201, adjudicative facts are simply the facts of the particular case, while legislative facts are established truths, facts, or pronouncements that do not change from case to case but apply universally. *See United States v. Wolny*, 133 F.3d 758 (10th Cir. 1998). "When a court finds facts concerning the immediate parties — who did what, where, when, how, and with what motive or intent the court is performing an adjudicative function and the facts are conveniently called adjudicative facts, whereas legislative facts are ordinarily general and do not concern the immediate parties." *United States v. Gould*, 536 F.2d 216 (8th Cir. 1976). An "adjudicative fact," is regulated by the Federal Rules of Evidence, and concerns the parties to a proceeding, as contrasted with "legislative fact" which is general and broad and related to the parties, not as individuals or particular entities, but unspecifically. *In re Digby*, 47 B.R. 614 (Bankr. N.D. Ala. 1985).

If legislative facts fall outside of Rule 201 and its judicial notice requirements, then what standards should be used to judge these legislative facts as worthy of judicial notice? The answer is that they are judged by "common law principles." These principles are not always clearly articulated.

Drawing on a survey of judicial notice afforded legislative facts in case law, one writer suggested that "[c]ourts would do better to hold themselves to the same standards used when they judge the factual support for legislation challenged as unconstitutional; that is, the facts must be those that a lawmaker could rationally believe. This standard seems implicit in decisions holding that "legislative facts" must be "relevant. Most of the cases seem to meet this standard, even if they do not proclaim it." Kenneth W. Graham, Jr., 21B Fed. Prac. & Proc. Evid. § 5103.2 *Scope of Rule 103; "Judicial Notice" — "Legislative Facts"* (2d ed. database updated Apr. 2015).

In this chapter, relevant evidentiary and ethical provisions are provided at the start. As you read the cases, you will find little or no mention of the terms adjudicative fact, legislative fact, or judicial notice. However, that analysis underlies the decisions; observe how that analysis influences the outcome. The lack of explicit terms in decisions is not unusual and has a long tradition. The 1976 case of *Gould*, cited above, had to review the lower court's ruling and derive from it that the district court below had taken judicial notice of a fact and that the fact noticed was a legislative fact, not an adjudicative fact.

In addition to supporting legislative and adjudicative facts, some judicial use of facts accompanied by Internet citations may offer background or context for the opinion or may simply be a show of judicial learning and wit.

## Federal Rule of Evidence 201.   Judicial Notice of Adjudicative Facts

**(a) Scope.** This rule governs judicial notice of an adjudicative fact only, not a legislative fact.

**(b) Kinds of Facts That May Be Judicially Noticed.** The court may judicially notice a fact that is not subject to reasonable dispute because it:

(1) is generally known within the trial court's territorial jurisdiction; or

(2) can be accurately and readily determined from sources whose accuracy cannot reasonably be questioned.

**(c) Taking Notice.** The court:

(1) may take judicial notice on its own; or

(2) must take judicial notice if a party requests it and the court is supplied with the necessary information.

**(d) Timing.** This rule governs judicial notice of an adjudicative fact only, not a legislative fact.

**(e) Opportunity to Be Heard.** On timely request, a party is entitled to be heard on the propriety of taking judicial notice and the nature of the fact to be noticed. If the court takes judicial notice before notifying a party, the party, on request, is still entitled to be heard.

**(f) Instructing the Jury.** In a civil case, the court must instruct the jury to accept the noticed fact as conclusive. In a criminal case, the court must instruct the jury that it may or may not accept the noticed fact as conclusive.

At the trial court level, the adversarial process and due process are firmly in place: A party opposing judicial notice of an adjudicative fact has the opportunity to be notified of the judge's intent and to heard on the issue. But judicial notice on appeal of what may be adjudicative facts raises concerns that the parties have been deprived of a chance to receive notice and to be heard on the issue.

## Federal Rule of Appellate Procedure 10.   The Record on Appeal

**(a) Composition of the Record on Appeal.** The following items constitute the record on appeal:

(1) the original papers and exhibits filed in the district court;

(2) the transcript of proceedings, if any; and

(3) a certified copy of the docket entries prepared by the district clerk.

**(b) The Transcript of Proceedings.**

**(1) Appellant's Duty to Order.** Within 14 days after filing the notice of appeal or entry of an order disposing of the last timely remaining motion of a type specified in Rule 4(a)(4)(A), whichever is later, the appellant must do either of the following:

(A) order from the reporter a transcript of such parts of the proceedings not already on file as the appellant considers necessary, subject to a local rule of the court of appeals and with the following qualifications:

(i) the order must be in writing;

(ii) if the cost of the transcript is to be paid by the United States under the Criminal Justice Act, the order must so state; and

(iii) the appellant must, within the same period, file a copy of the order with the district clerk; or

(B) file a certificate stating that no transcript will be ordered.

**(2) Unsupported Finding or Conclusion.** If the appellant intends to urge on appeal that a finding or conclusion is unsupported by the evidence or is contrary to the evidence, the appellant must include in the record a transcript of all evidence relevant to that finding or conclusion.

## ABA Model Code of Judicial Conduct (2011 Edition)

## Rule 2.9.  Ex Parte Communications

\* \* \* \*

(C) A judge shall not investigate facts in a matter independently, and shall consider only the evidence presented and any facts that may properly be judicially noticed.

> **Comment on Rule 2.9:** [6] The prohibition against a judge investigating the facts in a matter extends to information available in all mediums, including electronic.

> **Reporter's Explanation of Changes** [6] New Comment containing prohibition against independently investigating facts. Given the ease with which factual investigation can now be accomplished via electronic databases and the Internet, the risk that a judge or the judge's staff could inadvertently violate Rules 2.9(B) and (C) has heightened considerably. The need for vigilance on the part of judges has increased accordingly.

---

Statutory interpretation and contract interpretation are fertile grounds for trial courts to use judicial notice to recognize the common, ordinary meaning of terms. While a print dictionary may have once served this purpose, now the Internet may provide the meaning.

## FIRE INSURANCE EXCHANGE v. OLTMANNS
### 285 P.3d 802 (Utah Ct. App. 2012)

ORME, JUDGE:

Robert Oltmanns and Brady Blackner appeal the decision of the district court granting Fire Insurance Exchange's motion for summary judgment. The court determined that the term "jet ski" as used in a homeowner's policy was unambiguous and effectively excluded coverage for claims arising from the use of any and all personal watercraft. We reverse.

### BACKGROUND

Oltmanns, the insured, and his friend Blackner were operating a Honda F-12 AquaTrax personal watercraft on a lake in southern Utah. This kind of personal watercraft is designed for use by a seated driver and up to two additional seated passengers. A lawsuit resulted from injuries sustained in an accident that occurred during this use, and Oltmanns tendered the defense to Fire Insurance Exchange, with whom he was insured under a homeowner's policy. The insurance policy contained the following exclusion from its liability coverage:

We do not cover bodily injury [that] . . . .

. . .

    7. results from the ownership, maintenance, use, loading or unloading of:

      a. aircraft

      b. motor vehicles

      c. jet skis and jet sleds or

      d. any other watercraft owned or rented to an insured and which:

        (1) has more than 50 horsepower inboard or inboard-outdrive motor power; or

        (2) is powered by one or more outboard motors with more than 25 total horsepower; or

        (3) is a sailing vessel 26 feet or more in length.

Exclusions 7c and d do not apply while jet skis, jet sleds or watercraft are stored. . . .

Relying on this exclusion, the insurance company brought a declaratory judgment action against Oltmanns and Blackner, arguing that it had no duty to defend or indemnify Oltmanns or compensate Blackner because liability coverage was excluded by the above provision. The insurance company then moved for summary judgment, arguing that Oltmanns was operating a "jet ski," which is merely a synonym for personal watercraft, and that the policy unambiguously excluded coverage for use of all such watercraft. Oltmanns argued that the exclusion did not apply because it was ambiguous, pointing out that "Jet Ski" is a registered trademark for a particular model of Kawasaki personal watercraft, which was not involved in the accident. The trial court granted the insurance company's motion for summary judgment, and this appeal followed.

## ISSUE AND STANDARD OF REVIEW

Oltmanns and Blackner contend that the trial court erred in granting the insurance company's motion for summary judgment. A motion for summary judgment may be granted only when "there is no genuine issue as to any material fact and . . . the moving party is entitled to a judgment as a matter of law." Utah R. Civ. P. 56(c). "Where the moving party would bear the burden of proof at trial, the movant must establish each element of his claim in order to show that he is entitled to judgment as a matter of law." *Orvis v. Johnson*, 2008 UT 2, ¶ 10, 177 P.3d 600. Even " '[w]here the party opposed to the motion submits no documents in opposition, the moving party may be granted summary judgment *only . . . if he is entitled to judgment as a matter of law.*' " *Ward v. Graydon*, 2011 UT App 358, ¶ 15, 264 P.3d 764 (emphasis and omissions in original) (quoting *Olwell v. Clark*, 658 P.2d 585, 586 (Utah 1982)), *cert. denied*, 275 P.3d 1019 (Utah 2012). A trial court's ruling on summary judgment presents a question of law. *See Massey v. Griffiths*, 2007 UT 10, ¶ 8, 152 P.3d 312. The court's "legal conclusions and ultimate grant or denial of summary judgment are reviewed for correctness." *Id.* Also, "[i]nterpretation of an insurance contract presents a question of law" and we "accord the trial court's legal conclusions regarding the contract no deference but review them for correctness." *Bear River Mut. Ins. Co. v. Williams*, 2006 UT App 500, ¶ 7, 153 P.3d 798 (citations and internal quotation marks omitted).

## ANALYSIS

The insurance company argues that its use of the term "jet ski" was intended to refer to any and all personal watercraft. It contends that "jet ski" is common vernacular for such and thus is not ambiguous. Before we attempt to understand what "jet ski" means for purposes of this contract, however, it is helpful to review the rules governing contract interpretation, particularly in the insurance contract context.

"Insurance policies are generally interpreted according to rules of contract interpretation." *Utah Farm Bureau Ins. Co. v. Crook*, 1999 UT 47, ¶ 5, 980 P.2d 685. Because "an insurance policy is a classic example of an adhesion contract," Utah courts have long held that " 'insurance policies should be construed liberally in favor of the insured and their beneficiaries so as to promote and not defeat the purposes of insurance.' " *United States Fidelity & Guar. Co. v. Sandt*, 854 P.2d 519, 521–22 (Utah 1993) (quoting *Richards v. Standard Acc. Ins. Co.*, 58 Utah 622, 200 P. 1017, 1020 (1921)). "It follows that ambiguous or uncertain language in an insurance contract that is fairly susceptible to different interpretations should be construed in favor of coverage" and "provisions that limit or exclude coverage should be strictly construed against the insurer." *Id.* at 522–23. In strictly construing exclusions, we give them effect only when they use "language which clearly and unmistakably communicates to the insured the specific circumstances under which the expected coverage will not be provided." *Crook*, 1999 UT 47, ¶ 5, 980 P.2d 685 (citations and internal quotation marks omitted).

When faced with ambiguity in a written contract, courts do not interpret the provision to comport with what they think is most sensible or is most likely what one of the parties "really" meant or is what leads to the fairest result. Rather, they recognize the need to consider extrinsic evidence in an effort to resolve the ambiguity. *See Wilburn v. Interstate Electric*, 748 P.2d 582, 584–85 (Utah Ct. App. 1988). If the extrinsic evidence is not conclusive, then the last resort in contract interpretation is to construe the provision *against* the drafter. *See id.* at 585 ("Once a contract is deemed ambiguous, the next order of business is to admit extrinsic evidence to aid in interpretation of the contract. It is only after extrinsic evidence is considered and the court is still uncertain as to the intention of the parties that ambiguities should be construed against the drafter.") (footnote omitted).

As a practical matter, though, there is a different protocol in the case of insurance and surety contracts, where it is seen as appropriate to jump immediately to what is usually viewed as the "last resort," "tie-breaker" rule of interpretation, namely construction against the drafter. *See id.* at 585 & n.2. This is due to the probable dearth of relevant extrinsic evidence in these contexts. *See id.* (noting that while the usual rule is that extrinsic evidence must be considered before turning to the rule of construction that calls for ambiguities to be construed against the drafter, there are "arguable exceptions" in the case of insurance and surety contracts that "may be explained, at least in part, by the fact that such contracts are ordinarily not preceded by discussion or negotiation of specific terms and, thus, absent meaningful extrinsic evidence as to intent, recourse must be had directly to the maxim that ambiguities should be construed against the drafter"). As noted above, construction against the insurer is especially appropriate when an ambiguous term appears in an exclusionary provision because such provisions are "strictly construed against the insurer." *Sandt*, 854 P.2d at 523.

In the case at hand, it may be true that the insurer meant, through its use of the term "jet ski," to exclude from coverage all varieties of personal watercraft. And we are confident that the insurer did not intend to refer only to a particular Kawasaki model of personal watercraft, even though there is such a model named Jet Ski. But the provision in question is not a model of clarity and at least one additional interpretation is entirely possible. Another common use of the term "jet ski" is in reference to the stand-up variant of personal watercraft, in contradistinction to the sit-down variety, known colloquially — and also imprecisely — as wave runners. The subject is well-illuminated in that great repository of contemporary wisdom, Wikipedia.[1]

> Jet Ski is the brand name of a personal watercraft manufactured by Kawasaki Heavy Industries. The name is sometimes mistakenly used by those unfamiliar with the personal watercraft industry to refer to any type of personal watercraft; however, the name is a valid trademark registered with the United States Patent and Trademark Office, and in many other countries. The term "Jet Ski" (or JetSki, often shortened to "*Ski*") is often mis-applied to all personal watercraft with pivoting handlepoles manipulated by a standing rider; these are properly known as Stand-up PWCs. The term is often mistakenly used when referring to WaveRunners, but WaveRunner is actually the name of the Yamaha line of sit-down PWCs, whereas "Jet Ski" refers to the Kawasaki line.

Jet Ski, http://en.wikipedia.org/wiki/Jet_ski (last visited August 13, 2012) (footnotes omitted).

---

[1] In the past, we might have hesitated to cite Wikipedia in a judicial opinion given its reputation — perhaps not well deserved — for unreliability. *See, e.g., Wikipedia Survives Research Test*, BBC News (Dec. 15, 2005), http://news.bbc.co.uk/2/hi/technology/4530930.stm (finding rate of error in scientific articles to be about the same as between Wikipedia and Encyclopedia Britannica). But the increasing trend of using Wikipedia in judicial opinions over the last decade seems to demonstrate a growing recognition of its value in some contexts, as noted in one 2010 article that found that by that year Wikipedia had been cited in over four hundred judicial opinions. *See* Lee F. Peoples, *The Citation of Wikipedia in Judicial Opinions*, 12 Yale J. L. & Tech. 1, 1 (2009–2010) (reviewing several instances in which Wikipedia has been cited in judicial opinions and critiquing its usefulness, or lack thereof, in those contexts). Judge Posner argued in 2007 that "Wikipedia is a terrific resource . . . [p]artly because it [is] so convenient, it often has been updated recently and [it] is very accurate," after citing it in *United States v. Radomski*, 473 F.3d 728, 731 (7th Cir. 2007). *See* Noam Cohen, *Courts Turn to Wikipedia, but Selectively*, N.Y. Times, Jan. 29, 2007 at C3. While a prudent person would avoid a surgeon who bases his or her understanding of complicated medical procedures on an online source whose contributors range from expert scholars to internet trolls, where an understanding of the vernacular or colloquial is key to the resolution of a case, Judge Posner is correct that Wikipedia is tough to beat. A fuller explanation of the propriety of citing Wikipedia is set forth in Judge Voros's separate opinion.

Basically, then, the insurer was imprecise in using the term "jet ski" in its policy. Even discounting the bizarre possibility that it meant to refer only to one Kawasaki watercraft model, it still cannot be definitively said what the insurer intended: Did it mean all manner of personal watercraft? Or did it mean only the stand-up variety?[2] The provision, then, is ambiguous as a matter of law.[3]

## CONCLUSION

This provision fails to "clearly and unmistakably communicate[ ] to the insured the specific circumstances under which the expected coverage will not be provided." *Utah Farm Bureau Ins. Co. v. Crook*, 1999 UT 47, ¶ 5, 980 P.2d 685 (citation and internal quotation marks omitted). Because the exclusionary provision is ambiguous, it must be construed against the drafter, and thus the language relied on by the insurance company is not effective to exclude coverage for an insured's accident resulting from use of an AquaTrax personal watercraft of the sit-down variety. The summary judgment is reversed and the case remanded for trial or such other proceedings as may now be in order.

I CONCUR: Carolyn B. McHugh, Presiding Judge.

Voros, Associate Presiding Judge (concurring):

I concur fully in the lead opinion. I write separately to explain why I believe that opinion appropriately cites Wikipedia in construing the term "jet ski" in the insurance contract at issue here. Wikipedia has been cited in hundreds of American judicial opinions, including one issued by the Utah Supreme Court. *See State v. Alverez*, 2006 UT 61, ¶ 16 n.5, 147 P.3d 425 (citing a Wikipedia entry on Jesus Malverde). But today's lead opinion is the first time this court has cited it.

Wikipedia is a "free, collaboratively edited, and multilingual Internet encyclopedia" whose 22 million articles (over 4 million in English) are written by volunteers. Wikipedia, *Wikipedia*, http://en.wikipedia.org/wiki/Wikipedia (as of Aug. 13, 2012, 18:48 GMT). Most of its articles can be edited by anyone with access to the site. Wikipedia claims to be "the largest and most popular general reference work on the

---

[2] This does not seem like a terribly far-fetched proposition. Intuitively, at least, it seems that a motorized watercraft on which the rider stands up may be much more dangerous than one on which the rider is seated.

[3] The insurer's lack of care in drafting this provision is further demonstrated by its pairing of the term "jet sled" with "jet ski." The author of this opinion theorized at oral argument that perhaps "jet sled" was used in reference to the sit-down variants of personal watercraft while "jet ski" was used to refer to the stand-up kind. The idea had no takers, however, despite its apparent logic, and indeed, our research finds not a single instance where "jet sled" has been used synonymously with personal watercraft of any sort. Wikipedia does not even have an article, among its several million, on jet sleds. It appears that "jet sled" can refer to an unmotorized sled used for hauling ice fishing equipment, *see* Shappell, Multi-Purpose Sleds, http://www.shappell.com/sleds.html (last visited August 8, 2012), or to a large motorboat of the sort that would be readily and redundantly covered in the next subsection, subsection (d), of the exclusion in question, *see* Google Images for "Jet Sled Boat," http://google.com (follow "Images" option; then search "Jet Sled Boat") (last searched August 8, 2012).

Internet," with "an estimated 365 million readers worldwide" and "2.7 billion monthly pageviews from the United States alone." *Id.* (footnotes omitted).

Because Wikipedia is an open-source project, questions arise as to its reliability. Indeed, Wikipedia's own article on the subject references various studies as well as opposing views from librarians, academics, experts in science and medicine, and editors of other encyclopedias. *See* Wikipedia, *Reliability of Wikipedia*, http://en.wikipedia.org/wiki/Reliability_of_Wikipedia (as of Aug. 13, 2012, 18:51 GMT). In addition, most or all Wikipedia entries include a broad disclaimer on the entry's citation page:

> **IMPORTANT NOTE:** Most educators and professionals do not consider it appropriate to use tertiary sources such as encyclopedias as a sole source for any information — citing an encyclopedia as an important reference in footnotes or bibliographies may result in censure or a failing grade. Wikipedia articles should be used for background information, as a reference for correct terminology and search terms, and as a starting point for further research.
>
> As with any community-built reference, there is a possibility for error in Wikipedia's content — please check your facts against multiple sources and read our disclaimers for more information.

Wikipedia, *Cite Page: Jet Ski*, http://en.wikipedia.org/w/index.php? title= Special:Cite&page=Jet_Ski&id=493156065 (as of Aug. 13, 2012, 18:52 GMT).[1]

Citing Wikipedia is as controversial as it is common.[2] Some courts approve it, others condemn it. *Compare United States v. Lawson*, 677 F.3d 629, 650 (4th Cir. 2012) (stating that the court is "troubled by Wikipedia's lack of reliability"), *Bing Shun Li v. Holder*, 400 Fed. Appx. 854, 857–58 (5th Cir. 2010) (expressing "disapproval of the [immigration judge]'s reliance on Wikipedia and [warning] against any improper reliance on it or similarly unreliable internet sources in the future"), *Badasa v. Mukasey*, 540 F.3d 909, 910–11 (8th Cir. 2008) (noting Wikipedia's acknowledgment that, "at any given moment," an entry "could be in the middle of a large edit or it could have been recently vandalized" (citation and internal quotation marks omitted)), *and In re Marriage of Lamoure*, 198 Cal. App. 4th 807, 132 Cal. Rptr. 3d 1, 15 (2011) ("We

---

[1]  Reliability may also be an issue for the Wikipedia citation itself:

A defining feature of Wikipedia is that its entries are in a constant state of change. The impermanent nature of the information on Wikipedia has serious consequences when Wikipedia entries are cited in judicial opinions. Unless they are provided with a date-and time-specific citation, researchers who pull up a Wikipedia entry cited in a judicial opinion will never be absolutely certain they are viewing the entry as it existed when the judge viewed it . . . . This may ultimately lead to uncertainty and instability in the law.

Lee F. Peoples, *The Citation of Wikipedia in Judicial Opinions*, 12 Yale J. L. & Tech. 1, 38–39 (2009–2010). Fortunately, each Wikipedia entry has a "Cite this page" link showing citations to that entry in various styles, including the style prescribed by the Harvard Journal of Law & Technology. That journal's citation style, which I have followed in this opinion, is more specific than ordinary Bluebook citation style.

[2]  "Many citations by judges, often in footnotes, are . . . beside the main judicial point, [and] appear intended to show how hip and contemporary the judge is . . . ." Noam Cohen, *Courts Turn to Wikipedia, but Selectively*, N.Y. Times, Jan. 29, 2007, *available at* http://www.nytimes.com/2007/01/29/technology/29wikipedia.html. The lead opinion's citation to Wikipedia is obviously not of this type.

do not consider Wikipedia a sufficiently reliable source" for defining the term "noncustodial."), *with Prude v. Clarke,* 675 F.3d 732, 734 (7th Cir. 2012) (citing Wikipedia entry, in the context of an Eighth Amendment challenge, for the proposition that an anal fissure "is no fun at all"), *United States v. Brown,* 669 F.3d 10, 18 & n.12 (1st Cir. 2012) (citing Wikipedia for its definition of "sovereign citizen movement," one of a criminal defendant's "atypical legal beliefs"), *Murdock v. Astrue,* 458 Fed. Appx. 702, 705 n.3 (10th Cir. 2012) (citing Wikipedia for "some examples of block lengths from cities in this country"), *and State v. Ballard,* 2012-NMCA-043, ¶ 19 n.1, 276 P.3d 976 (N.M. Ct. App. 2012) (citing Wikipedia to define "peer-to-peer file sharing").

A recent law review article by Professor Lee F. Peoples examines in depth the issues surrounding the citation of Wikipedia in judicial opinions. *See* Lee F. Peoples, *The Citation of Wikipedia in Judicial Opinions,* 12 YALE J. L. & TECH. 1 (2009–2010). While Wikipedia is gaining acceptance among judicial writers, Professor Peoples notes that reliance on Wikipedia has occasionally been held to be erroneous:

> [A]ppellate courts have reversed or found error in lower court decisions [for] relying on Wikipedia entries for psychological research in a child custody case, for attempting to refute expert medical testimony with a Wikipedia entry, and perhaps most egregiously for denying an asylum seeker's request based on information obtained from Wikipedia.

*Id.* at 45 (footnotes omitted) (citing *Badasa,* 540 F.3d at 909; *Campbell v. Secretary of Health & Human Servs.,* 69 Fed. Cl. 775, 781 (2006); *D.M. v. Department of Children & Family Servs.,* 979 So. 2d 1007, 1010 (Fla. Dist. Ct. App. 2008), *reh'g en banc granted* (May 14, 2008)).

Professor Peoples extracts from the case law "several bright line rules for when a Wikipedia entry should not be cited in a judicial opinion." *Id.* at 28. For example, he suggests that "[c]ourts should not take judicial notice of Wikipedia content," because that content "is disputable and its accuracy can be reasonably questioned." *Id.* He also states that "Wikipedia should not be cited when a more authoritative source exists for the information." *Id.* at 29. In particular, Wikipedia is a poor source "to define technical or scientific terms." *Id.* at 46. And he cautions that "[a] Wikipedia entry should not be relied upon as the only basis for a court's holding, reasoning, or logic," given the encyclopedia's "numerous shortcomings" discussed in his article. *Id.* at 29.[3]

---

[3] Among its shortcomings — and strengths — is Wikipedia's fluidity. Anyone can edit a Wikipedia entry at any time, making it vulnerable to " 'opportunistic editing.' " *See* Noam Cohen, *Courts Turn to Wikipedia, but Selectively,* N.Y. Times, Jan. 29, 2007, *available at* http://www.nytimes. com/2007/01/29/technology/29wikipedia.html (quoting Professor Cass Sunstein). Thus, " 'an unscrupulous lawyer (or client) could edit the Web site entry to frame the facts in a light favorable to the client's cause.' " Peoples, 12 YALE J. L. & TECH. at 24 (quoting R. Jason Richards, *Courting Wikipedia,* Trial, Apr. 2008, at 63).

Opportunistic editing is detectable, however. Every article on Wikipedia has a "View history" tab with links to all previous edits, the dates of each edit, and the user name or IP address of each editor. The revision history also allows the reader to view an article in each of its previous iterations. By this method, we can see that the three possible meanings of the term "jet ski" discussed in the lead opinion were part of the Wikipedia article before the present dispute arose. *See* Wikipedia, *Jet Ski,* http:// en.wikipedia.org/w/index.php?title=Jet_Ski&oldid=14710157 (as of June 3, 2005, 06:32 GMT).

Further, as Professor Peoples notes, "[a] database called WikiScanner allows a researcher to dig deeper

However, Professor Peoples acknowledges "some limited instances where it is appropriate for a Wikipedia citation to appear in a judicial opinion." *Id.* at 30. Some are obvious, such as where the Wikipedia entry itself is at issue or where the court must address a Wikipedia entry cited by a party. *See id.* In addition, the evolving nature of Wikipedia "makes it a good source for definitions of new slang terms, for popular culture references, and for jargon and lingo including computer and technology terms." *Id.* at 31 (citing "tweaking," "phreakers," and "screenshot").

Relevant here, Professor Peoples also states that "Wikipedia entries can be useful in some limited situations . . . for getting a sense of a term's common usage." *Id.* at 50. In particular, he recognizes the utility of Wikipedia in the interpretation of terms appearing in insurance contracts:

> The collaborative process used to create Wikipedia entries makes them potentially useful to courts in specific situations. In several cases courts attempting to interpret insurance contracts have turned to Wikipedia entries for evidence of the common usage or ordinary and plain meaning of a contract term. This method of interpretation [i.e., looking to common usage] "has long been recognized, and has been applied in the context of various types of insurance." Wikipedia has been used in this context to define the terms "recreational vehicle" and "car accident."

*Id.* at 32 (footnotes omitted) (quoting 2 Couch on Insurance § 22:38 (2005), and citing *Laasmar v. Phelps Dodge Corp. Life, Accidental Death & Dismemberment & Dependent Life Ins. Plan,* No. 06-cv-00013-MSK-MJW, 2007 WL 1613255, at *4 n.5 (D. Colo. June 1, 2007); *Fergison v. Stonebridge Life Ins. Co.,* No. 271488, 2007 WL 286793, at *3 (Mich. Ct. App. Feb. 1, 2007) (per curiam)). *See also Colony Nat'l Ins. Co. v. Hing Wah Chinese Rest.,* 546 F. Supp. 2d 202, 209 n.9 (E.D. Pa. 2008) (citing Wikipedia in a discussion of the meaning of the term "restaurant" in an insurance policy).

Of course, getting a sense of the common usage or ordinary and plain meaning of a contract term is precisely the purpose for which the lead opinion here cites Wikipedia. Our reliance on this source is therefore, in my judgment, appropriate. Moreover, here Wikipedia does not stand alone. As appellants note, the Macmillan online dictionary defines "Jet Ski" as "a very small fast boat for one or two people that you drive standing up." Macmillan Dictionary, http://www.macmillandictionary.com/dictionary/american/Jet-Ski (last visited Aug. 13, 2012).

Finally, we need not nail down the one true meaning of "jet ski" in this case. Whatever meaning the drafters of the insurance policy may have intended, our task is to determine whether they employed "language which clearly and unmistakably communicates . . . the specific circumstances under which the expected coverage will not be provided," *Alf v. State Farm Fire & Cas. Co.,* 850 P.2d 1272, 1275 (Utah 1993), or whether, on the contrary, there is "a range of possible meanings" that the term may bear in this context, *see In re E.Z.,* 2011 UT 38, ¶ 103, 266 P.3d 702 (Lee, J., concurring in part and concurring in the judgment). Whatever its shortcomings in other contexts,

---

into the revision of a Wikipedia article." *Id.* at 25 (citing WikiScanner, http://wikiscanner.virgil.gr/ (last visited by Peoples Dec. 16, 2009)).

for this task, an open-source encyclopedia with many editors and millions of readers seems just the ticket.

# MENDLER v. WINTERLAND PRODUCTION, LTD.
### 207 F.3d 1119 (9th Cir. 2000)

KOZINSKI, CIRCUIT JUDGE:

In this case of contract interpretation we must answer the following riddle: When is a photograph no longer a photograph?

## I

Jeffrey Mendler is a professional photographer. In August 1991 he signed a licensing agreement with Winterland, a manufacturer of screen-printed apparel. Pursuant to the agreement, Mendler provided Winterland with numerous slides of photographs he had taken of the America's Cup yacht race. Among these was an image titled "San Diego's America's Cup," which depicts the "España" overtaking the "Spirit of Australia" in a tacking duel. *See* Appendix. The license allowed Winterland the use of the photos as "guides, models, and examples, for illustrations to be used on screenprinted T-shirts or other sportswear."

By 1992, Winterland had begun marketing T-shirts produced under this agreement. There were at least two different designs, each featuring drawings of two yachts with sails crossed, in a configuration modelled after Mendler's photo of the tacking duel. The drawings on these shirts are clearly identifiable as such, containing just enough detail to convey the desired image.[1] After receiving some samples of these T-shirts, Mendler had no further communication with Winterland for several years.

In 1995, Mendler learned that Winterland had put out a new line of America's Cup T-shirts. While depicting the same scene as the earlier series, these shirts were made using a very different technique. Instead of line drawings, the newer shirts display a digitally altered version of the image from Mendler's original photo. *See* Appendix. Mendler complained to Winterland that this use of his photo was not authorized by the licensing agreement. The ensuing negotiations failed. Mendler registered his photograph with the Register of Copyrights, and brought suit for copyright infringement and related claims against Winterland.[2]

The case was tried without a jury. The district court held for the defendants on the copyright claim, ruling that "Winterland's use of the slides was within the scope of the

---

[1] One of these drawings contained only bare abstract outlines of the two boats, placed in front of a background that appears to be a photographic image of ocean water. Another version adds more detail to the sails and hulls of the boats, including some silhouetted human figures. Instead of a solid background of water, there are some cartoon-style waves drawn around the bottom of each boat.

[2] The complaint also named the San Diego Yacht Club, which had hosted the America's Cup in 1995, and licensed its logo for use on the apparel in question.

license agreements." Mendler appeals.[3]

## II

Contract interpretation is a question of law we review de novo. *See Confederated Tribes of Siletz Indians v. Oregon*, 143 F.3d 481, 484 (9th Cir. 1998). While we are wont to defer when a district court relies on extrinsic evidence in interpreting an ambiguous contract, *see L.K. Comstock & Co. v. United Eng'rs & Constructors Inc.*, 880 F.2d 219, 221 (9th Cir. 1989), the district court here made no findings of fact with regard to the copyright claim. We know neither how it interpreted the contract nor on what extrinsic evidence, if any, it relied in concluding that the T-shirt fell "within the scope of the license agreements." Faced with a naked conclusion of law, we have nothing to which to defer.

Nevertheless, our task of interpretation is reduced substantially, because the parties agree, to some extent, about the contract's meaning. Though they dispute what they meant by "illustrations," the parties agree that the contract did *not* authorize Winterland to use photographic reproductions of Mendler's work. Thus, in order to affirm the district court's ruling, we must conclude that the image on the T-shirt is not a photograph.

Winterland created the T-shirt image by scanning — digitally reproducing — the photo Mendler gave them. It is conceded that a reproduction created in this fashion is photographic.[4] The case does not end here, however, because another term of the license gave Winterland the right to use "whatever illustration process" it found most appropriate. Winterland was thus allowed to make a scanned image, so long as it used the image only as a "guide[ ], model [or] example[ ]" to achieve an end result that was an "illustration" and not a photographic reproduction. The question we must answer, then, is whether Winterland's subsequent electronic modifications transformed the scanned photograph into something that was no longer a photograph.

## III

Winterland, no doubt, made noticeable alterations to the image from Mendler's original photo. The image was flipped horizontally, so that the vessel in the foreground is on the right rather than left. The sail of this craft, cut off by the frame in the original photo, has been extended and its missing tip reconstructed. A smooth background of

---

[3] The court also ruled against Mendler on his conversion and negligence claims. It found for Mendler on his breach of contract claim for failure to return the slides, but awarded only nominal damages. Mendler appeals only the copyright ruling.

[4] As indeed it must be, in an age when memory cards and LCD displays are quickly replacing silver nitrate and darkrooms. Indeed, the history of photography features many methods of capturing images, and everything from egg-white to raspberry syrup has been used to facilitate the process. *See* entries for Albumen process and Collodion process *in* Robert Leggat, *A History of Photography from its beginnings till the 1920s* (1999) http://www.kbnet.co.uk/rleggat/photo. It is not the precise method used that makes something a photograph, but the fact that the image is created by light reflected from the image one wishes to reproduce. *See* note 6 *infra*. That the light source is a scanner and the storage medium is electric rather than mechanical or chemical is of no consequence.

gently gradated blue has replaced the original sky with its strata of white and grey clouds. Shades of brown have been changed to shades of violet, whites to fluorescent blues. At the same time, the tonal range of the whole image has been compressed through posterization.[5]

Winterland argues that these changes have transformed the image on the T-shirt from a photograph into an illustration based on a photograph. The dissent agrees, asserting that while the T-shirt image is "obviously based on the photograph, it is not the photograph." *Infra*, at 2040 (Rymer, J., dissenting). The only reason the dissent gives for this conclusion is that "Winterland's manipulation of the photograph was significant." *Id.* at 2940. But what does "significant" mean? The dissent leaves unexplained why the changes made are such as to destroy the original image's photographic quality. If we are to give our judgment content beyond "I know it when I see it," we must attempt to articulate what kinds of changes are "significant" enough to render an image non-photographic. The contract itself does not address this issue, and neither party argues that the concept "photographic" had any idiosyncratic meaning in the context of their business relationship. It is therefore appropriate to look to common usage and understanding, taking judicial notice of such materials as may aid us. *See* E. Allan Farnsworth, Contracts § 7.11 (1990) ("When interpreting contract language, courts start with the assumption that the parties have used the language in the way that reasonable persons ordinarily do."). The parties have participated in this inquiry, providing supplemental briefing that addresses such topics as the history of photography and the nature of the technology utilized here.

What distinguishes photography from other visual art forms is that, as the name implies, the light itself does the writing.[6] The photographer can compose the shot, but once he triggers the shutter, anything visible to the eye is captured exactly as an observer would see it.[7] The reactions of the exposed film, like the workings of one's own retina, are not subject to direct control. This fact gives rise to the two qualities we most associate with photographic images: lifelike appearance and objective accuracy. The former is why we like photographs so much — they're the next best thing to seeing something in the flesh. Indeed, the association is so close that an extremely realistic drawing or painting is often described as "photographic."[8] The latter is why we trust photographs — since there's no willful agency intervening between the actual scene and its recording on the film, we tend to regard photographs as infallible and unimpeachable witnesses. We don't always trust the call of the live referee; but no one argues with the photo finish.

--------

[5] "The Posterize command lets you specify the number of tonal levels (or brightness values) for each channel in an image and then maps pixels to the closest matching level." Adobe Systems, Inc., Adobe Photoshop 5.0 User Guide (1998) 132.

[6] *Cf.* Webster's Ninth New Collegiate Dictionary 885 (1985) (defining "photography" as "the art or process of producing images on a sensitized surface (as a film) by the action of radiant energy and esp. light").

[7] *Cf.* Susan Sontag, On Photography 132–33 (1977) ("In most uses of the camera, the photograph's naive or descriptive function is paramount.")

[8] *See* Webster's, *supra* note 6, at 885 (defining "photographic" as "representing nature and human beings with the exactness of a photograph"); The American Heritage Dictionary 987 (1976) ("representing or simulating something with great accuracy and fidelity of detail.").

Of course, both of these characteristics of photography are subject to important caveats. While objective accuracy is a large part of what we mean by the term "photographic," we have also long been aware that photographs are not always to be trusted. The camera may not lie, but the person who develops the film or prints the image on paper can alter what it tells us.[9] Even before the advent of computers, an airbrush or a strategically placed thumb during the printing process could be used to erase a facial blemish or eliminate a purged Bolshevik. Digital technology makes such alteration child's play, and most of the photographs we see in the media today have been digitally tweaked to get the exact image desired.[10] Often important elements of the depicted scene are relocated, removed or replaced entirely with borrowed images.[11] Even though we are (sometimes) aware that these doctored photographs no longer accurately depict reality,[12] we nevertheless perceive and identify the images as photographic.[13]

Nor does an image have to look perfectly lifelike to be recognized as photographic. This is most obvious with regard to color. A black and white photograph is unquestionably a photograph, even though it is dissimilar in an important respect from what we normally perceive. Similarly, a color negative doesn't lose its photographic quality when a black and white print is developed from it. This obvious truth isn't changed when, instead of *removing* colors, we *change* them. From hand-painted daguerreotypes to colorized oldies, we have always regarded images as photographic

---

[9] Even such an austere purist as Ansel Adams was apparently not above a little darkroom legerdemain. *See* Kenneth Brower, *Photography in the Age of Falsification*, The Atlantic Monthly, May 1998, at 92, 95 (describing Adams's deletion of unwanted details and use of the "dodge and burn" technique to lighten selected areas of a print).

[10] *See, e.g.,* Stuart Wavell, *Exposed: The cameras' white lies*, The Sunday Times (London), June 27, 1999, at 14 ("One broadsheet picture editor admitted that up to 90% of photographs are now digitally enhanced or manipulated.").

[11] In fact, there is now a cottage industry dedicated to helping people improve their family photos by sending that better-forgotten ex-spouse down the oubliette of history. Or better yet, you can insert yourself into an old snapshot in place of your boyfriend's ex-girlfriend. *See* Wavell, note 10 *supra.*

*See also* Art Golab, *Picture Perfect? Don't Be So Sure*, Chicago Sun-Times, Mar. 3, 1996, at 32. Consumer Stalinism, one might call it.

[12] Presumably few were fooled when actor Leslie Nielsen's head was superimposed on the body of a nude pregnant woman imitating Demi Moore's notorious Vanity Fair pose. *See Leibovitz v. Paramount Pictures Corp.*, 137 F.3d 109 (2d Cir. 1998) (holding that this was a parody covered by fair use). The same may not have been true when the Harvard Lampoon attached the head of Henry Kissenger to the body of an unknown muscle-man for the centerfold of its 1972 Cosmopolitan parody. Indeed, there are apparently many willing to suspend disbelief when the composite image is of something they'd like to see. *See, e.g.,* Melissa Grego, *Skin Trade*, The Hollywood Reporter, March 3–9, 1998, at 16 (describing the thriving business in nude images featuring the superimposed heads of celebrities). For expert dissection of such images, *see* The Fake Detective http://lairofluxlucre.com/detective/index.html.

[13] Indeed, our instinctive tendency to assume that such images accurately reflect reality has led to no little ethical hand-wringing among journalists and nature photographers. *See, e.g.,* Mitchell Stephens, *Digital Wizards and Composite Reality*, Chronicle of Higher Education, January 9, 1998, at B9 (describing the "journalistic battles" over use of altered photos, including the proposal that a symbol of a camera with a slash through it be displayed whenever a photo has been digitally altered); Brower, note 9 *supra* (describing similar conflicts among nature photographers).

even though they contained coloring not derived from the original exposure.[14] Even an image whose overall chromatic appearance radically diverges from reality can be unquestionably photographic — as in the case of a negative print.

Thus, while lifelike appearance and faithful detail are the hallmarks of the photograph, an image can contain significant deviations in both respects while still remaining photographic. At the same time, an image may be extremely accurate and lifelike without being a photograph at all. A skilled artist can draw or paint an image that looks as real as a photograph — or even more so. Had Winterland engaged such an artist to create an image modeled after Mendler's photo, it would have stayed within the terms of its license, no matter how lifelike or how similar to the original the image looked. This doesn't help Winterland, however, for we know that whatever photographic elements remain in the T-shirt image were not created by Winterland's artistry — they were captured mechanically in the chamber of Mendler's camera. Unlike a painting, where every detail successfully reproduced on the canvas is a triumph of the artist, here every detail that tracks the original represents the extent to which Winterland created nothing.

The contract did authorize Winterland to select the illustration process pursuant to which it used Mendler's photographs "as guides, models, [or] examples." Winterland was thus within its rights in choosing to make its illustration by scanning Mendler's photograph and using computer software to digitally alter it to create an "illustration." In choosing this method rather than reconstructing the image from scratch, however, Winterland necessarily took on a burden of altering the image sufficiently so it would no longer exhibit those qualities that cause us to recognize it as a photograph. This must be so, for if the use of a photographic process to reach a recognizably photographic result is authorized, the parties' avowed understanding that photographic reproductions are not "illustrations" becomes meaningless.

## IV

Viewing the problem through this lens, we conclude that the alterations made by Winterland failed to destroy the essentially photographic quality of the image on its T-shirt. Were this question to hinge solely on the appearance of the T-shirt image when viewed alone, the case might be a close one. Changes in color alone do not render an image any less photographic, but here the addition of posterization has produced an effect such that at first glance it is unclear how the image was created. The question, however, is not whether the T-shirt image is readily recognizable as a photograph *standing alone.* To evaluate the degree of accurate, lifelike detail an image contains, we must necessarily compare it to the original. *See* Appendix.

Once we do this, all doubts disappear. The precise shapes of the two boats, their positions in the water, their spatial relationship to each other — all remain perfectly distinct and (apart from the horizontal flip) identical to the original. Though somewhat washed out by the posterization, even most of the finer details of the original photo —

---

[14] Indeed, the adding of color to selected elements of a photograph is a commonly-used technique in magazines and other print media. *See, e.g.,* Michael Bane, *Circuit Rider,* Snow Country, October 1996 at 39, 39 (featuring a photo by Dave Nagel of a snowboarder with greenish hair and a bright pink tongue).

the stitching and insignia in the sails, the positions of the crew members, the reflection of a boat in the sun-dappled water — remain visible and unaltered. The smoothing out of the background and reconstruction of the sail tip are within the range of cosmetic retouching we see in media photographs every day. Apart from the sail tip, none of the elements of the T-shirt image that can be said to "illustrate" anything were added by Winterland — they were simply scanned from Mendler's photo. Despite the differences in appearance, no one familiar with the original can fail to recognize this.[15] The T-shirt image thus remains essentially what it was the moment it was transferred from Mendler's slide to the hard drive of Winterland's computer: a photographic reproduction. It is now a filtered, posterized reproduction — but photographic nonetheless.

As we find that Winterland's use of the photo exceeds the terms of the license, it was an unauthorized use and therefore infringes Mendler's copyright. We REVERSE and REMAND for a determination of damages.

---

[15]  Indeed, Mendler received a complaint from someone who had purchased a limited edition of his photo and was disturbed to see it mass reproduced in this manner.

APPENDIX

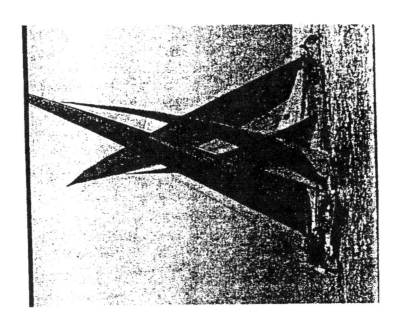

RYMER, CIRCUIT JUDGE, dissenting:

The real riddle in this case is: When is a record no longer a record?

The majority opinion cites no fewer than two web sites, one computer software user's guide, one book, two dictionary definitions, and six newspaper or magazine articles — none of which was referred to, introduced, validated, used or argued in the district court or to us. While it makes for interesting reading, I have no idea whether the parties' intent was shaped by the existence of a "cottage industry dedicated to helping people improve their family photos by sending that better — forgotten ex-spouse down the oubliette of history," much less colorized pictures of snowboarders with green hair and bright pink tongues. These things were not in the record, and I don't even know whether they existed at all when the contract was formed in 1991. In any event, these data are not the usual stuff of contract interpretation.

I would instead use more conventional tools to ascertain what the parties meant when they allowed Winterland to make "illustrations." *See* Cal. Civil Code §§ 1636, 1647; *City of Atascadero v. Merrill Lynch, Pierce, Fenner & Smith, Inc.*, 68 Cal. App. 4th 445, 80 Cal. Rptr. 2d 329, 349 (1998). Hunter argues that the scope of the copyright license was limited to "cartoon-style" or "graphic" illustrations. He also contends that the parties did not intend for Winterland to use computer-scanned images of his photographs. I don't agree. While it is clear that the parties intended the term "illustrations" to be limited to "graphic" illustrations (thereby excluding photographic reproductions), the evidence does not support Hunter's further limitation to "cartoon-style" illustrations. Nor does it support the exclusion of computer-scanned images as "guides, models, and examples" for computer-created artwork. The contract allows Winterland to "use whatever illustration process it finds most appropriate." Winterland had the technology (albeit less sophisticated) to scan and manipulate images at the time of the contract; thus, this case is distinguishable from *Cohen v. Paramount Pictures Corp.*, 845 F.2d 851, 854 (9th Cir. 1988), in which the relevant technology, home videocassette recorders, did not exist in any form at the time of the contract. Further, Winterland could have used the same technology to produce simple line drawings that Hunter admits are within the scope of the license.

As I see it the issue is not "when does a photograph stop being a photograph," rather it is whether *this particular* digitally-scanned and manipulated image is within the scope of the license. Having reviewed the record and exhibits, I am not firmly convinced that the district court erred in finding that the "Cross Sails" image is within the scope of the license. Winterland's manipulation of the photograph was significant. It was flipped horizontally, one sail was elongated, colors were changed dramatically, the sky was redrawn, and it was posterized in such a way as to destroy and compress tonality. While the resulting image is obviously based on the photograph, it is not the photograph. Rather, the photograph was used as a guide or model to produce a graphic illustration of sailing.

Given that Winterland did not infringe upon Hunter's license, I do not believe that the district court erred in finding that the San Diego Yacht Club was not liable for infringement. I would, therefore, affirm.

# RANDY DISSELKOEN PROPERTIES v. CHARTER TWP. OF CASCADE

## 2008 U.S. Dist. LEXIS 1504 (W.D. Mich. Jan. 9, 2008)

\* \* \* \*

[The text below is footnote 12 of the opinion. — Ed.]

[12] At oral argument, the parties discussed the history of Eller Outdoor and could not agree on whether Eller Outdoor and Eller Media were the same entity. Plaintiff CBS alleges Eller Outdoor was part of Combined Communications when it became part of Gannett in the largest media merger in history, at the time. Plaintiff alleges Eller Media was created years later. At oral argument, Plaintiff provided the Court with a number of documents attempting to establish ownership of the sign. (Dkt. No. 72). Defendant offers exhibits from the website Wikipedia indicating that Eller Outdoor was a predecessor to Clear Channel Outdoor, a competitor of CBS Outdoor. (Exhibits 35 and 36 attached to reply brief).

Under Federal Rule of Evidence 201, this Court takes judicial notice of the 1979 corporate merger of Gannett, Inc. and Combined Communications Corp. (CCC) which included Eller Outdoor. Eller Outdoor Advertising was founded in 1962 by Karl Eller. In 1968, Mr. Eller merged Eller Outdoor and formed CCC. In 1979, CCC was merged with Gannett, Inc. *See* http:// www.advertisinghallof fame.org/members/member_bio_ text.php?memid=612 & uflag=e & uyear= (Karl Eller's biography at the Hall of Fame for the American Advertising Federation, last checked December 14, 2007) and http://phoeniz.bizjournals.c om/phoenix/stories/2005/08/22/story3.html (article in the Phoenix (Arizona) Business Journal dated August 22, 2005, last checked December 14, 2007).

The documents submitted by Plaintiff are sufficient to create a genuine issue of material fact regarding ownership of the sign. For the purposes of this motion, the Court does not make credibility assessments of documents. That said, despite the proliferation of federal court opinions citing wikipedia, *see e.g. United States v. Bazaldua*, 506 F.3d 671, 673 n.2 (8th Cir. 2007), this Court is skeptical of relying on the anonymous and voluntarily edited website for anything more than general background information. *See* Burt Helm, *Wikipedia: "A Work in Progress,"* Business Week, Dec. 14, 2005 (available at http://www.businessweek.com/technology/content/dec2005/ tc20051214_441708.htm and last viewed Dec. 14, 2007) and Daniel Terdiman, *Wikipedia Faces Growing Pains,* Wired, Jan. 10, 2005 (available at http://www . wired.com/ culture/lifestyle/news/2005/01/66210 and last viewed Dec. 14, 2007). Although this Court has NO DOUBT that Defendant did nothing improper, this Court notes the ease with which wikipedia entries can be altered and further notes that others have edited entries for improper reasons. *See e.g.* John Borland, *See Who's Editing Wikipedia-Diebold, the CIA and a Campaign,* Wired, Aug. 14, 2007 (available at http:// www.wired.com/politics/onlinerights/news/2007/08/wiki_tracker? currentPage=1 and last viewed Dec. 14, 2007).

# IN RE KOGLER
368 B.R. 785 (Bankr. W.D. Wis. 2007)

*ORDER*

Thomas S. Utschig, Bankruptcy Judge.

There is an oft-quoted saying, ostensibly an ancient curse, which bestows upon the recipient the desire that they might "live in interesting times."[1] Certainly this notion fairly represents bankruptcy jurisprudence in the wake of the passage of the Bankruptcy Abuse Prevention and Consumer Protection Act of 2005, perhaps the most sweeping modification of American bankruptcy law since the enactment of the 1978 code. Legal changes tend to necessitate the reexamination of seemingly settled principles, and the BAPCPA is riddled with opportunities for such debate. * * *

## II.   IMAGES IN THE JUDICIAL PROCESS

### A.   Attorney-Created Images

# IN RE GLASMANN
286 P.3d 673 (Wash. 2012)

Madsen, C.J.

Edward M. Glasmann was convicted of second degree assault, attempted second degree robbery, first degree kidnapping, and obstruction arising from incidents that occurred while he was intoxicated. During closing argument, the prosecuting attorney made an electronic presentation to the jury that graphically displayed his personal opinion that Glasmann was "guilty, guilty, guilty" of the crimes charged by the State. The prosecutor's misconduct was flagrant, ill intentioned, and we cannot conclude with any confidence that it did not to have an effect on the outcome of the trial. We reverse the defendant's convictions and remand for a new trial.

## FACTS AND PROCEDURAL HISTORY

In celebration of his October 2004 birthday, Edward Glasmann and his fiancée, Angel Benson, rented a motel room in Lakewood, Washington. Over the course of the

---

[1] According to the online encyclopedia Wikipedia, "interesting" in this context is usually interpreted as "turbulent" or "dangerous." *See* Wikipedia, *May you live in interesting times,* http://en.wikipedia. org/wiki/May_you_live_in_interesting_times (last visited March 28, 2007). Efforts to verify the source of this "curse" as Chinese in origin have generally proved futile, though it has been attributed as such in a variety of publications. One of its first verified appearances was in a 1966 speech by Robert Kennedy in Cape Town, South Africa; it also appeared in a 1950 science fiction story called "U-Turn" by Duncan H. Munro. *Id.* While it serves as an appropriately ironic characterization of many situations, it does not appear that the phrase is truly Chinese, ancient, or necessarily even a curse.

evening, the two ingested methamphetamine, ecstasy, and alcohol. Glasmann and Benson had been arguing throughout that day and evening and around midnight, their argument escalated. Glasmann started punching and kicking Benson. He told Benson he wanted to go for a ride and then dragged her out of the motel room. Outside the motel room, another motel guest witnessed Glasmann punch and kick Benson before dragging her to the passenger side of his Corvette. This witness called 911 and provided an account of the events.

From the driver's seat, Glasmann reached over to open the passenger door and attempted to pull Benson into the car by her hair. Benson testified that she was partially in the car and stumbled when Glasmann ran the car up her leg, backed off of her leg, pulled her into the car, and drove out of the parking lot. Benson was then able to get the car into park. She next grabbed the car keys and ran into a minimart adjacent to the motel.

Inside the minimart, she hid on the floor behind the cashier's counter. Police soon arrived and attempted without success to apprehend Glasmann. Shouting at the officers to shoot him and claiming to possess a firearm, Glasmann ran into the convenience store. He ran behind the counter, held Benson in a choke hold, and threatened to kill her. As officers approached, Glasmann held Benson between himself and the officers. Benson was able to wiggle free enough to allow an officer to use a stun gun on Glasmann.

The officers subdued and arrested Glasmann. In the process, Glasmann was held down by one officer while another officer stomped on his head approximately five times. Glasmann continued to struggle as he was dragged out of the minimart. His booking photograph shows extensive facial bruising. The incident inside the minimart was recorded on the store's security camera.

The State charged Glasmann with first degree assault, attempted first degree robbery, first degree kidnapping, and obstruction. Exhibits admitted into evidence included the minimart security video, photographs of Benson's injuries, the 911 recording, recordings of telephone calls between Glasmann and Benson, and Glasmann's booking photo. The defense offered Glasmann's booking photo to display Glasmann's facial injuries sustained during arrest.

At trial, Glasmann did not deny culpability. Rather, he disputed the degree of the crimes charged. He argued the jury should convict only on lesser included offenses. The prosecution sought to establish that Glasmann acted with intent, a necessary element of all the crimes charged.

In closing argument, the State used an extensive PowerPoint presentation that included numerous slides incorporating the security camera video, audio recordings, photographs of Benson's injuries, and Glasmann's booking photograph. Each of the slides containing a video shot or photograph included a caption consisting of testimony, recorded statements, or the prosecutor's commentary.

One slide showed Glasmann crouched behind the minimart counter with a choke hold on Benson and a caption reading, "YOU JUST BROKE OUR LOVE." State's Resp. to Pers. Restraint Pet. (PRP), App. G at 1. Another slide featuring a photograph of Benson's back injuries appeared with the captions, "What was happening right before defendant drove over Angel . . . ," and ". . . you were beating the crap out of me!" *Id.* at 2. This slide also featured accompanying audio.

In addition, the prosecutor argued that jurors should not believe Glasmann's testimony. He told the jurors that the law required them to "[c]ompare Angel Benson's testimony and the testimony of the remainder of the State's witnesses to the defendant's." 8 Verbatim Report of Proceedings (VRP) at 458. The prosecutor then told jurors that in order to reach a verdict they must determine: "Did the defendant tell the truth when he testified?" *Id.*

At least five slides featured Glasmann's booking photograph and a caption. In one slide, the booking photo appeared above the caption, "DO YOU BELIEVE HIM?" State's Resp. to PRP, App. G at 5. In another booking photo slide the caption read, "WHY SHOULD YOU BELIEVE ANYTHING HE SAYS ABOUT THE ASSAULT?" *Id.* Near the end of the presentation, the booking photo appeared three more times: first with the word "GUILTY" superimposed diagonally in red letters across Glasmann's battered face. PRP, App. H at 8. In the second slide the word "GUILTY" was superimposed in red letters again in the opposite direction, forming an "X" shape across Glasmann's face. *Id.* at 9. In the third slide, the word "GUILTY," again in red letters, was superimposed horizontally over the previously superimposed words. *Id.* at 10. As best as we can determine, the prosecutor stated the following while the "GUILTY" slides were being displayed:

> You've been provided with a number of lesser crimes if you believe the defendant is not guilty of the crimes for which the State has charged him, but the evidence in this case proves overwhelmingly that he is guilty as charged, and that's what the State asks you to return in this case: Guilty of assault in the first degree; guilty of attempted robbery in the first degree; guilty of kidnapping in the first degree; and guilty of obstructing a police officer. Hold him accountable for what he did on October 23rd, 2004, by finding him guilty as charged. Thank you.

8 VRP at 465–66. Defense counsel did not object to these slides.

In closing argument, defense counsel emphasized the governing standard, proof beyond a reasonable doubt. He asked the jurors to focus on the actual charges, not Glasmann's drug use, reckless driving, or "hitting Angel Benson in the motel room." *Id.* at 470. Counsel reviewed the elements of each charge and argued that Glasmann's conduct did not meet the definition of the charged crimes:

> The issue for you to decide is[,] is there proof beyond a reasonable doubt that Mike Glasmann committed any crimes that night, and the answer to that is yes, but this case is overcharged.
>
> What do I mean by that? I mean that the charges that the State has leveled against Mr. Glasmann are not reflective of what, in reality, happened that night or reflective of what has been proven beyond a reasonable doubt happened that night. He's charged with Assault 1 when only assault in the third degree or assault in the fourth degree reasonably fit these facts, arguably, beyond a reasonable doubt. He's charged with attempted robbery in the first degree when only attempted robbery in the second degree fits these

facts beyond a reasonable doubt. He's charged with kidnapping in the first degree when only unlawful imprisonment fits these facts beyond a reasonable doubt. Obstructing a law enforcement officer is, I said, a proper charge.

*Id.* at 494.

The jury convicted Glasmann of first degree kidnapping and obstruction, and the lesser included offenses of second degree assault and attempted second degree robbery. Glasmann appealed. He was sentenced to 210 months in prison. The Court of Appeals affirmed in an unpublished decision. *State v. Glasmann*, noted at 142 Wash. App. 1041. Thereafter, Glasmann filed a personal restraint petition and we granted review limited to whether the prosecutor's closing argument deprived Glasmann of a fair trial and whether assistance of Glasmann's trial counsel was ineffective. *In re Pers. Restraint of Glasmann*, 170 Wash. 2d 1009, 245 P.3d 226 (2010).

## ANALYSIS

The right to a fair trial is a fundamental liberty secured by the Sixth and Fourteenth Amendments to the United States Constitution and article I, section 22 of the Washington State Constitution. *Estelle v. Williams*, 425 U.S. 501, 503, 96 S. Ct. 1691, 48 L. Ed. 2d 126 (1976); *State v. Finch*, 137 Wash. 2d 792, 843, 975 P.2d 967 (1999). Prosecutorial misconduct may deprive a defendant of his constitutional right to a fair trial. *State v. Davenport*, 100 Wash. 2d 757, 762, 675 P.2d 1213 (1984). "A ' "[f]air trial" certainly implies a trial in which the attorney representing the state does not throw the prestige of his public office . . . and the expression of his own belief of guilt into the scales against the accused.' " *State v. Monday*, 171 Wash. 2d 667, 677, 257 P.3d 551 (2011) (alteration in original) (quoting *State v. Case*, 49 Wash. 2d 66, 71, 298 P.2d 500 (1956); *see State v. Reed*, 102 Wash. 2d 140, 145–47, 684 P.2d 699 (1984)).

Although a prosecutor has wide latitude to argue reasonable inferences from the evidence, *State v. Thorgerson*, 172 Wash. 2d 438, 448, 258 P.3d 43 (2011), a prosecutor must "seek convictions based only on probative evidence and sound reason," *State v. Casteneda-Perez*, 61 Wash. App. 354, 363, 810 P.2d 74 (1991); *State v. Huson*, 73 Wash. 2d 660, 663, 440 P.2d 192 (1968). "The prosecutor should not use arguments calculated to inflame the passions or prejudices of the jury." American Bar Association, Standards for Criminal Justice std. 3-5.8(c) (2d ed. 1980); *State v. Brett*, 126 Wash. 2d 136, 179, 892 P.2d 29 (1995); *State v. Belgarde*, 110 Wash. 2d 504, 755 P.2d 174 (1988).

In order to prevail on a claim of prosecutorial misconduct, a defendant is required to show that in the context of the record and all of the circumstances of the trial, the prosecutor's conduct was both improper and prejudicial. *Thorgerson*, 172 Wash. 2d at 442, 258 P.3d 43. To show prejudice requires that the defendant show a substantial likelihood that the misconduct affected the jury verdict. *Id.*; *State v. Ish*, 170 Wash. 2d 189, 195, 241 P.3d 389 (2010); *State v. Dhaliwal*, 150 Wash. 2d 559, 578, 79 P.3d 432 (2003). Because Mr. Glasmann failed to object at trial, the errors he complains of are waived unless he establishes that the misconduct was so flagrant and ill intentioned that an instruction would not have cured the prejudice. *Thorgerson*, 172 Wash. 2d at 443, 258 P.3d 43; *State v. Russell*, 125 Wash. 2d 24, 86, 882 P.2d 747 (1994).

Our courts have repeatedly and unequivocally denounced the type of conduct that occurred in this case. First, we have held that it is error to submit evidence to the jury that has not been admitted at trial. *State v. Pete*, 152 Wash. 2d 546, 553–55, 98 P.3d 803 (2004). The "long-standing rule" is that " 'consideration of any material by a jury not properly admitted as evidence vitiates a verdict when there is a reasonable ground to believe that the defendant may have been prejudiced.' " *Id.* at 555 n.4, 98 P.3d 803 (quoting *State v. Rinkes*, 70 Wash. 2d 854, 862, 425 P.2d 658 (1967) (emphasis omitted)); *see also, e.g., State v. Boggs*, 33 Wash. 2d 921, 207 P.2d 743 (1949), *overruled on other grounds by State v. Parr*, 93 Wash. 2d 95, 606 P.2d 263 (1980).

In *Rinkes*, 70 Wash. 2d at 855, 425 P.2d 658, for example, a newspaper editorial and cartoon highly critical of what it claimed was lenient court decisions and liberal probation policies was inadvertently sent to the jury room. The court stated that the material in the newspaper should not have gone to the jury and observed that the article was "clearly intended to influence the readers of it [(the newspaper)] to be concerned about the purported leniency" of area judges and "may well have evoked a jury members feelings or convictions of the necessity for being stricter and less careful about observing legal principles and procedure in dealing with defendants accused of crime." *Id.* at 862–63, 425 P.2d 658. The court said the material was "very likely indeed" to be prejudicial and assumed that "the requisite balance of impartiality was upset." *Id.* at 863, 425 P.2d 658.

Here, the prosecutor intentionally presented the jury with copies of Glasmann's booking photograph altered by the addition of phrases calculated to influence the jury's assessment of Glasmann's guilt and veracity. In the photograph, Glasmann is unkempt and bloody, a condition likely to have resulted in even greater impact because of captions that challenged the jury to question the truthfulness of his testimony. While the State argues that it merely combined the booking photograph, admitted as exhibit 89, with the court's instructions and argument of the law and facts, the prosecutor's conduct went well beyond this. Indeed, here the prosecutor's modification of photographs by adding captions was the equivalent of unadmitted evidence. There certainly was no photograph in evidence that asked "DO YOU BELIEVE HIM?" *See* State's Resp. to PRP, App. G at 5. There was nothing that said, "WHY SHOULD YOU BELIEVE ANYTHING HE SAYS ABOUT THE ASSAULT?" *See id.* And there were no sequence of photographs in evidence with "GUILTY" on the face or "GUILTY, GUILTY, GUILTY." *See id.* Yet this "evidence" was made a part of the trial by the prosecutor during closing argument.

Although this is not a case where unadmitted evidence was sent to the jury room, as in *Pete* and *Rinkes*, these cases nevertheless establish that a prosecutor must be held to know that it is improper to present evidence that has been deliberately altered in order to influence the jury's deliberations. As in *Rinkes*, the multiple altered photographs here may well have affected the jurors' feelings about the need to strictly observe legal principles and the care it must take in determining Glasmann's guilt.

It is also well established that a prosecutor cannot use his or her position of power and prestige to sway the jury and may not express an individual opinion of the defendant's guilt, independent of the evidence actually in the case. The commentary on *American Bar Association Standards for Criminal Justice* std. 3-5.8 emphasizes:

The prosecutor's argument is likely to have significant persuasive force with the jury. Accordingly, the scope of argument must be consistent with the evidence and marked by the fairness that should characterize all of the prosecutor's conduct. Prosecutorial conduct in argument is a matter of special concern because of the possibility that the jury will give special weight to the prosecutor's arguments, not only because of the prestige associated with the prosecutor's office but also because of the fact-finding facilities presumably available to the office.

Likewise, many cases warn of the need for a prosecutor to avoid expressing a personal opinion of guilt. [citations omitted]. By expressing his personal opinion of Glasmann's guilt through both his slide show and his closing arguments, the prosecutor engaged in misconduct.

The case law and professional standards described above were available to the prosecutor and clearly warned against the conduct here. We hold that the prosecutor's misconduct, which permeated the state's closing argument, was flagrant and ill intentioned.

Moreover, the misconduct here was so pervasive that it could not have been cured by an instruction. "[T]he cumulative effect of repetitive prejudicial prosecutorial misconduct may be so flagrant that no instruction or series of instructions can erase their combined prejudicial effect." *State v. Walker*, 164 Wash. App. 724, 737, 265 P.3d 191 (2011) (citing *Case*, 49 Wash. 2d at 73, 298 P.2d 500).

Highly prejudicial images may sway a jury in ways that words cannot. *See State v. Gregory*, 158 Wash. 2d 759, 866–67, 147 P.3d 1201 (2006). Such imagery, then, may be very difficult to overcome with an instruction. *Id.* Prejudicial imagery may become all the more problematic when displayed in the closing arguments of a trial, when the jury members may be particularly aware of, and susceptible to, the arguments being presented. Given the multiple ways in which the prosecutor attempted to improperly sway the jury and the powerful visual medium he employed, no instruction could erase the cumulative effect of the misconduct in this case. The prosecutor essentially produced a media event with the deliberate goal of influencing the jury to return guilty verdicts on the counts against Glasmann.

We also believe there is a substantial likelihood that the misconduct affected the jury verdict. As noted earlier, the State charged Glasmann with first degree assault, attempted first degree robbery, first degree kidnapping, and obstruction. The mental state required for the charged offenses, specifically intent, was critically important. Glasmann presented evidence that he lacked both the opportunity and capacity to form the intent necessary to commit the charged crimes. There was evidence that he consumed alcohol, methamphetamine, and ecstasy the night of the offenses and evidence that the events involving Glasmann, Benson, and law enforcement unfolded rapidly. Glasmann defended on the basis that the facts only supported a guilty verdict as to third or fourth degree assault, attempted robbery in the second degree, unlawful imprisonment, and obstruction. The jury convicted Glasmann of second degree assault, attempted second degree robbery, first degree kidnapping, and obstruction.

A prosecutor could never shout in closing argument that "Glasmann is guilty, guilty,

guilty!" and it would be highly prejudicial to do so. Doing this visually through use of slides showing Glasmann's battered face and superimposing red capital letters (red, the color of blood and the color used to denote losses) is even more prejudicial. *See Gregory*, 158 Wash. 2d at 866–67, 147 P.3d 1201. "[V]isual arguments manipulate audiences by harnessing rapid unconscious or emotional reasoning processes and by exploiting the fact that we do not generally question the rapid conclusions we reach based on visually presented information." Lucille A. Jewel, *Through a Glass Darkly: Using Brain and Visual Rhetoric to Gain a Professional Perspective on Visual Advocacy*, 19 S. CAL. INTERDISC. L.J. 237, 289 (2010). Further,

> [w]ith visual information, people believe what they see and will not step back and critically examine the conclusions they reach, unless they are explicitly motivated to do so. Thus, the alacrity by which we process and make decisions based on visual information conflicts with a bedrock principle of our legal system — that reasoned deliberation is necessary for a fair justice system.

*Id.* at 293 (footnote omitted) (citing William J. Bowers, Benjamin D. Steiner & Marla Sandys, *Death Sentencing in Black and White: An Empirical Analysis of the Role of Jurors' Race and Jury Racial Composition*, 3 U. PA. J. CONST. L. 171, 261 (2001) (citing Jeffrey Ambramson, We, The Jury: The Jury System and the Ideal of Democracy (1994) (generally discussing the basic democratic principle for jury trials is that deliberations should be a rational and reasoned process))).

During the critical closing moments of trial, one of the last things the jury saw before it began its deliberations was the representative of the State of Washington impermissibly flashing the word "GUILTY" across an image of Glasmann's face three times, predisposing the jury to return a harsh verdict. Indeed, the entire 50-plus slide presentation used during closing argument was full of imagery that likely inflamed the jury.[4] The prosecutor's improper visual "shouts" of GUILTY urged the jury to find Glasmann guilty as charged, and without them, the jury might have returned verdicts on the offenses Glasmann agreed he had committed. Because Glasmann defended by asserting he was guilty only of lesser offenses, and nuanced distinctions often separate degrees of a crime, there is an especially serious danger that the nature and scope of the misconduct here may have affected the jury.

When viewed as a whole, the prosecutor's repeated assertions of the defendant's guilt, improperly modified exhibits, and statement that jurors could acquit Glasmann

---

[4] "Sometimes, we are unable to rationally consider how images affect our emotions or our decision-making process. As we are processing an image in our pre-conscious sensory system, that image can activate an emotional reaction in our mind without us even knowing about it." Jewel, *supra*, at 263 (citing ANN MARIE SEWARD BARRY, VISUAL INTELLIGENCE: PERCEPTION, IMAGE, AND MANIPULATION IN VISUAL COMMUNICATION 18 (1997); JOSEPH LEDOUX, THE EMOTIONAL BRAIN 165 (1996)). "[T]he danger in using emotionally vivid imagery is not that it is subliminally persuasive, but that it tends to generate emotionally driven reactions that can unconsciously affect a decision-maker's thought process." *Id.* at 254. "[T]here is evidence that gruesome photographs cause unconscious emotional reactions—reactions that may not be curable with a limiting instruction." *Id.* at 268-69 (citing Kevin S. Douglas, David R. Lyon & James R.P. Ogloff, *The Impact of Graphic Photographic Evidence on Mock Jurors' Decisions in a Murder Trial: Probative or Prejudicial?*, 21 LAW & HUM. BEHAV. 485, 499 (1997) ("[I]f jurors cannot even recognize the extent to which [graphic] evidence affects them, it will be impossible for them to reduce or control the impact of the evidence when instructed to do so by a judge." (second alteration in original))).

only if they believed him represent the type of pronounced and persistent misconduct that cumulatively causes prejudice demanding that a defendant be granted a new trial. [citations omitted].

\* \* \* \*

In this case, the use of highly inflammatory images unrelated to any specific count was misconduct that contaminated the entire proceedings. The prosecutor's unacceptable argument announced to the jury that the defendant was intrinsically GUILTY GUILTY GUILTY. The misconduct distracted the jury from its duty to consider the evidence unaffected by the overlaid message that emphatically and repeatedly conveyed the prosecutor's belief to the jury that Glasmann is "absolutely guilty!," and which constituted an appeal to passion and prejudice on all counts.

There is a substantial likelihood here that the jury returned guilty verdicts for the offenses the jurors found because they were influenced by the prosecutor's improper closing argument and the altered "evidence" presented during argument. We cannot say that the jury would not have returned verdicts for lesser offenses, or even acquittal, i.e., we cannot even presume the jury would have accepted defense counsel's concessions even as to the obstruction charged. The impact of such powerful but unquantifiable material on the jury is exceedingly difficult to assess but substantially likely to have affected the *entirety* of the jury deliberations and its verdicts. Even the dissent agrees that the misconduct mandates reversal of the assault conviction. The requisite balance of impartiality was upset. Mr. Glasmann's right to a fair trial must be granted in full. In this way, we give substance to our message that "prejudicial prosecutorial tactics will not be permitted," and our warnings that prosecutors must avoid improper, prejudicial means of obtaining convictions will not be empty words. *Charlton*, 90 Wash. 2d at 665, 585 P.2d 142.

\* \* \* \*

## CONCLUSION

The prosecutor's presentation of a slide show including alterations of Glasmann's booking photograph by addition of highly inflammatory and prejudicial captions constituted flagrant and ill intentioned misconduct that requires reversal of his convictions and a new trial, notwithstanding his failure to object at trial. Considering the entire record and circumstances of this case, there is a substantial likelihood that this misconduct affected the jury verdict. The principal disputed matter at trial was whether Glasmann was guilty of lesser offenses rather than those charged, and this largely turned on whether the requisite mental element was established for each offense. More fundamentally, the jury was required to conclude that the evidence established Glasmann's guilt of each offense beyond a reasonable doubt.

It is substantially likely that the jury's verdict were affected by the prosecutor's improper declarations that the defendant was "GUILTY, GUILTY, GUILTY!," together with the prosecutor's challenges to Glasmann's veracity improperly expressed as superimposed messages over the defendant's bloodied face in a jail booking photograph.

We reverse the defendant's convictions and remand for a new trial.

WE CONCUR: Charles W. Johnson and Debra L. Stephens, Justices and Gerry L. Alexander, Justice Pro Tem.

Chambers, J., (concurring).

I agree with the lead opinion that the prosecutor's misconduct in this case was so flagrant and ill intentioned that a curative instruction would not have cured the error and that the defendant was prejudiced as a result of the misconduct. *See State v. Stenson*, 132 Wash. 2d 668, 719, 940 P.2d 1239 (1997). I write separately because I was stunned that the State argued to this court there was nothing improper with the prosecutor showing the jury a photo of the defendant digitally altered to look more like a wanted poster than properly admitted evidence. It was the State's view in oral argument that the PowerPoint slide in question was merely an instance of using modern techniques to present stimulating closing arguments. It was the State's position that the State may add "guilty" to the text of a PowerPoint presentation and therefore that it does not cross the line to add the text "guilty" to the photograph itself.

Under the State's logic, in a shooting case, there would be nothing improper with the State altering an image of the accused by photoshopping a gun into his hand to illustrate the State's version of how the shooting must have occurred. In my view, the State in this case does not understand its role in ensuring a fair trial and the courts must establish the boundary lines. *See State v. Monday*, 171 Wash. 2d 667, 676, 257 P.3d 551 (2011) ("The prosecutor owes a duty to defendants to see that their rights to a constitutionally fair trial are not violated."); *State v. Thorgerson*, 172 Wash. 2d 438, 462, 258 P.3d 43 (2011) (Chambers, J., dissenting) ("The proper measure of the success of any prosecutor is the prosecutor's devotion to the law, fidelity to the rules of the court and rules of evidence, and dedication to guarding the protections our constitutions and laws afford every person, including the accused."). Adding the word "guilty" to the PowerPoint slide was improper, whether in the text or splashed across the defendant's photo.

Certainly, lawyers may and should use technology to advance advocacy and judges should permit and even encourage new techniques. But we must all remember the only purpose of visual aids of any kind is to enhance and assist the jury's understanding of the evidence. Technology should never be permitted to dazzle, confuse, or obfuscate the truth. The jury's deliberations must be based solely upon the evidence admitted and the court's instructions, not upon whose lawyer does the best job of manipulating, altering, shuffling, or distorting the evidence into some persuasive visual kaleidoscope experience for the jury.

This was not a "he said, she said" case. Edward Glasmann's actions were captured on videotape by the security camera of the minimart. The State also had the testimony of five police officers, the witness who called 911, the 911 tape itself, and the victim, which altogether gave a real time account of the entire incident. There was absolutely no need for the prosecutor to alter an exhibit to demonize the defendant. I can only conclude the prosecutor's misconduct was flagrant and ill intentioned and designed to inflame the passions of the jury. *See Stenson*, 132 Wash. 2d at 719, 940 P.2d 1239. Turning Glasmann's photo into a poster one might expect to see on the wall of an Old West saloon was completely unnecessary, and I cannot say the misconduct did not affect the verdict in this case. *See State v. Pirtle*, 127 Wash. 2d 628, 672, 904 P.2d 245 (1995). I agree with the lead opinion that Glasmann's conviction should be reversed and the case remanded for a new trial.

WIGGINS, J., (dissenting).

I agree with the lead opinion that the prosecutor in this case improperly expressed a personal opinion about Edward Glasmann's guilt when he superimposed the words "guilty, guilty, guilty" over Glasmann's mug shot in a PowerPoint display. But I disagree that all of Glasmann's convictions should be overturned as a result. While it may appear at first glance that the prosecutor's error is grave enough to warrant a new trial on all of Glasmann's convictions, a closer examination of the facts reveals a different story.

\* \* \* \*

C. Prosecutors May Use Visual Aids

Although I agree that the prosecutor's inclusion of an altered version of Glasmann's mug shot proclaiming Glasmann "guilty, guilty, guilty" was improper, I do not condemn the use of visual aids generally. When properly created and employed, visual aids can be both effective and helpful during closing argument and I would not discourage their use. I do not read the lead opinion as limiting the proper use of visual aids either. However, I join the lead opinion in condemning the improper use of these aids when they are tantamount to improper closing argument, as was the case here.

For the foregoing reasons, I dissent. I would reverse Glasmann's second degree assault conviction and remand for further proceedings consistent with this opinion.

WE CONCUR: SUSAN OWENS, MARY E. FAIRHURST, and JAMES M. JOHNSON, JUSTICES.

## B.   Court-Created Images

### SANDIFER v. U.S. STEEL CORP.
678 F.3d 590 (7th Cir. 2012)

POSNER, CIRCUIT JUDGE.

These appeals arise out of a class action (technically a "collective action," as it is brought pursuant to 29 U.S.C. § 216(b), a part of the Fair Labor Standards Act of 1938, 29 U.S.C. §§ 201 *et seq.*, rather than pursuant to Fed. R. Civ. P. 23) on behalf of 800 former and current hourly workers at U.S. Steel's steel works in Gary, Indiana. The plaintiffs argue that U.S. Steel has violated the Act by failing to compensate them for the time they spend in putting on and taking off their work clothes in a locker room at the plant ("clothes-changing time") and in walking from the locker room to their work stations, and back again at the end of the day ("travel time"). The collective bargaining agreement between U.S. Steel and the steelworkers union does not require compensation for such time, and apparently none of the previous collective bargaining agreements between U.S. Steel and the union since 1947, nine years after the FLSA was enacted, required it either. But the plaintiffs argue that the Act itself requires compensation; and if it does, it overrides any contrary contractual provision.

The district judge ruled that the Fair Labor Standards Act does not require that the clothes-changing time in this case be compensated, but that the Act may require that the travel time be compensated and he therefore refused to dismiss the suit. But he certified the issue of the compensability of the travel time for an interlocutory appeal under 28 U.S.C. § 1292(b) by U.S. Steel, and we accepted the appeal.

The plaintiffs have cross-appealed. They want to challenge the district judge's ruling that clothes-changing time is not compensable. U.S. Steel points out that the cross-appeal doesn't satisfy the procedural standard for an appeal under section 1292(b) because the plaintiffs did not ask either the district judge or us for leave to appeal. So we hereby dismiss the cross-appeal. But the dismissal has no practical significance. For if the ruling on clothes-changing time was erroneous, the plaintiffs' case for compensation for travel time is, as we'll see, irrefutable. And so they can certainly argue, in opposition to the appeal, that the ruling was indeed erroneous.

So on to the merits — and it will simplify exposition to start with the clothing issue. The Fair Labor Standards Act requires that workers be paid at least the federal minimum wage for all hours worked, and time and a half for hours worked over 40 hours in a week. But the statute does not define "work," a critical hole that the courts must fill — critical because the Act covers an immense variety of kinds of workplace, and by expanding the meaning of "work" courts could overrule agreements negotiated between labor and management and create unforeseen retroactive liabilities. To cut back on Supreme Court decisions believed to have done this, Congress in 1947 passed the Portal-to-Portal Act, 29 U.S.C. §§ 251 *et seq.*, and two years later, in the spirit of that Act, added section 3(*o*) to the Fair Labor Standards Act, 29 U.S.C. § 203(*o*). That section excludes, from the time during which an employee is entitled to be compensated at the minimum hourly wage (or, if it is overtime work, at 150 percent of his hourly wage), "any time spent in changing clothes or washing at the beginning or end of each workday which was excluded from measured working time . . . by the express terms of or by custom or practice under a bona fide collective-bargaining agreement applicable to the particular employee." *Id.* ("Washing time" is not at issue in this case, however.) The plaintiffs argue that the section is inapplicable because what the district court deemed "clothes" are not clothes within the meaning of the Act, but rather safety equipment. The statute does not define "clothes."

The alleged clothes consist of flame-retardant pants and jacket, work gloves, metatarsal boots (work boots containing steel or other strong material to protect the toes and instep), a hard hat, safety glasses, ear plugs, and a "snood" (a hood that covers the top of the head, the chin, and the neck). These work clothes are in the record, and since a picture is worth a thousand words, here is a photograph of a man modeling the clothes:

The glasses and ear plugs are not clothing in the ordinary sense but the hard hat *might* be regarded as an article of clothing, and in any event putting on the glasses and the hard hat and putting in the ear plugs is a matter of seconds and hence not compensable, because *de minimis*. "Split-second absurdities are not justified by the actualities of working conditions or by the policy of the Fair Labor Standards Act. It is only when an employee is required to give up a substantial measure of his time and effort that compensable working time is involved." [citations omitted].

The rest of the outfit certainly *seems* to be clothing, but the plaintiffs argue, no, it's "personal protective equipment." Actually it's both. Protection — against sun, cold, wind, blisters, stains, insect bites, and being spotted by animals that one is hunting — is a common function of clothing, and an especially common function of work clothes worn by factory workers. It would be absurd to exclude all work clothes that have a protective function from section 203(*o*), and thus limit the exclusion largely to actors' costumes and waiters' and doormen's uniforms. Remember that the section covers not only clothes-changing time but also washing-up time, and workers who wear work clothes for self-protection in a dangerous or noxious work environment are far more likely to require significant time for washing up after work than a waiter.

It's true that not everything a person wears is clothing. We say that a person "wears" glasses, or a watch, or his heart on his sleeve, but this just shows that "wear" is a word of many meanings. Almost any English speaker would say that the model in our photo is wearing work clothes. Given the subject matter of the Fair *Labor Standards Act* it would be beyond odd to say that the word "clothes" in section 203(*o*) excludes work clothes, especially since the section is about changing into and out of clothes at the beginning and end of the workday. Not all workers wear work clothes, but workers who change at the beginning and end of the workday are changing into and out of work clothes, and if they are governed by a collective bargaining agreement that makes such changing noncompensable the agreement must apply to work clothes, for otherwise the noncompensation provision would have virtually no applications.

The fact that the clothing exclusion is operative only if it is agreed to in collective bargaining implies, moreover, that workers *are* compensated for the time they spend changing into work clothes, and washing up and changing back. "Section 203(*o*) permits unions and management to trade off the number of compensable hours against the wage rate; the workers get more, per hour, in exchange for agreeing to exclude some time from the base." The steelworkers would not have given up their statutory entitlement to time and a half for overtime, when changing clothes or traveling to and from their work stations, without receiving something in return; and they will get to keep that compensation until the next collective bargaining agreement goes into effect, in addition to the back pay they're demanding, if they convince us that "clothes" don't include the work clothes worn by steelworkers at the Gary plant.

From a worker's standpoint any time spent on the factory grounds is time "at work" in the sense of time away from home or some other place where he might prefer to be if he weren't at work. But it is not time during which he is making steel, and so it is not time for which the company will willingly pay. If the workers have a legal right to be paid for that time, the company will be less willing to pay them a high wage for the time during which they are making steel; it will push hard to reduce the hourly wage so that its overall labor costs do not rise. The steel industry is international and highly competitive, and unions temper their wage demands to avoid killing the goose that lays the golden eggs. They don't want the American steel industry to go where so much American manufacturing has gone in recent years — abroad. The plaintiffs are adverse to their union, to the interests of other steelworkers, and to their own long-term interests.

* * * *

So the district judge was correct to rule that, given the terms of the collective bargaining agreement, U.S. Steel doesn't have to compensate its workers for the time they spend changing into and out of their work clothes. We add that the ruling accords with all but one reported appellate decision, and again the outlier is the Ninth Circuit's decision in *Alvarez*. [citations omitted]. And in *Spoerle v. Kraft Foods Global, Inc., supra*, 614 F.3d at 428, we adopted *Sepulveda's* reasoning and conclusion without undertaking a separate analysis.

* * * *

We resolve the specific issue that we have been asked to resolve in this interlocutory appeal in favor of U.S. Steel. On the basis of that resolution, the suit has no merit and should be dismissed by the district court.

————————

The photo did not go unnoticed by commentators or by the United States Supreme Court Justices when the *Sandifer* case went on appeal from the Seventh Circuit:

> [The photo] appears to have been conceived of, staged, created, curated . . . , and edited by someone in Judge Posner's chambers. The model, who looks suspiciously like a law clerk, is wearing only some, but not all, of the equipment at issue: His jaunty air of fashion might have been tarnished had he been wearing the leggings and wristlets also in contention, or perhaps the respirator. The image's background also enhances Judge Posner's analysis. Instead of standing amidst the sparks and flames of a steelworks, Judge Posner's model leans against what appears to be a (flameproof?) chambers door. What is presented in the Seventh Circuit's opinion as a neutral depiction of evidence — a complete picture — is in fact a purposefully crafted visual argument, subtly but persuasively advancing Judge Posner's interpretation of the Fair Labor Standards Act. And his strategy seems to have been effective. In the opening moments of oral argument in the Supreme Court, Justice Ginsberg made her views plain, stating, "[F]rom the picture, that looks like clothes to me."

Elizabeth G. Porter, *The Negotiated Structural Constitution*, 114 Colum. L. Rev. 1687 (2014).

Judge Posner defended its use:

> . . . [O]n the theory that a picture is worth a thousand words, our opinion includes a photograph of a man (one of my law clerks), dressed in the "Clothes."

> We concluded for a variety of reasons unnecessary to dwell on here that the outfit was better characterized as work clothes than as safety equipment. I think it was a help to the judges but also to the reader of the opinion to see the items of clothing or equipment that we discussed and the ensemble formed by the items. The picture helped to make the verbal description and analytic discussion intelligible.

Richard A. Posner, Reflections on Judging, 146 (2013).

# SANDIFER v. UNITED STATES STEEL CORP.
## 134 S. Ct. 870 (2014)

\* \* \* \*

### III. Analysis

#### A. "Clothes"

We begin by examining the meaning of the word "clothes. It is a "fundamental canon of statutory construction" that, "unless otherwise defined, words will be interpreted as taking their ordinary, contemporary, common meaning." *Perrin v. United States,* 444 U.S. 37, 42, 100 S. Ct. 311, 62 L. Ed. 2d 199 (1979).

Dictionaries from the era of § 203(*o*)'s enactment indicate that "clothes" denotes *items that are both designed and used to cover the body and are commonly regarded as articles of dress. See* Webster's New International Dictionary of the English Language 507 (2d ed. 1950) (Webster's Second) (defining "clothes" as "[c]overing for the human body; dress; vestments; vesture"); see also, *e.g.,* 2 Oxford English Dictionary 524 (1933) (defining "clothes" as "[c]overing for the person; wearing apparel; dress, raiment, vesture"). That is what we hold to be the meaning of the word as used in § 203(*o*). Although a statute may make "a departure from the natural and popular acceptation of language," *Greenleaf v. Goodrich*, 101 U.S. 278, 284–285, 25 L. Ed. 845 (1880) (citing *Maillard v. Lawrence*, 14 L. Ed. 925, 16 How. 251 (1854)), nothing in the text or context of § 203(*o*) suggests anything other than the ordinary meaning of "clothes."

\* \* \* \*

## In Court Reports

1.  Take a "technology survey" of your court and its operations. Consider if it appears to be high tech, low tech, or no tech. To gain a sense of history, interview members of chambers who have worked with the court many years. Trace technology through the processes of filing, motion practice, research, drafting, and editing of an opinion. Also review a history of how communications have taken place among staff members and the judge.

Try to imagine your current work in chambers performed with paper research only; with an IBM electric typewriter; with a telephone without voicemail; with a fax machine; with paper filings only; and without research databases.

2.  Evaluate the technology used in your court. Do you find it is consistently a benefit to the functions and processes of your court? What are some of the disadvantages, if any?

3.  How has technology affected your court in the courtroom itself — either as a trial court with bench and jury trials or as an appellate court with oral arguments?

Consider use of electronic media, videotape recordings, and digital images.

4.   Search your court or jurisdiction for trial and appellate opinions that include issues of judicial notice. How would you characterize these rulings' and the facts being noticed either explicitly or implicitly? What sources do they find proper and what sources improper for taking judicial notice?

5.   Has your judge or would your judge cite to Wikipedia or similar websites, solely or with other resources, to support taking judicial notice of an adjudicative fact? Or of a legislative fact? Or of a fact used for context?

6.   During your externship have you observed the use of images in the courtroom at trial, in pleadings, in motion practice, or in an opinion? What procedures are in place to ascertain the accuracy and authenticity of these images? If you have not seen images used, then can you suggest a trial, pleading, motion, or memo where an image would have been powerfully and persuasively used? Do you think you would you incorporate images into written legal work — as a law student, for your judge, as a practicing attorney?

> Visualizing important facts and arguments is just as important in briefs and pleadings, with dispositive motions steadily taking a greater role. Trial judges find visuals just as helpful and persuasive as juries do. Yet how many of us regularly incorporate pictures in our written work, sparing the thousand words?

William S. Bailey, *Trial Lawyers' Storytelling Techniques from Decades Ago Are No Longer Enough*, 51 Jun Trial 48 (2015).

## Out of Court Reports

1.   Review the quote from *Badasa v. Mukasey* that opened this chapter. Under what circumstances would you cite to Wikipedia or a similar resource or website as a law student, as an extern drafting an opinion or performing research for a judge, or as a practicing attorney? Under what circumstances would you urge a court to take judicial notice of an Internet resource? Would you adopt the reasoning used by Judge Voros, citing to Professor Peoples, in *Fire Insurance Exchange v. Oltmanns*?

2.   Although judges have relied on Wikipedia, should jurors be allowed to consult this source? The issue is raised in *United States v. Lawson*, 677 F.3d 629 (4th Cir. 2012) and analyzed further, Brittany M. McIntosh, *Gamecocks Spur Trouble in Jury Deliberations: What the Fourth Circuit Really Thinks About Wikipedia as a Legal Resource in United States v. Lawson*, 64 S.C. L. Rev. 1157 (2013) (juror seeking a definition of a legal term within a criminal statute and used Wikipedia).

Jurors are instructed not to conduct on line research. Judge Posner, himself a fan of Internet research, has suggested that simply forbidding research is not enough when jurors need to be engaged during the trial. He instead offers other options to engage jurors, including allowing jurors to ask questions during the trial and to take notes during the trial. Richard A. Posner, Reflections on Judging 310–11 (2013).

3.   Are websites like Wikipedia and others inherently unreliable because they keep changing or may become unavailable over time? "Link rot" may mean that a once

active website has rotted and is no longer available.

> Books are inert information repositories, and are therefore also immune to information retention problems. By contrast, the Internet is a volatile environment and information can be added or removed without any notice to the end user. One aspect of this problem is familiar to anyone who has clicked on a link to an apparently interesting website only to discover that the site is no longer available. This phenomenon [is] appropriately termed "link rot."

Ian Gallacher, *Forty-Two: The Hitchhiker's Guide to Teaching Legal Research to the Google Generation*, 39 Akron L. Rev. 151, 187 (2006).

4.   When a link cited within an opinion becomes unavailable, what are the possible consequences? *See* Arturo Torres, *Is Link Rot Destroying Stare Decisis As We Know It?: The Internet-Citation Practice of the Texas Appellate Courts*, 13 J. App. Prac. & Process 269 (2012).

5.   Professor Cass Sunstein has commented that Wikipedia citations in opinions may be the result of law clerks' research because "law clerks are using Wikipedia a great deal." Noam Cohen, *Courts Turn to Wikipedia, But Selectively*, N.Y. Times (Jan. 29, 2007). This notion reflects concerns we heard in earlier chapters that law clerks are over-influencing opinion drafting. Do you agree that judges may be influenced by law clerks of a younger generation to rely on Internet sources or do the facts of cases simply warrant such research? Consider if the *Mendler* majority opinion and its footnotes reflect law clerk influence.

6.   In the three cases below, where the [CITE] indicator appears, the court opinion cites to a Wikipedia entry. Consider if you find this citation appropriate — as notice of an adjudicative or legislative fact, as a context or background fact, or as a statement not requiring any citation. Can you offer a different resource to cite that would be more acceptable? Should it matter if the citation is in the body of the opinion or in a footnote?

> a. Making health care services more accessible to LEP patients, as one might expect, is a Herculean and glacial task. One reason is the sheer multiplicity of languages. About 337 languages are spoken in the United States, twenty-four of which have over 200,000 speakers; [CITE] Florida's language diversity is equally impressive. [CITE] Attempting to accommodate access to health care information and services to this wide-ranging landscape of languages is of obvious difficulty, requiring complicated policy decisions at the federal and state levels that take time to analyze, make, and then implement.

[*Trejo-Perez v. Arry's Roofing*, 141 So. 3d 220 (Fla. Dist. Ct. App. 2014) ("In this workers' compensation appeal, Jesus Trejo-Perez ("Claimant") challenges the denial of his request for referral to a Spanish-speaking psychologist as recommended by his authorized treating physician. He argues the Judge of Compensation Claims ("JCC") erred by denying the request despite unrebutted medical testimony that a Spanish-speaking psychologist is medically necessary.")]

> b. Throughout history, there is little question that many societies and cultures have relied on groups of twelve to make reliable decisions. Whether reliance

on such duodecuple decision-making has only been based on a religious or cultural tradition of twelve or on some intuitive sense that a group of twelve is reliable is probably an unanswerable question. [CITE] However, within the law, we quite reasonably give trust to solutions that have withstood the test of time, and the jury of twelve has clearly withstood that test.

[*Gonzalez v. State*, 982 So. 2d 77 (Fla. Dist. Ct. App. 2008) ("Robert Gonzalez appeals his judgment for second-degree murder and sentence of life imprisonment as a prison releasee reoffender. . . . We affirm, but write to address Mr. Gonzalez's argument that he was entitled to a twelve-person jury rather than a six-person jury to decide his case because he faced a mandatory life sentence, without possibility of parole, upon his conviction for the charged crime.")]

    c. The Mohajir Qaumi Movement first became a political party in the mid-1980s and quickly rose to prominence in Pakistani politics. It formed an early coalition with the dominant political party, but the relationship soured, leading to conflict and often violent confrontations. In 1992 the military initiated "Operation Clean-up" aimed at purging the City of Karachi of terrorists, though many Mohajirs viewed it as a disguised attempt to suppress the Mohajir Qaumi Movement. [CITE]

[*Khan v. Holder*, 766 F.3d 689 (7th Cir. 2014) (Review of alien's claim to knowledge exception to terrorist bar: an "alien has an opportunity to "demonstrate by clear and convincing evidence that [he] did not know, and should not reasonably have known, that the organization [the Mohajir Quami Movement] was a terrorist organization.")]

    7.   Should a court's independent research using not Wikipedia, but using a state government website, be deemed sufficiently reliable to warrant judicial notice as adjudicative fact? *See N.Y.C. Medical and Neurodiagnostic v. Republic Western Ins. Co.*, 8 Misc. 3d 33 (N.Y. Sup. Ct. 2004).

    8.   Compare *State v. Glasmann* with an *en banc* opinion from the same court, three years later, *State v. Walker*, 341 P.3d 976 (Wash. 2015). In *Walker*, the court opinion includes the slides from the prosecutor's Powerpoint presentation to the jury in a murder trial. Consider the effectiveness of reproducing the slides' images in the *Walker* opinion itself versus the written opinion without images in *Glasmann*.

    Also compare the images of the two Powerpoint presentations in the two cases and consider what alternate images and means of persuasion might have been used in each case.

    9.   The *Walker* court suggests that trial courts could review Powerpoint presentations in advance of their use in a closing argument. Other jurisdictions have already devised procedures for closing arguments in the context of video excerpts.

    The portions of the videotape testimony shown during summation should not be so lengthy as to constitute a second trial emphasizing only one litigant's side of the case. The court must exercise its discretion to limit the amount actually played by counsel during summation. . . . Further, the court must take precautions to guard against the edited portions of the videotape misstating the evidence. By editing portions of the trial testimony evidence could be presented out of context and could easily confuse the issues or mislead the jury. *N.J.R.E.* 403. In order to eliminate this problem, a hearing akin to a *N.J.R.E.* 104(a) hearing should be conducted. The court, out of the jury's presence, should therefore view the proposed portions of the videotape testimony in open court on the record to make sure that it accurately reflects the evidence.

*Condella v. Cumberland Farms*, 689 A.2d 872 (N.J. Super. Ct. Law Div. 1996).

What other factors might be relevant for a court to consider in reviewing a Powerpoint or video during closing arguments? Or, should rules be developed that these slide shows and videos simply have no appropriate place in closing arguments?

**10.** Rather than rely on the photo of the Seventh Circuit law clerk to illustrate the concept of "clothes," The United States Supreme Court opinion in *Sandifer* uses a Webster's dictionary from 1950 and an Oxford English Dictionary from 1933. Why does the Court rely on these sources?

**11.** In *Mendler*, the appellate court noted that the lower court had not made any findings of fact. Was the appellate right to keep the appeal or should it have sent it back to the lower court for fact-finding? What about the order for supplemental briefing on appeal and the Appendix? Has the appellate court wrongly expanded the record as Judge Rymer concludes in his dissent?

**12.** How do the exhibits offered by the plaintiff and the defendant in *Randy Disselkoen Properties* differ in their "credibility"? Why does the judge capitalize the words NO DOUBT?

**13.** Why is Wikipedia relied upon and cited to in the *Kogler* case? What sort of "fact" is being supported?

**14.** Federal Rule of Appellate Procedure Rule 10 defines the record on appeal as "(1) the original papers and exhibits filed in the district court; (2) the transcript of proceedings, if any; and (3) a certified copy of the docket entries prepared by the district clerk."

Technology will allow the appellate court to use the video recordings of the trial in place of the written transcript. Technology will also allow the appellate court to view a videotape exhibit filed in the trial court. Will this ability to experience the trial court proceedings and exhibits undermine the standard of appellate review?

[In] *Scott v. Harris*, the Court explicitly relied on a videotape of the events at issue where there were no allegations that the videotape had been doctored or altered. 550 U.S. 372, 379 n.1 (2007) ("We are happy to allow the videotape to speak for itself."). Therefore, this Court will rely on the videotape of the Council meeting, submitted as an exhibit to Defendant's Answer, to expand upon the pleadings' description about what occurred during the meeting. *But see* Dan M. Kahan, David A. Hoffman, and Donald Braman, *Whose Eyes Are You Going to Believe? Scott v. Harris and the Perils of Cognitive Illiberalism*, 122 HARV. L. REV. 838 (2009) (providing a critical analysis of Scott and reviewing results of a survey of 1,350 individuals that challenged the assumptions and conclusions of the Supreme Court majority).

*Mobley v. Tarlini*, 641 F. Supp. 2d 430 (E.D. Pa. 2009).

## SELECTED BIBLIOGRAPHY

Jeffrey Bellin & Andrew Guthrie Ferguson, *Trial by Google: Judicial Notice in the Information Age*, 108 Nw. U. L. Rev. 1137 (2014).

David J. Dansky, *The Google Knows Many Things: Judicial Notice in the Internet Era*, 39 Nov Colo. Law. 19 (2010).

Herbert B. Dixon, Jr., *The Lack of Effort to Ensure Integrity and Trustworthiness of Online Information and Documents*, 46 Judges' J. 42 (2007).

Jeffrey C. Dobbins, *New Evidence on Appeal*, 96 Minn. L. Rev. 2016 (2012).

Philip G. Espinoza, *A Word from the Future — The Virtually Paperless Court of Appeals*, 49 No. 3 Judges' J. 10 (2010).

Neal Feigenson & Christina Spiesel, Law on Display (2009).

Joseph L. Gerken, *How Courts Use Wikipedia*, 11 J. App. Prac. & Process 191 (2010).

Brianne J. Gorod, *The Adversarial Myth: Appellate Court Extra-Record Factfinding*, 61 Duke L.J. 1 (2011).

Lucille A. Jewel, *Through a Glass Darkly: Using Brain Science and Visual Rhetoric to Gain Professional Perspective on Visual Advocacy*, 19 S. Cal. Interdisc. L.J. 237 (2010).

Jeffrey L. Kirchmeier & Samuel A. Thumma, *Scaling the Lexicon Fortress: The United States Supreme Court's Use of Dictionaries in the Twenty-First Century*, 94 Marq. L. Rev. 77 (2010).

Lenora Ledwon, *Understanding Visual Metaphors: What Graphic Novels Can Teach Lawyers About Visual* Storytelling, 63 Drake L. Rev. 193 (2015).

Raizel Liebler & June Liebert, *Something Rotten in the State of Legal Citation: The Life Span of a United States Supreme Court Citation Containing an Internet Link (1996–2010)*, 15 Yale J. L. & Tech. 273 (2013).

Eric J. Magnuson & Samuel A. Thumma, *Prospects and Problems Associated with Technological Change in Appellate Courts: Envisioning the Appeal of the Future*, 15. J. App. Prac. & Process 111 (2014).

Nancy S. Marder, *The Court and the Visual: Images and Artifacts in U.S. Supreme Court Opinions*, 88 Chi.-Kent L. Rev. 331 (2013).

Ellie Margolis, *It's Time to Embrace the New — Untangling the Uses of Electronic Sources in Legal Writing*, 23 Alb. L.J. Sci. & Tech. 191 (2013).

Lee F. Peoples, *The Citation of Wikipedia in Judicial Opinions*, 12 Yale J. L. & Tech. L. 1 (2009).

Elizabeth G. Porter, *Taking Images Seriously*, 114 Colum. L. Rev. 1687 (2014).

R. Jason Richards, *Courting Wikipedia*, 44 TRIAL 62 (2008).

David B. Saxe, *"Toxic" Judicial Research*, 87 N.Y. ST. B.J. 36 (Sept. 2015).

Frederick Schauer, *The Decline of "The Record": A Comment on Posner*, 51 DUQ. L. REV. 51 (2013).

Donald E. Shelton, *Video Court Reporting — The Time Has Come*, 42 JUDGES' J. 32 (2003).

William E. Smith, *Judicial Opinions and the Digital Revolution*, 49 JUDGES' J. 7 (2010).

Joan Steinman, *Appellate Courts as First Responders: The Constitutionality and Propriety of Appellate Courts' Resolving Issues in the First Instance*, 87 NOTRE DAME L. REV. 1521 (2012).

David H. Tennant & Laurie M. Seal, *Judicial Ethics & the Internet: May Judges Search the Internet in Evaluating and Deciding a Case?*, 16 PROF. LAWYER 2 (2005).

James D. Theiss, *Protecting the Burden of Proof in Kentucky: Procedural Safeguards for the Use of Video Excerpts During Closing Arguments*, 50 U. LOUISVILLE L. REV. 527 (2012).

Elizabeth G. Thornburg, *The Lure of the Internet and the Limits on Judicial Fact Research*, 38 No. 4 LITIGATION 41 (2012).

Elizabeth G. Thornburg, *The Curious Appellate Judge: Ethical Limits on Independent Research*, 28 REV. LITIG. 131 (2008)

Michael Whiteman, *The Death of Twentieth-Century Authority*, 58 UCLA L. REV. DISCOURSE 27 (2010).

Jodi L. Wilson, *Proceed With Extreme Caution: Citation to Wikipedia in Light of Contributor Demographics and Content Policies*, 16 VAND. J. ENT. & TECH. L. 857 (2014).

# INDEX

[References are to chapters and sections within chapters.]

## A

**ADR** (See ALTERNATIVE DISPUTE RESOLUTION (ADR))

**ALTERNATIVE DISPUTE RESOLUTION (ADR)**
Rise of . . . 5[IV]

**APPELLATE PROCEDURES, DECLINE OF**
Generally . . . 5[V]
Oral arguments in appellate courts, decline in . . . 5[V][B]
Settlement on appeal before appellate briefs . . . 5[V][A]

**ATTORNEYS** (See COUNSEL)

## C

**CIVIL JURY TRIALS**
Complex litigation and civil jury competence
  Generally . . . 5[III]
  "Burdens," accompanying . . . 5[III][C]
  Federal courts . . . 5[III][A]
  State courts . . . 5[III][B]
Decline of . . . 5[I]
Seventh Amendment right to . . . 5[II]

**COMPLEX LITIGATION**
Civil jury competence and (See CIVIL JURY TRIALS, subhead: Complex litigation and civil jury competence)

**CONFIDENTIALITY OF CHAMBERS**
Generally . . . 1[III][A]
Judicial privilege . . . 1[III][A][3]
Past confidences, revealing . . . 1[III][A][2]
Present confidences, revealing . . . 1[III][A][1]

**CONFLICT OF INTERESTS**
Current employment as judicial clerk . . . 1[III][B][2]
Family relations . . . 1[III][B][1]
Former clerks/externs as counsel . . . 1[III][B][3]
Future employment . . . 1[III][B][1]

**COUNSEL**
Former clerks/externs as . . . 1[III][B][3]
Images in judicial process, attorney-created . . . 7[II][A]
Impartial judicial treatment of counsel and parties . . . 4[II]

## D

**DECISIONMAKING**
Court record, confinement to . . . 1[III][C]
Diversity, by courts lacking . . . 3[IV][B]

**DISQUALIFICATION OF JUDGE** (See JUDICIAL ETHICS, subhead: Recusal and disqualification, judicial)

**DIVERSITY AMONG JUDGES** (See JUDGES, subhead: Diversity, lack of)

**DRUG COURTS**
Generally . . . 6[II]
Adversarial process . . . 6[IV]
Due process . . . 6[IV]
Working parts of . . . 6[III]

## E

**EDUCATION**
Judges . . . 3[III]; 3[III][B]

**EMPLOYMENT RELATIONS**
Conflict of interests . . . 1[III][B][1]; 1[III][B][2]

**ETHICAL CONSIDERATIONS**
Generally . . . 1[III]
Confidentiality of chambers (See CONFIDENTIALITY OF CHAMBERS)
Conflict of interests (See CONFLICT OF INTERESTS)
Decisionmaking confined to record . . . 1[III][C]
Judicial ethics (See JUDICIAL ETHICS)

## F

**FAMILY RELATIONS**
Conflict of interests . . . 1[III][B][1]

**FRIENDSHIPS, JUDICIAL**
Generally . . . 4[I][B]

## G

**"GHOSTWRITERS"**
Judicial opinions drafted by clerk . . . 2[III]

## H

**HISTORICAL DEVELOPMENT**
Judicial clerks/externs . . . 1[I]

## I

**IMAGES IN JUDICIAL PROCESS**
Attorney-created images . . . 7[II][A]
Court-created images . . . 7[II][B]

**IMPARTIALITY OF JUDGES**
Generally . . . 4[II]
Recusal and disqualification, judicial (See JUDICIAL ETHICS, subhead: Recusal and disqualification, judicial)

[References are to chapters and sections within chapters.]

**INTERNET FACT RESEARCH**
Generally . . . 7[I]

# J

**JUDGES**
Confidentiality of chambers (See CONFIDENTIAL-
ITY OF CHAMBERS)
Diversity, lack of
    Generally . . . 3[IV]
    Influence on decisions, issues of . . . 3[IV][B]
    Legitimacy, issues of . . . 3[IV][B]
    Minority judges, number of . . . 3[IV][A]
    Women judges, number of . . . 3[IV][A]
Education . . . 3[III]; 3[III][B]
Impartiality
    Generally . . . 4[II]
    Recusal and disqualification, judicial (See JUDI-
      CIAL ETHICS, subhead: Recusal and disqualifi-
      cation, judicial)
Qualifications
    Generally . . . 3[II]
    Evaluation criteria . . . 3[III]; 3[III][A]
    Federal courts . . . 3[II][A]
    State courts . . . 3[II][B]
Selection
    Diversity, lack of (See subhead: Diversity, lack of)
    Federal courts . . . 3[I][A]
    State courts . . . 3[I][B]

**JUDICIAL ETHICS**
Impartial judicial treatment of counsel and parties
    . . . 4[II]
Recusal and disqualification, judicial
    Generally . . . 4[I]
    Friendships, judicial . . . 4[I][B]
    Model rules of judicial conduct . . . 4[I][A]
    Trial judge as appellate judge . . . 4[I][C]

**JUDICIAL OPINIONS**
Drafting by clerk "ghostwriters" . . . 2[III]
Multiple audiences, writing for . . . 2[II]
Public perception and recognition of "ghostwritten"
    opinions . . . 2[III]
Well-reasoned judgments, writing . . . 2[I]

**JUDICIAL PRIVILEGE**
Generally . . . 1[III][A][3]

# O

**OPINIONS** (See JUDICIAL OPINIONS)

**ORAL ARGUMENTS**
Appellate courts, decline of in . . . 5[V][B]

# P

**PAST CONFIDENCES**
Revealing . . . 1[III][A][2]

**PRIVILEGE**
Judicial privilege . . . 1[III][A][3]

**PROBLEM-SOLVING COURTS**
Generally . . . 6[I]
Drug courts (See DRUG COURTS)

# Q

**QUALIFICATIONS**
Judges (See JUDGES, subhead: Qualifications)
Judicial clerks/externs . . . 1[IV]

# R

**RECORD OF CASE**
Decisionmaking limited to . . . 1[III][C]

**RECUSAL OF JUDGE** (See JUDICIAL ETHICS,
    subhead: Recusal and disqualification, judicial)

**RESPONSIBILITIES**
Judicial clerks/externs . . . 1[II]

# S

**SELECTION**
Judges (See JUDGES, subhead: Selection)
Judicial clerks/externs . . . 1[IV]

# T

**TECHNOLOGY**
Images in judicial process
    Attorney-created images . . . 7[II][A]
    Court-created images . . . 7[II][B]
Internet fact research . . . 7[I]

**THERAPEUTIC JURISPRUDENCE**
Problem-solving courts
    Generally . . . 6[I]
    Drug courts (See DRUG COURTS)

**TRADITIONAL COURT PROCEDURES**
Transformed court procedures compared . . . 6[I]

**TRIALS**
Appellate judge, trial judge as . . . 4[I][C]
Civil jury trials (See CIVIL JURY TRIALS)